LEEDS TRANSPORT
Volume 1 – 1830 to 1902

By
J. Soper, Dipl.T.P., Dipl.Arch., A.R.I.B.A.

Published by the Leeds Transport Historical Society 1985

Printed by UPS Blackburn Limited, 76-80 Northgate, Blackburn BB2 1AB

To Valerie, for much patience and understanding.

Contents

First published July 1985

ISBN 0 9510280 06

Introduction

old steam and horse
ɛtors etc. in the early
ɾay.

ɪformation has been
ɔontradictory and there
nain unfilled. Perhaps
ɉay become available
ne subject. In spite of
l to be inaccuracies in a
ɉrateful to anyone who
ɾisions will be incorpo-

ɲ this work and, in par-
ɵssrs. B. Donald, I. M.
ɲ and A. K. Terry who
and made many valu-
Donald was also able,
ions, and by means of
ɵ dimensions of the var-
ɜtock, the drawings of
ɵrs. I. M. Dougill and C.
th the research.
ɵd anyone and should

its identity and merged with others to form the Passenger Transport Executive.

The research for this and other volumes has, for many years, occupied the writer and other members of the Leeds Transport Historical Society. Among the sources of information checked were the local newspapers: the Leeds Mercury, Leeds Intelligencer, Leeds Express, Leeds Times, Yorkshire Post, Yorkshire Evening Post and Leeds Daily News, the Council minutes, both manuscript and printed, the Tramways Company and Corporation cash books, staff records, Board of Trade reports, Parliamentary plans, Ordnance Survey and other maps, solicitor's records of the Tramways Company, Tramways Company inventory, Thomas Green and Sons' records etc. In addition many contemporary journals and books have been consulted, among them being the "Railway World,", later "Tramway and Railway World"; "Light Railway Journal"; "Electrical Review"; D. K. Clark, "Tramways, their construction and working," 1878 and 1894 editions; "Modern Electric Practice", 1904 edition; Fairchild, "Street Railways," 1892 edition, and various patent specifications. Modern publications consulted include Dr. Whitcombe, "History of the Steam Tram;" J. S. Webb, "The British Steam Tram", and J. B. Horne and T. B. Maund, "Liverpool Transport, Volume 1." Particularly valuable were the

like to thank the following for help in many different ways: Messrs. R. Atkinson, A. W. Bond, R. Brook, Miss A. E. Burbridge, Messrs. G. B. Claydon, A. Cowell, I. Fraser, Dr. M. Harrison, Messrs. H. Heyworth, J. B. Horne, P. D. Johnson, R. F. Mack, J. D. Markham, J. H. Price, J. R. Stevens, S. M. Swift, Dr. R. G. P. Tebb, Dr. R. Unwin, Messrs. R. Wilks, A. D. Young, the staff of the Leeds Reference Library, Thoresby Society, Leeds Archives Department, West Yorkshire Archives Department, Leeds Corporation, Leeds City Transport Department and the West Yorkshire Passenger Transport Executive.

In addition to its interest in the history of Leeds transport the Leeds Transport Historical Society, founded in 1956, is the sponsor of three of the Leeds tramcars at the National Tramway Museum, Crich, Derbyshire. It has restored one, rail derrick car No. 2 dating from 1930, and is currently rebuilding "Beeston Air Brake" car No. 399 of 1925. "Convert" car No. 345 of 1921 vintage has still to be tackled. In addition, it also owns the body of a Leeds 1898 Milnes double-deck horse car, No. 107, which is in storage.

J. Soper, *Leeds Transport Historical Society*
2 Eastbrook Court, Bramham,
Wetherby, West Yorkshire LS23 6QT.
May 1985

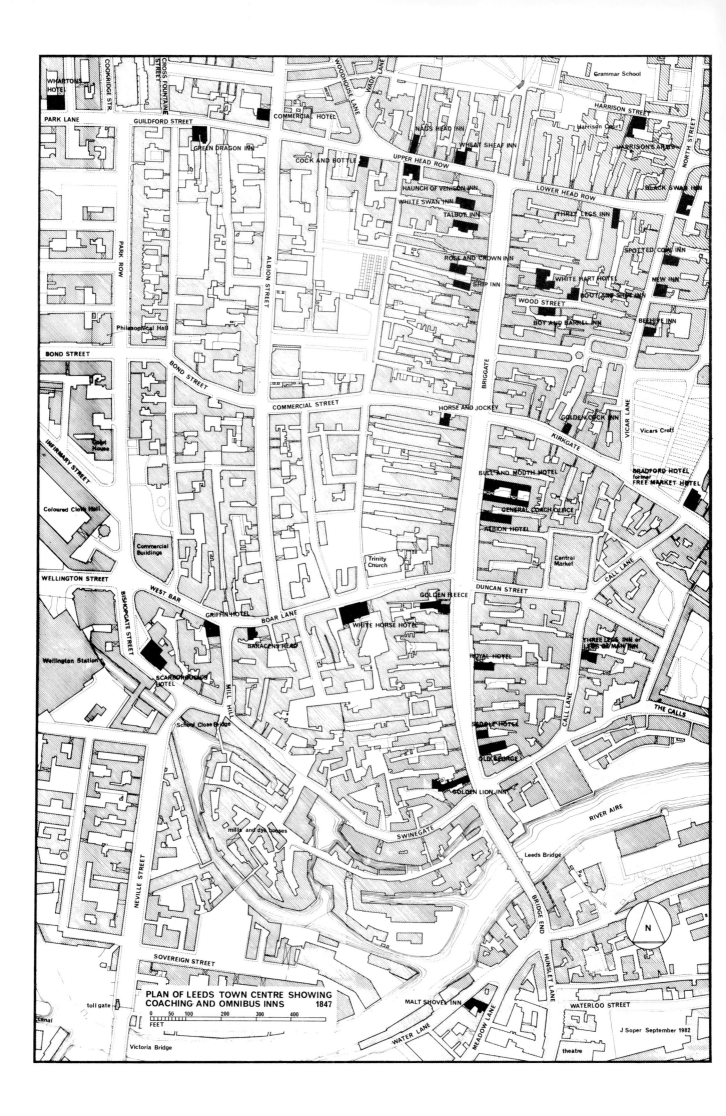

PLAN OF LEEDS TOWN CENTRE SHOWING
COACHING AND OMNIBUS INNS   1847

0   50 100   200   300   400
FEET

J Soper September 1982

CHAPTER ONE

The Beginnings

Cars and Railway Buses

It would appear that Leeds had a form of suburban passenger transport before any of the other towns in the West Yorkshire area. In 1830 it was a prosperous and rapidly developing manufacturing town and had become the woollen capital of England, being on the north eastern extremity of the great clothing district of the County of Yorkshire. The coming of the industrial revolution saw a big change in the face of the town and the most extensive expansion in its history. It was a "boom" town and by 1838 there were more than a hundred woollen mills employing 10,000 workers. From contemporary reports Leeds had by that time assumed the characteristic face of a West Riding town with a thickly sprouting forest of mill chimneys. Many other diverse industries developed in the 'thirties and 'forties of which engineering was the most important. South of the River Aire in Hunslet and Holbeck and in Armley and Wortley to the west, factories, mills and extensive housing for the workpeople were built. The nineteenth century was a period of great wealth for the town, but unfortunately it was also a period of great poverty for many of the workers who flocked to its growing industries.

The population of Leeds, according to the 1831 census, was 123,548 (including the out-townships); this had increased considerably over the previous thirty years by some 70,000 souls.

Lord Brougham praised Leeds in 1830 as "one of the first towns of the Empire, the seat of the greatest commercial community in Yorkshire", but Charles Dickens had a different opinion. As a fellow guest with George Stephenson, the railway engineer, at a Mechanics' Institute dinner in 1847, he referred to Leeds as "the beastliest place, one of the nastiest I know".

Industry generated goods traffic and this was catered for by the Aire and Calder Navigation and the Leeds and Liverpool Canal. Where there were no canals, local and far off towns were reached by turnpike roads on which private carriers conveyed goods in horse-drawn, frequently broad-wheeled, carts. Passenger traffic was served by the stage coach running over the turnpikes between towns.

In the early nineteenth century Leeds was a compact market town about two square miles in area and not large enough to support suburban transport services. At first the merchant and working classes lived side by side, but by the year 1800 Hunslet Lane and Meadow Lane, south of the river, were the residences of the more opulent. Thirty years later, however, the merchants had moved out and the poorer people were living in the

south or in the Quarry Hill area to the east. The better off lived mainly to the west and north. All lived within walking distance of Briggate, the principal shopping street and market, some 600 yards long running north from the river. It formed the town centre. Some of the more wealthy people, who lived further afield, used either their own carriages or hired a hackney coach, a popular mode of transport introduced into the town in April 1824.

At this time the quaint Sedan chair, originally introduced in Leeds in 1767, could still be seen in the streets and was usually hired by ladies. The actor Charles Matthews, in his reminiscences, told of an amusing story relating to a Sedan chair in which a brother actor – Mr. Holman – preferring to dress for the performance at his lodgings, was one night attired in the character of "Lord Townley", and as such, was being carried over the Leeds Bridge to the Hunslet Lane theatre in a Sedan chair. The novelty of the vehicle attracted the attention of some "croppers" (workmen who cropped wool). They stopped its progress and insisted upon seeing what was inside. "A mon wi' his fa-ace painted" – "It's a laker" (a player or actor) was the cry, followed by another cry of "Toss 'im ower't brig". And, but for timely assistance, said Matthews, "ower't brig" the erstwhile "Lord Townley" would certainly have gone.

(From lecture by J. B. Hamilton, 1916).

"The Leeds Improvement Act, 1824" enacted that all hackney coaches, cars, gigs and Sedan chairs plying for hire in the town, should be licensed. From 23rd August 1824 the licensing took place annually and maximum fares were fixed. The principal stand for the vehicles was in Briggate.

An important feature of the nineteenth century town was the public house or inn. It was the place where travellers rested on their journeys. It was the starting point for the stage coaches, where the coaches and horses were kept, where the ostlers and other persons connected with the coaches were stationed. It was also the place where the early 'buses in Leeds began and ended their journeys. The services which these 'buses gave were the compound activity of many small firms who usually had complementary interests. The innkeeper, cab proprietor or stage coach proprietor also owned and ran the local 'bus.

THE CARS

The seeds of suburban transport in Leeds were sown by John Cockill, a beer seller (later innkeeper of the "Woodman Inn", Kirkstall). By 1832 he was operating a number of cars on market days (Tuesdays and Saturdays) between the "Griffin Inn", West Bar (west part of Boar Lane to the west of Briggate) and the village of Kirkstall some three miles north west of Leeds. Shortly afterwards another car was running along the same route, but six miles further to Guiseley, a farming village of about 2,000 inhabitants. It made one journey on market days from the "Cock and Bottle", Upperhead Row (off Briggate to the west). These cars supplemented the regular stage coaches running between Leeds and the neighbouring town of Bradford through Kirkstall. By 1837 another car was running on the same road to Horsforth, a woollen village midway between Kirkstall and Guiseley. It ran from the "Green Dragon", Guildford Street (an extension of Upperhead Row), making one journey only on market days.

Cars had run from the middle 'twenties and early 'thirties to more distant sizeable villages and small towns such as Birstall, Cleckheaton, Heckmondwike, Idle and Pontefract. By 1837, they were also running from Leeds to Batley, Knottingley and Thirsk, the earlier cars to Cleckheaton and Pontefract being replaced by stage coaches.

The horses used on the Kirkstall market cars had a hard life. One passenger commented:—

"These vehicles carry six passengers beside the driver, are drawn by one horse, and their usual speed, after they have passed the Wellington Road is a hard gallop —the whip, of course is in pretty constant requisition, and the same horse is thus worked, with scarcely any intermission, from an early hour in the afternoon until there are no more passengers."

(Leeds Mercury, 4th August, 1832).

This is one of the few descriptions that has been found of a car, but advertisements show that the seating capacities varied from six to 12.

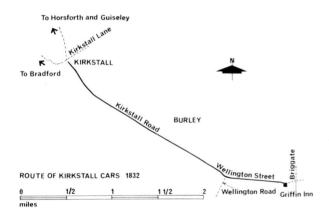

ROUTE OF KIRKSTALL CARS 1832

THE RAILWAY 'BUSES

Horse-drawn omnibuses were running in Manchester, London and Liverpool from the 1820's and early 'thirties. In Leeds we owe their introduction to the railway.

The opening of the first passenger carrying railway from Leeds to the inland port of Selby in the east on 22nd September 1834 resulted in the appearance, about a fortnight later, of a 'bus. It was operated by the Leeds and Selby Railway Company and ran between the Company's offices in Kirkgate (off Briggate), to the Marsh Lane Station and Depot, the Leeds terminus of the railway, to the east, described as "one of the most unpleasant and dirty parts of the town". As only one track of the railway was completed the train made one

departure (at 6.0 am to connect with the fast steam packets for Hull at Selby) and one arrival in the evening. Hence the 'bus made two journeys per day. An extortionate fare of 4d. was charged for the ride of just over a quarter of a mile. This fare, however, must be compared with the minimum fare of 1s. 0d. charged by the hackney coaches and 8d. by the cars.

The construction of the other railway track was completed and opened on 15th December 1834. The number of journeys made by the 'bus increased to four per day. During the summer season of 1835, commencing in June, an additional train was put on and the 'bus journeys increased to six daily.

The high fare ensured that the 'bus was used principally by the nobility and merchants. Sir George Head, writing in 1835 about a journey in the 'bus, commented:— *"It happened to be very shortly after the railway was opened that I made a journey from Leeds to Selby, having been conveyed from the centre of the town to the station in an omnibus, one of the most pre-possessing carriages of that description I remember to have met with. It was a well finished vehicle, fitted up inside with glazed pink lining, neatly plaited in festoons, a large looking glass at the end for the benefit of ladies, and what was better than all, it was carefully driven."*

(Sir George Head. A Home Tour through the Manufacturing Districts of Great Britain in the Summer of 1835).

This was certainly not the type of vehicle that would be used by an artisan or member of the working class.

In July 1835 a seasonal stage coach, the 'Safety', was introduced between Selby and Burlington Quay and ran in conjunction with the Leeds and Selby Railway. Passengers were booked on the coach at the Railway Booking Office in Leeds. During the 1836 season the coach ran through from Selby to Scarborough and, in order to entice passengers on to the coach, the proprietor – Joseph Smith of Market Weighton – offered free trips on the railway 'bus. In June the following year booking for the 'Safety' was changed from the Railway Office to the "Albion Inn" Coach Office, Briggate.

John and William Atkinson, two brothers, who were later to figure prominently in the development of the horse 'bus services in Leeds, ran stage coaches to various parts of the country from the "Albion". The Atkinson's had started a cab business in Leeds in the 1820's and, in 1836, took over a stage coach business at the "Albion". They carried passengers for the 'Safety' by their own 'bus from the "Albion" to the Marsh Lane Station, supplanting the railway 'bus. The latter continued to run from the Railway Company's offices, now situated at No. 147 Briggate, in connection with the ordinary trains.

Other stage coach proprietors expressed an interest in running 'buses in connection with the railway, and the Leeds and Selby Railway Company announced that, on and after 5th November 1838, the station yard would be open to all 'buses and cabs. Immediately, Matthew Outhwaite, of the "Bull and Mouth" and "Royal Hotel" in Briggate, the leading stage coach proprietor in the town, advertised that he was operating 'buses from the two inns to meet all trains. At the same time Outhwaite entered into an agreement with the Railway Company whereby passengers could book on the railway at the "Bull and Mouth" Coaching Office.

With the opening of the York and North Midland line between York and South Milford connecting with the

Leeds and Selby Railway, on 30th May 1839, passengers could travel direct to York from Leeds by railway. An increased number of train departures and arrivals at Leeds resulted. A further stage coach proprietor, Thomas Lee, of the "Golden Lion Hotel", Briggate, advertised 'buses to meet the railway trains.

Probably the most important date in the history of railways in Leeds was 1st July 1840, when the North Midland line was opened from Derby, giving a through railway connection to London. A new railway station was opened in Hunslet Lane, a quarter of a mile south of Briggate. Matthew Outhwaite made arrangements with the Railway Company to deliver parcels and run 'buses between the "Bull and Mouth" and "Royal Hotel" in connection with the new railway.

The Directors of the Leeds and Selby Railway Company leased their line to the York and North Midland Company in 1840. This was the result of pressure from the railway entrepreneur, George Hudson, who ruthlessly closed the railway to passenger traffic west of York Junction. The Leeds and York trains were transferred from the Marsh Lane Station to Hunslet Lane from 27th July 1840, and the Selby and Hull trains from 9th November the same year. This left only local passenger trains running to Garforth and Micklefield from Marsh Lane. There is no record of 'buses running regularly to Marsh Lane Station after this date.

On 1st March 1841 the Manchester and Leeds Railway was opened through to Hunslet Lane Station, further increasing the number of trains arriving at and departing from the town. As a result of this it appears that the various railway 'buses became very irregular. In October 1841 Outhwaite announced that he had been appointed sole agent to the North Midland Railway Company "in order to secure regularity in the conveyance of passengers to and from the station." He arranged the following route for 'buses to meet the trains, calling at the local hostelries as follows:—

"Bull and Mouth", Briggate; "Ship Inn", Briggate; "Commercial Hotel", Upper Albion Street; "Wharton's Hotel", Park Lane; "Scarborough Hotel" and "White Horse Hotel", Boar Lane; "Royal Hotel" and "Golden Lion", Briggate to the Hunslet Lane Station and returning by the same route.

William Morritt, of 27 Cobourg Street (off Woodhouse Lane), took over from Outhwaite at the "Bull and Mouth" in January 1842, and continued the railway 'buses. In November 1840 Outhwaite had taken up a carrier's business and continued his coaching interests at the "Royal Hotel". He ran stage coaches until late 1846, when he was joined in partnership for a few months with a Henry Littlewood, a coach proprietor, also of Cobourg Street (No. 22), who was later to become an important omnibus proprietor. In 1847 Littlewood took over completely at the "Royal" and formed a partnership with Morritt. Outhwaite continued a goods business at the Marsh Lane Railway Station for a few years. He went into semi-retirement at Harrogate and died there on 18th March 1865.

Only Morritt seemed to be able to maintain a regular 'bus service to meet every train, but this ceased to be advertised after 1842. Other coach and omnibus proprietors ran 'buses to order to meet specified trains, but in 1845 Dorothy Hollings, an old established stage coach proprietor of the "White Horse Inn", Boar Lane, was boldly advertising "omnibuses to the railway station for every train." A fare of 6d. was normally charged on all railway 'buses at this time.

The opening of the Leeds and Bradford Railway on 1st July 1846 put an end to any attempt to run a regular 'bus service in connection with each train. The Leeds and Bradford Railway Station was in Wellington Street

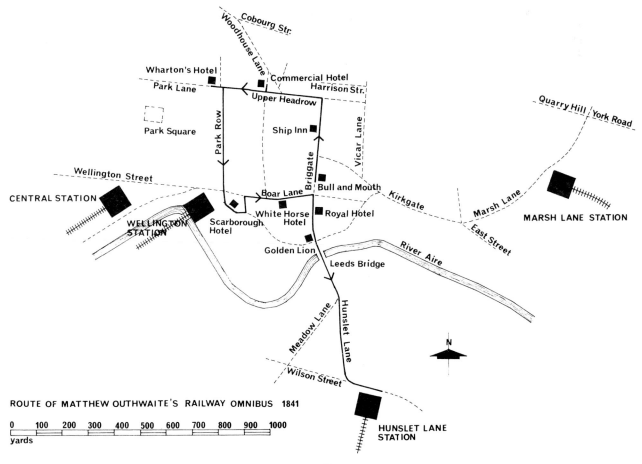

ROUTE OF MATTHEW OUTHWAITE'S RAILWAY OMNIBUS 1841

0 100 200 300 400 500 600 700 800 900 1000
yards

and officially known as the Wellington Station, but locally referred to as the "Bradford Station." From 2nd April 1849 all the passenger trains at the Hunslet Lane Station were transferred to the Wellington Station, as also were the 'buses.

The Leeds and Dewsbury Railway was opened for passenger traffic on 15th September 1848 and this resulted in a new railway station being built further west along Wellington Street. This station was to become the Central Station and not only served the Leeds and Dewsbury Railway, but also, later, the Leeds and Thirsk and Great Northern Railways.

By the early 'fifties the 'buses serving the two railway stations had become chaotic and the Great Northern Railway Company attempted to rectify this by running 'buses at fixed times in connection with certain of their trains. From 14th April 1851 they ran 'buses from the Central Station meeting trains from London due in Leeds at 2.30 pm, 4.30 pm and 6.30 pm. Unfortunately they did not advertise the route of the 'buses and they presumably went on a tour of the local inns. This attempt to run a regular service was apparently short lived. Thereafter, during the 'fifties and until the coming of the electric tramway, the concept of the railway 'bus as a public service vehicle, albeit carrying railway passengers only, but operating a fixed route and fixed timetable, disappeared and it ran more on the lines of a hackney coach. The Railway Companies, some of the later horse 'bus proprietors and many hotels and inns in the town operated railway 'buses, but these appear to have been entirely on a private hire basis.

A Railway 'bus loads outside the "Bull and Mouth", Briggate.

CHAPTER TWO

The Horse Omnibuses
1838—1860

In the 1830's the stage coach in Leeds was in its heyday. It reached its zenith in 1838 when 130 arrivals and departures were daily made from the town to all parts of the country. The stage coach proprietors were not interested in the provision of short distance transport and the inhabitants would not tolerate the rate of fares which could be coerced from railway passengers on the railway 'bus. 'Bus services would probably be unremunerative.

Earlier efforts to introduce stage coaches on short distance routes within the town had been abysmal failures. As early as 15th August 1818 a stage coach, the *'Woodpecker'*, was introduced by a James Sykes on a circuitous route to the west of Leeds to Wortley, Bramley and Pudsey. It made one journey daily from the "Talbot Inn", Briggate at 8.0 am in the morning and returned by the same route in the evening, but only ran for a short period.

A new westerly turnpike road was constructed from Wellington Road through Armley and Bramley to Stanningley during 1835 and 1836 and, on 1st November of

An advertisement for the Bramley coach, 1836.

the latter year, Isaac Morley, innkeeper of the "Cardigan Arms", Bramley, introduced a market coach making four journeys on Tuesdays and Saturdays from the "Griffin Inn", West Bar, to his establishment at Bramley. The coach also made one journey on Mondays, Wednesdays, Thursdays and Fridays. The fare was said to be 9d. each way, but this coach, too, was short lived.

Population movements were taking place in Leeds. The merchants and better off who lived west of Briggate in the Park Square and Park Row area were moving out of the town centre as commerce took over. They went to outlying villages some two miles to the north: Headingley, Chapeltown and Roundhay, where many large houses and villas were being built. Their houses in Park Row were pulled down and replaced by sharebrokers offices — a reflection of the railway boom of the late 'thirties and early 'forties — and later banks and insurance company offices. This area was to become the commercial and banking centre of the town.

By 1838 a demand for a service of some kind for transport of passengers from Headingley and Chapeltown to Leeds had become apparent and the residents of Headingley banded together to form a company to run a 'bus between their village and Leeds. The institution of this regular 'bus service on or about Monday 25th June 1838, just three days before the Coronation of Queen Victoria, can be said to mark the real beginning of suburban transport in Leeds. Press comment was brief:—

"A very neat omnibus has commenced running from Headingley to Leeds for the accommodation of merchants and others. The fare is only 6d."

(Leeds Mercury, 30th June 1838).

The 'bus was operated by John Wood, a cab proprietor of Headingley, and ran five journeys daily from the "Nag's Head", Upperhead Row, via Woodhouse Lane and Headingley Road (later Headingley Lane) to the "Three Horse Shoes" at Far Headingley, a distance of about three miles.

Popular legend, unsupported unfortunately by contemporary facts, states that the first Leeds 'bus conductor was a David Binns, who presumably conducted Wood's 'bus. He was a well-known character in Leeds and a noted huntsman, yeoman and musician. David died in 1886 in his 70th year.

"Of his versatility much might be written. As a cornet player he acknowledged no peer in Leeds, or in Yorkshire, for that matter, at that time. It was his custom to entertain his passengers with lively music on his favourite instrument on the way to Headingley, and every

morn he fairly made the welkin ring again as he trilled out his blatant brass notes while his chariot was rolling over Woodhouse Moor."
(Yorkshire Evening Post, 15th May 1905).

Wood's vehicle was well patronised and this did not escape the notice of Thomas Lee who instituted a similar 'bus service between the "Golden Lion", Briggate and Chapeltown, a 2½ mile journey, on 1st August 1838. The 'bus made five journeys daily and the fare was 6d.

With his profits Wood gradually cleared his debts to the company of residents and in November 1839 completed payment for the 'bus. He must have had some

A contemporary drawing of James Binns.
Courtesy Leeds City Libraries.

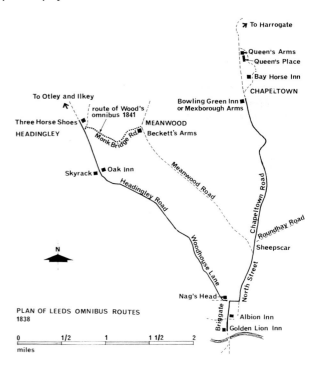

PLAN OF LEEDS OMNIBUS ROUTES
1838

A typical horse 'bus of the early 1840's.

6

altercation with the landlord of the "Nag's Head" as, on 2nd November 1839, he announced that his starting point was to be moved four doors away to the "Wheat Sheaf".

The stage coach proprietors were now beginning to feel the cold draught of railway competition. The Leeds and Manchester and Leeds and London lines were soon to be opened and John and William Atkinson took the opportunity to run an opposition 'bus from the vacated "Nag's Head" to the "Spen Lane Tavern", Far Headingley. The location of this inn is uncertain. The 'bus, known as the 'Mazeppa', which had been used in conjunction with Atkinson's stage coaches to Harrogate during the summer season of 1839, began operation in December performing six journeys daily. Whereas Wood stopped at the "Oak Inn", Headingley, en route, Atkinson's stopped at the "Skyrack" at the opposite side of the road. Wood charged 6d. any distance, but Atkinson's fares were Leeds to Woodhouse 4d. and Woodhouse to Headingley 4d. with a through fare of 6d.

On 17th August 1840 Atkinsons also instituted an opposition 'bus from the "Albion" to the "Mexborough Arms", Chapeltown, running four journeys daily (five on Sundays). At first the 'bus was operated jointly with a Thomas Gamble, but Gamble does not appear to have remained a partner for long, and Atkinson's took over sole charge.

An ambitious service was introduced in early October 1840 by John Moreton, the landlord of the "John O'Gaunts Inn", Rothwell Haigh, a village some 3½ miles south east of Leeds. He put on a 'bus between his inn and the "Old George Inn", Briggate, running twice daily. The return fare was 1s. 0d. and single fare 9d. The 'bus ran largely through open countryside and was not successful. On 27th October the service was reduced to run four days per week, Tuesday, Thursday, Saturday and Sunday, but shortly afterwards it was discontinued.

The tenth of March 1841 saw the death of Thomas Lee and the disposal of his assets. The coaching business passed to Dorothy Hollings of the "White Horse Inn", and the Chapeltown 'bus was taken over by

Matthew Pearson, cab proprietor and landlord of the "Bay Horse Inn", Chapeltown.

On 19th June 1841 Atkinson's announced that they were giving up running stage coaches due to railway competition and concentrating their efforts on the livery stable, hackney coach and omnibus business. They left the "Albion" and continued their activities from their stables in Harrison Street, off Vicar Lane. Their place at the "Albion" was taken by Messrs. Bradford, Wood, Forrest and Firth. This firm ran stage coaches and railway 'buses until 1842 when the partnership split up. Atkinson's stated that they had put on an "elegant new omnibus" called the 'Wellington' running to Headingley and serving the new Leeds Zoological and Botanical Gardens, Headingley, which were opened on 8th July 1840. These gardens, to the west of the 'bus route near to the "Oak Inn", were very popular with the Leeds inhabitants and regularly featured fêtes, galas, shows, bands, balloon ascents and, in June 1847, even witnessed the trial of a compressed air railway. They were an important generator of traffic for the Headingley area from their inception to closure on 1st July 1858. The 'Mazeppa' 'bus was apparently transferred to the Chapeltown route.

During September 1841, John Wood, who only owned one 'bus, had to take it off the road for repair and renovation and it returned to service on 4th October running an extra journey to Headingley, making a total of six daily. Two of the journeys were extended to the east to the "Becketts Arms", Meanwood, running from Headingley via Monk Bridge Road.

The following summer (from 4th July 1842), Wood increased the service to seven journeys per day owing to the increased demand for 'buses to the Zoological and Botanical Gardens. On 28th November the same year an increase of service also occurred on the Chapeltown route when Matthew Pearson announced that his 'bus, the 'Royal Sovereign', would undertake six daily journeys from the "Golden Lion" to the "Bay Horse", Chapeltown.

John Wood could not meet the competition from Atkinson's and, in February 1845, he was declared bankrupt. He did, however, retain his 'bus and ran it on a private hire basis for a year or two. Wood's place was taken by William Morritt whose 'bus left the "Wheat Sheaf" as before. The connection to Meanwood was apparently discontinued with the departure of Wood, but, by 1847, a 'bus was running twice daily to Meanwood from the "Wheat Sheaf" and "Commercial Inn", and was probably worked by Morritt. By 1849 the Meanwood 'bus is recorded as running from the "Nag's Head," "Wheat Sheaf" and "Black Swan" three journeys daily, but by 1851 it had been discontinued.

The Littlewood and Morritt partnership and Atkinson's, in co-operation rather than competition, operated the Headingley 'bus route until March 1853 when Littlewood and Morritt broke up due to the bankruptcy of Morritt. Littlewood paid off Morritt's debts incurred on his 'bus and coach activities. Littlewood, with Atkinson's, enjoyed the monopoly of the Headingley route for the next ten or so years.

During the period from 1845 to the early 'sixties the two firms provided a service of 12 journeys daily (six each) to Headingley, running approximately hourly. The first 'bus left Leeds at 9.0 am and the last at 8.30 pm (apart from a brief period about 1851, when the last 'bus is recorded as leaving at 9.0 pm).

Atkinson's continued to run to Chapeltown, Matthew

■ Nags Head

Briggate

■ Old George Inn

Leeds Bridge

Hunslet Lane

Low Road

Church Str

N

HUNSLET

◆ Crooked Billet Inn

Barnsdale and Leeds Turnpike Road

To Wakefield ↓

ROTHWELL HAIGH
John O'Gaunt's Inn ◆

To Pontefract

ROUTE OF MORETON'S OMNIBUS 1840

0   1/2   1   1 1/2   2
miles

Pearson's interests passing to his widow, Isabella, on his death on 16th March 1845. Isabella did not retain an interest in the 'bus for long, but ran cabs until about 1848. The 'Royal Sovereign' passed to Atkinson's who had the monopoly of Chapeltown until October 1846, when Morritt "in compliance with the request of the inhabitants" introduced a new 'bus making four daily trips from the "Bull and Mouth", Briggate to the "Bowling Green Inn", later known as the "Mexborough Arms", Chapeltown.

After their departure from the "Albion", Atkinson's changed the starting point for their 'buses to the "Black Swan" in North Street and, following the takeover of Pearson's business, they also ran from the "Golden Lion". By 1848, however, the "Golden Lion" starting point was changed to the "Old George Inn" on the opposite side of Briggate and, by 1851, Littlewood and Morritt started from the "Black Swan" in addition to their normal starting points of the "Bull and Mouth" and "Royal Hotel." By 1847 Atkinson's had extended their terminal point from the "Mexborough Arms" to the "Queen's Arms" ½ mile on the opposite side of Chapeltown village. Littlewood and Morritt altered their ter-

minus to Queen's Place, Chapeltown, near to the "Queen's Arms".

In 1847 Littlewood and Morritt's Chapeltown 'bus was known as the 'Mazeppa' and was presumably acquired from Atkinson's. The two proprietors were running a total of seven journeys daily to Chapeltown (five on Sundays), but, by 1848, this was increased to 11 per day (Atkinson's seven and Littlewood and Morritt four). An opposition 'bus was also running from the "Saddle", Briggate, proprietor unknown, making four daily journeys. It ran at similar times to the existing 'buses, but went out of business by the following year. In 1848, therefore, the Chapeltown residents had no fewer than 15 'buses per day, the first leaving Leeds at 9.0 am and the last at 9.0 pm (later changed to 8.45 pm). This good service was continued by the two proprietors with seven journeys each until about 1856 when Littlewood reduced the number of his journeys to four.

The Chapeltown service was operated by the two firms in a similar spirit to their Headingley route. Two 'buses, Atkinson's 'Royal Sovereign' and Littlewood's 'Mazeppa' dominated the scene on Chapeltown Road until the early 1860's.

Meanwhile on the Kirkstall route, John Cockill's cars, referred to in Chapter 1, were still running to the village in 1841, but, by 1843, they were apparently replaced by a 'bus driven and probably owned by Robert Johnson, a livery stable keeper of Swinegate, off Lower Briggate. Johnson's 'bus ran from the "Griffin" "several times a day."

Cockill owned a 'bus which ran along Kirkstall Road, but it appears to have been used solely on the Leeds

Typical horse 'bus and coach advertisements of the 1840's. Leeds and Chapeltown is from the 'Leeds Mercury' of 26th November 1842 and Leeds, Burley and Kirkstall from the 'Leeds Intelligencer' of 26th April 1845. The illustrations give a good idea of the type of vehicles used.
Courtesy Leeds City Libraries.

and Bradford service in competition with the stage coaches running to Bradford via Kirkstall and the Leeds and Bradford Road. In May 1850 the 'bus and Cockill's other rolling stock were offered for sale, but were apparently not sold. Cockill continued to run his Bradford 'bus until the opening of the direct railway link between Leeds and Bradford on 31st July 1854.

Cockill's 'bus was driven by his son Joseph, a well-known character on Kirkstall Road, who was often in court for minor offences in connection with his 'bus. On one occasion he was charged at Bradford with having driven his horses up the Leeds Road at a full gallop:–

"The defendant denied the charge, saying he defied all the men in Bradford to flog his horses onto a gallop, one of them being 29 years old and all four were not worth £5."

(Leeds Mercury, 29th September 1851).

John Cockill remained at the "Woodman", Kirkstall, advertising a coaching and cab business, until his death on 13th November 1863.

Robert Johnson seems to have gone out of business by 1845 for, at this time, Edward Beeston, a cab proprietor, and William Randall, a stage coach proprietor, were jointly operating a 'bus from both the "Cock and Bottle", Upperhead Row and the "Saracen's Head", Boar Lane, to Burley and the "Star and Garter" at Kirkstall. From 1st May 1845 the 'bus service was advertised to run five journeys daily with four on Sundays. The first 'bus left Leeds at 8.0 am and the last at 7.30 pm.

Although the Kirkstall 'buses were advertised to run to Burley and Kirkstall, it seems unlikely that they went directly along Burley Road and through the village of Burley to Kirkstall. This area was very sparsely populated and the 'buses would have had to negotiate Kirkstall Hill, which would be almost impassable for a horse-drawn vehicle. Unsuccessful attempts to run 'buses along Burley Road were made in the late 'fifties and early 'sixties. It seems most probable that the 'buses travelled along Kirkstall Road, which was fairly well populated as far as the "Cardigan Arms" and almost level the whole of the way – ideal for horse 'buses. The village of Burley was passed at a distance of a few hundred yards on the right.

Edward Beeston, whose premises were in Albion Street, had his licence as a cab proprietor revoked for assaulting the "Superintendent of Scavengers" (dustmen) in January 1849. Soon afterwards he left the partnership with Randall. Randall and his family were particularly notorious characters, frequently in court, and whose principal activity was the running of 'buses and stage coaches in fierce competition on the road from Leeds to Wakefield and Barnsley from 1845 until the railway took over in the middle 'fifties.

Randall continued to run the Kirkstall 'bus until about 1855 when it ceased operation probably due to railway competition, and also competition from a "twopenny 'bus" which ran over the most lucrative built-up part of the route as far as Cardigan Place, Kirkstall Road. This 'bus will be mentioned later.

A stage coach, later replaced by a 'bus, had been travelling along Kirkstall Road through Kirkstall and Horsforth to Guiseley replacing the cars introduced in the early 'thirties. This probably made a slight contribution to the closure of the Kirkstall 'bus service, although it only made one journey on each of the market days from the "Wheat Sheaf". It also made one journey on Thursdays from Guiseley to Bradford. By 1847 the 'bus was operated by James Crabtree of Guiseley.

We will now turn to the village of Roundhay.

"Roundhay is a township and genteel village in the parish of Barwick-in-Elmet, Wapentake of Skyrack, West Riding, situated on the main road from Leeds to Wetherby about 2½ miles north east from the former town. The views round here are very pleasing, the land well wooded and the air remarkable for its salubrity. These local advantages have attracted the notice of the merchants of Leeds whose elegant villas, walks and plantations form delightful adjuncts to the general scenery."

(Slater's Directory of the Northern Counties, 1848).

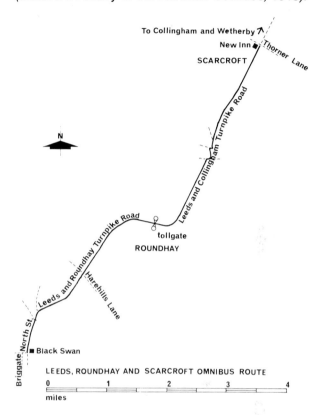

LEEDS, ROUNDHAY AND SCARCROFT OMNIBUS ROUTE

In 1831 the population of Roundhay was 314 and, by 1841, it had increased to 439. It was to this small village of wealthy residents, who invariably owned their own carriages, that Peter Outhwaite (possibly related to Matthew Outhwaite), a cab proprietor of Roundhay, hopefully instituted, on 23rd May 1843, a "light conveyance" running from the "Black Swan" to the toll bar at Roundhay, four journeys daily. By 1845 the vehicle was referred to as an "omnibus" and the service was reduced to three journeys daily. In addition to his Roundhay 'bus Outhwaite also ran a seasonal 'bus through Roundhay between the "Black Swan" and the spa village of Thorp Arch. This was some 14 miles north east of Leeds and the 'bus ran during the summer seasons of 1844 and 1845.

Advertisement for the Scarcroft and Leeds Omnibus, from the 'Leeds Mercury' of 5th July 1845.
Courtesy Leeds City Libraries.

An extension of the Roundhay 'bus service occurred when Outhwaite announced, on 5th July 1845, that he was operating a 'bus from the "Black Swan" to Scarcroft (a village some three miles beyond Roundhay on the Wetherby Road). The 'bus left the "New Inn", Scarcroft at 8.45 am and returned from the "Black Swan" at 4.15 pm. It would appear that Roundhay, with its small population, could not support a service of three 'buses per day. By a route extension to Scarcroft (population 240) and reducing the service, it would be financially viable. This surmise was later to be proved correct for other proprietors, as Outhwaite only ran the service until April 1847, when he advertised his 'bus and horses for sale.

There was no 'bus service to Roundhay for some months but, by June 1848, two competing firms of omnibus proprietors, Littlewood & Morritt and Wood & Germaine were working the route. Their 'buses left the "New Inn and "Black Swan" at the same times as Outhwaite's previous 'bus. Littlewood and Morritt have already been mentioned and Jacob Wood and John Germaine had been in partnership as stage coach proprietors from 1843. This was apparently their first venture as 'bus operators. Germaine appears to have left the partnership in late 1848. He carried on a business as a cab proprietor at his premises in Great George Street for a number of years, but there is no record of him running any further 'buses.

Wood, whose stables were in North Street, was a particularly notorious individual, of similar character to William Randall, and was involved in the reckless stage coach and 'bus competition on the Leeds, Wakefield and Barnsley road. Following court appearances in 1848 and 1849 for using unlicensed coaches, "racing" with other omnibus and coach proprietors, and finally having a stage coach seized by the court for "furious driving", he decided to pack up and his business was auctioned on 9th July 1849. His assets were listed as one stage coach, three 'buses, four hackney coaches, two cabs and 21 horses.

Three days prior to the sale Littlewood and Morritt, who had now formed a partnership with William Hollings of the "White Horse", in connection with the Roundhay service, advertised that they had acquired Jacob Wood's interest in the Roundhay and Scarcroft 'bus. Hollings had taken over the family coaching business from his mother, Dorothy, following her death on 2nd June 1847.

It is recorded that the 'bus carried the mail between Leeds and the two villages and in November 1850 the three partners stated that they would enter into "annual contracts for passengers and parcels on moderate terms." In 1850 Hollings took up the business of undertaking as an auxiliary to his 'bus and coaching interests and left the partnership at about the time of Morritt's bankruptcy in 1853. The coaching and omnibus firm of Hollings was established as early as 1815; it faded away when, in 1854, their one 'bus was sold and, in April the following year, their remaining coaches and cabs were disposed of. The purchaser was a former employee of 25 years standing, Edward Binnington. Binnington ran cabs, a railway 'bus and owned another 'bus, but the latter was apparently used solely on a private hire basis.

In 1851 the driver of the 'bus was a John Machan, employed by Littlewood and Morritt. Machan, stated by the Leeds Town Clerk to be "a steady driver and a civil man", had to contend with an opposition 'bus put on by Jacob Wood. Wood vacated his premises in North

A "race" between Machan and Wood.

Street in 1849 and moved with his son, William, to Scarcroft. He re-entered the omnibus business and his 'bus left both Scarcroft and Leeds at the same times as Machan's vehicle.

Machan appears to have gradually purchased his 'bus from Littlewood and Morritt and, by 1854, he was the owner. He courageously fought a continuous battle with Wood and Son (Jacob being the 'bus driver and William the guard). He was frequently in court for "racing" with Wood and, in virtually all the cases, Wood was found to be in the wrong. A race along North Street, in August 1853, in which Wood collided with a lamp post, fell from his 'bus, and was severely injured, did not stop the competition. It was not until the following incident took place that the opposition finally ceased:–

"The specific obstruction took place on 14th inst. when it was proved that both the defendant's omnibuses stood for at least 25 minutes in front of the Black Swan Inn, bottom of Lowerhead Row. During this time both the defendants were engaged in looking out for passengers, and a Mrs. Bramma who wished to go by Machan's 'bus, was, on making her appearance, seized by the defendant Wood, who wished her to patronise his 'bus. The two defendants did their best to secure the fare, and in the end they quarrelled, and it was alleged pushed at and struck one another, though Mrs Bramma said Wood only struck, and that she saw no fighting. However there was a blow from the defendant Wood, intended for Machan, which a woman named Woodruff, who came up at the time, received and was knocked down, Wood falling upon her. On being lifted up by the defendant Wood she fell sick and was taken into the Black Swan until she recovered. This stir, of course, attracted a great crowd, which added still more to the obstruction in the street" ——

(Leeds Mercury, 26th November 1853)

The two drivers were fined £2 each and had to provide securities of £30 each to keep the peace for six months. Wood now disappeared from the scene. No further mention has been found of him and he was not listed as a resident of Scarcroft in the 1861 census returns. Machan later established stables at Scarcroft and now had sole command of the 'buses on Roundhay Road. He was to retain this for almost 20 years.

When the Scarcroft service was introduced by Peter Outhwaite only one departure was apparently made from Leeds, but from 1847 onwards the service was operated as follows:–

Dep. "New Inn," Scarcroft for Roundhay and Leeds at 8.30 am.

Dep. "Black Swan," Leeds for Roundhay only at 11.45 am.

Dep. Roundhay for Leeds at 1.00 pm.

Dep. "Black Swan," Leeds for Roundhay and Scarcroft at 4.15 pm.

During the Littlewood, Morritt and Hollings involvement, departures were also made from the "Royal Hotel" and "White Horse". There were slight variations to the timetable but this arrangement continued through to the 'seventies.

From 1835 onwards William Adkin, a coach proprietor of Thorp Arch, ran a summer seasonal coach known as the 'Providence' from the "Three Legs Inn", Call Lane, Leeds to his spa village. The coach made one journey on Tuesdays, Thursdays and Saturdays; the Thursday coach usually ran via York Road, Seacroft, Thorner and Bramham and the Tuesday and Saturday coaches via Kiddal Lane. During the 1853 season Adkin put on a Monday morning coach from Thorp Arch via Collingham to Scarcroft and formed a connection with the 'bus to Leeds. There is no record of the 'Providence' running after the 1855 season or of this arrangement being repeated.

Seasonal coaches had been running from Leeds to Boston Spa and Thorp Arch from as early as 1792, but in the 1860's 'buses were largely used. Henry Littlewood ran a seasonal Sundays only coach from the "Royal Hotel" and "Black Swan" to "Dalby's Hotel", Thorp Arch from 1850 to 1865. The route was normally via Thorner and Bramham, but during the 1857 season it ran via Roundhay, Scarcroft and Collingham. On 1st May 1865 a seasonal daily service (Sundays excepted) was introduced by a Thomas Howard from the "Old George", "Saddle" and "Black Swan" to "Dalby's Hotel". Howard continued this seasonal service until 1870 and for a few days in July and August 1871. Sunday services could not have been very profitable for, during 1866, Thomas Cammage, a cab proprietor, ran the service for one Sunday only and then transferred his 'bus to a route between Leeds and Harewood. During 1868 a John Ramsden ran a Sundays only service. Both Howard and Ramsden and other services to Boston Spa will be mentioned in the next chapter.

By 1845, in addition to the Chapeltown, Headingley, Kirkstall and Roundhay services, buses were also running to Halton and Whitkirk to the east of Leeds and Morley to the south. Unfortunately the practice of advertising 'bus services was not undertaken as frequently in the middle 'forties as in the earlier period and no details are known when these services were started.

Halton and Whitkirk were two farming and mining villages on the Leeds and Selby Turnpike Road. The "pleasant village of Whitkirk" was four miles to the east of Leeds. Halton was smaller and nearer to the town. The villages were partly served by a station at Cross Gates, on the Leeds and Selby Railway, but this did not reduce the need for a 'bus service. The 'buses ran "several times a day" from the "Horse and Jockey", Commercial Street (off Briggate) and the "Free Market Hotel" later known as the "Bradford Hotel". By 1847 the

LEEDS, ROUNDHAY AND SCARCROFT OMNIBUS ROUTE									1843 TO 1876
proprietor	years of operation								notes
	1845	1850	1855	1860	1865	1870	1875	1880	
OUTHWAITE, Peter	▬▬								business sold April 1847
LITTLEWOOD AND MORRITT		▪							Hollings joined partnership c.1849
WOOD AND GERMAINE		▮							Germaine left ,, late 1848
WOOD, Jacob		▪ ▬▬							ceased running c.1854
LITTLEWOOD, MORRITT & HOLLINGS		▬▬							Machan took over c.1853
MACHAN, John			▬▬▬▬▬▬▬▬▬▬▬						Richard Machan took over 1873
MACHAN, Richard							▬▬		re-routed via Moortown 1876

11

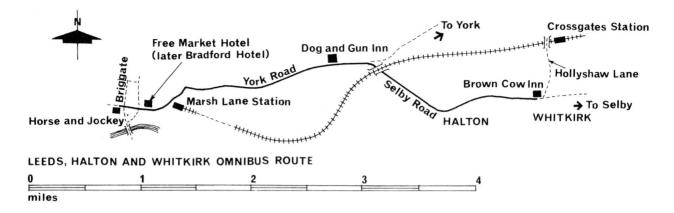

LEEDS, HALTON AND WHITKIRK OMNIBUS ROUTE

service was reduced to three journeys daily. No details have been traced of the proprietor.

By 1848 Littlewood and Morritt were running an opposition 'bus three times daily from the "Royal Hotel" and "Bull and Mouth", but this was withdrawn in 1849. The original service was unchanged during the 1850's but during the latter part of this period was being operated by a John Coates, cab proprietor of Leeds.

Parallel with the Halton and Whitkirk route was a 'bus or coach running to Garforth, a village two miles further to the east. This was in operation by 1847 and ran only once on market days from the "Horse and Jockey" and "Bradford Hotel". By the late 'fifties this 'bus was also run by John Coates.

The Morley 'bus service ran from the "Saddle" three times daily. It travelled along Elland Road to the large clothing village of Morley, four to five miles south west of Leeds. Morley boasted a large stone quarry, still in existence, and a population of 4,822. By 1847 the 'bus also ran from the "George", but the service was reduced to two journeys daily. An opposition 'bus running at the same times departed from the "Malt Shovel" and "New Cross", Meadow Lane, to the south of Briggate.

Two firms of omnibus proprietors, Messrs. Clark, Elam and Co. and Rayner, Mortimer, Garnett and Co. existed in Morley at this time and presumably ran the rival 'buses. It appears that their 'buses were well patronised as there were complaints, in 1847, of overloading and consequent cruelty to the horses. The 'buses continued in operation until the opening of the London and North Western Railway between Leeds, Dewsbury and Huddersfield on 18th September 1848, the railway station at Morley rendering them superfluous. "Two good omnibuses that lately ran between Leeds and Morley named 'Industry' and 'Free Trader'" were sold on 28th November the same year. William Smith in his book "Morley, Ancient and Modern", published in 1886, stated that the rival 'buses were "daily crowded" and one of them was known as the 'Cuckoo'.

With the exception of part of the Kirkstall route and possibly Morley, Halton and Whitkirk, all 'bus services in operation until 1847 had served middle or upper class districts.

Apart from Moreton's brief effort in 1840, an area which had been neglected by the omnibus proprietors was the rapidly expanding working class industrial district, two miles south of the river, known as Hunslet. Perhaps the proprietors felt that the labourers and artisans would not be able to afford the fares, but in January 1847, J. and W. Atkinson took the initiative and began a service from the "Nag's Head", calling at the various inns en route, via Hunslet Lane and Low Road to the

"Crooked Billett", Hunslet. The 'bus made five journeys daily. The timetable was operated in conjunction with their Headingley 'bus and, by a change of 'bus at the "Nag's Head", a direct connection between Headingley and Hunslet resulted.

The residents of Hunslet were apparently conscious of their class as the 'bus used was divided into first and second class sections. The fare was 3d. from Briggate to Hunslet, but was 4d. in the "first compartment". The 'bus was presumably single-deck and this is the only instance that has been found of a 'bus of this type running with first and second class compartments in Leeds. Inside passengers by stage coach always paid more than outside passengers and this practice was continued on the double-deck buses until about the 1870's. All the early 'buses in Leeds appear to have been of the saloon single-deck type of various seating capacities, and similar in construction to 'buses in London and other large towns. The smaller 'buses would have had three side windows with possibly up to six windows for the larger vehicles. The first double-deck 'buses fitted with "Knifeboard" seats (passengers sitting back to back), appeared in London in April 1847, but were not to be seen in Leeds until the early 1860's.

By 1847 a 'bus was running twice daily from the "Cock and Bottle" and "Saddle" to Holbeck, Armley and Wortley, working class areas to the south and west of Leeds, apparently operated by Messrs. Beeston and Randall. The route is uncertain and the service appears to have been discontinued shortly after the break up of the partnership in 1849, probably due to competition from the railways, which were spreading a network over this area.

In 1847 a 'bus called the 'Busy Bee' was running between the "Griffin" and Bramley, making four journeys on market days and one journey on the other days of the week. It was short lived and was discontinued by the following year.

An economic depression was prevalent in Leeds and the country as a whole in the late 1840's and this, together with railway competition, resulted in the early demise of some of these 'bus routes. The ten or so suburban 'bus services listed as being in operation in 1847 were reduced to six by 1851, as follows:—

Burley and Kirkstall.
Chapeltown.
Halton, Whitkirk and Garforth.
Headingley.
Hunslet.
Roundhay and Scarcroft.

Other 'bus services, however, appeared in the 'fifties. The first cross town 'bus route in Leeds was introduced at the end of May 1852. An enterprising livery stable

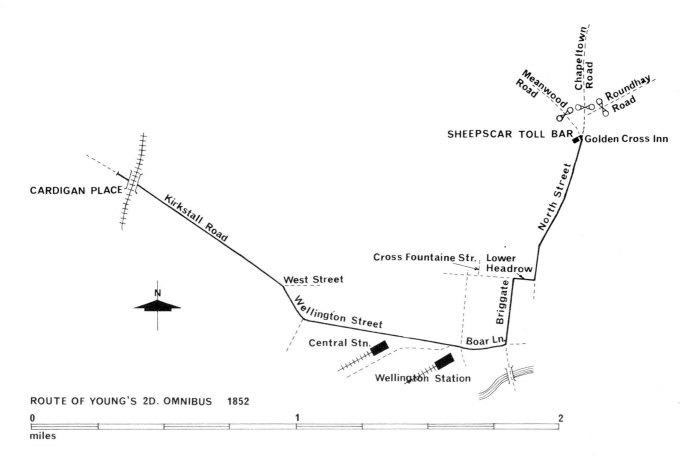

CARDIGAN PLACE

Kirkstall Road

West Street

Wellington Street

Central Stn.

Wellington Station

Cross Fountaine Str.

Lower Headrow

Briggate

Boar Ln.

North Street

SHEEPSCAR TOLL BAR | Golden Cross Inn

Meanwood Road

Chapeltown Road

Roundhay Road

N

ROUTE OF YOUNG'S 2D. OMNIBUS 1852

0   1   2
miles

keeper and horse riding instructor, James Young, of Cross Fountaine Street (off Guildford Street) started the service, which ran from the toll bar at Sheepscar to Cardigan Place, Kirkstall Road, a very moderate through fare of 2d. being charged.

The 'bus was in direct competition with the Chapeltown and Roundhay 'buses as far as Sheepscar and with the Kirkstall 'bus at the other end of the route, each of which charged a 6d. fare. It ran hourly from the "Golden Cross," Sheepscar from 8.0 am to 8.0 pm (13 journeys per day), and traversed North Street, Lowerhead Row, Briggate and Boar Lane, the central business part of the town, passed both railway stations, Wellington Street and Kirkstall Road.

This "twopenny 'bus" deserved to pay, but was not successful and was withdrawn by Young in 1856. A new proprietor, Joseph Hartley and Co. re-introduced the service on 23rd March 1857; the fare was increased, being 2d. from either terminus to Briggate with a through fare of 3d. The proprietor "begged to solicit the patronage of the public" but his 'bus also did not pay and was soon withdrawn. This was apparently both Hartley and Young's only venture into the omnibus business.

To the south east the township of Rothwell had neither a coach nor a bus service from the failure of Moreton's attempt to introduce a service in 1840. By 1857, however, John Squires, of Call Lane, Leeds, was running a 'bus from the "Elephant and Castle", Hunslet Lane, making one journey on each of the market days.

The Rothwell service paralleled the route of Atkinson's Hunslet 'buses giving some opposition, but was much greater when Squires began a daily service from the "Elephant and Castle" and Hunslet itself. Squires' 'bus made four journeys per day. Competition was not encouraged and in many cases not tolerated. The Hunslet district was an example of the latter where Atkinsons' had enjoyed a complete monopoly of the service since its inception. A "fine chase" resulted. Squires ran his

opposition 'bus until about 1861 when Atkinsons extended and increased the frequency of their service and forced him off the road. He continued to run to Rothwell for a number of years.

Burley, between Kirkstall and Headingley and 1½ miles north west of Leeds, was a "neat rural hamlet of scattered houses and villas" and in the 1850's had seen some new housing. Joseph Ackroyd, a cab proprietor of Waterloo Street, off Hunslet Lane, introduced a 'bus service in April 1858. The 'bus intended for "the gentry and inhabitants of Burley, Burley Lawn and the upper part of Kirkstall" made three journeys daily (9.45 am, 1.0 pm and 6.0 pm) from the "Golden Fleece Inn", Briggate to St. Anns Lane, Burley. There were two journeys on Sunday and the fare was 4d. from Leeds to Burley Lawn and 6d. to the terminus. The 'bus was soon withdrawn and appears to have been the first of several attempts by the 'bus proprietors to run a paying service to Burley. This was apparently Ackroyd's only endeavour to establish a suburban 'bus service, but he later ran a 'bus to Ilkley and ran cabs for many years.

The closure of the Royal Gardens (formerly the Zoological and Botanical Gardens) at Headingley, and near to Burley, in 1858, resulted in the formation of a new road from Burley through the park to Headingley. This road was later to be known as Cardigan Road and in the 'eighties and 'nineties boasted a horse 'bus route. The park was sold in small plots and many "desirable villas and houses" were built. Eventually the area became sufficiently built up to provide profitable 'bus services.

During the 1850's the traffic congestion in Briggate and Boar Lane became intolerable. Narrow Boar Lane was particularly bad and businessmen often missed trains. Complaints were frequent:—

"At one time you see a continuous string of coal carts and wagons, then a stream of wherries laden with goods of various kinds; and next, a succession of ve-

Boar Lane was frequently impassable on market days.

hicles —omnibuses, flies, cabs etc. and a crowd of foot passengers proclaiming the arrival of a railway train. This picture may also be reversed there being at all times also vehicles and passengers going west for the trains departing; and woe betide many an anxious traveller who flatters himself on seeing the clock at Trinity Church, that he may just reach the station in time to catch a train, not at all reckoning on finding his carriage blocked up amongst carts, and other vehicles further along the street. On the two market days, and the day of the fortnight cattle fair, every vacant space is filled up with cattle, sheep and pigs. This is no exaggerated statement, and those who are much in the street, see all the danger, especially to aged people and children, and the great inconvenience to the public at large."

(Leeds Mercury, 12th March 1853).

In an effort to improve matters the Town Council moved the fortnightly Cattle Market from Vicars Croft, Kirkgate to a field in North Street. The first market was held on the new site on 13th July 1853. The Tuesday and Saturday problems still continued, however, and the Corporation obtained an Act of Parliament for the removal of the market stalls from Briggate. A new permanent market was built in Kirkgate and there was also a small covered market in Duncan Street. Saturday 28th November 1857 was an historic day for Leeds as on that day the market stalls, which had stood in Briggate for centuries, were seen for the last time.

The removal of the market not only made things easier for the 'bus proprietors and traffic in general, but also had the important effect of reducing the need for market 'buses and coaches. Being on permanent prem-

OMNIBUSES,

To the Suburbs & surrounding Villages.

BRADFORD. (See preceding list.)

BURLEY & KIRKSTALL, from the Cock & Bottle, Saracen's Head, & Griffin Inns, at 8½ a.m., & 1, 5, & 8 p.m.

CHAPELTOWN, from the George, the Bull & Mouth, and the Royal Hotels, Briggate; & the Black Swan, North st. 7 times a day; only 4 times on Sun

HALTON & WHITKIRK, from the Horse & Jockey, Commercial street, and the Bradford Hotel, Kirkgate, at 8 a.m., and 1 & 6 p.m.

HEADINGLEY, from the Bull & Mouth & Royal Hotels, Briggate; the Nag's Head and Wheat Sheaf. Upperhead row, and the Commercial Inn, Upper Albion street. every hour, from 9 a.m to 8½ p.m. (Only 4 times on Sun.)

HUNSLET & THWAITEGATE, from the Nag's Head, Upperhead row, at 9 a.m., & 1¼, 4½, and 7 p.m.; also on Sat. at 8 p.m. (Sun. 8 p.m.)

ROUNDHAY & SCARCROFT, from the Royal Hotel, the White Horse and Black Swan, at 12 noon, & 4½ afternoon.

Part of a page from White's Directory of Leeds, 1853, indicating omnibus services.

ises the market was open on weekdays and the two official market days became less important. Some 'buses were later withdrawn. Examples were the Rothwell 'bus and a 'bus which ran between Leeds and the township of Gildersome between 1857 and 1861. Many of the coaches to local towns and villages were also discontinued, others varying their timetables. Outlying villages were slower to change and a Tuesdays and Saturdays only horse 'bus was still operating to Barwick, eight miles north east of Leeds, and Kippax, eight miles to the east, as late as the First World War.

During the 'fifties the 'bus scene in Leeds stagnated. The omnibus proprietors showed no interest in expanding or improving their services and the few new proprietors who appeared did not remain long. This was probably largely due to the existence of the turnpike roads which were penal to all who used them.

Prior to the construction of the turnpikes the roads in and around Leeds were in a deplorable state. Dr. Whitaker wrote *"They were sloughs almost impassable by single carts, where travellers who encountered each other sometimes tried to wear out each others patience rather than either would risk a deviation".*

During the late 18th and early 19th centuries the principal roads leading out of the town were put into a better state of repair. This was done by Acts of Parliament which enabled Turnpike Trusts to be set up for the various roads. The Trusts were enabled to repair existing roads or build entirely new roads. This system meant a great outlay of capital and a system of payment, or "tolls", was exacted from all vehicles using the turnpike. Toll bars were erected at strategic points to enable the money to be collected.

The traffic on the turnpikes had decreased considerably following the introduction of the railways and they became less important. Their revenue was lower and repairs nominal. Each year the revenue from the gates was let out to the highest bidder. This was accepted as the norm until the 1850's when the town expanded beyond the toll gates. The gates then became an intolerable imposition to those who used them daily. Bitter protests were frequent and "Pike", the toll collector, faced continual abuse. It was one thing to have to pay for the upkeep of a long section of road, all of which you were using; it was a totally different thing to have to pay daily for living less than a quarter of a mile past the toll bar.

All the early 'bus routes in Leeds traversed turnpike roads, resulting in high 'bus fares and consequently few passengers. The Leeds and Otley Turnpike Road, on which ran the Headingley 'buses, was the worst affected. A 'bus passenger travelling to the "Three Horse Shoes" passed through no fewer than five toll gates on his journey from Leeds. The omnibus proprietors made a daily payment and this became so high in 1851 that Messrs. Littlewood and Morritt and Atkinson objected:-

"Gentlemen, As we perceive your Turnpike Road is advertised to let, we take the liberty of informing you and also the future lessees that we shall no longer submit to the exorbitant demand of £1 per day extorted from us as toll.

When the omnibuses were first placed on the road a moderate composition was made with the proprietors on account of the great public accommodation they afforded, but since your present Surveyor was appointed we have been charged the highest toll the Act permits viz. 20 pence each double journey,

repeatedly paying the toll when the carriages are empty, and on applying for redress we have been requested (not very politely) to take the omnibuses off if they do not pay, the convenience of the inhabitants or justice to ourselves not being considered.

Private carriages pay toll once and pass as often as they please the same day. Of course we do not ask the same privilege, but we respectfully submit that a composition of £100 annually for each omnibus ought to be made with us.

If you still refuse to grant us redress, we have reluctantly come to the determination of withdrawing four double journeys daily, the inhabitants being deprived by your unreasonable demands of proper accommodation which we are anxious to afford.

We are Gentlemen, your obedient servants,
Littlewood and Morritt, J. and W. Atkinson, Leeds, 21st May 1851."
(Leeds Mercury, 24th May 1851).

The toll was reduced to ten shillings per 'bus per day.

In spite of the tolls there was room for improvement; the 'buses did not run to time and the old vehicles introduced in the 1840's were still running. The population of the town increased from 172,270 in 1851 to 207,165 in 1861, but there was no corresponding increase in any of the 'bus services. 'Buses were often overcrowded and so unreliable passengers turned to travelling by cab, the minimum fare of which was now 8d.

A bus ride to Headingley was often unpleasant:-

"I have had the misfortune to ride with people half drunk, three quarters drunk, quite drunk, noisy drunk, sleepy drunk, dead drunk. I have ridden with people who were 'the worse' for brandy, 'the worse' for beer, 'the worse' for gin, whisky, et hoc genus omne. The omnibus unfortunately for some of us, passes two or three places of resort in Briggate and elsewhere, where men in respectable positions congregate of an evening to talk and tipple, then ride home in a public conveyance to the disgust of all decent people. Could not a tipplers' omnibus be started for these should--be-gentlemen? I am not a teetotaller, but I hate to sit in a small compartment of about 4 feet wide by 6 feet long, with two, perhaps three redolent gentlemen trying to talk without stuttering, but none of whom could pronounce intelligibly the word "statistics", if it were to save his life. Let the omnibus for tipplers go round then, at some convenient hour, to the Royal, the Commercial, the Wheat Sheaf etc. etc. and pick up the intellectual ornaments of these several retreats. Punctuality would be a matter of no consequence to them," wrote 'Perambulator'.
(Leeds Mercury, 28th November 1857).

Another passenger 'Viator' commented:-

"The inconvenience and antiquated structure of the present conveyances cannot be too vividly described. If an unlucky gentleman, in an excess of politeness, should take the middle seat, to make room for a lady in the corner, and have to be the first to get out, it is almost a question for a civil engineer how it is to be done. If he get out on the lady's side he must inevitably carry with him almost an acre of petticoat. Or if he think egress that way impossible, he will very likely have to walk through a somewhat smaller space of sludge in the road, and then leap a miniature mountain of mud, which our road surveyors considerately leave at the road side from October to April. I must question if there be another town in the kingdom of the size of Leeds which

would tolerate such caricatures of omnibuses as these Headingley inconveniences. — But we must, somehow, have a new 'bus. One that will hold more and charge less; one that will start at the time it professes to do, and not keep you waiting 15 minutes in the wet and cold; one that will have a respectable and civil conductor, and not a little ragged dirty urchin from whose hands no decent person likes to take change; one that you can get out of without carrrying a large portion of your neighbour's clothes with you or treading on somebody's corns." (Leeds Mercury, 5th December, 1857).

A new 'bus was not provided; the omnibus proprietors sat and did nothing. It was to be John Greenwood, a Manchester proprietor who was to shake them from their complacency.

Stage coaches could still be seen in the 1890's. The picnic club of St. Martin's Church, Potternewton, Leeds, on an outing to Boston Spa. One of the passengers is blowing the horn.
Courtesy W. Nichols Photographer Leeds City Libraries.

CHAPTER THREE

The Sixties

Following the static period of the 1850's the position in 1860 was very similar to that of 1850. Suburban 'bus services in operation were as follows:–

CHAPELTOWN: From the "George", "Bull and Mouth", "Royal Hotel" and "Black Swan": 7 journeys per day (9.0 am to 8.30 pm) – 4 journeys on Sundays. Operated by J. and W. Atkinson and H. Littlewood.
HALTON AND WHITKIRK: From the "Horse and Jockey", "Ship Inn" and "Bradford Hotel": 3 journeys per day (9.0 am, 1.0 and 5.0 pm.) – Sundays 9.0 am, 2.0 pm and 8.0 pm. Operated by John Coates.
GARFORTH: From the "Bradford Hotel", Kirkgate: 1 journey daily at 5.0 pm – Sundays 2 journeys at 2.0 and 8.0 pm. Operated by John Coates.
HEADINGLEY: From the "Bull and Mouth", "Royal Hotel", "Nag's Head", "Wheat Sheaf" and "Commercial

Inn": 12 journeys per day (9.0 am to 8.30 pm) – 4 journeys on Sundays. Operated by J. and W. Atkinson and H. Littlewood.
HUNSLET: From the "Nag's Head" and "Elephant and Castle": 4 journeys per day (9.0 am to 7.0 pm). Operated by J. and W. Atkinson and J. Squires.
ROTHWELL: From the "Elephant and Castle" on Tuesday 5.30 pm and Saturday 8.0 pm. Operated by John Squires.
ROUNDHAY AND SCARCROFT: From the "Black Swan" twice daily, 12 noon and 4.30 pm. Operated by John Machan.
SEACROFT: From the "Beehive", Tuesday, Wednesday, Friday and Saturday at 4.30 pm. Saturday also at 10.30 am. Operated by William Mitchell.
GUISELEY: From the "Wheat Sheaf" on Tuesday and Saturday 3.30 pm. Operated by James Crabtree.

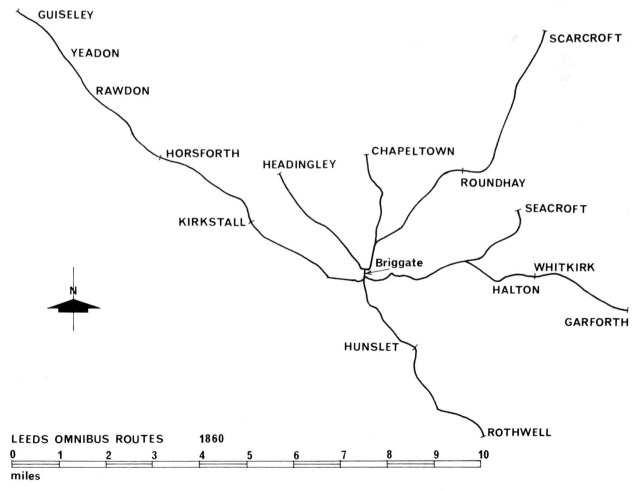

LEEDS OMNIBUS ROUTES   1860

It can be seen that a total of only 29 daily journeys (up to 32 on market days) were made from Leeds. The number of daily journeys in 1847 was approx. 35 and no routes had shown any improvement. The service to Hunslet was worse with one journey less than in 1847. The Headingley and Chapeltown services totalled 19 journeys, well over half the total number and these were by far the most important 'bus routes, and provided the greatest profit for the proprietors.

The earliest 'bus to leave Leeds was at 9.0 am and the last at 8.30 pm. The first journeys from the suburbs were the 8.20 am 'bus from Headingley and the 8.30 am 'buses from Chapeltown and Scarcroft. This poses a difficult social question as to who used these 'bus services and how.

The high fares, unchanged from the 'forties, and still 6d. to Chapeltown, Headingley and Roundhay, ensured that the bus was used almost exclusively by the middle and upper classes. The average weekly wage of a working man in 1860 was about 16s. 0d. and a 'bus ride was an unheard of luxury. An artisan or labourer would almost invariably walk to and from home to work. The late starting and early finishing times put 'buses out of the range of the working hours of people as the day usually began at 7.0 am or earlier. The 'bus could not, therefore, have been used for commuting and the middle class would also walk to work. It could not be used in the evening for entertainment as the last 'bus left Leeds long before the end of the performance at the theatre.

Stage coach and early 'bus advertisements were usually addressed to the "nobility, gentry, commercial gentlemen and members of the public", and it appears that it was to the wealthier that the omnibus proprietors directed their attention. By 1860 the 'bus was probably less used by the nobility and gentry who would take a cab, but was certainly extensively used by commercial travellers. Middle and upper class ladies and their servants used it on shopping expeditions; invalids, gentlemen, and members of the professions were also passengers. It is unlikely that the average male member of the middle class would use it regularly except possibly in wet weather. The working class would rarely, if ever, use a 'bus and it was not until the introduction of the tramcar, the "penny 'bus of the 'eighties and 'nineties and later still the halfpenny fare, that public transport in Leeds was extensively used by all classes.

Complaints about the inadequacy of the 'buses, referred to in the last chapter, continued, but no action was taken until July 1861. On 15th to 19th of that month the Royal Agricultural Show was held in Leeds on land at Armley, a large clothing village with several woollen mills, about 2 miles to the west. Beyond Armley, on either side of the Leeds and Bradford Railway, was the showground. Enormous crowds attended the show and on the busiest day, Thursday, 18th July, no less than 50,000 passengers entered Leeds by the Wellington Station, the terminus of the Midland, North Eastern and London and North Western Railway Companies. On the same day the Great Northern and Lancashire and Yorkshire brought 20,000 passengers into the Central Station. The Midland Railway carried 25,000 passengers to the show on the Leeds and Bradford line and the rest were carried by road transport.

"Cabs began to ply vigorously between Leeds and the Show Yard over that vile piece of road which runs from the Junction Inn to the boundary of the township and further on to the fields in Mrs. Tattersall's occupation. It was found necessary to augment the regular

coach and omnibus accommodation and Mr. Greenwood of Manchester placed on the road during the week a regular service of 'buses which ran from Briggate to the Show Ground every ten minutes. They were most commodious vehicles and afforded the inhabitants an opportunity of contrasting their comfort and ventilation with the miserable shake-downs which are frequently put on duty in Leeds. On Monday these 'buses carried 1,850 passengers, on Tuesday 4,850, on Wednesday 6,786, on Thursday 8,490 and yesterday 6,010."
(Leeds Mercury, 20th July, 1861).

Greenwood's 'buses were double-deck and of large seating capacity and this really brought home to the Leeds 'bus proprietors the inadequacy of their own vehicles and services. In Manchester and other large towns some of the omnibus proprietors owned the turnpike and people could travel twice the distance for the same fares as were charged in Leeds, in some places three and four miles for 3d. or 4d.

A contemporary sketch of one of Greenwood's 'buses. The brake blocks were an advanced feature for the time.

In apparent anticipation of the furore which would result from the demonstration of Greenwood's 'buses, two Leeds proprietors, Atkinson's and a Thomas Stork of Chapeltown took some action immediately prior to the Show. Atkinson's extended their Hunslet 'bus from Briggate along Lowerhead Row and North Street to the toll bar at the "Golden Cross", Sheepscar. This was a cross-town service and the 'bus made six journeys per day from 9.0 am to 7.0 pm from the "Golden Cross" with a stop at the "Old George", Briggate en route. A "better appointed" 'bus at a lower fare "3d. all the way" was introduced. Stork started a 'bus between Briggate and Moortown.

THOMAS STORK

Thomas Stork, a groom, took up the business of a beer seller in Regent Street, Chapeltown in the middle 'fifties, and by 1858 had established himself as a cab proprietor. His first venture into the omnibus world was the institution of the 'bus from Leeds to Moortown, a farming village on the Leeds and Harrogate Turnpike Road, 1½ miles beyond Chapeltown. The fare to Moortown was not stated, but the fare to New Leeds, an area about 1½ miles from the town centre, was 2d. and to Chapeltown 3d. The fare by both Atkinson's and Littlewood's 'buses to the same destinations was 6d.

Stork's 'bus daily made two journeys from the "Old George", Briggate at 2.40 pm and 6.30 pm to Chapeltown, and journeys from the station to Chapeltown at 9.50 am and to Moortown at 4.50 pm. On 24th March 1862 he put a "new and commodious" omnibus on the service but in December 1863 he was bought out, apparently by Atkinson's. His five "strong and powerful horses" 'Frenchman', 'Charley', 'Tom', 'Peter' and 'Jim' were sold on 22nd December.

Stork was a minor figure in the changing 'bus scene in Leeds, but to him goes the distinction of being the last proprietor to run a regular horse 'bus service between Leeds and the local town of Harrogate.

On 10th July 1849 the Leeds and Thirsk Railway was opened from Leeds to Harrogate, a spa town 16 miles to the north. The railway station at Harrogate was at Starbeck, two miles from the town centre, and passengers took a 'bus to Harrogate. Harrogate had been served by stage coaches from Leeds as early as the 1740's, and the three stage coaches still running from Leeds on the Harrogate Road, the 'Union' to Knaresborough, the 'Courier' to Ripon and the 'Telegraph' to Harrogate, all operated by William Hollings, ceased to run on 9th July 1849. The Mail Coach to Knaresborough, worked by Littlewood and Morritt, continued until 30th June 1852.

Other than the Mail there is no record of stage coaches running to Harrogate during 1850, but, during 1851, and for the following 12 years, a seasonal coach or 'bus was jointly worked by William Webster, a coach proprietor of Hunslet Lane, and a Thomas Howard. Howard had established himself as a coal merchant at Leeds Bridge in 1846.

On 1st August 1862 a new station was opened in the centre of Harrogate and the coaches or 'buses from Leeds began to lose money. Webster withdrew at the end of September 1863 and, during the 1864 season, a coach or 'bus, the 'Amity', was run between Leeds and Harrogate by Howard and a Pybus Allison, a milk dealer and omnibus proprietor of Boston Spa. A 'bus, probably the 'Amity', seating eight inside and three out, which had run to Harrogate for the season, was sold on 11th October 1864.

It had become uneconomical to run to Harrogate and when it was apparent in 1865 that no 'buses were to run, the following awkwardly worded notice appeared:–

"Harrogate and the public. The public not knowing of any accommodation by road to Harrogate this season calls upon Thomas Stork of Chapeltown to run his 'bus. I, Thomas Stork, do know the case with the intention to run daily from Leeds to the "Commercial", Harrogate and back and ensure the public that I will conduct it in my old style with civility and economy and recommend the 'bus as the most comfortable ever before the public for the purpose."
(Leeds Mercury, 11th April, 1865)

Stork's 'bus began on 1st May 1865 from the "Old George" and "Black Swan", traversing his old route via Chapeltown and Moortown, to the "Golden Lion", near the "Commercial Hotel", Harrogate. The 'bus made one daily journey at 10.0 am and on Sundays at 8.30 am. The fare from Leeds to Harrogate was 2s. 0d. inside and 1s. 6d. outside. Beginning 1st May the next year he ran his Harrogate 'bus, but it apparently lost money and was withdrawn on 10th September 1866. Stork's horses were sold and he was the last to run a service which had operated for over 120 years.

Many years later – on 12th July 1880 – a George Lowther of Swillington Hall, re-introduced a stage coach, 'The Rocket', from the "Bull and Mouth" to Harrogate. This nostalgic "coaching revival" was not successful and the coach was withdrawn after a few weeks.

ATKINSON'S, LITTLEWOOD AND FARNELL

Strangely the introduction of Stork's opposition 'bus to Chapeltown did not induce either Atkinson's or Littlewood to quickly lower their fares. From 29th April 1861 Littlewood had increased the frequency of the 'Mazeppa' from four to five journeys daily but on 14th October the same year it reverted to four again. There was no hint of any fare reduction. Littlewood did, however, take some action on his Headingley route. On 12th August 1861 the service was increased to nine journeys daily and the fares became:–

From Headingley to Leeds, inside 6d. outside 4d.

From Woodhouse to Leeds, inside 4d. outside 3d.

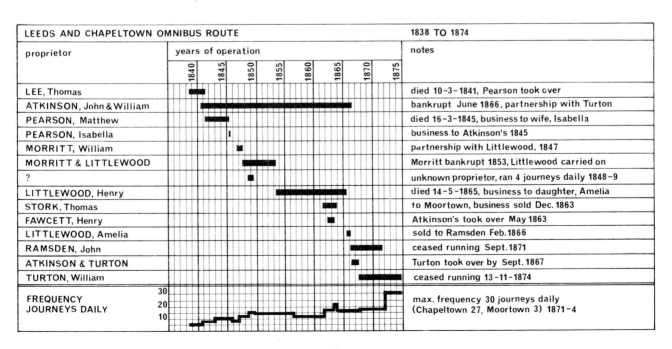

LEEDS AND CHAPELTOWN OMNIBUS ROUTE										1838 TO 1874	
proprietor	years of operation									notes	
	1840	1845	1850	1855	1860	1865	1870	1875			
LEE, Thomas										died 10-3-1841, Pearson took over	
ATKINSON, John & William										bankrupt June 1866, partnership with Turton	
PEARSON, Matthew										died 16-3-1845, business to wife, Isabella	
PEARSON, Isabella										business to Atkinson's 1845	
MORRITT, William										partnership with Littlewood, 1847	
MORRITT & LITTLEWOOD										Morritt bankrupt 1853, Littlewood carried on	
?										unknown proprietor, ran 4 journeys daily 1848-9	
LITTLEWOOD, Henry										died 14-5-1865, business to daughter, Amelia	
STORK, Thomas										to Moortown, business sold Dec. 1863	
FAWCETT, Henry										Atkinson's took over May 1863	
LITTLEWOOD, Amelia										sold to Ramsden Feb. 1866	
RAMSDEN, John										ceased running Sept. 1871	
ATKINSON & TURTON										Turton took over by Sept. 1867	
TURTON, William										ceased running 13-11-1874	
FREQUENCY JOURNEYS DAILY	30 20 10									max. frequency 30 journeys daily (Chapeltown 27, Moortown 3) 1871-4	

During the early 'sixties an opposition Chapeltown 'bus was introduced by a Henry Fawcett. Fawcett ran a coach or 'bus between Leeds and Wakefield from the late 'forties until it was discontinued about 1861. In May 1863 Atkinson's purchased Fawcett's 'bus and ran it on a through service between Chapeltown and Thwaite Gate, Hunslet. The 'bus ran hourly from Chapeltown from 8.0 am to 7.0 pm, but did not run for long.

After the introduction of Atkinson's through service, Littlewood increased his Chapeltown service again from four to five journeys daily. The alteration took effect from 1st June 1863 and the residents of Chapeltown were now well served with 'buses as there were three proprietors (Atkinson's, Littlewood and Stork), between them, running 21 journeys daily on the Chapeltown Road.

From 1st December 1863 the Hunslet to Sheepscar 'bus was altered to run hourly from the "Golden Cross" from 8.50 am to 7.50 pm. (This was presumably a curtailment of the Chapeltown to Hunslet through service). The fares were 3d. inside and 2d. outside and, at the same time, Atkinsons reduced the fares on their 'Royal Sovereign' Chapeltown 'bus. These were now:–

Briggate to New Leeds 3d.

Briggate to Chapeltown, outside 3d. inside 4d.

In April 1864 a new omnibus proprietor, James Farnell, made his appearance in Leeds. Farnell, a cab proprietor, had stables at Weetwood, Far Headingley (five minutes ride beyond the Headingley 'bus terminus). He introduced an opposition 'bus from Weetwood to Leeds making one journey daily leaving his stables in the morning at 9.40 am and returning from the "Albion Hotel", Briggate at 7.30 pm. The service began on 18th April 1864 but, within a short time, Farnell ceased to run in opposition and diverted his 'bus to run from Weetwood and along Otley Road and Monk Bridge Road to the "Beckett's Arms", Meanwood and presumably via Meanwood Road and North Street to Leeds. Three journeys daily were run from Weetwood and one from Meanwood to Leeds. An additional journey was run on Tuesdays and Saturdays.

Traffic increased on the Headingley route when an area of middle class housing was built west of Woodhouse Lane in the 'fifties and 'sixties. A steep hill, Mount Preston, some half a mile from the Headingley 'bus route, and about a mile from Briggate, passed through the centre. It was a long walk to Woodhouse Lane and the residents requested their own 'bus service. This was provided by Farnell in May 1864. His 'bus ran hourly from the "Albion" making 11 journeys daily on a circuitous route via Upperhead Row, Guildford Street, Calverley Street, (passing the new Town Hall), Great George Street, (passing the new Infirmary), Springfield Place, Mount Preston, Moorland Road, the Royal Park and Hyde Park Road to Hyde Park Corner.

Hyde Park was a new district of Leeds which came into being about 1860. Hyde Park Corner was the junction of five roads:– Hyde Park Road, Woodhouse Street, Victoria Road, Woodhouse Lane and Headingley Road. 'Buses passed it on their way to Headingley.

Immediately Henry Littlewood, "in consequence of the increasing requirements of the district", began an opposition 'bus from the "Royal Hotel". It ran at the same times as Farnell's 'bus. Bitter "racing" ensued and the 'buses accompanied each other at full gallop around the many sharp turns. Complaints appeared in the local press and within six months, Farnell appears to have worn out two 'buses. He put a new 'bus on the service on

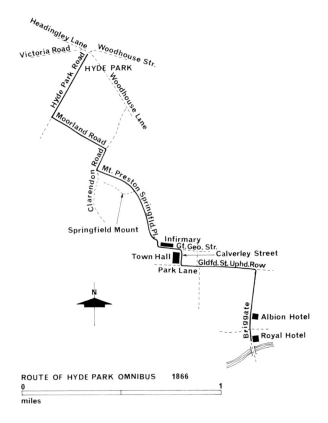

ROUTE OF HYDE PARK OMNIBUS   1866

21st June and a further on 19th December. 'Viator' made an informative comment:–

"The cause of all this is Mr. Littlewood's running in opposition to Mr. Farnell's omnibus. Mr. Littlewood was asked first to place an omnibus on this road and declined. Mr. Farnell was then induced to take this road and he did so and reduced the fare to 3d. The moment Mr. Farnell starts, Mr. Littlewood places also an omnibus on the same road at the same time, to run in opposition. Here then is the origin of all the mischief. The inhabitants of the neighbourhood of this road, having encouraged Mr. Farnell to run his omnibus, will not allow Mr. Littlewood to crush a small man, and therefore they support Mr. Farnell. If Mr. Littlewood would accommodate the public, he should start his omnibus at the half hour time as Mr. Farnell runs his full hour time and then the public would support him upon a fair equal basis. Mr. Littlewood has been asked to do this several times but he declines."

(Leeds Mercury, 31st December, 1864).

Littlewood refused to give way. He was determined to "run Farnell off the road" and the opposition continued.

A blow to both Littlewood's and Atkinson's monopoly of the Headingley route came when a John Emmott, livery stable keeper, of Far Headingley, introduced an opposition bus in April 1865. Ten journeys were daily made from 10.30 am to 9.0 pm (Saturdays 10.30 pm) from the "Albion". The new service apparently began on Monday 3rd April 1865 for on that day Littlewood reduced his fares to Headingley:–

Leeds to Richmond Road inside or outside 3d.

Leeds to "Three Horse Shoes". 4d. inside, 3d. outside.

The strain of the continuous battle with Farnell and this blow to his Headingley service was too much for Littlewood. On 14th May 1865 he was dead.

Littlewood and the Atkinson's dominated the 'bus scene in Leeds for a period of 18 years. Henry Littlewood was born in 1811 and apparently had a ruthless and stubborn streak in his character. He was more successful and opulent than the Atkinson's who always displayed a kindly image. He lived with his family in Hopewell House, Woodhouse Lane with three servants to run the house. He had a tragic life. His wife died in 1852, some of his children died in the 'fifties and 'sixties, and by the early 'eighties his entire family of near relatives had died out.

The Atkinson brothers lived modestly in adjoining houses in Harrison Court. They had no servants and lived, as most other horse 'bus proprietors, "on the premises", adjacent to their stables in Harrison Street.

Littlewood's business passed to his 15 years old daughter Amelia. Within three weeks of her father's death she had reached an agreement with Farnell and their 'buses ran alternately every half hour to Hyde Park. Although the Hyde Park 'buses were advertised to run via Springfield Place and Mount Preston, these two streets were not connected until October 1866. The 'buses had to make a diversion via a tortuous route which included Springfield Mount.

With the introduction of Emmott's 'buses the Headingley residents were well served with a half hourly 'bus service. Of greater significance, however, was the fact that they also had a late Saturday evening 'bus. Visitors to the town could now go to the theatre or attend a concert at the Town Hall and return home by 'bus. The improved facilties, however, had their disadvantages and a Headingley resident commented:–

"Some time ago, the conductors of the various omnibuses running between Leeds and Headingley were in the habit of blowing horns as a means of announcing their approach. It can scarely be conceived, except by those experiencing it, what a serious annoyance it was to the inhabitants of the houses on the route to have these unmusical horns blown past their doors at all hours of the day. In the case indeed, of young children and persons suffering from illness the consequences must have been much worse than merely annoying.

Some six or seven weeks ago, in consequence, I believe, of numerous complaints on the subject, the proprietors of the omnibuses put a stop to the practice, to the general satisfaction, no doubt, of the parties interested. A short time afterwards, however, the horn-blowing was recommenced without any apparent cause or necessity, by one of the omnibuses. This 'bus runs some four or five times each way during the day, and the small boy who occupies the post of conductor, blows the horn almost continuously through Headingley and seems to delight in producing as loud and discordant noise as he can. The practice is at present confined to this one 'bus, but there is no knowing how long this may continue to be the case if it is allowed to pass without notice, and if it should again become general, now that the omnibuses have become so numerous passing our doors, one way or the other, nearly every quarter of an hour from 8.30 am in the morning to 10.30 at night, it will be an intolerable nuisance both at the Headingley and Leeds ends."

(Leeds Mercury, 26th August, 1865).

It would appear that the tradition carried on from the stage coaches by David Binns on his original Headingley 'bus had been continued, but the standard of playing had deteriorated. In Leeds the use of horns and trumpets generally was discontinued with increased services, but the practice was continued on private 'bus and wagonette parties until the coming of motor transport. The vehicles left Leeds to the accompaniment of bugles and horns and returned in the evening to vocal strains of dubious origin.

Horn blowing conductors were a nuisance on the Headingley route.

A rapidly developing district of Leeds in the 1860's was the area to the west of Hunslet known as Hunslet Carr. Extensive working class back-to-back housing was built and the population had increased sufficiently by 1865 to support a 'bus service. Atkinson's increased the frequency of their Hunslet and Sheepscar service to half hourly. The 'buses leaving the top of Briggate at the hour ran to Thwaite Gate, Hunslet and on the half hour went from Low Road, Hunslet, via Church Street and Balm Road to a terminus at the "Bay Horse Inn", Hunslet Carr. The new service began on Monday 17th April 1865. At the Brewster Sessions later in the year, Mr. Lilley, the landlord of the "Bay Horse", applied for a licence to sell spirits. In support of his application the 'bus was mentioned:–

"It stopped at Mr. Lilley's house, and that gentleman had made considerable alterations in the formation of stables in order to accommodate the 'bus and horses. A large number of persons coming from Middleton and other districts waited for the omnibus at the "Bay Horse" and frequently asked for spirits."

(Leeds Mercury, 31st August, 1865).

Improvements were also taking place on the Chapeltown 'buses.

An area built during the 'forties and early 'fifties was a residential middle class district on Chapeltown Road known as New Leeds. New Leeds extended from Leopold Street in the south to Newton Lane in the north and by 1865 it had become extensive. On 25th September of that year Atkinson's introduced an hourly 'bus service between the top of Briggate and New Leeds running from 9.30 am to 7.30 pm. The terminus was

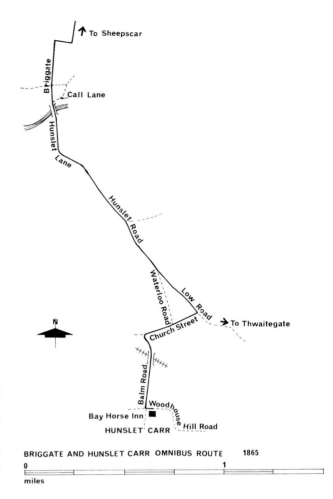

BRIGGATE AND HUNSLET CARR OMNIBUS ROUTE   1865

Bean's horse 'bus stands at the Hunslet Carr terminus about 1900.   *Courtesy R. F. Mack Collection.*

apparently Newton Lane. The following day Amelia Littlewood reduced her fares on the Chapeltown route as follows:–

Briggate to Newton Lane, inside or outside 3d.
Briggate to Chapeltown 4d. inside, 3d. outside.

Her 'bus was now running six journeys daily from 12.30 to 9.0 pm with the addition of a late 'bus leaving Leeds on Saturday nights at 10.15 pm. The Chapeltown residents now enjoyed the same facilities as Headingley with regard to late night transport. Amelia was operating three 'bus services, Chapeltown, Headingley and Hyde Park, and, in February 1866, she sold her interests in the 'buses, cab and coaching business to John Ramsden. Ramsden continued the services and took over Littlewood's stables at the "Royal Hotel".

The competition on the Headingley and Chapeltown routes was beginning to have a serious effect on Atkinson's. They still had to pay tolls on the turnpikes, but were forced to reduce their fares. The introduction of the Hunslet Carr and New Leeds services was an apparent attempt to diversify their interests in order to recoup their losses. On 26th February 1866 they instituted a 'bus on the route between Leeds and Kirkstall in opposition to a Matthew Jackson, already running a 'bus service. Jackson will be mentioned later. The 'bus ran from the top of Briggate to the "Star and Garter Inn", Kirkstall and made six journeys daily from 9.0 am to 7.15 pm. Atkinson's advertised that the 'bus would start at the times stated and the journey would not exceed 30 minutes. This was to be Atkinson's last attempt at diversification as four months later they were bankrupt.

John and William Atkinson were born in Northumberland in 1787 and 1792 respectively and their vehicles were a familiar sight in Leeds for over 40 years. Although the firm was always known under the title of John and William Atkinson, the elder brother John had died in the 'fifties. "Old Willie Atkinson", as he was popularly known, carried on the business, but the pressures of the 'sixties were apparently too much for him. His business was to pass to a William Turton. The name Turton dominated Leeds transport and the transport of many other towns for the next thirty years. William Turton became one of the great tramway entrepreneurs and accumulated vast wealth. He was a hay and corn merchant and was probably one of Atkinson's principal creditors.

"Old Willie" was not subjected to the indignities of a public examination, but was gradually taken over by Turton in 1867. A partnership was formed known as Atkinson and Turton, and by September 1867 Turton had taken over complete control.

No records have been traced of James Farnell after 1867 and it appears that he was taken over by Turton. Turton was running over Farnell's route to Hyde Park and on Meanwood Road by the early 'seventies.

MATTHEW JACKSON

One of the most important omnibus proprietors of the 'sixties and early 'seventies was Matthew Jackson. Jackson does not appear to have had any complementary interests, had a chequered career as a 'bus operator, and was to achieve notoriety. He was responsible for the re-introduction of the Kirkstall and Burley 'bus services.

Some new property had been erected in both Burley and Kirkstall and this encouraged Jackson to try his hand at running a 'bus service. The service was apparently introduced on or about Monday 9th December 1861 and the 'bus made five journeys daily from 8.30 am to 8.0 pm from the "Horse and Jockey", Commercial Street, to the "Star and Garter" at Kirkstall. The route was not stated but was presumably via Kirkstall Road. The 'bus was a success for Jackson but, in 1862, there were complaints of overcrowding. By 1866 the service was increased to seven journeys per day and, with the introduction of Atkinson's opposition 'bus, Jackson almost doubled his service running 13 journeys daily from 9.45 am to 9.15 pm. On Saturdays there was a half hourly service from 6.0 pm to the late hour of 10.30 pm. Three journeys were run on Sundays – shortly afterwards increased to four. The two proprietors were giving the Kirkstall residents a daily 'bus service of 19 journeys. After the withdrawal of Atkinson's 'bus Jackson increased his service to 14 journeys daily.

During the 'sixties Jackson made attempts to run a 'bus along Park Lane and Burley Road to Burley over part of the route of Ackroyd's short lived service in 1858. He ran buses for a few months in 1866 and withdrew them in August of that year. A "Rider on the Old 'Bus" gave the passengers viewpoint:–

"I would wish to give one or two reasons why the 'bus

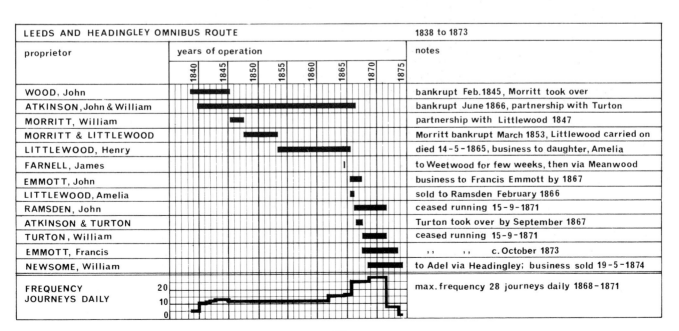

LEEDS AND HEADINGLEY OMNIBUS ROUTE									1838 to 1873
proprietor	years of operation								notes
	1840	1845	1850	1855	1860	1865	1870	1875	
WOOD, John									bankrupt Feb.1845, Morritt took over
ATKINSON, John & William									bankrupt June 1866, partnership with Turton
MORRITT, William									partnership with Littlewood 1847
MORRITT & LITTLEWOOD									Morritt bankrupt March 1853, Littlewood carried on
LITTLEWOOD, Henry									died 14-5-1865, business to daughter, Amelia
FARNELL, James									to Weetwood for few weeks, then via Meanwood
EMMOTT, John									business to Francis Emmott by 1867
LITTLEWOOD, Amelia									sold to Ramsden February 1866
RAMSDEN, John									ceased running 15-9-1871
ATKINSON & TURTON									Turton took over by September 1867
TURTON, William									ceased running 15-9-1871
EMMOTT, Francis									,, ,, c. October 1873
NEWSOME, William									to Adel via Headingley; business sold 19-5-1874
FREQUENCY JOURNEYS DAILY	20 / 10 / 0								max. frequency 28 journeys daily 1868-1871

did not suceed, as under different management I am convinced it would pay well. There are three things very essential: a good clean vehicle, a civil active conductor, and punctuality. We were treated to a variety of 'buses; but of the first and best the roof was not waterproof, the second varied the performance by letting in the rain at the sides under the windows, while the third was counteracting to the damp, being so small and stuffy as to be unbearable. Our conductors were also three in number; one lame, one very uncivil and sulky; and one a mere child, none of the three at any time betraying too great an intimacy with soap and water. The time was as the proprietor thought fit, and if convenient the 'bus was taken off all day and no notice given. Is it surprising that ladies refused to ride or that businessmen could not put up with such unpunctuality."

(Leeds Mercury, 24th August, 1866).

and Jackson's reply:-

"I have tried twice to support a good 'bus on that road before, and this is my third attempt, which shows very plainly that if it had been possible to keep the 'bus on the road I should, but I have run for days and days and have not received 8s. 0d. per day, out of which I must keep six horses, one man and a boy, pay 'bus duty, and keep my 'bus in repair."

(Yorkshire Post, 28th August, 1866).

Jackson does not appear to have made any further attempts to run along Burley Road.

The populous clothing village of Armley had a short lived 'bus service in the 1840's (previously referred to), but from that period until 1866 was entirely dependent upon the Leeds and Bradford Railway. On 15th October of that year Jackson instituted a 'bus from the "Horse and Jockey" to the toll bar on Armley Road via Wellington Street and Wellington Bridge. Seven journeys daily were operated from 8.40 am to 5.30 pm. There was no Sunday service.

The bridge over the River Aire, known as Wellington Bridge, was erected in 1818 and all vehicles and pedestrians crossing the bridge paid a toll. The toll for pedestrians was abolished in 1847, and on 1st March 1867 the bridge was made free for all vehicles. On this day Jackson extended his Armley 'bus along Armley Road and increased the service. The 'bus ran hourly from 10.0 am to 7.0 pm; there were three journeys on Sundays and the new terminus was at the "Nelson Inn", Armley.

Most 'bus proprietors were particular about the type of passenger they carried and several refused to carry drunks. Jackson carried anybody regardless of condition. John Hepper, a well known Leeds auctioneer and Dr. Goldie, later the Leeds Medical Officer of Health, had a memorable ride by the 8.45 pm Kirkstall 'bus on Friday 28th December 1866. Hepper commented that Jackson's 'buses were more of a public nuisance than a public convenience and Dr. Goldie wrote:-

"The night was wet, 'bus 15 minutes late out, crammed full. I with many others, had to stand three fourths of the journey. I may say that at least six seats were occupied by six of the most disgraceful and drunken men I have seen for some time. Two out of the six had the honour of entertaining us with a prize fight for so much a side. Such was the terms I heard. A third insulted three respectable females, for which he was courteously kicked out. A fourth, I wish to say little about him, simply that his countenance was a breach of the peace: this arose from past fights and past and present potations. The fifth threatened me that in some quiet

corner I shall be repaid for my assistance in easing No. 3 out. The sixth smoked for some time, counter to all wishes, until the conductor snatched the pipe out from the midst of the few teeth he had left, at their immediate risk."

(Yorkshire Post, 29th December, 1866).

In May 1867 Jackson suffered a tragedy as a virulent epidemic, glanders and farcy, infected his stables in the "Black Bull Yard", Lands Lane, near Briggate. He purchased a 'horse from a farmer of Burley and it developed what at first was thought to be influenza. The other animals were successively attacked and death or slaughterings took place almost daily. Within a fortnight 21 of Jackson's 26 horses died and his 'bus services were severely curtailed. Jackson's loss invoked sympathy from the other 'bus proprietors who opened a subscription and gave Jackson pecuniary assistance. His 'bus services were soon restored.

Thomas Stork ran the last 'bus on the Harrogate route. The honour of running the last 'bus on a similar service to the township of Ilkley, about 15 miles north west of Leeds, was to be Jacksons. From 1822 seasonal coaches and later 'buses ran from Leeds to Ilkley. During the 'fifties and 'sixties the service was worked by Webster and Howard and a George Brumfitt, innkeeper of Ilkley. The 'Raglan', 'Old True Blue' or 'Wellington' buses were normally used, but a 'bus, the 'Prince of Wales', ran during the 1863-4 seasons operated by a Henry Ward. The 'Old True Blue' and 'Wellington' did not apparently run in 1864, and in October of that year, as at the end of previous seasons, Webster and Howard auctioned off their horses. A "four-horse light omnibus to carry 8 inside and 16 outside passengers weighing 16cwt" was also sold. The 'bus was apparently the 'Raglan' and Jackson announced on 8th October that he was to run this 'bus from the "Old George" and the "Wheat Sheaf" (Webster and Howard's starting point) to Otley and Ilkley. He ran the 'bus in association with Brumfitt and it ceased to run for the season on 29th October.

Jackson ran the 'Raglan' during the 1865 season at reduced fares: Leeds to Otley 1s. 0d; Leeds to Ilkley inside 2s. 6d. and outside 1s. 9d. The 'Prince of Wales' also ran, but, in the meantime, on 1st February 1865, the North Eastern Railway Company opened a new branch railway from Arthington, on the Leeds and Harrogate line, to Otley, a distance of $3\frac{3}{4}$ miles. The line was extended through to Ilkley, a further $6\frac{1}{4}$ miles, on 1st August. There was now no necessity for a 'bus service.

The 'Prince of Wales' was not advertised to run in 1866, but Jackson announced that the 'Raglan' would begin running on Good Friday (30th March) and make one journey on Sundays to Brumfitt's hostelry, the "New Inn", Ilkley. The fares were reduced to 2s. 0d. inside and 1s. 6d. outside, but Jackson could not compete with the railway and his 'bus was soon withdrawn.

In 1864 Jackson also took over the Mail Coach from Leeds to Ilkley and this ceased to run on 11th October of that year. The "Leeds and Ilkley Mail" was the last Mail Coach of importance to run from Leeds, but what happened to the letters from its discontinuance to the opening of the railway is not certain. 'Buses from Leeds to the local villages carried the mail for many years afterwards, examples of which are Scarcroft and Thorner.

In the late 'sixties a 'bus was introduced to Bramley paralleling the route of the Armley 'bus. It made two journeys daily at 9.0 am and 1.0 pm from the "Horse and

Jockey". Three journeys were made on Tuesdays and four on Saturdays, which included a 'bus at 10.0 pm on Saturday night. The 'bus was probably worked by Jackson.

In March 1866 the Royal Society for the Prevention of Cruelty to Animals appointed an officer in Leeds. Cruelty to horses was wide-spread and it was not uncommon for a horse to suddenly drop dead in the street from overwork. Jackson was a particularly bad offender and was frequently brought to Court. In April 1872 an R.S.P.C.A. officer commented that for a long time past it had been a "matter of public notoriety and disgust" the way in which Jackson's horses were worked. His stables were inspected; all the horses were in bad condition and three were ordered to be destroyed. He was threatened with imprisonment if things did not improve. Owing to competition from the new horse tramway, Jackson withdrew his Kirkstall service and reduced his 'buses in service from four to one. He made some effort to clean up his stables and look after his horses in a better manner, but soon lapsed into his old ways. The crunch for Jackson came on 26th February 1874 when the Secretary of the R.S.P.C.A., John Colan took a ride on his Armley 'bus.

"He took occasion to see how the horses of the defendants were treated, as he had heard many complaints respecting their ill-usage. He got on Jackson's 'bus in Commercial Street and was driven as far as Wellington Bridge. The horses were very weak, and could not be started without a great deal of pulling at the reins and whipping. Albert Thurwell was the driver and the whipping almost incessant. Witness counted the number of lashes inflicted in the quarter of an hour occupied in going from Commercial Street to Wellington Bridge, and they were no less than 68. He admitted

that that was the case, and added that they were "dead beat". He also told witness that they were kept at work for several hours every day. One witness remonstrating with him for whipping one of the horses, the driver said he was obliged to do so in order to keep it up and to get through the journey. At the end of the whip was a gutta-percha thong, an instrument of torture which was not allowed to be used in London. The horses came to a standstill at the bridge, being unable to draw the 'bus over the bad piece of road there, and the passengers had to alight and turn the wheels."
(Yorkshire Post, 28th February, 1874).

Jackson was sent to prison for two months with hard labour and his driver was fined 40s. 0d. and costs.

After the glanders epidemic of 1867, Jackson moved his stables to Kirkstall Road, at the rear of the "Beckett's Arms", and, by 1872, also had stables at the "White Hart Yard", Briggate. On 24th March 1874, at his Kirkstall Road stables, an "important sale of 9 horses, 5 omnibuses, cab, wagonette" etc. took place. Jackson never ran a 'bus again but took up the business of a mineral water manufacturer at the "White Hart Yard". He died on 1st December 1891 at the age of 78 years.

COATES'S

An important firm of 'bus proprietors to emerge in the 'sixties was the Coates's. The name Coates appears frequently in the story of nineteenth century coach and 'bus transport in Leeds, but, in spite of research, the exact relationship between the various proprietors of this name has not been discovered. A Thomas Coates was an important stage coach proprietor from 1832 until 1840 when the railways forced him into bankruptcy. By 1843 he was running coaches again and eventually

Coates' 'bus No. 11 stands outside the 'Royal Hotel," Briggate in 1890.   *Courtesy The late D. Hunt, Photographer.*

went out of business about 1848. A John Coates of Sovereign Street was licensed to run cabs from 18th December 1857 and was apparently the first of the Coates's to run 'buses. He took over the operation of 'buses to Halton, Whitkirk and Garforth by the late 'fifties. In 1862 59 years old John was joined in partnership by Joseph, probably his nephew, aged 23, a carter and son of a farmer, also named Joseph, of Osmondthorpe. The partnership prospered with the injection of new blood and the cab side of the business expanded, but it was split up the following year, Joseph concentrating on the 'buses and John the cabs. John retired in January 1870 when his licence was revoked and some years later a John Coates Junior, presumably his son, appeared and ran 'buses to Meanwood.

On 1st January 1866 Charles Joseph Coates, Joseph's elder brother, who was to become the most important member of the family in relation to their 'bus activities, was given a licence to drive a cab by the Hackney Coach Committee and joined his brother in partnership. The firm was now known as Coates Brothers and their first action was to introduce a new 'bus service. Charles Joseph was born in Beeston and had stables at the bottom of Beeston Hill; Joseph had stables in Great Garden Street, Burmantofts, and they began a 'bus service between the two areas.

Beeston, "a pleasant village on a bold eminence two miles south by west of Leeds", boasted several collieries and many of the inhabitants were coal miners. The village was approached by Beeston Hill, a 1 in 9 gradient, too steep for horse 'buses, and the 'bus terminus was at Lady Pit Street at the bottom of the hill.

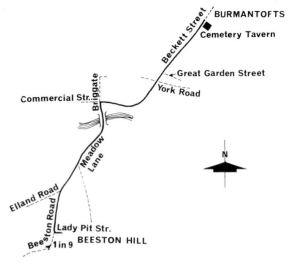

COATES'S BURMANTOFTS AND BEESTON HILL 'BUS ROUTE 1866

Burmantofts was a rapidly developing working class area about 1½ miles north of Briggate and the terminus was at the "Cemetery Tavern", Beckett Street. A through service was operated.

On 14th April 1866 a prominent advertisement for the Burmantofts to Beeston Hill service appeared in the local press and it is assumed the service was started about this time. Ten journeys daily from 10.0 am to 10.0 pm (11.0 pm on Saturdays and, up to this time, the latest 'bus to leave Briggate) were made from the corner of

Coates' Beeston Hill 'bus approaches the Lady Pit Street terminus in 1890.   *Courtesy The late D. Hunt, Photographer.*

26

Commercial Street, Briggate, to Beeston Hill and six journeys, from 9.0 am to 7.45 pm (10.0 pm on Saturdays), from Briggate to Burmantofts. The fare from Briggate to Beeston Hill was 3d.

The withdrawal of Jackson's Burley 'bus in 1866 resulted in the institution by Coates Brothers of a through service between Beeston Hill and Burley on 12th October the same year. They were able to make it pay. The timetable was not stated, but by 1870 eight journeys daily, from 9.0 am to 7.30 pm (Saturdays 9.30 pm) were made from Burley to Briggate, four of them running through to Beeston Hill. Possibly due to competition from the Kirkstall horse tram, the Burley 'buses were withdrawn about 1874.

During the 'sixties Coates's faced no opposition on either their Beeston Hill, Burmantofts or Burley routes, but the Halton, Whitkirk and Garforth 'buses were in competition with a 'bus running over the same route to Kippax. The Kippax 'buses are mentioned in the next chapter of this volume.

The Coates Brothers were pretty rough characters and Joseph has the dubious distinction of being the first omnibus proprietor in Leeds to be prosecuted for cruelty by the R.S.P.C.A. On 29th April 1866 he was in charge of the Garforth 'bus:—

"The complaint was preferred by Inspector Francis of the R.S.P.C.A. who stated that on Sunday night, on the 'bus arriving at the bottom of the hill just beyond the "Dog and Gun Inn", York Road on its return journey to Leeds, a fourth horse was attached for the purpose of assisting to gain the top of the hill. The assistance was simply temporary and the horse had no reins affixed. It first went on one side of the road and then the other, and the defendant, who was acting as conductor of the vehicle, left his place at the back, and with the whip which was handed to him by the driver, lashed the animal most unmercifully, causing great weals to rise upon its shoulders and flanks. Not content with this when half way up the hill he took a large stone and threw it with force at the horses head. He fortunately missed his aim. Several of the passengers were so afraid that they insisted on leaving the 'bus, some of them objected to pay their fares and a gentleman threatened to summon the defendant for cruelty."
(Leeds Mercury, 4th May, 1866).

Joseph was fined 20s. 0d. and costs. Shortly after forming the partnership he moved his stables to Beeston Hill and met an early death on 1st January 1868. The omnibus business was transferred to Charles Joseph who mellowed and, in later years, was regarded as probably the best of the horse 'bus proprietors in Leeds, who treated both his passengers and horses well. There were other members of the family who ran 'buses and these will be mentioned in a later chapter.

Apart from the carriers' 'buses, referred to later, the only other omnibus proprietor to appear in the 'sixties was William Newsome, a farmer of Far Headingley who started a 'bus service between Leeds and Adel about 1868. Adel or "Addle" – "a smelly place" – as it was referred to until about 1860, was a small scattered farming village five miles north west of Leeds and included the hamlets of Cookridge and Eccup. Newsome's 'bus ran from the "Albion", Briggate, making three departures daily, traversed the Headingley 'bus route, and ran via Weetwood Lane to a terminus at the end of Weetwood Lane near to Dunstarn Lane. Newsome moved his stables to Beck Farm, Adel, in April 1872 and about this time the service was increased to four departures daily. The service was discontinued in 1874 due to tramway competition and Newsome's rolling stock, two three-horse 'buses to seat 30 and 37 passengers respectively, and his ten horses, were sold on 19th May of that year.

Coates' 'bus No. 13 at the Beeston Hill terminus about 1895.

CHAPTER FOUR

The Carrier's Services

From the 17th century horse-drawn carrier's vehicles had run from Leeds to outlying towns. They later served the local villages and were used principally for the carriage of goods, but some also carried passengers.

White's Directory of Leeds for 1861 lists no fewer than 27 coaches "for goods and passengers" serving several towns and villages, Bedale and Thirsk, over 30 miles from Leeds, being the most distant. In some cases the carriage of passengers became the primary use for the vehicle and it became referred to as a 'bus. Some carriers used carts and waggons and others vans, and it is the latter which usually carried passengers. The dis-

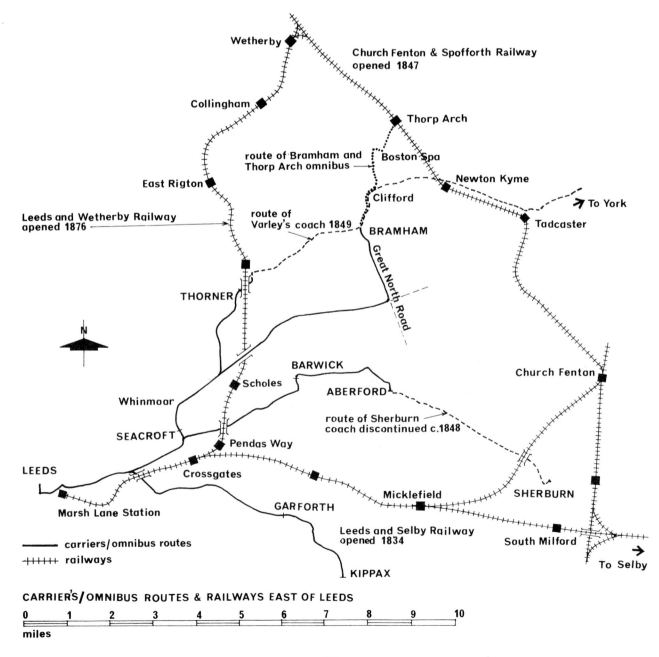

CARRIER'S/OMNIBUS ROUTES & RAILWAYS EAST OF LEEDS

tinction, therefore, between a van, coach or 'bus is often blurred.

Some 'bus routes in the immediate vicinity of Leeds developed from carrier's services and these included Aberford, Barwick, Bramham, Kippax, Seacroft and Thorner, all to the north east and east of the town. These villages were not at first served by rail whereas towns and villages to the south, west and north had intensive railway services. Although there were also carrier's services they did not develop into long established 'bus routes.

There was a carrier's van, also used for passengers, operated by a William Bickerdyke to Farnley, a village to the south west of Leeds, in the 1830's and 40's and Joseph Smith's passenger carrying van to Guiseley in the 'thirties. There was also a carrier's van worked by a Samuel Cooper to Guiseley in the 'forties, 'fifties and 'sixties which carried passengers. Crabtree's Guiseley 'bus, mentioned in a previous chapter, was apparently used for passengers only.

There had been a market coach 'The Nettle' running from the "White Hart Hotel," Briggate to Aberford by 1834, but it did not run long and was taken over by William Adkin (referred to in a previous chapter) in 1835. Renamed the 'Providence' it was diverted to a seasonal service between Leeds and Thorp Arch. There was no coach or 'bus service to Aberford for a few years, but by 1841 a coach, the 'Perseverance', was running from the

"Talbot Inn," Briggate, through Barwick and Aberford to the village of Sherburn, about four miles beyond Aberford.

Aberford and Barwick were served by four carriers running between Leeds and the two villages on market days. By 1845 a carrier named Grey was running a van from the "Black Swan," North Street to Aberford, but about two years later a proprietor named Dawson had taken over.

Presumably as a result of railway competition, the Leeds to Sherburn coach was discontinued in late 1848 or early 1849 and a Charles Wrigglesworth began to run a van between the "New Inn," Vicar Lane and Barwick. Dawson and Wrigglesworth carried both goods and passengers and their vehicles were referred to as 'buses or coaches in the local directories. By 1851 Wrigglesworth had changed his starting point from the "New Inn" to the "Black Swan" but a 'bus continued to run from the "New Inn" to Barwick, and was extended through to Thorner for a short while. By 1857 it was worked by George Perkin, a farmer of Barwick, who ran on market days (Tuesdays and Saturdays) whereas Wrigglesworth ran on Tuesdays, Thursdays and Saturdays at this time. By 1851 a market coach was running from the "Boy and Barrel", Wood Street to Aberford worked by a George Priestman.

From the 1820's, the Seanor or Senior family had run a market day carrier's service from the "Boot and

No room on this cheap-jack's van, but this type of vehicle was used for passengers. Photograph taken at Headingley about 1890.
Courtesy The late G. Bingley, Photographer. Leeds University Collection.

29

Shoe," Wood Street, to Aberford. Some directories refer to their vehicle as a coach which carried passengers. Dawson ceased to run to Aberford in the late 'fifties but both Senior and Priestman continued to run uneventfully through the remaining 'fifties and 'sixties. Similarly Perkin and Wrigglesworth ran from Leeds to Barwick during the same period.

In 1871 Priestman, Senior and Wrigglesworth withdrew their 'buses and Perkin had the monopoly of the service for a while and, by 1876, was running from Leeds to Barwick on Tuesdays only. Two years later, however, he was forced to improve the service when an opposition 'bus was put on by Henry Wrigglesworth, Charles' son. Henry Wrigglesworth ran from the "Black Swan" to Barwick and Aberford on three days weekly — the same days as his father had operated previously. Perkin also extended his service to Aberford running on three days weekly leaving Leeds at 4.0 pm, the same time as Wrigglesworth's 'bus, but, by October 1878, he had altered his departure time to 4.30 pm from the "New Inn." In the middle 'eighties Perkin died and Wrigglesworth also ceased to run. A Joseph Helm of Barwick and a proprietor named Morrell took over operation. In the middle 'nineties Morrell went out of business and Helm cut back his service to Barwick. The Barwick 'bus continued to run until the First World War and will be mentioned in the next volume.

The Aberford and Barwick 'buses passed through the village of Seacroft, a farming and mining village, some four miles from Leeds, with a population of 1,093. It included the hamlets of Killingbeck, Cross Gates and Coldcotes, the last of which contained only two houses. By 1847 Seacroft had its own carrier's service. It was worked by a James Mitchell from the "Beehive", Vicar Lane and at first ran on Tuesdays and Fridays only, but later ran on Wednesdays and Saturdays in addition. By 1856 the vehicle was referred to as a 'bus and about this time was being operated by a William Mitchell, presumably a relative of James. In the early 'sixties Mitchell's 'bus was withdrawn, but in the meantime a market coach was introduced from the "New Inn," Vicar Lane to Seacroft operated by a proprietor named Gaskin. After about two years William Mallinson, a former coal pit labourer of Seacroft, was running the service. Mallinson's vehicle was used for goods and passengers at first but in late November 1868 his 'bus was altered to run twice daily, including Sundays, and the town terminus was changed to the "Beehive," Mitchell's old starting point. The Seacroft 'bus was now used mainly for passengers.

About 1873 Mallinson gave way to an Edwin Brown, son of George Brown, farmer, omnibus proprietor and carrier of Thorner. The Seacroft 'bus terminus was at the "Lion and Lamb Inn," Seacroft and remained at this location until early 1887. About January 1887 Edwin Brown's brother, Alfred, sold an omnibus business which he had been working from Leeds to Shadwell and became innkeeper at the "Old Red Lion Inn," Whinmoor, at the far side of Seacroft village. Alfred Brown took over operation of the Seacroft 'bus which was now extended to run through to his hostelry. The fare from Leeds to the "Old Red Lion" was 6d. and to the "Lion and Lamb" 4d. on weekdays and 6d. on Sundays.

From 22nd November 1898 an alteration to the city terminus occurred due to building work at the "Beehive", and the 'bus was altered to run from the

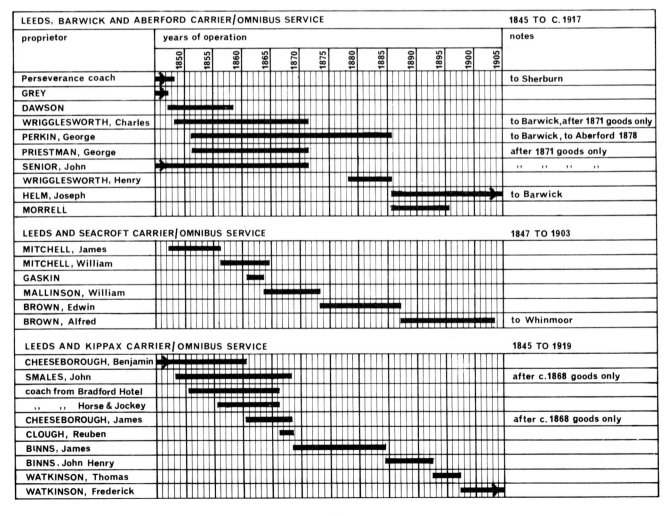

LEEDS, BARWICK AND ABERFORD CARRIER/OMNIBUS SERVICE	1845 TO C.1917

proprietor	years of operation	notes
Perseverance coach		to Sherburn
GREY		
DAWSON		
WRIGGLESWORTH, Charles		to Barwick, after 1871 goods only
PERKIN, George		to Barwick, to Aberford 1878
PRIESTMAN, George		after 1871 goods only
SENIOR, John		,, ,, ,, ,,
WRIGGLESWORTH, Henry		
HELM, Joseph		to Barwick
MORRELL		

LEEDS AND SEACROFT CARRIER/OMNIBUS SERVICE	1847 TO 1903

MITCHELL, James		
MITCHELL, William		
GASKIN		
MALLINSON, William		
BROWN, Edwin		
BROWN, Alfred		to Whinmoor

LEEDS AND KIPPAX CARRIER/OMNIBUS SERVICE	1845 TO 1919

CHEESEBOROUGH, Benjamin		
SMALES, John		after c.1868 goods only
coach from Bradford Hotel		
,, ,, Horse & Jockey		
CHEESEBOROUGH, James		after c.1868 goods only
CLOUGH, Reuben		
BINNS, James		
BINNS, John Henry		
WATKINSON, Thomas		
WATKINSON, Frederick		

"Wheat Sheaf", Upperhead Row. When the building works were completed the starting point reverted to the "Beehive." By 1900 the 'bus service had been reduced from twice daily to one journey only on Tuesdays, Thursdays and Sundays, presumably due to tramway competition on the inner part of its route. It remained at this frequency until its closure in 1903.

George Brown had worked a carrier's service from his village, Thorner, eight miles north east of Leeds from about 1849. His vehicle also acted as a 'bus and was known as the "Thorner Grand Express," and ran from the "New Inn," Vicar Lane to Thorner on Tuesdays, Thursdays and Saturdays. Brown was the first carrier to run between Thorner and Leeds only, but other carriers had passed through Thorner, on their way to Leeds, from Bramham, Boston Spa and Thorp Arch for many years previously.

By 1849 there was a coach or van running from the "Boy and Barrel," Wood Street, to York via Seacroft, Thorner, Bramham, Clifford and Tadcaster. The van ran on Tuesdays and Fridays and was worked by a farmer of Bramham, Bryan Varley. At the same time there was a coach operating from the "Harrison's Arms," Harrison Street via Seacroft to Thorner only. It was withdrawn about 1855 and about three years later Varley also ceased to run.

George Brown ran in opposition to these two vehicles and when they were withdrawn he had the monopoly of the Thorner route for three or four years. In the early 'sixties an R. Turton instituted a daily 'bus service from the "Three Legs," Upperhead Row, to Thorner in competition with Brown, but his 'bus could not have been economical for by 1866 it had been withdrawn. Turton's

place was taken by a John Pickles who, in turn, gave way to Edward Prentice, carter and coal dealer of Thorner, working from the "Three Legs" on Tuesdays and Saturdays only. Brown and Prentice appear to have co-operated with each other. Brown originally ran via Seacroft, but was now working via Moortown and Shadwell, and Prentice via Seacroft. Prentice apparently withdrew his 'bus when the Leeds and Wetherby Railway was opened through to Thorner in 1876, but Brown's 'bus, reduced from three to two departures from Thorner weekly, continued running until about 1882 when it apparently reverted to carrying goods only, but continued to carry the occasional passenger.

In 1881 Brown diversified his interests and, in addition to his omnibus, carrier and farming activities he was also recorded as an income tax collector! The Brown family continued their carrier's service from Thorner to Leeds until well into the 20th century.

Three miles beyond Thorner was the farming village of Bramham. A market day coach or van was advertised as running from the "Black Swan," Vicar Lane to Bramham in 1847 and was worked by a William Burton. The Burton family had operated a carrier's service from Bramham to Leeds, in competition with other proprietors, from the 1820's. By 1849 there was Varley's van or coach running through Bramham to York and a van from the "Spotted Cow" passing through Bramham, Clifford, and Boston Spa to Thorp Arch worked by a proprietor named James Bellwood. All three proprietors carried both goods and passengers.

In the late 'fifties Varley went out of business and by 1861 Burton had been replaced by a Charles Young running from the "Black Swan." By 1866 Young had

A carrier's van stands outside the "Red Lion Inn," Bramham.

31

An 1870 photograph of Bellwood's covered wagon. Bellwood is the driver.
Courtesy B. Scott.

given way to a J. Wright who in turn, was replaced by a Frederick Bovill in the late 'sixties. In October 1871 Bovill had his 'bus licence revoked but continued to carry goods only between Bramham and Leeds.

There were apparently no 'buses running between Leeds and Bramham for about a year and the Bramham residents had to rely on a 'bus connection from the "Red Lion Inn," Bramham, via Clifford and Boston Spa to the Thorp Arch Railway Station: This connection had operated from the time the Church Fenton and Spofforth Railway was opened in 1847, passengers for Leeds changing at Church Fenton.

On 2nd November 1872 a William Pearson announced that he was to run a 'bus from the "Beehive," Vicar Lane via York Road, Bramham Cross Roads and the Great North Road to Bramham. This 'bus ran on market days and it was apparently used solely for passengers. Bellwood's vehicle was withdrawn in 1875 and Pearson's about 1877. Thereafter, Bramham people had to rely on the Thorp Arch 'bus and railway or the Boston Spa seasonal 'buses if they wished to visit Leeds.

Two Directories, Kelly's for 1881 and White's for 1894, list a 'bus running from the "Black Swan" to Bramham. In February 1881 Frederick Bovill or a John Booker were running the Bramham carrier's service, but the carrier in 1894 was not indicated. The Bramham 'bus service petered out about 1895 and passengers had to revert to the Thorp Arch 'bus and railway. The Thorp Arch 'bus was running until the First World War.

In 1847 a market coach or van was advertised as running from the "Old White Swan," Swan Street, near Briggate, to Kippax. Kippax was a small mining community about two miles beyond the "Old George", Garforth Bridge (Coates's 'bus terminus) and near to the Leeds and Selby Road. The Kippax coach was operated by a Benjamin Cheeseborough who had been established for about 30 years as a carrier between his village and Leeds. By 1848 there was an opposition van worked by a John Smales from the "Three Legs," Call Lane, also on market days and, during the 'fifties a daily coach from the "Bradford Hotel," Kirkgate. During the latter part of this period there was also a coach from the "Horse and Jockey" to Kippax.

About 1860 Benjamin Cheeseborough gave way to a relative, James, and the Leeds starting point was altered from the "Old White Swan Inn" to the "Beehive," Vicar Lane. The daily coaches from the "Bradford Hotel" and "Horse and Jockey" were apparently discontinued about 1866 and a Reuben Clough introduced a 'bus, the 'Perseverance', running between the "Three Legs" and Kippax on Tuesdays, Thursdays and Saturdays. Clough was frequently in court for cruelty to his horses and ran to Kippax for about three years. His two 'buses and seven horses were sold on 4th November 1868. Smales continued to run from the "Three Legs" but his vehicle appears to have been used for goods only. Cheeseborough also seems to have reverted to carrying goods. James Binns, a farmer of Kippax, took over operation of the service from Cheeseborough, Clough and Smales and ran from the "Beehive." The 'bus at first made one journey on Tuesdays, Thursdays and Saturdays, but by 1882 this was reduced to Tuesdays and Saturdays only. Binns and later his son, John Henry, ran the Kippax 'bus without opposition for the following 20 years or so. By December 1892 a Thomas Watkinson of Kippax had taken over the service, but operating from the "New Inn," Vicar Lane in lieu of the "Beehive" and his 'bus was operating on three days weekly again. Thomas Watkinson gave way to a Frederick Watkinson in 1897 and Frederick's vehicle ran uneventfully until it was superseded by a motor 'bus in 1919. This was to be the last horse 'bus to run in Leeds.

The next chapter refers to the licensing of 'buses and omnibus proprietors in Leeds and this included 'buses running into Leeds from outlying districts. In 1869 Senior

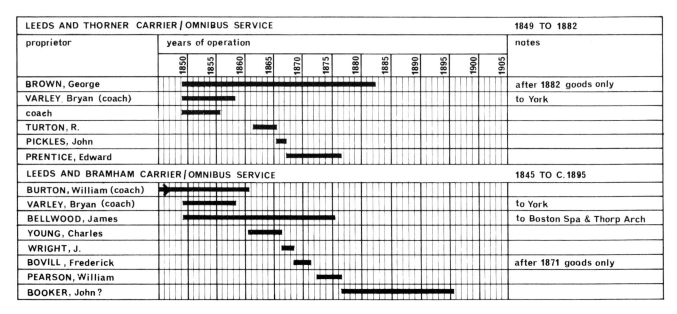

LEEDS AND THORNER CARRIER / OMNIBUS SERVICE													1849 TO 1882
proprietor	years of operation												notes
	1850	1855	1860	1865	1870	1875	1880	1885	1890	1895	1900	1905	
BROWN, George		▪▪	▪▪	▪▪	▪▪	▪▪	▪▪	▪					after 1882 goods only
VARLEY, Bryan (coach)		▪▪	▪										to York
coach		▪											
TURTON, R.					▪								
PICKLES, John				▪									
PRENTICE, Edward					▪▪	▪							
LEEDS AND BRAMHAM CARRIER / OMNIBUS SERVICE													1845 TO C. 1895
BURTON, William (coach)	▶												
VARLEY, Bryan (coach)		▪▪	▪										to York
BELLWOOD, James		▪▪	▪▪	▪▪	▪▪	▪							to Boston Spa & Thorp Arch
YOUNG, Charles				▪▪	▪								
WRIGHT, J.					▪								
BOVILL, Frederick					▪	▪							after 1871 goods only
PEARSON, William						▪▪							
BOOKER, John ?							▪▪	▪					

and Priestman (Aberford), Perkin and Wrigglesworth (Barwick), Bovill (Bramham), Binns (Kippax), Mallinson (Seacroft) and Brown and Prentice (Thorner) had their vehicles licensed as 'buses by the Hackney Carriages Committee. In 1871 Senior, Priestman, Wrigglesworth, Bovill and three proprietors: a George Blanshard operating a carrier/'bus service to Tadcaster and a John Hardcastle and William Naylor working a similar service to Wetherby, had their licenses revoked. The reason is uncertain, but the Leeds Corporation would not have jurisdiction over 'buses running beyond the borough boundary. After this date only Binns, Brown, Mallinson, Perkin and Prentice ran their 'buses as passenger carrying vehicles and are mentioned in the local directories and newspapers. The other proprietors either withdrew altogether or used their vehicles for goods only, as they would be liable for prosecution if they carried passengers within the Leeds boundary.

Sketch of Briggate about 1860. The old Corn Exchange, demolished in December 1868, is in the background.

CHAPTER FIVE

The Corporation Involvement

The Leeds Corporation took an interest in the Turnpike Roads and 'buses in the 'sixties. In common with many other towns throughout the country their first priority was to get rid of the punitive turnpikes. An Act, known as "The Leeds Improvement Act, 1866" was obtained. In addition to various road improvements, the Act enabled the Corporation to purchase all the turnpike roads within the borough and abolish the tolls. The Act received the Royal Assent on 28th June 1866 and the Corporation entered into negotiations with the various turnpike trusts with a view to their purchase.

The Leeds and Harrogate and Leeds and Roundhay Turnpike Roads were the first to be acquired and the tolls were abolished on 1st January 1867. These were followed a few days later by the Leeds and Meanwoodside Turnpike Road. The Chapeltown, Roundhay and Meanwood 'buses were thus freed from tolls and the toll bars at Sheepscar were quickly removed. The hated toll bar at Woodhouse on the Leeds and Otley Turnpike Road ceased to exist a month later. Midnight on Thursday, 31st January deserved a celebration:—

"Many of the inhabitants of Woodhouse and Headingley have manifested their pleasure in a somewhat singular manner. As midnight on Thursday approached, Emmott's 'bus, so well known on the road, was chartered, and with a full compliment of passengers drove through the bar towards Leeds. About five minutes to 12 o'clock the 'bus and its jubilant occupants — who to add to their festive mirth had with them the sundry instruments of music frequently more noisy than harmonious — in the vanguard some dozen or two cabs filled with 'fares' slowly approached the bar, where, however, this formidable midnight procession was brought to a halt for there "Pike" stood like a second Shylock and inexorably demanding his bond refusing to "ope the gates" unless he first received his "pound of flesh". There he kept them waiting until the sonorous midnight tones of the Town Hall clock as they were heard pealing forth like a death knell, warned him that his occupation was gone and throwing the gate open with a somewhat sorrowful air he permitted the boisterous procession to pass through rejoicingly, the "musical party" on the 'bus playing with all their skill and power "Hard times come again no more", etc.

(Leeds Mercury, 2nd February, 1867).

The tolls on Victoria Bridge ceased on the same day and on Wellington Bridge on 1st March. The following turnpikes and tolls within the borough remained to be acquired:—

Leeds and Whitehall Road.

Tong Lane End and Wortley and Pudsey Turnpike Road.
Shipley and Bramley Turnpike Road.
Kirkstall, Otley and Shipley Turnpike Road.
Leeds and Birstal Turnpike Road.
Wortley, Armley and Bramley Turnpike Road.
Leeds and Elland Turnpike Road.
Crown Point Bridge.
Leeds and Dewsbury Turnpike Road.
Leeds and Wakefield Turnpike Road.

Of these only the Wortley, Armley and Bramley and Leeds and Wakefield Turnpike Roads were traversed by 'buses. Dewsbury Road, Elland Road and Whitehall Road did not see 'buses until the 'seventies. The toll bars on the Kirkstall, Otley and Shipley Turnpike Road were at Kirkstall Bridge, Moorhouse Lane and at Tordoff Terrace, Abbey Road. Jackson's Kirkstall 'buses terminated at the "Star and Garter", near to Kirkstall Bridge and Tordoff Terrace and were not affected. Crabtree's Guiseley 'bus may have been, but was probably discontinued by this time. On 1st January 1868 the toll bars on this road were made free and Dewsbury Road was freed on the same day. Crown Point Bridge was made free on 1st March the same year and shortly afterwards the toll bar at the foot of Pepper Lane, Low Road, Hunslet, was moved 400 yards to the borough boundary. Hence Turton's Hunslet 'buses ceased to pay toll.

Tolls on the other turnpikes were successively abolished. The toll bar on Holbeck Moor on the Leeds and Elland Road was moved to the "Commercial Inn", Churwell, from 1st August 1868, and the Shipley and Bramley tolls finished on the same day. The Tong Lane End, Wortley and Pudsey tolls ceased on 1st October 1869 and the Wortley, Armley and Bramley shortly afterwards. Jackson's Armley 'buses thus ceased payments and after a lot of legal wrangling, the Leeds and Whitehall Road was freed on 1st January 1871. The Royds toll bar on Leeds and Birstal Turnpike Road was abolished in February 1872 and all the roads within the Leeds borough boundary were now free. Several of the turnpike roads retained their tolls outside the borough boundary for a number of years and the last to be abolished was the Leeds and Birstal Road in 1890.

Mention has not been made of the Leeds and Selby Turnpike Road on which ran the Halton, Whitkirk and Garforth 'buses. The toll gate was at Halton Dial at the junction of the York and Selby Roads. It was outside the Leeds boundary at the time and therefore of no interest to the borough. The tolls on this road were removed in October 1874.

The omnibus proprietors were now much better off and there was speculation that the fares would decrease. The Headingley residents did not receive a pleasant Christmas present in 1868. "Inquisitor" wrote:—

"Can you inform me why the omnibus fare to Headingley was advanced this week? It is a matter requiring some little investigation, as well as ventilation. The tolls have been taken off the road for the benefit, if not encouragement, of these conveyances, in consequence of which there has to be increased highway rates paid, and it does seem too bad for the public now to be required to bear the imposition of an increased fare also. If this is done under the plea of non-remuneration, because the abominable and indecent practice of overcrowding, which has prevailed for too long in these vehicles, has very properly been put a stop to, I should like to know, first, whether, to run 'buses to pay, it is necessary to cram and jam them to suffocation; and secondly, why was this plea never raised when the four omnibuses were paying annually something like a thousand pounds for tolls and mileage?"

(Yorkshire Post, 24th December, 1868).

Unfortunately details of the increased fares are not known and there was no reply from the Headingley omnibus proprietors – Messrs. Emmott (two 'buses), Ramsden and Turton (one 'bus each).

In addition to the abolition of the turnpikes, the "Leeds Improvement Act, 1866" contained an important street improvement, namely, the extension of Briggate through to North Street. This made a big change in the face of Leeds as also did the widening of Boar Lane and West Bar, authorised by a later Act, the "Leeds Improvement Act, 1869". At this time the North Eastern Railway Company was extending its line through Leeds from the Marsh Lane Station across Briggate to a station, known as the New Station, adjacent to Wellington Station. The New Station and extension line were opened on 1st April 1869 and the station was used jointly by the North Eastern Railway and London and North Western Railway Companies.

The widening of Boar Lane was essential to cope with the increased traffic as it formed a link between the two stations and Briggate. The intolerable congestion of former years was eliminated and 'buses travelling to the west to Armley, Burley and Kirkstall which usually avoided Boar Lane and ran via Commercial Street and Bond Street, now made their return journey via Boar Lane. The Boar Lane improvement involved the demolition of much of the property on the south side including two of the inns that coaches and 'buses used for their starting points. The "Saracen's Head" was demolished in February 1868 and the "White Horse" closed its doors on 18th September 1869.

Lowerhead Row was too narrow to take the large amount of increasing traffic safely from the north end of the town and it was decided that the old Corn Exchange be demolished and a direct link from Briggate be formed. Work began on the extension, some 380 yards long, in November 1867, the old Corn Exchange (replaced by a new building at the end of Duncan Street in 1863) being one of the last buildings to be removed – in December 1868. The extension, known as New Briggate, was opened the following year and made things easier for street traffic. This included the Chapeltown,

J. Soper 4/1984

A 'bus stands at the Sheepscar Turnpike.

35

Roundhay and Meanwood 'buses which formerly ran from North Street via Lowerhead Row. The Chapeltown and Meanwood 'buses now used New Briggate, but the Roundhay 'buses continued to run via North Street and Lowerhead Row and returned to Roundhay via New Briggate.

During the 'sixties, the number of 'buses and 'bus services increased considerably. The Corporation, however, had no control over the omnibus proprietors who ran when and where they pleased. The proprietors could run the most decrepit vehicles without fear of admonition. They could employ whom they liked as conductors and drivers; the former frequently children.

From 1824 to 1842 the hackney coaches, or cabs, in Leeds were under the control of the Improvement Commissioners, and from 1842 onwards by the Corporation. In September each year all the cabs in the town were lined up outside the Town Hall and inspected by members of the Hackney Coach Committee. If satisfactory they were granted a licence. Drivers were also licensed annually. If a driver committed an offence he was reprimanded or, in bad cases, had his licence revoked. A Hackney Coach Inspector was appointed and it was possible for the Corporation to have continuous control over the cabs.

The "Leeds Improvement Act, 1869" gave the Corporation similar powers over the 'buses, drivers and conductors. The Act became law on 13th May 1869. The Committee was renamed the Hackney Carriages Committee and in November, Capel A. Curwood, the Town Clerk, issued the following notice:–

"BOROUGH OF LEEDS.

1. Notice is hereby given that in pursuance of the "Leeds Improvement Act, 1869", the Hackney Carriages Committee of the Council of this borough will attend at the Town Hall on Wednesday 24th inst. at 9.0 o'clock in the forenoon to grant licenses to hackney carriage drivers, and on Thursday 25th inst. at 1.0 pm to grant licenses to owners of omnibuses, and to drivers and conductors of same.

2. Drivers of hackney carriages will be required to deliver up their existing licenses if they have not already done so, and in lieu thereof they will receive others without further charge, if the Committee shall consider them fit to be licensed.

3. Drivers of hackney carriages, and drivers and conductors of omnibuses are required to bring testimonials as to character and fitness with them.

4. Owners of omnibuses and drivers will have to pay a fee of 5s. 0d. each for their respective licenses, and in addition each conductor will have to deposit, on receiving his badge, the sum of 5s. 0d. to be returned to him upon the badge being given up.

5. Owners of omnibuses are required to attend with their omnibuses, with horses and harness in good condition and to bring with them statements of the places and times of starting of their several omnibuses, their routes and rates of fares.

6. As licenses will be granted for the term of one year only, all persons are required to attend punctually at the times herein appointed in default of which they will be proceeded against according to law, for acting without licenses.

(Yorkshire Post, 23rd November, 1869).

On 25th November 20 'buses, 29 drivers and 29 conductors were licensed. By the end of 1869 this had increased to 44 'buses and 59 drivers. No further conductors were licensed in 1869. Children no longer appeared as 'bus conductors, for no person under the age of 18 was permitted to drive or guard a 'bus. Carrier's vans, if they carried passengers, had to be licensed as a 'bus. The Corporation now had strict control over the omnibus proprietors who had fought between themselves over the years. Shortly they were to meet a new foe – the tramcar.

A contemporary engraving of Park Row showing a double-deck horse tram.

36

CHAPTER SIX

The Tramways
Initial Proposals

Tramways or street railways made their appearance in America by the 1830's. The first tramway in Britain was the "Line of Docks Railway" in Liverpool opened in 1859. The following year a go-ahead American, George Francis Train, introduced tramways into Birkenhead and on 23rd March 1861 opened a tramway in London. A few days after the opening of the London line the Town Clerk of Leeds received a letter from Train in which he offered to lay down one mile of street railway in Wellington Street, Leeds, or any other locality in the town. He promised that the work would be finished within three weeks after approval for construction had been obtained, and agreed to remove the line if it proved unsatisfactory. At their meeting on 30th March the Town Council referred the letter to the Highways Surveyors who took no action and the subject was dropped.

Train's experiments in this country were short lived as his tramways had an objectionable feature in that the rails projected above the surface of the road and inter-

fered with the ordinary street traffic. As a result of this and the fact that the track construction was very light and required constant maintenance, public opinion was prejudiced against tramways. In the late 'sixties a new type of rail was introduced which was flush with the road surface. Interest in tramways was re-kindled but public reaction throughout the country was generally hostile. It became necessary to make an application to Parliament to construct tramways and, during November 1869, Parliamentary applications to build lines up and down the country were made. Included were proposals for tramways in Leeds promoted by two separate firms. The horse 'bus proprietors had shown that the Headingley, Chapeltown, Kirkstall and Hunslet areas were the most profitable and could support a frequent service, and it was in these districts that the tramway promoters were interested.

Messrs. North and Sons, solicitors of Leeds, promoted a Bill on behalf of Messrs. Fisher and Parrish and

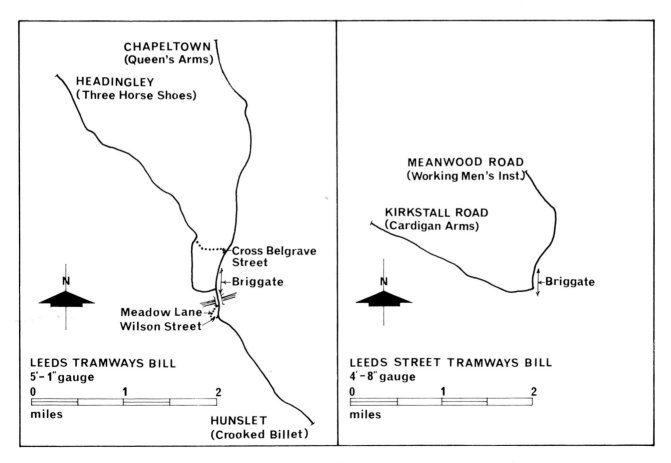

Partners, a firm of American origin, who were the contractors for the Liverpool tramways. This was known as "The Leeds Tramways Bill" and proposed the construction of a 5'-1" gauge system of tramway routes, these being:–

1. From Briggate to the "Queen's Arms", Chapeltown via North Street and Chapeltown Road.

2. From Boar Lane to the "Three Horse Shoes", Headingley, via West Bar, Park Row, Cookridge Street, Woodhouse Lane, and Headingley Road.

3. From Briggate to Hunslet, via Hunslet Lane, Hunslet Road and Low Road to the "Crooked Billet", Thwaite Gate.

The Headingley line was to have an alternative connection from Briggate via Cross Belgrave Street, Belgrave Street, Rockingham Street and Woodhouse Lane to connect at the top of Cookridge Street. An alternative link via Meadow Lane and Wilson Street was proposed for the Hunslet route. The Chapeltown and Headingley routes and Briggate connection were to be double track throughout, and the Hunslet and link route, single track with passing loops.

The other submission, "The Leeds Street Tramways Bill", was promoted by Ashurst, Morris and Co., solicitors, of London. They acted on behalf of a firm, some of whose members were connected with the Metropolitan Street Tramways, London, the Act for which was passed a few months earlier. The tramways proposed were to be laid down on the same principle as those in operation in Copenhagen and Brussels. Two tramway routes of 4'-8" gauge were proposed – one in double track from Briggate via Boar Lane, West Bar, Wellington Street and Kirkstall Road to a point about 200 yards past the Cardigan Arms, and a further route, also in double track, from Briggate via North Street and Meanwood Road to the Working Men's Institute in Meanwood Road.

The lower part of Meanwood Road had seen considerable building development in the late 'sixties and the promoters apparently thought a line in this direction would be remunerative. The 'buses running on Meanwood Road at this time, however, ran on only two days per week – Tuesdays and Saturdays.

Some members of the public were opposed to the "threatened tramways" but others spoke in favour. "J.T.N." had seen the tramways in Copenhagen and commented:–

"The draught is light for the horses, that trot along gaily, and they seem to know their business almost as well as their drivers. All classes of society freely use these vehicles which are very inviting; and they run at short intervals from eight in the morning to eleven at night".

(Yorkshire Post, 10th December, 1869).

Several of the local councillors were also in favour of the introduction of tramways, but, on the advice of the Town Clerk, it was decided to oppose the two bills. The Town Clerk, Capel A. Curwood, appears to have been one of the principal objectors to tramways and seems to have had considerable influence over the Town Council. He amassed a large number of objections from various sources, including complaints about the new Liverpool tramways – opened on 1st November 1869 – and constructed with the new type of flush rail and on the same principle as those proposed for Leeds.

The Corporation had almost completed the abolition of the tolls on the Turnpike Roads in the borough, at a cost of £60,000, and were in the process of acquiring possession of the local Gas Company's assets. Upon completion they would have control over all the streets in the town. At a meeting of the Council on 10th December 1869 some councillors felt that to give powers to a tramway company would mean that this control would be lost. Others considered that tramways were desirable but should be constructed by the Corporation. One or two spoke in favour of granting powers to one of the private companies. The principal champion of this course was Councillor Marsden who held shares in American tramway companies. Marsden compared the opposition to the tramways with that of 35 years earlier when railway construction was opposed on the ground that the smoke from the engines would blacken the fleeces of the sheep. He stated that tramways had proved a blessing to the countries where they were in operation and the promoters of them in England had had to fight a hard battle due to the fact that people were not acquainted with them. They also had the opposition of the omnibus proprietors to encounter – (one of whom in Leeds, William Turton, was a prominent Town Councillor). Marsdens' expostulations were to no avail; the Bills were to be opposed. If tramways were to be constructed the work would be carried out by the Corporation.

Messrs. Fisher and Parrish offered to lay down an experimental line 100 yards long in Oxford Street near the Town Hall. Similar proposals were made by the other promoters, but both were rejected. The Leeds based promoters, however, took the initiative and constructed a short length of line on private ground, a "barren and desolate area" at the bottom and on the east side of Cookridge Street. A circular was sent to each member of the Council inviting him to attend a demonstration. The Town Clerk made a strong public protest against this invitation for which he was later severely "ticked off" by Marsden. The demonstration took place on 26th January 1870 and, in spite of the Town Clerks' protestations, many members of the Corporation attended. The trial was conducted on a very short length of track and the car was drawn backwards and forwards. Several of the Councillors were impressed and intimated that "the feeling of the town was now moving decidedly in favour of the adoption of tramways".

A motion was put at the following Council meeting on 9th February that the Corporation should promote a Bill in Parliament to lay down tramways itself. The motion assisted the Corporation in its opposition to the two private tramway bills. Marsden again forcefully presented the case for a private company, but the motion was passed. The two Bills were successfully opposed by the Corporation and subsequently withdrawn.

A large number of applications to introduce tramways in the country were made and Parliament had under consideration a general Tramways Bill which covered all aspects of the institution and construction of tramways. The Bill received the Royal Assent and was known as the "Tramways Act, 1870". This Act gave full protection for the interests of Corporations in regard to tramway promotions by private companies. Its official title was "An Act to facilitate the Construction of and to regulate the working of Tramways" and its effects on tramway promoters were onerous. Briefly its clauses were:–

1. Promoters could apply for a Provisional Order to the Board of Trade instead of promoting a private Bill in Parliament as formerly. Tramway Order Confirmation

Acts confirmed the Provisional Orders at intervals.

2. The tramway operators were responsible for paving and maintaining the roadway between the tramway tracks and for a distance of eighteen inches on either side to the satisfaction of the local authority.

3. Local authorities had the power of veto if they objected to a line passing through their area and could use this power to impose such terms as they wished upon the promoters.

4. The local authority could purchase the tramway after 21 years from the date of authorisation. The purchase price was to be the "then value of the tramway and works" without any allowance for compulsory purchase, goodwill, prospective profits or other considerations.

Extensive litigation resulted with many tramway undertakings when this latter clause was applied.

The Corporation made no effort to promote its own Bill but two brothers, William and Daniel Busby of Liverpool, represented by Messrs. Barr, Nelson and Barr, solicitors, of Leeds, submitted new tramway proposals. Daniel Busby was the Chairman of the Liverpool Road and Railway Omnibus Co. Ltd. and had operated 'buses in Liverpool from 1834. He was also connected with the "Line of Docks Railway" and an early tramway in Liverpool. The consideration of Busby's proposals was referred to the Highways Committee. One of the Busby's, Mr. Nelson and Busby's engineer, a John Kincaid, attended a meeting of the committee on 12th October 1870. They presented a long report and proposals to construct four tramways. The gauge was to be 4'-8½" and the proposals a part combination of the two earlier promotions, as follows:–

1. From the Briggate end of Boar Lane and along Wellington Street to a point near the "Cardigan Arms", Kirkstall Road – largely double track.

2. From the west end of Boar Lane, along Park Row, Cookridge Street, Woodhouse Lane and Headingley Road to the "Three Horse Shoes", Far Headingley – a combination of double and single track.

3. From the Briggate end of Boar Lane along Briggate, North Street and Chapeltown Road to the "Queen's Arms", Chapeltown – single track with passing places.

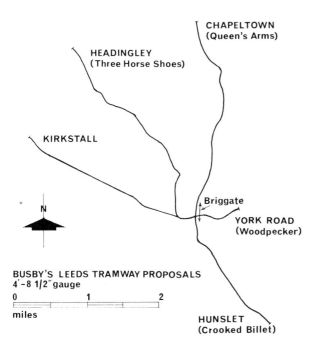

CHAPELTOWN
(Queen's Arms)

HEADINGLEY
(Three Horse Shoes)

KIRKSTALL

N

Briggate

YORK ROAD
(Woodpecker)

BUSBY'S LEEDS TRAMWAY PROPOSALS
4'-8 1/2"gauge

0   1   2
miles

HUNSLET
(Crooked Billet)

4. From the Briggate end of Boar Lane across Leeds Bridge and along Hunslet Lane and Hunslet Road to the junction of Low Road and Waterloo Road – largely double track.

At the suggestion of the Highways Committee, Busby's agreed to extend their "Cardigan Arms" terminus to Kirkstall. They were also to consider the construction of a tramway along Marsh Lane to Burmantofts.

The Highways Committee deliberated on the Busby's proposals and came to a rather surprising conclusion. They considered that it was "undesirable to give the consent asked for as it was probable street tramways would be superseded by some other invention". They presumably had in mind Thompsons' steam driven omnibus, which was undergoing trials in Edinburgh at the time.

Informed opinion was against the views of the Highways Committee. At a stormy meeting of the Council on 20th October 1870, they were censured for their inaction over the previous 12 months. At the meeting it seemed as if the Council would pass a resolution in favour of a private company constructing the tramways. This was again largely owing to Marsden, who had gathered support, principally from Councillor Gaunt. Gaunt pointed out that if the Corporation constructed tramways only in areas where they would be remunerative, rate-payers in other areas would complain. A private company could use its discretion. It was this view that settled the matter for Marsden and his supporters. The whole subject was deferred to a special meeting of the Council held on 28th October.

In the meantime Messrs. North and Sons noted the change of heart of the Council. On behalf of the promoters of the previous unsuccessful application, they resubmitted their scheme in an amended form.

Messrs. Thompson and Co., the proprietors of the Edinburgh Steam Omnibus, submitted tramway proposals. Councillor William Turton and John Ramsden, omnibus proprietors, submitted an application that in the event of tramways being constructed they should receive compensation from the Tramways Company.

At the special meeting of the Council it was agreed that a private company should carry out the work. The question of who was to construct the tramways was referred to the Highways Committee, and the Committee considered the four applications. Messrs. Busby's agreed to construct the four tramways proposed at their earlier meeting with the committee. They also agreed to compensate Messrs. Turton and Ramsden and pay £1,000 to the Corporation for the concession to build the tramways. Mr. Thompson, who appears to have suggested a combined goods and passenger tramway, talked for a long time, but the Committee could get no definite proposals out of him and his application was withdrawn. Messrs. North and Sons' clients would not offer any money for the concession to construct the tramways, but were, however, prepared to build tramways beyond the "Three Horse Shoes", Headingley (proposed by Busby's as their terminus) to Adel, and beyond the "Queen's" at Chapeltown (Busby's terminus) to the "Chained Bull" at Moortown. They also promised to make a tramway to the "Shoulder of Mutton Inn", York Road. These were rash proposals. The areas between the "Three Horse Shoes" and Adel, and the "Queen's" and "Chained Bull" were, with the exception of the odd villa and cottage, completely open countryside. No tramway could have possibly paid along these routes. Messrs. Fisher and Parrish realised this too late and irately withdrew their offer. The way was now clear for the Busby's. At their meeting on 9th November 1870 the Council unanimously gave their consent to Messrs. William and Daniel Busby to undertake the construction of the Leeds tramways.

The Leeds Tramways Company insignia as used on rolling stock in the 1880's and 1890's.

CHAPTER SEVEN

The Tramways

Inauguration and Formation of Company

The Busby's Tramways Bill, as agreed with the Town Council, passed through Parliament as an unopposed measure and became law on 14th August 1871. In anticipation of the receipt of the Royal Assent, Busby's began the construction of the Headingley tramway on Monday 5th June 1871, employing a local contractor, Messrs. A. Speight and Sons of the Canal Basin, Leeds. Ground was broken at the south eastern side of Woodhouse Moor proceeding towards Headingley, 30 men being employed, and within a week two other gangs in Boar Lane and Park Row were working. It was anticipated that the work would be completed by August, but there was some delay due to the construction of gas mains in Woodhouse Lane and poor weather.

The tramway, from the Briggate end of Boar Lane to the "Oak Inn", Headingley, was completed in early September. After leaving the busy shopping street of newly widened Boar Lane and West Bar, the tramway was single track in Park Row, the commercial centre, skirted St. Anne's Cathedral on the east side of the street, and then ran up Cookridge Street on double track – a 1 in 18 gradient, the steepest on the route. At the top of Cookridge Street was the sharpest curve – 50 feet radius – to the left into Woodhouse Lane. The lower part of Woodhouse Lane, a steady incline, was largely double track through a middle class residential area. On the west side was the site of the future Yorkshire College (later Leeds University) in Beech Grove (later renamed College Road and later still University Road). The tramway continued up Woodhouse Lane with, on the east side, the "Pack Horse Inn" a future horse 'bus terminus. The highest point of Woodhouse Lane was reached at Reservoir Street Police Station on the west side, and the tramway then descended on double track across Woodhouse Moor to Hyde Park corner. Cattle grazed on the Moor and at that time it was the only publicly owned recreation area in Leeds. At Hyde Park was a road connection with the working class area of Woodhouse. The line then ascended Headingley Road (shortly afterwards known as Headingley Lane) on single track with passing loops, serving middle and upper class villas, and terminated at the "Oak Inn" near to St. Michael's Church. Adjacent to the "Oak Inn" were the remains of a centuries old oak tree which did not finally collapse until 1941. The total length of the route was approximately $2\frac{1}{4}$ miles, of which one mile was single track.

Three of the tramcars to be used on the new tramway arrived from Birkenhead on 6th September, via the London and North Western Railway, and the following day,

Captain Tyler, the Government Inspector for the Board of Trade, made his inspection. John Kincaid, Busby's Engineer, had previously requested permission to lay down granite setts between the rails where areas of single track occurred, but this request was inadvisedly refused by the Highways Committee. Captain Tyler reported:–

"The roadway between, and at the sides of the tramway rails is paved with stone in some cases of granite, in some cases sand stone, for a distance of $\frac{3}{4}$ mile along the streets. The remainder of the roadway is formed of macadam. I believe that portions of the Birkenhead Tramway, and of the Staffordshire Potteries Tramways have been laid in macadamised roads, but this is as far as I am aware, the first instance, in which a tramway has been so laid in an important city of crowded traffic, and I fear that the inconvenience and expense attendant upon the repairs which undoubtedly will be pretty constantly required, will be found to be considerable. I understand that the Proprietor and Engineer of the Tramway were both desirous to employ a material of a more durable character, but that the Corporation of Leeds insisted, as they had the right to do, that the same material which was found in the roads by the Tramway Proprietor before he commenced his operations should be replaced in them during the construction of the tramway. This being the case, the roadway is in as good a condition as could probably under the circumstances be expected."

(Board of Trade Report, 7th September, 1871).

Captain Tyler passed the tramway as fit for traffic and on 13th September 1871 the tramway, cars, drivers and conductors were inspected by the Hackney Carriages Committee:–

"With the view of avoiding the inconvenience of a crowd the intention of the Committee to inspect the line and rolling stock had not been publicly announced, but the passage through the town of the novel cars, decorated with flags, speedily apprised the public of the event of the day. The four cars to be employed in carrying the traffic on the line, and the fifth, or pattern car, which is to be reserved for emergencies, were brought down the tramway from Headingley, two horses being attached to each, and in this way a sort of procession of cars was formed. The horses employed were supplied by Mr. Ramsden whose 'buses, along with those of other proprietors, are no doubt destined to disappear from the road as soon as the tramways cover the routes embraced in Messrs. Busby's scheme. It is hardly necessary to mention that the employment of Mr.

Starbuck car No. 28 stands outside Headingley Depot about 1880.

Courtesy R. Brook.

Ramsden's horses was only a temporary expedient. When the cars commence running Messrs. Busby will employ their own horses. As illustrating the resources of the Company it may be mentioned that in Liverpool where the tramways are in their hands, they have no fewer than 1,340 horses and 146 'buses, 96 of the latter being kept constantly running. ————

————Leaving Boar Lane the train of cars started for Headingley. Cookridge Street and Woodhouse Lane proved a somewhat heavy gradient for two horses, but at these points a chain horse will assist the team when the cars accommodate the ordinary traffic. It may also be observed that as soon as the tramway becomes settled by constant running the traction will become easier. Seeing the cars passing many persons were led to believe that the ordinary traffic had commenced. It was amusing to observe the puzzled air in which would be passengers regarded the cars as they passed on indifferent to their signals to stop and take them up." ————

(Yorkshire Post, 14th September, 1871).

The conductors were given a uniform of dark blue with the letters "L.T.Co." on the collar, supplied by J. T. Beer, a clothier of Boar Lane. The drivers had no uniform.

The line was opened for public service on Saturday, 16th September, the fares being from Boar Lane to Reservoir Street 2d. and beyond 3d. Cars ran from Leeds every 15 minutes from 9.0 am to 9.0 pm and every 30 minutes from 9.0 pm to 10.30 pm (52 departures daily). This service was a big improvement on the old 'bus service which, at its maximum with three proprietors, ran only 24 daily journeys. Within a week complaints were being received about the new tramway:—

"The extent of sticking fast, pushing, pulling, whipping and swearing between Boar Lane and Cookridge Street is a disgrace not only to the new and novel institution, but to civilisation. The fact is the dead, dull, stiff pull these low, solid metal-wheeled cars require on rising ground is too much for any three horses and more than enough for the occasional fourth horse put on."

(Yorkshire Post, 21st September, 1871).

Others however liked the tramways and one passenger suggested that they be extended to Shadwell, Scarcroft and Thorp Arch – some 14 miles! As Captain Tyler had anticipated, the tramway in Woodhouse Lane was soon in a "crippled" condition. Holes several inches deep appeared in the macadam and the tram rail stood out as prominently as that of a railway line. In December 1871, Arthur Lupton, a Leeds worthy, submitted an account for payment by the Corporation for repairs to his carriage damaged by the defective tramway and complaints came in thick and fast. John Bradley, a coach builder, submitted a list of vehicles that he had repaired, the damage being solely due to the tramways:—

"William Boothroyd, dog cart. W.B. thrown out and splashboard badly strained.

R. Shackleton, dog cart. Horse fell, passengers thrown out. Both shafts broken etc.

Henry Thorne, wagonette. Fore carriage broken, he was thrown out and damage to carriage £5 or £6." ——— etc. etc.

(Lupton files, Leeds Archives Dept.). There were many others.

The Corporation, of course, refused to pay Lupton's bill and referred him to Busby's. On 14th December 1871 notice was served on Busby's to put the line in order, but they declined and contended that "they were in no manner responsible" for the condition of the tramway and put the blame fairly and squarely on the Corporation. The legal wrangling started and at one stage the Corporation gave notice that they would repave the whole of the tramway themselves, charge the cost to Busby's, and discontinue the tramway service from 11th January 1872, in order to carry out the work. Busby's obtained an injunction from the Court of Chancery which restrained the Corporation from taking any such action.

Meanwhile, in November 1871, Busby's had applied to Parliament for a Bill – the "Leeds Tramways Act, 1872" – which proposed that their undertaking be transferred to a new Company to be known as the "Leeds Tramways Company." They also applied to build a new tramway extension, outside the Leeds boundary, to

42

Roundhay Park, a mansion and large park purchased by the Corporation a few weeks earlier. Roundhay Road was a narrow country lane and unsuitable for a double track tramway. Its average width was about 25 feet and at its narrowest point – the bridge over Gipton Beck – it was only 20 feet. The Highway Surveyors of Roundhay objected on the grounds of the narrowness of the road and the dangers to other road users as experienced on the Headingley tramway. Objections were also made by the Leeds Corporation.

Busby's and the Corporation eventually settled their differences with regard to the Headingley track problem and an agreement was reached in March 1872. The agreement included the withdrawal of the proposed tramways to Roundhay and New Wortley, the foregoing of the laying of the tramway to Chapeltown until it was proved by the working of the Headingley tramway that the road could be kept in good repair and not dangerous to horses and carriages, and to lay single track instead of double track in Wellington Street and Kirkstall Road until the traffic increased. In turn the Corporation consented to allow extra time for the making of the Hunslet and Marsh Lane tramways, to keep in repair the Leeds and Headingley and all other roads upon which tramways were laid, Busby's repaying the cost every quarter. The Company was also allowed to extend the track from the east end of Boar Lane along Duncan Street to the Corn Exchange to facilitate the changing of horses, and to make various minor track alterations. All legal proceedings were dropped.

Construction of the extension of the Headingley tramway from the "Oak" to the "Three Horse Shoes" proceeded soon after the tramway was opened, but upon reaching a point about 150 yards beyond Shaw Lane, the work stopped and the rails and sleepers transferred for use on the Kirkstall route. This was presumably owing to a shortage of materials for this latter route, and a probable reason why the Wellington Street and Kirkstall Road sections were constructed in single track in lieu of double as originally proposed.

The section of tramway between Boar Lane and the "Cardigan Arms", Kirkstall Road, was opened for traffic on 1st April 1872, a 20 minutes service operating from 9.0 am to 9.0 pm (37 journeys daily). The fare was 2d. each way. Again this frequency was a big improvement on Jackson's former 'bus service which normally ran 14 journeys daily – 16 on Saturday.

Owing to the Headingley track episode and the fact that for the first few months Busbys had no manager, things were disorganised and the image of the tramways was tarnished. The following was a common experience. In the words of a "Ratepayer":–

"About 4.0 pm car nos. 2 and 3 met on the same rails at the junction of Park Row and Bond Street, one of the busiest junctions in Leeds. Each driver began to abuse the other each declaiming he would stay there until midnight before he would move, and judging from the manner each was determined to keep his word. A large crowd soon assembled, vehicles could not pass the busy thoroughfare rendered more busy by it being market day and foot passengers were greatly annoyed and inconvenienced. The drivers continued to abuse each other for a quarter of an hour when the "up" car drove off the rails to allow the other car to pass. The driver of the "down" car went off at an almost unjustifiable speed much to the danger of the people in the street. It appeared from what passed between the drivers that these meetings are of common occurence

and I have seen several myself."
(Yorkshire Post, 27th June, 1872).

By April 1872 a manager, Charles Smith, had been appointed, and he immediately began to try and improve the tramway image. On May Day he put on a splendid display; all the trams were drawn by grey horses, the guards in immaculate uniform, the cars and horses decorated with flags and rosettes, and a procession of 25 grey reserve horses, gaily caparisoned, paraded through the streets of the town. A similar display was put on for the opening of the extension of the Kirkstall tramway from the "Cardigan Arms" along Commercial Road to Kirkstall village on Saturday, 18th May. Four cars were used to open the service.

A remarkably accurate engraving of car No, 5 in Wellington Street from "The Building News" of 21st March 1884. *Courtesy Leeds City Libraries.*

The Kirkstall route was ideal for horse trams being level and almost straight for the whole of its length. Leaving Boar Lane the tramway passed along Wellington Street with, on the south side, the railway stations and on either side commercial and industrial buildings. At Wellington Bridge the tramway veered to the right and at the end of Wellington Street made a turn to the left on to Kirkstall Road. This part of Wellington Street and Kirkstall Road, as far as the "Cardigan Arms", was heavily built up with industrial property, mills and working class dwellings. The tramway passed under the viaduct of the North Eastern Railway Harrogate line and further on the "Cardigan Arms" was reached on the north side. Beyond this point was countryside. A slight curve to the right brought Kirkstall Road on to Commercial Road and from there the line made a gradual descent into Kirkstall village. The terminus was near to the "Star and Garter Hotel" and about a quarter of a mile from the famous Kirkstall Abbey.

The "Leeds Tramways Act, 1872" received the Royal Assent on 6th August 1872 and the Leeds Tramways Company was incorporated. The capital of the Company was £160,000 divided into 16,000 shares of £10 each. Subscriptions were invited on 9th September 1872 and the directors of the Company were given as follows:–

William Bower Esq. Iron master, Drighlington, near Leeds.

William Coghlan Esq. Messrs. Coghlan and Drury, Ironmasters, Hunslet, near Leeds.

William Illingworth Esq. Messrs. Illingworth, Ingham and Co. timber merchants, Leeds.

Alexander McEwan Esq. Lombard House, Lombard Street, London.

William Turton, Esq. omnibus proprietor, Leeds.

Thomas Wright Esq. Chairman of the Liverpool Omnibus and Tramways Co. Ltd. Liverpool.

The solicitors were Barr, Nelson and Barr of Leeds, the Engineer John Kincaid and Secretary Edward Bellamy. Bellamy was also the Secretary for a Company known as the Continental and General Tramway Company. The offices were given as 3 Park Row, Leeds and Westminster Chambers, London.

Under an agreement authorised by the Act, the Company was to acquire from Busby's the undertaking so far opened with the freehold land, stabling, plant, rolling stock and horses, in consideration of the repayment to Busby's of their actual outlay and the issue to them of £13,000 of fully paid up shares in the Company.

The new Company entered into an agreement with the Continental and General Tramway Company under which that Company undertook to make the cash payments to Busby's. They also agreed to construct the remaining tramways, provide the required number of cars and horses, build ample stable accommodation and give 12 month's maintenance, all for the sum of £137,000.

The Company's prospectus forecast a net return of 11% on capital invested for passenger traffic alone and added:–

"By the construction of sidings into the large works on the Kirkstall and Hunslet Roads and into the goods yards of the railway companies who are anxious for the accommodation, there is no doubt that the greater part of the enormous traffic now carted along those roads would be brought in the railway wagons over the tramways and the line along the Kirkstall Road has been laid for some distance with heavier rails in view of this object."

(Yorkshire Post, 9th September, 1872).

It was intended that the goods traffic would be taken over the tramways at night to prevent disruption of passenger traffic and the track in Kirkstall Road was later doubled and a crossover put in at the "Beckett's Arms", possibly to facilitate shunting. There is no evidence, however, that railway wagons ever ran over the tramways, presumably due to the differences in the thicknesses of the wheel flanges.

Under the agreement with Busby's the Company would come into immediate possession and working of the existing tramways, as a going concern. The receipts would from then on belong to them; so that an early dividend on the paid up capital could be expected.

The Company stated that the construction of the remainder of the lines would be pushed on as rapidly as possible and anticipated that the whole of the lines would be completed during 1873. The share list was closed on 3rd October 1872 and the first meeting of the shareholders of the new Company took place on 5th February 1873. William Coghlan presided. It was stated that the total amount of shares subscribed, including the £13,000 to be issued to Busby's as fully paid up, was

£153,350. The Continental and General Company had already paid £10,000 to Busby's in advance and arrangements were in progress for the payment of further instalments when, in November, the Company were unexpectedly served with a notice by Fisher and Parrish, the promoters of the unsuccessful tramway scheme in 1870. It appears that there must have been some under cover financial dealing with Busby's for Fisher and Parrish claimed a partnership with them in the Leeds tramways. They asked the Company (and through them the Continental Company) not to make further payments to Busby's until the partnership rights could be settled. After about four months this legal difficulty was sorted out and more payments were then made to Busby's.

Starbuck single-deck horse cars Nos. 33 and 51 in Briggate about 1880. The dash of car No, 16 can just be seen in Duncan Street on the right.   *Courtesy J. Valentine.*

On 1st March 1873 a manager, William Bulmer of Liverpool, and a secretary and treasurer, William Wharam of Leeds, were appointed. Bulmer had connections with the Busby's and had experience of tramways in Liverpool. He was also an omnibus proprietor and innkeeper in that town. Wharam, for the previous 17 years, had been in the service of the Great Northern Railway Company and was the cashier in their goods depot at Leeds. Bulmer and Wharam replaced respectively Charles Smith and Edward Bellamy.

A partial transfer of the undertaking from Busby's to the Company took place on 15th March 1873. In May two cheques amounting to £12,192 were paid to Busby's and the Company's cash books indicate that from Whit Sunday, 1st June, the Company began to take the receipts from the cars. Later, after payment of a cheque to Busby's for £13,000, a public notice, dated 8th August 1873, appeared, signed by William Wharam, announcing the complete transfer of the tramways undertaking from Busby's to the Leeds Tramways Company. The Company was now secure and in a position to construct the remaining tramways authorised by the "Leeds Tramways Act, 1871."

CHAPTER EIGHT

The Tramways:
1873 to 1880

During 1873 the tramway traffic was increasing and one of the first actions of the new Company was to introduce a tramway service between Boar Lane and Hyde Park, a short working of the Headingley tramway. The service was in operation by July 1873 and two small one-horse cars were employed. An idea of the General Manager, William Bulmer, was the introduction in late July of a ticket system in which tickets were issued to each passenger. The tickets were collected by the passenger and returned to the Company, and for every 12 tickets received the Company paid 3d. This ticket system was short lived and on 31st October 1873 was discontinued, but was replaced with a system whereby passengers could purchase either a 2s. 6d. or 5s. 0d. book of tickets from the Tramways waiting room in Boar Lane and were allowed 5% discount. This, again, was short lived and the Company made their last payment for tickets on 22nd April 1874.

I No. 340
LEEDS
TRAMWAYS COMPANY.
Fare 3d.
3d. given for 12 of these Tickets returned to the Office.

Ticket of the type used in 1873-4 by the Leeds Tramways Company. It measured 3″ × 2 ¹/₁₀″ and was pink in colour. *Courtesy Leeds City Libraries.*

It was one of the conditions of purchase that Busby's would re-pave the Headingley line from Cookridge Street to Shaw Lane with granite and, by an agreement between them and the Corporation, this work was done in the summer of 1873. At the same time the Tramways Company doubled the track in Wellington Street and Kirkstall Road as far as the "Cardigan Arms" whilst, in late August, a start was made on the construction of the extension of the Headingley tramway from beyond Shaw Lane to the "Three Horse Shoes." The work was completed by 8th October and the tramway opened shortly afterwards. Cars ran from Boar Lane to the "Three Horse Shoes" every half hour from 9.0 am to

10.30 pm with a quarter hour service to the "Oak" from 8.45 am to 12 noon and from 8.0 pm to 10.30 pm (from 12 noon to 8.0 pm every ten minutes). On Sundays a morning half hourly and afternoon quarter hourly service was operated.

During the early 'seventies the old bridge over the River Aire, at the bottom of Briggate, was taken down and replaced by a new structure. This prevented the construction of the Hunslet tramway, but the official opening of the bridge on 9th July 1873 made it possible for work on the tramway to commence. Almost immediately a contractor, A. M. Child, started work. The Highways Committee approved variations to the Parliamentary plans in respect of the trackwork, but progress was very slow and the paving defective. The Kirkstall route was also not properly paved and in December, the Highways Surveyor, Thomas Wrigglesworth, issued a long report listing the defects on the Hunslet and Kirkstall tramways.

In order to overcome the problem, the Continental and General Tramways Company, who had sub-let the construction of the Hunslet tramway to Child, made an agreement with the Corporation whereby the latter would re-pave the tramway, the cost to be paid by Child. An agreement was also made that the Corporation should re-pave the Kirkstall route and also pave the York Road and Chapeltown tramways which had yet to be constructed. The paving of the latter two routes was to cost £10,760.

By November 1873 the Hunslet tramway had been completed as far as Waterloo Road, but it was not until late the following February that the Board of Trade inspector passed the line for traffic and it was officially opened on Monday 2nd March 1874. A large crowd "sufficient almost to have done honour to a royal procession" gathered along the route to see the cars which were decorated with flags. Marsden, now the Mayor, was present with Directors and officials of the Tramways Company and, at a dinner at the "Great Northern Hotel" afterwards, he remarked:–

"There were many persons who, at one time, said that the existence of tramways in their streets would be a nuisance, whilst they would be no improvement upon the old, slow, jog-trot omnibus traffic, but who now acknowledged that they were one of the greatest boons that had ever been introduced into the town and had added very much to the convenience and comfort of travellers. He sympathised with the Company in the trouble they had had in Leeds. They had had to educate the people to ride instead of walk, and to fight

for the establishment of something new as opposed to what had existed for a long time, and this was always difficult."

(Yorkshire Post, 3rd March 1874).

The Chairman, William Coghlan, said that the Headingley tramway, now repaired, was the "best piece of tramway in the kingdom," and Councillor William Turton admitted that he at first opposed the tramways, but finding, as an omnibus proprietor, he would soon be nowhere, he went in with the Tramways Company. Turton had an agreement with the Tramways Company that he would withdraw any of his 'buses which were in competition with the tramways. The Hunslet service had been the most profitable of his 'bus routes and the Tramways Company anticipated that it would be similarly successful as a tramway route.

The route, about 2½ miles long, ran from Briggate over the new Leeds Bridge on double track and continued along Hunslet Lane and Hunslet Road through densely populated working class areas, with factories and engineering works on each side, as far as the "Swan Junction" – the junction of Hunslet Road, Low Road and Waterloo Road. From here to the terminus the track was single with passing loops along Low Road. The area was less densely populated beyond Church Street, on the right, and at the terminus, the "Crooked Billet Inn," Thwaite Gate, was comparatively rural. This area was later built up with working class dwellings in the 'nineties.

On 3rd March 1874 the line was opened to the public and a 15 minutes (later increased to ten minutes) service was operated from 8.45 am to 10.30 pm from Briggate, the fare being 2d. from Briggate to the "Swan Junction" and through to Thwaite Gate 3d.

By February 1874 construction work had begun on both the Chapeltown and York Road lines. There were many complaints about the standard of paving carried out by the Corporation who were apparently no better than the Tramways Company. North Street was particularly bad and a memorandum was presented to the Chairman of the Highways Committee in which it was stated that horses were constantly falling down and blocking the street. On Saturday 25th April seven fell within an hour. The paving was later improved.

A Starbuck single-deck car stands in Duncan Street in 1890. *Courtesy The late C. R. Wood, Photographer.*

The short line to York Road was the first to be completed and opened for traffic on 29th August 1874. The tramway was virtually level throughout its length and ran on single track with passing loops. Travelling from the Boar Lane junction with Briggate the tramway passed along narrow Duncan Street and Call Lane through commercial property and then via Kirkgate, passing under the new railway bridge of the North Eastern Railway, and a hundred yards further on the right, the Leeds Parish Church. From there the route ran along Marsh Lane through a densely populated working class slum

A busy scene at the Boar Lane terminus of the Headlingley trams about 1893.   *Courtesy The late C. R. Wood, Photographer.*

area, demolished about 30 years later. The terminus was at the "Woodpecker Inn" at the junction of Marsh Lane, Quarry Hill, Burmantofts Street and York Road.

Cars ran every quarter of an hour from 8.45 am to 10.30 pm (Saturdays 11.0 pm) and the fare was 1d. from Duncan Street. The York Road service was intended to run through to Kirkstall, but if this arrangement was carried out, it was soon discontinued and a through service between Kirkstall and Hunslet instituted in lieu.

In April 1874 construction of the Chapeltown tramway had reached Mitchell Hill, but then ceased. Concern was expressed by the Corporation that a repetition of the state of affairs that had existed on the Headingley route was to take place. They insisted that they would not allow the tramway to be opened until the entire route to the "Queen's Arms" was completed.

Heavy double-deck cars were proving uneconomical, particularly on the hilly Headingley service where three and in places four horses were required to haul the cars. In winter and during bad weather people refused to ride on top and the Tramways Company were carrying the additional weight of an upper deck without any remuneration. The cost of feeding the horses was increasing and a large number of horses was required. In February 1874 there were 128 horses in stock. This was increased by 56 to work the Hunslet service and by a further 86 in November to work the York Road and Chapeltown routes making a total of 270 horses. The policy of the Tramways Company in 1874 was to run a lighter type of single-deck car and to run them more frequently. In the words of William Coghlan:—

"It was the general opinion of tramway managers that the time would come when they would have one-horse cars for flat roads and two-horse cars for hilly roads. The cars on the Chapeltown branch would require two horses and on some portions of the road, perhaps three."

The one-horse cars acquired for the hilly Boar Lane to Hyde Park service apparently did not run on this service for long. One is recorded as running on the level Kirkstall route in January 1874. Light single-deck cars were ordered for the Chapeltown service.

A variation occurred during the construction of the tramway as five additional passing places were put in, over and above those allowed for in the Parliamentary plans. On 11th November 1874 the official opening took place. Alderman Marsden was again present and the guests were entertained at Councillor Turton's imposing residence, Hayfield House, a large villa adjacent to Reginald Terrace, Chapeltown Road. The house was built for Turton and still exists but is now used for offices and a public house.

The Board of Trade inspection took place on 13th November and the following day the line was opened for public traffic. At first a quarter hourly service was operated from Briggate to the Cross Roads, Chapeltown (the junction of Stainbeck Lane and Town Street with Harrogate Road). This was half a mile short of the terminus at the "Queen's Arms" and cars ran from 8.45 am to 10.30 pm. A fortnight later, commencing on 1st December, the quarter hourly service was extended through to the "Queen's" with a short working, at the same frequency, to Cowper Street (111 journeys daily). The fare to Cowper Street was 2d. and beyond 3d. The Cowper Street short working appears to have been short lived and was probably discontinued after a few months.

The Chapeltown tramway was rather similar to Headingley in character. It ascended Briggate on double track and ran along New Briggate through a recently constructed shopping area and into North Street with the Smithfield Market on the left. North Street was partly single track and, prior to the 'sixties, in the early 'bus days, was rural with fine elm trees on each side. The removal of the trees caused the same opposition that exists with similar proposals today. It was now

A re-built eight window Starbuck double-deck car with garden seats stands in Lower Briggate en route to Hunslet, about 1890.
Courtesy The late C. R. Wood, Photographer.

built up densely with commercial property and working class housing. William Turton later had a corn merchant's shop on the left hand side near Sheepscar. The tramway descended slightly into Sheepscar with Meanwood Road on the left and Roundhay Road on the right. It then began the ascent of Chapeltown Road. New working class housing and shops were under construction at the lower part of Chapeltown Road. The new St. Clement's Church (built 1868) was on the left and Roscoe Place Methodist Chapel (built 1862) on the right. Just below the Chapel was a developing working class area of brick built terrace houses which included a street some 150 yards from Sheepscar on the east side of Chapeltown Road. This was quaintly named Tramway Street, built between 1871 and 1874 and demolished 100 years later in 1970–1. The street legend plates are now preserved at the National Tramway Museum, Crich, Derbyshire. Barrack Street was passed on the west side and just above were Joseph Walkers' 'bus stables (referred to in a later chapter). Leopold Street was on the east side and this formed the start of the middle and upper class residential area of New Leeds. Opposite Hayfield House on the west of the tramway, the road levelled out and continued on the level past Sholebroke Avenue – large brick built terrace houses. This was the upper limit of the New Leeds area. Passing the Congregational Church on the left the tramway reached the bottom of Mitchell Hill and was now in rural surroundings. There was a horse trough here used by the chain horse required to assist the tram up the hill. The line veered to the right and then to the left passing Harehills Lane on the right and the village of Potternewton on the left. The chain horse was detached and the line made a slight ascent to the "Mexborough Arms," Chapeltown. The site of the future Chapeltown

Tram Depot was on the left below the "Mexborough". An ascent and a curve to the right and the Cross Roads was reached. Again through middle class housing and shops the tramway ascended the Harrogate Road, passing on the summit of the hill Wood Lane on the west side. A descent of about 250 yards and the terminus at the "Queen's Arms" was reached. This marked the outer boundary of Chapeltown. Beyond was open countryside.

The opening of the Chapeltown tramway completed the system for which the Company had obtained Parliamentary powers and the mileage now in operation was 18 miles 3 furlongs and 8 chains of single track.

The middle 'seventies was a period of consolidation for the Tramways Company. From its inception the Company had paid a dividend of 6%, far short of the 11% originally forecast, but nevertheless a reasonably satisfactory return. A setback occurred during the last six months of 1874 when a dividend of 5% was paid. This was caused by a 25% increase in the price of hay and corn and also severe weather conditions. The weather not only caused a considerable falling off in traffic receipts, but also incurred a big labour cost in clearing snow from the lines. The horses needed extra attention and care under the trying conditions to which they were exposed. The Company used salt on the lines to clear the snow and this resulted in many complaints from, not only the Town Council, but also the R.S.P.C.A. who considered that the use of salt inflicted cruelty on the horses. There were conflicting views from veterinary surgeons but the Tramways Company eventually won the day and was allowed to salt its lines.

Traffic increased weekly during 1875 and the dividend paid for the half year ended 30th June 1875

"Horsfield" car No. 172 passes Tramway Street on 8th September 1956. *Courtesy A. K. Terry.*

48

had returned to 6%. The number of horses increased to 289.

The Company continued to pay a 6% dividend throughout 1876 and dispensed with the services of the Continental and General Tramway Company with whom they had been in dispute over payment for the work the Company had carried out. The Company cash books show that the Continental Company was paid off on 20th May 1876. The introduction of new cars, light in weight, enabled the Company to provide a 7½ minutes service on some routes, but this did not prove profitable and soon reverted to every ten minutes or quarter of an hour as before.

Things had progressed peacefully for the Company in its first three years of existence but some changes of directorship had taken place. William Bower died in 1873 and his place was taken by Councillor (later Alderman) Mason of Leeds. Alexander McEwan also ceased to be a director in 1873 and Daniel Busby, now a major shareholder in the Company, took his place. The Company meeting on 11th August 1876 was attended by a person named William Abbott, a sharebroker from London, an apparent unpleasant individual, who was responsible for a big shake-up of the directorship:–

"After disclaiming having any purpose hostile or antagonistic to the directors he expressed his confidence in the soundness of the Company, and said he had had considerable experience in joint stock companies, and especially tramway companies. He was about to allude to the working of the Dublin and Liverpool tramways, when Alderman Mason rose to order, and the Chairman ruled that these allusions were irrelevant. Mr. Abbott, however, proceeded to quote figures in reference to these two companies showing that the proportion charged for horse keep and the amount put to the renewal fund were very much larger than was the case at either Dublin or Liverpool and he contended that the difference in the cost of horse keep was equivalent to 3% upon the dividend of the Leeds Company. He complained that the aim of the Secretary seemed to be to make the Company a local one, he threatened that if his complaints did not have the effect he had in view he should follow them up by such means and practices – The Chairman – As you have done to others. Mr. Abbott: Yes, as I have done elsewhere, to bring about a proper administration of this Company. I believe that the Company is perfectly sound, but it is not as progressive as it might be."

(Yorkshire Post, 12th August 1876).

Over the next few months three directors retired from the Board – Alderman William Mason, William Illingworth and J. W. Maclure (the latter was a director for a very short period in late 1876). They were replaced by William Baxter, William Walker and John Eddison respectively.

At the following Company meeting on 24th February 1877 the dividend had dropped to 5% and this was blamed on wet weather. The price of corn had decreased. Other tramways, notably the Metropolitan Tramways Company, London and Dublin Tramways Company were paying a 9% dividend. Abbot was:–

"at a loss to understand why the Leeds Tramways Company was the only tramway company, which this half year exhibited a retrograde movement. He had gone all over the Leeds tramways and into all their stables, and the stables, permanent way and horses were second to those of no other tramway company in the kingdom. And yet there was a leakage somewhere,
and there could not be the slightest doubt that there was also a want of energy. His own opinion was that the leakage was in the keeping of horses. In Liverpool the horses were kept for 13s. 6d. per week, but in Leeds they cost 16s. 6d.

(Yorkshire Post, 26th February 1877)

Alderman Mason departed under a cloud as it transpired that, as a director, he had been selling corn to the Company, although he protested that it was at the "lowest price." Daniel Busby and the Chairman, William Coghlan, retired from the Board and offered themselves for re-election. Objections were made against Busby, but after an appeal from Eddison on Busby's behalf and an announcement that he held 780 shares, he was re-elected. William Turton proposed the re-election of Coghlan, but this was opposed by Abbott who said Coghlan "possessed neither the health, tact, nor temper necessary to be Chairman of the Company." The proposal to re-elect Coghlan was rejected by a large majority and the Chair was left vacant.

The changes at the top were unsettling for the General Manager, William Bulmer, and he left on 31st March 1877 to take up a post as Chief of the new Manchester and Salford tramways system (an undertaking promoted by Busby and Turton). Bulmer had maintained an active part in his interests in Liverpool throughout his period with the Leeds Tramways Company and in 1878 is recorded as being engaged in promoting a tramway in Liverpool in conjunction with Turton. There were upwards of 700 applicants for Bulmer's post and the successful one was a Matthias Smith of Leeds, formerly of Halifax. On 15th March 1877, at a meeting of the Directors, he was unanimously elected General Manager.

The alterations that Abbott forced on the Company did not have the effect he had intended. At the following Company meeting the dividend dropped to 3½% and Abbott was conspicuous by his absence. 1877 marked the beginning of a recession in Leeds when there was considerable unemployment and the tramway receipts, particularly on routes passing through working class areas, decreased considerably. William Turton was now Chairman of the Company and he attributed the low dividend to the depressed state of trade. He said that the Board and Manager had done all in their power to try and keep up the receipts; they had put more cars on two of the routes; they had reduced the intervals between the cars to ten minutes and, in some cases, 7½ minutes. He added that it was well known that the first half of the year never yielded as large a revenue as the second, there being more fine weather in the latter half and more people moving about. The cost of horse renewal was also more than had been anticipated.

The shareholders were critical. Some advocated the trial of penny stages on the Hunslet and Kirkstall route to try and improve the receipts and the new General Manager was criticised. One shareholder attributed the small dividend not so much to bad trade, but to the inefficiency of the new Manager, whose experience with regard to the value of horses, he questioned. The Manager was also accused of using a trap belonging to the Company for his personal pleasure and use. The Directors must also have had misgivings about Matthias Smith for on 30th September 1877 he left the Company. William Wharam was promoted to the post of Secretary and Manager in his place and Turton later said that the Directors "were not sorry for the change they had made."

Starbuck car No. 11 turns in Briggate for Reginald Terrace as the Burmantofts Penny 'bus passes, about 1890. *Courtesy A. K. Terry Collection.*

With the appointment of Wharam as manager things improved in spite of the recession. Although the receipts fell compared with the previous half year the price for feeding stuffs for horses also fell and the Company, "by the exercise of great economy," was able to declare a dividend of 6% for the half year ended 31st December 1877. Director John Eddison showed that the sums spent on car repairs and renewals and horses for the previous three years were:–

	Cars.	Horses.
June 1875	£699	£381
December 1875	£1,188	£745
June 1876	£871	£1,025
December 1876	£1,203	£1,608
June 1877	£1,268	£1,706
December 1877	£924	£1,398

Eddison said that if they had gone on increasing in this ratio, the time would soon come when there "would not have been a shilling to divide."

Abbot reappeared and complained about the "preponderating influence of the 'horse element' on the Board" and boasted that the prosperity of the Company dated from the time when he became intimately associated with it and through his exertions the Board had been improved by the retirement of some of its original members. He said he would approach the shareholders and show them that the "weeding" process could be further extended to their advantage. Threatening letters were sent by Abbott to the Directors, but this time they stood firm and Abbott's efforts to unseat them came to nought. Abbott then disappeared from the scene and must have presumably sold his shares with the Tramways Company.

On 1st January 1878 the system of penny fare stages was introduced on the Hunslet and Kirkstall route, but the results were not as satisfactory as was expected. It made little difference to the receipts but resulted in a great deal more wear and tear. In August 1879 Turton said that penny stages were "anything but a success" and in a court case they were termed an "abominable nuisance". Passengers could pay at each stage or at the end of their journey which was very taxing for the conductors' memory and led to disputes. The penny stage system was, however, continued.

Meanwhile, in November 1876, the Company had applied to Parliament for further tramway extensions and also proposed to ask for powers to use "locomotive, steam or other engines, or other mechanical or motive power on their lines." Three new tramway routes were proposed:–

1. From Wellington Bridge forming a connection with the Kirkstall tramway along Wellington Road to the "Crown Inn," New Wortley.

2. From the "Golden Cross Inn," Sheepscar with a connection from the Chapeltown tramway and proceeding along Meanwood Road to a point 12 yards south of the junction of Buslingthorpe Lane with Meanwood Road.

3. From the "Swan Junction", Hunslet Road, connecting with the Hunslet tramway and running via Waterloo Road, Church Street and Balm Road, Hunslet Carr and terminating near the "Bay Horse Inn," Hunslet Carr.

The proposal to run trams to Hunslet Carr met with immediate opposition. On 13th December 1876 a deputation attended a meeting of the Highways Committee

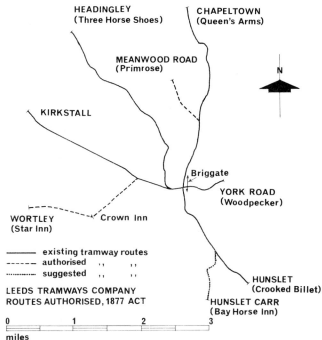

HEADINGLEY
(Three Horse Shoes)

CHAPELTOWN
(Queen's Arms)

MEANWOOD ROAD
(Primrose)

KIRKSTALL

N

Briggate

YORK ROAD
(Woodpecker)

WORTLEY
(Star Inn)

Crown Inn

———— existing tramway routes
------ authorised   ,,   ,,
············ suggested   ,,   ,,

LEEDS TRAMWAYS COMPANY
ROUTES AUTHORISED, 1877 ACT

HUNSLET
(Crooked Billet)

HUNSLET CARR
(Bay Horse Inn)

0   1   2   3

miles

with a requisition signed by 540 property owners and ratepayers asking the Committee to oppose the laying of rails in Waterloo Road. This was due to the narrowness of the road and the large number of vehicles that used it. In some places the road was only 16' - 10" wide and nowhere more than 19' - 5" wide. The Committee considered the Company's application on 10th January and refused permission for the Hunslet Carr tramway. They were also opposed to the New Wortley tramway as it only terminated at the "Crown Inn"; the 'buses running along Tong Road to the "Star Inn" would be withdrawn with nothing to replace them. They agreed to the construction of the Meanwood Road tramway so long as the Company paid £500 for the concession. The Committee objected to the proposed introduction of steam power unless clauses were included which allowed payment to the Corporation for the consent.

In reply to the Corporation the Tramways Company reluctantly agreed to extend the New Wortley line to the "Star Inn", but believed that the line, due to the gradient of Tong Road, would be very costly to work, and that its construction would not yield an adequate return to the Company. The Company said that they did not attach much importance to the provision enabling them to use steam power and were prepared to withdraw that provision from the Bill. Considering the great cost they would incur in completing and working the "Crown Inn" to "Star Inn" section and the advantages which the Meanwood and Wortley lines would confer on the districts through which they would pass and thereby increase the rateable value of the property, the Directors trusted that no money payment would be required for the Corporation's consent. If the Corporation persisted in their demand for payment the Directors said they would withdraw the Bill.

The Highways Committee recommended to the Council that the Tramways Company be not allowed to build any more tramways and that all future lines should be constructed by the Corporation. Following a Council meeting a compromise was reached which gave the Corporation the right to construct the tramways if they so chose within six months of the passing of the Bill. If they failed to do so the work would be carried out by the Company. The Company was also allowed to insert a clause enabling them to use steam traction with the

approval of the Corporation. The Bill as amended went through Parliament as an unopposed measure, but the clause relating to steam traction was struck out as a uniform Bill on the subject for the whole country was in preparation. The "Leeds Tramways Act, 1877" received the Royal Assent on 2nd August 1877.

The Corporation was approached with regard to the construction of the lines and at a special meeting of the Highways Committee on 1st October the question was discussed at length. It was contended that, as the whole of the tramways within the borough must, at the end of 14 years, be offered to the Corporation, as required by Act of Parliament, the wiser course would be to await that period before taking any direct responsibility. On the other hand, it was argued that the making of the new lines by the Corporation would be the means of keeping the roads exclusively in the control of the Town Council, and that the divided authority now existing was injurious to the public interests. In reply to this objection, it was contended that the Corporation had full power to compel the Tramways Company to keep the roads, on which their lines ran, in perfect repair and that such powers ought to be exercised. By nine votes to two it was agreed to allow the Company to construct the Meanwood and Wortley tramways.

The Company was worried about the state of the tramway track, which was now beginning to deteriorate considerably. Track repairs were an increasing burden. The Directors visited Manchester to see the tramway and a new form of track construction was inspected, stated to be far in advance of any other. The Directors decided to construct the new lines for Leeds on the same system.

Construction of the Meanwood Road tramway commenced at the beginning of April 1878 and a variation from the Parliamentary plans occurred in that the Company laid down double lines in lieu of single between Crawford Street and Meanwood Street, in Meanwood Road. Major Marindin of the Board of Trade inspected the line but withheld approval pending the consent of the Corporation to this additional double track. Approval was given on 10th July and the line opened for traffic on the 16th. A 20 minutes service was operated from Briggate from 8.05 am to 8.40 pm (39 journeys per day) with a fare of 2d. The short tramway, only 1,538 yards in length, ran on a level route largely single track with passing places through built-up working class brick housing with some industrial property. It formed a connection with the Chapeltown tramway at the "Golden Cross", passed along Meanwood Road, took a fork to the right at Cambridge Road and terminated at the "Primrose Inn," Buslingthorpe, near to the end of Buslingthorpe Lane.

Shortly after the opening of the Meanwood Road line the Company commenced the construction of the line to Wortley. This again varied from the Parliamentary plans in that nine additional passing places were inserted, but the Company obtained approval from the Corporation before the visit of the Government Inspector. By November 1878 the line was constructed as far as the Crown Hotel, New Wortley. Major Marindin officially inspected the line on 13th December 1878 and expressed himself "perfectly satisfied" with the tramway. It was opened to the general public on 1st January 1879 as far as New Wortley.

The New Wortley tramway ran on a level road largely on double track and passed through similar surroundings to the Meanwood Road route – working class hous-

Kitson engine No. 9 stands with modified Starbuck trailer No. 59 at the "Crown Hotel," New Wortley, about 1890. *Courtesy The late W. E. Cain.*

ing and industrial property. It left the Kirkstall tramway at Wellington Bridge, crossed over the River Aire on Wellington Road and on the right was the White Horse Hotel and Armley Road – the main road to Bradford. The line then passed under a railway bridge carrying the Midland Company's trains to Bradford and the Great Northern's to Harrogate. About 150 yards past the bridge was the New Wortley Gas Works and a railway level crossing, constructed in 1875, which was to be the only level crossing on the Tramway Company lines. The earlier proposed connections to the railways which may have involved level crossings in Kirkstall Road and Hunslet Road never materialised. The line terminated at the "Crown Hotel" at a cross roads – the junction of Wellington Road, Tong Road, Oldfield Lane and Copley Hill. Penny stages were employed on the route with a through fare of 2d.

Although the Company still managed to pay a dividend of 6%, the depression in Leeds became considerably worse in 1878 and 1879. One of the worst affected areas was the Buslingthorpe district where there was much unemployment and distress and free soup kitchens were set up by the Corporation to provide food for the needy. The poverty-stricken inhabitants could not afford a tram ride and the receipts for the Meanwood line – only £981 for the six months period ending December 1878 – were a sorry sight for the Tramways Company. The inhabitants on the Wortley route were similarly in a "distressed state" and the income from this line during 1879 was anything but satisfactory. The dividend dropped to 4% in the first half of the year when the recession was at its height. The

closure of Briggate for 7 weeks due to track repairs from late March to early May and the reduction of the 10 minutes service on the Hunslet route to 20 minutes due to road repairs exacerbated matters.

A start was made on the construction of the extension of the New Wortley tramway from the "Crown Hotel" up Tong Road to the "Star Inn," Upper Wortley, approximately 7/8 mile in length on 25th August 1879. It was said to cost £5,000 and was completed by February 1880 and on the 25th of that month was inspected by Major General Hutchinson of the Board of Trade. The Inspector considered that some of the paving was low and recommended that it be raised, but otherwise it was satisfactory. The Company carried out the remedial work and the line was opened for traffic on 5th April.

The extension ran entirely through working class terrace housing with a small amount of industrial building, and the line, of single track, made a gradual ascent of Tong Road. A half hourly service was operated and the through fare from Briggate to the "Star Inn" was 3d.; 2d. being charged from the "Crown" to "Star" on the up journey and 1d. down.

The new tramways to Wortley and Meanwood did not pay well and Turton said in 1880 that the directors did not propose to build any further tramway extensions as they were "a drawback rather than a help." No further lines were constructed but suggestions were made to construct a tramway to Roundhay Park in 1881. During the 'eighties the Company was concerned with the problems of the "penny 'bus" and a new form of traction – the steam tram.

A filthy Green tram engine No. 24 contrasts with newly painted Milnes trailer No. 41 at Wortley terminus about 1894. The driver is James Wade.
Courtesy The late J. Wade.

The Wortley route in August 1892 with Green engine No. 19 and Milnes Trailer. The driver is Billy Cain.
Courtesy The late W. E. Cain.

CHAPTER NINE

Mechanical Traction:

Wortley, Headingley and Kirkstall

Mechanical traction in the form of the steam tram appeared in Leeds in 1877. At the time Parliament was considering the introduction of legislation relating to steam tramways and several engineering companies were interesting themselves in the construction of suitable tramway engines. The "dullness of trade" in 1877 gave firms in Leeds the opportunity to devote their attention to the problem. Among them was a firm, Kitson & Co. of the Airedale Foundry, Hunslet Road, which had wide experience of railway locomotive construction. They built an experimental engine and it made trial runs on the Leeds tramways. On 24th October 1877 it was inspected by the Hackney Carriages Committee and began a fortnight's public trial. The engine had run previously on private trials when traffic was light.

"By one of the ordinary cars of the Tramways Company, drawn by four horses, the committee and other gentlemen interested were conveyed to the Hunslet Depot, where the new engine-car was to be seen. It is about half the size of the ordinary cars, and in the centre of it is a vertical boiler, with funnel passing through the roof. The wheels and brakes are shielded by sheet iron to within about 4" of the ground. The upper half of the engine-car except of course the top, is glass, so that the driver can see in any direction. Having been attached to one of the ordinary cars a start was made, the passengers being the Hackney Carriages Committee with Alderman Addyman (Chairman), Councillor Turton (Chairman of the Leeds Tramways Company), Mr. Eddison (Vice-chairman), Mr. Ashworth (one of the Directors) and Mr. Wharam (Secretary and Manager). They were driven at about the ordinary speed, which was occasionally slackened and stopped to show the control possessed. The bottom of Briggate was reached in little over a quarter of an hour, without hitch of any kind, but just as the vehicle got beneath the railway bridge, a joint in one of the pipes burst, and a delay of two or three minutes was occasioned. Another short halt was purposely made in Boar Lane, and then they proceeded to Kirkstall, Mr. James Kitson, junior, travelling in the engine-car. When this part of the journey had been completed, the boiler was replenished with water by means of an ordinary india-rubber tube connected with a tap in the depot, and a pipe underneath the engine-car, whence it was pumped into the boiler. Then they drove back to Leeds. Altogether the trial passed off very satisfactorily with the exception of the discomfort caused to outside passengers by the emission of fumes and grit from the funnel; but we understand this can easily be obviated. The funnel,

however, sends forth no smoke, and there need be no steam. The motion of the car is almost noiseless, and few horses passed on the road appeared to be disturbed by its appearance. The weight of the engine-car is 4 tons 15 cwt."
(Yorkshire Post, 25th October, 1877).

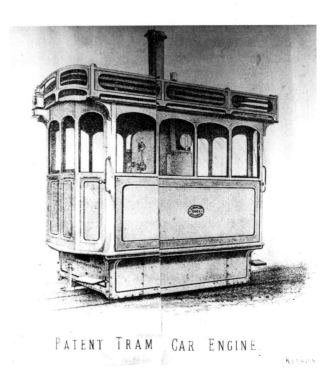

PATENT TRAM CAR ENGINE.

An engraving of the first tram engine manufactured by Kitson's in 1877.   *Courtesy Leeds City Libraries.*

Within a week, on 31st October, another Leeds firm, noted for the manufacture of traction engines, threshing machines etc, John Fowler and Co. of the Steam Plough Works, Hunslet, made a trial run with a tramway engine. Fowler's attempted a repetition of Kitson's trial and at 2.0 pm their engine left Hunslet with the intention of going to Kirkstall. It went very smoothly and almost noiselessly on the level or where there was a slight fall, but when the slightest gradient had to be climbed the noiselessness gave place to a whirring sound – like a threshing machine and this was somewhat alarming to the horses on the route. The whirring was said to be a "slight mishap" and when the ascent at the bottom of Briggate was reached, it was considered advisable to go no further. The engine was returned to Fowler's

Works and it was found that a joint in the casing of the steam chest had burst. One of the advantages of the engine was that the whole of its working parts, contained in a box, could be taken out in ten minutes, and that none of the working parts could be affected by dust, except the outside side rods which it was impossible to cover. It was said that prior to the official trial the engine had run over the Headingley and Chapeltown routes in the early morning of 31st October in a "perfectly satisfactory manner."

The firm of Fowler's is not mentioned in the late Dr. Whitcombe's admirable booklet "The History of the Steam Tram", as a manufacturer of tram engines, nor does it appear in literature relating to the firm. It must be assumed that this trial was probably their only venture into the tramway engine business. There is no record of any further trials with Fowler's engines on the Leeds tramways, but Kitson's, however, were to develop the tramway engine and become the most important builder of them in the country.

Kitson's engine was modified and in December 1877 made further trials on the Headingley line. The engine was said to run with greater steadiness and an "objectionable vibration" was eliminated. It had not been previously considered practicable to run a steam car up so steep a gradient as Cookridge Street (1 in 18), but the engine, hauling a car with a full load of passengers, repeatedly mounted the inclines on the route without the slightest difficulty and seemed to have solved the problem of adopting steam power for tramways. An objection was the emission of steam and smut from the funnel and there was a tendency for some horses to be frightened by the engine.

In spite of adverse comments, the Tramways Company was very interested in the adoption of steam as it was thought it would result in considerable savings in horse power and consequently increase the profits of the Company. The Company, however, could do nothing until the Government legislation was sorted out. During the 1878 Parliamentary session a Bill was passed by a Commons Committee but was thrown out by the House of Lords acting on the advice of a prominent member of that august body who stated that the "great highways of England, Ireland and Scotland would be converted into railways." Eventually, in August 1879, the "Use of Mechanical Power on Tramways Act" became law and, like the 1870 Tramways Act contained several restrictive clauses. The Board of Trade was permitted to grant special licences for a limited period for the experimental use of steam or other mechanical traction; the permanent way was to be constructed with sufficient solidity to bear the increased wear and tear; the engine should consume its own steam and smoke, should be virtually silent and should show no moving parts above 4" from rail level. A speedometer had to be fitted and also a governor that would apply the brake if the driver exceeded 8 m.p.h. The Kitson engine was said to answer these criteria, but in everyday service, as will be seen, they were difficult to maintain.

During the intervening period Kitson's had not been idle and completely redesigned their tramway engines. They built three experimental engines with vertical boilers in 1878, but abandoned this concept the following year and adopted a horizontal boiler of locomotive type and increased the size of the cylinders and wheels. Six of these engines were built and sent to New Zealand where one still exists.

The Meanwood and Wortley tramways were laid with heavier rails with a view to future use by mechanical traction but the Tramways Company was reluctant to rush into the immediate adoption of steam trams. Informed opinion was not enthusiastic and "The Engineer" for June 1880 made a scathing attack:—

"The reason why steam tramway engines cannot be made to pay is that they are never out of the repairing sheds for more than a very short period — they knock and cut themselves to pieces. At the best of times the profit made out of a tramway as compared with the working expenses is very small, rarely more than 7 or 8%, while at others the total expenditure comes to within 97% of the receipts. It will be seen that under such conditions the margin available for repairs and renewals is very little. The engines suffer severely because the roads they run over are extremely bad, and because it is impossible to keep the rubbing surfaces of guide bars, link motions, and so on clean. It would seem than an entirely new departure is necessary, and that quite enough has been done on the existing plans to prove that they cannot confer success, and must be abandoned. A remarkable similarity exists between the essential features of all tramway engines. No matter how they may be designed with sheds and cabs, or built on to with condensers or coal bunkers, they are still one and all very faulty copies of the railway locomotive."

(The Engineer, June 1880).

"The Engineer" recommended that tramway engines should be designed on the same lines as traction engines with large wheels and tyres set on india rubber. Their opinion was proved correct where tramway engines were run on lightly constructed horse tramway track, but on substantially constructed track the steam tramway engine was a financial success.

In spite of the despondent views of "The Engineer" the Tramways Company decided to experiment with a steam tram on their new line between Boar Lane and Upper Wortley. They applied to the Board of Trade for permission for a three month's trial and Major-General Hutchinson, of the Board, made an inspection of the proposed route on 7th May 1880. The engine to be used was said by Kitson's to be similar to the engines which had been sent out to New Zealand and which were worked with "very satisfactory" results. On Saturday, 5th June, the Major-General made a further inspection of the engine to be used, in Kitson's foundry yard. He carried out exhaustive tests and granted the Tramways Company and Kitson's permission to use the engine on the Wortley line for a period of three months beginning on 14th June.

Kitson's reached an agreement with the Leeds Tramways Company to test their engines on the Company's lines and in July 1879 were granted permission by the Highways Committee for a track connection from their works to the Hunslet Road tramway. This was soon constructed and the vast majority of Kitson's engines were tested on the Leeds lines. They made regular payments to the Company for the privilege, which in busy periods, such as the middle 'eighties, was about £40 per month. Fowler's apparently had ideas of constructing more engines for, three months after Kitson's application, they approached the Highways Committee for permission to lay a tramway from their works along Dresser Street to connect with the Hunslet Road line. This, however, was refused on the grounds that Dresser Street was not a public highway.

During the week prior to 14th June 1880 the engine to

Kitson engine No. 1 with Starbuck horse car No. 22 in 1880. *Courtesy Kitson and Company.*

be used on the Wortley tramway was thoroughly tested on the line and, on 17th June, it was used for the first time in passenger service. Kitson's said that the weight of the engine was just short of six tons, less than that of any equally powerful locomotive invented, and it was capable of drawing two fully loaded cars up any of the gradients on the Leeds tramways. It ran with one car and covered the distance between Boar Lane and Upper Wortley in 20 minutes. It created a very favourable impression being almost noiseless and extremely smooth running and, in busy Boar Lane and Wellington Street, horses showed no fear of the engine.

The engine ran in conjunction with the Wortley horse cars and was rented from Kitson's at a mileage charge. However for the first three months Kitson's charged a nominal £20. William Turton was very pleased with it and said it was a great credit to Kitson's. He had seen all the other tramway engines at work in the United Kingdom and none were equal to it. He did not think, however, that engines could be worked as cheaply as one-horse cars and there would not be much saving as compared with two-horse cars, but where three and four-horse cars had to be employed, steam power had a decided advantage. He thought that the Company would be able to work the Headingley and Chapeltown routes by steam, but did not think it worth while on the other routes.

On 11th September the three months trial came to an end and full horse car operation resumed to Wortley. The Tramways Company said the trial was "eminently satisfactory" and applied to the Board of Trade for a licence for a further trial of one or more of Kitson's engines on the Headingley, Chapeltown and Wortley tramways for a period of 12 months. A trial trip was made to Chapeltown and the engine ascended the steep gradients without difficulty, but on the return journey it was derailed while passing over some points in North Street. No damage was done but the Board of Trade inspector considered that the points should be lengthened before he could pass the line for steam traction. As the pointwork on the Headingley route was similar to that of Chapeltown, the inspection did not extend further than the latter branch.

The Company was now convinced that the steam tram was the answer for hilly routes and would also be financially viable on other lines. In November 1880 they made application to Parliament for sanction to use steam on all their lines and proposed to raise additional capital of £17,750, part of which was to be used to pay the cost of 40 tram engines that would be required at about £550 each. The Bill gave the Company authority to run steam tramways and, on 18th July 1881, the "Leeds Tramways Act, 1881" became law.

The work of lengthening the points on the Chapeltown section was completed by the date of the Company meeting in February 1881, when it was said that the Headingley line would be similarly dealt with as soon as possible. The directors were full of praise for the Kitson engine and John Eddison said that he knew of no town more suited to the adoption of steam than Leeds. There were cheap coal, engineering works on nearly all the tramway routes, and plenty of practical engine drivers in the district who would work a tramway engine without difficulty.

By August 1881 Kitsons had put a further two engines on the Wortley route and it was now entirely steam operated. Rental payments to Kitsons in 1881 rose from £37 8s. 4d. in January to £107 15s. 10d. in August and were thereafter about £110 per month. An increase in rental payments shows that the second engine was put on the line in March 1881 and the third in May. The horse trams were withdrawn when the third engine appeared and there is no record of them running to Wortley again.

Turton said that the Company could work a tramcar with steam power at 10s. 0d. per day less than for a tramcar drawn by three horses. This represented about 2% of the cost of working which in future would go to dividend. Later it was stated that the three cars on the Wortley route gave a saving of at least 25% compared with horse power. Efforts were made to improve the track on the Headingley and Chapeltown routes with a view to the adoption of steam traction. Reversing triangles for the use of engines were laid at both termini in September 1881 and, in December, Major-General Hutchinson made a further inspection. He said that an improvement had been made on the level of the paving

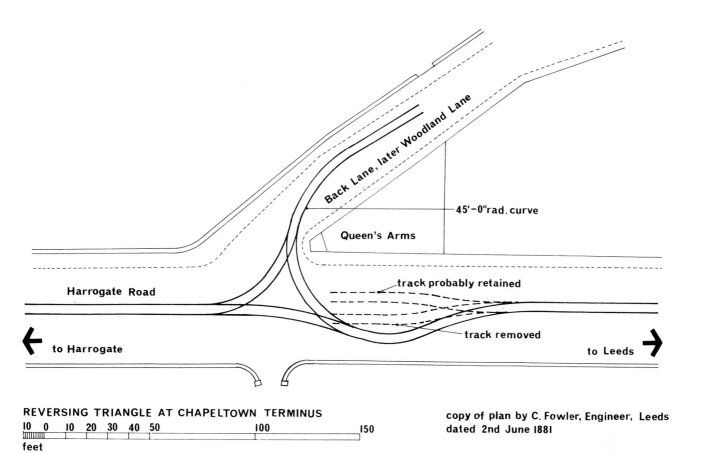

Back Lane, later Woodland Lane

45'-0" rad. curve

Queen's Arms

Harrogate Road

track probably retained

track removed

to Harrogate

to Leeds

REVERSING TRIANGLE AT CHAPELTOWN TERMINUS

10 0 10 20 30 40 50   100   150

feet

copy of plan by C. Fowler, Engineer, Leeds
dated 2nd June 1881

Green engine No. 23 and Milnes trailer, probably No. 38, at Headingley, about 1890.
Courtesy Science Museum, South Kensington, London, Whitcombe Collection.

setts in some of the points and crossings, but was concerned that the condition of many of the rail fastenings, rail joints and crossings was unsatisfactory. He questioned whether any improvement could be made without relaying large portions of the permanent way, which would very soon be seriously damaged if engines were allowed to run over it. He also considered it imperative that the speed of the engines be restricted to 3 m.p.h. in passing round the corners of Briggate and Boar Lane and also the corner near the Exchange Building.

The Board of Trade said they were not prepared to sanction the use of steam on the two lines until the track was relaid. Beginning in February 1882 and for the following nine months the rails on the Headingley route were replaced with heavy section steel-girder rails at a cost of about £3,000. On 2nd December the Headingley line was again inspected by Major-General Hutchinson. This date saw the appearance of the first tramway engine manufactured by Thomas Green and Son of the Smithfield Ironworks, North Street, Leeds. Green's were noted for the construction of, among other things, lawn mowers and their "celebrated sausage chopping and mincing machines" were exported all over the world. They also had experience of the building of steam traction engines and were to become one of the largest manufacturers of tramway engines in the country and strong rivals to Kitson's. Two of their directors, William Turton and William Baxter were also directors of the Leeds Tramways Company, and their engine was built to the design of William Wilkinson, an engineer of Wigan.

"On Saturday morning a car left Boar Lane about 9.10 am containing 16 gentlemen, including Major-General Hutchinson, Mr. W. Wilkinson, Mr. Thomas Green, Mr. Baxter, vice-chairman of Thomas Green and Son, Councillor North, Chairman of the Hackney Carriages Committee, Mr. Turton, Mr. Hebblethwaite, Mr. Mason, Mr. Eddison, Chairman of the Tramways Company, Mr. Ashworth, a director, Mr. Wharam, secretary of the company etc. The weather was extremely cold and foggy. The car ran easily and smoothly into Cookridge Street, when passing the Mechanics' Institute, on a steep incline of 1 in 17, the inspector ordered a stoppage. When the car was at a standstill he gave the word to go forward, but when the driver put on steam the car made a rearward movement, which was repeated on the second attempt. With the third effort, however, the journey was resumed, and on reaching the Yorkshire College buildings a good speed was again attained. The Inspector pointed out that the car was lightly laden, and there should have been no difficulty in restarting, but various reasons were assigned to account for this — the wet state of the rails, the greasy condition of the wheels, and the wetness of the sand on the line, which should have been dry. Stoppages were also made on the incline by the Girls' Schools and Buckingham Road, at the declivities near the Wesleyan College, and at other points, but in all cases the car was brought up and restarted without any apparent delay or difficulty. The journey up to the Moor was accomplished in about 19 minutes, including stoppages, and thence to the stables at Far Headingley in another 17 minutes — a total of 36 minutes, including one or two stoppages of some duration. During the journey the inspector remarked upon the emission of steam from the engine, but said it all appeared to come from the safety valve, and not from the cylinder. On arriving at

the terminus a stoppage was made while fuel and water was taken on the engine, advantage of which was taken by the Chairman of the Company to explain the Company's position with respect to the use of steam as a motive power. He said the Company had now for nearly three years employed steam upon the Wortley route with most satisfactory results. While the line had been almost free from casualty it had been worked at a saving of over 20% compared with horse power. With the latter it had cost them 9d. per mile, but Messrs. Kitson had supplied engine power at 5½d. per mile. As the result of that three years working the Company had purchased from Messrs. Kitson three engines, which would come into their possession on January 1st next. They had also arranged with Messrs. Green and Sons Ltd. (who are the manufacturers of Mr. Wilkinson's engines for Yorkshire), to hire the new engine for three months. The Wilkinson engine had been most successful in Wigan and some other large towns, but had not before been made by Messrs. Green. —— On returning to town the car proceeded up Briggate to the works of Messrs. Green and Sons Ltd. in North Street. Here Major-General Hutchinson made a most minute and thorough examination of three engines in various stages of erection. The inspection which had occupied about 3½ hours, was completed at 12.30 pm, when the party lunched together at the "Queen's Hotel".

(Yorkshire Post, 4th December, 1882).

It was intended that as soon as the sanction of the Board of Trade was obtained the new engine together with two others of similar construction were to be put on the Headingley route. When the track on the Chapeltown section was relaid the three engines were to be used on a through service between Headingley and Chapeltown. The approval of the Board of Trade was received but various restrictions on the use of the engine were imposed – a speed not exceeding 6 m.p.h. was to be observed on the sharp descending gradients and compulsory stops were to be made in Boar Lane at the crossing with Albion Street, at the sharp turn opposite the Exchange Building (junction of Boar Lane and Park Row), and at the Bank of England at the bottom of Cookridge Street. Bye Laws for the regulation of steam tram traffic were also introduced.

Steam tramcars thus began regular service between Boar Lane and Headingley on 1st January 1883, but two engines only were supplied by Green's and ran in conjunction with the horse cars. Green's Order Book still exists and shows that the two engines were Order Nos. 1 and 2. Order No. 3 was for four similar engines to be supplied to the Leeds tramways. These were partly constructed, but never delivered. The gauge was apparently altered to 3'-6" and the engines sold to the Manchester, Bury, Rochdale and Oldham Tramways Company in February 1884. It appears that they became M.B.R.O. engines Nos. 9-12. The M.B.R.O. tramways were of different gauges and a 4'-8½" gauge engine for this company was tested on the Headingley line and delivered to Bury on 9th April 1883. It performed very well in Bury, pulling three cars each weighing 3¼ tons with 290 school children and 20 adults up a gradient of 1 in 21 with 116lbs steam pressure.

It was not usual for Green's engines to be tested on the Leeds tramways as there was no track connection from their works to the tramway. They did, however, apply to the Highways Committee in February 1883 to construct a line along Back Byron Street to connect with

Green engine No. 19 and an immaculate Milnes trailer No. 21 at Headingley terminus in the summer of 1889.
Courtesy Science Museum, South Kensington, London, Whitcombe Collection.

the North Street tramway, but, as with Fowler's earlier application, it was refused.

The highly successful Kitson engines on the Wortley route passed through a working class area, where few people owned private carriages, and there were no grumbles. On the Headingley route the story was entirely different and the newspapers were flooded with complaints as vividly described below:–

"Last evening I rode up to Headingley on the top of the tramcar drawn by the engine and whatever our authorities are doing to allow such a nuisance as this diabolical machine to travel another time up that road I do not know. Up Cookridge Street and Woodhouse Lane, the engine did not send an odd spark or two out of the chimney, but one continuous stream of sparks 10 or 12 feet high, and covering passengers on the top with pieces of cinder insomuch that some put up their umbrellas to protect themselves. How horses will be got to face such an infernal machine goodness only knows." wrote W. H. Maude.

(Yorkshire Post, 18th January, 1883).

"On Thursday last (4th January) my coachman was riding across Woodhouse Moor when he met one of these steam engines. The horse planted his feet firmly on the ground for a few seconds, and, as the engine glided nearer he sprang in terror on the footpath, to the danger of foot passengers, rider and horse. Yesterday my son was riding through Headingley and came upon an engine at a stand. His horse became excited; and to make matters worse, the engine driver thoughtlessly blew off steam, when the horse jumped upon the footpath to the great peril of several persons walking thereon."

(Yorkshire Post, 10th January, 1883).

Another writer said that a walk from town to Headingley and back used to be pleasant and enjoyable, but was now unbearable owing to the sickening fumes given off by the tram engines. However, there was a solitary voice, accused of being a shareholder, in favour of the steam tram who made:–

"an earnest plea for patience and forbearing on the part of carriage owners in the use of the steam tramcar as a substitute for the late long enduring sufferings of that most hard-worked and short-lived animal, the tramcar horse, whose desperate struggles to take Leeds humanity homewards, the tram horse had had quite enough of and must for ever hope to be a thing of the past."

(Yorkshire Post, 13th January, 1883).

On 11th January 1883 a meeting of the Highways Committee was held to discuss the problem and consider whether they should immediately instruct the Town Clerk to write to the Board of Trade, but thought that it was better in the first instance to contact the Tramways Company. At the "Oak Inn", Headingley, the engines took in water from a hydrant and in the process discharged large amounts of steam. This was a cause of many complaints and the Committee instructed that the water point be moved to the "Three Horse Shoes" terminus. Court cases resulted in which the Tramways Company was summoned for allowing steam to be emitted from the engines which they pleaded was "hot air". In spite of all the protests, the "jangling, wheezing, flaring" steam trams continued to run to Headingley. Green's made determined efforts to improve the two engines and apart from complaints about speeding (exceeding 8 m.p.h.) the opposition subsided.

On 3rd July 1883 a serious accident occurred on the

59

newly opened Huddersfield tramways where Wilkinson's patent engines were employed. There were seven fatalities and among the recommendations made by the Board of Trade at the resulting inquiry was one recommending that an independent hand screw brake be fitted on each engine. Faith in the automatic brake, fitted to Wilkinson's engines, was shaken, and in the hope of meeting the emergency many experiments were tried by the various tramway engine manufacturers. The Board of Trade decided to formulate an entirely new set of rules to regulate the use of steam on tramways and Major-General Hutchinson visited the foremost engineering firms and tramway systems in the country. He was invited to visit Leeds by the Highways Committee who were worried about the possibility of an accident and was asked to make a thorough inspection of all the tramways in Leeds on which steam was used.

In August 1883 the new brakes were fitted on the two Green engines, but they did not inspire confidence with the public. On 15th August the 5.20 pm steam car to Headingley was ten minutes late leaving Boar Lane and was consequently followed immediately behind by the 5.30 pm three-horse car. On going up Cookridge Street the engine failed and came to a standstill and then began to move backwards. The passengers in a panic got out as quickly as possible and, by putting their shoulders to the engine and car, managed by brute force to bring it to a halt. What could have been a serious accident was fortunately averted. The incident was blamed on the "greasy" state of the rails.

The following day Major-General Hutchinson visited Leeds and rode to Headingley and back in a new Ashbury built Eades Reversible car hauled by Green's engine No. 1. The new brake was thoroughly "tested and performed well". It was said to work independently of the Board of Trade automatic brake and was of simple construction. Steam turned on from the boiler by a lever forced clams tightly on the wheels, and the brake was found to stop the engine even when in full steam.

The Inspector's report was received in October and stated that the engines should be provided with an efficient mechanical brake acting on each of the four wheels, so that there would be no need to reverse the engine for ordinary stops. The means for preventing the driver tampering with the governor should be most carefully attended to, and not allowed to fall into disuse. He suggested that the Corporation should appoint a special officer to inspect the tramways on which steam was used and ensure that the Bye-Laws and Regulations were carried out. The track on the Headingley route was said to be in a bad state in various places and should be relaid as soon as possible. The Inspector advised that compulsory stops be made before crossing Park Lane, Cobourg Street and Hyde Park Road and that the speed should be limited to 4 m.p.h. on the curved parts of the line at Spring Bank, and to 6 m.p.h. on the inward journey down the hill at Blenheim Terrace, Carlton Hill and Cookridge Street. Also recommended were alterations to the rolling stock; these are referred to in a later chapter.

At the half yearly meeting of the Tramways Company on 17th August 1883 the dividend was greatly reduced. The Company had had to pay £626 17s. 9d. in compensation – equal to 1% of the dividend – partly the result of claims from accidents due to steam trams. Turton said that expenses had been incurred which had not been anticipated and Eddison, vice-chairman, was now opposed to steam trams. He said that the cost of work-

Kitson engine No. 7 and Starbuck horse car No. 18 with top cover pose at Headingley "Oak" in the autumn of 1884. No. 18 reverted to its horse car status later.
Courtesy F. Davison.

ing the engines on the Wortley section was 7d. per mile and apart from the depreciation of the engines and cars and wear and tear there was also the enormous damage done to the trackwork. He thought that if the Company acted cautiously in the adoption of steam or abandoned it altogether, they might increase the dividend paid to shareholders.

Eddison's views, however, were not shared by the other directors and at the following Company meeting in February 1884, Turton, possibly influenced by his financial connections with Green's, said that his confidence in steam trams had increased and that they "answered better in every way" than horses on steep gradients. The cost of horses on the Headingley route had been, over the previous three years, 9 1/8d. per car mile. Green's only charged 6½d. per car mile for their two engines and the three Kitson engines owned by the Company cost 6d. per car mile. Eddison admitted that if they could keep clear of accidents they could make a saving by the use of steam, but he was still concerned about the damage to the rails.

The Directors were now satisfied that steam was proving successful and ordered a fourth tramway engine from Kitson's. This was of a more advanced design than the three previous engines and was delivered about March 1884. The Company was very pleased with it and promptly ordered a further six similar engines for use on the Headingley route. There had been continued complaints about Green's engines, particularly with regard to their erratic speed and there was a storm of protest when it was learnt that the number of steam trams was to be increased. The comments of a "Headingley Householder" were quite poetic:–

"What can be more formidable than a moving monster, clad in a panoply of steel, rolling and rattling along with puffs and gasps, and at night vomitting a blue flame, and glaring at you with a red eye (the route colour light), approaching swiftly and suddenly, and leaving no means of escape? No wonder horses tremble and quake at their approach."

A Councillor said that he had seen a steam car travel a mile in 3½ minutes (17 m.p.h.) and the Hackney Carriages Committee endeavoured to appoint an inspector to check that the Bye Laws and Regulations were being observed. This was one of the Board of Trade recommendations, but was opposed by the Council on the ground that the Corporation would be "exposing themselves to unnecessary responsibility." Alderman North, the Chairman of the Committee, had a meeting with Turton about the tramway engine complaints generally

A Kitson engine stands at Headingley "Oak" with the Headingley Church horse 'bus on the left, about 1890. *Courtesy R. Brook.*

and received the following interesting letter dated 31st May 1884:–

Dear Sir,

In reference to the conversation I had with you a few days ago respecting tram engines and the speed they run at, we have at the present four of Messrs. Kitson and Cos. engines running on the Wortley section and two of Messrs. Green and Cos. running on the Headingley section. The two latter will come off in about 14 days from now, and will be succeeded by six new engines now being made at Messrs. Kitson and Cos., and will have all the latest improvements, with automatic brake power, which prevents the engines running at more than 8 m.p.h. and when it reaches that speed, it will shut off to 4 m.p.h. This is self-acting and cannot be tampered with by the engine drivers, so the makers say, and has been tested by Major-General Hutchinson on the Dudley tramways within the last seven days, and spoken of by him very highly. As to a speed indicator, it can be so placed on the engine that the passengers can see it when riding in the car, if needful; but as the brakes are now brought to such perfection, it may not be necessary to apply the indicators. I have every confidence in the six new engines we are getting, as we have one of the same type now working on the Wortley section, which has complied with all the above conditions.

I am etc. William Turton, Chairman, Leeds Tramways Company.

Hyde Park about 1890 with a Kitson engine and Starbuck trailer. *Courtesy J. Soper Collection.*

The Green engines were very unpopular with the public and the Company was probably pleased to get rid of them. This, however, was denied by Turton who said that Greens had sold their engines to "other parties" and could not allow them to remain on the Headingley line any longer. Green's Order Book does not indicate how the engines were disposed of, but it is possible they were dismantled and servicable parts used on other engines.

The introduction of Kitson's engines on the Headingley route did not provoke a reaction from the residents who must have found them acceptable. The protests ceased and in 1885 the Company said that the time was approaching where the public was looking on the steam tram as a necessity where there was heavy traffic. The cost of the Headingley engines was now 6d. per car mile as on the Wortley route, but it was considered that this would be reduced to 5d. when the entire route was worked by steam.

Eight engines were said to be allocated to the Headingley line, but in February 1885 it was reported that only four or five were working. The use of both horse cars and steam on Headingley enabled a cost comparison to be made between the two forms of traction. It was found that the savings were 3⅝d. per mile in favour of steam engines or 18s. 1½d. per car per day – £45 per week. At the following Company meeting six months later it was said that the difference between horse and steam traction was now 4⅝d. in favour of steam. A further two tramway engines were ordered, one from Kitson's and another, to a new design from Green's followed by a further four engines from Kitson's. With the delivery of these – about May 1886 – the Company was able to withdraw the remaining horse cars from the Headingley route. They now had 16 tram engines and two routes, Wortley and Headingley, steam operated, and forecast that they would soon by able to run steam cars through from Headingley to Chapeltown in penny stages. The Chapeltown route, however, required extensive track re-construction, but this was never carried out and steam cars did not usually run on Chapeltown Road in Company days.

In snow conditions steam tram engines were used on all routes to assist in clearing the rails. On only two other routes did the Company run a regular steam car service: Roundhay, covered in a later chapter, and Kirkstall. By 1884 steam cars were reported to be running to Kirkstall in conjunction with the horse cars. Following a complaint by the Hackney Carriages Committee in May 1885, Wharam said that the Company had made use of steam power occasionally on the Kirkstall line under the power conferred by the Act of Parliament, 1881, but that the line had not been inspected by the Board of Trade.

The reason why the Company ran steam cars on the level Kirkstall route is uncertain, as it contradicted their policy that steam cars were only economical on hilly routes.

At first, the Tramways Company hauled double-deck or single-deck horse cars as trailers, but trailers specially built to protect passengers from smoke and fumes were later introduced. When horse cars were used the tram engines frequently hauled two as trailers. In the early and middle 'eighties there was a short working to the "Cardigan Arms", Kirkstall Road, usually worked by steam with two trailers, and known as the "Cardigan Arms Special Car". Two trailers were also regularly used on the Wortley route at this time. There were two conductors, one to each car, and the conductor of the first car signalled for the driver to stop or move on. The Company, however, never had authority from either the Corporation or Board of Trade to adopt this practice. The Board of Trade frowned on it and, in some towns, banned the use of two trailers. The Company continued to run occasional steam cars to Kirkstall with no further objection from the Corporation. Nor did the Corporation comment when the Company's seven years authority to use steam (granted by the 1881 Act) expired on 18th July 1888. This was forgotten and it was three years before they realised that the Company was running steam trams illegally, and then insisted that the Company re-apply to the Board of Trade for a renewal of its authority.

Steam traction was now regarded in a favourable light by the Directors of the Tramways Company, but Eddison was never enthusiastic. His forecast of future

Kitson engine No. 15, Milnes trailer No. 41, Driver Billy Cain with oil can and a Conductor with fare box on the Wortley route about 1900.
Courtesy The late W. E. Cain.

major track problems was later proved correct. The steam trams, however, with their large seating capacity, were undoubtedly responsible for the satisfactory dividends paid by the Company in the late 'eighties. Following a decline to 2% for the half year ended 31st December 1884, mainly due to horse 'bus competition and the cost of track repairs, the dividend gradually increased with the greater use of steam. For the following half year it was 3% and Turton declared that but for steam there would have been no dividend at all. In 1887 the dividend reached 6% and for the half year ended 30th June 1889 was 6½% – the highest ever.

For his doubts about steam Eddison faced criticism from the shareholders. His term as a Director expired in February 1887 and he was nominated for re-election, but failed and Wilson Sharp, a dyer of Meanwood Road, Leeds, was elected in his place. A poll was demanded and a Special General Meeting of the Company was held on 18th March 1887 on the question of directors. The retiring Directors were Eddison, William Baxter and a James T. Simpson. Simpson was originally elected to the Board in February 1884. The last two named were re-elected at the half yearly meeting but Eddison was out-voted.

At the Special Meeting a shareholder said that Eddison had been persistent in his opposition to steam trams and had, in other ways, obstructed the business of the Company. If Eddison had had his way the increased dividends would not have been realised and it was added that he did not "cordially and actively" work with his colleagues. Eddison "emphatically denied" the allegations but the shareholders were not convinced, and the result of the poll was announced as follows:– Simpson 1,427; Baxter 1,405, Sharp 1,036 and Eddison 491. Over the remaining years of the Company, Eddison confined his activities to asking awkward questions at the half yearly meetings. On 12th June 1895, at the age of 70, he died.

Two further tramway engines were purchased from Kitson's and several to a new design from Green's. These are discussed in a later chapter.

How did the operation of steam trams affect the passengers on the routes on which they worked? In late 1883 a reduction of fares occurred on the Wortley route when, in order to encourage traffic, the line was divided into three penny stages either way instead of 2d. stages up and 1d. down. The following year it was reduced to two stages of 1d. each, the fare stage being at the "Crown". This was a desperate attempt to increase the number of passengers, but the Company blandly stated that the reduction was made "with a view to meet liberally the requirements of the working population" of the Wortley district. They added that the low fares would not have been remunerative if the line was worked by horse cars. The original service was half hourly, but by December 1882, was 20 minutes from 7.47 am to 9.27 pm and, in late 1884, this was further increased to 15 minutes. By 1887 trams were running every 12 minutes with a ten minutes service on Saturdays with a late departure from Boar Lane at 10.20 pm. The following year a ten minutes service was worked on weekdays also and, except for a period from 1889-91, this frequency and fare structure was apparently maintained until the takeover of the tramways by the Corporation.

Similar fare reductions took place on the Headingley route and from 13th April 1885 the "outside" fare was reduced to two stages of one penny each, instead of stages of 2d. and 1d. The "inside" fare remained at 3d.

from Boar Lane to Headingley. There were, in the 'eighties, frequent minor alterations and inconsistencies in the fare structure on the Headingley tramway and this led to many complaints. By 1888, however, the 3d. through fare was discontinued and, with the exception of the Chapeltown route, the maximum fare anywhere on the tramways was 2d. This resulted in an increase in the number of passengers carried. For the period July to December 1886 the number carried on the whole of the tramways was 3,356,014 and for the similar period, four years later, it had increased to 4,988,384 or 13 times the population of Leeds. The total car mileage for the same periods respectively was 427,484 (steam 142,783) and 485,337 (steam 160,750).

Turton was very pleased with these results and considered it "wonderful" that a person could get a ride under cover from Boar Lane to the "Three Horse Shoes", Headingley for 2d. This could be done and still pay expenses, but it could only be done by "strict economy and carefulness." The 2d. inside fare, however, did not last long and by 1891 had reverted to 3d. The outside fare remained at 2d. until 1st January 1893 when it, too, was increased to 3d. With the use of steam the frequency on the Headingley route was also increased, but this was not as marked as Wortley. In December 1882, just prior to the introduction of steam cars, 73 departures were made daily from Boar Lane to Headingley from 8.30 am to 10.30 pm. By August 1887 this had increased to 82 and three years later a further increase to 105 departures daily took place.

Milnes trailer No. 21 in Boar Lane about 1890.
Courtesy The Thoresby Society Collection.

One of the social effects of the improved financial position of the Company in 1889 was the introduction of cheap early morning workmen's cars on the Wortley, Hunslet, Kirkstall and Meanwood Road routes. This was one of the stipulations of section 11 of the "Leeds Tramways Order, 1871" and required the Company to run "carriages on the tramways each way morning and evening for artisans, mechanics and daily labourers at tolls or charges not exceeding ½d. (the Company nevertheless not being required to take any less fare than one penny)." The Corporation never showed much interest in the introduction of workmen's cars, but when the subject was discussed the Company always maintained that the cars would be little used and it would not be worth their while to put them on. However, a request for workmen's cars made at a Council meeting on 2nd October 1889 was almost immediately complied with by the Company who did not argue and jeopardise their position. As will be seen later, they were negotiating with the Corporation for an extension of their authority to operate the tramways – due to expire in 1892. An early morning workmen's steam car began to run from the "Star Inn", Wortley at 5.30 am on Monday 28th October 1889 and, on the same day and at the same times horse cars from Kirkstall to Hunslet and Hunslet to Kirkstall were also started. On 25th November a workmen's horse car was also instituted from Briggate to Meanwood Road and back. The Wortley, Kirkstall and Hunslet services appear to have been moderately successful, but the Meanwood car frequently had only two passengers and was probably soon discontinued.

On both the Wortley and Headingley routes the Company suffered several setbacks partly due to severe wear and tear on the track and also by problems caused by the Corporation. As the Wortley route was originally laid on an improved type of track there were few complaints for this reason, but the service was suspended on three occasions because of Corporation activities. A "great and unexpected calamity" occurred when the line was closed from December 1884 to 23rd May 1885 due to the construction of a sewer in Wellington Road. This not only caused a loss in the receipts of £490 9s. 3d. but also damaged the line and gave the Company considerable expense in the construction of temporary tracks in their efforts to work a small portion of the line. The route was stopped for eight weeks from early May to early July 1886, also due to sewerage works in Wellington Road. On this occasion the loss was £280 but opportunity was taken to completely relay the section between Canal Street and the "Crown Inn", about 700 to 800 yards of double track. This was previously part single track. The biggest suspension, however, was the closure of Tong Road from 10th March 1890 to late July

1891. This was again due to sewerage works and the line was so badly damaged that it had to be relaid completely by the Corporation who charged the cost to the Company. In the process some of the loop lines were extended and some stretches of single line doubled. During the period of closure the steam trams ran to the "Crown Hotel" only, but the same number of cars was used as the number formerly employed on the through service to the "Star Inn". Hence an increased service to the "Crown" (125 journeys daily) was operated during this period. Even this intensive service resulted in complaints from passengers:–

"After walking the length of unused rails from the "Star" to the "Crown" one deliberates whether the tramcar or the 'bus will depart first. As the tramcar makes a start first you elect to travel by it. He goes ahead about 30 yards and then stops when on the double line of rails. You begin to feel impatient, for be it known the Wortley cars at present have no fixed timetable. The car starts and dribbles gently down to Wellington Bridge. It is usual to take on coke here, which is carried by shedmen to the great inconvenience of pedestrians. While this is done the 'bus runs gaily past, which makes you feel very unamiable indeed. Having got fuel you resume the dribbling style ——"
(Yorkshire Post, 16th February, 1891).

On 27th July 1891 the Tong Road line was re-opened as far as Strawberry Lane, being extended through to the "Star Inn" about a month later.

Although the Headingley route was said to have been completely relaid with girder rails in 1882, it appears that the timber foundations of the old horse car track were used and it soon deteriorated. The cold winter of 1890-1 played havoc due to frost action and there were many

Kitson engine No. 11 and a Milnes Trailer at the "Crown" terminus, New Wortley about 1890.
Courtesy The late J. Houghton Photographer.

Green engine No. 27 and Milnes trailer No. 33 at Wortley about 1892.   *Courtesy C. Heaton.*

complaints. In literally hundreds of places there was a difference of 2″ and 3″ between the level of the rails and adjoining setts, and in some cases the rails were 4″ below the road surface. There were gaps of 1″ or 1½″ between the rails at rail joints and they were so awry that it was said to be "surprising" that the cars remained on the track. Passengers were frequently almost jolted off their seats and private carriages were "torn to pieces".

On 7th January 1891 the question was discussed at a meeting of the Council, and it was reported that several ratepayers in Headingley had instructed a firm of solicitors to undertake Court action to compel the Corporation and the Tramways Company to immediately take action to repair the lines. Although the Company was responsible for the repair, the Corporation could, if it wished, under the "Tramways Act" carry out the remedial work and charge the full cost to the Company. The threat of legal action had the desired effect for the following day the Company set all their available platelayers to work in Cookridge Street, one of the worst sections. The Corporation also put on staff in order that the work could be carried on night and day. Much of the work, however, was patching using the existing timber foundations, but the section between Buckingham Road and the "Oak" was relaid with girder rails on a concrete foundation. During the work of relaying the passing places were lengthened and, from 6th February 1891, the tram service was curtailed to Buckingham Road. This resulted in many complaints as the Company continued to charge the full fare of 3d. for the journey and provided no connection at the "Oak" to take passengers through to the "Three Horse Shoes". Eventually, however, on 12th March, a shuttle service between the "Oak" and "Three Horse Shoes" was opened, passengers walking to their connection at Buckingham Road. The route was re-opened throughout later in the month.

Turton, commenting on the Headingley problems, said that it was most difficult to work a steam tram service on lines intended for horse cars and remarked that the Manager, Wharam, had had a lot of trouble and worry. At the August 1891 half yearly meeting of the Company a shareholder was upset about the unpleasant "grumbling and growling" that was made against the Tramways Company.

"The other day he happened to be coming down in a Headingley car when there was a breakdown, and everybody got out amidst general laughter at what they considered a not unusual occurrence. It was quite humiliating to listen to the amount of abuse poured on to the Company as one travelled along the lines".

(Yorkshire Post, 15th August, 1891).

As a result of the Headingley track problem, it was realised that the Company's licence to run steam cars had expired some three years previously; Major-General Hutchinson was invited to inspect the Wortley, Headingley, Kirkstall routes and the North Street tramway with a view to its renewal. On 10th July 1891 the inspection took place and the Inspector was "gratified" to note that North Street was being relaid. (This was in conjunction with the Roundhay steam cars referred to in a later chapter). He described the Headingley route as being in "fair condition" except for Boar Lane, used in common with other routes, which he advised be completely relaid. He made no comment on the Wortley or Kirkstall lines. Steam trams were now only running on

65

the Kirkstall line for the early morning and evening workmen's cars. He recommended that Wellington Street and Briggate be also relaid and was unwilling to sanction the renewal of the licence until the repairs were completed. The Company agreed to relay the tracks in question but took no action, no doubt in view of the fact that their authority to run the tramways was due to expire in 12 months.

There were heavy snowfalls in January 1892 and the Headingley track became even worse, being in places 5″ to 6″ below the road surface. The engines and cars "wobbled alarmingly" and it was extremely dangerous to travel along the tramway in a carriage after dark. In desperation the Highways Committee wrote to the Board of Trade asking that a further inspection be made. They received a reply to the effect that the Tramways Company did not have authority to use steam power and they could see no point in making another inspection. Legal action was again threatened by the Headingley residents and the Highways Committee was forced to "take the bull by the horns" and carry out the track repairs itself. They called in two firms of local contractors, Towler and Speight, and David Speight and, on 1st February, 100 men began work relaying the section of track between Boar Lane and Wellington Bridge. New steel girder rails, supplied by the Tramways Company, were used on a concrete foundation and Boar Lane was closed to trams for several weeks. The Headingley cars worked a quarter hourly service from the Royal Exchange building and the Wortley and Kirkstall cars ran from the top of Aire Street. In spite of the large labour force the progress of the work was described as "leisurely". It took over a week to relay the Briggate/Boar Lane junction in mid-February and just before Easter work came to a standstill when the supply of rails dried up. However, in late April, an assignment of rails for the

extension of the Beckett Street tramway (described in a later chapter) arrived and was immediately diverted for use by the Tramways Company in Wellington Street, to whom they were sold by the Corporation. Further delays occurred when the paviors employed on the work formed themselves into a union and from 6th to 31st May went on strike. The work was completed about a month later.

Meanwhile it was reported that the havoc which heavy engines and cars, together with the effects of frost and snow, had wrought upon the permanent way between Boar Lane and Headingley was "filling the minds of the leading representatives of the Tramways Company with regret that they ever ventured upon steam hauled cars". The service to Headingley had been reduced by about half and the cars still running were fitful and uncertain. The Highways Committee and the solicitors representing the Headingley ratepayers eventually managed to persuade Major-General Hutchinson to visit Leeds again. On 1st March 1892 the Inspector walked over most of the Headingley route. In many places the rails were lost to sight in mud and at Shaw Lane the inspector witnessed a rail snap in two as a car passed over it.

In his report, the Inspector emphatically described the Headingley line as being in an extremely unsatisfactory condition and said that it was rapidly deteriorating. "In the interests of public safety," he added, "the use of steam haulage should be at once discontinued, and should not be resumed until the tramway has been relaid." On 9th March a meeting of the Highways Committee was held to discuss the report and it transpired that the Company's Act of 1881 included a clause to the effect that they were liable to a penalty of £10 and a continuing penalty of £5 per day if steam or other mechanical power were used contrary to the provisions

Kitson engine No. 8 and Starbuck car No. 62 stand on the reversing triangle at Kirkstall terminus, about 1895.
Courtesy Science Museum, South Kensington, London, Whitcombe Collection.

of the Act. Although the Company had been running steam cars for three years without the licence or authority of the Board of Trade, the Committee decided not to invoke this clause but gave the Company 24 hours notice to discontinue the use of steam cars on the Headingley route. Hence, the last steam tram ran to Headingley on 10th March 1892.

For some time there was chaos for Headingley passengers. It was intended that the steam cars be transferred to the Kirkstall route and the horse cars on that route transferred to Headingley. This was impossible, however, as, due to track reconstruction, there was no rail connection at the Royal Exchange, and the best the Company could do was to put on two horse cars and a 'bus running between the Exchange and the "Oak" every 20 minutes. After a month or so the Kirkstall horse cars were transferred to Headingley. The Company estimated that to maintain the service previously operated by steam (105 journeys daily) would require the purchase of 100 additional horses and new stable accommodation at Headingley. Although some horses were purchased and temporary stables erected the frequency was only just over half that of the steam trams.

The Kirkstall to Hunslet through horse car service was discontinued and the Kirkstall section was now entirely steam operated. The steam cars had generally run about 5,000 miles annually on the Kirkstall line in the late 'eighties, but in 1890 this was increased with the arrival of more rolling stock. During 1890 the Kirkstall steam trams ran 20,774 miles as compared with about 156,000 for the horse cars. To provide improved turning arrangements for steam, a reversing triangle was constructed adjacent to the Police Station, Kirkstall, during the latter part of 1889. The partial introduction of steam cars on the service made little difference to the frequency. A ten minutes service from 8.40 am to 10.30 pm (84 journeys daily) was in operation in 1882. It was slightly increased to 88 journeys daily in the late 'eighties. The penny fare stages introduced in January 1878 were unchanged until late 1885, when the penny stage was extended from Wellington Bridge to Ventnor Street and the 2d. stage from the "Cardigan Arms" to Burley Wood. The through fare to Kirkstall remained at 3d. but, by 1889 had been reduced to 2d. with a 1d. stage at the "Cardigan Arms" (later altered to the "Beckett's Arms"). The Kirkstall line did not have the same problems due to Corporation activities as other routes, and the only suspension of service that has been traced was early in 1877 when a sewer was constructed, necessitating the

insertion of a crossover at Lloyd Street to facilitate working. In the first part of 1885 a loss of £264 was recorded due to sewer repairs.

As Turton frequently stressed, the steam tram would have been more successful in Leeds had the tramway tracks been constructed at a later period as in other towns.

In addition to steam various other forms of mechanical traction existed in the 'eighties and 'nineties such as cable, accumulator, gas and compressed air. The Leeds Tramways Company had a brief encounter with the latter.

A product of Manning, Wardle and Co., steam locomotive and, to a lesser extent, steam tramway engine manufacturers, Jack Lane, Hunslet, Leeds, was a tramway engine driven by compressed air. The engine was to the design and patents of Colonel Frederick E. Beaumont, R.E. and M.P. for South Durham, who was well known for his work with compressed air drills and tunnelling machines. He was involved with the drilling of the Channel Tunnel in 1880 until the politicians put a stop to his work. An engineer named Mekarski had carried out trials with a compressed air tram in Paris in 1876 and about this time Beaumont turned his attention to the design of a similar vehicle. It appears that Greenwood and Batley Ltd. of Armley Road, Leeds, did some preliminary construction work on the engine in the late 'seventies, but it was Manning, Wardle and Co. who brought the design to fruition in 1880.

A compressed air tramway engine was similar in construction to its steam counterpart except that it had a high pressure air reservoir in place of a boiler and fire box. The reservoir was charged from a stationary air compressor and the locomotive returned periodically to be re-charged. Stationary steam driven plant tended to be very efficient and several locomotives could draw their supplies of energy from one plant. Being odourless and almost silent, compressed air was considered to be the answer to the steam tram. The reservoir capacity was 65 cubic feet with a pressure of 1,000 lbs per sq. inch and the engine was designed to draw a loaded tram a distance of ten miles on a straight and level road without being re-charged with air. Colonel Beaumont employed a compound engine of four cylinders in which the air was successively expanded down from the initial pressure. The volumes of the cylinders were in the ratios 1:3:9:27 and were progressively cut out as the pressure fell. The expansion of air at such a high pressure caused a refrigerating effect and, in order to

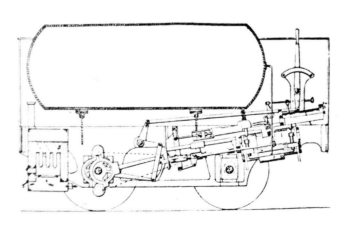
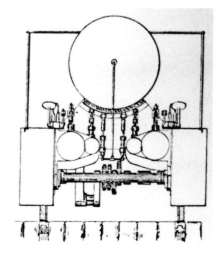

Drawing showing the layout of Beaumont's compressed air engine. From a patent specification.

obviate this, a small boiler was provided to keep the cylinders warm. This was done by surrounding them with a cast iron steam jacket, exhaust air from the engine providing a forced draught to the boiler.

The first trial took place on 9th January 1880 in Manning, Wardle's works and was said to be successful although the engine was without its wheels. The wheels were fitted and further trials took place in the same Company's works on 13th February. The engine was tested on a short length of track 96 yards long and afterwards was sent to London for trials. A further locomotive was built by Manning, Wardle and the "shapely and small" engine made a trial on the Leeds tramways on 23rd September 1880.

"The locomotive was charged with air giving the enormous pressure of 1,000 lbs per sq. inch and with this power it started with one of the heavy cars from Hunslet terminus. When it arrived at Boar Lane the air pressure had been reduced to about 700 lbs per sq. inch. *It proceeded as far as the "Crown Inn" at Wortley and by that time the gauge stood at about 500 lbs pressure. There was some shunting necessary at that point, but the remaining pressure sufficed to take the engine and car back to the Hunslet terminus. The engine ran with remarkable steadiness and was perfectly under the command of the driver. It was quietly stopped and easily started."*

(Leeds Mercury, 24th September, 1880).

It was reported that the Leeds Tramways Company was intending to use compressed air on the gradients of Chapeltown Road and experiments were later carried out on the route. On one occasion the engine ran out of air half way along the line and was unceremoniously hauled back to Leeds by a team of horses. Following this the Company quietly dropped the idea. Experiments with compressed air were carried out in several towns, but it did not prove economical and was not extensively adopted in Great Britain.

Two steam trams, a horse tram, band, and lifeboat can be seen on this photograph of City Square, taken on Lifeboat Saturday, 6th July 1895.
Courtesy J. Soper Collection.

CHAPTER TEN

The Tramways Company and the Penny 'Bus Problem

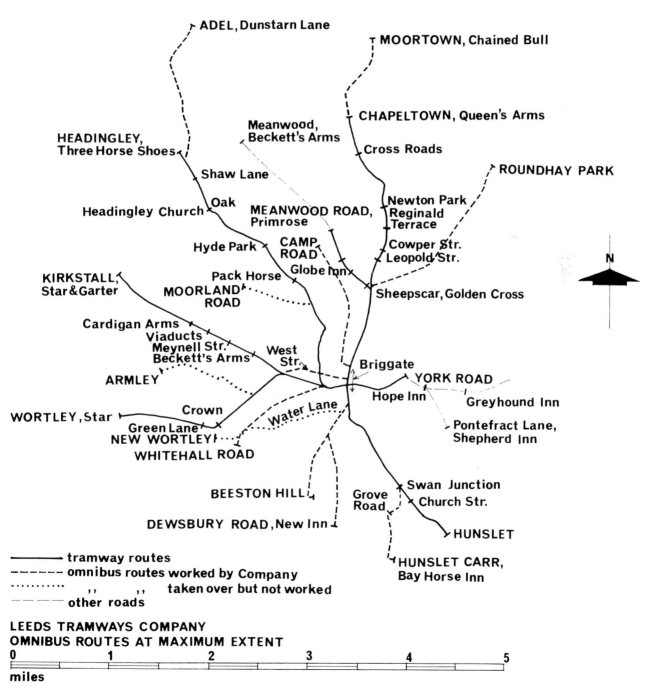

ADEL, Dunstarn Lane

MOORTOWN, Chained Bull

CHAPELTOWN, Queen's Arms

Meanwood, Beckett's Arms

Cross Roads

HEADINGLEY, Three Horse Shoes

ROUNDHAY PARK

Shaw Lane

Oak

Headingley Church

MEANWOOD ROAD, Primrose

Newton Park Reginald Terrace

Hyde Park

CAMP ROAD

Cowper Str. Leopold Str.

Globe Inn

KIRKSTALL, Star & Garter

Pack Horse

MOORLAND ROAD

Sheepscar, Golden Cross

Cardigan Arms

Viaducts Meynell Str. Beckett's Arms

West Str.

Briggate

ARMLEY

YORK ROAD

Hope Inn

Greyhound Inn

WORTLEY, Star

Crown

Water Lane

Green Lane

Pontefract Lane, Shepherd Inn

NEW WORTLEY

WHITEHALL ROAD

BEESTON HILL

Grove Road

Swan Junction Church Str.

DEWSBURY ROAD, New Inn

HUNSLET

HUNSLET CARR, Bay Horse Inn

N

———— tramway routes
−−−−− omnibus routes worked by Company
············ ,, ,, taken over but not worked
− − − other roads

LEEDS TRAMWAYS COMPANY
OMNIBUS ROUTES AT MAXIMUM EXTENT

0   1   2   3   4   5
miles

In common with many other tramway companies, the Leeds Tramways Company also ran 'buses. At first the 'buses were run in conjunction with their tramways, but in the 'eighties the Company expanded its operations and ran on other routes in opposition to various omnibus proprietors.

The Corporation had insisted that a clause be inserted in the "Leeds Tramways Order, 1871" to the effect that if, after the construction of a tramway, any 'bus service was permanently discontinued, the Company, if requested by the Corporation, had to provide a replacement service. This clause proved to be a source of continuous annoyance to the Company.

In September 1871, when the tramway was opened to Headingley "Oak", the Company introduced a one-horse 'bus, running at half-hourly intervals to the "Three Horse Shoes", in connection with the tramway. The 'bus was apparently discontinued when the tramway was opened as far as Shaw Lane and, in April and May the following year, it was used to form a connection from the "Cardigan Arms" to the "Star and Garter", Kirkstall, while the tramway was being constructed.

These temporary 'bus services caused no problem to the Company, but the opening of the Hunslet tramway in March 1874 resulted in the withdrawal of Turton's 'buses to Hunslet and Hunslet Carr. The Company was forced to open a permanent 'bus route connecting the Hunslet tramway at the "Swan" Junction with the "Bay Horse Inn", Hunslet Carr. The same one-horse 'bus was apparently used, but at the half yearly meeting of the Company, held in August 1874, it was reported that the receipts on the Hunslet tramway and 'bus were disappointing. It was said that the 'bus was losing £100 a year and by October it was withdrawn. This resulted in immediate protests from the local inhabitants who met the Directors of the Company in an endeavour to have the 'bus restored. The Company was referred to the clause in their Tramways Order, but they ignored the pleas of the residents.

As a result of the Company's action a local man, John Guy of Lower Carr Place, Hunslet, began to run a 'bus to Hunslet Carr. Guy ran his 'bus through to Briggate during the long and severe winter of 1874–5. This competition evidently affected the tramway receipts for, in May 1875, the Company ran two 'buses on a half hourly service between Briggate and Hunslet Carr in an attempt to put Guy out of business. This action resulted in a massive protest from the local people when, on 8th May, between 1,000 and 2,000 held an open air meeting on Penny Hill, Church Street, Hunslet. "Great indignation" at the behaviour of the Tramways Company was expressed and the meeting promised to give Guy all possible support for his enterprise. The Company, however, won in the end. On 1st January 1878 they purchased Guy's business for £200 and had the monopoly of the Hunslet area for a time.

The withdrawal of Newsome's Adel 'bus in 1874 resulted in the Company being approached by the Corporation to provide a replacement service. On 1st October 1874 a twice daily 'bus was introduced running in connection with the Headingley tramway. It always lost money but ran uneventfully throughout the remainder of the Company's existence.

Shortly after the introduction of the Adel 'bus, the Chapeltown tramway was completed and Turton's Chapeltown and Moortown 'buses withdrawn. On 14th November 1874 the Company began a 'bus, running at approximately hourly intervals, in connection with the tramway to the "Chained Bull", Moortown. This 'bus also proved to be a financial burden on the Company.

To work the Hunslet Carr, Adel and Moortown services the Tramways Company had six 'buses. The 'bus bought from Guy was not required and was sold for £50 in October 1878. In February 1879 it was said that of the six 'buses only four were working, one each on the Adel and Moortown services and two on Hunslet Carr. In October 1880 only one 'bus, said by the Hackney Carriages Committee to be in a "very unsatisfactory condition", was being worked to Hunslet Carr. The 'bus and Hunslet tramway were facing stiff competition from a 'bus introduced by a Thomas Hawkes of Larchfield Road, Hunslet, from Leeds Bridge to the "Swan" Junction. This was introduced in August 1880 and was followed two months later by another 'bus operated by a Joseph Walker of Chapeltown Road over the same route. Penny fares were probably charged on the opposition 'buses and the tramway 'bus lost money; the service was reduced to hourly and eventually in 1882 cut back to the "Swan" Junction.

Hawkes, a contractor, had served terms of imprisonment in the 'seventies for cruelty to horses and was a particularly notorious character. He regularly had disagreements with his conductors over payment of wages, one of them being killed in a pay day fight with Hawkes. For this offence Hawkes was imprisoned for manslaughter in August 1883. In February 1881 his licence had been revoked for cruelty and was transferred to a relative, Arthur James Hawkes, Thomas acting as 'bus driver.

The cut back of the Company's 'bus to the "Swan" Junction resulted in protests from the residents who requested that Walker be allowed to extend his service through to the "Bay Horse Inn". In August 1882 a licence granting this extension was given, Walker operating an hourly service between Briggate and Hunslet Carr. At the same time Hawkes instituted a 40 minutes service between Briggate and Hunslet Church, a short working of the Hunslet Carr route.

The 'bus stands at the "Swan" Junction and Hunslet Church termini were abolished by the Hackney Carriage Committee in December 1882 and a new terminus was fixed on the west side of Church Street, between the "Green Man Inn" and Grove Road for four 'buses belonging to the Tramways Company, Walker and Hawkes. A regular 'bus service between Briggate and Grove Road was instituted by the two latter proprietors, but the Tramways Company did not take up the Grove Road licence and continued to run 'buses to the "Swan" Junction at busy periods, particularly on Saturday afternoons. This was now illegal and following cautions and threats of proceedings from the Corporation they were forced to discontinue the practice. The Company later made several applications to reintroduce 'buses to the "Swan" Junction but all were refused. The Company did, however, introduce a regular tramway short working known as the "Swan Junction Special Car." This operated until March 1892 and the service varied from 34 to 66 journeys daily. During 1887 "Special Cars" are also recorded as running to Church Street, Hunslet. The ten minutes tramway service to Hunslet introduced in the 'seventies remained virtually unchanged through the Company's period of operation. 'Bus competition, however, brought a reduction of fares. The original 3d. fare from Briggate to the terminus was reduced to 2d. by 1880 and shortly afterwards to 1d. In 1893 it reverted to 2d. for a short while, later being reduced to 1½d.

Walker's 'bus waits at the "Pack Horse" 'bus terminus as a Headingley steam tram passes.

Although the Tramways Company could not make the Hunslet Carr 'bus service pay, Walker and Hawkes apparently could. In 1881 Walker caused further trouble to the Tramways Company when he introduced a penny 'bus running a 20 minutes service from Briggate to the "Pack Horse Inn", Woodhouse Lane. The 'bus ran via newly widened Upperhead Row and Woodhouse Lane, a densely populated section of the Headingley tramway, and could travel to the "Pack Horse" in less time than the tramcar running from Boar Lane via Park Row and Cookridge Street, which the Company said they "could not do under 2d."

The penny 'buses were mentioned at the Tramways Company meeting in August 1881, Turton saying that they might pay in the summer but would run at a loss in the winter. Eddison said that 'buses would never pay running alongside tramcars and the Company had nothing to fear from penny 'buses. A year later there was a different story when it was reported that the losses on the Headingley tramway due to 'bus competition were £1,000 and on the Chapeltown route £500 – the latter was facing troubles with a penny 'bus operated by a Joseph Bramfitt from Briggate to Cowper Street, Chapeltown Road.

In 1882 the Headingley tramway was facing severe competition from Walker's 'buses. The three early morning twopenny tramcars to Hyde Park, originally put on in 1874, were seriously affected by the "Pack Horse" 'bus as passengers tended to walk across Woodhouse Moor and ride by the 'bus to save a 1d. Only on wet days did the trams have any passengers and they were soon withdrawn. Following representations from the local residents the Tramways Company put on a replacement 'bus to Hyde Park in August 1882. Soon after-

wards Walker introduced an opposition early morning 'bus to Hyde Park. The Company's 'bus received the same treatment that the early morning trams had received and was withdrawn on 29th April 1883, but to compensate for its withdrawal, the Company increased the frequency of the morning service of trams between Boar Lane and Headingley from quarter-hourly to ten minutes.

A 'bus introduced by Walker in February 1883 between Briggate and Headingley Church (near to the "Oak") and traversing the tramway route created more problems for the Company. Walker's Headingley Church service must have been profitable for, in April 1885, he was granted permission to run two additional 'buses on the route. The three vehicles worked a 20 minutes service from Briggate and were worked in conjunction with the "Pack Horse" 'bus giving a ten minutes service to the latter terminus. An improving service of steam trams to Headingley in the middle 'eighties provided effective opposition by the Company for, by 1888, the Headingley 'buses were reduced from 35 to 26 journeys daily. In March 1892, however, following the withdrawal of the steam trams, the two "Pack Horse" 'buses were extended through to Headingley Church giving a ten minutes service with shortworkings to the "Pack Horse" at 20 minutes intervals.

The Moortown 'bus was never remunerative and, in May 1880, was withdrawn, the Company using the excuse that, as there was already a 'bus running to Shadwell via Moortown (referred to in a later chapter), there was no need for their vehicle. Following complaints from the Corporation, the Moortown 'bus was restored in September, but, in retaliation, a week or so afterwards, the Tramways Company cut back the ter-

71

The Briggate 'bus stand with Walker's Headingley church 'bus, about 1890.   *Courtesy The Thoresby Society Collection.*

Three tired horses wait with their vehicle at the Headingley church 'bus terminus in the 1880's.
Courtesy The late G. Bingley, Photographer. Leeds University Collection.

minus of the Chapeltown tramway from the "Queen's" to the "Cross Roads" – about half a mile. The Moortown 'bus formed a connection between the two points and, "to evade legal proceedings", one tram per day was run through to the "Queen's." This section of route was uneconomical for the Company and Eddison said that they didn't think it necessary to run the trams for the full length of the route either for themselves or the public. Following objections the Company replied that as soon as they were in a position to use steam cars on the Chapeltown route they would run through to the "Queen's" and added that passengers were carried to the "Queen's" by the Moortown 'bus without charge. The steam trams never materialised and the through service was eventually reintroduced in 1885.

The Tramways Company, worried at the rapid increase of 'bus competition, felt that the only effective way to meet the opposition from the omnibus proprietors was to run competing 'buses themselves. Accordingly they included in the "Leeds Tramways Act, 1881," a provision for the Company to work "omnibuses, coaches, hackney carriages and other vehicles." The Act had a difficult passage through Parliament as Lord Redesdale of the House of Lords Committee insisted that the Corporation pass a resolution in favour of the Company operating 'buses. At the Town Council meeting on 3rd June 1881, Eddison said:–

"It was the intention of the Company, if they got the power, to run omnibuses wherever they were required for the accommodation of the public. Additional omnibuses had been required and had been supplied by others, the Company not having the power to supply them. Seeing they were such large ratepayers they thought they ought to have this power ——— The omnibuses they now ran they were compelled to run by the Corporation under the provisions of the Act of 1871. They had no intention of running cabs, but they wished to have the power to do so."
(Yorkshire Post, 4th June 1881).

The Company made no mention of the losses it was sustaining and said that it wished to run 'buses as branch connections for the tramways on the main lines and to utilise the horses and stables which would be displaced by the steam trams.

Alderman Emsley said that the town was indebted to the Tramways Company for the improved facilities for getting from one part of the town to another as compared with a few years previously and thought that a "further public benefit would ensue if the Company had the powers they were now seeking." The Council, however, declined to pass a resolution. The Company then made an application to the Mayor to have the matter reconsidered as they felt that many members were under a "considerable misapprehension" as to the intentions of the Company. The Company's proposals were reconsidered at a further meeting of the Council on 15th June. A deputation from the Tramways Company attended, preceded by a deputation of omnibus proprietors objecting, and stating that the powers already possessed by the Company were ample. Robert Chapman, omnibus proprietor, said:–

"The Company were seeking for additional powers not in the interest of the public, but in order to enrich themselves. The Company wanted to get in the thin end of the wedge, and then they would drive it home by driving all other competitors out of the field."
(Yorkshire Post, 16th June 1881).

The Company agreed to insert a clause in its Act placing the operation of its 'buses under the jurisdiction of the Hackney Carriages Committee and eventually the Council approved the Company's proposals by a majority of 23 to 17.

Following passage of the Bill the Company decided to purchase six new 'buses and an additional 60 or 70 horses to work them. However, their Chairman, Turton, then the major omnibus proprietor in the town proposed that they buy the whole of his 'bus undertaking at a valuation. The Company was facing competition largely in the inner part of the town, and, as Turton's routes traversed this area, the offer was gratefully accepted. During the purchase negotiations Turton resigned his position on the Board of Directors, Eddison, and later William Baxter, taking his place as Chairman. Following unsatisfactory financial results Turton was re-elected to the Board in February 1883, replacing Daniel Busby who had ceased to play an active part in the Company.

At the August 1882 Company meeting Eddison said that in taking up the 'bus business, the Directors were not anxious to extend their operations; they had done so merely in self defence. Turton's undertaking was valued by John Hepper and the sum agreed was £4,537 10s. 0d., said by Eddison to be a "fair price."

"They were now in a position to cope with any opposition which presented itself. They had no wish to interfere with other people in any way until they came behind a tramcar, and he was convinced that no omnibus could run alongside a tramcar and pay its way."
(Yorkshire Post, 26th August 1882)

At least 13 'buses and 100 horses were purchased from Turton and the following 'bus routes were taken over:–

Briggate to Armley –
(no competing service).
Briggate to Beeston Hill –
(in competition with C. J. Coates).
Briggate to Dewsbury Road –
(no competing service).
Briggate to Moorland Road –
(no competing service).
Briggate to New Wortley ("Queen Inn") via Water Lane –
(no competing service).
Briggate to Roundhay Park –
(in competition with J. Bramfitt and J. Walker).
Camp Road to Whitehall Road and New Wortley through service –
(no competing service).

Included in the sale were Turton's cab business and the rental of his stables in Sheepshanks Yard, North Street. The Tramways Company began to take the receipts from Turton's 'buses on 12th May 1882, but the actual date of purchase was 28th July 1882. Turton was bound by agreement not to operate 'buses in Leeds again as long as he lived. He apparently ran his 'buses efficiently and profitably and at first the Tramways Company seemed to do likewise. Eddison said, in August 1882, that the weekly 'bus receipts were £138 against an average of £120 when they took them over. The public, however, did not take kindly to the Tramways Company running 'buses as it felt that the Company were trying to secure domination of the streets in the town. As a result there was a tendency to boycott the Company and patronise their competitors' vehicles. The Company apparently made no attempt to run the Armley, Moorland Road or New Wortley via Water Lane services. Other proprietors later ran 'buses to Armley and Moorland Road, but 'buses never again ran to New Wortley via Water Lane.

The Roundhay Park 'bus soon succumbed to passenger resistance, "Justice" wrote:–

"I ask you to give publicity to the scandalous proceedings of the Leeds Tramways Company with regard to their omnibuses at present being run from Briggate to Roundhay Park. It is well known to those who travel that way that the usual fare from Briggate to the "Prince Arthur," or by some 'buses as far as Leopold Street, is a penny, and passengers never think of asking the fare before entering the 'bus, but taking it as a matter of course, expect the fare will be 1d. The Leeds Tramways Company charge the unsuspecting passenger 2d. for the same distance, giving no notice except by a small card inside the 'bus, where it is impossible to see it after dark, and what can a passenger do after he has taken his seat? If the conductor does his duty, the passenger is compelled to pay the full fare. Mr. Bramfitt and I think Mr. Walker run their 'buses that way for a penny, and I believe I echo the wish of many that their courage will outlive the opposition of the Leeds Tramways Company."

(Yorkshire Post, 27th July 1882).

Through passengers to Roundhay, however, were in favour of the higher fares for the short distance as it enabled them to get a seat and avoid the annoyance of arriving at Kirkgate corner, Briggate, on a wet day and finding the Roundhay 'bus "crowded to repletion with penny fares," and hence a three miles walk home in the rain. There is no record of the Company running a regular Roundhay 'bus service after September 1882. Bramfitt and Walker retained the monopoly of the route.

The Camp Road 'bus service was also short lived and the Company seems to have adopted a deliberate policy of diverting traffic from the Camp Road 'bus to the Meanwood Road tramway. The tram terminus was only a short distance from the 'bus terminus and the public was said to be "educated" to use the tram by the Company making the 'bus unreliable in time so that passengers were forced into the Meanwood Road trams as the lesser of two evils. After thus "educating" the public, on 29th April 1883, the Company withdrew the 'bus and the day after increased the tram fare from Briggate to the Meanwood Road tram terminus from 1d. to 1½d. with a 1d. fare stage at the "Golden Cross". The through tram fare, originally 2d., was later halved to encourage traffic.

The Meanwood Road tramway faced problems with penny 'buses. In 1881 a half hourly 'bus service was running from Briggate to the "Globe Inn" Meanwood Road, but by late 1882 was discontinued. The Tramways Company enjoyed a monopoly of traffic until December 1883, when a Thomas Blakey of Lodge Street reintroduced the half-hourly service to the "Globe Inn." The town terminus was at the Corn Exchange, changed to the "Greyhound," Vicar Lane on 9th January 1886. By 1887 Blakey appears to have gone out of business for, in June of that year, John Coates Junior, referred to in a previous chapter, took over as proprietor. His 'buses ran from the "White Swan," Call Lane in lieu of the "Greyhound" and the route was via Vicar Lane, North Street, Meanwood Road and extended to the "Beckett's Arms," Meanwood with short workings to the "Junction Inn". Coates objected to the Vicar Lane route and in September 1888 was granted permission to run his outward journey via Duncan Street and Briggate and inwardly via Vicar Lane.

John Coates's stables were in Nelson Street and he was a notorious alcoholic who served several terms of imprisonment for drunkenness. He died in early 1890 and in March of that year the licence to operate the Meanwood routes was transferred to his wife, Elizabeth. She outlived her husband by five years, passing away on 24th July 1895; their children, John and Sarah Coates, took over the business. In February 1896 they sold out to 18 years old Frederick Spurdens who used their stables in Nelson Street. The introduction of steam trams to Meanwood in 1898 marked the death knell for the 'buses and on 16th February 1899 they were auctioned off.

With the introduction of Blakey's 'bus the Tramways Company was forced to reduce the tram fare to 1d. but it reverted to 1½d. again in January 1893. The original 20 minutes frequency was increased to ten minutes about 1881, but reduced to 15 minutes by 1887. It remained at this level until the Corporation takeover.

Although Charles Coates's penny 'buses to Beeston Hill were probably the most profitable in Leeds, the Tramways Company found that the Beeston residents tended to boycott its vehicles and patronise Coates. Coates had a reputation for keeping good time and his 'buses were among the best kept in the town. The Company's Beeston Hill 'buses were withdrawn in the latter part of 1884, their report of February 1885 complaining that there was "a factious opposition on the part of many residents about Beeston Hill, who persistently refused to ride in the Company's 'buses." The low dividend of 2% was blamed on the penny 'bus competition which "harrassed the Company on all sides;" the 'buses only ran where traffic was good whereas the trams had to run the full length of their lines.

The Tramways Company had lost all the routes taken over from Turton with the exception of two: Whitehall Road and Dewsbury Road. On Whitehall Road, Joseph Walker introduced an opposition 'bus shortly after the Company began operation of the service. Walker's 'bus ran at the same times and over the same route to the "Smyth's Arms", Whitehall Road but, following complaints, the proprietors were instructed by the Hackney Carriages Committee to run alternately every 15 minutes. In October 1883 both Walker and the Tramways Company put on a second 'bus on weekdays and a third 'bus on Saturdays giving a very good 7½ minutes weekday service and a five minutes Saturday service. There was also an opposition 'bus running from 1882 and operated by Amos Kirby. He had the habit of starting late and immediately before the Company's 'buses, much to the consternation of the latter. The very frequent service, resulting from the competition between the three proprietors, was obviously beneficial to the residents of Whitehall Road, but the Tramways Company 'buses now lost money and they were withdrawn in the latter part of 1885. The opening of a new Cattle Market in Whitehall Road, near to the 'bus terminus, the following year and the prospect of increased traffic, induced the Company to reintroduce their 'buses on 1st June 1886. The Hackney Carriages Committee, however, objected as they were of opinion that there were already enough 'buses on Whitehall Road. The Company was forced to take its 'buses off after a few days.

The Dewsbury Road route was the only 'bus service acquired from Turton which turned out to be reasonably successful. There were complaints about the Com-

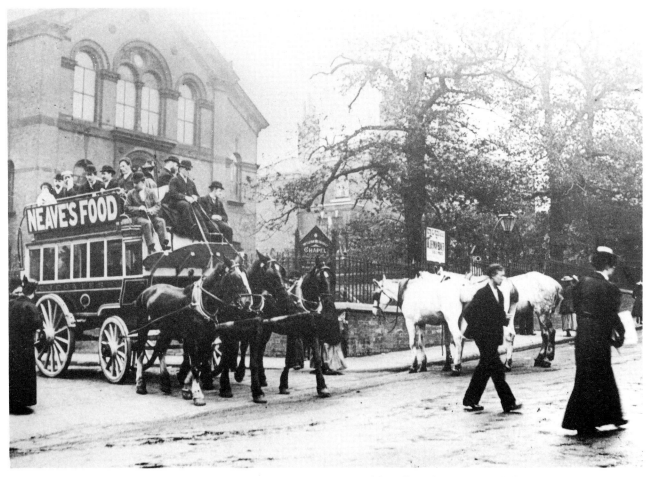

The reserve horses wait at the bottom of Beeston Hill as Coates' 'bus No. 6 leaves Lady Pit Street for Briggate.
Courtesy Leeds City Libraries.

pany's method of running the service, particularly during the summer months:–

"Whenever there is a fête at Roundhay Park or any stir in Leeds, off go two of the 'buses usually plying between Briggate and the 'New Inn'. I never found this to be the case when Turtons supplied the district. Today there have been 200 volunteers at the rifle range, who would have travelled both ways if there had been 'buses, but who now had to walk. Several parties on this date went and asked for the 'buses to run as usual, but 'No thank you,' a few more coppers might be made by running to the Park, and the convenience of the public was nothing when placed in the balance."

The Tramways Company ran a 15 minutes service of penny 'buses in spite of fierce competition from other proprietors in the late 'eighties and 'nineties. The Company 'buses ran until 1894 and the opposition they faced is referred to in a later chapter.

There were other factors which caused problems to the Tramways Company. The widening of Upperhead Row and other road improvements took place which gave the 'buses an advantage over the tramways. The extension of Hunslet Road through to Bridge End in 1880, and opened in January 1881, by-passed Hunslet Lane and gave a short cut for the Grove Road and Hunslet Carr 'buses. Also in 1880 the York Road tramway suffered a blow when the line was closed from 5th February to 30th October due to the construction of a large sewer along virtually the whole of the route. The line was relaid and during its closure the Tramways Company ran two 'buses via York Street to the tram terminus at the "Woodpecker". In spite of this the total loss in receipts was estimated at £1,242. The widening

and opening out of York Street about this time gave the omnibus proprietors the opportunity to introduce penny 'buses on the more direct route which "greatly prejudiced" the tramway via Marsh Lane.

In October 1881 an opposition penny 'bus was introduced by a Henry Cook from Kirkgate via York Street to the "Hope Inn", York Road. Cook, however, showed little interest in running the service and the licence passed to a George Henry Clayton in February 1882. Clayton ran for a year or so but must have found it uneconomical in competition with the trams and his 'buses were withdrawn. A more successful proprietor was a David Horton of Spring Street who instituted, in February 1886, a 'bus from the "Borough Arms Cocoa House," Kirkgate to the "Shepherd Inn", Pontefract Lane via York Street and, shortly afterwards re-introduced a 'bus service along York Road to a terminus at the 'Greyhound Inn." The Pontefract Lane 'bus ran at 15 minutes intervals but was reduced to half hourly by 1888. The "Greyhound" service was more successful with a 15 minutes frequency, increased to ten minutes by 1894. Horton owned a number of small single-deck 'buses and his son, Manasseh, was one of the drivers. Horton's smallest 'bus, a six seater, was called the *'The Pearl'* and on one occasion it is recorded that, for a joke, four of the stoutest passengers on the route, including Mr. Stocks, landlord of the "Greyhound", took their seats on 'The Pearl'. They called to the driver that he could start as he was "full".

Manasseh took a peep through his little window then got down and approached the 'bus from the back, and demanded that some of them should get out. They kept their seats wanting their joke, but Manasseh said "I'll see you in hell before I take you four up York Road for four fares," and straightaway unyoked his horse and took it down Wharf Street to be shod. That was the end of the joke for the four stout men had to get out, take the tram to the bottom of York Road and walk the remaining half mile or so to the "Greyhound."

David Horton died in January 1895 and a James Dean of Timber Place took over the "Shepherd Inn" service. The "Greyhound" 'bus was taken over by a Fred Tate and Ben Briggs who sold out to Dean in September 1896. The "Greyhound" 'bus ceased to run when the horse tramway was extended up York Road and the "Shepherd Inn" service lasted until the coming of the electric trams.

The tram fare on the York Road service was always a 1d. in Company days. With competition the frequency was increased from 56 to 75 journeys daily in 1882, a ten minutes service being operated in the afternoon and evening. It remained at this level until 1897.

A further tramway to suffer from penny 'bus competition was that to Kirkstall. A half-hourly penny 'bus service between Briggate and the "Junction Hotel," West Street, at the bottom of Kirkstall Road was in operation as early as 1878 and, by later in the year, was extended through to the "Beckett's Arms, Kirkstall Road, a densely populated area, and formed a through service with Little London (Camp Road) for a time, being changed in the early 'eighties to run through to Cowper Street, Chapeltown Road. The proprietor was Joseph Bramfitt who, in December 1885, extended the service to Meynell Street, Kirkstall Road. Two months later an extension to the Viaducts further up Kirkstall Road was authorised. Although the Tramways Company suffered from the competition, Bramfitt also found his 'buses uneconomical and they were withdrawn in July 1886.

The Tramways Company and a John Thomas Lister took over from Bramfitt and jointly ran the Kirkstall Road via West Street service. It appears that Lister ran through to Camp Road but neither operator ran for long, and both had ceased to run by the following year. In July 1887 a John Newton Sharp was granted permission to run two 'buses from St. James Hall, York Street to the end of St. Philip Street in West Street via Call Lane, Duncan Street, Boar Lane and Infirmary Street. Two months later he extended the service to the "Junction Hotel", but in December the same year, his 'buses were withdrawn and diverted to another short lived service running in opposition to the steam trams on Wellington Street and Wellington Road to the foot of Armley Road. This service ceased in May 1888. The Tramways Company had the monopoly on Kirkstall Road for three months when, in March 1888, a Joseph T. Wilkinson began a wagonette service from the Corn Exchange to the Viaducts. The wagonettes were still running in September 1888 but were withdrawn shortly afterwards.

Following the sale of his undertaking in June 1893, a Henry Harrison, who had operated 'buses on Burley Road, referred to in a later chapter, made an attempt to start up business again in October 1893. He began two pair-horse 'buses on a route between the Corn Exchange and Green Lane, Wortley and a month later ran them to the "Cardigan Arms," Kirkstall Road, in competition with the steam trams. He could not compete and his 'buses were withdrawn by March 1894 and Harrison gave up running 'buses for good.

No further 'buses ran in opposition to the Kirkstall tramway and on this route the Tramways Company won their battle.

The section of tramway along Tong Road between the "Crown" and the "Star", Upper Wortley, although well populated, was never profitable for the Tramways Company. The working class inhabitants tended to walk to the penny stage at the "Crown" and, with the exception of Turton, mentioned in a later chapter, Tong Road was also avoided by the omnibus proprietors. The densely populated section between Boar Lane and the "Crown Inn," New Wortley was a different matter however. An opposition 'bus was running to New Wortley, worked by a Benjamin Elsworth in 1881, but it was short lived and the trams had no opposition during 1883.

A 'bus service which caused considerable embarrassment to the Tramways Company was the Wellington Road penny 'bus instituted by Robert Chapman of Preston Terrace. In April 1884 he introduced a half-hourly service between Briggate and the "Crown", increased to quarter-hourly the following month. The time of starting of Chapman's 'bus was within two minutes of the tramcars and the Company lost a lot of traffic. Following complaints from the Company the timetable was altered, but the competition continued and there were several cases of obstruction of the tramway engines by Chapman's vehicles. The 'bus service was reduced in frequency by March 1890 and with the death of Chapman's widow later in the year the two 'buses operating the service were sold off. No other proprietor showed an interest in re-introducing 'buses to New Wortley. This was not wholly due to the tramway, but also owing to an intensive service of wagonettes, operated by various proprietors according to demand, from New Briggate to the "Crown." There were said to be six wagonettes to every tram and they ran from the late 'eighties to the coming of the electric trams. Their terminal point was on the north side of Oldfield Lane (changed to the south side in 1897).

To return to the Chapeltown tramway, Bramfitt's penny 'bus to Cowper Street was apparently cut back to Leopold Street, Chapeltown Road by 1882. It ran through to West Street and the "Beckett's Arms", Kirkstall Road and two 'buses, the 'Gem' and 'Pearl' ran the service. The Tramways Company had a crossover at the "Beckett's Arms" from 1872 and it is possible that there were tramway shortworkings to this point. Bramfitt may have discontinued the Chapeltown Road section of his route in the middle 'eighties but, in February 1886, was granted a licence to run a penny 'bus from Briggate via Chapeltown Road to Reginald Terrace. The 'buses ran every 40 minutes and did not present much opposition to the tramway. The frequency of the trams was increased from quarter-hourly to ten minutes by 1881, but reverted to quarter-hourly about 1885 and remained at this level throughout the remainder of the Company's period of operation.

There was an opposition 'bus run by John Newton Sharp from St. James' Hall via Kirkgate, Briggate and North Street to the "Sheepscar Hotel," in May 1888, but it was withdrawn after only three months.

A tramway short working to Reginald Terrace was in use by 1880, although it was not regularly used until the introduction of the Reginald Terrace opposition 'bus. The Reginald Terrace trams were run in conjunction with those to Chapeltown giving a $7\frac{1}{2}$ minutes service to Reginald Terrace. Following the cessation of the Headingley steam trams, from 19th March 1892, the Chapeltown cars were run through to Headingley. In May a Reginald Terrace to Hyde Park through service was also introduced, giving a $7\frac{1}{2}$ minutes service bet-

Bramfitt's penny 'bus No. 107 at the Reginald Terrace terminus in 1887.
Courtesy The late W. Nichols, Photographer. Leeds City Libraries.

ween these points and a 15 minutes service between Chapeltown and Headingley.

'Bus competition had little effect on the Chapeltown tram fares. The through fare remained at 3d., but there were some alterations to stages. The fare from Briggate to Sheepscar was reduced from 2d. to 1d. in late 1884, but this was said to have benefited the public only as there was a reduction in receipts of £8 to £10 per week. The following year the 1d. stage was extended to Leopold Street with a 2d. stage at Reginald Terrace. In December 1889 the 2d. stage was extended through to Newton Park and short workings were operated to this point. In November 1892 a down fare of 1d. was introduced from Reginald Terrace to Briggate, but from 1st January 1893 the down journey from Chapeltown was divided into three penny stages at Newton Park, Leopold Street and Briggate; the stages on the up journey being at Leopold Street and Reginald Terrace. This resulted in objections from the Newton Park residents, who tended to walk and, hence, there was a reduction in receipts on the route.

Starbuck single-deck car Nos. 14 and 11 in Briggate about 1892. No. 14 is on the Hyde Park to Reginald Terrace through service. *Courtesy Hudson's Series R. Brook Collection.*

Mention should be made of the Tramways Company's only venture into the hackney carriage business. The Company purchased five cabs from Turton, and these were operated on a daily basis from 15th May 1882. The cabs, however, made only a token visit to the cab stands as the receipts were usually under £1 daily. The daily cabs ceased on 3rd October 1882 and for the following few weeks a weekly visit to the cab stands was made, usually a single trip. The Company sold its cabs to a Frederick Thornbury on 21st December 1882 for £120, the last running on 27th December. Its total receipts for that day were 1s. 6d.

The competition from penny 'buses had the effect of forcing the Tramways Company to reduce fares and increase frequencies on most of its tramway routes. Although a severe blow to the Company at first, the number of passengers increased, and their finances recovered. The number of Company 'buses in use in 1883 was eight and the following year was reduced to five. In 1894 the Company owned ten 'buses of which six were in regular use, four on the Dewsbury Road service and one each on Adel and Moortown. The purchase of Turton's business in 1882 turned out to be a waste of money. The Company had little success in forcing competing 'buses off the road; it was their own 'bus services which were discontinued. On no route could the Company make 'buses pay. The Moortown and Adel 'buses struggled on throughout the Company's existence acting purely as a service to the public. Figures for the six month period July to December 1883 are available and show that the takings on Moortown were £24 and on Adel £11 10s. 8d. Following the takeover by the Corporation it transpired that the Dewsbury Road 'buses were also losing money and they ceased to run on 30th April 1894. Five 'buses were sold to a George Horsfall and Thomas Robinson for £250 and these two proprietors took over operation of the Dewsbury Road service.

CHAPTER ELEVEN

By, 'Bus, Train and Tram
to Roundhay

The 'bus service that John Machan was working to Roundhay and Scarcroft in 1851 was still in operation 20 years later, running at the same frequency. The only alteration that had taken place was a change in the terminal point in Leeds from the "Black Swan" to the "Three Legs," Lowerhead Row about 1868. In the early 'sixties Machan, a single man, moved to lodgings in Scarcroft and his stables were situated adjacent to the toll bar at Scarcroft on the Leeds and Collingham Turnpike road. Machan always appears to have driven his own 'bus and the census returns for 1861 list ten years old John Foden of Scarcroft as a 'bus conductor. He was presumably employed by Machan.

There had been no building development in Roundhay. The population in 1861 was 570, increasing by a mere 13 inhabitants to 583 in 1871. The population of Scarcroft was now 336. The bulk of the land in Roundhay was owned by the Nicholson family and this prevented any expansion of the village. However, on 19th September 1868, William Nicholson died and his mansion, large park and estate passed to his wife. The whole estate was offered for sale in 1871 and due to pressure from, and influence of the Mayor, John Barran, an eminent Leeds clothier of Chapeltown, the 774 acre park and estate were purchased for the people of Leeds on 4th October 1871. The idea was to use the park for recreation and sell the remainder as building plots for housing in order to "open up the area."

The Park was opened to the public for the two Saturdays preceding the sale and C. and J. Dacre of Albion Street advertised two 'bus journeys to the Park from the "Albion," Briggate on Saturday 23rd September and an hourly service the following Saturday from 1.0 pm to 7.0 pm. For a few days after the sale the Park was open to the public and Dacres' provided 'buses. During Easter 1872 the Park was again opened and William Turton ran a 15 minutes 'bus service from Briggate. Many people used the 'buses but the majority "preferred to walk."

The official opening of the Park by Prince Arthur on 19th September 1872 was an impressive affair and between 100,000 and 200,000 people went to Roundhay. Prince Arthur also laid the foundation stone of the new Royal Exchange building at the corner of Boar Lane and Park Row and the town was illuminated. Turton ran special 'buses from Briggate to "tour the illuminations" for a fare of 6d. Roundhay Park was now permanently open to the public and this had an immediate effect on traffic to Roundhay. Literally thousands of people visited the park weekly during fine weather and the demand for transport was immense. Machan continued to operate

his regular 'bus and this was supplemented at weekends by innumerable wagonettes and cabs.

In 1871 Roundhay Road, between Sheepscar and Roundhay, passed through open countryside. It had paving over only part of its length, did not boast street lighting until 1873, and was described as "the most beautiful road in the vicinity of Leeds." The application of the Tramways Company to build a tramway on Roundhay Road had been rejected and the North Eastern Railway Company considered making an extension of their system to Roundhay Park, but in November 1872 abandoned the idea. During 1873 Roundhay Road was dominated by wagonettes and in May Machan advertised his business for sale. There were no takers, however, and the operation of the 'bus service was taken over by a relative, Richard Machan, the driver being a Michael Machan.

The idea of constructing a railway to Roundhay Park was brought up again by John Barran who called a special meeting at the Town Hall to discuss the question. The meeting was held on 26th August 1873 and three alternative schemes were discussed but were not taken very enthusiastically. On 20th October a further meeting was held and six schemes prepared by Martin and Fenwick, Engineers of Leeds, were considered. A scheme was also presented by Usill, Willcocks and Peggs, Civil Engineers of London. C. Fowler and J. Fox, Engineers of Leeds, also prepared schemes but these were not considered.

After careful consideration and further meetings one of Martin and Fenwick's schemes was chosen. Their railway was to be standard gauge with the principal station in North Street, and running via Burmantofts and Harehills to the north west side of Roundhay Park, the length being 3¾ miles. A proposed branch line was to run from Gipton Farm, near Roundhay, to join the Leeds and Selby line at Osmondthorpe; its length was 1¼ miles. Besides the station in North Street it was proposed to have stations at Burmantofts, Harehills Lane, the intended new Park entrance, near the Horse Shoe Cottages, Roundhay and in Park Road within a short distance of the mansion.

Application was made to Parliament in the 1874 session for Parliamentary powers to construct the "Leeds, Roundhay Park and Osmondthorpe Junction Railway," and a Company was formed with a capital of £160,000 in 16,000 shares of £10 each. The Company's prospectus stated that the large Corporation estate and other properties in Roundhay would be "considerably benefited" by the railway and it would be possible to sell plots as

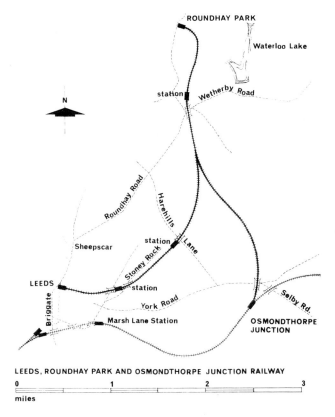

ROUNDHAY PARK

Waterloo Lake

station Wetherby Road

N

Roundhay Road

Harehills Lane

Sheepscar

station

Stoney Rock

LEEDS

station

York Road

Briggate

Selby Rd.

Marsh Lane Station

OSMONDTHORPE
JUNCTION

LEEDS, ROUNDHAY PARK AND OSMONDTHORPE JUNCTION RAILWAY

0   1   2   3
miles

building sites. As the railway did not pass through residential property there were no objections from landowners. There were, however, few subscribers to the railway as the prospective traffic was purely seasonal, being almost non-existent in the winter months and weekdays in summer. Only on summer weekends and at Bank Holidays was the traffic really heavy. On 16th December 1873 a meeting of the subscribers to the Bill unanimously resolved that no further action be taken and the Bill be withdrawn. The promoters led by Alderman Barran and Marsden rejected the suggestion of the subscribers and the Bill passed through Parliament as an unopposed measure. On 7th October 1874 the first meeting of the Company was held and the amount of capital subscribed towards the £160,000 was said to be £26,640. Very little further money was forthcoming but the Company lasted for another two years. An application was made to Parliament for the abandonment of the railway and it was granted during the 1877 Parliamentary session. At a meeting of the Company on 6th February 1877, attended by 20 shareholders, Barran sadly remarked:– *"From the first they had found a great reluctance on the part of the public to join in the undertaking. Many held back because they did not see a prospect of its being made a profitable scheme, and others had said they did not think the proposed line would meet the requirements of the borough. One strong objection had been that the railway did not go far enough, and some had said that if the scheme had provided a railway connecting the town with Headingley and Moortown, they would have supported it. They would all know, however, who carefully thought over the matter, that a scheme of that kind presented far greater difficulties than the undertaking proposed. The population beyond Roundhay Park was very thin, and the prospect of traffic on the independent line was very small."*

(Yorkshire Post, 7th February 1877).

During the middle 'seventies wagonettes and 'buses running to Roundhay Park were operated on a hire

basis with no fixed timetable and all types of vehicles were used to try to cope with the traffic. Wagonettes, omnibuses, spring carts, warehouse wagons etc. were brought into use and many of them appeared anything but safe as they whirled along the road, their rusty springs in many instances creaking loudly under the heavy loads of human beings they had to carry.

One passenger had an unforgettable ride:–

"A few days ago, while walking to Leeds with a friend from Wetherby, on reaching the gate of Roundhay Park we agreed to take the two spare seats in a wagonette about to start. This we did the more readily as the party seemed highly respectable, the driver a decent looking fellow, and the horse a quiet one. We jogged along pleasantly until we reached the top of Gipton Hill, when I imagine the weight caused by eight people forced the trap against the horse. This he did not relish and started off full tilt down the long steep hill. The driver could not keep in the centre of the road and the vehicle swerved from side to side, first shaving one kerb and then the other, until at last there was a horrid crash against a telegraph post. My first thought as I gathered myself from the middle of the road with clothing torn and bleeding freely, was, What of my friend? He suffered the same fate 50 yards further on, while further back were a heap of sufferers huddled together, all having been injured, one lady I fear seriously. The driver also must have suffered very much. After getting our wounds dressed at the 'Gipton Inn', where the landlady was unusually kind and attentive, refusing any remuneration; I made an examination of the vehicle and found what I considered to be the cause of the whole disaster. The brake seemed almost worn through, while an old slipper or shoe tied with a piece of string was used as a substitute."

(Yorkshire Post, 10th August 1875).

Some wagonette proprietors did attempt to establish a regular service to Roundhay Park, of whom the most important was a Joseph Bramfitt. Bramfitt is recorded as being a 'bus driver in 1874, and on Saturday, 17th April 1875, instituted a regular service of wagonettes from the "Black Swan," North Street, via Lowerhead Row and New Briggate to Roundhay Park. His wagonette ran hourly from 10.30 am and the fare was 4d. The service could not have been economical for, from 22nd April, it was reduced to run every hour and 20 minutes from 11.30 am. Bramfitt was to run wagonettes and later 'buses to Roundhay Park for the following 23 years. On 14th June 1875 a William Harrison began a wagonette service from the "Horse and Jockey," Commercial Street, to the park making five departures daily (weather permitting). The fare was 4d. but the service was short lived. About the same time a more permanent service was introduced by Peter Outhwaite – possibly related to the proprietor of the same name who started the original 'bus service to Roundhay in 1843. In 1876 Bramfitt and Outhwaite were reported as running 'buses to Roundhay Park all the year round whereas other proprietors ran irregularly. The latter had to queue for passengers with their vehicles in a similar manner to cabs and the Hackney Carriages Committee ordered Bramfitt and Outhwaite to do likewise. However, on 12th July 1876, after representations from the Surveyors of Roundhay, they agreed to allow the two proprietors to ignore the queue system. Outhwaite ran 'buses to Roundhay until 1878 when his assets – three horses, one old 'bus, wagonette, etc. were sold on 22nd October. A "nearly new" 'bus was sold the previous week. Outhwaite

79

An early Bramfitt's 'bus with 'knifeboard'' seats at Roundhay Park about 1885. *Courtesy J. Soper Collection.*

apparently set up business again for one of his wagonettes was recorded as being in a collision en route to the Park in 1882.

Joseph Walker, omnibus proprietor of Chapeltown Road, was running wagonettes to Roundhay Park during the middle 'seventies and one of his drivers is recorded as racing with Bramfitt's wagonette in 1876. Walker's vehicle was travelling at 12 m.p.h. and veered from side to side so much that two of the ten occupants were thrown out.

In spite of Bramfitt and Outhwaite's regular 'buses to Roundhay and Machan operating to Scarcroft, at busy periods the wagonettes were by far the dominant form of transport on Roundhay Road. The wagonette proprietors charged a 6d. fare for the ride to Roundhay and their ire was aroused in early July 1878 when Joseph Walker introduced a 'bus from Boar Lane to Roundhay Park for a fare of 4d.

"It was stated by the police that the wagonette drivers were completely masters of the road, acting as they liked with their vehicles, and insulting visitors to the Park who refused to patronise them," ——— *"On the day in question the defendants and a number of other wagonette drivers vented their spleen on people leaving the Park who patronised the 'bus, calling out they could not afford a 'sixpenny ride', but were obliged to have a 'fourpenny one.' One of the party, a driver named Tom Brook, also remarked that it could soon be stopped by them drawing their vehicles across the road, and thus preventing the 'bus from turning. Acting upon this hint the roadway was completely blocked on the 'bus coming back again, and, in consequence, the vehicle had to be driven into the Park and, at the same time, a man named Simpson, who was driving his own trap along the road, was stopped. It was stated that there were no less than 50 wagonettes at the gate at the time; but as soon as the police interfered and began to take down the names of the offenders they all drove off apart from three or four, and in a few minutes the road was cleared."*

(Yorkshire Post, 17th July 1878).

Walker's 'bus ran four afternoon journeys daily to Roundhay Park. A fortnight after the above incident he increased this number to five and further rubbed salt into the wounds of the wagonette proprietors by reducing the fare to 3d. Children under seven years paid a half fare.

A nationwide depression in 1878–9 presented the Corporation with the opportunity of carrying out its policy of "opening up" the Roundhay Park area. Three major road schemes were carried out using able-bodied men

who applied to the *'Distress Relief Fund'*. The construction work cost the town comparatively little whilst at the same time those employed upon it were saved from the degradation of receiving either poor-law relief or charity. During 1878 a road was built from the Horse Shoe Corner to the Canal Gardens. In the vicinity of Horse Shoe Corner was a large house named *'Oakwood'* and the area soon afterwards became known by this name. The new road was named Prince's Avenue and brought visitors to the Park nearer to the Mansion. A further road, Park Avenue, was constructed into the Park about the same time and the two roads afforded "ample choice of pretty drives in the confines of the park."

In March 1879 a start was made on the construction of a new road half a mile in length and 40 feet wide from Burmantofts, at the top of Beckett Street, across the fields to a point where Harehills Lane crossed Roundhay Road. Burmantofts was virtually a dead end and the new road, Harehills Road, provided an alternative route from the town centre via the working class district of Beckett Street and Burmantofts, to Roundhay Park. It relieved the pressure of traffic on the lower part of Roundhay Road and North Street. A new road 1½ miles long was also built the following year from the western boundary of Roundhay Park to a point near the "Chained Bull Inn," Moortown, a horse 'bus terminus. This road, 36 feet wide ran mainly across fields, "one of the most charming drives in Leeds," and traversed part of an old lane, known as Street Lane, for some of its length. When completed the road took this name and was gated at each end; the gates being removed in September 1898. Of these major roads, Prince's Avenue, Street Lane and Harehills Road, only Harehills Road had a regular horse 'bus service, but each was later to become an important tramway route.

Traffic on Roundhay Road during 1879 was "thin" due to the depression and the Corporation's efforts to dispose of its surplus lands were unsuccessful. 31 villa sites were offered for sale by auction in July and not one was sold. This was largely blamed on the lack of an adequate public transport service to the area and in September a big demonstration against the Corporation was held at the Park. The Park was causing an annual loss to the ratepayers of £10,000 and the Corporation was censured.

The wagonette competition between Leeds and Roundhay and the opening of the North Eastern Railway line between Leeds and Wetherby on 1st May 1876, which passed near Scarcroft, resulted in Richard Machan re-routing his Scarcroft 'bus via Chapeltown, Moortown and Shadwell. He ran one journey daily from

ROUNDHAY PARK
FARE
EACH WAY 3D.

Walker's traffic notice dating from the late 1890's. *Courtesy Leeds City Museums.*

Open countryside at the junction of Harehills Road with Roundhay Road as Roundhay Electric car No. 76 passes about 1893. *Courtesy H. Heyworth.*

the "Brunswick Hotel" and was still running in October 1878, but apparently withdrew his 'bus shortly afterwards. Machan disappeared from the scene and Scarcroft was no longer a 'bus terminus but merely a stopping place used by the seasonal 'buses running between Leeds and Boston Spa.

Easter 1880 saw another omnibus proprietor, William Turton, running to Roundhay Park and it was reported that the number of 'buses now operating to the Park was larger than ever before. Turton owned many fine horses and as he charged a fare of only 3d. his 'buses were well patronised and offered severe competition to the wagonettes. On this occasion both 'buses and wagonettes ran over the new Prince's Avenue to the far entrance to the Park. Turton continued to run a regular service to Roundhay Park until his takeover by the Leeds Tramways Company. The latter's abysmal attempt to run 'buses to Roundhay was mentioned in the last chapter.

To accommodate the large number of 'buses and wagonettes, the Corporation laid out an area, three acres in extent, at Horse Shoe Corner. Following the opening of Prince's Avenue, however, vehicles tended to run along this road to the far entrance of the Park. The parking space was deserted and referred to as a "howling wilderness." In 1881 the area was reduced to one acre and later a lodge and gates were built to form an imposing entrance to the Park. From then on this formed the regular terminus of the Roundhay Park 'buses. At holiday times the transport situation to the park continued to be hopeless:–

"From an early hour in the forenoon, the omnibuses and wagonettes plying between Briggate and Roundhay Park were freighted to their fullest capacity, whilst hundreds of young people made their way on foot to the same destination. As the day wore on Briggate was crowded with persons desirous of obtaining a conveyance to the Park, and on the rare occasions when an omnibus or wagonette appeared it was quickly surrounded by five or six times as many people as it could possibly accommodate. At the same time the stream of pedestrians wending their way up Briggate along North Street, and thence by way of Roundhay Road to the Park Gates increased in volume. Many of these persons were unwilling walkers and returning empty vehicles were for the most part taken possession of by them a little beyond Sheepscar, and the horse's heads turned parkwards again."

(Yorkshire Post, 11th April 1882).

The conditions were such that the wagonette proprietors could charge 6d. each way. It was not unusual at holiday periods for almost all the 'buses in Leeds to be withdrawn from their regular routes and placed on Roundhay Road, but even they were unable to cope with the literally tens of thousands of passengers. Many of these passengers were from outside the borough and paid their 6d. fare without grumble, but for the Leeds artisan with a large family, earning a small wage and living south of the river, the Park was practically unapproachable. The economy of the country was still depressed and working men had little money. With the existing 'bus and wagonette service a visit to the Park meant the spending of half a day at a cost that many people could not afford. To obviate this the tramway and railway proposals were revived.

The heavy Roundhay Park traffic rekindled the interest of the Directors of the Leeds Tramways Company in the possibility of constructing a tramway to the Park. In January 1881 they had discussions with the Corporation

Both Walker's and Chapman's 'buses can be seen on this photograph of Roundhay 'bus terminus in 1887.
Courtesy The late W. Nichols, Photographer, Leeds City Libraries.

"Street arabs" perform cart wheels for pennies as a Roundhay bound wagonette passes.

and agreed to construct a line if the Corporation would arrange for road widening to be carried out. On 14th February 1881 a special meeting of the Town Council was held to discuss the matter, but no action was taken and the suggestions came to nought. More promising were railway proposals made the following year. It was felt that if a direct railway service could be established, the journey to Roundhay would be made in less than a quarter of the time and at a greatly reduced expense. In September 1882 a group of residents met and submitted proposals. A route was surveyed and it was suggested that the station at Leeds should be near the Kirkgate Market near to which the line would join the North Eastern Railway and then branch off towards Beckett Street, passing the Burmantofts workhouse and running across the fields to Roundhay Park. There were to be stations at Beckett Street and the Park and the line was to continue through Chapeltown, Moortown and join the North Eastern Railway at Headingley. The directors of the North Eastern Railway Company were approached with a view to constructing the line but they showed no interest.

A more hopeful scheme was the "Leeds, Church Fenton and Hull Junction Railway Bill" which came before Parliament the following year. The railway was to begin in George Street with a station in Vicar Lane and run on a viaduct from Lady Lane to Gipton Beck and, keeping to the south east side of the beck, pass under Harehills Road and Harehills Lane, and then on to Roundhay Park, Seacroft, Scholes, Barwick and Aberford to Church Fenton – a distance of 15 miles. There were to be stations at Sheepscar and Roundhay Park. A special meeting of the Town Council was held on 19th March 1883 and a unanimous vote in favour of the Bill was passed. A large meeting of landowners and others interested passed a similar resolution at the "Queen's Hotel" the following week. However, the East and West Yorkshire Union Railway Company was promoting a rival railway from Leeds through the southern part of the town to Drax. This was passed by Parliament and the Bill for the proposed railway through Roundhay was withdrawn.

The 'buses and wagonettes continued to reign supreme and a common feature of a holiday 'bus journey to Roundhay in the 'eighties was the immense number of "street arabs and urchins" who "played their antics at the rear of vehicles in quest of pence, turning somersaults and otherwise asserting their presence and their nimbleness of limb." They were warned many times by the police but persisted until the coming of the tramcar.

Walker does not appear to have run an all-the-year round service to Roundhay after about 1883. The only proprietor running regular 'buses during the 'eighties and 'nineties was Bramfitt, supplemented for a short period by Turton and the Leeds Tramways Company. In 1881 Bramfitt's 'buses were running from Kirkgate corner, Briggate, in lieu of his former starting point at the "Black Swan," making 15 journeys daily from 9.10 am to 7.10 pm (Saturdays to 9.45 pm). As can be seen in the accompanying chart, the number of journeys from Briggate had increased to 45 by late 1882. With the withdrawal of the Tramways Company 'buses, Bramfitt increased his service to 20 minutes, running 36 journeys daily and the inhabitants were said to be "well provided for." There were, however, no late weekday evening 'buses to Roundhay and two large meetings of the residents were held to try and obtain an improvement. They agreed to subscribe moneys towards an improved service and Alfred Lamb, a cab proprietor and landlord of the "Gipton Wood Inn," was granted a licence by the Hackney Carriages Committee to run an early and two late 'buses from Briggate to Roundhay. His later 'buses left Briggate at 8.40 and 10.0 pm and began operation on Monday 15th December 1884. The late 'buses were a boon and a saving to the residents who could now attend lectures, concerts or the theatre without the expense of cabs.

In March 1885 Lamb put on two additional 'buses at 5.0 pm and 7.0 pm, but did not run for long after that. By 1887 Bramfitt was running an improved service at a frequency of from 16 to 20 minutes, but the service was reduced to 20 minutes by the following year. Bramfitt continued this service with slight variations until his 'buses ceased to run due to electric tramway competition in 1898.

Bramfitt's 'buses were, of course, supplemented by the wagonettes and 'buses running, when required, from New Briggate, but complaints about the inadequacy of the service continued to be made. In 1884 the Lord Mayor, Alderman Woodhouse, said that Leeds had one of the most magnificent parks in the Kingdom, but it was "so far from the town that it was of little service to the community." The building land at Roundhay was unsaleable and the civic rulers were accused of waiting "Micawberlike" for something to turn up. Requests were made for the Corporation to construct either a railway or tramway to the Park. In March 1886 a deputation, led by estate agent, John Hepper, waited on the Council. They said that the time had now arrived when some improved means of communication should be

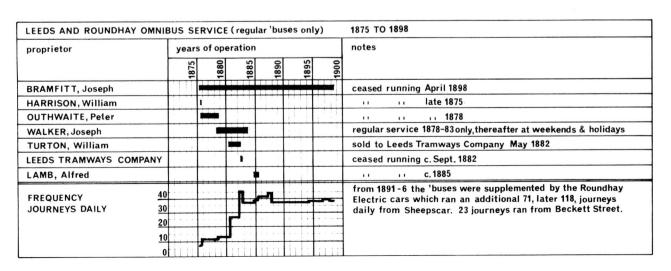

LEEDS AND ROUNDHAY OMNIBUS SERVICE (regular 'buses only)   1875 TO 1898

proprietor	years of operation						notes
	1875	1880	1885	1890	1895	1900	
BRAMFITT, Joseph							ceased running April 1898
HARRISON, William							ʼʼ ʼʼ late 1875
OUTHWAITE, Peter							ʼʼ ʼʼ ʼʼ 1878
WALKER, Joseph							regular service 1878–83 only, thereafter at weekends & holidays
TURTON, William							sold to Leeds Tramways Company May 1882
LEEDS TRAMWAYS COMPANY							ceased running c. Sept. 1882
LAMB, Alfred							ʼʼ ʼʼ c. 1885
FREQUENCY JOURNEYS DAILY	40 30 20 10 0						from 1891-6 the 'buses were supplemented by the Roundhay Electric cars which ran an additional 71, later 118, journeys daily from Sheepscar. 23 journeys ran from Beckett Street.

made between Leeds and Roundhay Park, not only for the purpose of providing easy access to the Park, but also to bring on to the market the large amount of surplus land owned by the Corporation. They asked the Council to try and induce the North Eastern Railway Company to build a loop line from Killingbeck through Roundhay and Moortown to Headingley, but should that prove impracticable, they recommended the widening of Roundhay Road, and that a double track tramway be laid on one side so as to keep the tram lines away from the centre of the road.

There was opposition from other deputations protesting against the proposals to widen Roundhay Road due to the cost that would have to be borne by ratepayers, but they were overruled and the Corporation agreed to widen the road for a distance of 2,400 yards. They also agreed to make a fresh approach to the North Eastern Railway Company. On 3rd June 1886 Council representatives met the Directors of the railway company. The Town Clerk, Sir George Morrison, presented the Corporation's case. He quoted the "vast increase" in the 'bus traffic but to no avail. The Directors promised to give the proposal their "careful attention" and that is as far as it went.

Meanwhile, however, others were showing an interest in the Roundhay problem. Magnus Volk, the patentee of an electric tramway in Brighton submitted a scheme for a railway or tramway in which he estimated that three miles of double track, 14 cars (each to carry 46 passengers), two compound engines, boilers and dynamos would be required. The cost would be £12,700 and although Alderman Scarr was in favour of Volk's scheme, it was not brought before the Council.

A new railway proposal, the "Leeds Suburban Railway Bill" was presented to Parliament in November 1886. The terminus was to be at the Leeds New Station and it was to run over part of the North Eastern line and

branch off at Osmondthorpe and run pass Killingbeck and Seacroft to Roundhay, terminating in Roundhay opposite the church. The total length was to be 2½ miles with a gradient of 1 in 120 and throughout its whole length it touched no buildings except a small villa at Roundhay where the terminus was to be. The cost of the railway was to be £50,000, a big saving on Barran's earlier railway of 1873 which was to cost £160,000. An enabling clause in the Bill made it possible for the Corporation to subscribe £15,000 towards the cost. At their meeting on 5th January 1887 the Council voted 33 to 6 to support the construction of the railway, but it was the enabling clause that led to the downfall of the scheme. The Local Government Board, who reported on the Bill stated that "it was undesirable that local authorities should be empowered to subscribe to railway undertakings and to charge their rates with the repayment of money for that purpose." The Bill was therefore abandoned.

An unusual proposal, which reached a fairly advanced stage, was submitted to the Council in 1887. It was to construct an elevated railway to Roundhay Park on a system that had been recently patented by J. Clark Jefferson and J. T. Pullon, Engineers, of Leeds. An illustrated brochure was prepared and showed that the scheme consisted of a monorail supported longitudinally on the top of a row of lattice girders. These girders, of an average span of 45 feet, were supported on steel or wrought iron columns fixed in cast iron pedestals on foundations of concrete or brick, similar to the New York elevated railways. There was to be double track and the uprights or columns were to be connected in pairs by cross girders and where necessary by diagonal bracing. The centre entrance carriages were 23' long by 7' 6" wide accommodating 28 to 38 passengers and capable of going round curves of 100 feet radius. Both the carriages and the engines were supported on two-wheeled

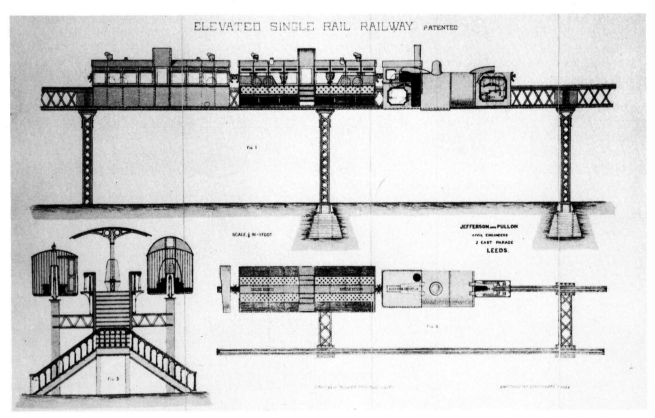

Plan and sections of proposed elevated single rail railway.

Courtesy Leeds City Libraries.

84

PLATE II

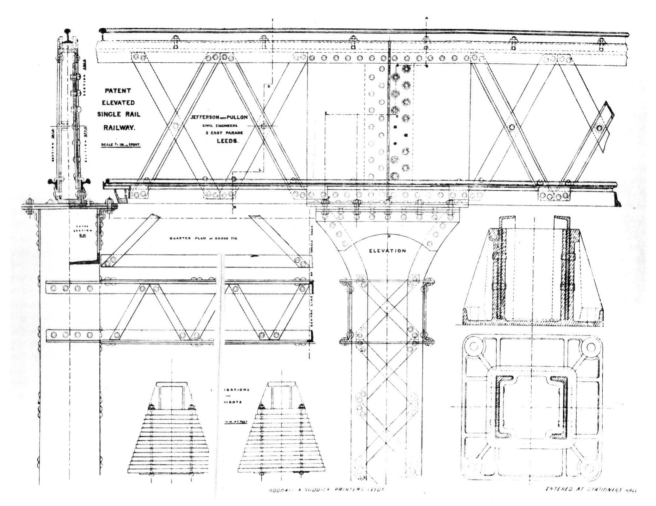

Constructional details of the proposed elevated single rail railway. *Courtesy Leeds City Libraries.*

bogie trucks astride the rail, the greater part of the weight being well below the top of the rail. In order to prevent surging when going round curves, or owing to unequal loading, inclined guide wheels running on guide rails fixed near the bottom of the girder on each side were provided. The steam engine was of a special design with a large heating surface in the boiler, weighing about nine tons and capable of pulling eight to ten fully loaded cars. The intermediate stations were covered platforms reached by stairs and of "very inexpensive" construction. No booking office or officials were required as the system was arranged to be worked similarly to a tramway; the conductor, who could pass from one car to another, could collect the fares while the train was moving. The route proposed started from a station in North Street near its junction with Briggate, passing parallel with Regent Street, to and along Gipton Beck to near the Park Avenue entrance, and then to near the Canal Gardens where the Park Station was to be. Optimistic proposals were made to extend the line round the upper side of the Park to "open out" the far side and also to link up with Chapeltown, Meanwood and Headingley. There were to be numerous intermediate stations on the route, and the estimated cost was £60,000, but the scheme did not find much support in the Council.

The Chairman of the Highways Committee, Alderman Firth, favoured a tramway and commented that the elevated railway would, like all the other previous railway proposals, be a "financial failure," and would "practi-

cally ruin the scenery and picturesqueness of the park." In 1887 the Council was fairly equally divided between those who favoured a railway or tramway to the Park. Councillor Arnold Lupton and Councillor Gordon were in favour of the elevated railway scheme, but when others showed little interest in it, Lupton proposed an underground compressed air railway running from Briggate to Benson Street in a subway and then across the fields and partly in a cutting and partly subway to the Park. It would be out of sight "so as not to mar the beauty of the scene," and Lupton proposed that the whole question be discussed at a special meeting of the Council. The meeting was held on 16th August 1887 and the promoters of the elevated railway attended and stated that their railway would carry people to the Park in 12 minutes whereas a tramcar would take 35 minutes. It would be impossible during the rush of the holiday period to work a tramcar every minute due to the enormous cost of the additional cars. Also present at the meeting was Holroyd Smith of Halifax, an electrical engineer who had constructed an electric tramway in Blackpool a short time previously. He proposed the construction of an electric railway. Alderman Firth pushed the case for a tramway, but some councillors felt that the construction of a tramway was "absurd" or of "no use." The split in the Council was emphasised by the two contradictory resolutions which were passed. Lupton proposed, "That it is desirable to have a railway that does not run upon the high road between Leeds and Roundhay Park," and this was passed almost unanim-

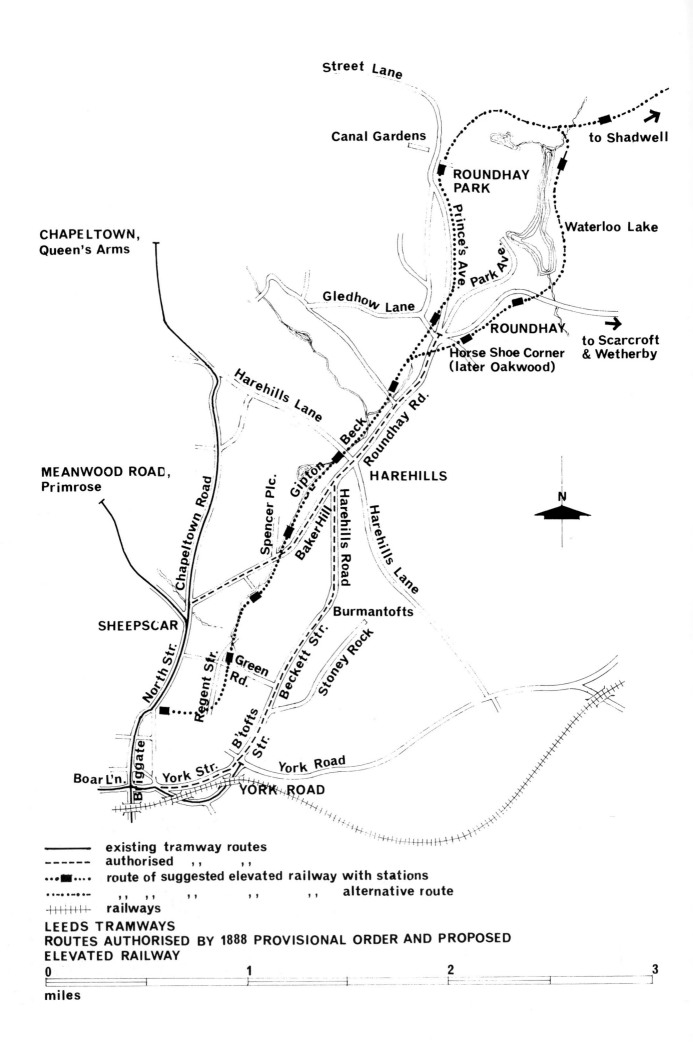

Street Lane

Canal Gardens

ROUNDHAY PARK

to Shadwell

Prince's Ave.

Park Ave.

Waterloo Lake

CHAPELTOWN, Queen's Arms

Gledhow Lane

ROUNDHAY

to Scarcroft & Wetherby

Horse Shoe Corner (later Oakwood)

Harehills Lane

Gipton Beck

Roundhay Rd.

MEANWOOD ROAD, Primrose

Chapeltown Road

Spencer Plc.

Baker Hill

HAREHILLS

Harehills Road

Harehills Lane

N

Burmantofts

Beckett Str.

Stoney Rock

SHEEPSCAR

North Str.

Regent Str.

Green Rd.

B'tofts Str.

York Road

Briggate

Boar L'n.

York Str.

York Road

YORK ROAD

———— existing tramway routes
- - - - - authorised   ,,   ,,
•••■••• route of suggested elevated railway with stations
•••—••— ,, ,, ,,   ,,   ,, alternative route
++++++ railways

LEEDS TRAMWAYS
ROUTES AUTHORISED BY 1888 PROVISIONAL ORDER AND PROPOSED
ELEVATED RAILWAY

0   1   2   3

miles

ously. Alderman Harrison proposed, "That it is expedient that the Corporation forthwith provide tramway communication between Leeds and Roundhay Park, to be leased." This resolution was passed by 16 votes to 14.

At the following meeting of the Council on 29th September the subject was again discussed at length. Alderman Firth proposed that the Council should make an application to Parliament for a provisional order authorising the construction of two tramways; a double line from Sheepscar along Roundhay Road to the new entrance to the Park at an estimated cost of £14,776, and a tramway from York Street, at the junction with Kirkgate, along Beckett Street and Harehills Road to the junction with Roundhay Road. The estimated cost of this was £5,237 making a total of £20,013 for the two lines. Firth remarked that they could not get people to invest money in a railway and it would be "insane" for the railway proposal to go ahead. The only feasible plan was a tramway. Councillor Lupton said that he still favoured the elevated railway scheme and stated that a majority of the Council was in favour of a railway. If Firth's tramway scheme was approved it would put an end to the railway scheme as no investor would support a railway unless the Corporation put some money in it. Lupton said that a tramway was "bad in itself" and commented that the charges were high, the speed slow, and at present the public could get to the park quicker and cheaper than they would do by a tramway, and on occasions of public holidays a tramway would be a block rather than otherwise. He contended that if there were traffic for a tramway to pay, a railway would pay still better. If a tramway paid 3%, a railway would pay 6%. Government returns showed that the working expenses of tramways were three quarters of the gross receipts, whilst railway working expenses for passenger traffic were 50%, and in some cases as low as 40%. He continued that if the Corporation would contribute £20,000 or £30,000 to a railway there were investors ready who would put up the remainder of the money. The Town Clerk reminded the meeting of the decision of the Local Government Board with regard to the "Leeds Suburban Railway". Alderman Scarr described Lupton's scheme as that of an "amiable enthusiast" and it would never pay. Lupton drew a laugh when he remarked that Scarr had told them a few years previously that they ought to have a cable tramway to the Park via Beckett Street and that when the cars passed the cemetry they would collect a great deal of traffic. Some councillors thought that if they voted for a railway it would be years before it could be built, whereas a tramway could be constructed quickly. Years of procrastination were ended when, after much further discussion, the meeting voted by 25 votes to 20 to apply for a provisional order to construct a tramway. There were several abstentions.

On 12th December 1888 a start was made on the road improvements and construction of the tramway from Sheepscar to Roundhay Park and by February 1889 most of the road widening was completed and the gradient, just beyond Spencer Place, eased. Several contractors were employed and the first rails were laid at the top of Baker Hill, Roundhay Road. The rails were not in the centre but on the north west side of the road. This scheme was adopted in deference to the wishes of the residents who originated the idea in 1886, "in order to reduce to the minimum the damage likely to be inflicted upon horses and vehicles through the existence of tram lines." In spite of protests, no work was done on the second tramway along Beckett Street and Harehills Road. The 'Yorkshire Post' commented that there "was a feeling that a more convenient route could be arranged."

Progress was rapid and it was hoped to have the tramway completed by Whitsuntide. In May it was almost finished but a number of delays occurred. There was a strike at the works in Bochum, Germany, from

Track construction in Roundhay Road showing the Gathorne Terrace crossover, 14th May 1889.
Courtesy The late W. Nichols, Photographer, Leeds City Libraries.

where the rails were obtained; the contractors ran out of stone for paving the road and, although negotiations were proceeding with the Leeds Tramways Company to work the line, they had got nowhere at this stage. Satisfactory terms for a lease had to be agreed with the Company before they would order the additional rolling stock required. On 7th June 1889 a meeting between the Tramways Company and Highways Committee was held, when it was reported that discussions were also taking place for the renewal of the existing "leases". It was said that an agreement was reached but before it could take effect, it had to be ratified by the shareholders of the Company and the Town Council.

The connection of the tramway with the Chapeltown line was made on 25th July 1889 and the first trial took place.

"The car, which was one of the large 'saloon' vehicles, was drawn by one of Messrs. Green's engines. A start was made from Briggate shortly after six o'clock. Unfortunately, before many yards of the new line had been traversed the engine ran off the metals, owing to the accumulation of grit in the grooves at that particular point. After a considerable delay all was put right again, and the remainder of the journey was accomplished without any untoward incident occurring. Most favourable opinions were expressed by the passengers about the manner in which the line has been put down. It is, undoubtedly, vastly superior to any other tramway in Leeds. The metals rest on a thick bed of concrete, and there is none of that jolting over the joinings of the rails so noticeable on other routes. The return from the Park to Sheepscar Police Station was made in fourteen minutes."

(Leeds Mercury, 26th July 1889).

So pleased was the Corporation with the line that they immediately invited Major-General Hutchinson, of the Board of Trade, to make his inspection. They were particularly anxious that the line be in operation for a Hospital Gala due to be held at Roundhay Park on Monday, 5th August. On the first of the month the line was inspected. The Highways Committee was congratulated on its "splendid piece of work" and the inspector announced that the Board of Trade certificate would be given immediately. The first tram ran in passenger service on 3rd August. Monday, 5th August, however, was a "wash out" as far as the weather was concerned, but still 50,000 to 60,000 persons visited the Park. The efforts of the Tramways Company were not impressive:—

"Every available omnibus and wagonette in the town seemed to have been put on the Roundhay route and still there were thousands of people who were obliged to tramp the whole distance. The feeble efforts put forth by the Tramways Company to cope with the traffic are scarcely deserving of passing notice. Instead of ten steam cars which it was said they intended bringing forth for the occasion there were three which started at irregular intervals from opposite the Dispensary in North Street and covered the journey to the new entrance to the Park in an unconscionably long time. The rails were in a slippery condition and at each rise in the ground the conductor had to strew sand in front of the engines in order to make the wheels 'bite'."

(Yorkshire Post, 6th August 1889).

Steam trams probably ran to Roundhay on the following day and also carried representatives of the British Medical Association to the Park on 15th August, but after this no trams were to run to Roundhay for nearly two years. The Tramways Company did not have the rolling stock to run the additional service and was unable to obtain an agreement with the Corporation.

Negotiations between the Corporation and Tramways Company were very protracted and the inhabitants of the town and the press became very impatient. The 'Yorkshire Post' referred to the "peddling incompetency" of the Highways Committee and made many attacks on Alderman Firth. The Corporation was accused of making the blunder of building the Roundhay tramway without arranging with the only persons who were in a position to work the lines – the Leeds Tramways Company. "They found to their surprise that they were at the mercy of the Company who could dictate terms." Proposals were made that the Corporation should purchase the whole of the Company's lines and then lease them to the Company for 21 years at a fixed rental of £290 per mile offered by the Company, which would include repairs. The Company would retain the land, depots and rolling stock and operate the tramways.

The negotiations at first went in favour of the Company and were helped in October 1889 by the introduction of the cheap early morning cars on the Wortley, Kirkstall and Hunslet routes. The Highways Committee, however, had a change of mind and in December 1889 decided to invite general competition for the working of the entire tramway system of the borough. Immediate possession would be given for the Roundhay Park line and the proposed Beckett Street section, when the latter was constructed, and the other sections would be taken over in 1892 when the Tramways Company's licence, under its 1871 Act, expired. An advertisement for tenders was approved, competitors being asked to stipulate terms for leases extending over 7, 14 or 21 years and the Town Clerk prepared a draft agreement.

The Corporation was preparing an Improvement Bill to be presented during the next session of Parliament and it was pointed out that in the event of an agreement being entered into with the proposed lessees, this should be included in the Bill. However, it was later realised that the Corporation could only lease the Roundhay Park line; it could not advertise to let property which it did not own, and was dependent upon the Tramways Company for allowing tramcars to run over its lines from Sheepscar to Briggate. The Corporation did not want to place itself in a position where the Company would have a whip hand and at its meeting on 25th April 1890 the Highways Committee decided to appoint a sub-committee to continue the negotiations with the Tramways Company, the agreement between the Corporation and Company to be included in the proposed Bill.

Several meetings between the sub-committee and the Company were held and eventually an "amicable arrangement" was reached. The terms were approved at a meeting of the Highways Committee on 18th June 1890, and were that the Corporation would acquire the tramway lines at a valuation from the Company and then, lease the whole of the tramways for 14 years to the Company, at a rental of £300 per mile per annum for the first seven years and £310 per mile per annum for the following seven years. The powers of the Tramways Company had still two years to run under its 1871 Act and about seven years under its 1877 Act, but these powers would lapse with the signing of the 14 years' lease. It was hoped that by August Bank Holiday, 1890, trams would be running to Roundhay Park, and it was suggested that the line be extended on double track along Prince's Avenue to the Canal Gardens, the yearly rental for this section being £310 per mile. Other future extensions would be rented on terms to be agreed and it was felt that steps should be taken to relay the track in North Street to make it suitable for tramway engines.

Before the scheme could be finally adopted it had to be approved by both the Council and shareholders of the Tramways Company. On 22nd July 1890 an Extra-ordinary General Meeting of the Tramways Company was held to discuss the agreement.

"The Chairman said they were aware that the pro-moters got the Leeds Tramways Act for 21 years and that at the expiration of that term the Corporation could take the lines, plant, rolling stock, and everything the Company had at their value. Of the 21 years 19 had expired and the Corporation had obtained an Act of Parliament to work a tramway line to Roundhay Park. On completion of the line the Corporation approached them, and asked if they would take it at an amount to be agreed upon. An undertaking to work the line would have involved a great expenditure in rolling stock and he felt he could not go before the shareholders and ask them to lay out the money that would be required espe-cially having regard to the fact that their term had only 2½ years to run. The directors decided to refuse to take the line over such a period, though they came to the conclusion that they would not object to having a lease of it, if the Corporation would take all their lines at a valuation, and then lease them to the Company for 21 years. Negotiations had been pending for some time, and there had been anxiety on the part of the directors, as well, no doubt, as on the part of the Corporation. In the negotiations the directors did not want to steal a march over the Corporation, nor did the Corporation wish to take advantage over them. The directors en-deavoured to get a 22 year lease, but the Corporation came to the conclusion that whatever terms were agreed upon the lease should not be more than 14 years. It had been agreed that the Corporation should take the lines of tramways at a valuation –the Company now held the plant, rolling stock and freehold, but at the expiration of 14 years the Corporation would have power to take over the property."
(Yorkshire Post, 23rd July 1890).

John Eddison, the former vice-chairman of the Com-pany, was against the proposed agreement and "strongly advised" the Directors not to consent to any sale unless the Corporation took over the whole under-taking. He said that if they separated the tramway from the stock they would form a precedent for the loss of millions of pounds in England, and hoped the meeting would reject the proposals. Eddison's "advice" was ignored and the agreement was approved with one vote against – presumably Eddison's.

The following day a special meeting of the Council was held to discuss the same subject. At the beginning of the meeting it was announced that a letter had been received from North and Sons, Solicitors, of Leeds, asking on behalf of a syndicate (not named) if there would be an opportunity of tendering for the lease of the tramways when they became Corporation property. This letter was ignored and Alderman Firth submitted the proposed agreement for approval and said that the Roundhay line had cost £15,232, or an average of £4,352 per mile. He remarked that it had been said that the Committee made a blunder in laying the lines before they had arranged to lease them to any company. That was all very carefully considered by the Committee, and taking into account that Roundhay Road was to be widened, and a portion of it reconstructed, the Commit-tee thought it was by far the cheaper and wiser plan to lay down the lines then, even though arrangements could not be made for the lines to be worked until the end of the Tramways Company's present lease. The agreement was for the purchase of the tramway lines at their "then value" only, the value to be ascertained by two valuers, one appointed by the Corporation and the other by the Company. Failing their agreement the Board of Trade would appoint an arbitrator whose deci-sion would be final, each party to pay their own costs. Firth stated that when the York Street and Beckett Street route was constructed the York Road (Marsh Lane) route would probably cease operation and the

A busy holiday scene in Roundhay Road in the early 1890's. The building on the right is the old toll house which stood on the corner of Harehills Lane.

rental would cease, and that no valuation would be made for that line. After "careful calculation" the Committee had come to the conclusion that the purchase of the existing lines, the relaying of the lines which were out of repair, and the cost of the Roundhay Road line, would amount to £81,982.

An "animated discussion" followed and Councillor Petty, a member of the Highways Committee, and also a shareholder of the Tramways Company, was accused by Councillor Battle of influencing the other members of the Highways Committee to support the agreement. This was strongly denied by Petty, whose "honour and integrity were at stake," but he was shouted down by Battle. Councillor Willey strongly objected to the granting of a 14 years' lease as he believed that at the expiration of that time, Leeds would have a population of 500,000 (in 1891 it was 368,929) and the value of the tramways would have largely increased. The agreement appeared to him to be one-sided with all the advantages to the Company. After further discussion the Council agreed to adjourn the question until their September meeting.

A "stiff tussle" was expected at the September meeting of the Council and many members believed that the sooner a bargain was struck with the Company the better the terms would be, as far as the ratepayers were concerned. On the other hand the belief prevailed that if the Corporate authority waited for a year or two until the lease of the Company ran out, the Corporation would be in a better position to insist on more of its own way. The Highways Committee, however, at its next meeting, presumably as a result of North and Sons' letter, decided to change their mind as they said that there was a strong probability of an offer of an increased rate beyond that already received from the Tramways Company. They voted to recommend the Council to advertise for tenders for the tramways "as soon as possible." The resolution was brought up at the next Council meeting on 3rd September 1890 and after a short discussion was passed unanimously.

The prospect of a tramway to Roundhay seemed to be as far away as ever, but the "goings-on" in Leeds had not escaped the notice of others who, no doubt, dropped hints to the Highways Committee via North and Sons. If the Council had approved the original resolution of the Highways Committee at its meeting on 23rd July, the whole course of the history of tramways in Leeds would have been altered and, almost certainly, the town would not have had the honour of being the first in Great Britain and Europe to operate electric tramways on the overhead principle. On 10th September 1890 the Highways Committee received a letter from C. H. Wilkinson of the Thomson-Houston International Company "expressing a desire to enter into negotiations with the Corporation for the running of electric tramcars on the Roundhay Park route."

An artisan crosses the Briggate/Boar Lane junction. In the background, behind the carriage, is a Kitson tram engine and Milnes trailer bound for either Roundhay or Leopold Street.
Courtesy The late C.R. Wood, Photographer.

90

CHAPTER TWELVE

The Roundhay Electric Tramway

In 1890 it was only 11 years since the electric incandescent lamp had been invented and electricity was a new and mysterious form of energy whose potential was just beginning to be appreciated. The technical problems of designing an electric tramway were numerous and difficult and nearly a decade of effort by engineers and inventors, beginning with Siemens and Edison in 1879-80, was required before solutions to the major problems of electric traction were found.

The most fundamental problem of the electric tramway was to supply the motor, mounted on a moving vehicle, with electric current. The first experiments successfully used a third rail or conduit and examples in the United Kingdom were at Brighton (Volks Electric Railway), Portrush, Ryde Pier, Bessbrook and Newry and Blackpool.

In 1885, in the U.S.A., a Belgian immigrant, Charles J. Van Depoele, invented a new form of current collection which employed an overhead conductor with an underrunning trolley attached to the end of a pole which was mounted on the roof of the car. A strong spring pressed the pole upward and thereby kept the trolley wheel

continuously in contact with the overhead conductor.

Another American, Frank J. Sprague, was also involved with trolley poles at about the same time, but concentrated his efforts mainly on the production of an efficient means of mounting an electric motor in a tramcar truck and transmitting the power to the car axles. Van Depoele's company was bought out by the Thomson-Houston Electric Company of Lynn, Massachusetts, in 1888. This highly efficient concern had entered the field of electric power in 1887 and opened their first electric tramway on the overhead principle at Lynn on 4th July 1888. A problem with this tramway and other early electric tramways was brush sparking and in 1889 Van Depoele solved the problem by suggesting carbon instead of copper for the brushes. The success of the brushes was phenomenal and electric motors could now run for a month without attention. Van Depoele's patents put the Thomson-Houston Company in the lead in the electric traction field. Reliable and economical operation had been achieved and within a short time an electric tramway mania spread across the United States.

A Thomson-Houston car, elaborately painted, stands at Roundhay terminus about 1892. *Courtesy Thomson-Houston Company.*

An overhead line had been demonstrated in Britain at an exhibition at Edinburgh in 1890. The problem of the Roundhay Road tramway presented the Thomson-Houston Company with an opportunity of staging a more durable demonstration of their new system in Britain. The Manager of the Company, C. H. Wilkinson, attended a meeting of the Tramways Sub-Committee on 17th September 1890 and explained the system to the members present. The cars were to be worked by electricity transmitted to them by means of overhead wires erected along the tramway route, via a trolley pole carried on the car roof, into the motors and returned by the running rails. He offered to put six cars on the line as quickly as possible for the period up to the termination of the lease of the Leeds Tramways Company (August 1892) and undertook to pay the Corporation a nominal rental of 100 guineas per year on the understanding that the local authority would erect sheds for cars, offices etc. If, after the expiration of two years, the Corporation decided to adopt electric traction, they would take over the rolling stock at a valuation; if the experiment was unsuccessful they would remove their plant. Should the Corporation accept the terms, it had to give notice, six months before the expiration of the two years, of its intention to purchase the Company's cars etc. and should any disagreement as to price occur, the point in dispute would be referred to the Board of Trade. The outcome of the meeting was that the Highways Committee and the Town Council were to be recommended to accept Wilkinson's proposals.

The Thomson-Houston scheme interested Holroyd-Smith (referred to in the last chapter) and he approached the Tramways Sub-Committee and tried to persuade them to adopt his system of electric traction. He failed and negotiations continued with Wilkinson. On 15th October 1890 the Highways Committee unanimously accepted the proposals.

This "step into the unknown" and "latest freak" of the Corporation was not welcomed by many members of the public. One ratepayer said that the flashes of fire emitted from the wheels and track were similar to lightning and would be exceedingly dangerous to horse traffic. Another stated that overhead wires were ugly, a death trap, and arranged on the same principle as the latest mode of execution in America. The Highways Committee was accused of insanity. In spite of these and other objections and, acting on the motto "Leeds leads," the recommendations were accepted by the Council at its meeting on 10th November 1890. In addition to those already referred to, the proposals of the Thomson-Houston Company were subject to the following terms and conditions:—

1. Not to charge more than one penny for any fare.

2 To run a car each way for the whole length until 11.00 pm.

3. To run early cars for artisans and labourers except on Sundays, Good Friday and Christmas Day.

A week later the Highways Committee decided that the Company would be required to begin running cars on the line within three months after signing the agreement, under penalty of £20 per week in case of default. It stipulated that the necessary posts should be fixed so that all wires would be at least 20 feet above the highway. The Sanitary Committee was asked to allow a portion of its land at the Beckett Street dust destructor to be used for the erection of a tramway shed, and the General Committee was recommended to proceed with the laying of a portion of the Beckett Street tramway,

authorised by the Provisional Order of 1888, from the top of Green Road, Beckett Street, to the end of Harehills Road at its junction with Roundhay Road. Application was to be made to the Board of Trade for permission to work the tramway by electricity. The sanction of the Board of Trade was given on 2nd March 1891 and the only variation from the application that the Corporation made was a request by the electrical engineer to the Board of Trade that the voltage be reduced from 500 to 300 volts. The Thomson-Houston Company agreed to this reduction, immediately made preparations for the institution of the electric tramway, and appointed an agent, a W. S. Graff-Baker, to look after its affairs. William Sebastian Graff-Baker was an electric traction engineer of Fulton Junction, Baltimore, U.S.A., and was to become a noted tramway entrepreneur in both the United Kingdom and abroad.

Graff-Baker was not happy with the proposal to charge a penny fare, and after consultation, the Highways Committee reluctantly agreed that it be increased to one penny per mile or two pence from Sheepscar to Roundhay Park. He also requested that the time allowed for the installation of the electrical equipment be extended. Again the Highways Committee agreed and the Chairman, Alderman Firth, came in for considerable criticism for the tardy progress of the negotiations. He countered the criticisms by saying that the proposed tramway would put Leeds in a unique position; it would give a chance of testing whether electricity as a motive power was of any service and that would be of far more importance than the charging of even three pence per mile. He was later proved correct.

In the meantime, in spite of the promises of an electric tramway, complaints from the public about the lack of tramway facilities to Roundhay were continuing. Eventually the campaigning bore fruit and on 13th May 1891, the date when the agreement between the Corporation and the Thomson-Houston Company was signed, the Corporation also came to an agreement with the Leeds Tramways Company to run steam cars temporarily to Roundhay until electrification was complete. Hence, two days later, on 15th May, steam tramcars began to run between the Public Dispensary in North Street and Roundhay Park. The cars for the service came from the "Crown Hotel" to "Star Inn" section of the Wortley route, closed due to sewer construction in Tong Road. The Dispensary to Roundhay Park service continued until early June when a through service between the "Crown Hotel," Wortley and Roundhay was introduced; the fare from Briggate to Roundhay being 2d. each way. It was soon found that the steam trams were playing havoc with the tram rails in North Street and, beginning on 9th July and finishing in August, these were relaid on a concrete foundation by the Tramways Company, except for the section between Trafalgar Street and Skinner Lane, relaid a short time previously. Single line working was operated during the repairs.

One effect of the introduction of steam trams was to bring down fares. The competition between trams, 'buses and wagonettes was fierce and 'buses were now charging 2d. instead of 3d. and the wagonettes, which formerly charged 6d. were asking 3d. "or 4d. if they could get it" – to quote a 'bus conductor of the time – for the journey.

The steam tram service to Roundhay ran at 15 minute intervals, but after the re-opening of the "Crown Hotel" to "Star Inn" section of the Wortley route in August 1891, the service was reduced.

Meanwhile, visible progress was evident in the construction of the new electric tramway. In July work started on rail bonding and, during September, Graff-Baker's employees were busily engaged in erecting tramway poles, overhead wires and the machinery for the power station in a lane, (the access road to the dust destructor), later known as Stanley Road, off Beckett Street. Construction of the Harehills Road and Beckett Street section which had begun on 15th June 1891 was completed on 30th September. The total cost of the electrical installation was said to be between £5,000 and £6,000 and progress was so good that by the end of September, Graff-Baker was able to announce that the electric trams would be running in a fortnight.

The six cars to be used on the tramway arrived in Leeds on 5th October and the day after were inspected by the Highways Committee. An inspection was also made of the power station. Graff-Baker assured the Committee that trials would begin in a few days, and it was hoped to perform the opening ceremony on the 22nd. However, owing to inclement weather, the first trials did not take place until 26th October, when they were stated to be a complete success. The official opening was fixed for the 29th, and so Thursday, 29th October 1891, was to become the great day when Leeds was to formally open the first electric tramway, operating on the overhead wire system, in Europe.

On the morning of the 29th, the line was inspected by Major-General Hutchinson and Major Cardew of the Board of Trade, and was said to be "satisfactory." The opening ceremony in the afternoon, however, was a different matter and makes interesting reading:–

"It is unfortunate that the Thomson-Houston Company did not perfect their arrangements before having a public opening ceremony on so large a scale as that which took place in Leeds yesterday, unfortunate for the simple reason that many people, seeing the delay that was only too apparent in this particular trial trip, would probably jump to the conclusion that the Highways Committee of the Leeds Corporation had perpetrated another blunder in relying upon the overhead system of electric traction to convey the thousands of persons who daily wish to journey from Leeds to Roundhay Park. As a matter of fact, no one will deny that there is a future for electricity as a motive power; the question is whether everyone who witnessed the trial trip yesterday would be satisfied with the results so far attained by this particular system. As an experiment the trip may be considered fairly successful. Unhappily, however, for the temper and endurance of the hundred or more gentlemen who had been invited to take part in the function there was an impression abroad that the trip would partake more of the nature of an opening ceremony than an experiment. Aldermen, councillors, representatives of the Tramway Companies, and other interested persons were assembled in such large numbers at the appointed hour of 1 o'clock yesterday expected to find everything arranged to perfection. They understood that General Hutchinson and Major Cardew from the Board of Trade had inspected the line

Thomson-Houston car No. 79 at the Sheepscar terminus about 1893.
Courtesy The late W. Nichols, Photographer, Leeds City Libraries.

that same morning and had expressed themselves satisfied. General Hutchinson, it was said, had inspected the tram road in Beckett Street and Harehills Road and Major Cardew had looked over the electrical arrangements as far as they had gone, and both had approved what was done. True it was shown that only one overhead line had been completed, but the other, it was stated, would be ready in a day or two and the inspector would then make an additional inspection and at the same time, it was hoped, express entire approval of the undertaking. The fact that the line was not finished, too, was said not to be a bar to the running of the tramcars at a public opening ceremony.

With the knowledge of such things the crowd that went on foot, in tram, cab or 'bus to the Sheepscar terminus naturally expected a successful fillip to the new project, and it was galling to them to have to wait an hour and a half before anything like a start could be made. The delay was partially explained by the circumstance that a number of London guests could not arrive until nearly 2 o'clock, but what was nearer the truth – as the company's servants honestly admitted – was that it was not easy to get up the power necessary for running the tramcars at the stated time, 1 o'clock. Accordingly more than one Alderman, several councillors, as well as other visitors, went away disappointed, tired of waiting, and on all sides were heard complaints as to waste of time, unpunctuality and mismanagement. A certain worthy Alderman went so far as to propose that the Corporation should retire in a body and leave the alleged opening ceremony to itself. In patience, however, the assembly possessed their souls, even if they did not, as one councillor put it, 'possess their bodies,' until at last about 2.25 pm, nearly an hour and a half behind time, the elegantly designed tramcars appeared in sight, and the crowd made a rush to obtain seats therein. Inside no fault could be found with the arrangements made for the comfort of passengers, for besides being nicely cushioned, every conveyance is lighted with five incandescent lamps each of about 12 candle power, and there are useful contrivances for obtaining both fresh air and window shade in summer. Another good feature is that the man who has charge of the brake and the switch can, by simply moving one foot, ring the alarm bell and caution travellers ahead on the same road. Each car, by the way, is supposed to accommodate 22 persons. All six cars put upon the rails were crowded with the invited guests, and the Mayor (Mr. Alf Cooke) having released the lever of the first vehicle, the procession was soon in full progress. Exclamations of delight at the apparent triumph of the system were quickly in evidence until suddenly the lights went out in the cars and the vehicles themselves came to a standstill a few yards short of the Harehills Road junction. Then there were various remarkable comments and explanations offered by both the passengers themselves and the amused concourse of spectators who lined Roundhay Road. It was interesting for instance, to hear Councillor Atha declare that nothing would please him better than to have the 'buses come and pick the company up, and convey them back to town. These observations, however, did not lessen the time of waiting, which stretched out to 17 minutes before the cars could be induced to move again. At the end of this 'wait,' the motive power reasserted itself and it was possible to run for a couple of hundred yards. Then another dead halt took place, and this time the delay was so prolonged – nearly half an hour – that many persons got off and walked back to town. All at once the power came on once more, and putting on the spurt as it were, the cars ran down the incline and up to Gipton Wood Hill to the new park entrance, the whole journey from Sheepscar being accomplished in 1 hour 10 minutes. ——

—— The two 'breakdowns' mentioned were

Two electric cars stand side by side at the Roundhay terminus.   *Courtesy A. K. Terry Collection.*

94

explained by the overheating of the cross heads of the engine and the necessity of a stoppage in order to cool them. With the perfecting of arrangements those in charge state that there will be no more of the unfortunate incidents which spoiled the trial trip yesterday. The return from the park was made in good style, the cars running with smoothness and speed, notwithstanding some further delay at the Harehills Road junction. After inspecting the power station the company proceeded in wagonettes to the Town Hall where dinner was served."

(*Yorkshire Post, 30th October 1891*).

Graff-Baker, fortunately perhaps for his peace of mind was confined to his house through illness and was not at the opening.

During the following week or so the other overhead wire was installed in Roundhay Road and, on 10th November, the line was again inspected by Major-General Hutchinson and Major Cardew. They gave permission for the running of cars on all the lines, with the exception of Beckett Street, the use of which could not be sanctioned until the space between the metals was slightly increased. A few days later, on 18th November, permission was given conditionally upon these alterations being carried out, and it appears that cars began to run on the Beckett Street section the following day.

On 10th November 1891 the Leeds Tramways Company ceased to run its steam trams on Roundhay Road and the next day the electric service was opened to the public. Cars ran at 15 minutes intervals from Sheepscar

Interior of the power station showing the two Thomson-Houston dynamos.
Courtesy The late W. Nichols, Photographer, Leeds City Libraries.

to Roundhay Park from 6.0 am to 11.35 pm (71 journeys daily). A 45 minutes service operated on the Beckett Street section, cars leaving Green Road, Beckett Street from 5.56 am to 10.26 pm (23 journeys daily). Soon afterwards the Sheepscar to Roundhay Park service was increased to a nine minutes frequency. (118 journeys daily).

The power station measured 85 feet by 36 feet and contained a 192 h.p. Babcock and Wilcox water-tube type boiler fitted with a mechanical stoker and supplying a MacIntosh and Seymour, American horizontal type, single cylinder, $18 \times 18\frac{1}{2}$ in., high speed engine of 200 hp. This drove by means of endless perforated leather belts, running at 4,500 feet per minute, two Thomson-Houston 80 h.p. motor type dynamos. These supplied direct current at 315 volts giving a nominal line voltage

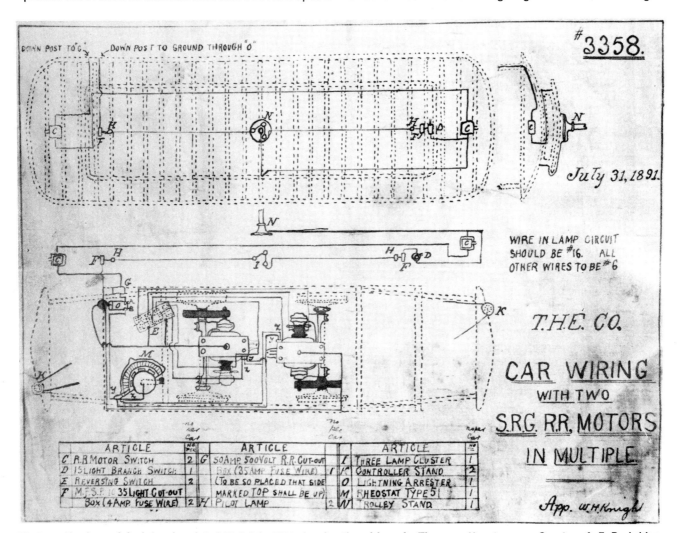

Photograph of an original drawing dated 31st July 1891 showing the wiring of a Thomson-Houston car. *Courtesy A. E. Burbridge.*

of 300. The switch board was placed at one end of the station. The generating plant was the bare minimum owing to the expected shortness of tenure. It is, however, fair to point out that the Company was hoping to be awarded a contract for the electrification and operation of the Leeds tramways on the completion of a successful demonstration and never regarded the generating plant as anything more than temporary.

The tubular steel standards, supporting the overhead wires, were 21'-6" high and set into the ground 6'-0" with a concrete surround. They were spaced at 125'-0" intervals along the route and the overhead wires were constructed on what was known as the cross suspension method, the span wires being placed on top of the poles, the poles being insulated by means of a wooden plug driven into the top of the pole. The trolley wires carrying the current were placed centrally over the tracks and were of .34" dia. hard drawn copper soldered to ears with hard rubber insulators and suspended on cast iron hangers. The current was carried to the overhead wires by means of an overhead feeder line carried on poles in the streets and the power fed into the overhead lines at more than one point.

The six tramcars were the objects that really sold the line to the general public. They were four wheel, single-deck, unvestibuled cars, licensed Nos. 75 to 80 by the Hackney Carriages Committee and painted in a very ornate American style livery of chocolate and white. The waist panels and end dashes were in chocolate and the words "Roundhay Park" were painted in gilt on both the dashes and white rocker panels. The window frames were white and the ornamental lining to the waist panels was of an intricate fretwork pattern on the corners. They carried the Leeds coat of arms. The car bodies were built to the designs of John Stephenson and Co. of New York and were based on Stephenson's standard 16'-0" horse car body modified with the addition of a trolley plank etc. for electric traction. There is no reference to the cars in the Stephenson records and the actual builder is uncertain. The cars had wooden sashes whereas Stephenson-built cars incorporated patent brass stile sashes. Contemporary references call them "standard American pattern" cars and John R. Stevens of the Shore Line Trolley Museum, East Haven, Connecticut, U.S.A. (the American authority on the Stephenson Company) thinks that they were probably constructed by the Lewis and Fowler Manufacturing Co. of Brooklyn, who built almost identical cars. The weight of the cars was $6\frac{1}{4}$ tons and seating was provided for 22 passengers on longitudinal upholstered benches. There were 34 swivel windows in the clear-storey of decorative stained glass coloured to tone with the bodywork; the 12 drop sash side windows could also be opened. A removable destination board was placed above the saloon windows and bore the words "Sheepscar" with "Beckett Street" on the reverse side. Each car was mounted on a Bemis Standard No. 26 truck of 6'-0" wheelbase. This truck, manufactured by the Bemis Car Box Company of Springfield, Massachusetts, U.S.A. was of a brand new design only coming into use in the U.S.A. in 1891. There it was one of the most widely used truck types until the advent of the Brill 21E design in 1895. In these trucks were fitted two 15 h.p. Thomson-Houston motors driving through single-reduction spur gears one to each axle. The motors were series wound but connected in parallel with each other. In running the car, the speed was regulated by means of a rheostat which was mounted under the car body and consisted of

thin plates of iron insulated from each other with mica. It was in the form of a semi-circle, and was operated by a steel cable passing round a drum and connected to the controller stand at each end of the car. The controller stands were fitted with sprocket wheels and chain, which were attached to the ends of the cables passing round the drum; by this method the amount of resistance was regulated by the motorman. The direction of the car was changed by means of a reversing switch controlled in the same manner as the rheostat. The trolley poles and bases were "live", unlike those used on practically all subsequent British installations which, with their predelection for double-deck open top cars, had of necessity to have insulated trolley poles. The trolley pole was mounted on a stand and was held in contact with the overhead wire by means of springs. The base was pivoted on a vertical pin which permitted some lateral deflection, but the overhead wire was generally suspended over the centre line of the track.

The tramway was leased to Graff-Baker for a term extending to 31st October 1892 and, after a month of successful operation, he asked the Corporation to allow the construction of the Beckett Street tramway from Green Road to Kirkgate via Burmantofts Street and York Street. The Highways Committee agreed and asked the General Committee to proceed with the work. Another Committee was to carry into effect the widening of Burmantofts Street, near to Grimston Street, to facilitate the work. Arrangements were also made to contact the Leeds Tramways Company with regard to the track intersection of their York Road horse tramway in Marsh Lane. By 6th April 1892 progress with the extension was well under way. Standards were being erected, the rails on order, and it was hoped to have the extension completed by Whitsuntide, so giving a direct connection from Kirkgate, one of the busiest parts of the town centre, to Roundhay Park. Unfortunately, the Corporation had not purchased the land for widening Burmantofts Street and was faced with claims of £35,600 from property owners to which it could not agree. To expedite the tramway extension the Corporation had to reduce the pavement to the dangerous width of 3'-8". This, along with the fact that standards were being erected within 2'-6" of shop windows and doorways, led the owners to consult the 1870 Tramways Act, a section of which reserved to owners and occupiers the right to object to tram rails being laid within a prescribed distance of the kerbstone along their frontages. On 13th April a letter was read to the Highways Committee from North and Sons, solicitors, regarding the width of the footpath. It was rejected by the Corporation and, hence, the solicitors threatened an injunction with the result that, within a few days, work on the extension was stopped. The rails were delivered about a week later and immediately diverted for track relaying in Wellington Street. The property in Burmantofts Street was acquired and the extension eventually constructed some years later. Thus, throughout their life, the electric cars had to work an uneconomic and almost useless line.

The tramway was very popular with the public and an immediate and lasting success in spite of the inconvenient termini at Sheepscar and Green Road. To obviate the termini problem, from mid-December 1891, John Newton Sharp, omnibus proprietor, ran 'bus services from Sheepscar to Briggate and Green Road to Kirkgate in connection with the electric cars. He ran these until August 1893, when he went out of business, and thereafter passengers either had to walk into town,

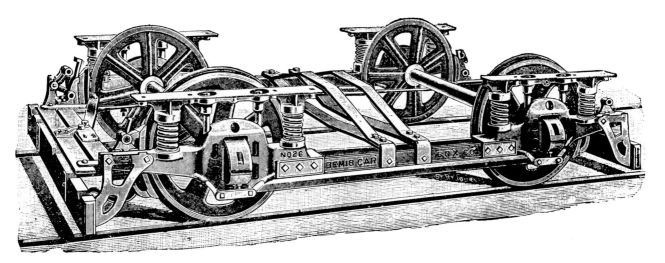

Engraving of a Bemis Standard No. 26 truck.
Courtesy C. B. Fairchild, "Street Railways," 1892.

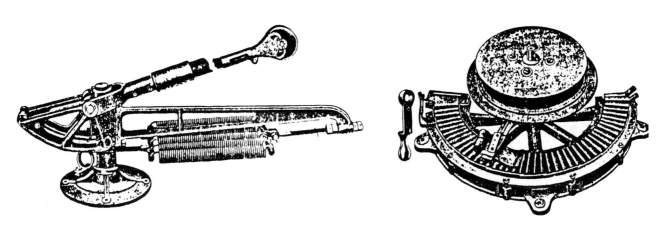

Illustration of Trolley stand and rheostat.
Courtesy C. B. Fairchild "Street Railways," 1892.

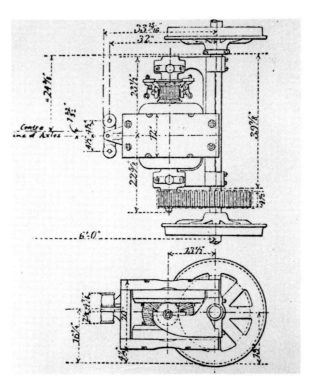

Details of electric motor.
Courtesy D. K. Clark, "Tramways, Their Construction and Working," 1894.

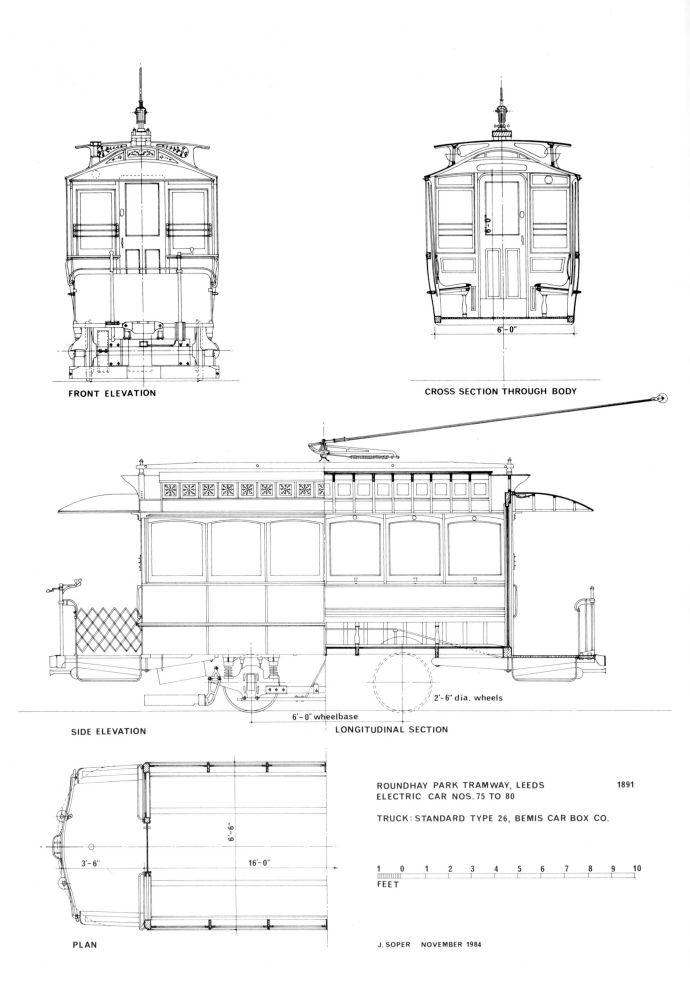

FRONT ELEVATION

CROSS SECTION THROUGH BODY

6'-0"

SIDE ELEVATION

LONGITUDINAL SECTION

2'-6" dia. wheels

6'-0" wheelbase

PLAN

6'-9"

3'-6"

16'-0"

ROUNDHAY PARK TRAMWAY, LEEDS   1891
ELECTRIC CAR NOS. 75 TO 80

TRUCK: STANDARD TYPE 26, BEMIS CAR BOX CO.

1 0 1 2 3 4 5 6 7 8 9 10
FEET

J. SOPER   NOVEMBER 1984

98

rely on the horse tramway, or other 'bus services.

The construction of the tramway gave rise to an important lawsuit when complaints were received from the National Telephone Company with regard to the interference on their telephones. This was due to the fact that the electric tramway was using the same earth for its current as was the Telephone Company. There was apparently a sound "like a sawmill" in the phone, but the electric tramway authorities were unable to do anything about it. Eventually, on 13th December 1892, the matter was brought before the High Court of Justice. The plaintiffs recommended that the problem would be solved by the tramway adopting a double wire system as in Budapest, Hungary, or on the Montreux-Vevey-Chillon electric railway in Switzerland, which used Siemens' slotted tube overhead. The court was adjourned and reassembled about a month later. The hearing lasted about a fortnight and, on 4th February 1893, the case was dismissed by the Judge, Mr. Justice Kekewich. The Judge considered that the land, into which both the plaintiffs and defendants discharged their current, did not belong to either. Hence the Telephone Company had to put in an insulated return.

Car No. 77 in Beckett Street. Note the overhead wire suspended centrally over the track.
Courtesy D. K. Clark, "Tramways, Their Construction and Working," 1894.

Of the six electric cars, five were used to run the service and the other was kept as a spare. In 1893 two trailer cars were added to the fleet and, on 22nd March 1893, were licensed as Nos. 81 and 82 by the Hackney Carriages Committee. They seated 46 passengers, weighed 2 tons 10 cwt., and were used mainly at weekends and holidays. The electric cars were said to pull them with ease. They appear to have been disposed of towards the end of 1895 and were delicensed from March 1896. No photographs have been discovered and their fate is unknown. In March 1896 a further two single-deck trailers 21'-6" long, and seating 32 passengers inside, were ordered from the Brush Company of Loughborough. Only one of these was delivered and licensed from 20th May 1896. It was a low open-sided vehicle and the Hackney Carriages Committee gave instructions that the Company should adopt means for preventing passengers alighting from the wrong side. It does not appear to have been given a number.

The lease allowing the operation of the electric tramway was renewable from 31st October 1892, and Graff-Baker's lease was renewed for a further year. Following 31st October 1893 Graff-Baker relinquished control and it passed to the Thomson-Houston Company. He had wanted to renew the lease with the addition of three new clauses, which were at variance with the requirements of the Thomson-Houston Company, who wished to continue with the existing arrangement. The Corporation accepted the offer of the Thomson-Houston Company for a period of six months and afterwards the arrangement was to be continued, subject to one month's notice on either side. Graff-Baker later submitted a claim to the Corporation asking to be reimbursed if electric traction was adopted in the city (Leeds had achieved the status of a city in 1893). His claim was dismissed by the Highways Committee.

Graff-Baker left under a cloud and, in addition to the above, it could also have been partly due to the fact that the tramway was operating at a loss. The Company never published any reliable figures and the local press always suspected that the tramway was unprofitable. The public, however, was very pleased with it and many letters praising the tramway were written stressing how courteous and polite the staff were. The following is a typical example:—

"The tramway itself was laid by the Leeds Corporation and well done. The cars are attractive, well lighted and ventilated, free from advertisements and complete even to the smallest details." (They even boasted a clock) "At night they are brilliantly lighted, so that reading is easy. In fact they run so smoothly and are so comfortable that one is often sorry to be so soon at the journey's end, a feeling not ordinarily excited by a tramcar ride. They start punctually, easily average 8 m.p.h. up hill, including stoppages, and rarely or never lose time. If one misses a Headingley car in Park Row, the chances are one may walk to the Moor before being overtaken. But if you miss an electric car and walk the next speedily glides after and overtakes you. The driver stands on a low platform in front where he can clearly see everything. His foot is on a warning bell, and his hands on the controlling gear. The driver can stop, start, or slow down to any speed with surprising promptitude. In fact the cars are more under command than any other vehicle" —— *"The personal service is well managed, both drivers and conductors are civil — one may say polite. The conductor usually dismounts to assist a lady to alight. Notwithstanding the long hours that the cars run, each man can dine at home — for there are two sets of men per day — so that the Roundhay tram service is also a model as to hours of labour".*

———

"The benefit of this line is evidenced not only by the hundreds of houses built on Roundhay Road, but by the building of houses near the tramway terminus — two are already built in the Park estate land, previously practically unsaleable" ——
wrote Wilson Hartnell of Roundhay.
(Leeds Mercury, 15th February 1894).

The tramway was at first under the managership of Isaac Evison Winslow, brought over from America by Graff-Baker. An early employee of the Company was a Charles Herbert Bent who joined the undertaking in July 1891. He was promoted to Chief Clerk in March 1892 and in November of that year succeeded Winslow as Manager. However, he was accused of falsification of the accounts and was suspended from 25th August

Leaves Sheepscar	Leaves Roundhay Park	Leaves Sheepscar	Leaves Roundhay Park	Leaves Sheepscar	Leaves Roundhay Park	Leaves Sheepscar	Leaves Roundhay Park	Beckett Street	
								Leaves Green Road	Leaves Roundhay Park
A 6 0	B 6 2	E 11 3	D 11 4	D 3 33	B 3 34	E 8 3	D 8 4	C 6 55	C 6 15
B 6 20	A 6 22	A 11 13	E 11 12	A 3 42	B 3 43	B 8 12	B 8 22	C 6 35	C 6 55
A 6 40	B 6 42	D 11 21	E 11 22	D 3 52	D 3 52	D 8 21	B 8 31	C 7 15	C 7 35
B 7 0	A 7 1	E 11 30	B 11 31	B 4 0	A 4 1	A 8 30	D 8 40	C 8 35	C 8 15
D 7 9	E 7 10	B 11 39	D 11 40	D 4 9	A 4 18	E 8 39	E 8 49	C 9 55	C 9 35
A 7 18	B 7 19	A 11 49	A 11 49	A 4 18	B 4 27	B 8 48	B 8 58	C 10 15	C 10 15
E 7 27	D 7 28	E 11 57	E 11 58	E 4 37	A 4 37	D 8 57	D 9 7	C 10 35	C 10 55
B 7 36	A 7 37	A 12 6	B 12 7	A 4 46	B 4 46	A 9 6	A 9 16	C 11 15	C 11 35
D 7 45	E 7 46	D 12 15	D 12 16	A 4 54	E 4 55	E 9 15	E 9 25	C 11 55	C 12 15
A 7 54	B 7 55	B 12 24	A 12 25	E 5 3	B 5 3	B 9 24	B 9 34	C 12 35	C 12 55
E 8 3	D 8 4	E 12 33	E 12 34	B 5 12	D 5 21	D 9 33	D 9 42	C 1 55	C 1 35
B 8 12	A 8 13	A 12 42	B 12 43	D 5 13	A 5 21	A 9 42	A 9 46	C 2 35	C 2 15
D 8 21	E 8 22	E 12 51	D 12 52	E 5 22	C 9 55	E 9 50	B 9 45	C 1 55	C 1 35
A 8 30	B 8 31	B 1 0	A 1 1	B 6 31	C 9 55	B 9 50	D 9 52	C 2 15	C 2 55
E 8 39	A 8 40	D 1 9	E 1 10	D 5 40	B 10 2	E 10 6	E 10 6	C 3 15	C 3 15
B 8 48	E 8 49	A 1 18	B 1 19	E 6 49	D 10 7	E 10 13	C 10 13	C 3 65	C 4 15
D 8 57	B 8 58	E 1 27	D 1 28	B 6 7	A 10 14	C 10 14	C 10 13	C 4 35	C 4 55
A 9 6	D 9 7	B 1 36	A 1 37	A 6 6	E 10 21	B 10 20	B 10 2c	C 5 15	C 6 15
E 9 15	A 9 16	D 1 45	E 1 46	D 6 15	C 10 28	C 10 25	C 6 15	C 6 55	C 6 15
B 9 24	E 9 25	A 1 54	B 1 65	B 6 24	B 10 35	A 10 32	C 6 16	C 6 15	C 6 66
D 9 33	B 9 34	E 2 3	D 2 4	D 6 33	D 10 42	E 10 39	C 7 15	C 7 15	C 7 36
A 9 42	D 9 43	B 2 12	A 2 13	A 6 42	A 10 49	C 10 46	C 7 15	C 8 15	C 8 55
E 9 51	A 9 52	E 2 21	E 2 22	B 6 51	E 10 t6	B 10 53	C 7 65	C 8 35	...
B 10 0	A 10 1	A 2 30	B 2 31	A 7 0	C 11 3	D 11 0	C 8 35	C 9 18	...
D 10 9	B 10 10	E 2 39	A 2 40	D 7 9	E 10 10	A 11 7	E 11 14	...	...
A 10 18	B 10 19	B 2 48	A 2 49	A 7 18	B 11 10	A 11 7	...	...	...
E 10 27	D 10 28	D 2 67	E 2 58	B 7 27	A 11 24	E 11 30	...	...	...
B 10 36	A 10 37	A 3 6	B 3 7	A 7 36	E 11 30	...	...	...	...
D 10 45	E 10 46	E 3 15	D 3 16	A 7 45	...	...	...	...	...
A 10 54	B 10 55	B 3 24	A 3 25	A 7 64	...	...	...	...	...
				B 7 55					

Between the hours 9.50 and 11.30 p.m., the Cars will leave Sheepscar every seven minutes.

SUNDAYS.

1st Car leaves Sheepscar 9, 6 a.m., last car 10.35 p.m.   Cars must not pass Harehill's Road sooner than
  "   Roundhay Park 9.7   "   "   10.29   "   10½ minutes after leaving Sheepscar.
  "   Green Road - 9.15   "   "   9.18   "   Cars must not pass Harehill's Road sooner than
                                        7 minutes after leaving Roundhay Park.
Any irregularities in fulfilling the above to be reported to the Manager, 1, Roseville Rd., Roundhay Rd.
During the Winter months, the First Car will leave Sheepscar at 7 o'clock; Roundhay, 7.1 o'clock; Beckett Street, 7.15 o'clock.

Timetable of the Roundhay Electric Tramway dated January 1st 1894. *Courtesy A. E. Burbridge.*

1893, Winslow resuming control. The system of bookkeeping adopted by the Company was said to be very complicated and at Bent's trial on 10th January the following year a "not guilty" verdict was returned.

There was a total of 32 staff and, in addition to the Manager and Chief Clerk, there were two assistant clerks, two inspectors of motors, three engine drivers, ticket inspectors, timekeepers, drivers, conductors and cleaners. The drivers earned 31s. 0d. per week and conductors between 24s. 0d. and 25s. 0d., and these wages compared very favourably with other undertakings and places of employment in Leeds. The platform staff were 18 in number (nine drivers and nine conductors) working a shift system. The motor inspectors were Englishmen who had been trained in the United States and were said to be well paid. Also well paid were the three engine drivers. As the generating plant was of the absolute minimum, if a breakdown occurred the entire tramway ceased to run. The chief engine driver and his two assistants had to work round the clock if required. The Chief earned £3 10s 0d per week. The plant, however, gave very little trouble and records indicate that there were only four major breakdowns or overhauls when the service was stopped:–

27th to 29th March 1892 due to a burst cylinder on the engine.
1st to 2nd September 1892 due to reconstruction of engine.
13th to 14th July 1893 due to general overhaul.
28th to 29th November 1894 due to general overhaul.

On the occasion of the last closedown, the Corporation ran a steam tramway service between Wortley and Roundhay.

After its takeover of the Leeds Tramways Company's assets in 1894, the Corporation adopted the practice of loaning cars, usually double-deck horse cars, to the Roundhay Company during busy periods for use as trailers. The Corporation accounts do not indicate that the Electric Tramway Company paid any money for the privilege and it would appear that the Corporation took the receipts on its own cars. There was little traffic in the winter, but on summer weekends and holiday periods the traffic was immense. Graff-Baker said that if he had 50 or 60 cars he would not be able to cope and admitted that on occasion the 16'-0" electric cars had carried 100 passengers in contravention of the Board of Trade regulations. When the Corporation became tramway operators, they supplemented the electric cars on Bank Holidays by introducing a steam tram service, paying 20% of their receipts to the electric tramway. This occurred on four occasions. On 6th and 7th August 1894, a Wortley to Roundhay steam tram service was operated

An electric car hauls a double-deck horse car in Harehills Road about 1895. *Courtesy H. Heyworth.*

in place of the Wortley to Leopold Street service. A Wortley to Roundhay and Kirkstall to Roundhay steam service was worked on 15th and 16th April 1895, and similar services on 5th and 6th August 1895 and 6th and 7th April 1896. It should be noted that only Corporation steam trams ran in conjunction with the electric cars. There is no record of steam trams running with electric cars when the steamers were in the possession of the Leeds Tramways Company.

During the Corporation's deliberations in 1895 and 1896 on the form of traction to be employed on the tramways, the Thomson-Houston Company (now the British Thomson-Houston Company) patiently waited, hoping to be given the order for equipping the city with electric tramways. They were, however, ignored by the Corporation who did not like to have a "foreign firm controlling the streets" and were more interested in patronising local firms. When it became patently obvious that the Company was not to become involved, it gave a month's notice of its intention to withdraw the electric service.

Summary of earnings and expenses for a typical fortnight in 1893. *Courtesy A. E. Burbridge.*

In 1894 Winslow gave up as manager and his place was taken by John Burbridge, one of the motor inspectors. Born on 4th February 1861 in Stourbridge, Worcestershire, Burbridge, in his early twenties went to the U.S.A. and Canada proposing to get a job in every state. He had all sorts of employment and in Victoria, British Columbia, obtained a job driving Thomson-Houston electric trams. Being of an inquisitive nature, he was curious as to the working of the trams and, lifting the floor trap of his car, he received a severe electric shock. This was the start of his interest in electric traction and he was given a job in the power station of the electric tramway company. While in Victoria he met Dr. John Hopkinson, the eminent electrical engineer. Hopkinson had a high opinion of Burbridge and recommended him for the post of electrical engineer to the Roundhay Electric Tramway. Burbridge drove the first trial car on the Roundhay tramway and thus had the honour of driving

the first electric tram on the overhead principle in Europe. He was responsible for training staff to drive the electric cars.

John Burbridge. A photograph taken in 1913 when he was aged 52. *Courtesy A. E. Burbridge.*

Burbridge made a frank statement to the press and admitted that the Company had expected more consideration than they had received from the Corporation of Leeds. The Company had been keeping the cars going, at a loss, in the hope of being asked to extend their working area into the centre of the city. The electric cars had not produced an adequate return for capital invested, taking one part of the year with another.

"In summer, we have sometimes made as much as £200 per month profit, but we have always run the cars at a loss in the winter; and the loss has more than swallowed up the profits of summer" ——

—— *"With our experience gained at great cost, we could make overhead electric cars pay all the year round, had we the whole city as our area"* ——

—— *"Considering that we have only one engine, one boiler, and one spare car, engineers who come to see us are kind enough to say that we have maintained our service remarkably well. The total value of our plant now stands on the books at about £23,000. I have not the least idea where we are going to take it or what the 32 men we employ will do after this month. Of course, the Corporation will have a better chance of making cars running through Briggate and Boar Lane pay than we who are restricted to Roundhay Road. We should for anything I know, have been willing to continue running our cars till the Corporation start theirs, but I have never heard of our being asked to. We gave them a month's notice and they straightaway accepted it"* ——

(Yorkshire Post, 10th July 1896)

The local residents of Roundhay and district were very concerned about the impending closure of the electric tramway. Three days before the closure the 'Yorkshire Post' commented that the change was regarded with deep dissatisfaction by the residents of Roundhay. The service of cars had been frequent, the rate of travelling quick, the accommodaton luxurious, especially in comparison with the often filthy steam cars running between Wortley and Leopold Street. The Thomson-Houston employees had been distinguished by a

The Roundhay Electric Tramway staff pose outside Beckett Street Depot. On the extreme left is John Burbridge the Manager and, next to him, J. Kidd, who became Power Station Superintendent. Seated in the front row wearing a bowler hat is J. Ramsey, Overhead Lines Superintendent, and the boy in the centre of the group is A. W. Maley who later became assistant Engineer with the Leeds City Tramways Undertaking. *Courtesy J. Soper Collection.*

smartness, civility, and a desire to oblige that the servants of the Corporation would do well to imitate.

A ticket system, including contract tickets, was employed on the tramway and it was reported that the cost of running the cars was 5.76d. per car mile. The run of 3,379 yards in Roundhay Road, a steady rise all the way from Sheepscar with two stretches about a quarter of a mile long of 1 in 20 gradient, was normally done in 12 minutes, including stops. However, the cars were known to have completed the journey in $7\frac{1}{4}$ minutes. The average speed for the normal 12 minutes journey was 9.6 m.p.h., the running speed being generally 10 to 12 m.p.h., while from Gipton Wood to Harehills Lane

(downhill) a speed of 20 m.p.h. was often reached. The cars covered about 112 miles each per day (85 miles on Sundays) compared with 60 to 80 miles per day for a steam tram. Throughout their life the cars carried a total of approximately 4,210,000 passengers. Although the number of passengers carried increased from 733,823 in the period 26th March 1892 to 25th March 1983 to 1,036,264 in the period 26th March 1895 to 25th March 1896, the line still lost money. The total number of car miles run for the whole period of operation was approximately 956,000.

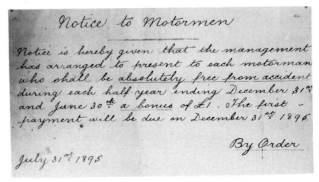

A " Notice to Motormen" dated 31st July 1895. *Courtesy A. E. Burbridge.*

The last Thomson-Houston car ran without ceremony on 31st July 1896. The redundant employees, including John Burbridge, were absorbed into the Corporation system and the rolling stock was later acquired by them. A steam tram service was substituted on 1st August between Briggate and Roundhay Park. The Harehills Road and Beckett Street section did not run again until the route was extended to Kirkgate in 1898.

A carefully posed photograph of car No. 79 outside Beckett Street Depot about 1894. On the platform step is I. E. Winslow, the Manager. *Courtesy The late W. Nichols, Photographer, Leeds City Libraries.*

CHAPTER THIRTEEN

The Tramways Company
and the Corporation Takeover

The Leeds Tramway Company's licence under its 1871 Act expired on 14th August 1892, and following the abortive negotiations of 1889 and 1890, nothing further transpired for two years.

The appalling condition of the tramway track culminating in the withdrawal of the Headingley steam trams was occupying the minds of both Corporation and Company in early 1892. Large sections of track required immediate renewal and the Company could not be expected to lay out "thousands upon thousands of pounds" in reconstruction prior to August. The cost of relaying a mile of tramway on a bed of concrete with a granite pavement was said to be £4,500. Accordingly, three members of the Corporation, Alderman Firth, Chairman of the Highways Committee, Alderman Sir Edwin Gaunt, Chairman of the Corporate Property Committee and Councillor Teale decided to approach the Tramways Company to determine if the Company would relinquish possession of the tramways immediately instead of waiting until August. The idea was that if the Corporation could obtain early control of the tramways, they could put them all in good condition and then re-let their working by tender. A meeting with the Company's representatives was held on 22nd March 1892.

The principal difficulty to overcome was that of valuation. That the Company would ask a higher price than the Corporation was inclined to pay was certain. The Company, in assessing the value of its undertaking could not be expected to lose sight of the amount of capital it had expended, or of the fact that some of the land it owned was worth three times the price paid for it. It was equally certain that the Corporation was only interested in the actual present value of the lines, cars and plant, as a going concern, which required a large outlay before it could be considered satisfactory. The Tramways Act empowered the Corporation to take possession of the tramways at their "then value", and these two words were subject to various interpretations. It was said at the meeting that as two arbitrators seldom agreed it would be as well to go straight to the Board of Trade and ask them to send to Leeds a valuer in whom all concerned would have confidence. He would be able to sort out the problem. Turton said that no definite course of action could be taken without the consent of the Company's shareholders, but thought that the course suggested by the Corporation was the best for the local authority, the inhabitants, the Company and all interested.

The matter was discussed at a meeting of the Highways Committee and the Town Clerk was instructed to prepare a draft agreement transferring the tramways from the Company to the Corporation at an early date. A meeting of the Directors of the Company was also held and, as a result, the following letter dated 26th March, was sent to Alderman Firth:–

"Dear Sir, With reference to the interview which took place between a committee of my directors and a sub-committee of the Tramways Committee of the Corporation on 22nd inst. I am now instructed by my directors to say that, having fully considered your proposal to anticipate the 14th August 1892, and to enter into negotiations for the sale and purchase at once of the Leeds tramways undertaking, they are disposed without prejudicing their position, and providing there is no legal impediment, to favour the view of the Corporation, so that the work of putting the Headingley lines into a satisfactory condition may not be delayed till the approach of another winter.

My Board is prepared, as soon as the County Council has passed the necessary resolution to purchase the tramways undertaking, to call a special meeting of the shareholders of the company, and to submit to them for their sanction such proposals as may have been by that time framed.

In the meantime we shall be glad to have a draft agreement to lay before our solicitors.

Yours etc, William Wharam, Secretary and Manager."

(Yorkshire Post, 31st March, 1892).

Three days later a meeting of the Tramways Sub-Committee was held and the Company's letter was discussed. The Committee took exception to the wording of the letter and stated that it was not prepared to proceed with the negotiations. It also instructed the Company to put the whole of its lines in a proper state of repair and to resume the running of cars or 'buses from Headingley "Oak" to the "Three Horse Shoes" (this section was closed when the steam trams ceased running), otherwise legal action would be taken.

"At first sight this ultimatum of the Tramways Committee seems to be as mysterious as it is sudden and unlooked for. What the 'conditions' are to which exception is taken is not clear. It is regarded as highly probable, however, by interested onlookers, that the Corporate representatives have taken umbrage at the tone of the Tramways Company's communication. It is said that some of those present at yesterday's meeting would have been disposed to press for a continuance of negotiations had the company been willing to show its hand with a little more confidence in the Committee.

A Starbuck double-deck horse car in Briggate about 1890.   *Courtesy Leeds City Libraries.*

It was pointed out that the directors had not mentioned whether they had unanimously agreed upon the response which they authorised their manager to make to the Committee, or whether they would be ready to recommend the proprietors to adopt the scheme; also, that they did not propose to submit the offer of the Corporation to the shareholders of the Company until the Borough County Council had "passed the necessary resolution to purchase the undertaking". As one member of the Tramways Committee puts it, the local authority would, in complying with these requirements, be revealing the whole of its policy on the entire subject of acquiring the tramways now or at a later date, while the Company, instead of making a sign of some sort, simply looked on, and noted points that might prove useful to it, reserving to itself all the while the right to reject the final proposals of the County Council".

(Yorkshire Post, 31st March, 1892).

Negotiations were now at a total deadlock. "In the interests of the public", said Alderman Firth, "the Tramways Company had better run out its full course". A formal resolution, authorising the Corporation to acquire the tramways, constructed under their 1871 Act, was passed by the Council on 4th May 1892. This covered the whole of the tramways with the exception of the Meanwood Road and Wortley lines, the licence for which terminated in 1898. It was felt, however, that the Corporation would have no difficulty in obtaining these additional lines, as they would be uneconomical for the Company to operate independently.

On 12th May a meeting was held at the Board of Trade offices in London at which John Kincaid, the engineer who had originally designed the tramway lines, was present. The differences which had arisen between the Tramways Company and Corporation were discussed and it was agreed that a referee be appointed at once. The Wortley and Meanwood Road lines were to be included in the purchase and the Board of Trade appointed Sir Douglas Galton K.C.B. as arbitrator. A date for the hearing of 4th July 1892 was fixed, but this had to be changed to 28th July owing to an intervening General Election. However, things came to a standstill due to a delaying tactic introduced by the Tramways Company. It had been arranged that the arbitration would take place under section 43 of the Tramways Act, 1870. The Corporation had complied with all the provisions of that section including the holding of a special meeting of the Council after a month's notice. The Tramways Company now withdrew from that arrangement and proposed a purchase under section 44 of the Act. To adopt this section, however, would mean more delay, a further meeting of the Council after a month's notice being necessary, while in addition it would be a departure from the course so far adopted. There was also a claim for compensation raised by the proposed new agreement which had been previously considered and withdrawn. The Corporation declined to recognise the claim and decided to proceed under section 43 of the 1870 Act, leaving the Wortley and Meanwood Road sections under the control of the Tramways Company.

104

A Special Meeting of the shareholders of the Company was held on 13th July 1892 to approve the draft of the agreement between the Company and Corporation. Clause 43, Turton explained, only empowered the Company to sell and the Corporation to buy, after 14th August next, and therefore the Directors had to proceed under the 44th clause, which was a voluntary clause empowering the Company to sell and the Corporation to buy at any time. After a long, and at times "excited" discussion, the agreement was approved unanimously. The agreement included the provision enabling the Company to claim compensation based on past profits, but was flexible in that it allowed the Directors to alter it as they wished for the benefit of the Company. The Corporation was totally opposed to the compensation clause and negotiations came to a standstill. The Yorkshire Post was upset.

"As a sample of diplomacy, all this manoeuvreing may possess interest for those immediately concerned. In the meantime, however, the public are not so much concerned whether Alderman Firth or Mr. Turton is the more skilful hand at driving a bargain, as they are anxious to know when the borough tramways will be regulated with some regard to the requirements of the people for whose convenience they are supposed to exist".
(Yorkshire Post, 20th July, 1892).

At the Company meeting on 31st August it was reported that the matter was in abeyance as the Corporation refused point blank to discuss the compensation question. The Corporation was interesting itself in the case of the London County Council who was preparing to take over the undertaking of the London Street Tramways Company, paying the "present value" of the lines and plant, no allowance being made for past profits. It was felt that whichever side lost in London would bring the question before the House of Lords for final decision, and the Leeds authorities were prepared to wait for this rather than give way to the Tramways Company.

The Company had originally asked for compensation for the Wortley and Meanwood Road lines, but later it was discovered that they had been losing money on these lines for years. The Corporation pointed out that it would be relieving the Company of a "deadweight" if it took them over, and instead of the Company being compensated, the Corporation ought to be compensated in lieu. Eventually the whole question of compensation for past profits and for the two lines was dropped and the Company asked that they be included in the purchase. In the meantime the Corporation had obtained approval from the Board of Trade to serve notice on the Company for the compulsory purchase of its undertaking, with the exception of the Wortley and Meanwood Road sections. However, following receipt of a draft agreement from the Company's solicitors, the Corporation agreed to their inclusion, and served notice on the Company on 15th September 1892. The purchase of the two lines required a special resolution of the Council and this was passed on 16th November, and thereafter nothing happened for several months. An agreement was reached between the Company and the Corporation, but the Company was slow to sign and, in February 1893, the Corporation again threatened to exclude the Meanwood Road and Wortley sections if the Company did not take some action. The Corporation, however, was also dilatory. One member of the Council is said to have exclaimed:—

"Oh there is no hurry; the London County Council and the Street Tramways Company are fighting our battle, let us wait".
(Yorkshire Post, 22nd February, 1893).

On 27th February the Company's solicitors submitted the estimate of the value of their undertaking to the Corporation. This was in the sum of £240,136 and at a Council meeting two days later was greeted with laughter and ironical cheers. Alderman Firth said that the Company was trying to take advantage of the people of Leeds and it would be prudent to wait for the London case to be settled. In the meantime the Company was instructed to carry out immediate remedial work on defective track.

The London case was eventually settled, the arbitrators award being in two parts, one figure being given for the "present value" and another for the "rental value" of the lines; a higher court to decide which mode of valuation was to apply. The Corporation, whilst not concurring in some parts with the decision, decided to ask the Company to proceed with the arbitration and fix a date for the hearing. A date could not be fixed until the Company prepared an inventory of the items which they intended the Corporation to take over. The Company, however, was reluctant to do this as it felt it would prejudice its case, and the Corporation had to obtain an order from Sir Douglas Galton before it was forthcoming. All obstacles now out of the way, the date for the arbitration was fixed to commence on Tuesday 25th July 1893. The counsel for the Tramways Company were the ex-Attorney General (Sir Richard Webster, Q.C.), Mr. Cripps, Q.C. and Mr. Henry Sutton, while the Corporation was represented by Mr. Lockwood, Q.C., Mr. Lawson Walton, Q.C. and Mr. Kershaw.

The Leeds Tramways Company

AND

The Corporation of Leeds.

Particulars of the Tramways, Lands, Buildings, Works, Materials, and Plant of the Company.

Amount of Claim.	Tramways.					M.	F.	Chs.
	Single Line and Crossovers	...	...	...	...	6	0	5·43
	Double Line	...	...	...	...	8	0	8·23
£152,900						14	1	3·66
	Reduced Single Line of Permanent Way	...	...	...	22	2	1·89
	Lines connecting with Depots and in Car Sheds	...	...		8	5·53

Land and Depots.

Headingley Depot.

Including Car Shed, Engine Sheds, Painting Shop, Fitting Shops, Store
£9,000 Rooms, Yard, Smithy, Dwelling-houses, &c.

Freehold.

Area purchased by Company in 1875, 5587 square yards.

Chapeltown Depot.

Including Car Shed, Stables, Smithy, Shed, Manure Pit, Dwelling-house,
£7,500 Yard, &c.

Freehold.

Area purchased by Company in 1875, 3970 square yards.

Front page of the Leeds Tramways Company Inventory.
Courtesy Leeds Corporation.

TRAMWAY DISPUTE.

WILLIE F-R-H : " Nah then, just let's hev hod o' that Tramcar ! "
JENNIE WH-R-M : " Ger art !   What ar' yer baarn to go' me for it ? "
MOTHER G-LT-N : " Nar then childer, let me settle this matter for yer."

Cartoon about the Tramways Arbitration from "The Yorkshire Owl."   *Courtesy Leeds City Libraries.*

Sir Douglas Galton made a thorough inspection of the tramway lines and depots the day before the arbitration. The arbitration lasted three days and agreement was quickly reached on the valuation of the depots, offices, and rolling stock – the latter valued by John Eades, manager of the Manchester Carriage and Tramways Company and J. Waugh of Bradford. There was some argument with regard to the value of the tramway engines, which were said to have cost £18,240. The Company's cash books showed a depreciation of £10,163 yet T. Pogson of the Huddersfield tramways valued them at £12,844 5s. 0d. for the Company; the Corporation at £7,945. The horses, harness and stores were to be valued immediately before the Corporation takeover. The main area of disagreement was the value of the tramway lines themselves. The Corporation maintained that the value was the original cost of the tramways, less depreciation, and valued them at £46,013 3s. 0d. This was considered to be the structural value of the lines and a figure of £58,000 for this was later agreed between the two parties. The Company submitted that the basis of valuation should be the rental value of the tramways for 20 years less a certain percentage, and calculated a figure of £155,000.

The Arbitrator's award was received in September 1893 and was said to be "distinctly in favour of the Corporation". The lines were valued on the same basis as the London tramways, the "present" or structural value being the agreed £58,000, and the "rental value" £119,000. The tramway engines were valued at £12,100 and the Corporation was to pay the costs of the arbitration. The Corporation immediately accepted the award and queried if the Company intended to go to Court for a decision on the principle of valuation. The Company was slow to reply and the Corporation had second thoughts and objected to the rental value award of £119,000. It claimed the right, either before the Arbitrator or elsewhere, to further argue and question witnesses with a view to reducing the figure. The Company replied that under the Tramways Act, the award of Sir Douglas Galton was final and binding and that the local authority ought to pay either £58,000 or £119,000 as the higher court would determine. The outcome of the London appeals and a similar case between the Edinburgh Tramways Company and Edinburgh Corporation was awaited. An agreement between the two parties was formulated and approved by the Council on 9th November 1893, but the Company refused to put the agreement before its shareholders until this legal difficulty was sorted out. It was later agreed that the Court that made the decision on the method of valuation would also be asked to decide whether the award of the Arbitrator was final.

An Extraordinary General Meeting of the Tramways Company was held on 19th December at which it was proposed to accept the agreement and hand over the tramways to the Corporation. Sir Douglas Galton's award was made up as follows:–

Tramway lines.	£58,000.0s.0d.
Land and depots.	£23,250.0s.0d.
Tramcars.	£8,900.0s.0d.
Omnibuses.	£638.0s.0d.
Office furniture, safes, clocks, etc.	£231.3s.3d.
Telephones.	£250.0s.0d.
Machinery and fixed plant.	£823.16s.6d.
Tramway engines.	£12,100.0s.0d.
TOTAL	£104,192.19s.9d.

Turton was disappointed:–

"The arbitrator was very painstaking over the inquiry, although he did not come up to the Company's idea of the value of the property, and he thought the shareholders must abide by his estimate. ——the arbitrator had allowed nothing for the undertaking, which was another thing. The undertaking was the Act of Parliament — there had been three Acts altogether — and for this Sir Douglas Galton had not allowed sixpence. It ought to have been valued. The arbitrator had valued the plant at what might be called structural value, and the difference between that calculation and the Company's estimate on the rental basis amounted to £61,000. The directors were therefore not satisfied with the award, and at a later stage would ask the authority of the shareholders for taking steps to recover the difference."

(Yorkshire Post, 20th December, 1893).

Eddison was very upset. "They had brought the tramways to Leeds, and were now asked to sacrifice them at half the cost. It was simply scandalous." The solicitors to the Company advised the shareholders to accept the agreement as the Company would be placed in a disastrous position because the Corporation could "set them at defiance in every way". The agreement was accepted with only four dissentients.

The Corporation made application to the Board of Trade to borrow £130,000 to cover the cost of the purchase plus legal charges, and Major General Hutchinson held an inquiry at the Leeds Town Hall on 28th December. The Town Clerk pointed out that of the 22 miles 3 furlongs and 128 yards of tramways which were to be taken over, it was necéssary to relay 16 miles 4 furlongs and 112 yards for which a further £77,000 would be required. Application for this latter sum was to be made at a later date. Board of Trade approval was soon received for the £130,000. There remained to be valued the 368 horses, harness etc. The horses were valued at £7,297, harness, engine duplicates and stores £3,095 1s. 11d. and there was an allowance of £5 5s. 0d. in respect of articles of furniture removed. With the £104,192 19s. 9d. already agreed this made a total of £114,590 6s. 8d. and a cheque for this sum was formally handed to the Tramways Company on 2nd February 1894. The Corporation took possession from this date.

At the Company meeting three weeks later it was stated that the valuation had cost £11,000 and it was agreed that the assets of the Company be disbursed to the extent of £4 10s. 0d. on each share. This was paid on 21st March and the total amount distributed £72,000. Shortly afterwards the Company took steps to recover the £61,000 – the difference between the structural and rental value of the tramways – and served a writ on the Corporation. This was resisted and the Company was forced to await the result of the London and Edinburgh appeals. The two appeals were taken to the House of Lords and judgement given against the tramway companies on 30th July 1894. The Leeds Company, therefore lost its £61,000 and withdrew its action. It now only remained for the Company to pay the costs of the abandoned action and the Corporation the costs of the arbitration for the transaction to be completed.

The Company meeting on 31st August 1894 was stormy and there were at times as many as half a dozen shareholders shouting at the Chairman simultaneously. Turton was:–

"Sorry that he had not a more favourable prospect to hold out to them. The directors had endeavoured all through to maintain and get what they considered right

and just for the shareholders. Their effort however, had unfortunately not been as successful as they had anticipated, inasmuch as they had not thought that there was an Act of Parliament which he could only term as giving a means of confiscating the property of the people".
(Yorkshire Post, 1st September, 1894).

Objections were made that fees were still being paid to the Directors who were said to be in no hurry to wind up the Company's affairs. Although Turton said that he was prepared to work without fees, the other Directors were not and the meeting broke up in disorder.

The 45th half yearly meeting of the Tramways Company was held on 28th February 1895. There was no business to transact, but the meeting had to be held according to statute. The Directors, with the exception of Turton, were still receiving fees though now at half their original rate and came in for a lot of criticism. The final meeting was held on 20th May 1895 and it was agreed to wind up the Company's affairs. Of the share capital of £160,000 in 16,000 shares of £10 each, £72,000 had been repaid and a resolution was passed in favour of a further and practically final distribution of 11s. 0d. per share. The remaining surplus after liquidation proceedings was expected to be small but whatever the amount it would be distributed later. The shareholders had therefore lost almost half the money they had invested in the Company. Turton said that it was especially hard upon poor people with whom he heartily sympathised.

*"He and the Secretary (W. Wharam) had received many piteous letters. Only yesterday morning a shareholder, 79 years of age, and unable to earn a living, wrote that the earnings of a lifetime had been invested in the company". Another shareholder said "A lady shareholder, 60 years of age, had gone to him almost broken hearted. This shareholder had saved £600, and invested it in the company, but now she would have a little over one half of that sum for her future mainte-*nance. It was such cases as those which imparted a painful aspect to the winding-up of the company."
(Yorkshire Post, 21st May, 1895).

Turton was appointed liquidator and the meeting terminated with a hearty vote of thanks to him for his long service to the Company.

Upon the Corporation takeover the Company moved out of their offices in Boar Lane and took a small office on the balcony (No. 2) of the Corn Exchange. The office furniture was sold for £42 10s. 0d. on 5th February 1896 and the following day payments of £20 0s. 0d. and £35 0s. 0d. made respectively to Nelson, Barr and Nelson (the Company's solicitors) and William Wharam, their manager. These were the final entries in the Company's cash books. The Leeds Tramways Company had ceased to exist.

Turton retired from the tramway scene in Leeds but continued to take an active interest in other tramways with which he was associated. On 6th August 1900, at the age of 76, he died.

"He was an old and respected Leeds citizen. Everybody had a good word for William Turton, he was a plain speaking and plain mannered Yorkshireman, but with it all there was a quiet tone in his speech and in his demeanour which made people like him."
(Yorkshire Post, 7th August, 1900).

At the time of his death he was Chairman of the Bradford Tramways Company, Deputy Chairman of the Manchester Company and a director of the Leicester tramways, and was at one time or another up to their acquisition by Corporations, officially connected with the Nottingham, Newcastle and South Shields systems. Turton maintained to the end his businesses as a hay, straw, horse, corn and coal merchant and died a wealthy man. He had lived at Hayfield House, Chapeltown Road throughout his association with the Leeds Tramways Company, and until his death. He was interred at Chapel Allerton Burial Ground on 10th August 1900.

Kitson engine No. 18 taking in water at Wortley terminus. The trailer is Milnes car No. 13.   *Courtesy The late W. E. Cain.*

CHAPTER FOURTEEN

The Tramways:
The Period of Uncertainty 1894–5

Throughout the whole of the existence of the Leeds Tramways Company and, from as far back as 1840, the Town Council in Leeds had been under the control of the Radical or Liberal Party. This party took over the responsibility of operating the tramways on 2nd February 1894. During the purchase negotiations with the Tramways Company, the Radical Highways Committee had been trying to decide the action it would take when it took over the tramways. It was faced with two alternatives: it could operate the tramways itself or could relay the lines and lease the undertaking to a private company. Both sides of the press – the Leeds Mercury representing the Radicals and the Yorkshire Post the Conservatives – were in no doubt that the Council would be incapable of running the tramways and advocated that they be worked by a private company.

On the day of the takeover the Yorkshire Post, in a leading article, predicted "failure, odium and financial disaster" if the Corporation tried to run the tramways. Most of the Council were of the same opinion and stood by their earlier resolution of 3rd September 1890 to lease the tramways. The only municipality in Britain operating its own tramways was Huddersfield which, since 1882, had run at a loss of £29,864 which had to be met from the rates. The concern was therefore justified. Alderman Firth, Chairman of the Highways Committee, thought that the less labour the Corporation employed the better for the city. Provided they could get a responsible company to work the lines, a company that would try to meet the wishes of the Corporation as to workmen's cars, workmen's fares, service of cars, and would be prepared to work any extensions that the Corporation may construct from time to time, it would be preferable for the operation of the tramways to be in private hands.

A sub-committee of the Highways Committee was formed in December 1893 to take charge of the transfer of the tramways and the temporary working of them by the Corporation. It was also to consider the future working and mode of traction to be adopted. In spite of Alderman Firth's remarks it was obvious that if the Committee controlled the tramways until it had decided upon the system of traction to be employed, and had relaid the lines, it would be in "temporary control" of the tramways for a long time.

There were certain aspects of the tramways which worried the new Tramways Sub-Committee. It wanted to improve the tramway service throughout the city by running earlier and later cars. It was felt that workmen's cars ought to start earlier in the morning. People attending the theatre, concerts or other night entertainment

should be able to go home to the suburbs by cars leaving the town centre at a later hour at night. The repair of defective track was an urgent consideration and the Highways Surveyor, T. A. Prince, was instructed to engage a large staff to put the tramways into "reasonable repair" beginning on Monday 4th February 1894.

The Tramways Sub-Committee's first apparent concern, however, was to get rid of its responsibilities. A report was prepared and proposals made that tenders be invited by advertisement to work the tramways, beginning on 1st June 1894, when it was thought the Corporation would gain control of the Roundhay tramway. The lessees would rent 27 miles 6 furlongs 103 yards of single track and the Corporation would relay those portions which it thought necessary. The lease was to be for a term of 7, 14 or 21 years to be agreed upon. A long list of conditions was imposed which effectively put the Corporation in almost complete control of the tramways and was off-putting for prospective lessees. The Corporation retained the permanent way and freehold estates, but the lessees were required to take over everything else including rolling stock. They were allowed to charge fares not exceeding one penny per mile but no terminus or stopping place was allowed within one mile of the Briggate/Boar Lane junction. Cars had to be painted different colours depending on the route; the Corporation was not liable in case of accidents caused by any portion of the tramways including permanent way and could make any alteration to the track and charge the lessees a rental. Virtually every aspect of operation, timetables, routes, destination boards, advertisements, parcels, staff conditions, disruption due to the construction of gas, water mains etc. was covered. On the determination of the lease the Corporation refused to be under any obligation to purchase buildings, or other assets of the lessees. These were stringent conditions indeed.

The Board of Trade frowned upon the idea of municipal tramway operation and would only grant it if it was impossible for the local authority to lease the tramways to a private firm (as was the case at Huddersfield). One suspects that the Highways Committee by imposing awkward conditions were hoping that no firm would tender.

The proposal to let the tramways was strongly opposed by the Leeds Trades Council, representing the trades unionists who called upon the local authority to work the tramways for the benefit of the ratepayers and staff. They felt that it was the modesty of the Corporation which caused it to doubt its ability to run the tramways. Many members of the public and a few councillors who had suffered due to the activities of the Leeds Tramways Company, and the Corporation's inability to do anything about it, were also opposed to private operation. They contended that if the tramways could be worked at a profit by a private firm, surely the Corporation could do the same.

Following requests from the public the Lord Mayor called a meeting at the Town Hall on the night of 6th February 1894 to discuss the question of municipal or private operation of the tramways. All ratepayers were invited. The meeting was said to have been attended by 900 to 1,500 persons mainly "unemployed or working men". Speakers advocating municipal operation were cheered vociferously; those in opposition were treated with derision and the meeting overwhelmingly voted for Corporation management. The Yorkshire Post dismissed the meeting as "worthless and unrepresentative"; the Leeds Mercury said that it was an "emphatic decision for municipal management".

A meeting of the City Council was held the day after the town's meeting to discuss the question but was deferred to a special meeting of the Council on 14th February. Alderman Firth put up a strong case for leasing but some councillors, led by Alderman Baker, opposed. After a lengthy discussion the Council decided by 41 votes to 13 to lease the tramways.

In the meantime a start was made on repairing the track. The Leeds Tramways Company employed 16 men on track maintenance, but when the Corporation took over they were dismissed and replaced by 80 men who were set to work by the Highways Committee. The Kirkstall route was the first to be tackled followed simultaneously by Headingley and Chapeltown. All the work was of a temporary nature as no permanent track reconstruction could take place until the system of haulage was decided. It took two years to settle this question. The Tramways Sub-Committee found it difficult to carry out any major revisions to services but some minor improvements were carried out. It was easy to provide additional staff and horses, but engines and their drivers, cars and stabling for horses, could not be obtained at a few days' notice, nor was it desirable to add to plant which could soon be completely superseded.

The first improvement was on the Headlingley to Chapeltown through route where a 10 minutes service (in lieu 15 minutes), and earlier and later cars, was introduced on 26th February 1894. The number of through journeys per day was increased from 58 to 90. The introduction of this service, however, resulted in the withdrawal of the existing $7\frac{1}{2}$ minutes through service to the shortworkings at Hyde Park and Reginald Terrace, the two-horse cars on this service being utilised on the through route. The penny fare to Leopold Street was also abolished. Although of benefit to passengers at the outer termini, the passengers in the highly populated Hyde Park and Chapeltown Road districts soon objected. The number of passengers carried increased, but the passengers using the inner parts of the routes were crowded out of the cars. To obviate this, the Wortley steam cars, from Saturday, 10th March 1894, instead of reversing at Boar Lane, were altered to run via Briggate, North Street and Chapeltown Road to Leopold Street, giving a six or seven minutes service to Leopold Street. The fare reverted to a penny and the alteration had the added advantage that congestion at the Briggate/Boar Lane junction was reduced. The

Tramways Sub-Committee had originally intended to run steam cars through to Meanwood Road but the Manager advised against this due to the poor state of the track. The track was better in Chapeltown Road, but some repairs and alterations had to be done before the steamers could be run.

The Tramways Sub-Committee now turned their attention to the Hyde Park section and decided that from 21st March 1894 a through service between Hyde Park and Meanwood Road would be introduced. The Manager, however, said that the proposal was impractical, the Committee could not agree on the fares to be charged and no action was taken. Complaints from passengers continued and the Committee reconsidered the question. On 4th May they decided to institute a service between City Square and Hyde Park, running alternately with the through cars to give a five minutes service to Hyde Park. To avoid interruption to the through cars a spur was to be constructed in City Square to facilitate turning, and shortly afterwards the spur was inserted and the service introduced. From 11th June 1894 five two-horse cars were put on, running between Duncan Street and Hyde Park instead of three cars from City Square. There was a penny fare stage at Blackman Lane.

From 3rd March 1894 the penny fare stage on the Kirkstall route was changed from the "Beckett's Arms" to the "Cardigan Arms" and this resulted in a slight increase in the receipts. A further improvement took place on 11th June with the introduction of an early morning workmen's car leaving Kirkstall at 5.10 am. The improved services led to an increase in receipts but also extra expenditure due to the additional staff required.

The Tramways Sub-Committee also turned its attention to the 'bus services taken over from the Leeds Tramways Company. The Dewsbury Road service lost £275 during the year 1893-4 and it was decided to close it down. This resulted in protests from the ratepayers of the area, but to no avail, for the service was withdrawn on 30th April 1894. The Moortown and Adel 'bus services also lost money, but the Corporation was bound to run these (as was the Leeds Tramways Company) under the Tramways Act, 1870.

In April 1894 tenders were invited for the working of the tramways. Each tenderer had to state the motive power he intended to use and tenders were to be returned by 5th May 1894. Three were received. One was from the Thomson-Houston Company operating the Roundhay Electric Tramway, who intimated that the conditions to be imposed by the Corporation were such that it was not prepared to say what it would pay per mile for the right to work the undertaking. It was willing to extend for the Corporation or any other proprietors its Roundhay Park electric system throughout the city.

W. S. Graff-Baker, who had superintended the Roundhay tramway for the Thomson-Houston Company, submitted two offers. In the first tender he undertook on behalf of the Electric and General Contract Corporation to work the lines by electricity with overhead or underground wires at £220 per mile for 21 years on the local authority's terms. As an alternative the Company Graff-Baker represented said that if the Corporation did not insist that the existing plant be taken over and would undertake to accept the Company's plant 21 years hence, they would pay £500 per mile for the right of working.

The third offer came from Graff-Baker personally and

it was said to be a repetition of the tender of the company he was acting for with these alterations; he was willing to give £300 instead of £220 per mile on the Corporation's stipulations and £520 instead of £500 if he did not have to be saddled with the existing plant.

It was reported that Alderman Firth and his colleagues were "extremely surprised and disappointed" with this feeble response to their endeavours to get the undertaking off their hands. They were not inclined to take the tenders seriously and decided to think over the matter. No doubt it was the stringent conditions that had frightened tenderers. One of the main problems was the existing rolling stock and plant that would have to be taken over which, in all probability, would be unsuited to the form of traction to be selected by the Corporation. At a meeting of the Highways Committee on 25th May 1894 the question was discussed but no action taken. A special meeting of the Committee was held on 18th June to consider the matter further. It transpired that another offer had been received from Graff-Baker. He asked to be entrusted with working the lines by electricity, partly on the conduit system in the city centre, and by overhead wires in the outskirts. He was now prepared to work the system in the manner indicated on the Corporation's terms and to pay rent at the rate of £615 per mile of single track per annum for 21 years. The matter was discussed and consideration of the tenders adjourned pending the settling of the question of haulage. The tenders were soon forgotten. The meeting became involved with a long and exhaustive discussion on the question as to the method of haulage to adopt. Some members of the Committee favoured the cable system and the choice of this form of traction by the Edinburgh and Newcastle Corporations was cited in its favour. It was decided to visit these two towns on 25th June. The Committee was favourably impressed with what it saw in Edinburgh and it was felt that it would recommend cable haulage on one or two of the more hilly routes in Leeds. It now became bogged down with the problem of the type of traction to be employed.

Leeds had had experience of three methods of traction – horses, steam and electricity. There were many objections to the continued use of horse trams. They were very slow and, from humane considerations alone, many wanted to relieve the horses of their cruelly severe work. Steam engines were admitted to be useful in drawing heavy loads up hill, but it was thought they were an abomination to be got rid of as soon as possible. As to the overhead wire electrical system, as used on Roundhay Road, it was universally favoured both for the smoothness of running, the speed attained, and the comfortable cars; but there was just as widespread a conviction that the overhead wires were objectionable in busy thoroughfares, and it was felt unlikely that the system would be extended into the town centre. There were two other methods of electrical traction of which Leeds had no experience, viz, the accumulator system and the conduit system. There was also the cable system of traction which many spoke highly of. In finding an acceptable form of traction the Highways Committee were face-to-face with a question of no small difficulty.

The Tramways Sub-Committee decided to obtain as much experience as possible in order that a report could be submitted to the Council recommending the type of traction to be adopted. It had already visited Edinburgh and Newcastle and on 13th October 1893 had inspected the new South Staffordshire Electric Tramway using double-deck cars and the overhead system

with single traction poles. From 29th to 31st August 1894 it went over the new electric tramway running between Douglas and Laxey in the Isle of Man. This tramway used a bow form of current collection instead of the trolley and employed cut-out switches at intervals of $\frac{3}{4}$ mile, the advantage of this arrangement being that in the event of failure of the current only the section between the point of the breakdown and nearest cut-out was affected. Alderman Firth remarked that he and his colleagues were "highly pleased" with the Manx undertaking. In December 1894 Firth and the City Engineer, T. A. Hewson, visited Paris for the purpose of obtaining information on tramway traction. On their return Hewson was asked to prepare a detailed report on the various systems of traction listing the advantages and disadvantages of each and recommending a system for adoption in Leeds.

The Corporation was now growing in confidence with its tramway operations. The receipts were an improvement on those achieved by the Tramways Company – up to £150 a week more – and the press was no longer hostile. The Corporation now began to look into the question of extending the tramway system.

An obvious route for extension was the Roundhay tramway from its terminus at Horse Shoe Corner along Prince's Avenue to the Canal Gardens, Roundhay. On 7th February 1894, only a few days after the Corporation takeover, Alderman Gaunt moved at a Council meeting that the tramway extension be carried out. The extension would enable the Corporation to sell its surplus lands at Roundhay, but the level of Prince's Avenue would have to be raised 25 feet and a cutting formed prior to the construction of a tramway. This was carried out between September and October 1894 and provided work for 120 unemployed men, but the road was not finally completed until September 1895.

Street Lane was also receiving the attention of the Council. Although still rural in character there were many plans for housing. A tramway extension along this road would give a connection with Moortown and the Chapeltown tramway, forming a circle and giving an alternative access to Roundhay Park. In October 1894 the Council decided to increase its width from 36 feet to 60 feet to allow the construction of a tramway and make it "one of the finest roads in the suburbs".

In September 1894 the Tramways Sub-Committee made a series of visits to various parts of the city with a view to the construction of tramway extensions. It visited Kirkstall in response to requests that the tramway be extended to the Abbey. Many new areas of housing had been built in the city during the past 10 or 20 years and the Committee concentrated its attention on these locations. Meanwood, Armley, Wortley and Dewsbury Road were visited and also York Road where a new housing estate at East End Park had just been constructed.

At the City Council meeting on 14th November 1894 it was decided to make application to Parliament for a Provisional Order for the following tramway extensions:–

1. Horse Shoe Corner to Canal Gardens, Roundhay Park.
2. Extension of York Road tramway along York Road to Victoria Avenue.
3. Extension of Meanwood Road tramway to the Beckett's Arms, Meanwood.
4. Extension of Wortley tramway from Star Inn along Tong Road to the New Inn.
5. A tramway from the New Inn extension along Whin-

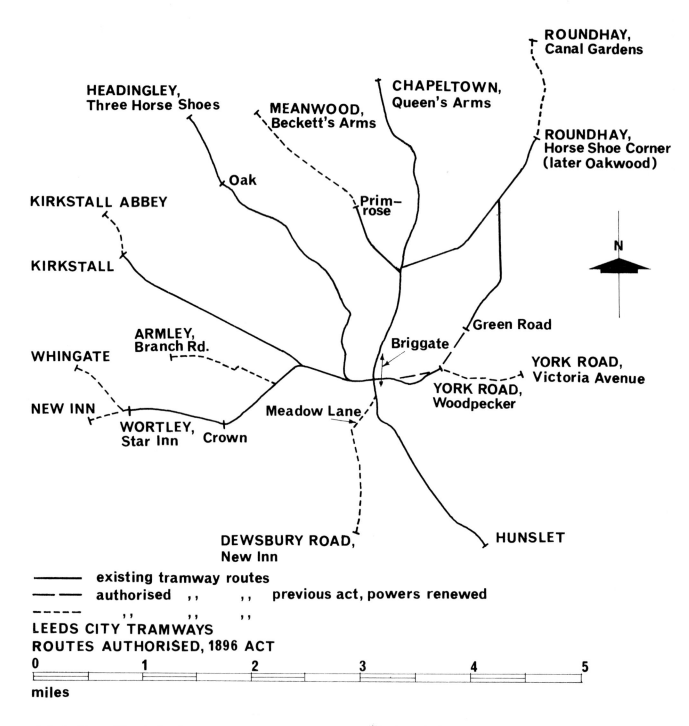

HEADINGLEY,
Three Horse Shoes

MEANWOOD,
Beckett's Arms

CHAPELTOWN,
Queen's Arms

ROUNDHAY,
Canal Gardens

ROUNDHAY,
Horse Shoe Corner
(later Oakwood)

Oak

KIRKSTALL ABBEY

Prim-
rose

KIRKSTALL

N

Green Road

ARMLEY,
Branch Rd.

Briggate

YORK ROAD,
Victoria Avenue

WHINGATE

YORK ROAD,
Woodpecker

NEW INN

Meadow Lane

WORTLEY,
Star Inn   Crown

DEWSBURY ROAD,
New Inn

HUNSLET

——————— existing tramway routes
— — — authorised ,,   ,,   previous act, powers renewed
— — — — ,,   ,,   ,,

**LEEDS CITY TRAMWAYS
ROUTES AUTHORISED, 1896 ACT**

0   1   2   3   4   5

miles

gate to Town Street, Armley.

6. A tramway from Wellington Road along Armley Road to Branch Road.

7. Extension of the Kirkstall tramway along Abbey Road to Kirkstall Abbey.

8. A line along Meadow Lane and Dewsbury Road to the New Inn, Dewsbury Road.

The Provisional Order, authorised in 1888, to build a tramway from the junction of Kirkgate and Call Lane along York Street and Burmantofts Street to connect with the Beckett Street tramway at Green Road had lapsed and application was made for renewal. A clause was inserted that the rails would not be less than 9′ 6″ from the kerb – the Board of Trade minimum.

It will have been noted that only one tramway extension was proposed in the heavily populated districts to the south of the River Aire. This was owing to the fact that all the principal roads in this part of the city were too narrow for the construction of tramways. Considerable widening and purchase of property would have to be

carried out before tramways could be contemplated. It was also a very close-knit area of working class housing and industry intermixed. Workers went to work on foot and a walk of one or two miles was not unusual. Dewsbury Road, the one southerly route proposed, was no exception and was only included in the application due to pressure from certain members of the Council. Meadow Lane and the railway bridge in Dewsbury Road would have to be widened before tramways could be built.

In the application to Parliament, authority was sought to convert all single track tramway routes to double track where the space between the rails and kerbs was not less than the statutory Board of Trade 9′ 6″. The tramway extensions proposed by the Corporation would therefore result in a big improvement to the roads in the city. Powers were also sought to erect overhead wires and poles in case electricity was adopted as the motive power on the tramways. Alderman Firth confirmed that no extensions would be carried out until the method of

A Conductor delivers a mail bag to Chapel Allerton Post Office.

haulage was agreed. The most controversial clause was one authorising the Corporation to work the lines, but it was said that the Corporation need not adopt this power. It would not stop them leasing the tramways if they so desired. The London County Council was applying for similar powers at the same time. To grant this clause the Board of Trade would have to alter its policy of forbidding local authorities to operate tramways and Imperial leave would be required if Leeds was to keep the undertaking in its own hands for good. The Corporation could, however, work the system on a yearly licence from the Board of Trade as was done with the Huddersfield tramways. To carry out the works in the Order, application was made to borrow the sum of £213,000.

A blow to the Corporation's confidence occurred in October 1894 when the City Accountant reported that during the period 2nd February to 29th September 1894 the tramways had been operating at a loss. Although the receipts had increased considerably on every route, the expenditure had grown further resulting in a deficit of £404 7s. 6d. The public, however, was not dissatisfied. Improvements had been carried out, service frequencies increased, nearly half a million more passengers carried, staff conditions and rolling stock improved, some track relaid and 31 new horses purchased.

In an attempt to recoup some of the loss, the Tramways Sub-Committee decided to penalise the Post Office! From its inception the Tramways Company had carried mail bags and in 1883 was charging the Post Office £105 per annum. This was gradually increased and by November 1891 was costing them £141 yearly. Postmen also travelled on the cars free and, due to more frequent postal deliveries, the sum paid was increased to £250 and was at this figure when the Corporation took over the tramways. From observations,

the Tramways Sub-Committee considered it totally inadequate and felt that postmen should be charged a penny per journey, which they estimated would produce an annual income of £1,000. The G.P.O. suggested that the annual payment be increased to £400, but this was rejected and the agreement was terminated by the Committee from 20th October 1894, the postmen having to pay the ordinary tram fares. Many felt that this was unfair as other tramway companies, including the Roundhay Electric Tramway, did not charge postmen, telegraph messengers or policemen. Following long discussions a figure of £500 per annum was eventually agreed in September 1895.

It was nearly a year since the Corporation had taken over the tramways and, in January 1895, the City Council and press were becoming impatient that the report on the future of the tramways, under preparation by the City Engineer, had not appeared. On 26th January the gist of the report was made available to the press and, after modifications suggested by the Tramways Sub-Committee, it was finally completed and released on 1st March 1895.

Hewson opened his report with comment on systems of motive power – compressed air, gas and oil engines – that had been used but had not proved practical for tramway purposes. He stated that the existing system of combined horse and steam power, the cable and electricity were the only forms of tramway traction calling for comparison. With a view to preparing a common basis for comparison, he reviewed the existing position of the lines in Leeds, the work of reconstruction required on them and the capital cost to the Corporation of the tramways. He compared the systems of traction, submitted estimates of cost for the installation of each, costs of working, discussed the advantages and dis-

THOMAS HEWSON, M.I.C.E.,
City Engineer of Leeds.

Courtesy "The Railway World"

ROUTES.	Miles.	Total Miles.	No. of Cars.
Headingley to Chapeltown.			17
Headingley to Boar Lane	2·965		
Length along Boar Lane	·180		
Boar Lane to Chapeltown	2·970		
		6·115	
Hyde Park to Meanwood.			9
Hyde Park to Boar Lane	1·532		
Length along Boar Lane	·180		
Boar Lane to Meanwood	1·591		
		3·303	
Chapeltown to Hunslet.			8
Reginald Terrace to Briggate	1·680		
Briggate to Waterloo Road	1·200		
		2·88	
Kirkstall to Hunslet.			14
Kirkstall to Briggate	2·980		
Briggate to Hunslet	1·950		
		4·930	
Wortley to Roundhay Road.			12
(via Beckett Street.)			
Wortley to Wellington Street	1·660		
Wellington Street to Boar Lane	·577		
Length along Boar Lane	·180		
Boar Lane to Beckett Street	·911		
(via York Road.)			
Beckett Street to Roundhay Road	1·120		
		4·448	
Roundhay to Boar Lane.			9
Roundhay to Sheepscar	2·170		
Sheepscar to Briggate	·954		
		3·124	
Total length of Car route, say 25 miles		24·800	

Cars required for ordinary service		69
Do. do. special days		7
Cars in repair		8
Total		84

A page from Hewson's Report indicating the number of cars required to run a 7½ minutes service.
Courtesy Leeds Corporation.

advantages of cable and electric traction and concluded by advising that electric traction be adopted in Leeds. The conclusion was controversial and cable v. electric traction became the big question of the day. There was long and heated correspondence in the press, the cable system being supported by Prof. Arnold Lupton, C.E. and John Sturgeon, C.E. of Leeds who advocated the adoption of the Wilson Patent Cable System. They produced their own printed report as a counter to that of the City Engineer.

The cable system was generally admitted to be the cheapest to work but was expensive to lay owing to the deep channel required between the rails. With the Wilson system the cable was laid at a depth of 6", no greater than the depth of the granite setts and would therefore be much cheaper to lay. The principal advocate of the electric system was Alfred Dickenson, engineer to the Birmingham Central Tramways Company, which operated a successful cable line in Birmingham. He considered that the Wilson System was impracticable and quoted figures showing that the South Staffordshire electric tramways cost less to run than cable traction. If the Wilson system was adopted,

Lupton and Sturgeon stood to gain £5,000 per annum in royalties from the Leeds Corporation! Dickenson was the patentee of the side running trolley pole as used on the South Staffordshire tramways and also stood to gain if electric traction was employed.

It was no secret that Alderman Firth favoured electric traction and he was accused of influencing the conclusions of the report. The comparison between the cable and overhead electric systems was said to be strained in an endeavour to make the objections to the

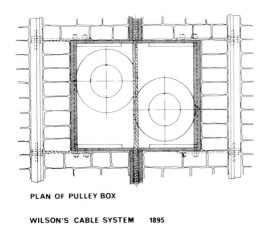

PLAN OF PULLEY BOX

WILSON'S CABLE SYSTEM 1895

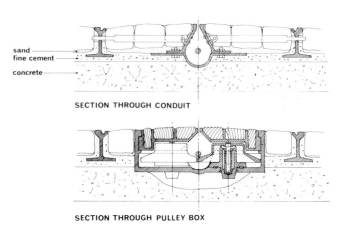

sand
fine cement
concrete

SECTION THROUGH CONDUIT

SECTION THROUGH PULLEY BOX

cable out-number those of electric traction. The Yorkshire Post was sceptical:–

"The foregoing report of the City Engineer of Leeds is very deficient in the qualities which cautious business men look for when they are asked to commit themselves to a vast and novel enterprise, the history of which has so far been little more than a history of sanguine experiment, expensive failure, and financial mystery. We should all like to have tramcars drawn by electricity, but it is useless to ask a great community to spend a quarter of a million sterling upon an experiment in electrical development at a time when it can only be done at the expense of the comeliness, safety, and convenience of its streets, when the capital expenditure may, in a few years, prove to have been half wasted, and when the working expenses may turn out to be 50% more than a less pretentious but safer, simpler, and more trustworthy form of traction. No other English municipality has been induced to even look at the scheme of overhead wire tramways for its busy thoroughfares, all of them treating it merely as an ephemeral and repulsive link in the chain of electrical development, tolerable enough as a side track in a wide Continental boulevard, or in Transatlantic cities where life and money and the amenities of civilisation are no object, but grotesquely out of place in a crowded manufacturing English city."

(Yorkshire Post, 1st March 1895)

In view of such comments, it must have taken courage on the part of Firth to stick to his conviction that overhead electric traction was the answer for Leeds. Neither the Roundhay Electric tramway or the South Staffordshire tramways had published any reliable figures as to costs and people were suspicious. The cable v. electric traction question then became conducted on party lines, the 'Leeds Mercury', and the Radicals favouring electric traction; the 'Yorkshire Post' and most of the Conservatives, the cable system.

A sub-committee of four members of the Highways Committee was formed to consider the City Engineers' Report and prepare its own report and recommendations for submission to the Council. It took six months for this to be done. The Tramways Sub-Committee was more concerned with its Tramways Bill which was having a difficult passage through Parliament.

Objections to the Tramways Bill were made by the railway, telephone and electricity companies and there were problems with the renewal of powers for the York Street and Beckett Street section as new plans would have to be submitted. There were other problems, but the main apparent difficulty was the request of the Corporation to run the tramways themselves. The Corporation did not wish to work under a licence – as at Huddersfield – which could be withdrawn at any moment by the Board of Trade, but wanted statutory powers to work the tramways without being required to let them except by a resolution of the Corporation itself. On 22nd February 1895 members of the Council had an interview with the President of the Board of Trade. It appeared that the idea in the minds of the framers of the Tramways Act, 1870, was to prevent Corporations entering speculative trading transactions which ultimately could end in a loss to the ratepayers. It was pointed out that since 1870 great advances had been made in tramways and the growth of the population in Leeds ensured success for the undertaking if carried out on business lines. At the close of the meeting it was decided that joint committees from both Houses of Par-

liament should consult on the matter. Meanwhile the "Tramways (Local Authorities) Bill" was proceeding through Parliament, the main object of which was to do away with the obstacle to local authorities working the tramways and charging fares to passengers. A decision on the Leeds Bill could not be taken until this measure had passed through Parliament. The problem that killed the Bill, however, was in connection with the proposed generating stations for electric cars. The Bill as it stood provided that the generating stations should be within a certain distance of the tramways, but the Examiners on Standing Orders at the House of Commons said that it was necessary to state definitely the actual sites proposed to be appropriated which the Corporation was unable to do. The Bill was therefore thrown out and the Corporation had to await the next parliamentary session.

A Milnes double-deck car outside "The Woodman," Headingley, about 1898.
Courtesy Science Museum, South Kensington, London, Whitcombe Collection.

What of the tramway services during 1895? Very little happened; there were no route alterations or improvements due to the shortage of rolling stock and no efforts were made to obtain additional vehicles. From 12th August 1895 the fare from Boar Lane to Meanwood was reduced from 1½d to 1d. There was also a minor alteration of fares on the Chapeltown route. Complaints were forthcoming from the public due to the apparent inactivity of the Tramways Sub-Committee:–

"On Saturday night I stood watching the traffic in Boar Lane, and I am not exaggerating when I say that at least six times as many wagonettes as cars passed me carrying passengers to Wortley at the same fares as the cars — traffic simply lost to the Corporation through lack of rolling stock to put on the lines" ———

——— *"When the Corporation took over the tramways we were promised more frequent services and lower fares. What are the facts? Some districts are, perhaps, favoured with a more frequent service, but it is at the expense of others. Hunslet used to have a five minutes service to the "Swan Junction" under the old company, but now it is only a ten minutes service. Again when the steam cars ran to Headingley there was a car carrying 60 passengers every ten minutes; there is now a car carrying 36 to 40 passengers, also every ten minutes; but whilst one could formerly travel to Far Headingley for 2d, the fare is now 3d. We also had cars to Reginald Terrace then; now they only go as far as Leopold Street, so that I don't see that we are so very much better off now than we were before the steam cars were stopped on the Headingley line. The lines were also to be put in good repair, but I fail to see much improvement in this respect"* ———— wrote "Progress".

(Yorkshire Post, 25th September 1895).

In spite of the above comments, the number of passengers carried and the receipts on the cars increased. The annual report of the Tramways Sub-Committee was published in May 1895 and showed a slight surplus over the year's working of £133 7s. 5d. During the year ended 25th March 1895, 9,489,797 passengers were carried and 1,047,133 car miles run; an improvement on the efforts of the old Tramways Company.

The report of the sub-committee appointed to consider the City Engineer's report on tramway traction was completed and a 77 page octavo volume printed. One half consisted of the report on the various systems of tramway haulage by the City Engineer and the remainder was devoted to the report of the Tramways Sub-Committee of the Highways Committee. The sum and substance of the two reports was that the Committee's preference was in favour of electric traction, on the conduit system in Boar Lane, Park Row and Briggate, with overhead wires for the remainder of the city. It was presented to a special meeting of the City Council on 15th October 1895.

In his opening remarks Alderman Firth said the Committee was faced with two alternatives: cable or electric traction. These were looked at from two stand points: the initial capital cost and the working expenses. In the case of the cable system, the initial cost would be £428,922, and the working cost £101,819, but with the electric system the initial cost was £378,490 and the annual working cost £90,072. These showed a saving in favour of electric traction of £50,432 in the initial cost and £11,747 in the annual working. In discussing the merits and drawbacks of the two systems, Firth said that in the opinion of the majority of the members of the Committee "the electric system beat the cable hollow". The residents in Roundhay Road had complained when the tramway poles and wires were erected but now there was scarcely an inhabitant in that district who objected.

One of the principal opponents of electric traction was Councillor Hannam who favoured Wilson's cable system. He moved that the question be referred back for further consideration. Alderman Scarr contended that the Roundhay Road line had converted everybody while he believed the cable system never could advantageously do anything for Leeds. He maintained that electricity ruled every other system out of existence. Some councillors advocated that the cable system be tried out on the Headingley route. Others complained of the length of time it had taken to produce the report, Councillor Tweedale commenting that "the mountain had been a very long time in labour, and had brought forward a rather unsatisfactory mouse." Complaints were made about the timing of the meeting, said to be for political purposes and within a month of the municipal elections when there could be a change of Council. The present members of the council could commit their successors to a step which was one of the most important of any they had taken.

Re-built double-deck horse car at Chapeltown terminus about 1890. *Courtesy H. Heyworth.*

Councillor Hannam's amendment was narrowly defeated and Alderman Firth remarked that the Committee was not unanimous about the conduit system and said it was intended to try a short length as an experiment. With this proviso the report was accepted by 40 votes to 11. The Council rose after a sitting of close on six hours.

At a meeting shortly afterwards, the Leeds and Yorkshire Architectural Society was not happy about the decision:–

"He was sorry to say the effect of the little that was beautiful in our streets was soon to be obliterated by the erection of poles at very frequent intervals for the overhead electric power to drive the tramcars. These, of course, would do away with the hideous steam engines at present in use, but even that would not compensate for the permanent disfigurement of an overhead arrangement and it was a great pity our main thoroughfares should be so disfigured." ———
(Yorkshire Post, 12th November 1895).

The Tramways Sub-Committee now began to show signs of action. It met on 25th October to take steps to carry into effect the resolution of the City Council. Various suggestions were made and eventually it was decided to seek the advice of Dr. John Hopkinson, one of the foremost experts in the country on electricity as a motive power. Dr. Hopkinson was to visit Leeds and advise the Committee as to the feasibility of working a service of cars by electricity from the Canal Gardens, Roundhay Park, via North Street, Briggate, Boar Lane, Wellington Street and Kirkstall Road to Kirkstall. The idea of the Committee was to extend the exisiting overhead wires from the present terminus to the Canal Gardens. The overhead wires would then be carried along North Street, New Briggate, and Briggate to the junction with Boar Lane. From this point to the "Queen's Hotel" an experiment with the conduit system was to be carried out and from there to Kirkstall the overhead system was to be employed. Dr. Hopkinson was also to advise on the location for the generating station and attended a meeting of the Tramways Sub-Committee on 30th October 1895. He agreed to make a thorough examination of the proposed route and to prepare a report for the consideration of the Committee. His appointment was subject to the approval of the City Council at its next meeting but, in the meantime, a change was to take place in the political situation in Leeds.

At this time there was a reaction throughout the country against radical policies and at the General Election of 15th July 1895 the Conservatives gained a landslide majority of 152 seats. At the local Council elections, on 1st November 1895, the Conservatives also gained control in Leeds and, after nearly 60 years, the Radicals were swept from power. What was euphorically termed the "dawn of a new era" in the civic life of the town began. The Radicals had been undistinguished in their operation of the tramways but had done the cautious groundwork on which the Conservatives were to rapidly expand and improve the tramways during the next few years.

Kitson engine No. 15 and Milnes trailer No. 41 in L.C.T. livery with another engine and trailer in the background. Although the background is blanked out the photograph is taken at Meanwood terminus.
Courtesy A.D. Packer.

Greenwood and Batley electric car No. 13 at Roundhay Park, 1898.
Courtesy R. Brook

Milnes double-deck horse car at Briggate junction with B.T.H. car No. 140 in the background, 1901.
Courtesy "Tramway and Railway World".

CHAPTER FIFTEEN

The "New Era" and Electrification 1896–1897

The new Conservative chairman of the Highways Committee was the principal opponent of electric traction, Councillor Thomas Hannam, and elected unopposed in the Mill Hill Ward was a new councillor, Robert Alfred Smithson, also bitterly against electric traction. He was elected to the Highways Committee, was later to be chairman of the Tramways Committee, and dominated the transport scene in Leeds for almost 30 years. The controversial Alderman William Firth remained a member of the Highways Committee but took a back seat and retired from the Council and politics in October 1896 when his family firm went into liquidation. He died at the age of 80 on 12th April 1917.

The first City Council meeting under the new regime was held on 14th November 1895. The appointment of Dr. Hopkinson was discussed. Alderman Firth had said that Hopkinson was appointed as he was one of the leading electrical engineers in London and was not in any way connected with manufacturers and therefore not interested in patents. A letter appeared in the press from "Roundhay Road" – presumably the Thomson-Houston Company – listing a large number of patents that Hopkinson had taken out and saying that the Thomson-Houston Company would not get "fair play" from his appointment. Dr. Hopkinson wrote saying that he would not claim any royalties and after a long discourse his appointment was approved by the Council. Also approved was the construction of the proposed Roundhay Park to Kirkstall electric tramway.

Dr. Hopkinson's recommendations were received by the Highways Committee on 8th January 1896 and in them he advised the erection of centre poles 40 to 50 yards apart on the tramway from Roundhay Road to Briggate, and from the Yorkshire Banking Company's premises in City Square to Kirkstall Abbey. In Boar Lane he recommended an installation of the Westinghouse Enclosed Conduit System. This system of electrical traction was said to be very simple but had not been put into practical operation in England. It had been successfully tried on a line of tramways in Washington D.C., U.S.A. over the previous 18 months and a large model had been working for some time in Victoria Street, Westminster, London.

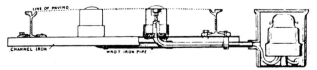

The Westinghouse Enclosed Conduit System.
Courtesy "Modern Electric Practice," 1904 Edition.

In his report, Dr. Hopkinson stated that a minimum of 16 cars with four spares would be required, and that the distance between the tramway tracks should be increased from the existing 3' 3½" to 4' 6" to allow wider cars. He mentioned that the Westinghouse System was more costly than overhead wires but less costly than conduit slots. With regard to the generating station, he suggested that this be built on Corporation land in Crown Point Road adjacent to the River Aire. This was a central site, a very important fact from the point of view of economy, and had the added advantages that condensation water could be obtained for nothing and coal could be delivered by water cheaply. Accumulators, he stated, should be placed at the most distant parts of the line, at Roundhay Park and at Kirkstall. He did not consider it practical to utilise the engines and dynamos belonging to the Thomson-Houston Company at Burmantofts, but thought that the overhead conductors could be usefully employed. He said that the cars should have two motors, each capable of developing 33 h.p. and that the series/parallel control system should be used. This system was "universally used" in the U.S.A. and latterly used on one or two cars of the Roundhay Electric Tramway. He suggested that the voltage should be the maximum that the Board of Trade would sanction – 500 volts, and estimated that £37,882 17s. 6d. would be required to finance the construction of the scheme. This sum did not include buildings, trackwork and roadworks.

Members of the Tramways Sub-Committee visited the Westinghouse Company's model tramway at Westminster on 10th January and were said to be favourably impressed. The chief feature of the Westinghouse system (later known as a "surface contact" system) was an electro-magnet arrangement underground. At road level were metal studs slightly raised above the road surface. Near the studs, but outside the track was an iron box which contained the magnetic switching gear. These studs and boxes were placed about 13 feet apart, the distance varying with the length of car. The studs were connected underground to the boxes by means of wires. The car was minus the trolley and suspended beneath were two spring contact skates mounted the same distance apart as the contact studs. The contact skates were long enough to come into contact with two studs at the same time and by means of this arrangement the car was supplied with current. Four days after their London visit the Tramways Sub--Committee inspected another type of surface contact system, mechanically actuated, known as the "Anderson Closed Circuit Electric System," on the Hunslet section of the Leeds tramways. Discussion of the trials of this system is given in a separate chapter.

The Westinghouse Company offered to put down a length of closed conduit in Boar Lane at a cost of £1,389, and, after completing it, they would allow the experiment to be continued for six months. If it proved to be unsuitable they would remove it at no cost to the Corporation. On 5th February 1896, at the following Council meeting, members were worried about the effect of the studs on horses' feet and, after much discussion, decided that Boar Lane was too busy a thoroughfare for the trial and suggested that a uniform system be adopted. There were also complaints generally about the proposed overhead system from the new Conservative councillors, led by Councillor Smithson, who opposed it from a commercial standpoint. Dr. Hopkinson, in his report, had stated that the plant of the Roundhay Electric Tramway, only four years old, was of no use in the construction of the new tramway. This was massive depreciation and the councillors were understandably concerned. Smithson asked the Council to hesitate before plunging into a speculation which would entail a capital expenditure considerably more than the figure in Dr. Hopkinson's report with no definite estimate of working expenses. The adoption of the report was referred back to the Highways Committee.

Dr. JOHN HOPKINSON, F.R.S.
Courtesy "The Railway World"

The report was discussed at the next meeting of the Highways Committee on 12th February and it was decided to adopt a uniform overhead system, using centre poles where possible, between Roundhay and Kirkstall. It was found that some streets, such as Wellington Street, were not wide enough for centre poles and side poles and brackets were suggested. These had been adopted on the new electric tramways in Bristol, where the overhead was said "in its simplicity, solidity and neatness" to be a "veritable triumph". On 24th and 25th February the Tramways Sub-Committee visited Bristol, was most impressed with what it saw, and decided to recommend the City Council to adopt the Bristol system for Leeds. Councillor Smithson was the only dissentient. In Bristol they noticed that stopping places for cars were placed at intervals of 300 or 400 yards. The tramways in Leeds had no fixed stopping places, but stopped anywhere for the convenience of passengers. This was said to be impossible with electric cars due to the wear and tear on rolling stock and consequent expense. At their meeting on 4th March 1896 the City Council approved the proposals of the Highways Committee.

During March 1896 the route from Roundhay Park to Kirkstall was inspected by the Committee. It was decided to adopt side brackets from the Canal Gardens to Sheepscar and from Aire Street to Kirkstall. Centre poles were to be used from Sheepscar to Aire Street. The installation of centre poles would necessitate the taking up of the lines and increasing the distance between the tracks to 5' 0". On 1st April the appointment of Dr. Hopkinson as the electrical engineer for the new tramway was confirmed by the Council. He was to prepare specifications and tenders for the new tramway and was to receive a commission of 5% of the total contract. The City Engineer was asked to prepare plans of the proposed power station at Crown Point, on land to be appropriated from the Sanitary Committee.

The Leeds Tramways Bill, thrown out in the 1895 Parliamentary session, and now revised slightly, passed through both Houses of Parliament and became law in 1896. The Corporation was now able to carry out tramway extensions, electrification of the Roundhay to Kirkstall route, and borrow money for the purpose. Dr. Hopkinson completed his specifications and tenders were invited. The local electricity company – the Yorkshire House-to-House Electricity Company – offered to supply electricity to work the tramways at favourable rates. The offer was declined by the Tramways Sub-Committee who felt it was better to generate its own electricity. Two years later the Corporation bought out the electricity company. Tenders were received on 22nd June 1986 and on the 26th the Tramways Sub-Committee recommended the following be accepted:–

1. Pillars and brackets; James Russell and Sons, Leeds	£3,607
2. Conduits and conductors; Greenwood and Batley, Leeds	£4,553
3. Trolley wires and attachments; Crompton and Co., London	£3,370
4. 25 electric motor cars; Greenwood and Batley, Leeds	£14,000
5. Accumulators and switches; Chloride Electrical Storage Syndicate	£1,341
6. Steam engines; Greenwood and Batley, Leeds	£3,507
7. Dynamos and switch boards; Greenwood and Batley, Leeds	£3,200
8. Boilers; Clayton and Sons, Leeds	£1,371
9. Building for generating station; J. T. Wright, Leeds	£5,815
TOTAL	£40,764

The tender for trolley wires and attachments by Crompton and Co. of London was later withdrawn and that of Laing, Wharton and Downes of London in the sum of £5,740 was accepted. The City Council was delighted that nearly 90% of the successful tenders had come from Leeds firms. Councillor Smithson, however, was not satisfied and advised that in order to save the cost of the generating station and plant, which would be useless if the Roundhay to Kirkstall experiment were a failure, the offer of the Yorkshire House-to-House Electricity Company be accepted. His suggestion was rejected by the Council.

On 21st July 1896 Councillor Hannam and the City Engineer formally began work on the extension of the Roundhay tramway to the Canal Gardens. Towler and Speight of Leeds were the contractors for this stretch of tramway. The route from the Canal Gardens to Kirkstall Abbey was seven miles but, although five and a half miles were already laid, the whole of the track would have to be lifted for either renewal or repositioning. This work was split into several contracts so that most of the paving contractors in the city had a share of the work. The trackwork in the city centre was to be carried out day and night and it was anticipated that the work would be completed in four months. Work began on the "Cardigan Arms" to Kirkstall Police Station section during the middle of August. This section was single track with passing places and was reconstructed as a double line.

John Burbridge, former manager of the Roundhay Electric Tramway, was appointed Clerk of Works for the electrical installation of the tramway for a weekly salary of £3 3s. 0d. At the same time he was also retained by the British Thomson-Houston Co. on a reduced salary of £1 per week to supervise the dismantling of the Roundhay Electric Tramway.

The new Tramways Sub-Committee was also interested in other tramway routes in the city. One of its first actions was a decision on 9th December 1895 to re-introduce the "Swan Junction" shortworking on the Hunslet tramway, giving a five minutes service to the "Swan Junction." To facilitate the turning of steam and horse cars in the city centre and reduce congestion in Boar Lane, a turning circle for steamers and a spur for the York Road horse cars was planned adjacent to the Corn Exchange. Duncan Street was to be made double track at the same time and, on 11th March 1896, the scheme was approved and constructed shortly afterwards. A reversing triangle for tramway engines was also constructed at the bottom of Oldfield Lane near the "Crown Hotel," New Wortley. It came into use on 5th June 1896. As an experiment, from 9th April 1896, the Headingley and Chapeltown routes were divided into penny stages. On the Headingley section the stages for the double-deck horse cars were Boar Lane to Reservoir Street, Reservoir Street to "Oak," and "Oak" to "Three Horse Shoes." In the case of the two-horse

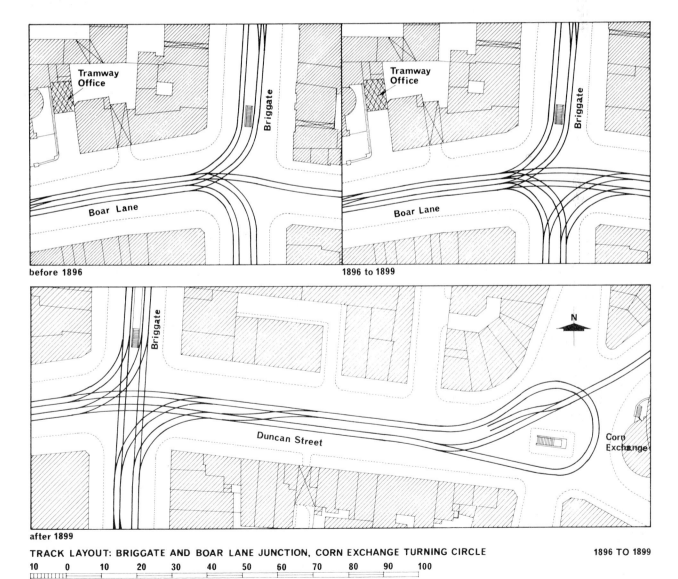

before 1896

1896 to 1899

after 1899

TRACK LAYOUT: BRIGGATE AND BOAR LANE JUNCTION, CORN EXCHANGE TURNING CIRCLE   1896 TO 1899

10   0   10   20   30   40   50   60   70   80   90   100
yards

A double-deck Milnes horse car at the "Queen's Arms" terminus, Chapeltown about 1898. *Courtesy J. Soper Collection.*

single-deck cars which did not run beyond Hyde Park, there were two stages: Boar Lane to Blackman Lane and Blackman Lane to Hyde Park. In May 1896 the Blackman Lane stage was changed to Reservoir Street. The Chapeltown route was divided as follows:– Briggate to Leopold Street, Leopold Street to Newton Park, and Newton Park to the "Queen's." The experiment was for a period of three months but was inconvenient for both passengers and crew as a penny had to be collected at each stage.

At the City Council meeting on 3rd June complaints were made about the Headingley service. Although the method of collecting fares was awkward, the alterations led to more passengers and increased receipts, with the result that people at the outer end of the route could not get on cars. It was becoming difficult to let property at Headingley. Councillor Clark "knew two gentlemen at the present time who had between them £400 worth per annum of property lying idle at Far Headingley, and the estate agents gave as the reason simply this, that people would not take houses at Far Headingley because they could not get trams to take them home."

Headingley business men were moving out to the nearby towns of Harrogate and Ilkley. It was quicker to travel 16 miles from Harrogate to Leeds by train than $2\frac{1}{2}$ miles by horse tram from Headingley to the city centre. Complaints were also made about the inadequacies of the York Road and Kirkstall services. The problem was acute and the Tramways Sub-Committee was advised

not to wait for electrification, but to purchase additional rolling stock as soon as possible. Soon afterwards the service to Headingley was improved by extending the five minutes Boar Lane to Hyde Park service to the "Oak", the fares being 1d. from Boar Lane to Reservoir Street and a further 1d. to the "Oak". Further horses were purchased.

The closure of the Roundhay Electric Tramway on 31st July 1896 caused difficult problems. From 1st August the Corporation took over operation of all the tram services in the city with the introduction of a steam tram service from Briggate to Roundhay, running every 12 minutes from 5.48 am to 11.0 pm (86 journeys daily). The fare was 2d. with a penny stage at Harehills Board School (in lieu of Gathorne Terrace on the electric cars). To serve Roundhay the steam car service to Leopold Street was withdrawn from 31st July and this resulted in immediate complaints from New Leeds and Chapeltown residents. During the previous few years the population of New Leeds had increased considerably and extensive building was taking place in the area of Harehills Avenue. The tram service between Briggate and Reginald Terrace, however, was now less than it was eight years previously – 90 journeys daily compared with 116 in 1888. On 7th September 1896 an "influential deputation" from the district attended a meeting of the Tramways Sub-Committee and said that from half to three quarters of the inhabitants of New Leeds, who used to crowd the steam cars, had to walk to and from the city. The Committee was accused of not making any contingencies pending the possible closure of the Roundhay Electric Tramway. After a fortnight spent in counting passengers, the Manager put on an extra car to Leopold Street in the morning and evening. A journey from Leeds to Chapeltown was said to be "most monotonous" and "Daily Passenger" reported:–

"A passenger cannot now, as in the past, quietly read his paper to pass away the time. I will as briefly as possible give you my experience. The car started with 14 inside passengers from Boar Lane. At the end of New Briggate the conductor came in shouting 'One penny each for the first stage.' When he had collected half a dozen pennies he passed down the car to ring the bell for a passenger to get in; he then reverted to collecting the remaining pennies. At Sheepscar two more passengers got in, and he came in again for a third collection. In giving change and collecting pennies I have seen the conductor pass up and down inside the car four times before the end of the first stage. This state of things is continued through the remaining two stages. Between the top of New Briggate and Potternewton Lane – a distance of two miles – I have seen the conductor make nine separate collections inside the car" ——

(Yorkshire Post, 19th October 1896).

At the City Council meeting of 7th October there were many complaints about "gross mismanagement," poor tramway services and the irritating system of collecting fares by stages. Some councillors pointed out that the tramways were in a state of transition and people who complained were "foolish and inconsiderate". Penny stages needed penny collections and the system protected conductors from false charges which were occasionally made against them. Alderman Scarr drew a laugh when he said there were 30,000 people in East Leeds without any tramway at all, but not a word was said about that district. He advised those who were unable to get a tram to do as he did – hire a cab.

At the Highways Committee meeting on 19th October the "obnoxious innovation" of collecting fares by stages was abandoned. In order to ease the rolling stock situation, two new steam tram engines and later some trailer and horse cars were ordered.

During 1896 many representations were made by councillors and residents to the Highways Committee for future tramway extensions. The Committee went over every suburb of the city where new tramways were suggested and some circular routes were proposed. At its meeting on 2nd October 1896 the Committee agreed that application be made to Parliament for authority to construct the following tramways:–

1. From the junction of Meadow Lane with Dewsbury Road via Meadow Road and Beeston Road to Town Street, Beeston.

2. From the junction of Elland Road with Beeston Road via Elland Road to the "Old Peacock Inn."

3. Tong Road to 50 yards past the "New Inn."

4. Oldfield Lane and Upper Wortley Road to connect the Tong Road tramway near the "Crown" and "Star Inn", (circular route).

5. From Wellington Street via Aire Street, Whitehall Road and Gelderd Road to the Cattle Market.

6. Dewsbury Road from the "New Inn" to Cross Flatts Park.

7. From Dewsbury Road along an intended new road at Hunslet Moor Road, Moor Road, Hunslet Carr, Balm Road and Church Street to join the Hunslet tramway, (circular route).

8. New Market Street, Vicar Lane and North Street when the intended widening had been carried out.

9. Infirmary Street, East Parade, Calverley Street, Great George Street, Clarendon Road, Moorland Road and Hyde Park Road to join the Headingley tramway at Hyde Park Corner, (circular route).

10. Park Lane, Burley Street, Cardigan Road and St. Michael's Road to join the Headingley tramway at the "Oak", (circular route).

11. From the intended new tramway in Cardigan Road via Victoria Road, Hyde Park, Woodhouse Street and Cambridge Road to join the Meanwood tramway, (circular route).

12. East Street, Cross Green Lane, Easy Road, Dial Street and Upper Accommodation Road to join the intended new tramway in York Road, (circular route).

At a special meeting of the City Council on 18th November 1896 the proposals were approved and application made to Parliament to construct the tramways. A large number of street widenings and improvements would have to be carried out before many of the tramways could be constructed. These included the following:– Meadow Lane, Vicar Lane, North Street, Duncan Street, New Market Street, Burmantofts Street, Meadow Road, Dewsbury Road, Beeston Road, Jack Lane, Pontefract Lane and Moor Road. Application was made for these road improvements and many others. The proposed tramway from Dewsbury Road to Hunslet Carr crossed the private land of the Middleton Colliery Company and, as this company made objections with regard to level crossings, this part of the tramway was withdrawn from the Bill. A double track had been intended in Aire Street, but following protests from property owners in the area, a single track was substituted. The "Leeds Corporation Act, 1897", which included the above extensions, became law on 6th August 1897.

The Tramways Sub-Committee was also considering which of the tramways authorised under its 1896 Act should have priority. It had already made a start on the Roundhay and Kirkstall sections and, largely due to pressure from Alderman Scarr and other councillors in the East Ward, turned its attention to the short York Road route. On 8th July 1896 the Committee decided to run a through service between Hunslet and York Road and this necessitated an alteration to the trackwork at the Briggate/Boar Lane junction. Photographs show that the track alteration was carried out but the Tramways Staff Records for 10th January 1899 contain an unusual entry concerning W. Welldon, a horse car driver:–

"When jumping his car off the lines in Duncan Street to get to Hunslet, the car came in contact with a hoarding, which is erected around a latrine, dislodging a portion of the boards. This was entirely owing to Welldon bringing the car too near the hoarding, a thing which he could easily have avoided."

(Leeds City Tramways Staff Records. Entry no. 449, 10th January 1899).

The reason for this apparently normal practice would indicate that the track connection was incomplete in some way, or there could have been some obstruction on the lines.

Suggestions had been made for some time that the fare on the York Road route be reduced from 1d. to ½d. so that the horse trams could compete more effectively with the 'buses running via York Street. The Committee

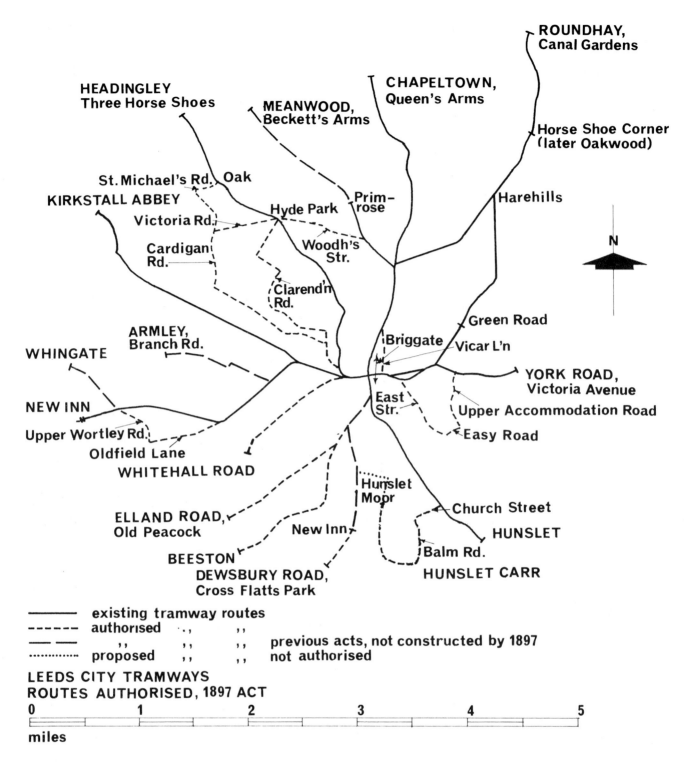

ROUNDHAY,
Canal Gardens

HEADINGLEY
Three Horse Shoes

MEANWOOD,
Beckett's Arms

CHAPELTOWN,
Queen's Arms

Horse Shoe Corner
(later Oakwood)

St. Michael's Rd. Oak

KIRKSTALL ABBEY

Victoria Rd.

Cardigan
Rd.

Hyde Park

Prim-
rose

Harehills

Woodh's
Str.

Clarend'n
Rd.

Green Road

ARMLEY,
Branch Rd.

Briggate

Vicar L'n

WHINGATE

YORK ROAD,
Victoria Avenue

NEW INN

East
Str.

Upper Accommodation Road

Upper Wortley Rd.

Easy Road

Oldfield Lane
WHITEHALL ROAD

Hunslet
Moor

ELLAND ROAD,
Old Peacock

New Inn

Church Street

HUNSLET

Balm Rd.

BEESTON
DEWSBURY ROAD,
Cross Flatts Park

HUNSLET CARR

───────── existing tramway routes
- - - - - authorised   ,,   ,,
── ── ── ,,   ,,   ,,   previous acts, not constructed by 1897
·············· proposed   ,,   ,,   not authorised

**LEEDS CITY TRAMWAYS
ROUTES AUTHORISED, 1897 ACT**

0   1   2   3   4   5

miles

obtained information from Glasgow where ½d. fares were in operation and on 12th August 1896 decided to reduce the fare for an experimental period of three months. The reduction took place from 5th September. In December it was agreed to make a start on the extension of the tramway along densely populated York Street and York Road to Victoria Avenue, a distance of about ¾ mile from the existing tram terminus at the "Woodpecker." By the end of April 1897 the section as far as the "Greyhound Inn" was completed and opened for traffic on 1st May. York Street was laid as a single line and cars travelled outwards via York Street and inwards via Marsh Lane from the same date. On 18th May a trial trip was made on the remainder of the tramway and a horse car service between Duncan Street and Victoria Avenue was introduced two days later on the 20th. The line was officially inspected by the Board

of Trade on 23rd July. The cars ran 74 journeys daily and the through fare was 1½d. with ½d. stages at the "Woodpecker" and "Greyhound".

On 22nd February 1897 a start was made on the extension of the Wortley tramway from the "Star Inn" to the "New Inn," Wortley. This was soon completed and opened for steam tram traffic on 24th April. Again the line was officially inspected by the Board of Trade on 23rd July.

Major track reconstruction was planned for the Headingley, Chapeltown and Hunslet routes and 3,000 tons of rails were ordered in January 1897. The routes were to be relaid as double track and be suitable for horse, steam or electric cars. Councillor Hannam said there was no intention of prejudging the question of electric traction. 12 steam trams would be available when the Roundhay to Kirkstall tramway was completed

124

Briggate/Boar Lane junction with part of Starbuck single-deck horse car No. 45. The tracks used by the Hunslet cars can be seen in the foreground. *Courtesy R. Brook.*

and they could be put on the routes if desired. The rails were to be bonded so that electric cars could be run if the electric experiment was successful. This was much less costly than pulling up the road and bonding them at a later date.

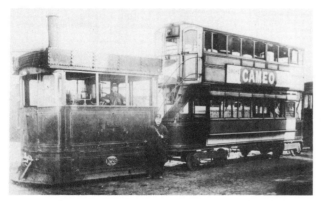

Green engine No. 26 and Milnes trailer No. 4, the first tram to "New Inn," Wortley, 24th April 1897. The Driver is George Dickenson. *Courtesy The late G. Dickenson.*

Work on the Roundhay to Kirkstall electric tramway was proceeding satisfactorily. A start was made on the erection of the power station at Crown Point during November 1896 and, at this time, the rails between Roundhay and the Canal Gardens were almost complete. On the Kirkstall route one pair of metals had been laid all the way from Wellington Bridge to Kirkstall. The first poles and brackets were erected in the vicinity of Wellington Bridge on 13th November, and the following month track relaying on the "Cardigan Arms" to Kirkstall section was completed. On 24th December the Boar Lane to Kirkstall steam trams used the new double track for the first time. A ten minutes service was worked and the through fare to Kirkstall was 2d., with a 1d. stage at the "Cardigan Arms." The Canal Gardens section was also complete apart from the connection with the existing track at the Park entrance. This work was carried out later and the first trial car ran on 22nd February 1897. At this time the tracks in Roundhay Road were being repositioned and relaid and single line working was in operation on several parts of the route. The tracks were relocated in the centre of the road, as the original position, on the north side of the road, was found to interfere with traffic travelling outwards from Leeds. It was not until April that the extension could be used by the public. The Board of Trade inspection took place on the 15th of the month, the Inspector being Major F. A. Marindin. He said he was "highly satisfied" with the tracks and the robust manner in which they had been laid and, the following day, a steam tram service between Briggate and the Canal Gardens was instituted. On Easter Monday and Tuesday (19th and 20th April), a Wortley to Canal Gardens steam tram through service was operated. By the middle of March the whole of the track between Wellington Bridge and Kirkstall Police Station had been relaid and, on the 29th, a start was made on the construction of the double track extension

125

An engine reverses around its car at "New Inn" terminus about 1900.   *Courtesy A. K. Terry.*

from the Police Station to the Abbey at Kirkstall. The reversing triangle for steam cars adjacent to the Police Station was removed. Of the 329 poles to be erected, 250 had been put up. The rails on the section between Aire Street and Kirkstall, and much of the Roundhay route had been bonded. The rails in Briggate were altered to allow a space of 5' 6" between them for the erection of centre poles.

In comparison with the work being carried out on other parts of the electric tramway, the work on the power station at Crown Point was very slow and by the middle of April was not even half finished. After strong letters from the City Engineer, the contractor, J. T. Wright, employed more brick layers and work proceeded at a greater pace. Progress was also slow in Briggate and there were many complaints. In order to ease the situation, from 4th May, until the work was finished a week or so later, all the horse 'buses were taken out of Briggate and had to operate from adjoining streets. The tracks in Boar Lane were relaid and paved in wood at the end of May and were completed in time for the Whitsuntide holiday when again, on 7th and 8th June, a service of steam trams ran between Wortley and the Canal Gardens. The Kirkstall Abbey extension was completed and on 4th June a trial trip took place, a regular service of steam trams being introduced the following day.

Work was now complete in connection with the trackwork with the exception of the relaying of track and bonding of rails in North Street, and on 9th June a start was made on this. After the City Engineer's promptings the power station was nearing completion and the two boilers were installed. The boilers were supplied by Clayton's and the steam engines and dynamos by Greenwood and Batley. The construction of the steam engines was sub-let to Fowler's of the Steam Plough Works and two engines of 400 h.p. each were fitted. The first engine was tested on 19th June and a fortnight later the two rope-driven dynamos were installed. Although the power station contained only two boilers and

dynamos, space was provided for an additional four boilers and six dynamos. The private telephone installation was moved to Crown Point. This had originally been set up by the Leeds Tramways Company in 1879. In May of that year a telephone line was laid from their office in Boar Lane to Chapeltown and Hunslet Depots, and shortly afterwards the remaining depots were connected by telephone. During 1898 the various depots and the homes of the chief officials of the Tramways Department were connected with the new Crown Point telephone exchange. In 1901 telephones were fitted to the tramway poles at each section box and this greatly facilitated communication in the case of a breakdown.

At the beginning of July 1897 a start was made on the erection of the overhead wires and, on the 7th, John Burbridge, formerly of the Roundhay Electric Tramway and Clerk of Works for the new electric tramway, was appointed Chief Electrical Engineer for the Tramways Department at a salary of £300 per annum. The electric tramway was now virtually complete.

Greenwood and Batley's had arranged to set up temporary premises in Kirkstall Road on a site, formerly occupied by a firm called Whithams, for the storage of electric cars. In January 1897 the Highways Committee agreed to contribute £100 towards the cost of the rails. £173 11s. 7d. was paid for car storage. In early July, the first two cars were delivered to a new tramway depot and works in Kirkstall Road. The depot was "far from complete" and the cars were transferred to Wellington Bridge Depot. From there, at 4.0 am on Saturday morning 17th July, one of the cars was quietly towed out of the depot by a steam tram engine. The "secret" trip, at the instigation of Dr. Hopkinson, was attended by only six other persons. The Manager, William Wharam, and Chairman of the Highways Committee, Thomas Hannam, were not present. The trolley was placed on the wires and the car made an "eminently successful" journey to Kirkstall Abbey and back. There were no hitches and the car travelled at speeds varying from 3 to 15 m.p.h. A temporary feeder cable was laid from the Crown Point power station to Wellington Bridge, as the overhead wires had not been installed on this section. The second and official trial trip took place at 5.0 am on 20th July in the presence of members of the Council and press. This time the trip was made from the new tramway depot in Kirkstall Road, and two cars were used for the trial. Two runs were made; the first from the depot to the Abbey and back and the second again to the Abbey and back to Aire Street. It was reported that there was a total absence of vibration even when the cars, "fitted and furnished in the most luxurious state," were at their highest speed of 15 m.p.h. On the 23rd July Sir Francis Marindin, formerly Major Marindin, of the Board of Trade inspected the trackwork of the route from the Canal Gardens to Kirkstall Abbey and three days later a trial run with an electric car was made over the route, the

journey, including stoppages, taking 40 minutes. On the 27th Major Cardew, the Chief Electrical Engineer to the Board of Trade, made a thorough inspection and found the line satisfactory.

At 12 noon on 29th July, with pomp and ceremony, the line was officially opened by the Lord Mayor, Sir James Kitson, Bart, M.P. Virtually all the members of the Corporation together with officials and contractors were present and a few visitors from other Corporations – Sheffield, Manchester, Bolton and the Mayor of Penzance. Those in the official party were driven in carriages to Kirkstall Road near to the viaduct, where three cars awaited them. They went first to Kirkstall Abbey then back to Roundhay and the Town Hall for lunch. Large crowds lined the route and the journey was said to be a "splendid success." Sir James Kitson joked about the tram engines which his family firm had built and Dr. Hopkinson commented that the power station was still

Kirkstall Road Works and Depot under construction in 1897.
Courtesy Leeds City Libraries.

The official opening of the Kirkstall and Roundhay tramway, 29th July 1897.
Courtesy J. Soper Collection.

Newly completed Kirkstall Road Depot with Greenwood and Batley cars Nos. 13, 16 and 12.   *Courtesy Leeds City Libraries.*

"very incomplete". He thought that the Highways Committee had been very bold in arranging the opening, but the result justified the boldness. A telegram was received from the Board of Trade stating that the tramway could be opened for public traffic. Six electric cars, accordingly, began running in passenger service on Bank Holiday Monday, 2nd August 1897, between Briggate and Roundhay Park supplementing the steam trams. The electric and steam cars ran alternately with a six minutes service, and this arrangement was repeated on the following day. The Kirkstall Road Depot and Works was sufficiently complete to accommodate the cars. The drivers and conductors, former employees of the Thomson-Houston Company, were said to look very smart in their new uniforms.

Owing to an engineers' strike at Greenwood and Batley's works, in Armley Road, only six of the 25 electric cars ordered were available for use. On 16th August the Tramways Sub-Committee yielded to pressure and ran them on a through service between the Canal Gardens and Kirkstall Abbey in conjunction with the steam trams, a ten minutes service being operated. New electric cars were delivered and the steam trams gradually supplanted. From 7th February 1898 the route was worked entirely by electric cars, the last steam tram running on the previous day. The Roundhay to Kirkstall electric tramway had to prove itself a success before any further electric lines could be constructed.

Up to this time there had been a considerable number of 'teething' troubles and breakdowns were frequent. As Leeds was the first Corporation to adopt overhead electric traction perhaps these were excusable. The "Railway World" attributed the problem to the fact that the contract for the construction of the tramway was divided among a large number of firms, there was no contractor who had overall responsibility and there

appears to have been little co-ordination between the various contractors. It was found that additional feeder cables were required, the cast iron trolley standards on the cars frequently broke and had to be replaced by standards of wrought iron or steel; the guard wires broke and there was trouble with the battery sub-stations. The "Railway World" commented that the electrical consultants, while they had theoretically mastered electric traction, had yet to acquire the practical knowledge of details which ensured complete and immediate success.

In addition to the above, 1897 generally saw a state of chaos on the Leeds tramways. There were long stretches of new track being laid in many parts of the city, services were dislocated, everything was in a state of transition and the Tramways Sub-Committee and Manager came in for much criticism. Mention has been made of the trackworks in connection with the Roundhay, Kirkstall, York Road and Wortley routes and other routes were also affected. Major reconstruction of the Chapeltown, Headingley and Hunslet routes was carried out and they were largely relaid with double track, though some stretches of single track remained on the Headingley and Hunslet routes. The rails were laid on a 9" thick concrete foundation with granite sett paving.

On 5th April 1897 work began on relaying the Chapeltown tramway from Sheepscar to the "Queen's Arms." The outer end of the route was dealt with first and the trams were gradually cut back as the reconstruction proceeded. By 3rd May the road from the top of Mitchell Hill to the terminus was out of action, not only to trams, but to other traffic as well. By 12th May the work had extended as far as Cowper Street and a temporary wagonette service was introduced over the section being reconstructed. In late May work on the Chapeltown tramway, although incomplete, ceased, and the labour

Greenwood and Batley car No. 7 at Kirkstall Abbey terminus about 1900.   *Courtesy The late W. E. Cain.*

was transferred to the Hunslet route and at the beginning of July to Headingley. Between 1,000 and 1,200 men were employed by four contractors working a 17 hour day in two shifts and these routes were soon in the same state as Chapeltown. At one stage two thirds of the Hunslet route was closed and, on 1st July, it was reported that cars could run no further than Kitsons's Works although "Whitehouse Street" was shown as the destination. By the end of July the route was completed as far as the "Swan Junction" and towards the end of August cars were able to run over the whole route.

The work on the Headingley tramway was stated by ratepayers to be a "monument to municipal incompetence." Again large stretches of road were closed and traffic was diverted via Cardigan Road. As on other routes, passengers had to walk over the incompleted sections, but between 13th September and 8th October 1897, when Cookridge Street and Park Row were relaid, a wagonette service was operated. Following the completion of the Headingley tramway on 8th October the labour force tackled the remaining quarter mile of Chapeltown Road and this was soon carried out. Horse cars ran over the completed double track for the first time on 26th October 1897, and about this time a through steam tram service between Reginald Terrace and Wortley was introduced.

The next tramway to be constructed was the new route from Kirkgate via York Street and Burmantofts Street to Green Road, Beckett Street. The route provided an alternative line to Roundhay Park and was formally opened by Councillor Hannam on 15th November 1897. A regular service could not, however, be instituted as Burmantofts Street had not been widened and this work was carried out over the next few months. Simultaneously, the laying of the new double

track extension to Meanwood was proceeding although the Corporation did not have any rolling stock for the service. They managed to run horse cars through as far as Ridge Villas in September 1897 and the trackwork for the remainder of the route was completed by the end of October. It was several months later when cars ran over the whole route.

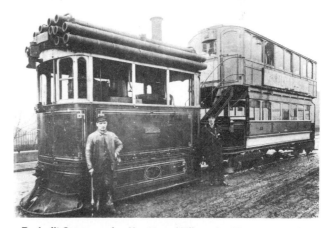

Re-built Green engine No. 12 and Milnes Car No. 26 at Wortley awaiting their return to Reginald Terrace.
Courtesy Science Museum, South Kensington, London, Whitcombe Collection.

Since the transfer of the tramways to the Corporation there were always complaints as to the management of the service. The Radicals had been criticised and so were the Conservatives. It was not that the service was more conspicuously different than it had been in private hands, but that the public expected marked improvement but did not get it. The '*Yorkshire Post*' commented that there was "little evidence of alert intelligence in the administration of the system." It added that there was hardly any limit to the development of tramway traffic in a great and thriving city like Leeds, and all that was wanted was a cheap and frequent service of cars so arranged that where the demand was greatest there would be the amplest accommodation. Penny stages had been introduced but were of little use when there was an interval of 10 or 15 minutes between the cars. People with a journey of half a mile or a mile before them would not wait about for a car with the prospect of having to fight for a seat among a crowd big enough to fill two cars. The result was that the streets were constantly full of people in whom the habit of riding had not been created. On the other hand, in towns such as Manchester and Glasgow, the tram service was frequent, rapid and cheap, and the proportion of people who rode on the trams was probably double what it was in Leeds. To take the example of the Sunday night summer traffic between Chapeltown and Headingley, the traffic between 6.0 pm and 10.0 pm was three times as great as between the same hours on weekdays, yet the same ten minutes service was operated. The result was that the cars carried about a third or quarter of the persons who wanted to ride, and the conductors were perpetually struggling to keep people off the cars. The same pattern was repeated whenever there was a cricket or football match at Headingley; the ten minutes service was worked and there were rarely any extra cars to carry the traffic. It was left to the wagonette and omnibus proprietors to provide the vehicles that the public wanted. The management argued that they could not put on rolling stock which they did not possess. The Radicals had been too cautious to "waste money" on horse and steam rolling stock which could soon become obsolete, but there is no doubt that if additional rolling stock had been purchased it would have paid for itself several times over. What was more important, the public would have had a frequent service of cars and would have been pleased with the tramways undertaking.

During 1896 and 1897 the Conservatives made great changes on the tramways and the 'Yorkshire Post' was very enthusiastic over this "gigantic enterprise.":–

"No public work accomplished by the Party of Reform during their two years of office has tended more remarkably to bring Leeds into the front rank of cities than that stupendous undertaking, the overhauling of the entire tramway system. By the relaying of miles upon miles of streets and roads, by the adaptation of electric traction to the old tramway system, by improving the cars, by shortening workmen's hours, increasing their wages, and supplying them with uniforms free of cost, by reducing fares, and effecting many minor reforms, the Highways Committee have made a contribution to the new and better epoch which, if not inclusive of all that needs to be done, is at least a pledge of what we may expect.

Green engine No. 28 and Milnes car No. 37 in the chocolate and white livery at Wortley terminus about 1896.
Courtesy Science Museum, South Kensington, London, Whitcombe Collection.

The most skilled tramway experts in the kingdom say that there is not in England a better laid tramway track than that approaching completion in Leeds, and the vigour with which this great enterprise has been pushed on will hardly be challenged. The whole of the extensions authorised by the Improvement Act of 1896, with the single exception of the tramway at Armley, where delay has arisen on account of drains, have been carried out within a year of that authority being obtained, although Parliament had allowed five years for the work to be done in."
(Yorkshire Post, 19th October 1897).

The 'Yorkshire Post' forgot to mention the Whingate and Dewsbury Road tramways which had not been started at this time. In the short space of two years the "new era" had seen big changes on the Leeds tramways, but the work had been carried out with a disregard for the needs of tramway passengers, the public and other traffic. There was disorganisation on many routes for weeks or months on end and the radical press was full of letters of complaint. Many Conservatives were also concerned at the manner in which the work had been carried out and the blame was directed to the management. The Manager, William Wharam, took the brunt of the complaints and was accused of being out of touch with modern tramway developments. The long drawn-out removal of Wharam is the subject of the next chapter.

A brand new Greenwood and Batley car No. 18 at Roundhay Park, 1898.
Courtesy "Cassiers Magazine".

Green engine No. 30 and Milnes car No. 38 in the chocolate and white livery at Meanwood terminus about 1899.
Courtesy Science Museum, South Kensington, London, Whitcombe Collection.

Green engine No. 26 and Milnes car of the same number en route to Whingate about 1900.
Courtesy The Science Museum, South Kensington, London, Whitcombe Collection.

CHAPTER SIXTEEN

Electrification:
Exit Wharam – Enter Hamilton

When William Wharam was Manager of the Leeds Tramways Company he had a relatively free hand to act on his own initiative in the best interests of the shareholders. He could make minor fare alterations and small alterations to services without reference to his Directors. He also had complete control over all matters relating to staff.

On one or two occasions he had acted in a similar manner when in the employ of the Corporation and the Tramways Sub-Committee took a strong disliking to this form of action. There had been constant criticism during the track reconstruction of 1897 as Wharam had seemed unable to surmount the problem of providing adequate alternative transport when the tramway services were disrupted and people had to walk long distances. The management situation came to a head in 1897 when, due to the "ineptitude" of Wharam, Leeds experienced its first tram strike (covered in a later chapter). At the City Council meeting on 2nd December 1897 the question of mismanagement of the tramways was brought up.

Councillor Henry said that Wharam was alright when horse traction was in vogue but was "quite out of sympathy" with the new part of the system. Wharam's style of management was a disgrace to the city and Henry advocated that a "really superior" manager be appointed. Councillor Wilson said he had nothing against the manager personally, but it was patent to all that there had been great complaints when fares had been altered without the knowledge of the Committee. Councillor Clarke said that the tramway system had developed beyond the powers of Wharam and he should be retired compulsorily or pensioned off. Things had become so intolerable that they could not continue. After further discussion the question of the General Managerial arrangements was referred to the Chairman and other members of the Highways Committee for a report. The report took a long time to appear and in the meantime the Committee turned their attention to the construction of the tramways authorised by their Act of 1897, which comprised 24 miles of single track.

In January 1898 the Committee decided to proceed with the extension of the Wortley tramway to Whingate, and to relay the Marsh Lane tramway as a single line to facilitate the inward working of the Beckett Street and Victoria Avenue horse cars. The single track and loop section from Sheepscar along Meanwood Road to the "Primrose Inn" was also to be relaid as a double line and when complete the route was to be operated by steam cars.

On 7th February 1898 a deputation from over 200 ratepayers in the Armley and Wortley area made an "emphatic protest" to the Tramways Sub-Committee against the irregular service on the Wortley tramway and asked that the line be doubled between the "Crown Inn" and "Star Inn" as soon as possible and a five minutes service operated. On the same day (7th February), the Committee placed four additional steam cars – displaced by the Roundhay to Kirkstall electric cars – on the route giving a ten minutes service from Boar Lane to the "New Inn" and a five minutes service between Boar Lane and the "Crown Inn". Additional horse cars delivered in January and February 1898 enabled the frequency of the "Swan Junction" service to be increased and, from 28th February, earlier cars were run on the Headingley and Chapeltown routes; the first car left the "Three Horse Shoes" at 7.0 am, a quarter of an hour earlier. The frequency on the Headingley route was also increased, a $2\frac{1}{2}$ minutes service running between Boar Lane and Reservoir Street, five minutes to the "Oak" and ten minutes to the "Three Horse Shoes."

The work of laying new tramways was delayed due to frost during February, but in early March the section of double track on Meanwood Road was completed and, on 13th of the month, the horse car service was extended from Ridge Villas to the "Beckett's Arms", Meanwood. 12 days later, on 25th March, the horse trams were withdrawn and a through steam tram service was introduced between Wortley and Meanwood. The Whingate extension was also proceeding satisfactorily and by mid-March was completed. It could not, however, be used until a coke shed and water supply had been installed at the Whingate terminus. This work was soon carried out and on 30th March 1898 the route was opened for steam tram traffic. The introduction of the Whingate and Meanwood steam trams resulted in the withdrawal of the through service between Wortley and Reginald Terrace and a through horse car service between the "Oak" and Reginald Terrace was introduced. At certain times in the morning and evening there was also a through service between Reservoir Street and Reginald Terrace.

Most of the property required for the widening of Meadow Lane had been removed and in late March a start was made on the construction of the tramway at Bridge End and proceeding along Meadow Lane. This was the first instalment of the new tramways to Dewsbury Road, Beeston and Elland Road and took a long time to complete. As with other routes the rails were laid on a concrete foundation and bonded for electric traction.

Between November 1897 and April 1898 Burmantofts Street was widened and on 25th April a horse car service was introduced from Kirkgate via York Street (outward) and Marsh Lane (inward), Burmantofts Street and Beckett Street to Green Road through one of the most densely populated parts of Leeds. The section of track from Green Road to Roundhay Road, closed when the Roundhay Electric Tramway ceased to run, was re-opened after nearly two years and Leeds now had an alternative tramway route to Roundhay Park. Halfpenny fares in three stages were introduced, namely, from the Corn Exchange to Green Road, Green Road to the Cemetery and the Cemetery to Roundhay Road. On the occasion of the Great Yorkshire Show held at Roundhay Park from 20th to 22nd July the whole of the available steam tram fleet (23 cars) was run on a special service from Wortley via Beckett Street and Harehills Road to Roundhay Park. This appears to be the only occasion that steamers traversed the route.

In March 1898 additional electric cars were delivered and this enabled the frequency of the Roundhay to Kirkstall service to be increased to five minutes between the "Cardigan Arms" and Harehills Lane and ten minutes between Kirkstall Abbey and the Canal Gardens. The electrical experiment was proving a success and the Highways Committee began to give serious consideration to the extension of the system. The electric cars were receiving an increasing patronage from the public and the residents from other parts of the city were clamouring for electric traction. Costs were submitted to the Committee and showed that for a sample week (the week ending 26th March 1898), the surplus per car mile on the electric cars was 2. 06d. At a special meeting on 26th April 1898 the Tramways Sub-Committee decided to recommend the extension of the overhead electric system to Chapeltown, Headingley, Hunslet and also to the new Meadow Lane and Dewsbury Road tramway in course of construction.

The 'Yorkshire Post', previously violently opposed to overhead electric traction, was still doubtful, and felt that the Committee should wait another six months before making a decision. While acknowledging that electric cars were a mechanical success, handsome, comfortable, travelled at an "exhilarating" speed and had lighting of "dazzling brilliance", it considered the Committee "bold and adventurous men". At the City Council meeting on 5th May Councillor Hannam predicted a "gigantic profit" and the proposed extension of the electric system was adopted. The Highways Committee lost no time and, four days later, decided to appoint Dr. Hopkinson as consultant electrical engineer under the same terms as were agreed for the Roundhay to Kirkstall tramway, and a sub-committee was set up to work in conjunction with Hopkinson.

The electric cars were fitted with attachments for trailers and in late 1897 a number of trailer cars were purchased and used in connection with the electric cars at busy periods. These placed considerable strain on the power station. Whereas one engine was adequate for normal use, trailer operation needed two engines, and, if a breakdown occurred, the electric service would have to be suspended. To obviate this problem, and also to provide power for the new extensions to the electric system, tenders were invited in June 1898 for further engines and dynamos of about 1,000 h.p. each. Tenders for 50 new electric cars were also invited. Greenwood and Batley Ltd. of Leeds submitted the

lowest tender for the two engines and dynamos – £15,586 – and Dick, Kerr and Co. of Glasgow, for the cars at £468 10s. 0d. each. The generating station also required extending and tenders of £4,083 from Isaac Gould of Leeds for building work and £830 from Clayton Son and Co. for steelwork were accepted. The Committee was not happy with the specification of the motors proposed for the new cars. The motors were of the Walker type. This motor was untried in Britain and the Committee refused to accept Dick, Kerr's tender. The tender of the British Thomson-Houston Company at £531 per car was accepted. In September 1898 tenders for poles in the sum of £5,058 from James Russell and Sons and £4,248 for overhead work from the B.T.H. Co. were accepted.

Greenwood and Batley car No. 20 and trailer No. 98 at Kirkstall Abbey about 1899.
Courtesy R. F. Mack.

Saturday, 27th August 1898, saw the tragic death of Dr. Hopkinson in a climbing accident in the Alps. Hopkinson's firm, later re-named Hopkinson and Talbot, continued with the consultancy.

One of the results of the inauguration of electric traction in Leeds was the introduction of stopping places for cars. In the horse and steam days, trams stopped anywhere for the convenience of passengers and it was normal for cars to stop at intervals of about 20 yards on some busy routes. With electric traction it was impossible to keep to a proper timetable with this system. There was also a wastage of current. From 1st September 1898 a system of fixed stopping places was introduced on the Roundhay to Kirkstall tramway. Attached to the tram poles or lamp posts were enamelled flag plates bearing the words "STOPPING PLACE FOR ELECTRIC CAR". The stopping place idea was found to work very well and was introduced on the remainder of the tramway system from 21st October 1898. The stops for the horse and steam cars were indicated by painting a lamp post white and these vehicles observed the electric car stopping places between Sheepscar and Wellington Bridge.

Meanwhile, by May 1898, the whole length of the Meadow Lane tramway had been laid and a start made on the construction of the section from "New Inn", Dewsbury Road, towards the city. The following month tramway construction began on the Beeston route beginning at the terminus and, in July, the Elland Road, Cambridge Road and Woodhouse Street to Hyde Park lines were started. Work, however, soon ceased on Dewsbury Road, Beeston and Elland Road as the

LEEDS CITY TRAMWAYS.

FIXED STOPPING PLACES.

Commencing FRIDAY, OCTOBER 21st, 1898, Tram Cars will only stop to take up or put down passengers at the places named below, which are indicated by the Lamp Posts being painted WHITE.

Horse and Steam Cars will observe the same stopping places as the Electric Cars between Wellington Bridge and Sheepscar.

CHAPELTOWN.	HEADINGLEY.	MEANWOOD.	WORTLEY.	HUNSLET.	YORK ROAD.	BECKETT STREET.	ROUNDHAY.	KIRKSTALL.
○ Briggate Terminus	○ Boar Lane Terminus	⊗ Briggate Terminus	⊗ Boar Lane Terminus	⊗ 24, Duncan Street	⊗ Call Lane Terminus	⊗ Call Lane Terminus	⊗ Briggate Terminus	○ Boar Lane Terminus
⊗ Commercial Street	⊗ Albion Street	⊗ Commercial Street	⊗ Albion Street	⊗ Duncan Street (Briggate End)	⊗ "City Arms Restaurant"	⊗ "City Arms Restaurant"	⊗ Commercial Street	⊗ Albion Street
⊗ Upperhead Row	⊗ Royal Exchange	⊗ Upperhead Row	⊗ "Queen's Hotel"	⊗ Briggate Terminus	× Harper Street	× Harper Street	⊗ Upperhead Row	⊗ "Queen's Hotel"
× Merrion Street	× Bond Street	× Merrion Street	⊗ King Street	× Swinegate	⊗ Duke Street	⊗ Duke Street	× Merrion Street	⊗ King Street
× Hartley Hill	× Bank of England	× Hartley Hill	× G.N.R. Station	× Meadow Lane	× Brick Street	× Brick Street	× Hartley Hill	× Great Northern Railway Station
× "Smithfield"	⊗ Great George Street	× "Smithfield"	⊗ Queen Street	× Great Wilson Street	× Plane Street Siding	× Plane Street Siding	× "Smithfield"	⊗ Queen Street
× Skinner Lane	× Top of Cookridge Street	× Skinner Lane	⊗ Wellington Street Depôt	Black Bull Street	⊗ "Woodpecker"	⊗ "Woodpecker"	× Skinner Lane	⊗ St. Philip Street
× Wintoun Street	× Carlton Hill	× Wintoun Street	⊗ Armley Road	× Leathley Road	× Edgar Street	× Edgar Street	× Wintoun Street	⊗ "Junction"
× "Golden Cross"	× Blackman Lane	× "Golden Cross"	× Canal Street	× 171, Hunslet Road	× Accommodation Road	× Great Garden Street	× "Golden Cross"	⊗ "Beckett Arms"
⊗ Sheepscar Police Station	⊗ College Road	× Crawford Street	⊗ Spence Lane	× Accommodation Road	× York Rd. Baptist Chapel	× Nippet Lane	⊗ Sheepscar	× Kennedy Street
× Barrack Street	× Bagby Road	⊗ Meanwood Street	× Skilbeck Street	× Goodman Street	⊗ "Greyhound"	⊗ Green Road	× "Queen"	× Ventnor Street
⊗ Leopold Street	× St. Mark's Street	× Sackville Street	× Havelock Street	× Larchfield Street	× Green's Farm	× "Beckett Arms" Siding	× "Prince Arthur"	⊗ Willow Road
× Francis Street	⊗ Reservoir Street	× Cambridge Road	⊗ "Crown"	⊗ Swan Junction	× Ivy Lodge	× Museum Terr Siding	⊗ Spencer Place	× Wellington Road
× Cowper Street	× Rampart Road	× Oxford Road	× Chapel Siding	⊗ Balcombe Street Siding	⊗ Victoria Avenue Terminus	× Glebe Street Siding	⊗ Gathorne Terrace	⊗ "Cardigan Arms"
⊗ Reginald Terrace	⊗ Hyde Park	⊗ "Junction Hotel"	× James Street Siding	⊗ Church Street	MARSH LANE.	⊗ Ashley Road	⊗ Whitfield Street	× Burley Mills
× Sholebroke Avenue	× Cumberland Road	⊗ "Primrose"	× Strawberry Lane Siding	× New Pepper Rd. Siding	⊗ Market	× Bayswater Grove Siding	⊗ Harehills Board School	⊗ Burley Wood
⊗ Newton Park	× Buckingham Road	× Horsfield's Tannery	× Wesley Road	× Pepper Lane	× Harper Street	× Elford Terrace	⊗ Harehills Road	× 387, Kirkstall Road
⊗ Bottom of Newton Hill	× Spring Road	× Clifdale Road	⊗ Thornhill Road	× Spring Grove Place	× East Street	× Banstead Street Siding	⊗ Harehills Lane	× "George Hotel"
× Potternewton Lane	⊗ "Oak"	× Oakdale Terrace	⊗ "Star"	⊗ Thwaite Gate Terminus	⊗ Duke Street	× Lowther Street	⊗ Gipton Lodge	⊗ Co-operative Stores
× Depôt	× North Lane	× Ridge View Terrace	⊗ Whingate Junction		× Mill Street	⊗ Harehills Road Terminus	× Harehills Avenue	⊗ Kirkstall Police Station
× "Mexbro' Arms"	× Shaw Lane	× Boothroyd's Mill	× Barden Street		× "Old Red Bear"	MARSH LANE.	⊗ Gledhow Wood Road	× Tordoff Place
× Dr. Carter's	× Burton Crescent	× Bentley Lane	⊗ "New Inn" Terminus		⊗ "Woodpecker"	⊗ Market	× "Gipton"	⊗ Kirkstall Abbey Terminus
× Cross Roads	× Cottage Road	⊗ "Beckett Arms" Terminus	WHINGATE.			× Harper Street	⊗ Gledhow Lane	
× Regent Street	⊗ "Horse Shoes" Terminus		⊗ Whingate Junction			× East Street	× Section Box	
× Short Lane			× Whingate Road			⊗ Duke Street	⊗ Canal Gardens Terminus	
⊗ "Queen" Terminus			× Aberdeen Walk			× Mill Street		
			⊗ Whingate Terminus			× "Old Red Bear"		
						⊗ "Woodpecker"		

NOTE.— ⊗ Denotes places at which all Cars stop.
× Denotes places at which Cars will stop if required.

Tramways Office, Leeds,
October 13th, 1898.

W. WHARAM,
Manager.

railway bridges in Dewsbury Road and Meadow Road were not wide or strong enough for tramcars. The bridge in Armley Road, Castleton Bridge, was also unsuitable. Complete renewal was required and, in October 1898, the Highways Committee made an agreement with the Midland Railway Company for the reconstruction of the three bridges to a width of 50 feet, the Corporation to pay £5,000 towards the total cost.

The Cambridge Road and Woodhouse Street tramway ran through a densely populated working class district and was completed by the end of October 1898. On the 28th a trial car ran over the line and, on 3rd November, the route was inspected by Sir Francis Marindin of the Board of Trade. The licence for the operation of steam trams in Leeds was on the point of expiration and Sir Francis also inspected the various routes on which steamers ran. On 20th November the Woodhouse Street line was opened for traffic and this resulted in a reduction of service on the Meanwood route. Steam trams had run every ten minutes to Meanwood but, due to a lack of rolling stock, this was now reduced to 20 minutes. A 20 minutes service also ran to Hyde Park via Woodhouse Street. The steam cars ran through to "New Inn" and Whingate and operated in rotation as follows:–

Whingate to Hyde Park.
Hyde Park to "New Inn".
"New Inn" to Meanwood.
Meanwood to Whingate etc.

A few days after the opening, the fares on the Meanwood and Woodhouse Street sections were modified by making the second penny stage on the Meanwood route between the "Primrose Inn" and the terminus into two halfpenny stages, the stage being at Ridge Villas. From Briggate to the Woodhouse Street end of Cambridge Road, a penny was charged and from there to Hyde Park a half penny.

No other tramways were constructed during 1898, but a problem which took much of the Tramways Sub-Committee's time was an application by a private company to build a tramway from the proposed tram terminus at Armley to Thornbury in Bradford. This was known as the "Leeds and Bradford Light Railway".

The light railway was brought to the attention of the Corporation in October 1897 when a preliminary notice of a Bill to be presented to Parliament to connect the tramways of Leeds and Bradford was submitted. It was said that the light railway was not intended to compete with or be a rival of either the Leeds or Bradford undertakings, but was to be a feeder to the tramway systems of the two cities. It was to be double track, 4'-8½" gauge, and be worked on the overhead electric system. The line was to be 5 miles 3 furlongs and 3 chains in length and was to cater for both passenger and goods traffic and a seven minutes service was contemplated. The promoters were the Power and Traction Co. Ltd. of London, the engineers A. and W. Hopkins, and the solicitors, Addyman and Evans of Leeds. On 16th November 1897 a sub-committee of the Parliamentary Committee was appointed to consider the proposed Bill and, at the City Council meeting on 1st December, it was instructed to oppose the scheme. After its experi-

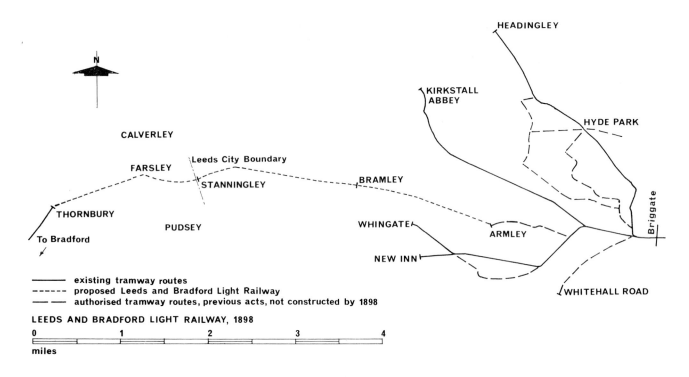

LEEDS AND BRADFORD LIGHT RAILWAY, 1898

0   1   2   3   4

miles

ence of the Leeds Tramways Company the Council was not prepared to let a private company run over its streets.

The Bradford Corporation was also opposed to the scheme but the local authorities through which the line would pass, Calverley, Farsley and Pudsey District Councils, were in favour. At a meeting at Leeds Town Hall on 4th January 1898, the Leeds and Bradford Councils decided to act jointly in their opposition to the light railway and, the following month, Leeds announced that it proposed to extend its own tramways to the boundary of the city at Stanningley. On 17th February 1898 a meeting of the Light Railway Commissioners was held in the Leeds Town Hall to consider the scheme and hear the various points of view. After the promoters had stated their case for the line, the Leeds representative said that if the portion of the scheme within the Leeds city boundary was withdrawn, Leeds would have no objections, but were in "absolute opposition" to any attempt to construct tramways within the city boundary. Bradford Corporation similarly objected and contended that the application of the promoters did not come within the scope and spirit of the Light Railways Act which was intended to relieve distressed agricultural districts, small fishing communities, etc. The Chairman of the Commissioners said that the need for the proposed line had been established, but the objections of the two Corporations would require very serious consideration.

In March 1898 the Commissioners forwarded a letter to Leeds stating that, in view of the fact that the Corporation proposed to extend their tramway from Armley to Stanningley, they were unable to recommend an order giving the promoters any powers within the city. They were, however, prepared to grant to the promoters an order for the construction of a tramway between the Leeds and Bradford boundaries. The promoters suggested a conference with the two Corporations but this was rejected and they then suggested to the Commissioners that the Corporations should be given a time limit to construct the tramways within their respective boundaries and if they failed the Company should be granted powers, working arrangements being left entirely to future agreement.

A shock move was made by Leeds in October 1898 when it was announced that application was to be made to extend the proposed Armley tramway, not to Stanningley as was originally suggested, but to the Bradford city boundary at Thornbury over the route of the light railway. This caused consternation, not only to the light railway promoters, but also to Bradford Corporation, who were said to be "unpleasantly surprised" at the move which was made without reference to the Bradford authorities. Bradford, therefore, decided to lay a counter application before Parliament for the extension of their tramway from Thornbury to Stanningley.

The Light Railway Commissioners were now faced with three conflicting applications. Since the two Corporations had proposed their own schemes, the light railway promoters revised their application for the construction of a tramway in the urban districts of Pudsey, Farsley and Calverley only. The Farsley and Calverley authorities, however, objected to the reduced scheme as it was felt that they would not have direct access to either Leeds or Bradford. It was suggested that the three authorities should construct the line through their districts and then lease it to the Leeds and Bradford Corporations, but this idea was not taken up. Meanwhile, Bradford held talks with the private syndicate and reached a provisional agreement with the promoters that they would purchase from the syndicate any concession they obtained so far as the section of the proposed line from Bradford to Stanningley was concerned. They were to withdraw all opposition to the private Bill. This was said to be done with a view to giving easy access to Bradford for the people of Stanningley, Farsley and Calverley. Access to Leeds, however, would not be as easy as, under the agreement, the gauge of the proposed light railway was to be altered to the Bradford gauge of 4'-0". The Farsley and Calverley Councils suggested that the tramway be jointly constructed by the Leeds and Bradford Corporations, but this did not receive much support.

In February 1899 the Commissioners stated that they had sanctioned the scheme of the private syndicate, including the clause giving the power to construct and work the line between Bradford and Stanningley to

136

Bradford Corporation. Bradford then dropped its own application to build the line. To become operative the scheme had to receive the sanction of the Board of Trade, and Leeds declared that it would appeal against the confirmation of the order. On 19th April 1899 a Board of Trade inquiry was held in London, where Leeds was accused of a "miserable piece of jealousy" and a "dog in the manger" attitude. Counsel for Leeds was bitter that the agreement between Bradford and the private company had been negotiated "behind the backs" of Leeds Corporation. Following the Inquiry the Board of Trade said it would suspend the Provisional Order and refer it to Parliament for a decision. From 10th to 12th May, before a Government Parliamentary Committee, the Leeds representatives proposed a joint working arrangement using a third rail for a through service. Bradford, however, objected saying that this system was "inconvenient". After lengthy consideration, the Committee came out in favour of Bradford, Leeds being given authority to build a line as far as Stanningley only. 18 months later, on 16th November 1900, Bradford formally opened its tramway extension from Thornbury to Stanningley.

The work of administering the tramways was proving too much for a sub-committee of the Highways Committee and at the City Council meeting on 9th November 1898 it was decided that a separate Tramways Committee be appointed. Councillor Hannam remained Chairman of the Highways Committee and Councillor Smithson was elected Chairman of the new committee. At the same time, due to the decline of the private horse 'buses and wagonettes, the Hackney Carriages Committee became a sub-committee of the Watch Committee.

The new Tramways Committee turned its attention to the management question. After an initial burst of enthusiasm in January 1898 when the Tramways Sub-Committee visited Glasgow, the question had lain dormant. In Glasgow they had been impressed with the system of halfpenny stages, the use of punched tickets and the two minutes service in operation in the town centre and, as has been seen, introduced halfpenny stages on some of the Leeds routes. In February and March 1899 discussions took place with regard to the appointment of a Traffic Manager to assist Wharam. The constantly growing traffic was said to be too much for one man and the Traffic Manager was to take charge of the outdoor work concerning the routes and services leaving Wharam with the indoor administration. Wharam drew up a specification of the duties for a Traffic Manager and, on 30th March, the Tramways Committee decided to advertise for a suitable person to take complete control of traffic in connection with the tramway service "comprising 180 cars, electric, steam and horse, and over 50 miles of single track." Within the last three years the number of cars and car mileage had doubled, the traffic trebled, and a Traffic Manager was certainly needed. He was to be appointed by the Tramways Committee and subject to dismissal by them. Wharam was to remain in charge of the general management of the office, responsible for the accounts, cash, correspondence, claims, stores, provender, supervision of the stables, depots and rolling stock etc.

The City Council meeting on 5th April 1899 was rather poorly attended due to the Easter holidays and the Radical party found itself in the majority. The meeting rejected the idea of a Traffic Manager and recommended that a man be appointed to have overall control of the

tramways. There would be friction between the Traffic Manager and Wharam, who was to be compulsorily retired. Councillor Smithson, however, appears to have got on well with Wharam; there had been few complaints during 1898 and he said that Wharam "had done well for the Committee and safeguarded their interests." On 24th April the Tramways Committee reconsidered the matter, the Radical members saying that Wharam should resign as a result of the Council vote. The Conservative majority, however, stuck to their earlier decision to appoint a Traffic Manager. Wharam had been silent throughout this controversy, but he now made a statement to the Committee and press which makes interesting reading:–

"If I resign my position I shall acknowledge that I have not done my duty, or that I have not done what any other man could have done. Further than that, I should be admitting that the complaints that have been made of mismanagement were justified. I altogether dissent from those views. On the other hand, I claim that I have done an immense amount of work that the Committee has never seen or known of, and has consequently not credited me with it.

Nothing definite has been pointed out as mismanagement, therefore I have had no chance of explaining or defending myself. The public who are very ready to complain, see every little hitch that occurs in the streets, but, considering the number of passengers carried (about 22,000,000), the complaints are not so numerous. But the public and, I fear, many members of the Corporation also, have no idea of the difficulties the Tramways Manager has to contend with ——

Many of our engines are the oldest in the country, and all, except the last four, have been written off in depreciation, and two of these four have only two years to run before they are written off, while the others are being written off a second time. This seems almost absurd, but it is a good financial position as regards the engine stock ——

I have also had to provide and fit up stabling for 218 horses, besides all other things in connection therewith, and the only help I have had has been that of the late Chairman, whose practical knowledge assisted me very much. Just over a year ago complaints were made of the condition of the steam bogie cars, but it was not explained, nor generally known, that the paint shop had been turned into a stable for horses, and that the cars had never been under cover night or day for four years. There is now a good paint shop, and most of the steam cars have been thoroughly repaired and repainted, and, unlike the engines, many of them are in first rate condition, although they have every one been entirely written off in depreciation, and are going on for the second time; and the same applies to many of the horse cars.

The office accommodation, too, was, and is yet, miserably inadequate, and the wonder is that in such surroundings the enormously increased business has been carried on so well ——

I must bow gracefully to the fact which has been referred to that I am not young, while at the same time I cannot be too thankful that in bodily vigour and capacity for business I feel equal to a great many men very much younger."
(Yorkshire Post, 25th April, 1899).

At the City Council meeting on 3rd May the proposal to advertise for a Traffic Manager was confirmed. Wharam was defended by Smithson and others and his defence was helped by the publication of the tramway accounts for the year ended 25th March 1899 which showed a net profit of £12,000. There were 60 applicants for the post of Traffic Manager and the Tramways Committee's choice fell, by a narrow majority of ten votes to nine, on 40 years old William Robert Spaven, the Chief Inspector of the Leeds City Tramways. He had started work as a conductor with the Leeds Tramways Company in 1879 and ten years later became Chief Inspector. It was his local knowledge that swayed the vote in his favour. Smithson was opposed to Spaven and wanted new blood, but Hannam, now an alderman, was in favour of "an old servant who has been in the service of the tramways for 20 years, and against whose character there was absolutely no stain." Spaven's appointment was approved by the Council and he was to administer the traffic very competently. Complaints of mismanagement disappeared.

Following the success of the Roundhay to Kirkstall tramway, Smithson was now converted to electric traction. One of the first actions of his Committee was a decision to electrically equip the Beckett Street and York Road tramways. The idea was to operate a through service from Thwaite Gate, Hunslet, to the Canal Gardens, Roundhay, via Duncan Street, York Street, Beckett Street and Harehills Road. The materials for the electrification of the Hunslet and Dewsbury Road routes were to hand but neither route could be proceeded with due to the construction of a large sewer on the one hand and the railway bridge on the other. The materials were to be transferred to Beckett Street and York Road and it was hoped that the work would be completed by July 1899, the anticipated completion date of the Headingley and Chapeltown electrification.

The battery stations used on the Roundhay and Kirkstall line were not working very satisfactorily and for the new electric routes it was decided to install boosters worked directly from the power station. They were much more economical than battery stations. The boosters, new switch boards and gallery were ordered from Greenwood and Batley Ltd. at a cost of £5,330.

The Committee also turned its attention to track improvements. Whereas the tracks on the Chapeltown route had been doubled during the summer of 1897, this had only partly been done on the Hunslet and Headingley routes. On 12th December 1898 it was decided to double the line between Pepper Lane and Thwaite Gate terminus and, three months later, the section between the "Swan Junction" and Church Street, on the Hunslet route. In January 1899 it was agreed to double the track from Spring Road to the crown of Headingley Hill. The doubling of the Headingley Lane line was, however, delayed, due to the high price asked for land required for the road widening. Harehills Road, originally laid as a single track through open countryside, became built up and the road was widened during the middle 'nineties. In January 1899 a decision was made to double this section, sufficient space being left between the tracks to allow centre poles to be adopted, and the work, including the erection of poles, was carried out in the first three weeks of February. During this period the horse car service along Harehills Road was suspended, but was resumed on 25th February.

In February 1899, a start was made on the erection of the tramway poles on the Headingley and Chapeltown routes, 186 poles being used on the Headingley and 100 on the Chapeltown section. By mid-March they had been erected and underground cables for the boosters were laid at the same time. A decision to double the track in Tong Road had been made in December 1898 and, on 13th March 1899, work began on this, was completed and the route re-opened for traffic in mid-April.

The work of electrification of the Headingley and

Starbuck car No. 31 passes another double-deck car at Headingley "Oak" shortly before electrification, 1899.
Courtesy A. K. Terry.

Chapeltown routes was progressing very well and on 17th June 1899 a trial run was made on the section from Boar Lane to Headingley "Oak". The experiment was an "entire success" and the gradients were climbed in "admirable style". However, work on the power station was delayed due to a dispute in the building trade and non-delivery of the engines and dynamos from Fowler's and Greenwood and Batley's, and it was to be another six months before a regular passenger service could be operated. On 27th June the Boar Lane to "Three Horse Shoes" section was inspected by Sir Francis Marindin and, on the occasion of the England v. Australia cricket test match at Headingley, a special electric car service was run. 12 to 15 electric cars were used, running a two minutes service from City Square to Headingley, in conjunction with the horse cars. Electric cars are recorded as running from 27th June to 1st July, 8th July, 24th to 26th July, 25th and 26th August 1899, prior to the operation of a regular electric car service to Headingley.

In January 1899 a double track tramway was laid in Victoria Road, but the connection with the Woodhouse Street tramway at Hyde Park was not made for some months later. Sir Francis Marindin inspected the line at the same time as Headingley and passed it for service. On 29th June steam cars began to run via Woodhouse Street to the bottom of Victoria Road, supplementing the Headingley test match "specials", as the terminus was only five minutes walk from the Cricket Ground. Victoria Road was a middle and upper class residential area and the inhabitants did not take kindly to the steam cars. There was a fear that property would be devalued through their operation and there were many complaints to the press and Council. The Tramways Committee took immediate action by removing the early and late cars on the route, but could not put on the horse cars requested. Rolling stock and horses would not be available until the inauguration of the Headingley and Chapeltown electric service.

From 3rd to 13th September 1899 one of the "most intricate pieces of tramway work in the country" was carried out, namely, the relaying of the Briggate/Boar Lane junction. The radius of the curve between Boar Lane and Briggate was increased from 45 feet to 60 feet and tracks provided connecting Briggate with Lower Briggate thus forming a north/south through connection. The tracks from Boar Lane to Lower Briggate, formerly used by the Hunslet to Kirkstall through horse tram service, were removed. It was said that an important feature of the new layout was that a car arriving there could continue to any point without the need for reversing or shunting. During the alterations, the Kirkstall and Wortley cars turned in Boar Lane; the Headingley and "Oak" cars in City Square; the Chapeltown, Roundhay, Meanwood and Victoria Road cars in Briggate and the Hunslet cars in Lower Briggate.

The financial report for the year ended 25th March 1899 showed that the total receipts for the Roundhay and Kirkstall electric cars were £48,032 15s. 0d., the mileage run 934,368 miles and the receipts per car mile 12.33d. The cost per car mile was 4.90d., excluding interest on loans and sinking fund charges which were roughly estimated at about 2½d. per mile, thus leaving a margin of slightly over 5d. per mile as profit, subject to deductions for depreciation and renewals. The receipts per car mile for steam cars were 11.08d. and cost 10.33d. The horse trams lost money, the receipts being 9.80d. and cost 10.17d., and this was largely due to the smaller carrying capacity of the vehicles. It was estab-

lished, beyond doubt, that electric tramways could be worked at a substantial profit and the Tramways Committee could, without hesitation, extend the method of traction to other branches of the system.

In September 1899 the Committee decided to hold a special meeting to ask the Council to sanction the electrification of the remaining tramway routes. The consulting engineers, Hopkinson and Talbot, were asked to consider the proposal to extend the system of electric traction to the following lines:– Vicar Lane; Beeston Hill; Elland Road; Whitehall Road; Wortley; Armley and Stanningley; Woodhouse Street and Victoria Road; Meanwood; Park Lane; Burley Street and Cardigan Road; and Hunslet Carr. The total route length was 17 miles and the tramways were the remainder of those being worked by horse and steam, lines in course of construction, or to be constructed under powers already obtained. Their electrification would involve a capital outlay of £160,000 and the engineers recommended that a total of 200 electric cars would be required. Of this number, 75 were in the possession of the Corporation, or on order, and tenders for a further 50 cars had been invited in August 1899. Hence, a further 75 cars were needed. Two additional sets of generating plant, each of 750 kw, were required and, in spite of problems which had been experienced on the Roundhay and Kirkstall tramway, the consultants recommended that additional battery stations be provided to cope with variations in load which occurred in everyday running.

At the City Council meeting on 4th October 1899 the Committee's proposals for electrification were passed without opposition. A question was asked about the Clarendon Road tramway, authorised under the Act of 1897, which was not included in the list of tramways to be constructed. Smithson said that there were difficulties owing to an awkward curve and steep gradient and added that the Park Lane tramway, near to and almost parallel with Clarendon Road was soon to be built. It was later admitted that the Clarendon Road tramway was hastily conceived, a "silly mistake" and "perfectly ridiculous" as a tramway route, both as regards gradients and the "scantiness of the population". The residents of Clarendon Road had not pressed for the line and, by resolution of the Council in August 1902, the powers for its construction were allowed to lapse.

Orders for 50 fully equipped electric cars were placed with Dick, Kerr and Co. of London at a cost of £550 each and two months later, in December, the order was increased to 100 cars.

Work was proceeding slowly on the extensions to the power station at Crown Point. There were labour troubles and the manufacturers of the generating plant were pressed with orders from all parts of the country. On 19th October 1899 Major Trotter of the Board of Trade made an electrical inspection of the Headingley and Chapeltown tramways. Sufficient current could be generated to enable an occasional car to run, but until the new plant was installed there could be no regular service and passengers had to be content with the horse cars. By the end of November it was said that the new engine at the power station was in working order, but it was to be another month before electric cars could run.

The long promised day, 3rd January 1900, arrived when a through ten minutes service of electric cars between Headingley and Chapeltown was inaugurated. A through service was also worked between the "Oak" at Headingley and Reginald Terrace giving a five minutes service to the two short workings. 11 cars ran between the outer termini and eight served the short workings. Cars ran from Briggate from 5.0 am to 11.05 pm to Headingley and to 11.02 pm to Chapeltown, and 20 minutes later on Saturday evenings. Residents in the neighbourhood of the "Oak" were now able to get a car home as late as 11.20 pm on weekdays and those at Reginald Terrace 11.27 pm. This was of benefit to people attending places of amusement in the city who previously had to crowd into small horse cars, the last of which left at 11.0 pm. Another benefit was the reduction in the fare from Briggate to the "Three Horse Shoes" from 3d. to 2d. with a penny stage at Hyde Park.

The introduction of the electric cars led to the release of 28 horse cars and 333 horses and a reorganisation of existing services. Coincidental with the start of the electric service, horse cars started to run on the new Dewsbury Road route. The Dewsbury Road tramway beyond the railway bridge to the "New Inn" and Cross Flatts Park had been laid for 18 months and, during the summer of 1899, the section from Meadow Lane to the railway bridge was laid down. The bridge was still incomplete and passengers had to walk over, transfer tickets being issued to all going beyond the bridge to the "New Inn". The "New Inn" to Cross Flatts Park section was opened later. The fare was 1d. and the service ran through in two directions; one set of cars running via Briggate to Victoria Road, Headingley, replacing the hated steam trams and the other to Meanwood also replacing the steamers. Cars ran to Victoria Road and Meanwood every 15 minutes and hence from Dewsbury Road to Cambridge Road there was a $7\frac{1}{2}$ minutes service. These re-arrangements resulted in a surplus of steam cars and, after repair, some were used to augment the Wortley service. From 29th January 1900, others were employed on a new tramway from Duncan Street via Armley Road to Castleton Bridge. During the period from 3rd to 29th January there was some disorganisation for the steam tram drivers and 11 were laid off work. The section of tramway beyond Castleton Bridge to the Armley terminus at Branch Road was completed and, on 30th April 1900, a horse car service was instituted running a 15 minutes shuttle service, in connection with the steam trams, from the bridge to the terminus.

Progress was being made with the electrification of other routes and on 12th April 1900 Colonel Yorke, of the Board of Trade, inspected the York Street, Beckett

Street, York Road, Dewsbury Road and Armley Road tramways, and also a new line which had been constructed in North Street, Vicar Lane and New Market Street. This line was intended to relieve congestion in Briggate by running the Dewsbury Road to Meanwood and Victoria Road through services this way. The track was, however, only regarded as "temporary" and was part single line as the road had not been widened.

On 24th April 1900 an electrical inspection of the York Road and Beckett Street tramways was made by Major Trotter of the Board of Trade. The imminent introduction of electric trams led the Tramways Committee to reconsider the question of halfpenny fares on the two sections. The halfpenny fares were causing a "heavy loss" and several members of the Tramways Committee recommended that they be abolished. The proposal was referred to a Sub-Committee to sort out. On 14th May the Sub-Committee met and it was said that when the cars were crowded in the morning and evening the halfpenny stages paid, but during the day there were few passengers. To pay halfpenny fares required a constant stream of passengers as was the case in Glasgow and some other large towns. It was decided that the three halfpenny stages on Beckett Street be discontinued and a 1d. fare be charged from Call Lane (Corn Exchange) to the end of Harehills Road. On the York Road line the experiment was to continue for six months after electrification with two halfpenny stages; Corn Exchange to Accommodation Road and Accommodation Road to the terminus.

Whit Saturday, 2nd June 1900, saw the introduction of electric trams on the Beckett Street section. Normally five cars ran from Corn Exchange via Beckett Street to Roundhay Park, but from 11.0 am this was increased to seven cars giving a ten minutes through service. On 6th June the York Road electric service was introduced, cars running every 15 minutes from 5.15 am to 11.30 pm.

In May 1900 work on the Dewsbury Road railway bridge was well advanced and from the 21st of that month horse cars were able to run over the bridge for the first time. On 14th June a trial run was made with an electric car. It went off very satisfactorily; the journey from Duncan Street to the new terminus at Cross Flatts Park took 17 minutes and, as this was the first electric car in the south of the city, it received a hearty welcome from the crowds gathered along the route. The regular service began on the following day, a five minutes service operating from Duncan Street to the "New Inn" and a ten minutes service to the terminus. The fare was 1d. for the two and a half miles journey, said to be "the cheapest ride in the city." The route was double track through a working class area as far as the "New Inn", with a sparse population from there to the terminus. There was a temporary single track over the bridge for a short time but this was doubled when the bridge was completed. The Meanwood and Victoria Road horse cars ceased to run through and now started from the Corn Exchange.

The inauguration of three electric routes within a fortnight resulted in a surplus of horse cars and some of these were utilised on a new tramway from City Square to the top of Cardigan Road which was opened on 18th June 1900. Construction of the City Square to Cardigan Road tramway via Infirmary Street, East Parade, Park Lane and Burley Road had begun in the summer of 1899. It was partly double and partly single track with passing places; construction had been leisurely. The Park Lane and Burley Road sections were the first to be

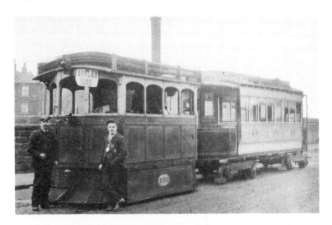

Kitson engine No. 10 and Starbuck car No. 60, converted to single-deck, at Castleton Bridge in 1900.
Courtesy Science Museum, South Kensington, London, Whitcombe Collection.

Milnes double-deck horse car No. 95 at Meanwood terminus, 1900.   *Courtesy D. W. Thwaites.*

laid down and, in April 1900, rails were laid in front of the Town Hall. A junction was laid into Calverley Street on the route of the abandoned Clarendon Road tramway. The reason is uncertain and perhaps there were second thoughts. It was removed about 1909. The laying of the tramway was said to be "difficult work" owing to the gradients of the route. The line passed through a densely populated fairly new residential lower middle class area in Burley Road and graduated to a middle or upper middle class district of large villas at the top of Cardigan Road. A 20 minutes service from City Square to the terminus was operated with a ten minutes service to the bottom of Victoria Road. The horse cars on the Corn Exchange to Victoria Road via Vicar Lane, Meanwood Road and Woodhouse Street service were extended from the Corn Exchange via Duncan Street and Boar Lane to City Square, thus forming the first of several circular routes which were planned. The through fare from City Square to the terminus at Cardigan Road was 2d., with a 1d. stage at the "Burley Hotel." There was a 1d. fare from the "Burley Hotel" to Hyde Park, via Victoria Road, on the circular route.

The Hunslet horse cars were the next to succumb to electric traction. The Hunslet tramway had suffered delays for a considerable time due to sewerage operations along the route. During the later part of 1899 Low Road had been partly closed and a temporary horse 'bus service operated. In February 1900 it was announced that horse cars could now run through, and shortly afterwards work began on electrification. On 20th August 1900 a trial run of an electric car took place and the route was opened to the public on the 24th. A 1d. fare was charged for the 3,515 yards journey to Thwaite Gate from the Corn Exchange. A ten minutes service was operated to Thwaite Gate with a five minutes service to the "Swan Junction" short working.

The following day, 25th August, the horse cars displaced by the Hunslet electric cars began to run on the new Beeston Hill and Elland Road routes. In October 1900 the five minutes service was extended to Thwaite Gate.

Probably no district of Leeds was looking forward to the introduction of tramways more than the popular and growing suburb of Beeston Hill. In anticipation of improved facilities for reaching the town, the neighbourhood was growing fast. From 1891 to 1899 the area on the Leeds side of Beeston Hill had entirely changed and

Electric car No. 143, a single-deck horse car and steam car at the Briggate/Boar Lane Junction, 1899. Trinity Church is in the background.   *Courtesy A. K. Terry*

141

now the Beeston side of the hill was being developed. Rows of streets, mostly of "superior working class" dwellings with occasional blocks of terrace houses and semi-detached villas were built. In 1899 a start was made on the development of the area beyond Cross Flatts Park and on the north side of Beeston Road, beyond the Common, housing was spreading towards the old village of Beeston. Coal mining was carried out in the area and new industries had sprung up in the late 'nineties. These areas had been inaccessible to the horse 'bus because of the 1 in 9 gradient of Beeston Hill, and their development was solely due to the promise of electric tramways.

By November 1899 both the Beeston and Elland Road tramways had been laid, but could progress no further until the railway bridge in Meadow Road was reconstructed, and Meadow Road itself sewered and widened. From 15th October 1899 traffic over the bridge was stopped, and a circuitous diversion via Jack Lane was operated. The bridge was partly re-opened in January 1900, but road works in Meadow Road continued to cause serious disruption. The Beeston Hill horse 'bus was withdrawn on 28th July 1900 and, from then until the horse trams began running, the Tramways Committee operated a combined electric car and wagonette service over the route. Special electric cars were run as far as the Dewsbury Road junction and passengers then transferred to a wagonette; a ten minutes service being run. On 25th August 1900 the

Meadow Road bridge was not complete and for a few weeks horse cars ran to the bridge, passengers walking across and connecting with horse cars on the other side. The cars ran to the "Duke of York", Malvern Road (the old horse 'bus terminus) and "Waggon and Horses", Elland Road. The Elland Road tramway was extended to the "Old Peacock" on 8th September 1900, the fare being 1d. from Briggate. It is recorded that a horse tram ventured up Beeston Hill as far as the Park Gates on a trial run, but, as far as is known, this was the only occasion.

In March 1900 orders were placed for an additional three engines and dynamos of a much larger type for the Crown Point generating station. The following month the Tramways Committee decided to electrify the Beeston, Elland Road, Meanwood, Woodhouse Street, Burley Road and Cardigan Road routes. These routes, however, could not be electrified until the new equipment was installed in the power station. It was reported in February 1901 that the work was "well in hand", and by the beginning of March at least one of the engines was in working order. The engines were of the cross-compound type direct-coupled to generators each giving 1,060 h.p. They were supplied by the Electric Construction Company at a cost of £10,149 each. The original rope-driven 400 h.p. engines and dynamos were sold, the larger engines occupying less space and being more economical. The two 1,000 h.p. engines supplied in 1899 were also of the cross-compound type

Dick, Kerr car No. 196 at Bridge End about 1901. The Hunslet 'bus is in the background. *Courtesy P. D. Johnson.*

direct-coupled to generators. In 1902, a 330 h.p. generator, direct-coupled to a steam turbine, was acquired from Messrs. Parsons for the sum of £2,613. This was principally used for lighting car depots etc. after midnight. In 1902, therefore, the total plant capacity was 5,510 horse power.

In January and February 1901 standards and overhead wires were erected on the Beeston route and, on 13th March, a trial run was made by the Tramways Committee over the Beeston and Woodhouse Street lines. On 18th March 1901 a service of electric cars was introduced over the whole length of the Beeston tramway and a through service was worked with Victoria Road via Vicar Lane, North Street, Meanwood Road and Woodhouse Street. Although the trams at first ran via Corn Exchange and Vicar Lane this was soon discontinued due to the width of New Market Street. A double track was laid but the clearance was only 18″ between the rails and kerbs, acceptable for slow moving horse trams, but dangerous with electric traction. The single track at the top of Vicar Lane and North Street was disconnected when the access track to North Street Depot was removed in November 1901. New Market Street was widened and electric cars resumed running via Vicar Lane on Good Friday 28th March 1902.

A 20 minutes service was operated to Beeston terminus, ten minutes to Park Gates and five minutes to Malvern Road. The fare was 1d. to Park Gates and a further ½d. from there to the terminus at Town Street. Later in 1901 a spur was laid into Lady Pit Street to facilitate the turning of the Malvern Road cars. On 4th April 1901 Major Pringle of the Board of Trade rode over the Beeston, Woodhouse Street, Elland Road and Meanwood routes for the purpose of fixing compulsory stops and speed restrictions on the gradients in accordance with the Board of Trade regulations. The introduction of electric traction on these routes led to a surplus of horses and cars and many were auctioned on 24th and 25th April. The electrification of the Elland Road and Meanwood routes was delayed as the Tramways Committee wanted its horses to be in top working condition immediately prior to the sale.

On 19th April 1901 the electric car through service between Elland Road and Meanwood, via Briggate, was introduced, cars running from Briggate to Meanwood every ten minutes from 4.47 am to 11.27 pm, and from Briggate to Elland Road every 20 minutes from 5.7 am to 11.27 pm. The fares were as formerly, except that there was a halfpenny fare between Ridge View Terrace and Meanwood terminus.

The horse trams were rapidly disappearing and their demise was near when the Burley Road and Cardigan Road section succumbed to electric traction on 3rd August 1901. This was the first electric car circular route, cars running to and from City Square via Park Row, Cookridge Street, Woodhouse Lane, Victoria Road, Cardigan Road, Burley Road, Park Lane, East Parade, and Infirmary Street. There was a ten minutes service in both directions, with a penny fare stage at the "Burley Hotel". A ten minutes service also ran via Burley Road to the top of Cardigan Road. The Victoria Road cars running from Beeston via Woodhouse Street were cut back to Hyde Park. 80 horses were released as a result of the electrification of this route and they were sold on 14th August 1901.

Castleton Bridge in Armley Road was completed in June 1901 and from the 13th of that month steam trams ran through to the terminus at Branch Road, replacing

the horse tram shuttle service running between the bridge and terminus. A 1d. fare was charged from the Corn Exchange to Branch Road, a distance of 3,561 yards. This was one of the cheapest rides in Leeds, being bettered by only two other routes: Briggate to Hyde Park, via Woodhouse Street, 3,770 yards for 1d. and Briggate to Cross Flatts Park, 3,581 yards for the same fare.

Looking down Branch Road to the Armley terminus; the only known photograph of a steam tram in this location. *Courtesy J. Soper Collection.*

One horse tram route was left running between the Corn Exchange and Whitehall Road. Construction of the Whitehall Road tramway had begun during the latter part of 1900 and was of double track throughout with a short single track section in Aire Street. It ran through an industrial area with factories and warehouses on each side with some residential development adjacent to the Cattle Market at the terminus. It used the horses and cars released by the electrification of the Beeston and Woodhouse Street routes and opened for traffic on 22nd March 1901.

In December 1900 the Tramways Committee had agreed to electrify the Whitehall Road tramway, the remaining steam tram routes to Armley and Wortley and the proposed extensions to Stanningley and Oldfield Lane. Hopkinson and Talbot were instructed to prepare specifications for the work. The first route to be completed was Whitehall Road. Horse trams ran without ceremony for the last time in Leeds on 13th October 1901. The new electric car service began the following day and was "much appreciated". It ran from the Corn Exchange every 15 minutes from 5.15 am to 11.15 pm with a 1d. fare.

Some widening of Oldfield Lane and alteration to Great Northern Railway bridges over the proposed tramway had to be carried out before the line from the "Crown Inn", New Wortley to Dixon Lane could be built. This work was undertaken during the latter part of 1900, and construction of the single track and loop tramway began in early 1901. The steam tram reversing triangle at the "Crown Inn" was removed and the route was opened for steam trams on 31st August 1901. The tramway traversed a working class residential area with a park on the south east side and was very welcome to the inhabitants as this area had no previous horse 'bus service. The fare from the "Crown" was ½d. and a service from the Corn Exchange to Oldfield Lane was operated, cars leaving Duncan Street from 4.25 am to 11.5 pm.

Meanwhile, in June 1901, a start was made on the

electrification of the Wortley routes. The work could not, however, progress owing to the height of the railway bridge over Wellington Road, which was too low for electric cars. The road was lowered under the bridge during November 1901 and the route, including the "New Inn", Whingate and Oldfield Lane branches, was electrified from 10th January 1902.

Dick, Kerr car No. 259 stands at the "New Inn" terminus shortly after electrification in 1902.
Courtesy A. K. Terry.

The Bramley and Stanningley tramway was laid during the summer of 1901, 700 men being employed on the work and, by the beginning of October, it was said to be almost completed. A successful trial trip was made as far as Town Street, Bramley, on 25th October 1901, but a regular service could not be operated as there was no steam rolling stock available. The electrification of the Wortley group of routes released rolling stock and, from 10th January 1902, the displaced steam trams were transferred to the extension of the Armley tramway from Branch Road to the "Daisy Inn", Bramley. A few weeks later, on 2nd March, the steam car service was extended to run through to the terminus at Stanningley. The route was the longest in the city – 5¼ miles – and there were penny stages, at Branch Road, and at Elder Road, Bramley. Electrification of the route had been progressing steadily and, on 27th March, a trial trip was made with two electric cars over the whole route. The trial "evoked the greatest interest among the residents on the route, cheer after cheer greeting the passengers". After congratulatory remarks from the Lord Mayor, it was announced that steam trams would run for the last time on 1st April 1902, Easter Tuesday. On 1st April there was no formal ceremony, but it was said that on Monday and Tuesday thousands of people went by tram to Bradford via Stanningley. The Leeds public had had their last ride on a steam tram.

What had electrification of the Leeds tramways achieved? A revolution in the lives of the inhabitants occurred. In comparison with horse and steam traction, electric trams provided a quick, comfortable and clean service, were more economical to operate and provided a much better profit. In the annual period ended 25th March 1902, the net profit was £48,241 5s. 11d., whereas in the same period ended 25th March 1895, when horse and steam trams were solely employed, there was a net profit of only £133 7s. 5d. Staff wages and conditions of working were vastly improved and fares were cheap. On some routes it was possible to travel two miles for a penny, and on certain routes half-penny stages were in use, although, as has been stated already, it was considered that these were not financially viable. Fixed stopping places were introduced and electric traction led to considerable suburban expansion. Good examples were in the Beeston and Roundhay areas which were neglected prior to electrification and, later, electric tramway routes led to further suburban expansion and ribbon development on routes through rural areas. Cheap tramways encouraged the population to move out of the inner city areas, reducing overcrowding, and there was an important effect on leisure and recreation which could now be more easily enjoyed. Later cars led to an increased use of theatres and places of entertainment in the city. Roundhay Park, Kirkstall Abbey and other places of recreation were now easily accessible and well patronised at weekends. The roads upon which the trams ran had to be of a prescribed width and this led to many road and bridge improvements which assisted the passage of other traffic. Virtually all the roads in the city, particularly to the south of the river, were improved owing to the introduction of the electric tram.

A side effect of the new system was the introduction of electric lighting to the streets of Leeds. On the section of tramway between the Dispensary in North Street, Briggate, Boar Lane and Wellington Street, to the Great Northern Railway Station, 40 electric arc lamps were fastened to the tram poles and, on 22nd December 1897, were ceremoniously switched on. The lamps were fed from the tramway electrical supply and were a big improvement on the old gas lamps. The improved lighting soon spread along other tram routes in the inner city area.

The most important result of the improved and cheap transport was that people who had previously walked had now adopted the habit of riding on a tramcar. During the first year of Corporation operation the number of passengers carried was 9,489,797. For the year ended 25th March 1902 it was 48,273,300, a considerable increase which included passengers who had travelled on the former horse 'buses, most of which had been withdrawn by this time. The average number of journeys per head of population per year in 1894-5 was 25.6 and by 1901-2 it had increased to 112.2, a percentage increase of 337. This was to increase still further with improvements effected by a new General Manager over the following years.

On 1st April 1902, coincidental with the abolition of steam traction in Leeds, a new General Manager, John Baillie Hamilton, took office. William Wharam had been asked to tender his resignation to make way for the younger man and, on 20th January 1902, the Tramways Committee received his letter of resignation.

"It has been represented to me in a manner to which I take no exception that on account of my age and the projected great extension of the tramway system, it is desirable that the Corporation should consider the question of future management. Looking at the matter from that same standpoint, I am not much inclined to disagree with that view. Therefore if it should be the wish of the Corporation that I should retire, I shall be glad if they will kindly give me some intimation as to the time and the conditions they propose. I may just mention that on 1st March next, I shall have held my position with the Leeds Tramways Company and the Leeds Corporation for 29 years." ——

(Yorkshire Post, 21st January, 1902).

WILLIAM WHARAM,
Manager of the City of Leeds Tramways.

The Committee accepted Wharam's letter and said that his resignation would take effect from 31st December 1903. Wharam was to continue in office until the new General Manager was appointed and afterwards to give assistance as and when required.

The Tramways Committee was impressed with Hamilton during its visits to Glasgow where he held the post of Traffic Manager, and invited him to accept the post of General Manager in Leeds. This he did at a salary of £900 per year – twice Wharam's salary. Hamilton was 46 years of age and was to make big improvements and changes on the Leeds Tramways. These are the subject of the next volume of this story of Leeds transport.

The post of General Manager was not advertised and the Traffic Manager, William R. Spaven, apparently took umbrage and, in the same month as Hamilton's appointment, he became manager of the Portsmouth tramways.

William Wharam lived at 41 Sholebroke Avenue, Chapeltown Road, and had caught the tram daily to work from 1874. On 24th February 1903 he briskly walked to Reginald Terrace and caught the 7.30 am tram to town. He was a little breathless and when the car had reached Louis Street the conductor, Bradbury, noticed he was gasping and, within a minute or two, he was dead.

"In his official capacity Mr. Wharam was always a strong disciplinarian. In private life he was the personification of geniality, and he counted his friends by the score. His death occurred from heart failure. For some

A festive scene in Boar Lane at the end of the Boer War in June 1902 with cars Nos. 267, 45 and 12. No. 267 bears the name W. Wharam on the rocker panel.

Courtesy Pickards, Leeds.

time past, however, his appearance has been that of a man with many years of active life before him. ——

His good constitution was doubtless due to his love for all outdoor pursuits, and in this connection it may be recalled that as a youth he was a capital skater and athlete. He leaves a widow and two sons, one of whom is a veterinary surgeon and the other an electrical engineer." ——

(Yorkshire Post, 25th February, 1903).

Wharam was 68 years old and probably the only tramway manager to die on one of his tramcars – perhaps a fitting end.

MEANWOOD. 430.

Ex-trailer car No. 130 converted for electric traction at Meanwood terminus about 1903. *Courtesy R. Brook.*

CHAPTER SEVENTEEN

The Buses: Seventies and Eighties, Turton and Walker

To continue with the story of the 'buses: by 1870 most services had late Saturday evening 'buses and some late journeys during the week. None, however, left Leeds or the suburbs before 8.0 am in the morning, the earliest being the 8.10 am from Beeston Hill. 'Buses from two of the outlying villages, about 12 miles from Leeds: Boston Spa (two 'buses at 8.0 am) and Bramham (one 'bus at 7.30 am) left at an earlier time. There had been some reductions due to competition, but fares were still high and the 'bus remained a middle and upper class form of transport.

The population of Leeds had increased from 207,165 in 1861 to 259,212 in 1871 and this was reflected in a similar expansion of the 'bus services. As areas of the town became built up, a need for a 'bus service arose and, as a result, the 'bus position in January 1870 was quite different from that in 1860. The Guiseley and

Rothwell services which were running in 1860 had ceased to operate, but other 'bus routes were instituted elsewhere. The Yorkshire Railway Guide No. 1 of January 1870 lists the following suburban services in operation:–

Adel, (Newsome); Armley, (Jackson); Bramley, (Jackson); Burley to Beeston Hill, (Coates); Burley and Kirkstall, (Jackson); Burmantofts to Beeston Hill, (Coates); Chapeltown, (Ramsden and Turton); Headingley, (Emmott, Ramsden and Turton); Hunslet and Sheepscar, (Turton); Hyde Park, (Ramsden and Turton); Meanwood and Woodhouse Carr, (Farnell?); Moortown, (Turton); New Leeds, (Turton); New Wortley, (Turton); Roundhay and Scarcroft, (Machan); Seacroft, (Mallinson); Weetwood, (Farnell?); Whitkirk and Garforth, (Coates).

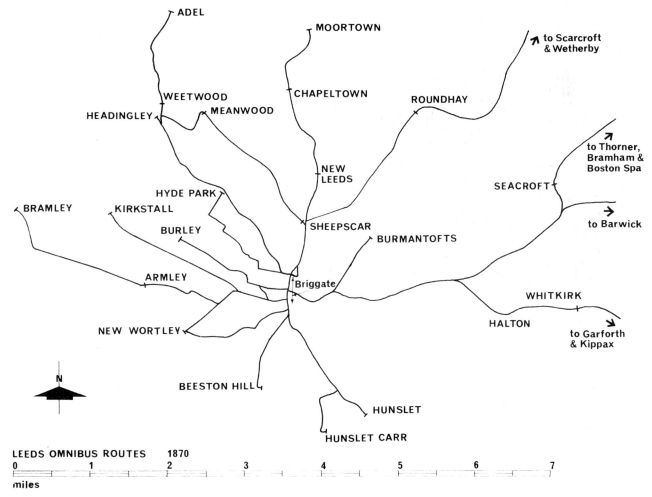

LEEDS OMNIBUS ROUTES 1870

In addition there were 'bus services to the outlying villages of Barwick, Boston Spa, Bramham, Kippax, Thorner and Wetherby.

These services made a total of 175 departures from Leeds daily, (198 on Saturdays), a big increase on the 29 departures of 1860. The busiest routes were Hyde Park, 24 departures, and Headingley with 23.

In the 'seventies and 'eighties there were many changes due to tramway competition. Several of the 'bus routes ceased to operate, but an intense network of short 'bus routes, frequently only a mile or so long, was built up to serve the heavily populated inner suburbs. They sometimes competed with the busiest sections of the tramway routes, charged low fares (usually 1d.), gave the Tramways Company many problems, but also provided transport which came within the pocket of the ordinary working man or artisan.

Of the various proprietors running 'buses in 1870 some did not continue long due to tramway competition. Jackson and Farnell have been mentioned in a previous chapter and John Ramsden retired from the scene in 1871. Ramsden never made such a success of the 'bus business as his predecessor, Littlewood. He advertised his business for sale in May 1869, but there were no takers, and the construction of the Headingley tramway gave him the opportunity to sell out. Ramsden's assets consisting of 18 horses, two saloon 'buses, wagonettes, hackney coaches, etc. were auctioned on 11th October 1871.

In the late 'sixties Emmott's 'buses were the most numerous on the Headingley route and, by 1867, were operated by Francis Emmott, who had taken over from the original proprietor, John. By agreement with the Tramways Company, Turton's and Ramsden's 'buses ceased with the introduction of the tramcar on the Headingley route, but Emmott ran in opposition for a time, his service being reduced from 12 to 5 departures daily from the "Three Horse Shoes". Emmott's 'buses apparently ceased when the tramway extension to the "Three Horse Shoes" was opened in 1873.

Boar Lane at the junction with Albion Street with one of Walker's 'buses about 1890.
Courtesy The late C. R. Wood, Photographer.

WILLIAM TURTON

19 years old Turton began in a modest way, in 1844, when he set himself up as a corn and seed merchant in The Calls, adjacent to the River Aire. He later obtained premises in North Street and, in 1860, he opened a coal business in Water Lane which was later transferred to The Calls. With the acquisition of Atkinson's 'bus busi-

ness in 1867 he entered the transport field. In the late 'sixties he introduced a three journeys daily service from his office in Briggate to Moortown and, about the same time, an hourly service, also from his office, to the "Crown Inn," New Wortley, alternately via Water Lane and Wellington Street. His 'bus activities then suffered a decline. Turton's partnership with the Leeds Tramways Company and his agreement that he would discontinue any of his 'buses in competition with the trams, have been mentioned in a previous chapter. He faithfully kept to this agreement. The Headingley 'buses were the first to succumb and when Ramsden sold out, Turton found himself with a monopoly of the profitable Chapeltown and Hyde Park routes. In the late 'sixties he appears to have taken over Farnell's Hyde Park and Weetwood via Meanwood services.

Turton's 'bus services:– Hunslet and Hunslet Carr to Sheepscar, Chapeltown, Moortown and New Leeds all ceased with the introduction of trams in 1874 and, in July 1878, his Meanwood 'buses were withdrawn. The Hyde Park via Mount Preston and Weetwood services were both discontinued about 1874, probably in agreement with the Tramways Company, as they gave some competition to the Headingley trams.

Although Turton closed most of his original services in the 'seventies he also opened several new ones. In 1874, when Jackson went out of business, he took over operation of 'buses to Armley and Bramley. The Bramley 'bus made one journey daily, but was apparently unprofitable for it was withdrawn about 1877.

In late 1871 an Alfred Burrows acquired stables at 35 Meadow Lane and began a 'bus service in opposition to Turton's Meanwood 'bus. The 'bus ran from the "Junction Inn", Meanwood Road to the "Green Man", Dewsbury Road. The lower part of Dewsbury Road was becoming developed with working class housing and industrial building and it soon became one of the most densely populated areas of Leeds and a profitable 'bus route. Burrows's 'bus at first made seven journeys daily along Dewsbury Road, but this was increased to 11 daily and the terminus in Dewsbury Road was altered to the "New Inn". About June 1875 Burrows's business was taken over by Turton and a half hourly service run between Dewsbury Road and Woodhouse Carr (Meanwood Road). When the Meanwood Road section closed, the Dewsbury Road 'buses ran from the "Royal Hotel", Briggate and, by 1881, were running at 20 minutes intervals. They were still at this frequency at the time of the Tramways Company take-over in 1882.

On 22nd July 1878 Turton introduced a service between the Horticultural Gardens, Moorland Road and Briggate. 'Buses ran from the "Royal Hotel", Briggate every half hour via Commercial Street, Park Row, South Parade, Park Lane and Belle Vue Road and the fare was 2d. both inside and outside. By 1881 the 'buses were running alternately via Belle Vue Road and College Road, traversing part of the Headingley tram route, although there seem to have been no objections from the Tramways Company.

By 1878 Turton opened an hourly service from the "Royal Hotel" to the "New Peacock Inn", Churwell Road (later known as Elland Road), a newly developing area of Leeds. By 1880 an opposition 'bus operated by a Henry Brown of Sidney Street, Vicar Lane, was running to Elland Road, but by the following year both Brown's and Turton's 'buses had been withdrawn as the area could not yet support a profitable 'bus service. By 1878 also, Turton had extended his New Wortley service from the "Crown Inn", along Tong Road to the "Star Inn", Upper Wortley, another area being developed with working class housing. A half hourly service was operated, the hour 'bus running via Water Lane to the "Crown Inn" and "Queen Inn", Oldfield Lane and the 'bus at half past the hour to the "Star". Following the opening of the New Wortley tramway to the "Crown" in 1879, Turton's New Wortley 'bus ran hourly via Water Lane only with the terminus at the "Queen Inn". 'Buses continued to run to the "Star Inn" until the extension of the tramway on Tong Road in 1880.

By October 1877 a half hourly 'bus service was operating from the "Horse and Jockey", Commercial Street, to the "Alfred Arms", Little London via Camp Road, a middle class residential area about half a mile from the town centre. The proprietor was Joseph Bramfitt who, by the following year, was running the service through to the "Junction Inn", West Street (extended through to the "Beckett's Arms", Kirkstall Road about November 1878). Bramfitt's Camp Road section was apparently discontinued for, by 1880, Turton had introduced a half hourly through service between Camp Road and Whitehall Road, an industrial area to the south west of the town centre. In 1880 also, Henry Brown began an opposition 'bus on Whitehall Road and there are reports of 'racing' between the two proprietors in Aire Street and Whitehall Road. Brown, however, was unable to compete with Turton and went into liquidation. On 18th April 1882 his 31 horses and:–

"three nearly new 'buses 'The Star', 'The Sunbeam' and 'The Violet' being licensed Nos. 77, 93 and 94 built by Brown of Leeds each for three horses and to carry inside 13 and 16 out, with painted claret body, vermillion carriage and pick with fine line black. Also two saloon 'buses by Brown of Leeds licensed Nos. 94? and 191 each carrying 21 inside and 4 outside passengers."
(Yorkshire Post, 15th April 1882).

were auctioned. This is one of the few instances where the livery of a horse 'bus is recorded. The coach builder referred to was a Gilbert Brown, a well-known Leeds man who built many of the horse 'buses in the town. His premises were in Brunswick Terrace, off Camp Road.

Henry Brown absconded with his remaining assets.

In addition to new routes that he opened on his own account, Turton also instituted opposition 'buses on established routes. By October 1878 he was running an opposition 'bus from the "Royal Hotel" to Beeston Hill, one of the most profitable routes in Leeds, in competition with Charles Coates. There was bitter rivalry between the two proprietors:–

"Joseph Leckenby, conductor of Turton's Beeston Hill 'bus was charged on remand before Mr. Bruce yesterday with unlawfully wounding Walter Guy, driver of Coates' Burmantofts and Beeston Hill 'bus — From the evidence of Guy and several other witnesses, it seems that on the 21st of this month Turton's 'bus was 'nursing' the 'bus of Mr. Coates, and that near Folly Lane, Beeston, the driver of Turton's 'bus pulled up suddenly, when the guard, Leckenby – so far as the evidence showed – without the slightest provocation jumped upon Coates' 'bus and made a terrible onslaught on Guy, who was strapped to the dickey with his knee sheet and unable to defend himself. —— Leckenby was committed to take his trial at the next

A busy scene at the Beeston Hill 'bus terminus with two of Coates' 'buses.   *Courtesy The late D. Hunt, Photographer.*

Coates was running an hourly service (15 journeys daily to Beeston Hill) and he increased this to half hourly. At first Turton's 'bus ran on Saturday, Monday and Tuesday only at half hourly intervals but, by 1881, both he and Coates had doubled the number of their departures, both 'buses leaving the termini at the same time. Each proprietor complained to the Hackney Carriages Committee about the other and the Committee instructed that they start alternately on and after 13th June 1881, each operating a 15 minutes frequency. This gave a $7\frac{1}{2}$ minutes service to Beeston Hill (110 journeys daily), by far the most frequent 'bus service in Leeds up to this time, and better than any of the services provided on the tram routes. There were still, however, no early 'buses, the first starting at $8.07\frac{1}{2}$ am from Beeston Hill and the last at 10.07 pm (Saturdays 11.27 pm).

As mentioned in a previous chapter, Turton ran to Roundhay Park in opposition to Bramfitt and Walker and, during the 'seventies, he also ran a Sundays summer only service between his Briggate office and the village of Harewood, eight miles north of Leeds.

From 30th September 1876 Turton moved his 'bus office and waiting room from the "Bull and Mouth", Briggate to the "Royal Hotel", also in Briggate. From there he ran his 'buses and a parcels delivery business until 3rd May 1880, when he moved to No. 3 Market Street. By 1882, when the Tramways Company took over his business, Turton had become the most successful omnibus proprietor in Leeds.

JOSEPH WALKER

Another omnibus proprietor to emerge in the early 'seventies was Joseph Walker of Chapeltown Road who, by the late 'eighties and 'nineties, became the major proprietor in Leeds surpassing Turton, and later the Leeds Tramways Company, in size and importance. Walker had been involved with the operation of cabs in Leeds from about 1857 and, in 1871, he had five plying for hire. His first venture into the 'bus field appears to have been in 1872 when, from 31st August, he advertised a daily wagonette from Boar Lane at 2.0 pm to Roundhay Park. After about two months the wagonette was withdrawn.

The 1st February 1875 saw the introduction of his first regular 'bus service: an hourly service (9.0 am to 8.0 pm) from Briggate to Spencer Place, Roundhay Road, returning to Briggate via Vicar Lane and Kirkgate. The fare was 2d. and the the 'bus served a new middle class housing area about $1\frac{1}{2}$ miles from the town centre. By March 1877 the route had been extended from Spencer Place along Leopold Street to Nassau Place, New Leeds. The 'bus used on this route must have been a second-hand one from Birmingham, as it showed "Aston Park" on the destination, much to the consternation of the Hackney Carriages Committee. The 'bus was still hourly, but must have been profitable for, by March 1878, the service was increased to half hourly and the fare reduced to 1d. about the same time. By 1881, however, the service had reverted to hourly and the following year increased to 45 minutes. In May 1887 Walker was given permission to put an additional 'bus on the route but timetables indicate that the 45 minutes was retained and it remained at this frequency until the route closed due to tramway competition.

One of Walker's Leopold Street Traffic Notices. *Courtesy Leeds City Museums.*

Walker's efforts to run a regular 'bus service to Roundhay Park are mentioned in another chapter, but, encouraged by the success of his penny 'bus to Leopold Street, on 15th November 1879, he introduced a penny 'bus on a short distance route from Briggate to the "Alexandra Hotel", Green Road, Beckett Street, a densely populated working class area about a mile from the town centre. The route from Briggate was via Duncan Street, Market, George Street, Quarry Hill, Regent Street and Green Road. The fierce 'bus competition in this area is referred to in the next chapter.

Walker's Reginald Terrace 'bus in Briggate. Kirkgate is on the right. *Courtesy Leeds City Libraries.*

Walker's Armley Traffic Notice. *Courtesy Leeds City Museum.*

SWEET STREET AND GREEN ROAD OMNIBUS ROUTE

BRIGGATE
TO
WELLINGTON BRIDGE 1
ARMLEY 2D.

Walker was one of the pioneers of the penny 'bus. His success with the Leopold Street and Green Road routes enabled him to buy more 'buses and start other short distance services, some of which, Headingley Church, Hunslet Carr, Hyde Park, "Pack Horse" and Swan Junction, were in direct competition with the tramways, and have been mentioned previously.

By 1881 Walker was running a half hourly (8.45 am to 8.15 pm) penny 'bus from Briggate to the "Commercial Inn", Sweet Street, Holbeck, via Boar Lane, Victoria Road, Manor Road and Marshall Street, an industrial area with few houses. A through service with Green Road was operated and the same half hourly service throughout the route's existence. In March 1882 an

opposition 'bus was introduced between the "Borough Arms", Kirkgate, via Duncan Street and Water Lane, over part of Walker's route. The proprietor was an Oliver Howard of 163 East Street, but his 'bus was discontinued after a few months. Walker used four 'buses on the route and, in May 1891, sold them to a Joseph Roberts, landlord of the "Old Parrot Hotel", Call Lane. Roberts, in turn, sold out to John Newton Sharp in October the same year. Sharp could not make the service pay and from November 1891 the Sweet Street 'buses were withdrawn.

Soon after the introduction of his Sweet Street service, Walker was running 'buses along Burley Road to the "Burley Hotel", in fierce competition with other proprietors. The complexities of the Burley Road services are dealt with in the next chapter.

Taking over from Turton, Walker ran the Briggate to Armley 'bus service without competition from August 1882 until its closure when the tramways arrived. The terminus was at the "Rose and Crown Inn," Armley, and the 'bus ran via Wellington Street, Wellington Road and

All traffic must have been stopped for this incredible photograph of Briggate taken in the 1880's. One of Walker's 'buses is on the right.

Armley Road. The service was half hourly, from 8.0 am to 8.0 pm, and fares were 1d. from Briggate to Wellington Bridge and 2d. to the "Rose and Crown."

In October 1885 Walker re-routed one of his Headingley Church 'buses via Woodhouse Lane and along Victoria Road, but this was not successful. In January 1886, he discontinued the route and ran via Woodhouse Lane and College Road to Moorland Road instead. Moorland Road had seen no 'buses since the withdrawal of Turton's vehicles in 1882 and there had been requests from the residents who said that a 'bus would now pay. The 40 minutes service ran from 9.10 am to 7.50 pm, the fare was 1d. and the terminus at the top of Belle Vue Road. In December 1887 Walker put on an additional 'bus increasing the frequency to 20 minutes (36 journeys daily) and, by 1888, the terminus had been extended along Moorland Road to the top of Hyde Park Road. By 1889 the afternoon service had been increased to 15 minutes (45 journeys daily) and this frequency was maintained until the closure of the route.

After the withdrawal of the Leeds Tramways Company 'bus to Whitehall Road in June 1886, Walker requested permission to put on an additional 'bus but this was refused. However, an application in January 1887 to alter the terminus from the "Smyth's Arms" to the "New Cattle Market Hotel" was granted. By the middle of 1887 an opposition 'bus run by Amos Kirby had been withdrawn, leaving Walker to run a 20 minutes service (8.40 am to 8.20 pm from Briggate). Walker now had the monopoly of the route and retained this for the remainder of its existence. The fare in 1894 was 1d.

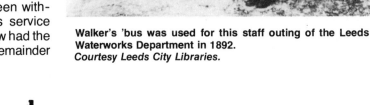

Walker's 'bus was used for this staff outing of the Leeds Waterworks Department in 1892.
Courtesy Leeds City Libraries.

DOMESTIC STREET, 1d. WHITEHALL ROAD, BRIGGATE,

J. WHITEHEAD & SON, Printers, ALFRED ST, BOAR LANE.

Walker's Whitehall Road Traffic Notice.
Courtesy Leeds City Museums.

In March 1891 Walker transferred his business to his three sons, Major, George Thomas and Benjamin. The firm became known as Walker Brothers, Major Walker being the leading partner. In 1893 Walkers took over operation of the Reginald Terrace 'bus service from Joseph Bramfitt and now ran on 11 routes:– Armley, Burley Road ("Burley Hotel"), Burley Road (via West-field Road), Cardigan Road, Headingley Church, Hyde Park, Moorland Road, New Leeds (Leopold Street), "Pack Horse", Reginald Terrace and Whitehall Road.

Walkers were, by far, the largest proprietor at this time as no one else ran more than four routes. They had their own inspectors and also used the "Bell Punch" ticket system, probably the only omnibus proprietor in Leeds to use tickets. All other proprietors appear to have used the fare box system. Walkers 'buses were easily recognisable, being painted with a red tartan decoration and were popularly known as the "Plaid 'o Laddie" 'buses.

OTHER ROUTES

Apart from the important Roundhay route few other 'bus routes emerged in the 'seventies. The most notable was that to Shadwell, running by 1872 and operated by George Brown of Thorner. His 'bus made one daily journey from Shadwell at 8.30 am, returning from the "New Inn", Vicar Lane at 5.0 pm. About 1876 the town terminus was changed to the "Black Swan" in Vicar Lane.

In 1873 a 'bus was running twice weekly from the "Horse and Jockey", Commercial Street to Farnley Iron Church, three to four miles south west of Leeds, but was soon discontinued. Christopher and James Dacre were also running from the "Horse and Jockey" to Lower Wortley about the same time but this service, too, was short lived. The Dacres split up in 1875, Christopher taking over the 'buses. The Lower Wortley 'buses were still running in March 1877 but disappeared when Dacre went into liquidation in October 1878. The Lower Wortley 'buses were not revived by other proprietors.

There were also 'bus routes to Churwell in 1875–6 and to Gildersome in 1878 which ran briefly. However, it was the short distance, cheap inner suburb services introduced by Walker and Bramfitt in the late 'seventies and copied by many other smaller proprietors in the 'eighties that revolutionised the horse 'bus traffic in Leeds for the remainder of its existence.

CHAPTER EIGHTEEN

The 'Buses:
Coates, Other Proprietors and their Demise

During the 'eighties and 'nineties the busiest 'bus routes were those serving the densely populated southern parts of Leeds and the inner city areas. There was a gradual expansion of the 'bus services in the 'eighties and by the 'nineties they were running slightly earlier in the morning.Many left their respective termini at 7.45 am instead of 8.15 am as formerly and thus were more useful to working people. These were the earliest 'buses that the proprietors could provide, and it was to be the Corporation steam and electric tram that gave early transport for all. After 1897 the 'buses suffered a rapid decline and within three to four years virtually disappeared due to increasing competition from the electric trams.

Throughout the 'seventies Charles Joseph Coates had operated his 'bus services, introduced some ten to 15 years earlier, with little alteration. From 17th November 1874 the fare on the Burmantofts to Beeston Hill route was reduced from 3d. to 2d. from Briggate to either terminus. Owing to competition from Turton and the Leeds Tramways Company the fare was later reduced to 1d. Like Turton, Coates operated a parcels service, his 'buses collecting parcels left at the "Horse and Jockey", Commercial Street. The charge, whatever the size of parcel, was 2d.

In March 1886 Coates opened a new 'bus service from the "Royal Hotel," Briggate to the "Waggon and Horses," Elland Road, over the route found uneconomical by Turton some years earlier and, in July of the same year, was granted permission to run an additional 'bus on "special occasions." Coates also ran seasonal 'buses to local beauty spots in the summer.He regularly ran to Boston Spa and is also recorded as running excursions to Ilkey. In addition to his 'bus interests, Coates also farmed at Brex Farm, Swillington.

One of Coates' 'buses stands at the Beeston Hill terminus. It is advertising an excursion to Ilkley.   *Courtesy The late J. Newton.*

Eli Spurdens, another omnibus proprietor, reminiscing in 1944, remembered "Old Charlie Coates" and described him as a "rare one for a deal" who dabbled in poultry, pigs and the like.

"One day," said Spurdens, "a number of pigs were sent by Charlie to the Royal Hotel Yard for delivery to Boston Spa. 'Where shall I put 'em?' asked the 'bus driver, 'Stick 'em inside and let the passengers get on top,'" was Charlie's reply.

(Yorkshire Evening Post, 27th December 1944).

Coates's stables were at 26 Charmouth Street, Beeston Road. On 11th December 1886, at the age of 53 years, he died. The business passed to his son, also named Charles Joseph.

Coates' faded gravestone in Swillington Church Yard proudly proclaims his occupation. *Courtesy J. Soper.*

Following the withdrawal of the Leeds Tramways Company 'bus to Beeston Hill in 1884 Coates had the monopoly of the service. He ran a 15 minutes service at first but, following an application from John Turton, son of William Turton, to run a through service from Spencer Place to Beeston Hill — fortunately for Coates junior, rejected by the Hackney Carriages Committee — he was induced, in May 1887, to increase the frequency to ten minutes. In 1891 a part day 7½ minutes service was introduced (104 journeys daily) and an earlier 'bus at 7.45 am from Beeston Hill was commenced about the same time. This arrangement continued until the 'buses ceased running.

As referred to later in this chapter, 'bus competition was very severe in the Burmantofts area and, about August 1887, Coates junior closed his Burmantofts section.

On 10th November 1890 a John Taylor applied for a licence to run a covered wagonette between Briggate and Lady Pit Lane, Beeston Hill. The licence was refused but on the same date a licence was granted to Coates to run two 'buses on a similar service via Call Lane, Duncan Street, Briggate and Dewsbury Road to a terminus on the west side of Lady Pit Lane to the north of Coupland Street, near to the terminus of the Beeston Hill 'buses in Lady Pit Street. There was no fixed terminus in Briggate but the 'bus was allowed to take up or set down passengers as required. Coates put a third 'bus on the service in December 1890 and in 1892 and 1893 it is recorded that 22 daily journeys were made. For some reason the route was discontinued in late 1893.

Coates junior briefly ran opposition 'buses on the Dewsbury Road and Hunslet Lake routes, but otherwise his main services were unchanged. Unfortunately, he

did not live long and died on 11th January 1894 at the early age of 29 years. The following month an attempt was made to sell his business which consisted of 80 horses and 11 'buses running on his Beeston Hill, Dewsbury Road, Elland Road, Halton and Whitkirk routes. The attempt was unsuccessful and the operation of the 'buses passed to his widow, Fanny Elizabeth. Although the number of 'buses offered for sale was 11, 12 'buses, licensed Nos. 1 to 12, were transferred to his widow. The Coates' were apparently "number collectors" and had gradually acquired the first 12 licence numbers from various omnibus proprietors over a period of 24 years. His widow added two more 'buses (licensed Nos. 13 and 14). On 18th October 1897 she married a Henry France of Holbeck and from then on the 'buses were operated under the name of Fanny Elizabeth France.

In January 1898 France instituted a new 'bus service between Briggate and Holbeck Moor via Meadow Lane, Sweet Street, Bridge Road and Stocks Hill to a terminus in Top Moor Side on the north west side of the street opposite the Conservative Club. Two 'buses operated the service. In June 1899 she withdrew her two Elland Road 'buses and diverted them to the Holbeck Moor route. At the same time the 'bus terminus was moved further along Top Moor Side nearer Elland Road.

Fanny France's 'buses were not to last long. The first to succumb was the popular Beeston Hill 'bus. Roadworks in connection with the new Beeston tramway made it impossible for the 'bus to continue and it ran for the last time on 28th July 1900. Just over a fortnight later, on 18th August, the Holbeck Moor route closed owing to competition from the new Elland Road horse trams.

There were opposition 'buses on Coates's Halton, Whitkirk and Garforth routes between 1875 and early 1877, operated by a William Harrison and, in the 1879-80 period, by a James Smith of Halton, but otherwise Coates's ran these services virtually unchanged for over 40 years. They ceased when France auctioned her remaining 31 horses and "seven garden chair, 'Jubilee' and rail seat omnibuses" on 22nd August 1900.

Another proprietor, probably E. Norbury of Whitkirk, took over operation of the Whitkirk service, but he sold out in July 1902 to another proprietor, whose name has not been traced. 'Buses are recorded as "wobbling" to Whitkirk as late as May 1905, but were probably discontinued soon afterwards.

A large five-window horse 'bus at the "Brown Cow Inn," Whitkirk about 1900. *Courtesy J. Soper Collection.*

154

Coates and Walkers provided a good service on most of their routes, stifled opposition and hence retained their monopoly. Other proprietors, such as Binns (Kippax) and Brown (Seacroft), provided a virtually unchanged service without opposition throughout the later horse 'bus era, but on other routes there were many smaller proprietors fiercely competing with each other. The routes are treated alphabetically:–

THE BURLEY ROAD OMNIBUSES

Following the withdrawal of Coates's Burley 'bus about 1874, due to competition from the Kirkstall tram, the omnibus proprietors abandoned the idea of running along Burley Road for a few years. Building development in the area in the late 'seventies and 'eighties encouraged another attempt to operate a 'bus service. On 5th January 1881, a William Hall Slater, of Skinner Lane, was granted a licence to run a 'bus from Briggate to the "Queen Hotel," Burley Road. About the same time Joseph Walker started a 'bus to the "Burley Hotel" and the following year both proprietors put additional 'buses on their routes. The two proprietors tended to start their 'buses at the same time, racing each other on the route, but, in 1882, the Hackney Carriages Committee put a stop to this practice. By December of that year 'buses were running to both the "Queen Hotel" and "Burley Hotel" at a 45 minutes frequency.

On 2nd September 1885 Slater was granted permission to change the terminus of his 'buses from the "Queen Hotel" to Westfield Road. At the same time, Robert Chapman opened a service to Victoria Road running via Park Lane, Westfield Road, Alexandra Road and Cardigan Road, traversing the route of Slater's 'bus. At first Chapman's bus ran half hourly, but was later reduced to hourly. The fare was 1d. to Woodsley Road and beyond 2d. Two of Slater's three 'buses were named 'Victoria' and 'Violet' and, in February 1886, his three vehicles were sold to a Joseph Tranter of 7 Hill Top Street, Hyde Park Road and to a Charles and Alfred Meek of 7 Holderness Terrace and 20 King's Avenue respectively.

The Victoria Road area was an upper middle class area where many of the inhabitants owned their own carriages and Chapman could not make his 'buses pay. On several occasions during 1886 and 1887 he applied to cut back the service to Westfield Road or Queen's Road, but each time the licence was refused. Eventually he curtailed the service on his own initiative to Westfield Road, but after being threatened with legal proceedings by the Corporation he had to reinstate his 'buses to Victoria Road. The constant harrassment from the Corporation and other 'bus proprietors was too much for Chapman and on 30th May 1887, at the age of 55, he died. The business was transferred to his widow, Caroline, who made applications to cut back the Victoria

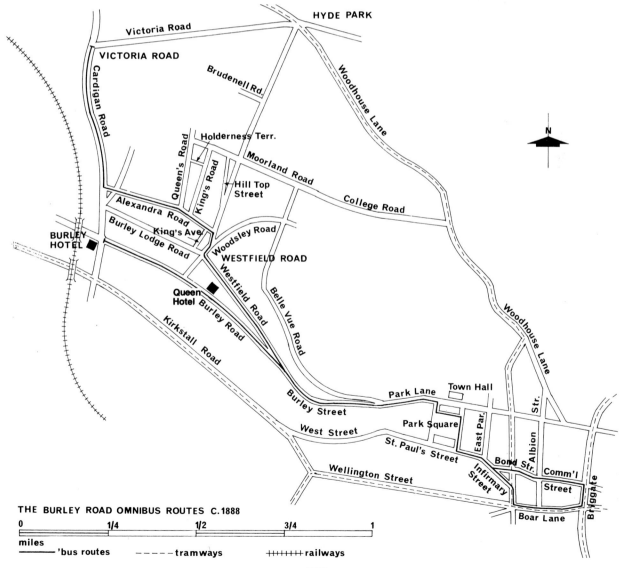

THE BURLEY ROAD OMNIBUS ROUTES C.1888

```
0            1/4          1/2          3/4           1
miles
——— 'bus routes    – – – – tramways    ++++++ railways
```

155

Road service to Burley Lodge Road or Owens Road, but was also refused permission. However, building developments in the late 'eighties brought increased traffic and the Victoria Road 'buses began to make a profit. In March 1890 Caroline put on a second 'bus, increasing the frequency to half hourly. In October 1889 she had re-routed the service via Burley Lodge Road instead of Alexandra Road and, as traffic improved, a year later she applied to put a third 'bus on the route.

In the meantime, in January 1887, Joseph Walker sold his interest in Burley Road to a Henry Harrison of 2 Grant Street. Harrison, in conjunction with the Meeks and Tranter, objected to Caroline Chapman's application. While her application was refused, Harrison was granted permission to run two 'buses to Victoria Road and there were now four 'buses giving a 15 minute service. Harrison, who used to drive his own 'buses, ran to Victoria Road for only six months before disposing of the licence to Walker's, whose 'buses reappeared in Burley Road. Harrison had had a lot of bad luck with his horses. In January 1887 he lost 18 horses due to glanders and, in December 1890, a further seven due to 'pink eye'.

At first Walker's ran only one 'bus to Victoria Road but in 1893 a further 'bus was put on.

In November 1890 Caroline Chapman died. On 17th March the following year, her 33 horses and four 'buses, were sold. All the 'buses had been built by Brown of Leeds, two having run to the "Crown Inn," New Wortley, and two to Victoria Road. No omnibus proprietor took over Chapman's stables at 7 Preston Terrace or her New Wortley 'buses, but the two Victoria Road 'buses (licence Nos. 199 and 231) passed to a Mary Sherwin of Cankerwell Lane. She did not run long and sold out to Eli Spurdens in August 1892. There is evidence to suggest that Harrison and Walker's may have run a slightly different route to Victoria Road than Sherwin or Spurdens but this is not indicated in the Hackney Carriages Committee minutes or reports.

Mary Sherwin's 'bus at the Cardigan Road terminus in 1892. The 'bus, No. 231, was built by Gilbert Brown of Leeds. *Courtesy Leeds City Transport Department.*

On 29th May 1893 Tranter's two Westfield Road 'buses were auctioned and purchased by Walkers. His stables in Hill Top Street were taken over by Charles Meek. Three weeks later, on 22nd June, Harrison's three 'buses, two wagonettes and ten horses were sold; Walkers buying his Burley Road 'buses. Thus, within a month, Walkers had obtained the monopoly of the

"Burley Hotel" service and a part interest in the routes to Westfield Road and Victoria Road. On 1st July 1893 the Alfred and Charles Meek partnership split up and Charles took over the 'buses. Following a conviction in April 1895 for cruelty to four of his "old, emaciated or mangy" horses, he sold out to Eli Spurdens. Meek's 'bus 'Victoria' (licence No. 105) was one of the last named 'buses to run in Leeds. David Horton, mentioned in a previous chapter, had six decrepit 'buses, four of which were named 'Favourite', 'Gem', 'Pearl' and 'Ruby', but these were largely scrapped following his death in 1895. The three Burley Road services were operated uneventfully by Walker Bros. and Spurdens throughout the late 'nineties.

The route of the Burley Road 'buses from Briggate was via Commercial Street, Bond Street, St. Paul's Street, Park Square, Park Lane and Burley Street to their respective destinations. The return journey to Briggate was via Infirmary Street and Boar Lane. Horses were changed at the top of Park Square and a well known local landmark was the horse trough, removed in 1938.

On 6th September 1897 Spurdens suffered an accident with one of his Victoria Road 'buses. The 'bus was negotiating the sharp bend from Cardigan Road into Burley Lodge Road when one of the wheels disintegrated and the 13 passengers on top, plus the driver, were pitched into the road and several were seriously injured. Tranter had experienced a similar accident with one of his 'buses in Park Lane on 29th March 1886 but his 'bus did not overturn and there were no injuries.

In 1899 the construction of the Burley Road tramway was imminent and Walker's ceased to run while they could still get a reasonable price for their rolling stock. In March 1899, John William Wilks, a well-known local horse dealer, took over from them on the Victoria Road service and Spurdens replaced them on the "Burley Hotel" and Westfield Road routes, the "Burley Hotel" section being apparently without 'buses for about six months. The opening of the horse tramway along Burley Road to Cardigan Road in June 1900 put great pressure on Spurdens and Wilks and frantic switching of routes took place in order to run an economical service. In May 1900 Spurdens extended his Westfield Road 'buses to Cardigan Road and the following month cut them back to Queen's Road. The Queen's Road service provided a short respite for Spurdens, and Wilks was encouraged to try an opposition 'bus in October the same year, but, after only three weeks, withdrew it and ran to Hyde Park Road via College Road instead. (Walker's Moorland Road via College Road 'bus had been withdrawn some months earlier.).

The introduction of the electric trams on Burley Road and Cardigan Road in August 1901 marked the death knell of the 'bus. Wilks had already ceased to run, but Spurdens foolishly thought he could compete with electric traction and finished up in the bankruptcy court.

"Debtor said that when he was making a good profit he only took 20s. 0d. or 30s. 0d. per week out of the business, and increased his stock from the remaining profit. When the electric tramway was introduced in Cardigan Road his omnibuses did not earn wages and people would not ride on them, though he reduced the fare to 1d. He had no idea at that time that the electric tramway service would be so energetically developed, and thought that he would always be able to run omnibuses on a few routes in Leeds. ——— The debtor

stated that he had two of the latest type of omnibuses, which at the time of the sale were comparatively new. They cost £145 each, but at the time of the sale only fetched £4 10s. 0d. and £7. Nobody wanted 'buses now in Leeds or anywhere else."

(Yorkshire Post, 10th June 1902).

Spurdens assets were auctioned on 30th October 1901. In the late 'nineties he had around 100 horses and ran excursions to various parts of the county. Along with Coates and other proprietors, he ran 'buses from Leeds to Doncaster on St. Leger Day. He usually employed six 'buses and 60 horses on the run. Ten horses were allowed per 'bus and five went to Pontefract the day before and relieved the five that pulled the 'bus from Leeds. The relief team took the 'bus to Doncaster and brought it back in the evening and then the first five pulled the 'bus back to Leeds, the other five walking home the following day.

Spurdens 'buses were brightly painted in vermillion and gilt with primrose wheels and must have formed a startling contrast with Wilks' 'buses painted in a green, gilt and cream livery.

Spurdens finished up as a garage proprietor at Lawnswood and was one of the characters of the horse 'bus era in Leeds. He was known to the writer's late grandfather who recalled an incident when Spurdens

had one of his 'buses repaired at Sammy Platts' (coach repairer's) yard in Burley Road. Spurdens was slow to pay bills and Platts refused to let Spurdens have his 'bus until the bill was paid. In the middle of the night Spurdens went to the yard with a couple of horses whose hoofs were muffled with several pairs of socks to avoid awakening Platts. Spurdens stole the 'bus from the yard and it was running in service the next day.

THE BURMANTOFTS 'BUS SERVICES

Of similar complexity to Burley Road were the Burmantofts 'buses. Throughout the 'sixties and 'seventies Coates had the monopoly of the Burmantofts area. There was no opposition until 1879, when Walker instituted his penny 'bus to Green Road, Beckett Street. Although Walker's 'bus did not travel the same route as Coates, the termini were close to each other and Coates must have lost some traffic to Walker.

In February 1883 William Hall Slater was given a licence to run a 'bus in opposition to Walker, but it did not run regularly and his licence was withdrawn in July 1885. In September of the same year a well known Leeds property speculator and notorious "jerry builder," John Newton Sharp, entered the omnibus business with a 'bus running from Kirkgate Market to near St.

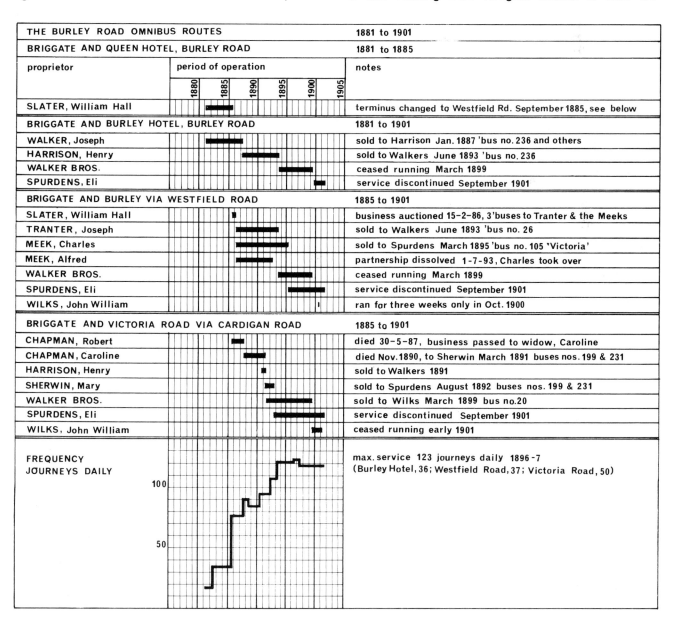

THE BURLEY ROAD OMNIBUS ROUTES		1881 to 1901
BRIGGATE AND QUEEN HOTEL, BURLEY ROAD		**1881 to 1885**
proprietor	period of operation	notes
	1880 · 1885 · 1890 · 1895 · 1900 · 1905	
SLATER, William Hall		terminus changed to Westfield Rd. September 1885, see below
BRIGGATE AND BURLEY HOTEL, BURLEY ROAD		**1881 to 1901**
WALKER, Joseph		sold to Harrison Jan. 1887 'bus no. 236 and others
HARRISON, Henry		sold to Walkers June 1893 'bus no. 236
WALKER BROS.		ceased running March 1899
SPURDENS, Eli		service discontinued September 1901
BRIGGATE AND BURLEY VIA WESTFIELD ROAD		**1885 to 1901**
SLATER, William Hall		business auctioned 15-2-86, 3 'buses to Tranter & the Meeks
TRANTER, Joseph		sold to Walkers June 1893 'bus no. 26
MEEK, Charles		sold to Spurdens March 1895 'bus no. 105 'Victoria'
MEEK, Alfred		partnership dissolved 1-7-93, Charles took over
WALKER BROS.		ceased running March 1899
SPURDENS, Eli		service discontinued September 1901
WILKS, John William		ran for three weeks only in Oct. 1900
BRIGGATE AND VICTORIA ROAD VIA CARDIGAN ROAD		**1885 to 1901**
CHAPMAN, Robert		died 30-5-87, business passed to widow, Caroline
CHAPMAN, Caroline		died Nov. 1890, to Sherwin March 1891 buses nos. 199 & 231
HARRISON, Henry		sold to Walkers 1891
SHERWIN, Mary		sold to Spurdens August 1892 buses nos. 199 & 231
WALKER BROS.		sold to Wilks March 1899 bus no. 20
SPURDENS, Eli		service discontinued September 1901
WILKS, John William		ceased running early 1901
FREQUENCY JOURNEYS DAILY	100 · 50	max. service 123 journeys daily 1896-7 (Burley Hotel, 36; Westfield Road, 37; Victoria Road, 50)

157

Eli Spurdens' Burley Road 'bus rounds the corner from City Square into Boar Lane in 1895. The New Post Office is under construction in the background.

Courtesy The late D. Hunt, Photographer.

Stephen's Church, Burmantofts, but it was short lived.

An Oliver Howard, who was running 'buses in the East Street area, ran a brief service from George Street to the "Moulder's Arms", Newtown, during January 1886 but this was uneconomical and, instead, on 4th February 1886, he was given a licence to run to the "Fleece Inn," Green Road, in competition with Walker. This did not last long and Howard had ceased to run to Green Road by the middle of 1887. The competition from Walker was also too great for Coates who gave up his "Cemetery Tavern" service about August of the same year.

THE BURMANTOFTS PENNY 'BUS ROUTES CIRCA 1894

0   1/4   1/2   3/4   1
miles
———— 'bus routes   - - - - tram routes

Henry Harrison took the place of Coates on the "Cemetery Tavern" route, but was soon pushed out of business, for Sharp put two 'buses on a new service from St. James Hall, York Street, via Burmantofts Street to the "Beckett's Arms," Beckett Street. Sharp ran over Harrison's route and his 'bus terminus was near to the terminus of Walker's Green Road 'buses, giving strong competition to both proprietors. To meet this opposition, in March 1888, Walker put two additional 'buses (Tuesdays and Saturdays only) on his Green Road service, further increased the following year to give 48 journeys daily. The route through the town centre for these additional 'buses was via Market Street, Duncan Street, Briggate and Kirkgate.

By 1888 Sharp had introduced a 'bus service from Kirkgate to Shakespeare Street, Burmantofts, and the competition between Walker and Sharp became very heated. The public benefited, Sharp giving a ten minutes service to Beckett Street, half hourly to Shakespeare Street and Walker 15 minutes to Green Road. However, neither proprietor could now make his 'buses pay. In August 1888 Sharp withdrew his Shakespeare Street service and Walker took his place, but he also found it uneconomical and withdrew his 'buses in September 1890, to be promptly replaced by Sharp again. Sharp ceased to run after a few weeks.

Mention has been made in a previous chapter of the sale of Walker's Green Road to Sweet Street 'buses to Joseph Roberts who, in turn, passed them on to Sharp. Sharp withdrew the service and had the monopoly of the Burmantofts area with his Beckett Street 'buses. Not for long, however, for a William Burnett, apparently operating from Slater's old stables in Skinner Lane, re-introduced a 'bus on the Green Road service and

Sharp himself went out of business when he was imprisoned for cruelty to his horses.

A James Dean, of 15 Timber Place, off East Street, whose 'buses were giving good service in the East Street area, was quick to take over Beckett Street with the immediate introduction of four 'buses. At the same time Burnett introduced a 20 minutes service along Nippet Lane and Stoney Rock Lane to Rock View Road, Burmantofts, later extended along Rock View Road to Shakespeare Street, but now referred to as the "Stoney Rock" route. There were now three 'bus routes serving Burmantofts and each charged a penny fare. In October 1894 Burnett re-routed his Green Road 'buses via Mabgate instead of The Leylands, and two months later disposed of his "Stoney Rock" route to an Ernest Scrubbs. Unfortunately, Burnett was of a similar disposition to Sharp. In February 1895 he was forced out of business owing to cruelty to his horses and the bad condition of his 'buses. Burnett lost 30 horses within a year due to skin disease, became bankrupt and had a spell in gaol.

The Burmantofts omnibus proprietors were rough characters in the extreme, for Scrubbs was also convicted for cruelty and was forced to sell out to a Tom Jagger in July 1895.

With the demise of Burnett the Green Road 'buses ceased to run and, owing to the condition of his rolling stock, Burnett had difficulty in selling his business. His wife, Fanny, obtained a licence to run two 'buses on a 20 minutes service from Kirkgate to Beckett Street, near the corner of Glebe Street, taking over from Dean who appears to have moved out of the area about this time. In April 1895 she sold the two 'buses and the remainder of Burnett's business to Tom Jagger. Jagger was no angel. His stables were said to be a "Hell's hole" and there were complaints about his 'buses running with broken windows. On 3rd April 1897 the off hind wheel of one of his 'buses came off and he was sued for injuries received by one of the passengers. He was also probably the only horse 'bus proprietor in Leeds to suffer a strike by his employees. On 15th November 1897 his eight drivers and conductors came out on strike in

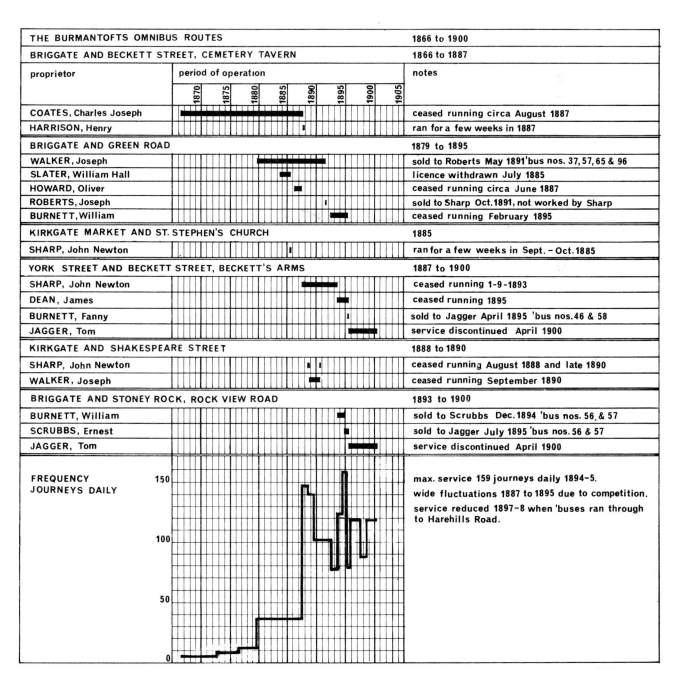

THE BURMANTOFTS OMNIBUS ROUTES	1866 to 1900
BRIGGATE AND BECKETT STREET, CEMETERY TAVERN	1866 to 1887

proprietor	period of operation	notes
COATES, Charles Joseph		ceased running circa August 1887
HARRISON, Henry		ran for a few weeks in 1887
BRIGGATE AND GREEN ROAD		1879 to 1895
WALKER, Joseph		sold to Roberts May 1891 'bus nos. 37, 57, 65 & 96
SLATER, William Hall		licence withdrawn July 1885
HOWARD, Oliver		ceased running circa June 1887
ROBERTS, Joseph		sold to Sharp Oct. 1891, not worked by Sharp
BURNETT, William		ceased running February 1895
KIRKGATE MARKET AND ST. STEPHEN'S CHURCH		1885
SHARP, John Newton		ran for a few weeks in Sept. – Oct. 1885
YORK STREET AND BECKETT STREET, BECKETT'S ARMS		1887 to 1900
SHARP, John Newton		ceased running 1-9-1893
DEAN, James		ceased running 1895
BURNETT, Fanny		sold to Jagger April 1895 'bus nos. 46 & 58
JAGGER, Tom		service discontinued April 1900
KIRKGATE AND SHAKESPEARE STREET		1888 to 1890
SHARP, John Newton		ceased running August 1888 and late 1890
WALKER, Joseph		ceased running September 1890
BRIGGATE AND STONEY ROCK, ROCK VIEW ROAD		1893 to 1900
BURNETT, William		sold to Scrubbs Dec. 1894 'bus nos. 56 & 57
SCRUBBS, Ernest		sold to Jagger July 1895 'bus nos. 56 & 57
JAGGER, Tom		service discontinued April 1900

FREQUENCY JOURNEYS DAILY

max. service 159 journeys daily 1894–5.

wide fluctuations 1887 to 1895 due to competition.

service reduced 1897–8 when 'buses ran through to Harehills Road.

protest against the appointment of a checker of fares who received a higher wage than they were paid.

After the competition between several proprietors a period of comparative calm settled on the Burmantofts 'bus services. Jagger retained a monopoly for the remainder of their existence. In October 1895 he re-routed the "Stoney Rock" 'buses via Accommodation Road, Green Road, Regent Street and George Street from a new terminus in the town centre at Ludgate Hill. In February the following year the route was changed to run via Mabgate instead of Regent Street and, in March 1897, the Beckett Street 'buses were extended along Harehills Road over the route of the abandoned Roundhay Electric tramway to a terminus on the west side of Harehills Road at the end of Back Elford Grove. The introduction of horse trams along Burmantofts Street and Beckett Street in April 1898 resulted in the service being cut back to Beckett Street again. The 'buses continued to run in opposition to the horse trams before going under to the electric tram in 1900. Jagger's assets, consisting of "25 horses, six 'buses, two wagonettes, char-a-banc, pony trap etc" were sold at his stables, 14 Carver Street, at the bottom of York Road, on 25th April 1900.

THE CAMP ROAD 'BUSES

Camp Road ran parallel with and very close to Meanwood Road, as near as 100 yards in places. Hence, the 'bus proprietors always faced stiff competition. The terminus was also within easy walking distance of the town centre and the route was probably never very profitable.

Following the departure of the Leeds Tramways Company 'buses in 1883, there were apparently no 'buses to Camp Road for two years, but in May 1885 a John Thomas Lister, of 18 Spring Street, was granted a licence to operate a 40 minutes service along Camp Road as far as Oatland Road, and, in August 1888, the route was extended to the end of Servia Road. In May 1890 Lister sold his business to a Joseph Poole, landlord of the "Irwin Arms Inn," Holbeck. Poole had a lot of trouble with his horses and had 18 affected with "pink eye" soon after he bought the business. In April 1891 he

was convicted for ill-treating his horses and sold out to a William James Hanson.

On the east side of Camp Road was an extensive tract of vacant land said to have been the site of an old quarry or brick kiln. During 1891, and the following year, the land was laid out with streets and housing and portions of it were at a lower level than Camp Road. On Christmas Day 1891 a dense fog prevailed throughout Leeds and "through no fault of the driver" Hanson's 'bus fell into a large hole left in connection with the new development. "Miraculously", the 'bus did not overturn and the passengers were uninjured, but a workman was killed in trying to extricate the 'bus from the excavations.

Hanson ceased to run to Camp Road when his 30 horses and five 'buses were sold on 6th April 1892. From then until the following year there were several changes of proprietor, some only operating for a few weeks. As can be seen in the chart below things did not settle down until 1893, when Eli Spurdens and a Henry Adamson were the competing proprietors. When Adamson withdrew in March 1899, Spurdens put two additional 'buses on the route. The 'buses probably continued to March or April 1901, when the Woodhouse Street and Meanwood electric trams began running.

THE DEWSBURY ROAD 'BUSES

Burrows', Turton's and the Leeds Tramways Company 'buses to Dewsbury Road have been mentioned in previous chapters. On 23rd May 1887 John Turton, son of William Turton, was granted a licence to institute a service of eight 'Jubilee' 'buses on a through route between Spencer Place, Roundhay Road and Dewsbury Road. John Turton had previously carried out scavenging (dust removing) contracts for the Leeds Corporation. His 'buses ran in opposition to the Tramways Company vehicles and the fare from Briggate to both termini was 1d. A ten minutes service was operated. Turton's stables were in Grant Row and Beaufort Place, Roundhay Road, but he did not live long, meeting an early death on 3rd March 1888. On 14th August 1888 his business was auctioned and the purchaser was a John Marshall who sold out to John Newton Sharp the following year.

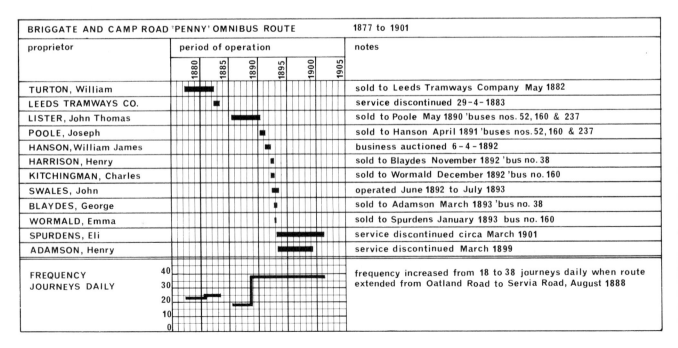

BRIGGATE AND CAMP ROAD 'PENNY' OMNIBUS ROUTE							1877 to 1901
proprietor	period of operation						notes
	1880	1885	1890	1895	1900	1905	
TURTON, William							sold to Leeds Tramways Company May 1882
LEEDS TRAMWAYS CO.							service discontinued 29-4-1883
LISTER, John Thomas							sold to Poole May 1890 'buses nos. 52, 160 & 237
POOLE, Joseph							sold to Hanson April 1891 'buses nos. 52, 160 & 237
HANSON, William James							business auctioned 6-4-1892
HARRISON, Henry							sold to Blaydes November 1892 'bus no. 38
KITCHINGMAN, Charles							sold to Wormald December 1892 'bus no. 160
SWALES, John							operated June 1892 to July 1893
BLAYDES, George							sold to Adamson March 1893 'bus no. 38
WORMALD, Emma							sold to Spurdens January 1893 bus no. 160
SPURDENS, Eli							service discontinued circa March 1901
ADAMSON, Henry							service discontinued March 1899
FREQUENCY JOURNEYS DAILY 40 30 20 10 0							frequency increased from 18 to 38 journeys daily when route extended from Oatland Road to Servia Road, August 1888

Sharp's Jubilee 'bus waits at the Spencer Place terminus as an electric car loads in Roundhay Road.

Sharp's 'Jubilee' 'buses became well-known on Dewsbury Road. The 'Jubilee' 'buses, nine of which were originally bought by Turton, were London built and a new design of single-deck 'bus operated by one man. They took their name from Queen Victoria's Golden Jubilee of 1887. The first 'Jubilee' 'buses appeared in London in the spring of 1887 and soon became very numerous on short distance penny routes in the metropolis. They seated 14 passengers, ten inside on longitudinal seats and two on each side of the driver on top. The 'bus was usually drawn by one horse and the driver opened and shut the door at the rear of the vehicle by a foot lever and strap passing through the 'bus. To stop or start the 'bus the passengers pulled the same strap. The fare box system was used and the driver collected the fares through a hole in the roof of the bus.

Sharp was a ruthless character who had many con-victions for 'jerry building' and cruelty to his horses. The end came for him in August 1893:–

"John Newton Sharp, builder and 'bus proprietor of Leeds was charged along with his 'bus manager, John William Sommers, with having cruelly ill-treated 16 horses in a stable at Beaufort Place, Roundhay Road. ——— The dimensions of the stable were — length 61' 6"; width 18' 0"; height 6' 6". There were six stalls, each containing two horses, and there was a narrow passage down the centre in which six horses stood lengthwise, 18 horses being thus crowded into the place. Each horse in a stall had 5' 1½" width of space to itself, being divided from the other horse by a loose bar. ——— The stable was entirely underground, and was approached by a steep gradient. At the time of his visit it was in a very dirty condition, and almost like a ploughed field. There was very little ventilation, and the animals were all huddled together. In order to see to the further end it was necessary to light the gas. The whole of the stalls were full — 18 horses altogether. The food smelt bad, and he wondered the horses could eat it at all. The bedding consisted of dirty sawdust; there was

no straw down, only a few shavings, not sufficient to cover the stones. The heat was almost unbearable. The horses could not stand still a minute; they were continually swishing their tails, and stamping their feet, worried by flies. ——— A good many were suffering from mange, others from sores, and others from lameness." ———

(Yorkshire Post, 31st August 1893).

Sharp was imprisoned for one month with hard labour and the 'buses on all his services ran for the last time on 1st September 1893. He had increased the number of his 'Jubilee' 'buses to 14. In addition to the original nine ex-Turton 'buses, Sharp obtained four from Gilbert Brown and one from J. Walker, coach builders of Leeds. They were sold on 2nd November 1893 and dispersed among various proprietors. Charles Coates took over two and ran them to Dewsbury Road and later Elland Road. James Dean and William Burnett also bought some, the latter taking over Sharp's stables in Beaufort Place.

In the early 'nineties the intense competition on Dewsbury Road resulted in the route being the busiest in Leeds. In the earliest part of the period 177 departures daily left Briggate for the "New Inn", but, by 1894, had reduced to 164. On 1st May 1894 Horsfall and Robinson took over from the Leeds Tramways Company and Coates, and the service was reduced to 102 departures daily. George Horsfall and Thomas Houlden Robinson operated the service in co-opera-tion, rather than opposition. Robinson had been in business as a cab and wagonette proprietor in Leeds from the 1860's and unsuccessfully tried to sell out in May 1895. In January 1899, in conjunction with Horsfall and two cab proprietors, John Wardle and Johnson Flintham, he floated a company known as the "Leeds Carriage, Omnibus, and Motor Car Company Ltd" with a nominal share capital of £30,000. The aim of the Company was to purchase the businesses of the four proprietors, but beyond that the prospectus was very

BRIGGATE AND DEWSBURY ROAD OMNIBUS ROUTE	1871 to 1900
proprietor / **period of operation** (1875 1880 1885 1890 1895 1900 1905)	**notes**
BURROWS, Alfred	sold to Turton circa June 1875
TURTON, William	sold to Leeds Tramway Company May 1882
LEEDS TRAMWAYS CO.	sold to L.C.T. 2-2-1894
TURTON, John	died 3-3-1888; to Marshall Aug.1888 'buses nos. 256-263 & 286
MARSHALL, John	sold to Sharp 1889 'buses nos. 256-263 & 286
SHARP, John Newton	ceased running 1-9-1893; business auctioned 2-11-1893
COATES, Charles Joseph	ceased running 30-4-1894
LEEDS CITY TRAMWAYS	,, ,, ,, sold to Horsfall & Robinson
HORSFALL, George	business auctioned 25-1-1900
ROBINSON, Thomas Houlden	sold to Bean April 1899
BEAN, Thomas Richard	service discontinued September 1900
FREQUENCY JOURNEYS DAILY (150, 100, 50)	max. frequency 177 journeys daily 1890-1

vague. The introduction of the electric tram meant that the Company was a non-starter and few, if any, shares were sold.

After one of his 'buses had overturned on 25th March 1899, due to the "appalling" condition of Dewsbury Road, Robinson sold out to a Thomas Bean. A horse tramway was opened along Dewsbury Road on 3rd January 1900 and Horsfall did not attempt to run in opposition. His 24 horses and four 'buses were auctioned three weeks later on 25th January.

From April 1899 the 'bus terminus was changed from the "New Inn" to Woodview Grove, and in October the same year to Middleton Crescent. With the introduction of the electric tram in June 1900, Bean cut back the service to Moor Road. By September of the same year Bean's firm was known as "Bean and Son" and their Dewsbury Road 'buses were withdrawn and diverted to Holbeck Church, replacing the Holbeck Moor 'buses which had just been taken off by Fanny France. These have been referred to previously. Bean and Son continued to run to Holbeck Church until the electric tram took over on Elland Road in 1901.

THE EAST STREET AND ELLERBY LANE 'BUSES

There were two short distance penny 'bus services that operated in the East Street area. One ran from Kirkgate to the "Robin Hood Inn," East Street and the other to the "Cross Green Lane Hotel," also in East Street.

The "Robin Hood Inn" service had small beginnings when, in January 1881, Oliver Howard was granted a licence to run a Saturday evening 'bus from the junction of York Street and Kirkgate. This must have been successful, for the following month a daily service was instituted. In October 1881 the town terminus was fixed on the north side of York Street opposite the "Borough Arms Cocoa House" and, by 1882, a half hourly service was in operation.

In the early 'eighties 500 houses were built in Long Close Lane and the population increased in proportion.

In March 1887 Howard extended his route to Long Close Lane, Ellerby Lane, the fares being 1d. to the "Robin Hood Inn" and 1½d. to Ellerby Lane. By 1891 the operation of the route passed into the hands of James Dean who ran it without apparent alteration until 1900. In May of that year an extension to the top of Long Close Lane was authorised and the 'buses apparently continued until the introduction of electric trams to Easy Road in March 1902.

The early history of the "Cross Green Lane Hotel" service is obscure, but it was certainly in existence by August 1887 and was probably worked by Oliver Howard. The 'buses traversed much of the route of the Ellerby Lane service and ran half hourly from the "Borough Arms," Kirkgate, thus giving a 15 minutes service to the "Robin Hood Inn." By 1891 the route was operated by James Dean and apparently continued until the opening of the Easy Road tramway. Dean sold odd 'buses and horses at intervals and it is impossible to ascertain exactly when his 'buses were withdrawn. He finally went out of business in 1903, when his stables were bought by Leeds Corporation. He was given notice to quit and on 25th May 1903 ten horses, three 'buses and four wagonettes were offered for sale.

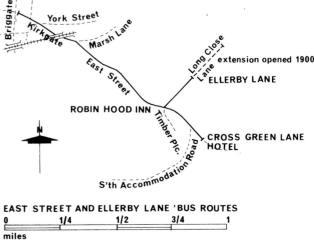

EAST STREET AND ELLERBY LANE 'BUS ROUTES

0   1/4   1/2   3/4   1
miles

THE HUNSLET 'BUS SERVICES

Mention has been made in previous chapters of the early history of the Hunslet and Hunslet Carr services, and the attempts of the Leeds Tramways Company to run 'buses to the latter district. When the Tramways Company departed from the route in 1882 there were two competing proprietors, Joseph Walker and Arthur James Hawkes, operating to Grove Road and Hunslet Carr. At this time Walker put on an additional 'bus and ran alternately with Hawkes, giving a 15 minute service to the "Bay Horse Inn," Hunslet Carr.

In April 1885 Amos Kirby introduced an opposition 'bus to Hunslet Carr. His 'bus ran uneventfully until Kirby's licence was revoked for drunkenness in August 1891.

Hawkes died in September 1886 and the licence passed to his notorious relative, Thomas. Thomas Hawkes was only allowed to run to Grove Road, but made unsuccessful applications to run to the "Bay Horse Inn." On 27th September 1887 his business was sold and his Grove Road route passed to a Robert Sowden of 10 Stafford Street, Hunslet. Walker ceased to run shortly afterwards and his Hunslet services were taken over by a John Swales. In September 1891 Sowden died and his widow, Sarah, took over. Three months after her husband's death she managed to obtain an extension of her Grove Road service to Hunslet Carr. This was apparently uneconomic, for after only 12 weeks she applied for it to be cut back to Grove Road again. This was granted, Grove Road having a ten minute service and Hunslet Carr half hourly.

In April 1893 Sowden sold her business to a John Henry Stephenson, the price paid being £270. Three months later, on 17th July, Swales' assets were sold at his stables, Chadwick Street, Hunslet. His two 'buses running to Grove Road were bought by Stephenson and his two Hunslet Carr 'buses passed to Eli Spurdens. Spurdens ran for about two months, selling one of the 'buses to Stephenson and the other to a James Gill. Gill ran the bus for a short time, replacing it with a new bus built by John Marston & Co. of Birmingham. Stephenson took over Swales' stables and during 1894 had the monopoly of the Grove Road section and ran to Hunslet Carr in conjunction with Gill. By December 1894 Stephenson had had enough and sold out to Thomas John Bean.

The many changes of proprietor in the early 'nineties indicate that the Hunslet Carr and Grove Road services were uneconomical to run. Stephenson, at his bankruptcy hearing, several years after he had finished running, attributed his failure to the losses he had sustained on his Hunslet 'buses.

By 1888 a Benjamin Riley of Cotton Mill Row set up business as a cab and wagonette proprietor in Hunslet. In late 1894 his widow, Elizabeth, bought one of Stephenson's 'buses and she began to run to Hunslet Carr in opposition to Gill and Bean. In May 1898 Bean bought her out but she retained some wagonettes which were sold on 5th April 1900.

On 2nd November 1896 Bean suffered a fire at his stables in Chadwick Street which were in joint occupation with a firm of sand, coal and limestone merchants, John Smith and Co. Two of his horses were killed and

Bean's 'bus outside the "Bay Horse Inn,' Hunslet Carr about 1905.   *Courtesy J. Soper Collection.*

163

Hunslet Lake 'bus terminus with two little girls at the drinking fountain, about 1890. *Courtesy The Thoresby Society, Leeds.*

he lost much of his harness, but his 'buses were saved.

Bean and Gill managed to make the route pay and continued their 'buses until the coming of the electric tram. In March 1901 the Grove Road section ceased to run, but the Hunslet Carr route lingered on until 1st June 1905, when it was replaced by the Balm Road electric tramway.

A third service to Hunslet was introduced in May 1887 running from Briggate via Hunslet Road and Glasshouse Street to the lake on Hunslet Moor. The service was initially operated by Thomas Hawkes, in partnership with another rough character, Jacob Matthias Lofthouse, who had convictions for assault. On 24th June 1887 the Hawkes and Lofthouse partnership of "omnibus proprietors, carters and hay dealers" was dissolved. When Hawkes sold up in September the same year, one of his 'buses was purchased by William Preval, a packing case dealer, who was noted as having been sentenced four times for felony and had served a term of penal servitude. Preval didn't last long and went into liquidation, his 'bus running for the last time on 5th January 1888. There is a possibility that Preval may have run to Hunslet Carr in addition to the Lake, but this is not certain.

Lofthouse had the monopoly of the Hunslet Lake service for a while and on 8th October 1887 one of his passengers, John Armistead, had a memorable ride:–

"It was stated that on the night of Saturday 8th inst. shortly before 11 o'clock, Armistead and a bookmaker named Septimus Austin, left Briggate with the intention of going to the "lake" at Hunslet. They entered an omnibus owned by the defendant Lofthouse and were driven by one of the defendants (Buckley). In the course of the journey they discovered they were not

being taken in the right direction and ultimately found themselves at Lofthouse's stables (in Stafford Street). Austin then went to lay a complaint at the police station. Armistead was left with the defendants in the stable yard where it was alleged the defendants seized him and ducked him in the horse trough, which was full of water and left him to struggle out as best he could. Austin returning with a police constable found Armistead in the stables wet through. In cross examination complainant admitted having been in a "dram" shop with Austin on the evening in question, and both men refused to pay the 'bus fare when they found they were being driven in the wrong direction. Mr Warren: You say you never got to the "lake" that night? Witness: Yes I got into the trough instead, that must be the way they deliver their last customers for the lake district." ———

(Yorkshire Post, 22nd October 1887)

Fortunately, Armistead could see the funny side of his predicament and Lofthouse had to pay one guinea costs. In December 1888 Lofthouse sold out to a William Stoner of Iron Street, Hunslet, who ran the service for 18 months before selling his 'buses to George Horsfall. After six months Charles Coates took over from Horsfall and the last proprietor to run to Hunslet Lake was John Swales, from February 1892 to July 1893. Swales ran two 'Jubilee' 'buses on the route.

No timetables have been discovered for this route but it is recorded that 26 daily journeys were made in 1889 increasing to 40 by the following year. The frequent changes of proprietor indicate that the route was difficult to run economically. The 'bus service was re-introduced by Bean's about 1902, apparently over the same route, and continued until the opening of the Balm

John Armistead emerges from the horse trough.

Road electric tramway. The very last 'bus to Hunslet Lake left Briggate at 11.30 pm on Saturday night 27th May 1905.

A short lived service to the "Wellington Hotel," Church Street, Hunslet, ran between 1888 and 1890. The proprietors appear to have been Lofthouse and Sowden. Little information has been traced but it is recorded that there were 18 departures daily from Briggate.

There was a brief service operated by James Dean to the "Queen Hotel," South Accommodation Road, from York Street via Crown Point Bridge, Hunslet Road and Sayner Lane. The service began in May 1889, but by August the same year had been discontinued.

Another short lived service was an extension of Bean's Grove Road route via Grove Road and Beza Street to the "Old Engine," Hunslet, instituted in April 1897. Bean could not make it pay and reverted to his old terminus after only two months operation.

The route of the Hunslet 'buses in the town centre was via The Calls, Call Lane, Duncan Street and Lower Briggate to their stand near the railway bridge. The various parts of Hunslet, their destination, although densely populated, was a poor working class area and the omnibus proprietors had great difficulty in making the 'buses pay. From about 1880 onwards, the fares on the different routes were only 1d. but as the routes were short it seems probable that many of the inhabitants walked into town.

VENTNOR STREET AND BLACKMAN LANE

On 16th July 1890 a licence was granted to a John Burnett to run a 'bus between Blackman Lane and Briggate via Fenton Street, Great George Street, Infirmary Street, returning via Commercial Street, Park Row and South Parade. The route was under a mile in length and was unsuccessful. In October of the same year Burnett transferred his Blackman Lane 'bus to a new route via Market Street, Kirkgate, Commercial Street, Bond Street, St. Paul's Street, West Street, Kirkstall Road, Adelphi Street and Somerby Street to the top of Ventnor Street. The return journey was by the same route as far as Infirmary Street and then along that street, Boar Lane and Duncan Street to Market Street. The terminus was at the east side of Ventnor Street, adjacent to Burley Road. At the same time a Wright Simison put on an opposition wagonette running every 50 minutes from the Corn Exchange to Ventnor Street.

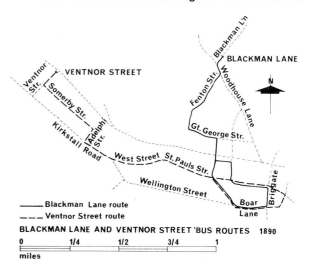

BLACKMAN LANE AND VENTNOR STREET 'BUS ROUTES 1890

165

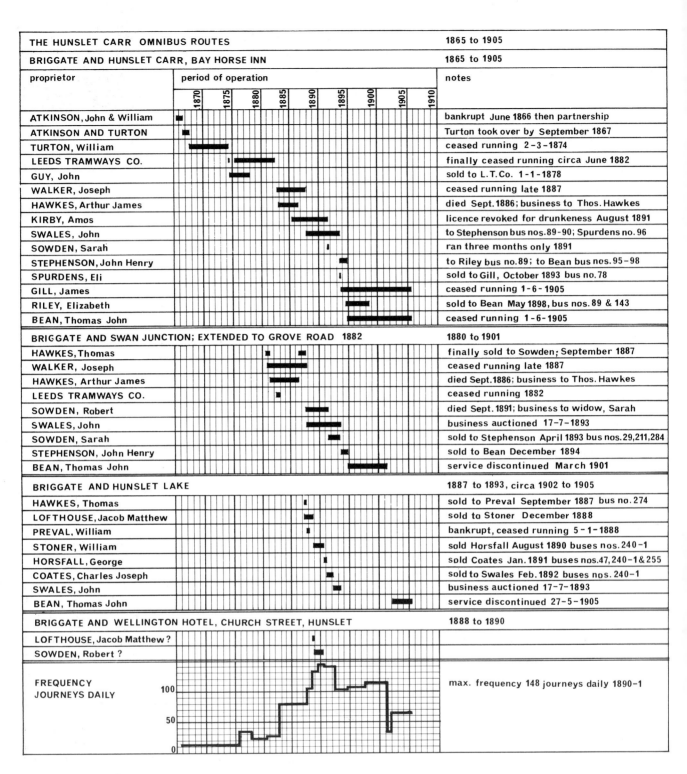

THE HUNSLET CARR OMNIBUS ROUTES											1865 to 1905
BRIGGATE AND HUNSLET CARR, BAY HORSE INN											**1865 to 1905**
proprietor	period of operation										notes
	1870	1875	1880	1885	1890	1895	1900	1905	1910		
ATKINSON, John & William											bankrupt June 1866 then partnership
ATKINSON AND TURTON											Turton took over by September 1867
TURTON, William											ceased running 2-3-1874
LEEDS TRAMWAYS CO.											finally ceased running circa June 1882
GUY, John											sold to L.T.Co. 1-1-1878
WALKER, Joseph											ceased running late 1887
HAWKES, Arthur James											died Sept. 1886; business to Thos. Hawkes
KIRBY, Amos											licence revoked for drunkeness August 1891
SWALES, John											to Stephenson bus nos. 89-90; Spurdens no. 96
SOWDEN, Sarah											ran three months only 1891
STEPHENSON, John Henry											to Riley bus no. 89; to Bean bus nos. 95-98
SPURDENS, Eli											sold to Gill, October 1893 bus no. 78
GILL, James											ceased running 1-6-1905
RILEY, Elizabeth											sold to Bean May 1898, bus nos. 89 & 143
BEAN, Thomas John											ceased running 1-6-1905
BRIGGATE AND SWAN JUNCTION; EXTENDED TO GROVE ROAD 1882											**1880 to 1901**
HAWKES, Thomas											finally sold to Sowden; September 1887
WALKER, Joseph											ceased running late 1887
HAWKES, Arthur James											died Sept. 1886; business to Thos. Hawkes
LEEDS TRAMWAYS CO.											ceased running 1882
SOWDEN, Robert											died Sept. 1891; business to widow, Sarah
SWALES, John											business auctioned 17-7-1893
SOWDEN, Sarah											sold to Stephenson April 1893 bus nos. 29,211,284
STEPHENSON, John Henry											sold to Bean December 1894
BEAN, Thomas John											service discontinued March 1901
BRIGGATE AND HUNSLET LAKE											**1887 to 1893, circa 1902 to 1905**
HAWKES, Thomas											sold to Preval September 1887 bus no. 274
LOFTHOUSE, Jacob Matthew											sold to Stoner December 1888
PREVAL, William											bankrupt, ceased running 5-1-1888
STONER, William											sold Horsfall August 1890 buses nos. 240-1
HORSFALL, George											sold Coates Jan. 1891 buses nos. 47, 240-1 & 255
COATES, Charles Joseph											sold to Swales Feb. 1892 buses nos. 240-1
SWALES, John											business auctioned 17-7-1893
BEAN, Thomas John											service discontinued 27-5-1905
BRIGGATE AND WELLINGTON HOTEL, CHURCH STREET, HUNSLET											**1888 to 1890**
LOFTHOUSE, Jacob Matthew ?											
SOWDEN, Robert ?											
FREQUENCY JOURNEYS DAILY											max. frequency 148 journeys daily 1890-1

The two proprietors could not make the service pay and by May 1891 it had been withdrawn.

THE SHADWELL 'BUS

George Brown's 'bus, introduced about 1872 from Shadwell to the "New Inn", (later to the "Black Swan"), Vicar Lane, ran unchanged during the 'seventies. Brown ran via Chapeltown and Moortown and, after Richard Machan's short-lived opposition Scarcroft 'bus was withdrawn, he retired from business and was succeeded by his son, Alfred. Alfred ran one journey daily only from Shadwell and, from October to December 1886, advertised his business for sale. It was purchased by a Joseph Greenwood of Shadwell who, by 1893, had increased the number of daily departures from Shadwell to Leeds to four, but this was halved the following year. Greenwood charged 7d. for the journey.

The Shadwell 'bus was bedevilled by a notorious steep hill, 1 in 10 Holly Bank, referred to by Lord Macaulay, M.P. for Leeds, in his book "History of England", p. 291:

"A 'bus crosses this 'Mauvais pas' daily, and whatever kind of weather there is, the passengers have to alight and walk up the hill. When this is covered with ice or it is snowing or raining hard, then they have literally to put their shoulders to the wheel and help to push the 'bus along. Such a thing, although almost incredible, is, in winter time, an every day occurence."

The Leeds Corporation discussed the removal of the hill for over 20 years and it was finally removed in 1906, the gradient being reduced to 1 in 20. By this time Greenwood's 'bus made only one journey weekly (on

A contemporary sketch of a typical winter's "journey" on the Shadwell 'bus in 1880.　　　　*Courtesy Leeds City Libraries.*

Saturdays). In 1902, upon the introduction of the Moortown electric tram, the 'bus was cut back to run between Moortown and Shadwell only. It continued to run until the introduction of a Corporation motor 'bus in 1913.

BRAMFITT'S DEMISE

Mention has been made of Bramfitt's Roundhay, Cowper Street, Kirkstall Road and Reginald Terrace 'buses in previous chapters. He also ran a 'bus service to Gathorne Terrace, a short working of his Roundhay route. Gathorne Terrace and Spencer Place, Roundhay Road, were areas of middle class terrace housing erected in the 'seventies and 'eighties and by November 1883 the district had become sufficiently developed for Bramfitt to start a 'bus service. By 1888 36 journeys daily were operated. John Turton's (later Marshall and Sharp's) opposition 'buses have been mentioned elsewhere and, when Sharp was forced to go out of business in 1893, Bramfitt transferred his 'buses from Reginald Terrace to supplement his Gathorne Terrace route, increasing the frequency to ten minutes.

Bramfitt's well-known Roundhay 'bus ceased to run in April 1898 when the electrification of the Roundhay to Kirkstall tramway was completed. The Gathorne Terrace 'bus finished at the same time; Bramfitt's assets consisting of 65 horses and nine 'buses were auctioned on 6th April. Bramfitt went into retirement at his home, Lily Villas, Roundhay Road. A few months later, on 16th January 1899, at the age of 74 years, he died.

Some of Bramfitt's 'buses were bought by John William Wilks, who ran the Gathorne Terrace route for about two years before being driven off the road by the improving service of electric trams.

WALKER'S 'BUS SERVICES

The fate of the other 'bus proprietors and their routes has been discussed, but what of the major omnibus proprietor in Leeds, Walker Brothers?

Walker's were always business conscious and never attempted to run 'buses when it was obvious the services would be uneconomic. When the steam trams stopped running to Headingley in March 1892 some of their "Pack Horse" 'buses were extended to Headingley Church, but some continued to short work to the "Pack Horse". Following their peak in 1892-3 the first of their 'bus services to close was that to Leopold Street. This route closed in late 1894 due to competition from the Leopold Street to Wortley steam trams.

In 1897, due to an improved Headingley horse tram service, Walker's Headingley Church 'buses were reduced in frequency. Walker's could see the writing on the wall and in 1898 hopefully approached the Corporation, suggesting that the Tramways Committee pay £150 per 'bus for the withdrawal of each of Walker's 'buses running in opposition to the Headingley and Chapeltown tramways. The Committee would not entertain the idea.

In early 1899 horse 'buses were still selling at about £150 each and in March of that year Walker's withdrew their Headingley Church, "Pack Horse", Hyde Park, Victoria Road and Burley Road 'buses; five 'buses and 32 horses being auctioned on 18th and 25th March 1899. It was a wise move by Walker's; in one stroke they had halved their 'bus interests. A year later, like horse and steam tramcars, horse 'buses were virtually unsaleable. The remainder of their routes disappeared one by one. In January 1900 the Reginald Terrace 'bus succumbed to the electric tram and their Armley 'bus ran for the last time on Saturday 28th April the same year, being replaced by steam trams on the following Monday. Moorland Road closed on 5th May 1900.

The withdrawal of the Moorland Road 'bus resulted in many complaints from local residents who were comparatively isolated from the tram. They made requests to the Corporation to re-instate the service but, owing to a shortage of rolling stock, the Tramways Department could not help. It was left to John William Wilks to re-introduce the route in October of the same year. He could not make the route pay and by May 1901 had taken his 'buses off. On 17th May Walker's made a come back and were given permission to take over from Wilks. They ran their 'buses for a short time but could not hope to compete with the Headingley electric trams.

Wilks' Victoria Road 'bus crosses Albion Street from Commercial Street to Bond Street in 1900.
Courtesy Leeds City Libraries.

Walker's Briggate and Victoria Road Traffic Notice.
Courtesy Leeds City Museums.

On 18th October 1901 Wilks had the last fling on Moorland Road when he was allowed to re-introduce the service extended to Brudenell Road. With the possible exception of Bean's Hunslet Lake 'bus, this was apparently the last attempt by a private operator to introduce a new horse 'bus service in Leeds. Alas for Wilks it was short lived. Wilks gave up and his business was sold "due to expiration of lease" on 29th October 1902. Wilks continued as a cab and wagonette owner and later became a garage proprietor with premises in Sheepshanks Yard, North Street, on the site of what became the Ritz (later the A.B.C.) Cinema. This became a starting place for private motor 'buses in the 1920's. The Wilks family later ran motor 'buses and coaches.

Walker's were still running to Whitehall Road, and in September 1900 were given permission to cut back the service to Domestic Street. The following month they re-introduced their 'buses to the Cattle Market, Whitehall Road, running on Tuesdays and Saturdays only. The introduction of horse trams on Whitehall Road in March 1901 resulted in the withdrawal of Walker's 'buses four months later. Two 'buses and six horses were auctioned on 30th July.

Walker's suffered only one major accident during the whole of their period of operation. This occurred on 17th February 1896 when a packed Reginald Terrace 'bus overturned in North Street when the near fore wheel ran off the axle. There were several injuries but no one was killed. Walker's said that their 'buses were inspected every morning before they left the yard and this was the first accident of this type that they had had during the 40 years that they had run cabs and 'buses.

During the horse 'bus era there were several cases of 'buses overturning, probably the most serious occuring on 9th July 1870. The accident involved a seasonal 'bus running from Leeds to Boston Spa and operated by Pybus Allison who ran 'buses on the route in the late 'sixties and 'seventies. The accident happened in Roundhay Road, opposite the Cavalry Barracks, and was due to the spokes of one of the wheels disintegrating. Several persons were seriously injured and one later died. Allison had been told about the defective wheel a day or two previously but took no action and he was committed for manslaughter.

Walker Bros. continued in business as cab proprietors, undertakers and removal contractors. The removal business survived until their premises in Chapeltown Road were demolished in 1963.

Within a few years the "lumbering tumbling" omnibuses of Leeds had become a memory. In 1897, within the confines of the city boundary, there were 24 'bus routes worked by 60 'buses, viz:—

Armley, two; Beckett Street, two; Beeston Hill, four; Burley Hotel, two; Camp Road, two; Cross Green Lane Hotel, two; Dewsbury Road, four; Elland Road, two; Ellerby Lane, two; Gathorne Terrace, two; Harehills Road, two; Headingley Church, four; Hunslet Carr, two; Hunslet, Grove Road, two; Meanwood, two; Moorland Road, two; Pontefract Lane, two; Reginald Terrace, two; Roundhay Park, four; Stoney Rock, four; Victoria Road, four; Westfield Road, two; Whitehall Road, two; and York Road, two.

By June 1905 all had disappeared.

Although 60 'buses were regularly working in 1897 considerably more than this number were licensed for use. The licensing records for this period indicate that no fewer than 327 'buses and wagonettes were licensed.

Mention should be made of the wagonettes. These played a very important part in supplementing the 'buses and trams. They paralleled the routes and usually terminated near to the 'bus or tram termini. They did not run to a fixed timetable but ran on a hire basis like taxi cabs. If the 'bus or tram was full prospective passengers would take a wagonette. Some of the omnibus proprietors ran wagonettes, but the majority were owned by a multitude of small firms who complemented the 'bus and tram services rather than ran in opposition. The wagonettes were not allowed to stand in Briggate but were lined up in various side streets.

Walker's Reginald Terrace 'bus overturns in North Street in 1896 as a steam tram passes.

Fully loaded wagonettes in Leeds Terrace, Sheepscar, in 1902.

Courtesy P. D. Johnson.

Albion Street, Brunswick Street, Cross Belgrave Street, Great George Street, Hartley Hill, Quebec Street, Wellington Street and Wilson Street were wagonette starting points. The 'buses and wagonettes were licensed in the same numerical series and frequently exchanged numbers. The highest number reached was 340 and it is usually not possible to tell a 'bus from a wagonette. In only four years, 1897-1900, did the licensing authorities split the two, and even these figures are not complete. In 1897 there were at least 90 'buses; 1898, 85; 1899, 65 and 1900, 56 licensed to run in Leeds.

A wagonette, believed to be in the Dewsbury Road area, about 1890. *Courtesy The late C. R. Wood, Photographer.*

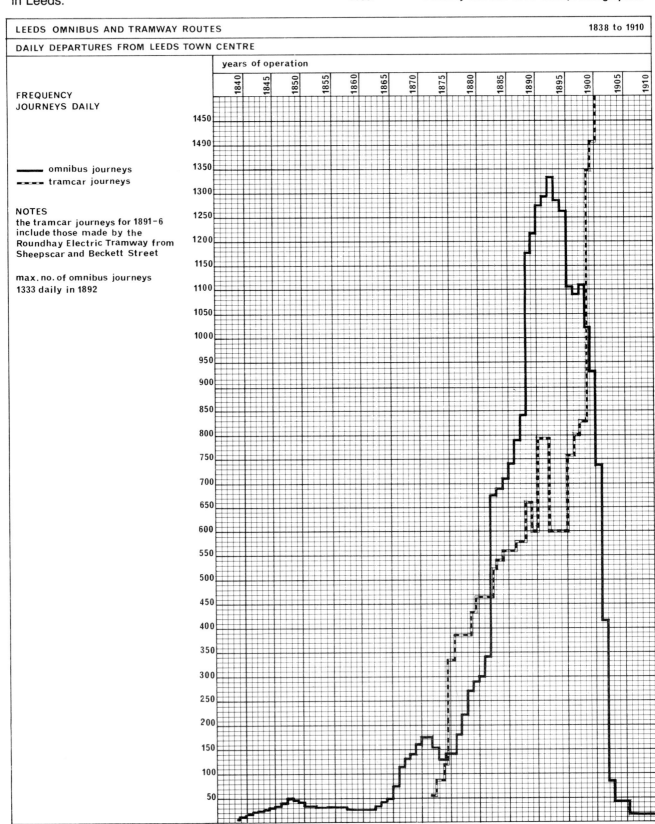

LEEDS OMNIBUS AND TRAMWAY ROUTES — 1838 to 1910

DAILY DEPARTURES FROM LEEDS TOWN CENTRE

years of operation

FREQUENCY JOURNEYS DAILY

—— omnibus journeys
▪▭▪▭▪ tramcar journeys

NOTES
the tramcar journeys for 1891-6 include those made by the Roundhay Electric Tramway from Sheepscar and Beckett Street

max. no. of omnibus journeys 1333 daily in 1892

The graph covering the whole period of horse 'bus operation in Leeds shows that the 'buses reached their zenith in 1892 with 1,333 departures from the town centre daily. The first 20 years were relatively stationary followed by a gradual climb in the 'sixties and 'seventies to the rapid expansion of the 'eighties. At that time they surpassed the tramcars in importance, but suffered a swift decline in the 1898-1901 period.

In the early days 'buses stuck rigidly to their own routes due to the fact that the destinations were permanently painted on the vehicles. It was not until April 1891 that removable destination boards were allowed on the wagonettes and the 'buses soon followed.

Both 'buses and trams displayed coloured lights for use at night. This system was introduced on 10th January 1870 and the colours allocated for the various routes were as follows:– Leeds to Armley and Bramley, blue with white star; Beeston Hill, Burmantofts, Halton and Whitkirk, yellow; Burley, blue with white cross; Chapeltown, green; Headingley, red; Holbeck and New Wortley, dark claret; Hunslet and New Leeds, green with a white cross; Hyde Park, pink with white diamond; Kirkstall, blue; Meanwood, red with white star. All 'buses coming from outside the borough had to show un-coloured glass.

On the trams the colours became:– Chapeltown, green; Headingley, red; Hunslet, Kirkstall and York Road, blue; Meanwood, red with white star; and Wortley, blue with the words "The Star". By 1887 the Wortley cars were showing a green light and York Road no light at all, but by 1891 the York Road trams showed a green light. When the Roundhay Electric Tramway opened in 1891, cars running between Sheepscar and Roundhay displayed a red light and on the Harehills Road and Beckett Street section, yellow.

The introduction of new routes, and route alterations, resulted in the coloured lights system becoming disorganised. On 18th December 1895 the Hackney Carriages Committee adopted a system using three colours only, red, green and white. On the 'buses the red light was adopted on the Armley, Beeston Hill, Gathorne Terrace, Hunslet Carr, Pontefract Lane, Reginald Terrace, Roundhay Park and Victoria Road routes; green on the Camp Road, Cross Green Lane Hotel and Headingley Church routes. The remainder were white. The Headingley and Meanwood trams showed a red light; Chapeltown, Hunslet, Kirkstall and York Road, green and Leopold Street, Wortley and the Roundhay Electric Tramway, white. There were colour variations on the electric trams but the coloured lights arrangement was retained until November 1912.

It was the practice of the Hackney Carriages Committee to erect a cast iron plate to mark the various 'bus and cab stands and some remained for many years after the vehicles ceased running. A plate inscribed "Stand for one omnibus" could be seen at the old Westfield Road 'bus terminus until the early 1930's, but the last plates of all were the two large cab and wagonette plates erected at the Whitehall Road Cattle Market terminus in June 1886. These were removed on 27th May 1970, one now being in the possession of the Leeds City Museum and the other displayed at the National Tramway Museum, Crich, Derbyshire.

Although the last 'bus, operating within the city, ran in 1905; weekly or twice weekly market 'buses from outlying villages could still be seen for many years afterwards. The Tramways Department ran horse 'buses to Adel until 1906 and to Farnley from 1907-11. In 1905 Helm's 'buses were still running to Barwick, Watkinson's to Kippax and Greenwood's to Shadwell. The demise of these remaining horse 'bus services will be discussed in the next volume.

The Leeds Cattle Market plaque shortly before removal, 27th May 1970. *Courtesy J. Soper.*

For all its advantages, the electric tram had put out of business many enterprising and hardworking 'busmen. Several of the proprietors were ruthless individuals who deserved to disappear. Many of the drivers and conductors became employed on the trams. Fanny France's employees, for example, were taken over by the Corporation in September 1900.

The horse 'bus driver, like the stage coach driver before him, was a highly respected person. To drive a three-horse 'bus required a great deal of skill and the passengers who came down with the driver each morning and returned each night sought a seat alongside him, especially if there was a "funny" horse in the team. A "funny" horse was an awkward horse that kicked and was good for nothing but 'bus work.

The omnibus proprietors were forced to take up other occupations, but some, unfortunately, finished up in the bankruptcy court. In the case of Eli Spurdens the Judge was sympathetic:–

"The system of Corporations entering into trading is perfectly justifiable, but it always brings with it a great deal of personal hardship and suffering, and I think where a municipality by undertaking things like tramways, by entering into competition with private traders of the town, ruins the business of those traders, although, it may be, no compensation either honorary

or in law can be given to them, yet I do think if it leads to bankruptcy, they ought to be treated with great consideration." ——
(Yorkshire Post, 10th June 1902).

We will leave the last word on horse 'buses to the *Yorkshire Evening Post*, reporting a trip on the last 'bus to Hunslet Carr on 1st June 1905:–

"Gill's 'bus — the last but one — should have left Briggate at nine o'clock, but it lingered twenty minutes after its appointed time, "Johnnie on the Road," the driver, being apparently loth to hasten its eclipse. On a pole in front of the vehicle drooped a big Union Jack. A painted sheet on one side of the 'bus bore the phrase — "Well played, Hunslet Carr." and on the other side, daubed in black letters on a big square piece of cardboard, was the inscription — humorous, had it not been sad — "Are we down-hearted? No." ——

—— Meanwhile , I spied Mr. Bean across the road, shaking hands with Mr. Daggett, the tramway traffic manager.

"I suppose it had to be," Mr. Bean was remarking, "and I don't blame people for riding on the trams."

After a talk, Mr. Daggett was persuaded to become a passenger on the last trip, and he, Mr. Bean, and myself took our seats on the top of the old 'bus.

There was no rush for places. There were three or four vacant seats on the top, and inside there were only two or three passengers.

Promptly at 9.30 Harry Long pulled the reins, and we were off ——

—— Mr. Bean too was sad.

"This business," said he, has cost me close on £2,000. Four years ago I'd ten 'buses and 160 horses and paid fully £80 a week in wages. And these 'buses cost me about £150 each." ——

—— Not until we got opposite Hunslet Church were there any marked evidences that an important era in the history of Leeds was just closing. Here a group of some fifty or sixty women were assembled, and as we passed they raised vigorous feminine squeals and waved their aprons. Balm Road was still livelier. All the residents in the neighbourhood turned out to see the last 'bus, and when at length we finished our journey at the "Bay Horse Hotel", it was in the midst of a cheering, hilarious crowd of fully five hundred people".

(Yorkshire Evening Post, 2nd June 1905)

A party of ex-busmen was held at the "Bay Horse" which temporarily broke up in order to witness the final departure of the 'buses, for Gill's vehicle was also there. A great cheer was raised, "Johnnie of the Road" pulled his reins, Harry Long did likewise, and the two 'buses passed away (via the stables) into history. The following morning electric trams took over.

Gill's 'bus stands at the Hunslet Carr terminus on the last day of operation, 1st June 1905. The 'bus, licence number 26, was built by John Marston and Company of Birmingham.
Courtesy The late J. Gill.

CHAPTER NINETEEN

The Anderson Closed Circuit Electric System

In the 1894-6 period, during the electric v. cable traction controversy, attempts were made by inventors to eliminate one of the principal objections to the electric system – the unsightly overhead wires. The open slot conduit and the Westinghouse Surface Contact System are mentioned in other chapters, and it was with the latter form that many engineers were interested. The most successful of the surface contact systems, such as the Dolter, Diatto or Lorain types, worked electromagnetically. An example of the Lorain system can be seen at the National Tramway Museum, Crich, Derbyshire. Electrical contact was made between a skate fixed to the underside of the car and a series of metal studs set into the road surface at fixed intervals down the centre of the track. An electromagnetically operated switch connected the underground supply to the stud while the skate was passing over it, and the tramcar was thus supplied with electric power. Of the many surface contact systems, very few were actually adopted for service. A number made electrical contact by mechanical means. One of these, the Anderson Closed Circuit Electric System, was constructed in Leeds.

Christopher Anderson was a Leeds man and, on 11th July 1894, he attended a meeting of the Highways Committee and asked for permission to lay a 400 yards length of tramway for the trial of his patent system. He prepared plans and in January 1895 the Highways Committee agreed to lay 100 to 200 yards of his system, at Anderson's cost, and loan a car for experiments. The experiment was made on 13th January 1896 and Thwaite Gate, Hunslet was the site selected.

Current was passed to the skate under the car by means of a rising contact stud worked mechanically by a lever system. The working of the system is shown in the illustration below. The switch mechanism was contained in a cast iron box, 3'-0" long by 1'-0" wide by 1'-8" deep. The distance between the boxes was regulated by the length of the car; this being in the Leeds experiments 17'-0". The boxes were provided with a checker plate cover, which could be removed with lifting keys. No attempt was made to keep the boxes watertight. The boxes were connected together by a three-way Doulton conduit laid on edge. The two steel wires, W and W, were carried through the upper and lower ducts, the electrical conductor through the middle duct. The electrical part was simple. The stud A was a hollow casting provided with an insulating bushing at each end, and an air-space between. A renewable cap of brass was fitted to the top of the upper insulating bushing, and the conductor carried down through the stud and

connected to a brass terminal which formed the lower portion of the stud. A second brass terminal was secured to the side of the box, but insulated therefrom and electrically connected with the main feeder. As the stud was forced up by the switch mechanism, these brass terminals came into contact and closed the circuit between the feeder and the brass cap on top of the contact stud. The collector-skate, which was carried on the car, consisted of sheet copper riveted to a channel steel frame. The collector-skate was considerably wider in the centre than at the ends, to enable it to keep in contact with the contact-stud even when going around sharp curves. This skate was rigidly attached to the car and carried about 4" from the ground, and was provided at the rear end with a ramp, which was carried down to within $\frac{1}{2}$" of the setts. The rear half of this ramp was insulated from the rest of the collector.

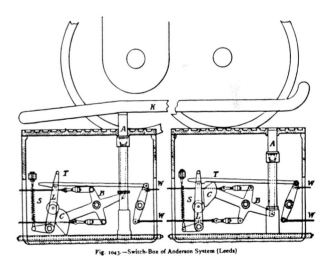

Fig. 1043.—Switch-Box of Anderson System (Leeds)

An illustration showing the working of Anderson's System. *Courtesy "Modern Electric Practice," 1904 Edition.*

The working of the system was as follows:– The first contact stud was raised by hand, or by a suitable lever, into contact with the skate. The car was then started, the current flowing through the brass cap on the contact stud, the collector-skate through the motors to the rail. As the car proceeded the ramp on the collector-skate K depressed the contact stud A, which actuated the double bell-crank lever B. The lever B carried on its end a cam C, bearing on a roller carried on a single bell crank L. The upward movement of the cam C forced the lever L to the left; thus by means of the rod T and wires

W W the double bell-crank lever B in the advance box was moved in the reverse direction to the lever B in the first box, thus forcing the advance stud A upwards. When the centre point of the cam C in the first box passed the centre of the roller on lever L, the spring S came into action, causing the cam C to be forced upward quickly, which forced the contact-stud A sharply down to its lowest point. At the same time the cam C, in rising, disengaged the rod T from the lever L. In the advance box the action of the cam was reversed. The centre point of the cam having passed the centre of the roller L, the spring S forced the cam C sharply down, and the lever L to the right so that it engaged the rod T, which fell and caught lever L by its own weight. The rapid downward motion of the cam threw the advance contact-stud A sharply upward, and made contact with the collector-skate K, against which it was held by the spring S acting through the roller on lever L, cam C, and double bell-crank lever B.

The pressure against the collector-skate was a flexible one, and capable of following any irregularities in the skate. The forcing down of the contact-stud A in the first box broke the electrical contact between the contact-stud and the feeder wire with absolute certainty, and as the collector-skate was so proportioned that the advance stud came into contact with the collector-skate before the first stud reached the insulated portion of the ramp, the electrical circuit to the car was never broken.

The action was then repeated in the succeeding boxes, and when installed on a single track, as in Leeds, two sets of mechanism and two contact-studs were provided in each box, the mechanism so arranged as to work in opposite directions.

The experiment at Hunslet was not satisfactory as there was no current to drive a car. A horse car was equipped with a skate and Anderson was able to demonstrate the theory only of his invention. He claimed that his system was cheaper, simpler and more positive in action than other forms of electric traction and indicated that the cost of installation would be £1,200 per mile. The Tramways Sub-Committee said it could not make any recommendation on a partial trial and wanted to see the invention practically tested – that is, a car propelled by electricity. On 22nd January 1896 members of the Bradford Corporation Tramways Committee visited Hunslet and were said to be very impressed with the "apparent simplicity, ingenuity and practicability" of Anderson's idea but also wished to see a proper demonstration. Encouraged by this apparent favourable response to his experiments, the following month Anderson asked the Highways Committee to lay a section of track, at his expense, on the Harehills Road line. The Thomson-Houston Company was to supply the cars and current for the trial. Four months later the Thomson-Houston Company had ceased to run electric cars and Anderson offered to lay a length of his system, provide a car, current and everything necessary to operate the trial car for 12 months. He asked the Corporation to take the system over at cost price if it was found to work as well as the overhead system. This they refused to do but allowed him to lay a half mile length in Harehills Road beginning at the Roundhay Road end with a 1 in 24 gradient.

It took two years for Anderson to lay down the section of track, provide a car and electrical supply. On 3rd October 1898 a trial run was made in the presence of members of the Tramways Committee. The car was taken along the track two or three times and ran with

View of track in Harehills Road showing contact studs.
Courtesy "The Electrical Engineer," J. D. Markham.

"remarkable smoothness and the regularity of the current was proved by the extreme steadiness of the electric lights". Councillor Hannam said he was quite satisfied with the demonstration as far as it went and regarded the experiment as a practical one well worthy of a trial by any local authority or company contemplating the adoption of electric traction. He could not, however, give a definite opinion until the system had been tried for a long period in wet, snow and frosty conditions. It appears that some runs were made during the winter of 1898-9 and the winter of the following year. They proved that the system was a failure.

The serious inherent drawback to the system was its inability to run backwards farther than the length of the skate, and if the current should be cut off momentarily while a car was ascending a gradient, and the car

Anderson's bogie car outside Kirkstall Road Depot in 1899.
Courtesy "Tramway and Railway World."

Car on curve of 30′-0″ radius showing skate.
Courtesy "The Electrical Engineer,' J. D. Markham.

allowed to run back, as might easily happen, a contact-stud would be left sticking up in the street and alive, and a serious danger to traffic. It was only possible to start the car again by pushing it by hand to the live contact-stud. It was also impossible to cut the current off from the live stud, for if it was forced down an advance stud promptly rose. The details of the system, particularly the electrical portions, were not well worked out and to this must be credited the failure of the system. The mechanism was also sluggish in action, particularly when starting a car. The cast iron boxes had to be electrically connected to the rails in compliance with Board of Trade requirements and short circuits were frequent.

The track in Harehills Road was doubled in February 1899, and it appears that some of the studs remained in position. This is implied in an article which appeared in the *"Tramway and Railway World"* for November of that year. The electric car used for the experiments, described in detail in a subsequent volume, was a Brush built bogie car equipped with both a skate and trolley. It was used by the Corporation at busy periods to assist the Roundhay to Kirkstall electric cars and appears to have carried passengers for the first time on 20th July 1898 on the occasion of the Great Yorkshire Show at Roundhay Park. It spent most of its first two years existence at the back of Kirkstall Road Depot and Works and on 16th November 1900 was purchased by the Corporation for £400. It became No. 52 in the electric car fleet.

Anderson's car under test in Harehills Road.

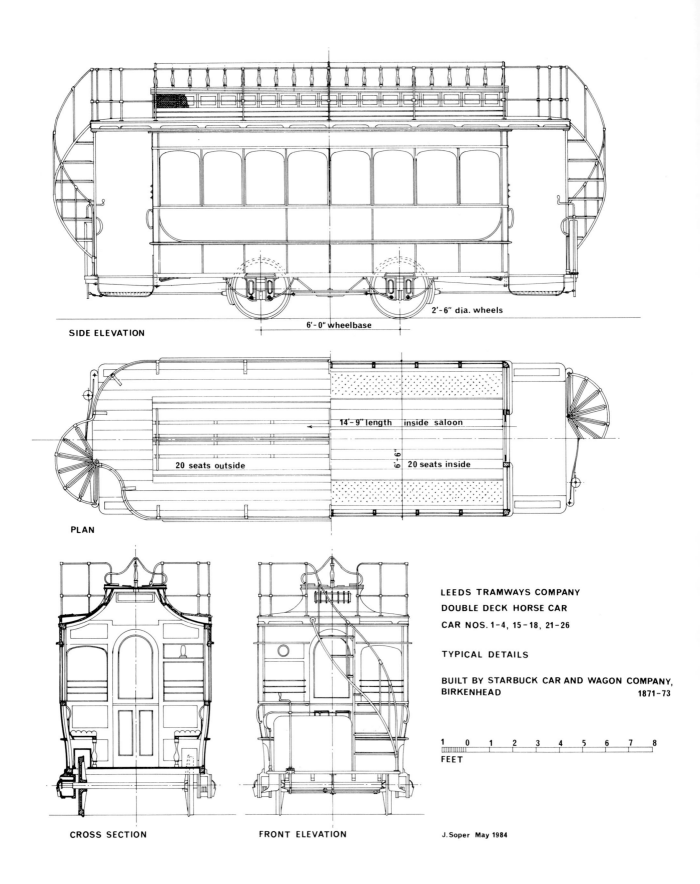

SIDE ELEVATION

2'-6" dia. wheels

6'-0" wheelbase

14'-9" length   inside saloon

6'-6"

20 seats outside

20 seats inside

PLAN

CROSS SECTION

FRONT ELEVATION

LEEDS TRAMWAYS COMPANY
DOUBLE DECK HORSE CAR
CAR NOS. 1-4, 15-18, 21-26

TYPICAL DETAILS

BUILT BY STARBUCK CAR AND WAGON COMPANY,
BIRKENHEAD   1871-73

1   0   1   2   3   4   5   6   7   8
FEET

J. Soper May 1984

CHAPTER TWENTY

The Tramway Rolling Stock

Several contemporary records concerning the early Leeds tramway rolling stock have survived. The Tramways Company cash books, inventory, staff records, annual reports, hackney carriage licensing records etc., still exist and it is possible to build up an almost complete picture. The licensing records give a large amount of information for most years, but are incomplete for the year 1876 when six old cars were replaced by new vehicles. Ambiguities occur with regard to the cash books of 1879, and small contradictions occur between the various sources of information. The City Engineer's report of 1895 states that the 69 cars taken over from the Tramways Company consisted of 25 double-deck horse cars, 20 single-deck horse cars and 24 trailers. All other sources of information show that there were 23 double-deck horse cars and 22 single-deck horse cars. The report is considered to be incorrect.

THE COMPANY HORSE CARS

The original rolling stock supplied by William and Daniel Busby to operate the tramways consisted of four-wheel, three-horse, double-deck cars. Five cars were supplied to inaugurate the service to Headingley in September 1871. They comprised four cars (Nos. 1-4) built by George Starbuck and Company of Birkenhead with 15'-3" long bodies and eight side windows and seating 20 inside and 20 outside on "knifeboard" seats (passengers sitting back to back on a longitudinal seat). A further car (No. 5) referred to as the "Pattern" car, for use as a spare car to supplement Nos. 1-4, to Busby's design and said to be manufactured by the John Stephenson Company of New York, was delivered. It appears to have been identical to similar cars supplied to Liverpool a year or so earlier. It was well finished and received very high praise, the "Yorkshire Post" commenting that it "must commend itself to the approval of the most critical." The car was larger than Nos. 1-4, having a 16'-0" long body and seated 22 inside and 24 outside. This proved to be the largest horse car purchased by the Company with the exception of a short-lived car, No. 7, which seated 48 passengers. For some unknown reason the "Pattern" car was re-numbered 6 in November 1871.

Three horses struggle to haul fully-laden Stephenson car No. 5 up Cookridge Street in 1871.

As shown in the rolling stock tables, late 1871 and early 1872 saw the delivery of various types of cars with odd seating capacities, which probably indicates that they were transferred from one of Busby's other undertakings, most probably Liverpool. These cars were used to open the service to Kirkstall in April and May 1872, and by August of that year, 14 double-deck cars had been delivered. In 1873, following the formation of the Leeds Tramways Company, four (Nos. 5, 7, 9 and 10), were withdrawn and presumably returned to Busbys. There was apparently no cash transaction.

Four double-deckers (Nos. 15-18) built by Starbuck and similar to Nos. 1-4 were delivered in January 1873. One of these cars was used on the trial run of the Dewsbury, Batley and Birstal Tramways Company – a Busby/Turton enterprise – on 20th July 1874. The car probably remained at Dewsbury as two cars, almost certainly Nos. 15 and 16, were sold to this Company in November 1874 for £359. In June 1873 two small single-deck one-horse cars (Nos. 19 and 20) were bought from Starbuck by Busby's and passed to the Leeds Tramways Company via the Continental and General Tramways Company. No. 19 was a very small car seating 14 passengers and No. 20 seated 16. The cars cost £160 each and appear to have had a short life. They were purchased specifically for use on the Boar Lane to Hyde Park service.

A further six cars (Nos. 21-26), similar to Nos. 1-4 and 15-18 were delivered from Starbuck in November 1873. On 1st April 1874 three of the cars, Nos. 24-26, were re-numbered 5, 7 and 9, not necessarily respectively, occupying the numbers vacated by withdrawn cars.

To open the Hunslet route in April 1874, the Company purchased nine rather smaller double-deck cars from Starbuck (Nos. 10, 25-31). They were delivered between March and May 1874 at a total cost of £1,452 – £161 per car. They were bought through the Continental and General Tramways Company and were similar in appearance to the 40-seater double-deckers, but had seven side windows and seated 16 inside and 16 outside passengers. They weighed 44 cwts and the bodies were 12'-0" long.

The gradients of the Headingley route were putting a severe strain on the horses required to draw the heavy double-deck cars. Four horses were sometimes necessary to pull a car up Cookridge Street, and the Tramways Company felt that it would be more economical to institute single-deck cars on the new Chapeltown route which ran over similar terrain to that of Headingley. Accordingly, Starbuck supplied nine-single deck cars, seating 18, and of light construction, weighing 31 cwts as opposed to 47½ cwts (40-seater No. 21 was stated to be of this weight in 1876). The cars (Nos. 15, 16, 32-38) "neatly and substantially built," delivered in October 1874, had turtle back roofs with seven arched side windows, and were used to open the Chapeltown service the following month. These cars required only two horses under normal usage but a chain horse was added on gradients such as Mitchell Hill. The cars cost £167 each, strangely some £6 more than the 32 seater double-deckers supplied earlier. In December 1874 the cars were fitted with an additional four seats – two on each driver's platform. Following a fatal accident this was reduced to one on each platform in March 1875. A further fatal accident on 10th September 1875 resulted in the abandonment of platform seats.

During 1875 some of the rolling stock was fitted with lifeguards to protect people falling in front of the cars.

A seven window Starbuck double-deck car.

178

These were said to be similar to those known as "cow catchers" used on cars in America and Glasgow. By July 1876, 34 cars had been fitted with lifeguards and shortly afterwards the complete tram fleet had been dealt with.

It was apparently not the intention of the early tramcar designers that ladies should travel upstairs, as all the double-deckers had removable ladders for access to the top. For a lady in a crinoline the upper deck was inaccessible and following complaints in September 1875, the ladders were permanently fixed. Staircases were fitted in the 'eighties and ladies were then able to travel outside. At first the sides of the upper decks were open but in the 'eighties advertisement or "decency" panels were fitted for the benefit of ladies.

During the severe winter of 1874-5 the Company found that there were few outside passengers on the double-deckers. Costs increased due to the additional horses required in snow and icy conditions and the receipts fell. To provide for the extra inside accommodation in winter conditions, 12 further 18-seater single-deck cars were ordered from Starbuck. They were delivered in mid-November 1875. Actually 13 cars (Nos. 39-51) arrived and were immediately utilised on the Hunslet to Kirkstall through service. The price paid for these cars, and some others, is not known exactly as the Company paid for them in instalments, and included were payments to Starbuck for spare parts.

All new cars delivered up to this time appear to have had the traditional curved decorative moulding to the waist panel, but during rebuilding and body modifications in the 'eighties, these were removed.

Six further Starbuck cars of the same seating capacity and similar appearance but of lighter construction, with the curved moulding omitted, and requiring only one horse to draw them, were delivered later the same year. The total cost was £1,015 10s. 0d., approximately £169 per car. The Tramways Company said that the cars

were purchased with a view to reducing the cost of working, and at the same time providing better accommodation for the winter months when the number of outside passengers was small.

This purchase resulted in the withdrawal of some of the earlier heavy double-deck cars, Nos. 11-14, and apparently the two small single-deckers, Nos. 19 and 20. The new cars occupied the vacant numbers. The disposal details of the six withdrawn cars is uncertain. Three cars "to seat 20 inside and 20 outside" were advertised for sale in September 1876 and the Company accounts for 30th June 1877 show a sum of £420 depreciation on the three cars. They were recorded as being broken up in late 1885. One car was sold in late 1876 and three car "tops", presumably bodies, were sold in 1879, one on 5th March for £3 0s. 0d., another on 14th March for £2 10s. 0d. and a third on 14th April for £5 0s. 0d. A double-deck scrap car body usually fetched about £5 or £6 and a single-decker rather less. The smaller sums received could be for car Nos. 19 and 20 and the £5 for a double-deck car.

The Company records thus show that seven cars were disposed of and the odd car cannot be explained. It is presumed that the three cars broken up in 1885 included a later withdrawal as many cars were scrapped in the 'eighties. The Cash Books show receipts of £130 (5th October 1875), £47 10s. 0d. (3rd October 1876), £34 12s. 6d. (7th December 1880) and £45 0s. 0d. (17th April 1885) from the Leicester Tramways Company – a Busby/Turton enterprise – which could indicate the sale of old rolling stock to this Company.

The fleet now totalled 51 cars, and no further vehicles were added until 1879 when the Company built, at Headingley Depot, three light open cars specifically intended for summer use only. The cars (Nos. 52-54) entered service on 20th May 1879, seated 24 passengers, and the "Yorkshire Post" commented that they were "especially intended to accommodate ladies and

The earliest known photograph of a Leeds tram shows Starbuck single-deck car No. 45 in 1875. Probably at the Starbuck Works.
Courtesy The Science Museum, South Kensington, London, Whitcombe Collection.

corpulent old gentlemen, who unable to climb to the top of the cars at present running would still like on a fine day to enjoy a ride in the open air instead of being couped up in a large box." It is assumed that the trucks for these cars came from under the three car "tops" disposed of a few weeks previously. No photographs have been discovered and the cars appear to have been little used and were withdrawn after a few years service.

All the horse cars built up to this time had four wheels, but were not mounted on "trucks" in the later, accepted sense of the word. There were four cast trunnions bolted to the body underframe. They accommodated the axle boxes and springs. The earliest double-deck cars had curved bracing, which cannot have been very effective, and the single-deck cars diagonal bracing. The brake rigging was bolted directly to the car underframe. The action of braking tended to force the trunnions away from the car body resulting in great strain. By the middle 'eighties the bracing had all been removed and replaced by a sturdy iron bar, about $1\frac{1}{2}''$ in diameter which was bolted between the two trunnions. The brake rigging was supported on the iron bars. This was a much better arrangement as shocks caused by braking, poor track and frequent derailments, were now more evenly spread through the car body. The trunnions were apparently manufactured by the Starbuck Company and were of 6'-0" wheelbase for the 40-seater double-deckers and 5'-6" for the single-deck cars and 32-seater double-deckers. Two types, both very similar in appearance, were used. The earlier trunnions had straight sides to the hornway castings and from about 1874 onwards the sides were tapered towards the bottom. Springing was by means of india rubber blocks, but when these later perished, coil springs were used in lieu. 30" diameter chilled iron disc wheels were employed and the axles were 3" diameter of "best scrap iron."

The Chapeltown route was apparently restricted to the small single-deckers from its inception and complaints about the stuffy atmosphere of the "ill-ventilated machines" were very prevalent in hot weather. In order to alleviate this problem, three double-deck cars of a light construction, designed on the "Eades Patent Reversible System," and supplied by the Ashbury Railway Carriage and Wagon Company of Manchester, were delivered, the first one entering service on the Chapeltown route on 3rd July 1883 and the second a week later. The "Eades Patent Reversible" car was patented in 1877 and was extensively used on the Manchester and other undertakings. D. K. Clark describes a car of this type as follows:—

"The body of the car is swivelled centrally on the underframe and can be turned round whilst the horses remain in harness and the driver retains his seat. The body is secured in position by a simple locking apparatus. There is but one entrance to the car at one end, and two staircases to the roof, one at each side of the entrance. The entrance is reached by three steps, one more step than there are in ordinary cars as the body is more elevated than usual. The windows are at a higher level than is usual and they are considered to be safer. The driver occupies an elevated seat in front. The body is seated for 16 inside passengers and 18 outside passengers, in all 34 passengers. The body is 12 feet long and $6\frac{1}{2}$ feet wide outside measure. It is $11\frac{1}{2}$ feet long inside giving $17\frac{1}{4}$ ins. per seat. The seat room outside is 12 feet long and for 18 passengers is equivalent to 16 ins. per passenger. The total length from the front of the dash board to the end of the staircase is 17 ft. 6 ins. There are four 30 ins. diameter wheels to the car constructed with cast iron nave, wood spokes and rim and a flanged steel tyre. One wheel on each axle runs loose and it is said that the traction is sensibly eased by the additional freedom of movement thus secured. The side springs are ordinary laminated steel springs as used in omnibuses. A brake block is provided for each wheel constructed of wood secured by four 1 ins. iron bolts which take a bearing with the wood on the wheel. This construction of wood and iron, it is stated, bites more keenly than either wood or iron alone.

Eades Reversible Car No. 58 at Headingley terminus about 1890.   *Courtesy H. Heyworth.*

At Chapeltown terminus the Eades Reversible cars overhung the pavement by 5'-4".

The weight of the car empty is 34 cwt, equivalent for 34 passengers to 1 cwt per passenger. So low a ratio as this has not been attained in any other English car of the same capacity. The comparative lightness of the car is attained by employing framework of light scantling, wheels of wood and smaller axles. It is reported that there is by the use of the reversible car a saving of over 30% in horse power inasmuch as the car can be worked with a stud of eight horses as efficiently as the ordinary car with twelve horses."

(D. K. Clark, "Tramways, their construction and working," 1878).

The cars (Nos. 56-58) supplied to Leeds were of a later and larger type than the one described by Clark as the seating capacity was stated to be 18 inside and 20 outside and there was only one staircase. The "Eades Reversible" car never became popular in Leeds due to the narrowness of the roads at the tram termini. At Chapeltown terminus the car overhung the pavement by 5'-4" when being turned and accidents were not uncommon.

Following the introduction of the Eades cars, the Company interested itself in the acquisition of steam rolling stock and it was not until 31st January 1887 that the next horse car (No. 67) made its appearance on the Chapeltown route. It was proudly announced that the Leeds Tramways Company had introduced a new industry into the town – the manufacture of tramcars.

During the 'eighties the Tramways Company had done a considerable amount of work on re-building and refurbishing their cars, much of this being done at the Headingley Depot and Works. In the early and middle 'eighties many new cars produced by the Starbuck Company had square topped windows in lieu of the arched windows previously employed. Some of the horse cars re-built by the Leeds Tramways Company, both double-deck and single-deck, employed this new form of fenestration, and, in some cases, the number of windows was reduced. Due to the withdrawal of the Company's 'buses, there was space at North Street Depot and plant was laid down for the building of horse cars. No. 67 was built there and the Company felt

confident enough to announce that it was to build similar cars for its own use and also for sale to other companies. No. 67 had a novel arrangement of seating, known as "garden seats" on the upper deck (seats side by side with a central gangway) instead of the old "knifeboard" seats used on all the earlier double-deckers. The car had seven side windows and could easily be distinguished by its deep rocker panel and narrow waist panel.

"They are built to carry 40 passengers — 20 inside and 20 outside. Above, the passengers face the horse and sit in pairs on each side of a passage that runs up the middle. There are ten of these seats which are provided with reversible backs and waterproof aprons. The great advantage of this arrangement is that persons can pass on or off the car without running the risk of stepping upon the toes of others or putting them to any other inconvenience. In summer, especially, these outdoor seats will be much appreciated, alike for the view they afford of the surrounding country and for their ease and comfort. The interior of the car is ventilated from the sides upon a principle similar to that adopted in railway carriages, and is lighted from lamps which open from outside, and through which the fumes from the wicks cannot penetrate into the car. The coaches which have been designed by Mr. Wharam, the Manager of the Company, upon the plan of some in use in London and Leicester with several improvements introduced, are a little heavier than those which have hitherto run upon the Chapeltown route."

(Yorkshire Post, 1st February, 1887).

The Company's venture into tramcar building was not a success and only one other car (No. 68) was produced. Apparently, no vehicles were constructed for other undertakings. Later in 1887 two double-deck cars with garden seats (Nos. 69 and 70) and a single-deck car (No. 74) were purchased. The builder of these three cars was George F. Milnes and Company of Birkenhead, who had taken over the old Starbuck Company the previous year. Originally known as George Starbuck and Company Ltd., the company was later known as the Starbuck Car and Wagon Company Ltd. In 1888 and

Double-deck car built by the Leeds Tramways Company at Headingley "Oak" about 1894. Note the deep rocker panel. *Courtesy The late Godfrey Bingley, Leeds University Collection.*

View of car No. 67 at the Corn Exchange shortly before electrification, about 1900. *Courtesy A. K. Terry.*

1889 the Tramways Company took delivery from Milnes of its last horse cars. These were three small one-horse cars (Nos. 1, 7 and 9) seating 16 passengers and weighing only 28 cwts. Milnes re-introduced the arched windows and the cars had five side windows of this type and were purchased at a cost of £108 13s 5d. each. They were for use on the short York Road route.

Many of the earlier cars were either broken up or sold and, at the time of the Corporation take-over in 1894, 45 were left consisting of 23 double-deck and 22 single-deck cars.

THE STEAM CAR TRAILERS

During the period of hire of Kitson's tram engines, from 1880 to 1883, ordinary horse cars, usually double-deckers, were hauled. Suitable couplings were fitted

and the braking was modified in order that the brakes could be operated from the engine. Due to the smoke and dirt from the engines the open toppers were not popular and at least one, No. 18, was fitted with a covered top to give protection for passengers. There may have been others, but no evidence has been found. New rolling stock was needed and in 1882 the Company took delivery of a four-wheel double-deck car from the Ashbury Company. The car was of a reversible type similar to horse cars Nos. 56-8 and had, in addition, an awning at the top of the front portion which was intended to divert the smoke from the engine. The car (No. 55) carried passengers for the first time on 25th November 1882 and had an eventful first day in service.

"On Saturday night an accident of a very alarming character occurred on the Wortley branch of the Leeds Tramways Company. That branch is worked by steam and for the first time on Saturday a new class of car was introduced on this route. It is somewhat after the style of those in use at Bradford and can be turned round by means of a swivel fixed in the centre of the body of the car. Tong Road, which is the terminus, is a continuous and heavy gradient and, as the line is only single, with one or two loop lines for the convenience of passing cars, it is usual when within about 200 yards of the "Star Inn", for the engine to be uncoupled, and by means of the loop line to get to the reverse end of the car, and to push it to the stopping place ready for the return journey, and this is a practice which has been followed with safety from the opening of the line. On Saturday the car left Boar Lane at 9.27 pm and was as usual well laden with people returning from the market. The journey was performed in safety until the last loop line was reached near the top of Tong Road. At this time the greater number of passengers had alighted, there

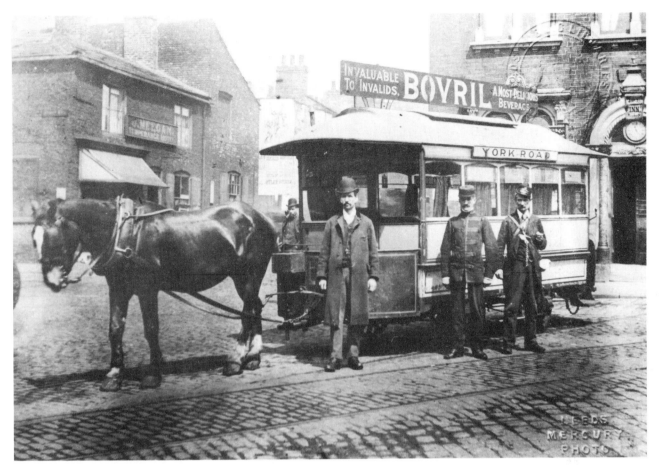

16-seater Milnes car No. 1 at York Road terminus about 1890.

being only two or three males on top and several females inside. The process of uncoupling was gone through, and the engine started off to get on the loop line and so work itself into a position to push the car the remaining part of the journey. The car had been turned round on its swivel to await the engine when, probably from a failure of the brakes, it started off down the incline, which is here very steep. The ponderous vehicle gathered more way every yard, and the position of the passengers became an alarming one. Those on the top jumped off and one of them was injured. So great had become the speed at which the car was travelling that it left the rails and ran into a gas lamp about 400 yards from the point where it started. The heavy gas lamp was snapped in two like a carrot, but the collision fortunately had the effect of considerably reducing the speed of the car. It, however, continued to run until it came in contact with another lamp post some 50 or 60 yards lower down. The top of it was completely smashed but the post proved strong enough to bear the strain of the collision and the car was thus brought to a standstill. Several of the passengers who jumped off the car whilst it was in motion received nasty falls but those who had sufficient presence of mind to retain their seats escaped with a good shaking. The car itself was not much damaged having only a little glass broken."

(Yorkshire Post, 27th November, 1882).

No. 55 cannot have been popular with the crews as, upon reaching the terminus, after being uncoupled, it had to be manually reversed on its swivel and then re-coupled to the engine. It was the only trailer of this type used in Leeds although reversible trailers were fairly common on other steam tramways which did not have reversing triangles to facilitate the turning of cars.

In September 1883 two further cars (Nos. 59-60) entered service. These vehicles were of an improved specification, built by Starbuck, and seated 46 passengers – 22 inside and 24 outside and cost £210 each. They had eight square-topped windows on each side, were about 18″ higher and larger than No. 55, more strongly built, and weighed about half a ton more. They had sole bars of channel iron, and the draw bar, instead of extending from the platform, projected from underneath the car and worked on a swivel. The staircases were said to be constructed with a view to their being used by ladies. The tops of the cars were covered in and the ends and a portion of the sides were glazed. This afforded protection from the weather and from anything which could escape from the funnel of the engine. Improved ventilators and blinds were fitted to the windows. Cushioned seats were employed and the internal decoration was said to be "artistically pretty." Instead of being fixed on india rubber or spiral steel springs as used on earlier cars, ordinary railway carriage springs were employed by which it was hoped to "secure a greater steadiness of motion," on the four-wheel trucks.

As a result of the Board of Trade report of October 1883, referred to in Chapter 9, the four-wheelers were condemned. Major-General Hutchinson recommended that cars with a "flexible wheel base" i.e. bogie cars, be substituted, or that single-deck cars only be employed as trailers. The three trailers, 55, 59 and 60, were soon fitted with bogies, and the upper saloons to Nos. 59 and 60 were completely glazed in, but it does not appear that No. 55 received this treatment. There is no evidence that No. 18 was ever fitted with bogies as the car body was probably unsuitable. It reverted to its horse car status and it is likely that the top cover was later removed.

Sketch showing the probable appearance of car No. 55, hauled by Kitson engine No. 3

Green/Wilkinson engine No. 2 and Starbuck trailer No. 60 about 1883.
Courtesy Science Museum, South Kensington, London, Whitcombe Collection.

In August 1884 two further cars (Nos. 61-2) were delivered by Starbuck. They were totally enclosed bogie cars similar to the modified earlier cars, but had eight arched side windows to the lower saloon as opposed to square topped, and the upper saloons had rounded ends whereas 59 and 60 were square. In 1885 another two cars (Nos. 63-4) were supplied by Starbuck. They were larger than Nos. 59-62 having 54 seats (28 upper saloon, 26 lower saloon) and nine arched windows to the lower saloon. The upper saloon ends were rounded, and there were four opening windows on each side, whereas Nos. 59-62 had only two. They cost £260 each. Nos. 65-6, apparently identical to Nos. 63-4, but costing £20 each less, were delivered in 1886.

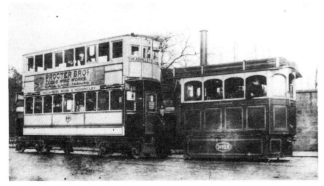

Kitson engine No. 13 and Starbuck trailer No. 66 at Headingley "Oak" about 1890. *Courtesy P. D. Johnson.*

The steam tram trailer was becoming, with competition and development, larger and larger and also less expensive. In August 1887 Ashburys delivered three 60-seater cars (34 upper saloon, 26 lower saloon), at a cost of only £225 each. These cars had nine arched windows on each side of both saloons, four windows on each side of the upper saloon being sliding. They were numbered 71-3. However, the ultimate in trailers as supplied to the Leeds Tramways Company were 12 cars manufactured by Milnes, and delivered between 1888 and 1890 at costs varying from £237 to £245 each. They were very substantial looking structures and became Milnes' "standard" design for a time and were purchased by several other operators in the country. They weighed 4½ tons and seated 28 passengers in the lower saloon and 38 in the upper on garden seats. The cars were about 4″ higher than the other trailers and were "prettily decorated" inside and well ventilated. They had seven arched windows to each side of both saloons, three on the upper saloon being sliding. These cars occupied fleet numbers vacated by withdrawn horse cars (Nos. 4, 5, 13, 20, 21, 26, 33, 35-8 and 41). There is photographic evidence that at one period, for some unknown reason, cars Nos. 5 and 21 exchanged numbers. The accompanying photograph shows a car at Wortley with the number 5 on the dash and a combination of the number 21 and 5 on the waist panel. No doubt the paint had faded.

All the trailers were mounted on plate frame bogies of similar design and had 24″ diameter solid wheels, with the exception of Nos. 61 and 62 which were 21″ in diameter. In order to reduce the problems caused by the sideways pull of the engine draw bar on curves, the bogies were mounted on the extreme ends of the car. This arrangement meant that the platform steps and entrances were placed on the corners to give clearance for the bogies. The underframes consisted of a 4″ × 2″ rolled steel channel carried through to the platform ends and, as a result, the floor of the saloon was on the same

Kitson Engine No. 5 and Milnes trailer at Wortley about 1890. The trailer bears the number 5 on the dash and a combination of the numbers 5 and 21 on the waist panel. *Courtesy Science Museum, South Kensington, London, Whitcombe Collection.*

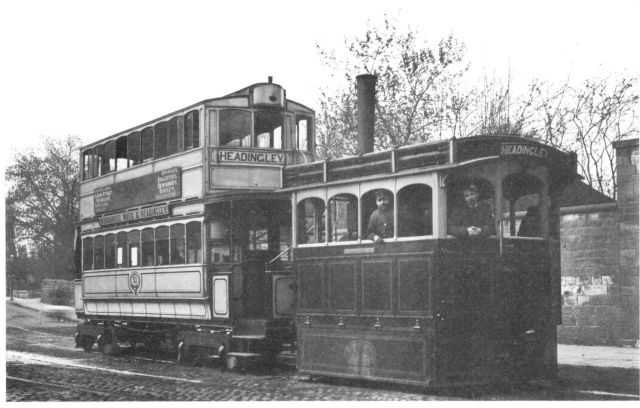

Kitson engine No. 4 and Ashbury trailer No. 71 at Headingley "Oak", 10th May 1888. The Ashbury trailers were the most unpopular trams in the Company's fleet. *Courtesy The late Godfrey Bingley, Photographer, Leeds University Collection.*

level as the platform. There was no step up to the saloon as was the case with the horse cars and later electric cars. "Direct" stairs (i.e. anti-clockwise up) were used and short canopies were provided to enable passengers to pass round the ends of the knifeboard seats on the upper deck.

With the knifeboard seat arrangement the ceiling height in the upper saloon was about 5'-8" in the gangways, but, when garden seats were employed to increase the seating capacity, the flooring was simply taken straight across the gangway and clerestorey resulting in a massive reduction in ceiling height. In the case of the Ashbury trailers (the first in Leeds to have garden seats), the height was reduced to 4'-9" at the perimeter and 5'-3" in the central gangway. The drawing at the end of this chapter clearly shows this, and it is no wonder that these claustrophobic dimensions resulted in complaints in the press, and Nos. 71-3 being the most unpopular cars in the Leeds fleet. The Tramways Company bought no more cars from Ashbury. The later Milnes trailers were rather better having a height of about 5'-3" at the perimeter and 5'-8" in the central aisle. Ventilation of the lower saloon was via the clerestorey, by means of slots cut into the side of the car. The roof construction was simply canvas stretched across the roof sticks. No doubt this was done for lightness, but it also possibly minimised damage to heads!

No further cars were added to the rolling stock after 1890 and the number of trailers in stock at the Corporation takeover in 1894 was 24.

THE TRAMWAY ENGINES

Kitson and Company had constructed a trial steam engine/car to the design of a W. R. Rowan in 1876 for use on the Copenhagen tramways, and it is recorded that on 15th November 1876 a Kitson engine was tested on the Dewsbury, Batley and Birstal Tramways. "Private" trials of a Kitson engine took place on the Leeds tramways in 1877, prior to its official public appearance in October of that year. This engine and the three experimental engines built in 1878 were on an entirely different principle to the Rowan design. They were fitted with vertical boilers and had two cylinders of 6" diameter and 10" stroke in an elevated position outside the frame and inclined slightly from the horizontal. Motion was provided by a modified Walschaerts valve gear of Kitson's patent to four coupled wheels of 2'-0" diameter and a 4'-6" wheelbase. A lever attached to the footplate operated a regulator and also an automatic brake, and a governor was worked from the wheel axle. Each engine was housed in a cab of timber and steel to conceal the machinery and wheels, and had four arched windows at the sides and five at the front. The condensing system consisted of a series of copper tubes placed longitudinally on the roof of the cab. Exhaust steam passing from the cylinders was condensed by air cooling and returned to the water storage tank where it was re-used in the boiler. This form of air condensation with various modifications became standard practice on tramway engines throughout the world.

The three engines (Nos. 1-3) supplied for use on the Wortley line in 1880-1 were constructed with horizontal boilers, larger cylinders and wheels, similar to engines already supplied by Kitson's to New Zealand. However, with the possible exception of engine No. 1, the longitudinal pipes forming the air condenser on the roof of the cab were replaced by slightly arched transverse tubes, an improvement on the earlier arrangement. On 20th January 1883 the Tramways Company purchased them from Kitson's for the sum of £1,520.

View of Milnes trailer No. 4.   *Courtesy Science Museum, South Kensington, London, Whitcombe Collection.*

The experimental Green engines built to Wilkinson's patent were numbered 1 and 2. The Wilkinson engine was patented by William Wilkinson, an engineer who opened a small foundry at Wigan with three or four employees. In 1881 he arranged with the Wigan Tramways Company to experiment with a tramway engine of his design. The engine had a vertical boiler and cylinders of small bore and stroke ($6'' \times 7''$) acting on a crankshaft connected to cog-wheel gears which transmitted motion to four coupled wheels. No condensation system was used, the exhaust steam being super heated in a special device in the firebox and then passed through the chimney. The engine was small and light and received high praise from tramway engineers, and orders were placed by several tramway companies. Wilkinson was unable to cope with this influx of orders and was com-

pelled to sublet the manufacture of the engines to three other firms of engineers, namely Thomas Green and Sons of Leeds, Black, Hawthorn and Company of Gateshead and Beyer, Peacock of Manchester. Beyer Peacock and Company produced a very satisfactory engine and one still exists at the National Tramway Museum, Crich, Derbyshire. The two engines, however, supplied by Green's to the Leeds Tramways Company were, as referred to in Chapter 9, anything but a success, and the Company had nothing further to do with Wilkinson patent engines. They interested themselves in the more reliable Kitson design.

The original three engines supplied by Kitson's to Leeds had remained their standard type of engine until 1884, when several improvements were introduced of which the most important was a big increase in the size of the boiler and firebox. A body alteration gave improved vision by the use of three windows in lieu of five at the front. Tramway engines Nos. 4-10 purchased from Kitson's at a cost of £702 each in 1884 were to this design and No. 11 delivered in October of the following year at £720, was apparently identical. In the new design the general external features of the engine were retained, but the cylinders were increased from $8''$ to $8\frac{1}{2}''$ in diameter, stroke to $12''$ and wheels from $2'-4\frac{1}{2}''$ to $2'-5\frac{1}{2}''$. The boiler was $2'-9''$ diameter, $4'-5''$ long and had 73 flue tubes of $1\frac{5}{8}''$ diameter. The firebox was $2'\ 9''$ long, grate area 6 sq. ft., heating surface 129 sq. ft., and the tank under the footplate was of 90 gallons capacity. The condenser comprised 260 $1''$ diameter thin copper tubes in four tiers in an arch form fixed transversely across the cab roof and connected with each other by two tubular chambers running along both edges of the roof. Exhaust steam passed into the upper chamber and condensate returned to the tank from the lower chamber. The condensing surface was about

Kitson engine No. 1, 1880.   *Courtesy Kitson and Company.*

400 sq. ft. and the engine weighed about 8½ tons. It could be driven from either end as the hand gear was duplicated but was usually driven backwards, firebox leading, ideal where triangular termini were adopted as it eliminated the need for uncoupling. The driver was able to sit at the side of the firebox and had complete control and a good view of the road ahead.

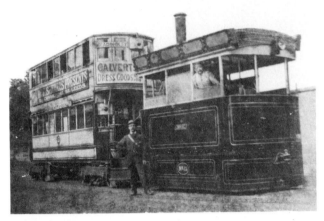

Green engine No. 12 in original condition with a Starbuck trailer at Headingley "Oak" about 1886.
Courtesy Science Museum, South Kensington, London, Whitcombe Collection.

Meanwhile Green's, who had experienced trouble with their Wilkinson patent engines, not only in Leeds but elsewhere, produced an entirely new engine to their own design. The arrangement was similar to the standard Kitson design, but had air condensers resembling those used on engines manufactured at the Falcon works in Loughborough. The cab was similar to that on a Wilkinson engine and the cylinders were 8½″ diameter with 12″ stroke and had reversing link gear.

One of the new engines was delivered to the Tramways Company on 25th August 1885. It was numbered 12 and the cost was £670, some £50 cheaper than the Kitson engines. The Tramways Company must, however, have had some doubts about the new locomotive for their next order for four engines was placed with Kitson's again. The engines, Nos. 13-16, apparently identical to Nos. 4-11, were delivered at a cost of £710 each in 1886. Two similar engines, Nos. 17-18, were supplied in 1887 and these proved to be the last Kitson engines bought for use on the Leeds tramways.

Green's made further improvements in the design of their engines and, in 1889, produced a compound tramway engine which met with considerable success and was highly competitive with the Kitson locomotive. There were four coupled wheels of 2′-6″ diameter, 5′-0″ wheelbase, overall length 11′-6″, width 6′-0″, height from rails to roof 9′-0″ and to top of condenser 10′-4″. On 24th January 1889 the Tramways Company placed an order for two of these engines and delivery of Nos. 19-20 was effected on 13th May and 14th June 1889 respectively, at a cost of £750 per engine. A further six similar locomotives, Nos. 21-26, were supplied in 1889 and 1890. Green's Order Book shows that Nos. 21-23 were identical to Nos. 19-20, but there were some "additions and alterations" to Nos. 24-26, unfortunately not specified.

1890 saw the abandonment by Green's of their "box" type condenser in favour of a system patented in 1887 by Charles Burrell and Sons of Thetford. This system consisted of double pipes running longitudinally over the roof of the engine. There were usually 18 pipes and each was a tube within a tube. Exhaust steam passed into the space between the two tubes, while cooling air passed through the centre pipe and surrounded the whole. The two engines with this improved condenser, Nos. 27-28, were delivered on 20th August and

Kitson engine No. 16 and a Milnes trailer about 1890.
Courtesy Science Museum, South Kensington, London, Whitcombe Collection.

5th November 1890 respectively at a cost of £780 each. Engine No. 12 was returned to Green's in 1890 and was rebuilt, compounded, fitted with Burrell type condensers and then closely resembled Nos. 27-28.

As a result of the introduction of these new engines, the three oldest engines in the fleet, Kitson's Nos. 1-3, which had become very much the worse for wear, were withdrawn, Nos. 1-2 in late 1890 and No. 3 in early 1891. During 1891 Kitson engine No. 4 was thoroughly overhauled and the body rebuilt with three side windows instead of four, and other earlier engines, including No. 6, received major overhauls. The fleet of engines now totalled 25 and this state of things persisted until the Corporation takeover in 1894. Lifeguards had been fitted to the engines some years earlier.

Green engine No. 19 and trailer No. 36 in L. C. T. livery at Meanwood terminus about 1899.
Courtesy Science Museum, South Kensington, London, Whitcombe Collection.

During 1894 the Corporation rebuilt and re-tested several engines at a cost of £1,000 and included were Nos. 13 and 15, both overhauled by Kitson's. An addition to the stock of steam engines was made by the purchase of two further engines from Green's in January and February 1897 for £700 each. They were numbered 29-30 and were similar in appearance to Nos. 27-28 and had Burrell condensers. Considerable trouble was experienced with the two new engines, and also the rebuilt No. 12, by the breakage of crank axles and many complaints were made to Green's. The Highways Committee set up a special sub-committee to deal with the problem but the axles continued to break and, in 1898, the Committee decided not to buy any more from Green's. The tramway engines generally were getting into a deplorable state. In April 1899, when Inspector Spaven was promoted as Traffic Manager, William Wharam, in answer to complaints that he was responsible for mismanagement of the tramways, said:–

"Notwithstanding the unsatisfactory condition of at least half of the engines, we are continually being pushed to get more mileage out of them with the result that there are innumerable breakdowns, which upset the whole of the traffic, and bring the manager into discredit, although he is personally not responsible. I do not blame the locomotive superintendent, because he cannot do what is impossible. I asked the Committee a year or two ago to break up No. 12 engine, but I am sorry to say it was thought advisable to extensively repair it, and that engine alone has broken six crank axles in the streets. Then again over two years ago I asked for four new engines of the Kitson type, but got

two only of other types, not both alike, and which have been of little use to us – one of them (No. 30), broke five crank axles up to the end of 1898 and the other (No. 29) the locomotive superintendent is afraid to send out."
(Yorkshire Post, 25th April, 1899).

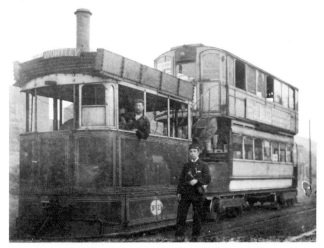

Green engine No. 21 and trailer No. 33 about 1890.
Courtesy Science Museum, South Kensington, London, Whitcombe Collection.

Later in 1899 the Locomotive Superintendent, Burton, wrote to the Tramways Committee complaining of the tramway engines and recommending that six of them be broken up. He was instructed to keep them going until electrification of the tramways. The fleet of 27 engines struggled on and remained almost complete until the demise of the steam tram in Leeds in 1902. One engine was withdrawn in 1899, another in 1900, and the other 25 engines, (with the exception of No. 12, sold separately), were all sold on 21st April 1902 to J. W. Hinchliffe, scrap merchant of Kirkstall Road, Leeds, for £1,000. Hinchliffe advertised the engines for sale over the following few months, but there appear to have been few buyers and they were eventually broken up for scrap.

THE CORPORATION HORSE, STEAM AND TRAILER ROLLING STOCK 1894-1902

At the takeover of the tramways on 2nd February 1894, the Corporation found itself the owner of a mixed bag of 69 cars of various ages and types, occupying the fleet Nos. 1-46, 48, 50, 51 and 55-74. The rolling stock consisted of 22 single-deck horse cars Nos. 1, 7, 9, 11, 12, 14-16, 19, 32, 34, 39, 40, 42-46, 48, 50, 51 and 74; 23 double-deck horse cars Nos. 2, 3, 6, 8, 10, 17, 18, 22-25, 27-31, 56-58 and 67-70; and 24 double-deck steam car trailers Nos. 4, 5, 13, 20, 21, 26, 33, 35-38, 41, 55, 59-66 and 71-73. An interest was immediately shown by the Highways Committee in the steam car trailers and instructions were given that five of them be converted to single-deck by the removal of the top deck. At least three (Nos. 60, 63 and 66) were converted for use on the newly opened Leopold Street steam car service in order to reduce the wear on the old track of the Chapeltown tramway. Single-deck and double-deck cars ran alternately. The original steam trailer, No. 55, was de-licensed on 22nd March 1893 and must have been in very bad condition as the Corporation paid the Tramways Company only £15 for it. It was soon scrapped. In March 1894 clocks were fitted in 12 cars to assist the conductors in keeping time, but no other alterations were made to the rolling stock until 1897.

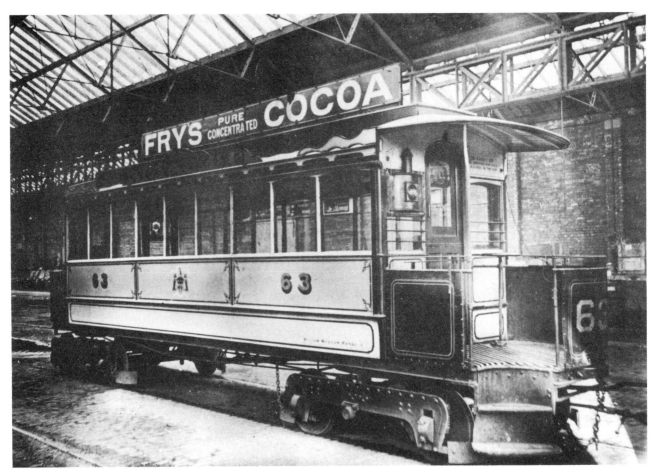

Starbuck trailer No. 63, converted to single-deck, in Kirkstall Road Depot about 1898. *Courtesy The Thoresby Society.*

Upon the delivery of the first Corporation electric cars, Nos. 1-25, from Greenwood and Batley Ltd., the horse and steam car trailers occupying those numbers were re-numbered, the 68 cars being allocated, in March 1897, the numbers 26-93. Licensing details and photographs suggest that the cars were re-numbered in numerical order occupying the vacant numbers, i.e. No. 1 became 47, No. 2 became 49 and so on. They were not re-numbered immediately as complaints were made by the Hackney Carriages Committee in July 1897 that the re-numbering had not yet been carried out. Little work was done on the maintenance of rolling stock for the last years of Company ownership and for the first three years after the Corporation took over. As mentioned in a previous chapter, the paint shop at Headingley Depot was converted into stables, and many cars had to stand outside. The rolling stock deteriorated so much that the Hackney Carriages Committee submitted a report in March 1897 listing the following cars which required urgent attention:–

No. 3 Very shabby, steps bad.
No. 4 Very shabby, wants painting.
No. 7 Hand rail at back broken.
No. 8 Two squares of glass broken.
No. 10 Wants repairing, very shabby for paint.
No. 13 End badly damaged.
No. 15 End panel damaged.
No. 21 Shabby for paint.
No. 25 ,, ,, ,,
No. 29 ,, ,, ,,
No. 31 Very shabby, wants painting.
No. 43 Very shabby.

In September 1897 car Nos. 10 and 25 were so bad that the Highways Committee decided that they be broken up, and they were apparently never re-numbered. It appears that the other cars, with the possible exception of No. 15, which was scrapped in 1898, were eventually overhauled and repainted, after the new depot and workshops were opened in Kirkstall Road.

1897 saw a big change in rolling stock, not only in the introduction of new electric cars, but also additional horse cars and trailers, for use with the electric cars, were ordered. Both horse cars and trailers were of a similar body type to the new electric cars, double-deckers of the latest Milnes design with four "tudor arch" windows and fitted with reversible garden seats on the upper deck. The horse cars were very small, measuring only 11'-2" inside the lower saloon and seating 34 passengers, 18 upstairs and 16 on longitudinal wooden seats in the saloon. The width of the car body was 6'-6" and overall length 19'-0". The trailers measured 15'-4" inside with an overall length of 26'-6" and width 7'-0". Ten cars were delivered at first, four horse cars, Nos. 94-97, and six trailers, Nos. 98-103, the latter being on Brill trucks and entering service on 27th November 1897. A further 10 similar horse cars, Nos. 50, 78, 93, occupying numbers of withdrawn cars (78 ex-10, 93 ex-25) – and 104-110 were delivered in 1898. These were followed by ten 18-seater single-deck cars, Nos. 111-120, supplied by Milnes for £125 each, and five further trailers. Nos. 128–132. These latter trailers had bodies built by the Brush Electrical Company, Loughborough. They had round top windows as opposed to the "tudor arch" of the Milnes cars.

The "trucks" to the horse cars were of a similar type as the earlier horse cars, having trunnions bolted at 5'-0" centres to the car body with a connecting bar on which was mounted the brake rigging. The overall appearance of the trunnions, however, bore a slight resemblance to a Brill truck and they were probably manufactured by Milnes. A rigid steel shoe was placed in front of the wheels to act as a rudimentary life guard.

Re-numbered Starbuck single-deck car No. 87, probably ex-19, at Victoria Avenue about 1898.
Courtesy P. D. Johnson.

In November 1897 the Corporation bought for £250 from the British Thomson-Houston Company the six redundant single-deck motor cars and the Brush trailer car which had formerly operated on the Roundhay Electric Tramway. The trucks and obsolete electrical equipment were removed, the cars fitted with horse tram trucks, and utilised as trailers at peak periods, Saturdays, Bank Holidays etc. They entered service in April and May 1898 and all were in use on the Roundhay route at Whitsuntide (29th to 31st May). They occupied the fleet Nos. 121-127 and this brought the number of trailers for use with electric cars up to a maximum of 18. Thereafter, all new cars were electric and the subject of future volumes.

The Brush trailer with Greenwood and Batley car No. 7 at Roundhay Park in 1899. The trailer was numbered in the 120's. *Courtesy A. D. Packer.*

Odd horse cars were withdrawn between 1898 and 1900 and five were converted into salt sprinklers. Upon the electrification of the Elland Road and Meanwood routes on 19th April 1901, the remaining early horse cars, with the exception of No. 29 (possibly a recent overhaul) were withdrawn. 15 one-horse cars, seating 18 passengers and 15 double-deckers, some "nearly new", were offered for auction by John Hepper and Sons at Headingley Depot on 25th April, but it was reported that there was little interest and only three were sold for a total of £33 1s. 6d. After April 1901 only 14 horse cars (Nos. 29, 50, 78, 93, 94, 96, 97, 104, 106, 107, 109, 110, 117 and 119) were licensed for service. The introduction of electric cars on Cardigan Road and Burley Road on 3rd August 1901 resulted in the withdrawal of most of these. A few lingered on until 14th October the same year when the last horse car ran along Whitehall Road.

Milnes double-deck horse car No. 78 outside Headingley Depot about 1899. *Courtesy A. K. Terry.*

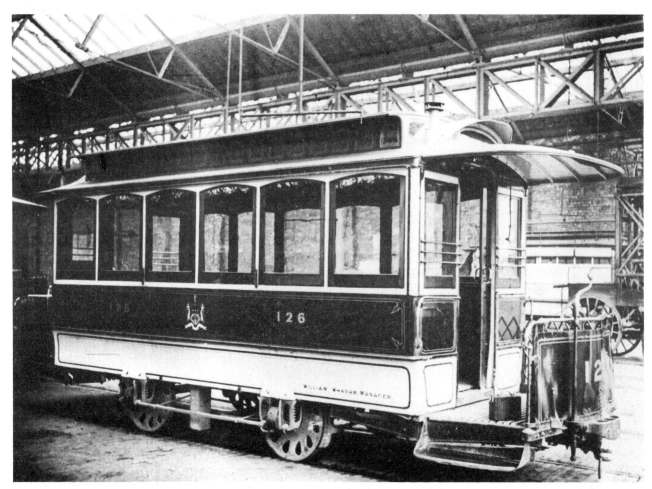

Ex-Roundhay electric car converted into trailer No. 126 in Kirkstall Road Depot, 1898. In the background is a tower wagon and horse car No. 49 (ex-2) apparently converted for works use. *Courtesy The Thoresby Society.*

Greenwood and Batley car No. 1 hauls the Brush trailer in Roundhay Road in 1899. *Courtesy A. D. Packer.*

Two or three of the horse cars were retained for preservation and were kept in the old stables at Hunslet Depot still bearing William Wharam's name on the side. They remained there throughout the Hamilton era. About 1926, a new General Manager, Chamberlain, ordered their destruction. One car, Ashbury steam trailer No. 73, was converted into a bungalow at Rodley, near Leeds, but was destroyed by vandals; the last traces disappearing in the middle 1970's. The body of one of the Milnes double-deck horse cars of 1898 vintage, No. 107, still exists, and is in store pending eventual restoration by the Leeds Transport Historical Society.

The Corporation did not immediately dispose of the remaining horse cars as many were only three or four years old and they were presumably hoping for a buyer. 32 were listed as being still in stock on 25th March 1902. 22 steam trailers were in stock on the same date, one having been disposed of a short time earlier. The Tramways Committee decided that the old rolling stock be offered for sale at not less than £5 per vehicle and failing that price being obtained they be broken up. Some cars were sold as caravans etc. and others passed to Hinchliffe of Kirkstall Road. In September 1902 Hinchliffe was advertising "18 double-deck tramcars, upper deck suitable for four single beds, lower deck suitable for living room, store room or office, gauge 4'-8½", also quantity of lesser tramcars, suitable for contractors offices, summer houses, or store rooms, same gauge."

One of the last horse cars at Briggate Junction in 1901. It was probably bound for Whitehall Road. *Courtesy P. D. Johnson.*

192

Trailer car No. 100 converted for electric traction at Briggate Junction, 1901.　　　*Courtesy Pickards, Photographers, Leeds.*

Of the 18 trailers, Nos. 98-103 and 128-132 were fitted with Peckham Cantilever trucks and converted into electric cars in 1900. The six ex-Roundhay single-deckers were all converted into salt sprinklers, two apparently being used for the first time in the snowy conditions which prevailed on Saturday, 10th February 1900. The annual reports indicate that seven trailers were still in stock on 25th March 1901. These were Nos. 121-127 which were re-licensed for service on 17th May 1901, and the cars which appeared in February 1900, although referred in the local press to as "old trailer cars" were probably converted horse cars. Following fatal accidents, the last trailer car ran on 6th April 1901 and it would appear that 121-127, although licensed the following month, never ran after April. In July the Tramways Committee decided to convert them into salt sprinklers. The fate of the Brush toast rack trailer is unknown.

THE WORKS VEHICLES

Information on the works vehicles owned by the Leeds Tramways Company is sketchy, but it is recorded that they had several carts for distributing salt and sand on the lines in snowy weather. The Company's inventory of 1893 indicated that there were six carts, three drays, four sand carts, one timber wagon, one horse float, one brougham, one gig, one whitechapel cart and three tar pans. The half yearly report for February 1888 shows that two patent "cars" for distributing sand and salt on the lines were added to the fleet. Presumably,

this should have read "carts" and an illustration of one of the sand carts used by the Company is shown on the next page. The brougham and gig were used by the General Manager and senior staff on official business. The brougham was sold by Hepper's for the Corporation on 24th February 1894 for £7. 15s. 0d.

THE OMNIBUSES

Although the Tramways Company became the largest operator of horse 'buses in the town for a short period in the early 'eighties, no photographs of their vehicles have been discovered, and the licensing records and Company cash books are either incomplete or ambiguous.

The first 'bus was acquired by Busby's in September 1871 to work the "Oak" to "Three Horse Shoes" service and was a small one-horse single-deck vehicle. It was transferred to the temporary "Cardigan Arms" to Kirkstall service in April and May 1872, and was then apparently out of use until March 1874, when it began the shuttle service between the Swan Junction and Hunslet Carr. After the withdrawal of this service it appears to have been transferred to the "Three Horse Shoes" to Adel route. A 'bus was required to work the Chapeltown to Moortown service and thus, by the end of 1874, the Company must have owned at least two 'buses. In May 1875 two further 'buses were acquired (licence Nos. 161 and 162) and put on the Briggate to Hunslet Carr service.

193

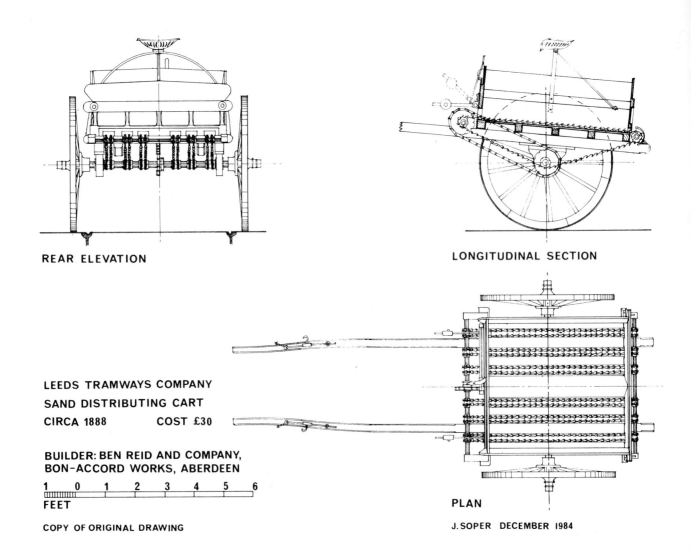

REAR ELEVATION

LONGITUDINAL SECTION

LEEDS TRAMWAYS COMPANY

SAND DISTRIBUTING CART

CIRCA 1888   COST £30

BUILDER: BEN REID AND COMPANY,
BON-ACCORD WORKS, ABERDEEN

```
1    0    1    2    3    4    5    6
|IIIIIIIII|         |    |    |    |    |
FEET
```

PLAN

COPY OF ORIGINAL DRAWING

J. SOPER   DECEMBER 1984

The Company cash books show that five 'buses were added to the fleet during the six months ended 31st December 1875, and these presumably included Nos. 161-2, probably paid for during this period, No. 198 and two others, one of which was a small 'bus purchased from the Liverpool Omnibus Company. The 'bus (No. 59) purchased from John Guy in 1878, was sold later in the same year and a 'bus (No. 195) was also licensed by the Company in 1878 but seems to have been disposed of after a few weeks. One of the earlier 'buses must have been scrapped for, in the period 1879 to 1881 the Company had six 'buses in stock.

The 'bus fleet was considerably augmented by the acquisition of Turton's business in 1882. There were at least 13 'buses purchased including Nos. 4-8, 16, 17, 46, 61, 72, 75, 110 and 193. Some of these and the six earlier 'buses were sold in the 'eighties. The Company cash books show that three 'buses were sold in 1883, one saloon 'bus and a wagonette in 1885, five 'buses in 1887, the old Adel 'bus and another in 1889 and an unspecified number of 'buses in 1890. Two further 'buses, Nos. 184 and 233, were added to the fleet and by 1894 the Company was left with six serviceable and four withdrawn 'buses which passed into the hands of the Corporation. The serviceable 'buses were listed as Nos. 6, 16, 75, 184, 193 and 233, but the numbers of the others, presumably de-licensed, were not recorded. They were not valued on the Company's inventory and were probably soon scrapped. The inventory also included a wagonette 'bus but the licence number (if any) was not recorded.

Five of the six good 'buses were double-deck and the other, No. 184, was a ten-seat single-deck vehicle. Messrs. Horsfall and Robinson purchased five of the 'buses and these included Nos. 75, 193 and 233. Nos. 6 and 16 presumably also passed to them but No. 6 must have been de-licensed as, by March 1894, Charles Coates was running a 'bus with this licence number.

The working of the Adel 'bus service was let to a William P. Walker, the Corporation paying him £18 per annum and allowing him the 'bus receipts. Hence they were left with one solitary 'bus, presumably No. 184, running between Chapeltown and Moortown. The Moortown 'bus, said to be "small" got into a "rickety" condition and was condemned by the Hackney Carriages Committee at its inspection on 24th March 1897, and was withdrawn from service three days later. A new 'bus was purchased and was apparently also numbered 184.

During the period of electrification of the tramways the Corporation found itself short of 'buses to work the temporary services required on some routes due to trackworks. In 1900 two 'buses were hired from Walker Bros. for a longish period and a 'bus was also hired from J. W. Wilks. Later in the year advantage was taken of the many bargain 'buses which were coming on the market due to tramway competition. Three 'buses were bought at auction in August 1900 for a total of only £35 19s. 0d. W. P. Walker ceased running the Adel 'bus on 19th August 1900 and the following day the Corporation took over operation of the service. On 19th May 1902 the Chapeltown to Moortown 'bus was discontinued when

194

the electric trams were extended through from Chapeltown and a month later, on 23rd June, Hepper and Sons auctioned at Chapeltown Depot, six horses, two "light and dandy one-horse 'buses to carry 10 and 12 respectively, and a strong 'bus to carry 32," 14 carts and wherries, etc.

The Corporation was left with one 'bus again and this was a ten seat saloon 'bus, licence No. 255, presumably acquired second-hand in 1900. It was usually drawn by two horses and ran to Adel and later Spen Lane Golf Ground until 1906, when it was replaced by a motor 'bus. In 1907 it was transferred to the Farnley route, replacing a motor 'bus, and carried on until the introduction of the Farnley trackless cars in 1911.

Farnley horse 'bus No. 255 near the Woodcock Inn, in 1907. The Driver is C. Smith.
Courtesy D. Broughton.

THE LIVERIES

Horse Cars.

The livery of the rolling stock of the Leeds Tramways Company was chocolate, primrose and white in various permutations. The original horse cars supplied to the Company had chocolate dash panels, primrose waist panels and the panel above the windows; white rocker panels and window frames. The rocker panels bore the words "LEEDS TRAMWAYS CO." in ornamental red lettering. There was simple gilt and chocolate coloured lining with a central gilt numeral on the waist panels and double lining on the rocker panels. The panel above the windows and the dash panels were lined in gilt, the latter having large gilt numerals. The corner pillars were vermillion with a gilt decoration, although some cars later had plain white or primrose corner pillars. The lettering on the rocker panels was discontinued in the early 'eighties and no cars with a higher fleet number than 51 appear to have received lettering.

In November 1898 the Corporation Tramways Committee decided to adopt the Tramways Company livery as standard and the only variation was the substitution of two numerals in lieu of a single one on each waist panel and the incorporation of the city coat of arms centrally.

Steam Car Trailers.

The first steam car trailers were painted in the same livery as the later horse cars, i.e. without lettering on the rocker panels, but the Ashbury trailers (Nos. 71-73) and

some of the Milnes cars of 1888-90, when new, had primrose dashes with chocolate coloured numerals. When the Corporation took over the tramways all the trailers received chocolate dashes again and, from about 1896-7, some were painted in a drab overall chocolate livery with white rocker panels with no lining on the upper saloons. Photographs show that cars Nos. 37, 38, 59 and others were painted in this livery. From November 1898 the trailers were painted in the standard Leeds City Tramways livery. The ceilings to the cars were lined out and an inspection of the remains of No. 73 in 1965 revealed that originally it had a white ceiling with vermillion lining.

Steam Tramway Engines.

A chocolate livery with white or ivory window frames was generally employed on all engines, but there were variations to the lining. The first Kitson engines, however, had an overall dark coloured livery with light coloured lining around each side panel. A gilt numeral was centrally situated on the side lower panel. Later Kitson engines had white window frames and each side panel was lined out with a thick line, probably primrose, and thin white line with simple square corners. The central red numeral was on a white background. The Green engines also had two lines but the corners were rounded. In Corporation days Green's engines had three lines, an outer thin white line being added. At least one Green engine (No. 12) and rebuilt Kitson No. 4 latterly had ornamental double square corners to the lining.

Kitson engine No. 10 and a Starbuck trailer. The trailer is in the chocolate and white livery.
Courtesy Science Museum, South Kensington, London, Whitcombe Collection.

Electric Car Trailers

The electric car trailers Nos. 98-103 and 128-132 were all painted in a royal blue and white livery similar to that adopted on electric cars Nos. 1-25. The livery was based on that of the Bristol tramways, which the Tramways Sub-Committee had inspected in 1896. The waist panels and dashes were in royal blue and the rocker panels and windows white. The words "LEEDS CITY TRAMWAYS", in gilt, were painted on the rocker panels and there were large ornamental gilt numerals on the dashes and two on each waist panel with a central coat of arms. There was ornamental lining to the waist panels, and the corner pillars were decorated. The trailers, when converted into electric cars, retained their blue livery for a year or two afterwards.

The ex-Roundhay trailers, Nos. 121-127, were painted in a similar livery, but the lettering on the rocker panels was omitted and the numerals and lining were of a simpler pattern.

DESTINATION INDICATORS

In the early days of the Leeds Tramways Company, it was mandatory that the destination must be permanently painted in a prominent position on all trams and 'buses in Leeds. It was usually painted in large letters above the lower saloon windows, and photographs show "Woodhouse Moor and Headingley", "Boar Lane and Upper Wortley", "Kirkstall and Hunslet", and "Kirkstall". Presumably, the other routes received similar treatment. As a result of this practice certain cars were used on the same routes for years. The Company staff records show, for example, that in the early 'eighties, cars Nos. 11-14 were solely used on the Chapeltown route; 35, 50 and 51 were also regular Chapeltown cars. After 1883 56-58 and 31 were also on Chapeltown. The Headingley route was usually operated by cars Nos. 10, 18, 20, and 23-30. Car Nos. 15, 32, 46 or 48 were usually on Meanwood and worked from Chapeltown Depot. The Hunslet and Kirkstall route had a variety of cars:– Nos. 1-9, 16, 19, 33, 34, 37-45, 47 and 49. York Road was served by cars Nos. 2, 4, 17 and 36 working from Hunslet Depot, and, after 1888, Nos. 1, 7 and 9 were the regular York Road cars. The remaining large double-deck cars such as 21, 22 and the largest car No. 6 were popular on the Wortley route, being towed by steam tram engines. No. 6 later ran from Hunslet Depot.

The introduction of removable destination boards in the 'eighties led to greater flexibility and there was a much greater movement of cars between the various depots and routes. The boards used on the trams hooked on to two metal lugs at each side of the car and were reversible. For example the boards used on the through service between Headingley and Chapeltown service in the 1892-4 period showed "CHAPELTOWN AND HEADINGLEY" on one side and "REGINALD TERRACE AND HYDE PARK" on the other, and other routes were presumably similarly treated. Latterly, when horse and steam trams were employed temporarily on routes prior to electrification, the destination often consisted of printed notices pasted inside the windows.

Former trailer car No. 128 at Meanwood terminus shortly after electrification in 1901. The car is still in its royal blue livery and carries temporary paper destination indications.
Courtesy A. K. Terry.

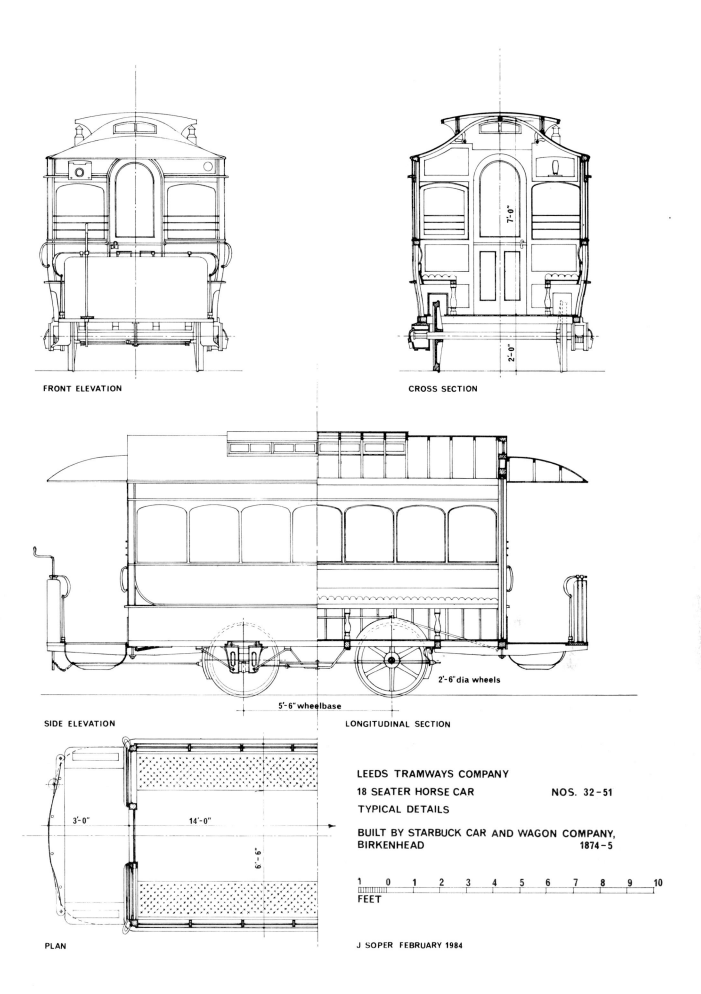

FRONT ELEVATION

CROSS SECTION

7'-0"

2'-0"

SIDE ELEVATION

LONGITUDINAL SECTION

2'-6" dia wheels

5'-6" wheelbase

PLAN

3'-0"   14'-0"

6'-6"

LEEDS TRAMWAYS COMPANY

18 SEATER HORSE CAR   NOS. 32-51

TYPICAL DETAILS

BUILT BY STARBUCK CAR AND WAGON COMPANY,
BIRKENHEAD   1874-5

1 0   1   2   3   4   5   6   7   8   9   10
FEET

J SOPER FEBRUARY 1984

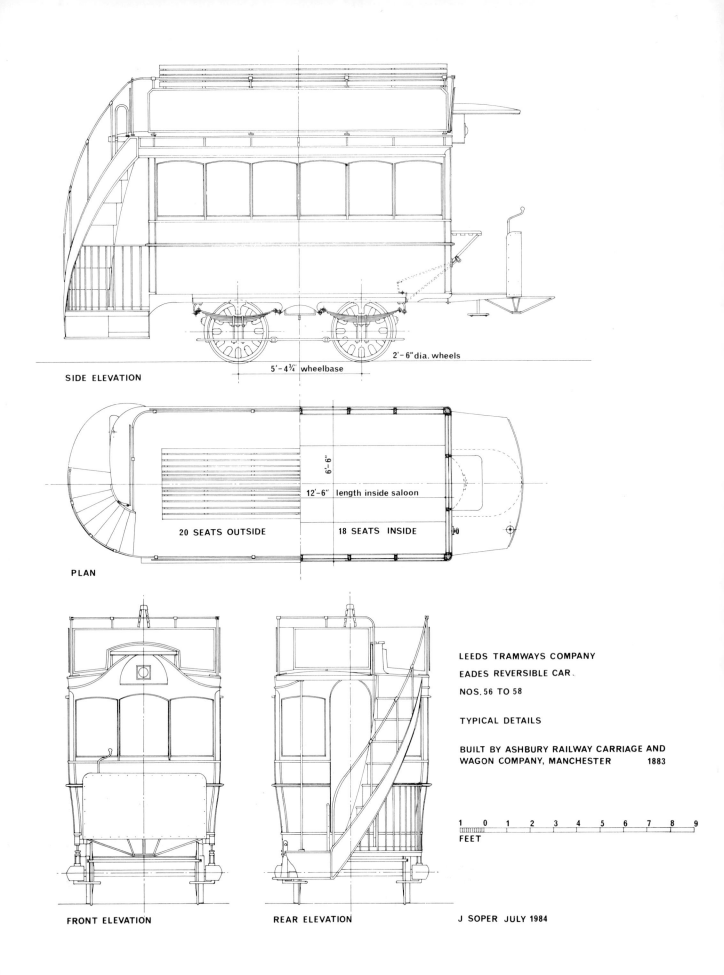

SIDE ELEVATION

2'-6"dia. wheels

5'-4¾" wheelbase

PLAN

6'-6"

12'-6" length inside saloon

20 SEATS OUTSIDE

18 SEATS INSIDE

FRONT ELEVATION

REAR ELEVATION

LEEDS TRAMWAYS COMPANY

EADES REVERSIBLE CAR.

NOS. 56 TO 58

TYPICAL DETAILS

BUILT BY ASHBURY RAILWAY CARRIAGE AND
WAGON COMPANY, MANCHESTER   1883

1 0 1 2 3 4 5 6 7 8 9
FEET

J SOPER JULY 1984

198

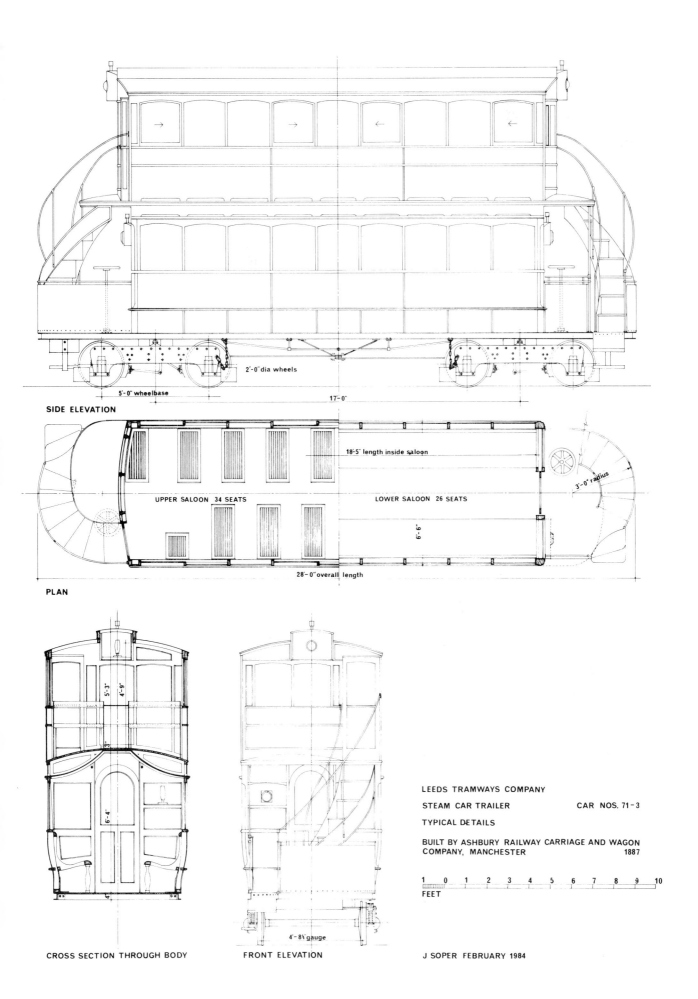

SIDE ELEVATION

2'-0" dia wheels

5'-0" wheelbase

17'-0"

18'-5" length inside saloon

UPPER SALOON 34 SEATS

LOWER SALOON 26 SEATS

3'-0" radius

6'-9"

PLAN

28'-0" overall length

CROSS SECTION THROUGH BODY

5'-3"

4'-9"

3'-3"

6'-4"

4'

FRONT ELEVATION

4'-8½" gauge

LEEDS TRAMWAYS COMPANY

STEAM CAR TRAILER   CAR NOS. 71-3

TYPICAL DETAILS

BUILT BY ASHBURY RAILWAY CARRIAGE AND WAGON
COMPANY, MANCHESTER   1887

1 0 1 2 3 4 5 6 7 8 9 10
FEET

J SOPER FEBRUARY 1984

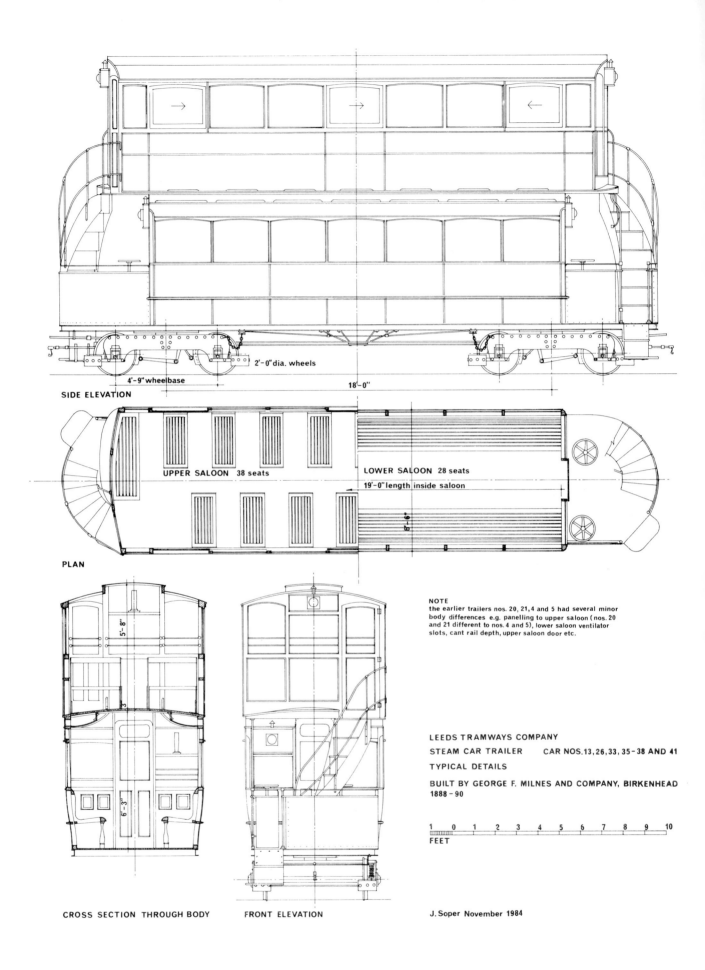

SIDE ELEVATION

2'-0" dia. wheels

4'-9" wheelbase

18'-0"

PLAN

UPPER SALOON 38 seats

LOWER SALOON 28 seats

19'-0" length inside saloon

5'-6"

5'-8"

6'-3"

CROSS SECTION THROUGH BODY

FRONT ELEVATION

NOTE
the earlier trailers nos. 20, 21, 4 and 5 had several minor
body differences e.g. panelling to upper saloon (nos. 20
and 21 different to nos. 4 and 5), lower saloon ventilator
slots, cant rail depth, upper saloon door etc.

LEEDS TRAMWAYS COMPANY

STEAM CAR TRAILER   CAR NOS. 13, 26, 33, 35-38 AND 41

TYPICAL DETAILS

BUILT BY GEORGE F. MILNES AND COMPANY, BIRKENHEAD
1888 - 90

1 0 1 2 3 4 5 6 7 8 9 10
FEET

J. Soper November 1984

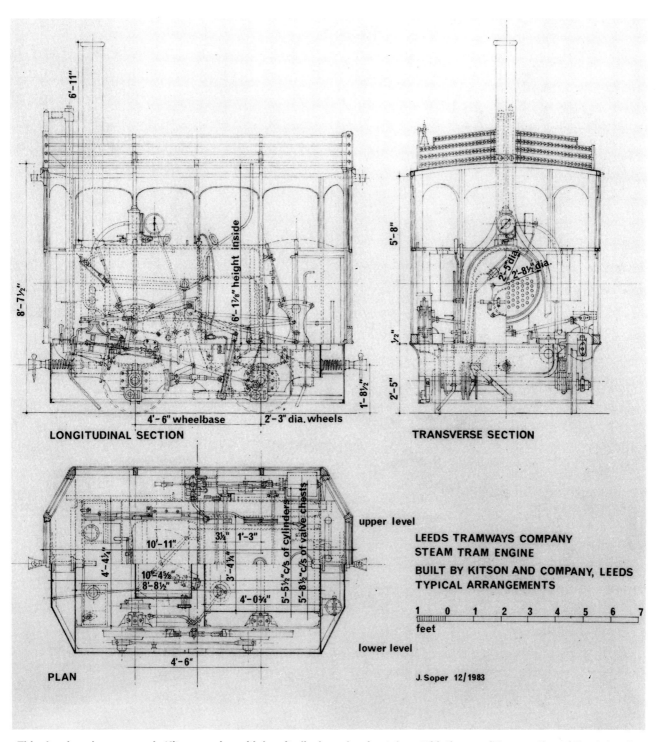

LONGITUDINAL SECTION

6'-11"

8'-7½"

6'-1⅛" height inside

1'-8½"

4'-6" wheelbase   2'-3" dia. wheels

TRANSVERSE SECTION

5'-8"

½"

2'-5"

2'-5" dia.
2'-8½" dia.

PLAN

10'-11"

3½"   1'-3"

3'-4¼"

10'-4½"
8'-8½"

3'-4¼"

4'-0¾"

4'-4¾"

5'-5½" c/s of cylinders

5'-8½" c/s of valve chests

4'-6"

upper level

lower level

LEEDS TRAMWAYS COMPANY
STEAM TRAM ENGINE

BUILT BY KITSON AND COMPANY, LEEDS
TYPICAL ARRANGEMENTS

1   0   1   2   3   4   5   6   7
feet

J. Soper 12/1983

This drawing shows an early Kitson engine with longitudinal condensing tubes. With the possible exception of No. 1, Leeds engines had transverse tubes.

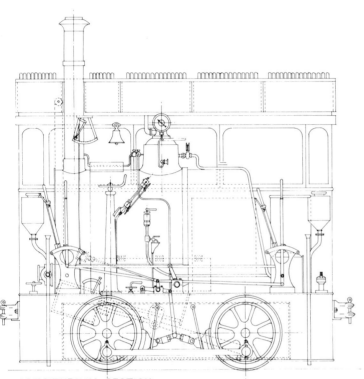

LONGITUDINAL SECTION

LEEDS TRAMWAYS COMPANY
STEAM TRAM ENGINE

BUILT BY THOMAS GREEN AND SON LTD., LEEDS
TYPICAL DETAILS

1 0 1 2 3 4 5 6 7 8 9 10
FEET

CROSS SECTION

copy of original blueprint dated 1-7-1891

J. Soper November 1984

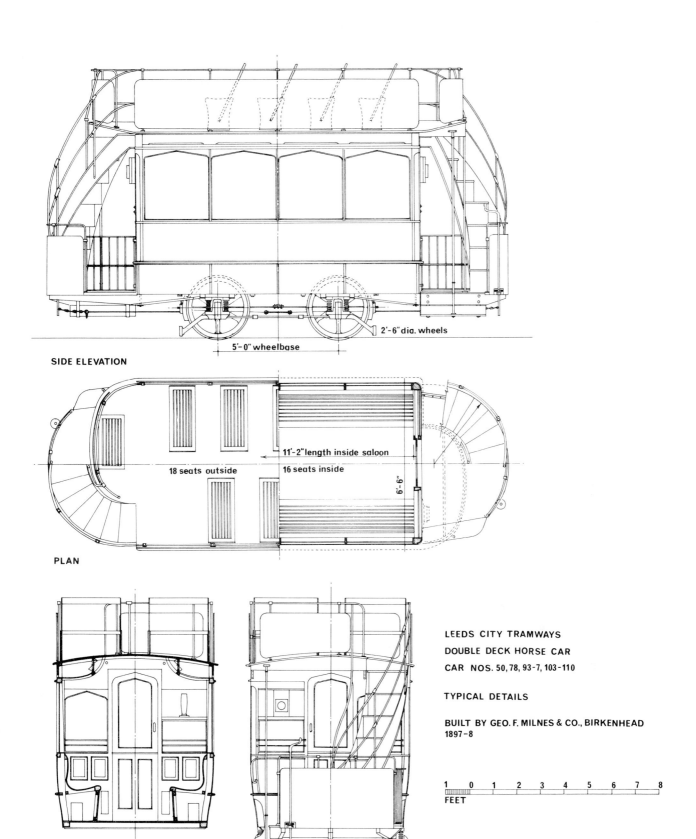

SIDE ELEVATION

2'-6" dia. wheels

5'-0" wheelbase

PLAN

11'-2" length inside saloon

18 seats outside

16 seats inside

6'-9"

SECTION THROUGH BODY

FRONT ELEVATION

LEEDS CITY TRAMWAYS
DOUBLE DECK HORSE CAR
CAR NOS. 50, 78, 93-7, 103-110

TYPICAL DETAILS

BUILT BY GEO. F. MILNES & CO., BIRKENHEAD
1897-8

1 0   1   2   3   4   5   6   7   8
FEET

J SOPER MARCH 1984

203

HORSE TRAMS

NO.	TYPE	BUILDER	COST	seating up	seating d'n	DATE IN SERVICE	DISPOSAL	NOTES
1	d.d.	Starbuck	?	20	20	16-9-1871	withdrawn c.1885	rebuilt c.1880-1
2	"	"	?	"	"	"	to L.C.T. 1894	" "
3	"	"	?	"	"	"	" "	
4	"	"	?	"	"	"	body sold 23-11-86	rebuilt c.1880-1. body sold for £6
5	"	Stephenson	?	24	22	"	to L.C.T. 1894	re-numbered 6, Nov. 1871. rebuilt c.1888
5	"	?	?	22	22	16-11-71 licensed	withdrawn 1873	possibly ex-Liverpool? returned late 1873?
7	"	?	?	24	24	7-3-72 "	" "	" " " " "
8	"	?	?	22	20	" "	to L.C.T. 1894	" "
9	"	?	?	20	18	4-4-72 "	withdrawn 1873	" " returned late 1873?
10	"	?	?	"	"	" "	" "	" " " " " "
11	"	?	?	22	22	8-5-72 "	" 1876	" "
12	"	?	?	"	"	4-7-72 "	" "	" "
13	"	?	?	18	18	1-8-72 "	" "	" "
14	"	?	?	22	22	" "	" "	" "
15	"	Starbuck	?	20	20	1-1-73 "	sold 16-11-1873	sold to Dewsbury, Batley & Birstal Tramways Co.£179 10s.
16	"	"	?	"	"	" "	" "	" " " " " " " "
17	"	"	?	"	"	" "	to L.C.T. 1894	rebuilt c.1890
18	"	"	?	"	"	" "	" "	top covered c.1883, cover later removed?
19	s.d.	"	£160		14	2-7-73 "	withdrawn 1876?	body sold 1879?
20	"	"	"		16	" "	" "	"
21	d.d.	"	?	20	20	28-11-73 "	" 1884	damaged in collision, broken up c.October 1884
22	"	"	?	"	"	" "	to L.C.T. 1894	rebuilt c.1889-90
23	"	"	?	"	"	" "	" "	
24	"	"	?	"	"	" "	5 withdrawn 1886-7	24-26 re-numbered 5, 7 & 9, not necessarily respect-
25	"	"	?	"	"	" "	7 " 1884	ively on 1-4-1874
26	"	"	?	"	"	" "	9 " 1886-7	7 in collision, broken up c. September 1884
10	"	"	£161	16	16	March 1874	to L.C.T. 1894	
24	"	"	"	"	"	" "	" "	
25	"	"	"	"	"	" "	" "	rebuilt c.1889
26	"	"	"	"	"	April 1874	withdrawn 24-12-88	damaged in collision, Meanwood Rd. broken up 1889
27	"	"	"	"	"	" "	to L.C.T. 1894	
28	"	"	"	"	"	" "	" "	
29	"	"	"	"	"	6-5-74 "	" "	rebuilt c.1888
30	"	"	"	"	"	" "	" "	
31	"	"	"	"	"	" "	" "	
15	s.d.	"	£167		18	14-11-74	" "	
16	"	"	"		"	" "	" "	
32	"	"	"		"	" "	" "	
33	"	"	"		"	" "	withdrawn 1889	
34	"	"	"		"	" "	to L.C.T. 1894	
35	"	"	"		"	" "	withdrawn 1887-8	
36	"	"	"		"	" "	" "	
37	"	"	"		"	" "	" 1886-7	
38	"	"	"		"	" "	" "	
39	"	"	?		"	24-11-75 "	to L.C.T. 1894	
40	"	"	?		"	" "	" "	rebuilt c.1887
41	"	"	?		"	" "	withdrawn 1887-8	
42	"	"	?		"	" "	to L.C.T. 1894	rebuilt c.1889
43	"	"	?		"	" "	" "	" c.1890
44	"	"	?		"	" "	" "	
45	"	"	?		"	" "	" "	
46	"	"	?		"	" "	" "	
47	"	"	?		"	" "	withdrawn 1886-7	
48	"	"	?		"	" "	to L.C.T. 1894	
49	"	"	?		"	" "	withdrawn 1887-8	
50	"	"	?		"	" "	to L.C.T. 1894	
51	"	"	?		"	" "	" "	
11	"	"	£169		"	1876	" "	
12	"	"	"		"	"	" "	

HORSE TRAMS CONTD.

NO.	TYPE	BUILDER	COST	seating up	seating d'n	DATE IN SERVICE	DISPOSAL	NOTES
13	s.d.	Starbuck	£169		18	1876	withdrawn 1888-9	
14	,,	,,	,,		,,	,,	to L.C.T. 1894	
19?	,,	,,	,,		,,	,,	,, ,,	
20?	,,	,,	,,		,,	,,	withdrawn 1885-6	
52	open	Leeds T. Co.	?		24	20-5-1879	,, ,,	built at Headingley Depot, seating later 22
53	,,	,,	?		,,	,,	,, 1881	,, ,, ,,
54	,,	,,	?		,,	,,	,, 1885-6	,, ,, ,,
56	d.d.	Ashbury	£185	20	18	2-8-83 licensed	to L.C.T. 1894	Eades Reversible car 1st. car of class in service 3-7-83
57	,,	,,	,,	,,	,,	,, ,,	,, ,,	,, ,,
58	,,	,,	,,	,,	,,	,, ,,	,, ,,	,, ,,
67	,,	Leeds T. Co.	?	20	20	31-1-1887	,, ,,	built at North Street Depot, garden seats
68	,,	,,	?	,,	,,	1-6-1887 licensed	,, ,,	,, ,, ,, ,, ,,
69	,,	Milnes	?	?		,, ,,	,, ,,	,, ,,
70	,,	,,	?	,,		,, ,,	,, ,,	,, ,,
74	s.d.	,,	?		18	,, ,,	,, ,,	
1	,,	,,	£108		16	July 1888	,, ,,	
7	,,	,,	,,		,,	22-8-88 licensed	,, ,,	
9	,,	,,	,,		,,	,, ,,	,, ,,	

STEAM TRAM TRAILERS

NO.	TYPE	BUILDER	COST	seating up	seating d'n	DATE IN SERVICE	DISPOSAL	NOTES
55	d.d.	Ashbury	£206	?		22-11-1882	to L.C.T. 1894	Eades Reversible car, bogies fitted c.1884
59	,,	Starbuck	£210	24	22	September 1883	,, ,,	four wheel truck ,, ,, ,,
60	,,	,,	,,	,,	,,	,, ,,	,, ,,	,, ,, ,, ,, ,,
61	,,	,,	£235	,,	,,	7-8-84 licensed	,, ,,	plate frame bogies
62	,,	,,	,,	,,	,,	,, ,,	,, ,,	,, ,,
63	,,	,,	£260	28	26	2-4-85 ,,	,, ,,	,, ,, delivered late March 1885
64	,,	,,	,,	,,	,,	,, ,,	,, ,,	,, ,, ,, ,, ,,
65	,,	,,	£240	,,	,,	10-6-86 ,,	,, ,,	,, ,,
66	,,	,,	,,	,,	,,	,, ,,	,, ,,	,, ,,
71	,,	Ashbury	£225	34	26	1-6-87 ,,	,, ,,	,, ,,
72	,,	,,	,,	,,	,,	,, ,,	,, ,,	,, ,,
73	,,	,,	,,	,,	,,	,, ,,	,, ,,	,, ,,
20	,,	Milnes	£242	38	28	22-3-88 ,,	,, ,,	,, ,,
21	,,	,,	,,	,,	,,	,, ,,	,, ,,	,, ,,
4	,,	,,	£237	,,	,,	17-4-1889 ,,	,, ,,	,, ,,
5	,,	,,	,,	,,	,,	,, ,,	,, ,,	,, ,,
35	,,	,,	£245	,,	,,	18-9-1889 ,,	,, ,,	,, ,,
36	,,	,,	,,	,,	,,	,, ,,	,, ,,	,, ,,
37	,,	,,	,,	,,	,,	,, ,,	,, ,,	,, ,,
38	,,	,,	,,	,,	,,	,, ,,	,, ,,	,, ,,
33	,,	,,	,,	,,	,,	19-2-90 ,,	,, ,,	,, ,,
41	,,	,,	,,	,,	,,	,, ,,	,, ,,	,, ,,
13	,,	,,	,,	,,	,,	19-3-90 ,,	,, ,,	,, ,,
26	,,	,,	,,	,,	,,	,, ,,	,, ,,	,, ,,

HORSE 'BUSES

NO.	TYPE	BUILDER	COST	seating up	seating d'n	DATE IN SERVICE	DISPOSAL	NOTES
?	s.d.					16-9-71	sold 14-3-89	used mainly on Headingley to Adel service
?						November 1874		
161						May 1875	withdrawn 1883	possibly sold to D. Busby Oct.1883
162						,, ,,	,, ,,	,, ,, ,, ,,
198						July 1875	,, ,,	,, ,, ,, ,,
?						late 1875		
?	s.d.		£45			19-10-75 bought		purchased from Liverpool Omnibus Company
59	d.d.			16	14	1-1-78 ,,	sold 8-10-78	ex-John Guy, sold for £50
195						4-9-78 licensed	delicensed 22-11-78	
4	d.d.			20	17	May 1882	,, 24-11-84	ex-Turton, licence to C.J. Coates 1885
5	,,			18	18	,,	sold 18-4-87	,, to G. Stockdale for £30
6	,,			12	14	,,	to L.C.T. 1894	,, valuation 1893 £65
7	,,			12	14	,,	withdrawn 1883	,, licence to J. Wilks 1884
8	,,			12	12	,,	sold 11-6-87	,, to Miller for £20

HORSE 'BUSES CONTD.

NO.	TYPE	BUILDER	COST	seating up	seating d'n	DATE IN SERVICE	DISPOSAL	NOTES
16	d.d.					May 1882	to L.C.T. 1894	ex–Turton valuation 1893 £65
17	,,			21	17	,,	sold 19-4-87	,, to W. Parker for £25
46						,,	delicensed 1893	,,
61	d.d.			20	23	,,	sold 8-6-87	,, to H. Harrison for £18
72						,,	withdrawn 1885	,, licence revoked 6-8-1885
75	d.d.					,,	to L.C.T. 1894	,, valuation 1893 £60
110						,,	withdrawn 1888	,,
193	d.d.			4	19	,,	to L.C.T. 1894	,, valuation 1893 £75
184	s.d.				10	c.1885	,, ,,	,, ,, £45
233						c.1886	sold 18-4-87	to G. Stockdale for £35
233	d.d.					c.1891	to L.C.T. 1894	valuation 1893 £60

LEEDS CITY TRAMWAYS   ROLLING STOCK TABLES

HORSE, STEAM TRAM TRAILERS AND ELECTRIC TRAM TRAILERS   1894-8

NO.	TYPE		BUILDER	cost/valu-ation 1893	seating up	seating d'n	DISPOSAL	NOTES
1	s.d.	horse tram	Milnes	£ 90		16	17-5-01 delicensed	ex–L.T.Co. renumbered 47, 24-3-97
2	d.d.	,,	Starbuck	100	20	20	24-3-99 ,,	,, ,, 49 ,,
3	,,	,,	,,	85	,,	,,	1900 ,,	,, ,, 52 ,,
4	,,	steam trailer	Milnes	205	38	28	8-5-02 ,,	,, ,, 53 ,,
5	,,	,,	,,	205	,,	,,	,, ,,	,, ,, 54 ,,
6	,,	horse tram	Stephenson	135	24	22	24-3-99 ,,	,, ,, 55 ,,
7	s.d.	,,	Milnes	90		16	17-5-01 ,,	,, ,, 75 ,,
8	d.d.	,,	?	110	22	20	,, ,,	,, ,, 76 ,,
9	s.d.	,,	Milnes	90		16	12-4-01 body sold	,, ,, 77 ,, sold for £5 to F. Dalby
10	d.d.	,,	Starbuck	75	18	16	c.Oct.97 scrapped	,, ,, 78 ,,
11	s.d.	,,	,,	60		18	13-6-01 body sold	,, ,, 79 ,, sold for £5 2s.6d.
12	,,	,,	,,	60		,,	17-5-01 delicensed	,, ,, 80 ,,
13	d.d.	steam trailer	Milnes	205	38	28	8-5-02 ,,	,, ,, 81 ,,
14	s.d.	horse tram	Starbuck	80		18	17-5-01 ,,	,, ,, 82 ,,
15	,,	,,	,,	80		,,	24-3-99 ,,	,, ,, 83 ,,
16	,,	,,	,,	70		,,	17-5-01 ,,	,, ,, 84 ,,
17	d.d.	,,	,,	85	20	20	24-3-99 ,,	,, ,, 85 ,,
18	,,	,,	,,	75	,,	,,	17-5-01 ,,	,, ,, 86 ,,
19	s.d.	,,	,,	80		18	,, ,,	,, ,, 87 ,,
20	d.d.	steam trailer	Milnes	215	38	28	8-5-02 ,,	,, ,, 88 ,,
21	,,	,,	,,	210	,,	,,	,, ,,	,, ,, 89 ,,
22	,,	horse tram	Starbuck	90	20	20	24-3-99 ,,	,, ,, 90 ,,
23	,,	,,	,,	90	,,	,,	17-5-01 ,,	,, ,, 91 ,,
24	,,	,,	,,	110	18	16	,, ,,	,, ,, 92 ,,
25	,,	,,	,,	90	,,	,,	c.Oct.97 scrapped	,, ,, 93 ,,
26	,,	steam trailer	Milnes	210	38	28	8-5-02 delicensed	,,
27	,,	horse tram	Starbuck	110	18	16	17-5-01 ,,	,,
28	,,	,,	,,	120	,,	,,	,, ,,	,,
29	,,	,,	,,	70	,,	,,	late'01 withdrawn	,,
30	,,	,,	,,	75	,,	,,	17-5-01 delicensed	,,
31	,,	,,	,,	120	,,	,,	,, ,,	,,
32	s.d.	,,	,,	85		18	,, ,,	,,
33	d.d.	steam trailer	Milnes	205	38	28	8-5-02 ,,	,,
34	s.d.	horse tram	Starbuck	75		18	17-5-01 ,,	,,
35	d.d.	steam trailer	Milnes	205	38	28	8-5-02 ,,	,,
36	,,	,,	,,	215	,,	,,	,, ,,	,,
37	,,	,,	,,	215	,,	,,	,, ,,	,,
38	,,	,,	,,	215	,,	,,	,, ,,	,,
39	s.d.	horse tram	Starbuck	80		18	17-5-01 ,,	,,
40	,,	,,	,,	70		,,	,, ,,	,,
41	d.d.	steam trailer	Milnes	205	38	28	8-5-02 ,,	,,
42	s.d.	horse tram	Starbuck	60		18	17-5-01 ,,	,,

HORSE, STEAM TRAM TRAILERS AND ELECTRIC TRAM TRAILERS CONTD.

NO.	TYPE		BUILDER	cost/valuation 1893	seating up	seating d'n	DISPOSAL	NOTES
43	s.d.	horse tram	Starbuck	£ 60		18	17-5-01 delicensed	ex – L.T.Co.
44	,,	,,	,,	75		,,	22-5-00 sold	,, sold to W.T. Carter for £3
45	,,	,,	,,	60		,,	17-5-01 delicensed	,,
46	,,	,,	,,	75		,,	16-3-00 ,,	,,
48	,,	,,	,,	60		,,	17-5-01 ,,	,,
50	,,	,,	,,	60		,,	late 1897 withdrawn	,,
51	,,	,,	,,	70		,,	17-5-01 delicensed	,, sold to S.Broughton 30-11-1901 for £5
55	d.d.	steam trailer	Ashbury	15	?		1895 scrapped	,, Eades Reversible car
56	,,	horse tram	,,	110	20	18	17-5-01 delicensed	,, ,, ,, ,,
57	,,	,,	,,	65	,,	,,	,, ,,	,, ,, ,, ,,
58	,,	,,	,,	110	,,	,,	,, ,,	,, ,, ,, ,,
59	,,	steam trailer	Starbuck	185	24	22	8-5-02 ,,	,,
60	,,	,,	,,	185	,,	,,	,, ,,	,, converted to s.d. 1894
61	,,	,,	,,	200	,,	,,	,, ,,	,,
62	,,	,,	,,	200	,,	,,	,, ,,	,,
63	,,	,,	,,	205	28	26	,, ,,	,, converted to s.d. 1894
64	,,	,,	,,	190	,,	,,	,, ,,	,,
65	,,	,,	,,	205	,,	,,	,, ,,	,,
66	,,	,,	,,	205	,,	,,	,, ,,	,, converted to s.d. 1894
67	,,	horse tram	L.T.Co.	140	20	20	17-5-01 ,,	,,
68	,,	,,	,,	140	,,	,,	,, ,,	,, sold to S. Benson 12-2-02 for £7
69	,,	,,	Milnes	140	?		,, ,,	,,
70	,,	,,	,,	140	?		,, ,,	,,
71	,,	steam trailer	Ashbury	210	34	26	8-5-02 ,,	,,
72	,,	,,	,,	210	,,	,,	,, ,,	,,
73	,,	,,	,,	210	,,	,,	,, ,,	,, body sold as caravan at Rodley
74	s.d.	horse tram	Milnes	70		18	17-5-01 ,,	,,
94	d.d.	,,	,,	160	18	16	late 1901 withdrawn	in service late 1897, purchased 13-8-1897
95	,,	,,	,,	,,	,,	,,	17-5-01 delicensed	,, ,, ,, ,,
96	,,	,,	,,	,,	,,	,,	late 1901 withdrawn	,, ,, ,, ,,
97	,,	,,	,,	,,	,,	,,	,, ,,	,, ,, ,, ,,
98	,,	elect. trailer	,,	170	28	20		,, 27-11-97, converted to electric car 1900-1
99	,,	,,	,,	,,	,,	,,		,, ,, ,, ,, ,,
100	,,	,,	,,	,,	,,	,,		,, ,, ,, ,, ,,
101	,,	,,	,,	,,	,,	,,		,, ,, ,, ,, ,,
102	,,	,,	,,	,,	,,	,,		,, ,, ,, ,, ,,
103	,,	,,	,,	,,	,,	,,		,, ,, ,, ,, ,,
50	,,	horse tram	,,	160	18	16	late 1901 withdrawn	licensed 23-3-98, purchased 4-2-1898
78	,,	,,	,,	,,	,,	,,	,, ,,	,, ,, ,, ,,
93	,,	,,	,,	,,	,,	,,	,, ,,	,, ,, ,, ,,
104	,,	,,	,,	,,	,,	,,	,, ,,	,, ,, ,, ,,
105	,,	,,	,,	,,	,,	,,	17-5-01 delicensed	,, ,, ,, ,,
106	,,	,,	,,	,,	,,	,,	late 1901 withdrawn	,, ,, ,, ,,
107	,,	,,	,,	,,	,,	,,	,, ,,	,, ,, body sold, now owned by L.T.H.S.
108	,,	,,	,,	,,	,,	,,	17-5-01 delicensed	,, ,, purchased 4-2-1898
109	,,	,,	,,	,,	,,	,,	late 1901 withdrawn	,, ,, ,, ,,
110	,,	,,	,,	,,	,,	,,	,, ,,	,, ,, ,, ,,
111	s.d.	,,	,,	125		18	17-5-01 delicensed	,, 27-4-98 ,, 13-5-1898
112	,,	,,	,,	,,		,,	,, ,,	,, ,, ,, ,,
113	,,	,,	,,	,,		,,	,, ,,	,, ,, ,, ,,
114	,,	,,	,,	,,		,,	,, ,,	,, ,, ,, ,,
115	,,	,,	,,	,,		,,	,, ,,	,, ,, ,, ,,
116	,,	,,	,,	,,		,,	,, ,,	,, ,, ,, ,,
117	,,	,,	,,	,,		,,	late 1901 withdrawn	,, 15-6-98 ,, 10-6-1898
118	,,	,,	,,	,,		,,	17-5-01 delicensed	,, ,, ,, ,,
119	,,	,,	,,	,,		,,	late 1901 withdrawn	,, 13-7-98 ,, 12-8-1898
120	,,	,,	,,	,,		,,	17-5-01 delicensed	,, 21-4-99 ,, ,,
121	,,	elect. trailer	?	£35 14s. 4d.		22	8-5-02 ,,	,, 27-4-98 ex-Roundhay, to salt car 1901
122	,,	,,	?	,,		,,	,, ,,	,, ,, ,, ,, ,,

HORSE, STEAM TRAM TRAILERS AND ELECTRIC CAR TRAILERS

NO.	TYPE		BUILDER	COST	seating		DISPOSAL		NOTES
					up	d'n			
123	s.d. elect.trailer		?	£35 14s. 4d.		22	8-5-02 delicensed		licensed 27-4-98 ex-Roundhay, to salt car 1901
124	"	"	?	"		"	"	"	" " " " "
125	"	"	?	"		"	"	"	" " " " "
126	"	"	?	"		"	"	"	nos.121-7 included a small trailer built by Brush, fleet
127	"	"	?	"		"	"	"	no. uncertain
128	d.d.	"	Brush	£200 12s.0d.	28	20			licensed 13-7-98, converted to electric car 1900-01
129	"	"	"	"	"	"			" " " " "
130	"	"	"	"	"	"			" " " " "
131	"	"	"	"	"	"			" " " " "
132	"	"	"	"	"	"			" " " " "

LEEDS TRAMWAYS COMPANY AND LEEDS CITY TRAMWAYS

STEAM TRAMWAY ENGINES

NO.	TYPE		BUILDER	COST	DATE IN SERVICE	PURCHASED	NOTES
	cylinder	stroke					
1	8 in.	10 in.	Kitson	£506	14-6-1880	20-1-1883	on hire 1880-2, withdrawn late 1890
2	"	"	"	"	c. March 1881	"	" " " "
3	"	"	"	"	c. May 1881	"	" " , " early 1891
1	6 in.	7 in.	Green		1-1-1883		Wilkinson's patent, on hire to June 1884
2	"	"	"		"		" " " "
4	8 1/2 in.	12 in.	Kitson	£702	1884	12-5-1884	rebuilt 1891, valuation 1893 £350
5	"	"	"	"	c. August 1884	9-9-1884	" " "
6	"	"	"	"	"	"	valuation 1893 £325
7	"	"	"	"	"	"	" " £400
8	"	"	"	"	"	20-9-1884	" " £325
9	"	"	"	"	"	"	" " "
10	"	"	"	"	"	"	" " £425
11	"	"	"	£720	1885	1-10-1885	" " £375
12	"	"	Green	£670	25-8-85 delivered	"	rebuilt & compounded 1890, valuation 1893 £500
13	"	"	Kitson	£710	1886	24-5-1886	valuation 1893 £440
14	"	"	"	"	"	"	" " £400
15	"	"	"	"	"	5-6-1886	" " £425
16	"	"	"	"	"	12-7-1886	" " £400
17	"	"	"	£660	1887	15-10-1887	" " £450
18	"	"	"	"	"	"	" " £500
19	9 1/4 in.	14 in.h.p.	Green	£750	13-5-89 delivered	26-6-1889	compound 14 1/2 in.14 in. l.p., valuation 1893 £650
20	"	"	"	"	14-6-89 "	"	" " " " £640
21	"	"	"	£747	23-9-89 "	30-12-1889	" " " " £700
22	"	"	"	"	11-11-89 "	"	" " " " "
23	"	"	"	"	29-11-89 "	"	" " " " "
24	"	"	"	£780	4-4-90 "	5-12-1890	" " " " "
25	"	"	"	"	2-5-90 "	"	" " " " "
26	"	"	"	"	24-5-90 "	"	" " " £725
27	"	"	"	"	20-8-90 "	30-4-1891	" " " £690, Burrell
28	"	"	"	"	5-11-90 "	15-7-1891	" " " £725 "
29	"	"	"	£700	1897	15-1-1897	" " Burrell condenser
30	"	"	"	"	"	"	" " " "

Style of interior numeral on horse car No. 107.

CHAPTER TWENTY-ONE

The Track

The track construction used by the Busby's for the Headingley line was to the design of Joseph Kincaid, their engineer. Kincaid was an eminent tramway engineer at the time and had designed the trackwork for the Pimlico, Peckham and Greenwich section of the London tramways, opened in August 1871. The track on the Headingley route was identical to that used in London. It consisted of a series of transverse timber sleepers, 6″ × 4″, placed at intervals of 3′-0″ with longitudinal rebated timber sleepers, also 6″ × 4″, laid to gauge over and cleated to the transverse sleepers by means of cast iron brackets spiked on to the outside of

each longitudinal sleeper, forming an abutment. The flat grooved rails were spiked to the longitudinal sleepers and had two fillets to firmly bed the rail on to the sleeper. The rails were 4″ wide, $1\frac{1}{4}$″ thick, had a sectional area of $4\frac{3}{4}$ square inches, and weighed $47\frac{1}{2}$ lbs per yard.

Longitudinal timber sleepers buried in the ground were subject to movement due to moisture and this type of track construction soon got into a deplorable state. In order to eliminate the problem Kincaid patented, in March 1872, a new system of track construction which he called "Kincaids Iron Way". An experimental section of a quarter of a mile in length was laid on the Head-

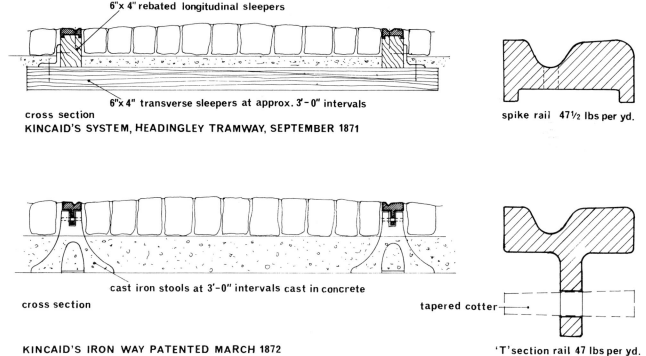

6"x 4" rebated longitudinal sleepers

6"x 4" transverse sleepers at approx. 3'-0" intervals

cross section
KINCAID'S SYSTEM, HEADINGLEY TRAMWAY, SEPTEMBER 1871

spike rail 47½ lbs per yd.

cast iron stools at 3'-0" intervals cast in concrete

cross section

KINCAID'S IRON WAY PATENTED MARCH 1872

tapered cotter

'T'section rail 47 lbs per yd.

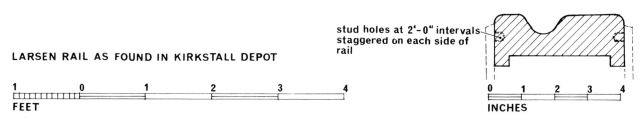

LARSEN RAIL AS FOUND IN KIRKSTALL DEPOT

stud holes at 2'-0" intervals staggered on each side of rail

FEET

INCHES

ingley route. Rails of the same section were used but instead of timber sleepers, were supported on a series of cast iron stools or supports at 3'-0" centres, seated on and embedded in concrete. The rail was fixed to the stool by a vertical spike through the groove driven into a hardwood plug forced into a round hole in the top of the stool. The Kirkstall route was probably constructed with this form of permanent way, but the later routes to Hunslet, York Road and Chapeltown were built to a similar system, but with a modified rail section and a different design of stool. This system, illustrated below, used rail lengths of 24 feet and was also employed on the Hull Street Tramways and Leicester tramways in 1874 and the Bristol and Sheffield tramways in 1876.

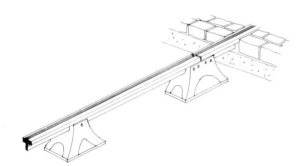

DETAIL OF KINCAID'S IRON WAY AS FOUND IN HEADINGLEY DEPOT

Kincaid also used on some of the earlier portions of track, his "iron way", using a tee-shaped rail section weighing 47 lbs per yard. A small section of this track was discovered in Headingley Depot during the reconstruction of the floor and showed that it was cottered into cast iron stools every 3'-0", one cotter per stool and four at a joint stool, the rail ends having two holes. Points and crossings were of cast iron, chilled with stool ends and fluted filler blocks to fill the openings between the ends. Excavations at the Kirkstall horse tram depot in 1966 revealed that two types of rail were used. There was a Larsen rail and a broad heavy guard spike-rail, both with two fillets below. The Larsen rail was similar in appearance to the earlier Kincaid rail and

was patented by Jorgen David Larsen in February 1871. It got rid of the disadvantage of the vertical spike used on Kincaid's system by substituting a lateral fastening consisting of a short rectangular piece of iron fixed by means of a stud into a hole in the fillet and fixed to the side of the longitudinal sleeper by means of a long spike. The fixings alternated on the head and check sides of the rail at 24" intervals. The spike-rail, although badly corroded, appeared to be identical to the rails used on the Headingley tramway in 1871.

Since Kincaid was still employed as Engineer by the Leeds Tramways Company when the Kirkstall Depot was built, it seems strange that a rail not of his patent was used. It was probably a later replacement. The Tramways Company paid off Kincaid in January 1878, following innumerable complaints from the Highways Committee with regard to the state of the track, and used their own discretion. They later used Larsen rails extensively in track replacements on the horse-operated lines.

During the latter part of 1877 a new passing loop was laid on the Headingley route using a new type of rail patented by Benjamin Barker in 1876. This rail had been used on the Manchester tramways – a Turton/Busby enterprise – and was of much more substantial construction than Kincaid's systems. The peculiar features of Barker's system were the longitudinal cast iron sleepers which gave a continuous bearing for the rail and the adjacent paving setts. The grooved rail was indented along its lower surface to fit the head of the sleeper, to which it was fastened by a cotter pin. Each sleeper, 2'-11½" long, weighed 137 lbs and the rails, of Bessemer steel, were 3" wide, weighed 40 lbs per yard and were in lengths of 18, 21 and 24 feet. The rail must have proved satisfactory for the whole of the new Meanwood Road and Wortley routes, about four miles in length, were laid on Barker's system. Three different sections of rail were employed. First a section for 6" paving having a rail of 40 lbs per yard and sleepers of 137 lbs; second, a section for 5" paving, with sleepers of 102 lbs and rails of 34 lbs, and third, a section for 4" paving, with sleepers of 90 lbs, and rails of

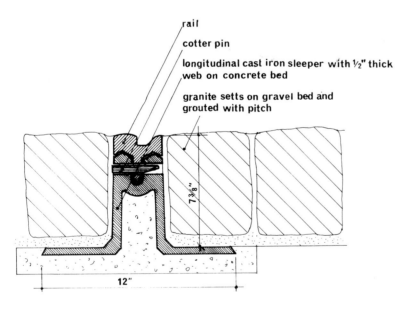

rail
cotter pin
longitudinal cast iron sleeper with ½" thick web on concrete bed
granite setts on gravel bed and grouted with pitch

7 ⅜"

12"

CROSS SECTION

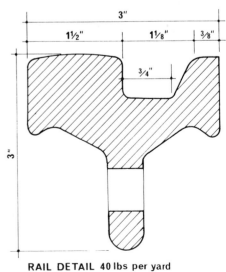

3"

1½"   1⅛"   ⅜"

¾"

3"

RAIL DETAIL 40 lbs per yard

BARKER'S SYSTEM AS USED ON THE LEEDS TRAMWAYS FROM 1877 TO 1881

34 lbs. The Tramways Company accounts show that £5,898 18s. 4d. was paid to Barker for rails between November 1877 and December 1878. Barker's rails were used for the extension of the Wortley line to the "Star Inn", and the relaying of Marsh Lane in 1880. A further £2,465 8s. 8d. was expended between June 1879 and December 1881. Thereafter, no further rails were purchased from Barker and the Tramways Company interested themselves in a new type of girder rail patented by a J. Gowan in 1878, a modification of a similar rail originated in Paris by M. Archille Legrand in 1877. Gowan's rail bore a close resemblance to the later rails adopted as a British Standard and was to supersede all other forms of rail construction. The rail was 7″ high, 7″ wide at the base and 3″ wide at the head and the web was perforated to lighten the weight, the rail weighing 85 lbs per yard. The perforated web, although perfectly satisfactory with a steady load, was subject to fracture under heavy blows caused by bad rail joints, and was soon abandoned.

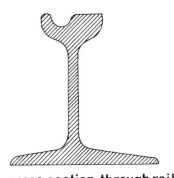

cross section through rail
85 lbs per yard

GOWANS' GIRDER RAIL AS PATENTED 1878

During the latter part of 1881 the tramways in Hunslet Lane, Wellington Street and Park Row were relaid with Gowan's rails supplied by the Darlington Iron Company (referred to as the Darlington Steel and Iron Company from June 1882). A small number of Barker's rails were also used. The Darlington Company also supplied Gowan's rails for the reconstruction of the Headingley tramway in 1882. The cost was about £3,000 and the rails were apparently laid on the old transverse wooden sleepers of Kincaid's system. Gowan's steel rails on sleepers and a 9″ concrete foundation were used for the 800 yards of track relaid in Wellington Road between April and July 1886. The rails were apparently supplied by a Douglas Elliott and Co. After 1886 all track-work carried out by the Tramways Company was largely of a cosmetic nature, Gowan's rails being used for the steam operated routes to Headingley and Wortley, and Larsen's rails for the remaining lines. Points and crossings to Kenway's design were used on some sections of the tramways.

The construction of the Harehills Road to Green Road via Beckett Street tramway, the major reconstruction of Tong Road in 1891 and the new trackwork in Boar Lane and Wellington Street, the following year, were carried out by the Leeds Corporation at the cost of the Tramways Company, Girder rails supplied by Dick, Kerr and Company at prices varying from £6 12s. 0d. to £6 17s. 6d. per ton, laid on a concrete foundation, were employed.

Due to lack of maintenance the state of the tramway track generally, was deplorable by 1893. The Headingley route was discussed at the arbitration and it transpired that there were as many as 213 rails ranging from 1′-0″ to 14′-0″ in length and also 109 split, broken or defective rails. William Wharam said that where rails had been damaged by engines, the defective portion

Relaying the Briggate/Boar Lane Junction in 1892. Rails supplied by Dick, Kerr and Company to Gowan's pattern were used.
Courtesy The late C. R. Wood, Photographer.

211

was repaired by a good cutting from another rail. Mr. Lockwood, Q.C., for the Corporation, commented that it was like "cutting up two old pairs of trousers to make a new pair". Wharam agreed, and several years later, after the tramways had been reconstructed by the Corporation, it turned out that about 2,000 pieces of rail measuring 1'-6" or less in length had been found.

Statement shewing construction of present Tramways, and quantity of needful re-construction to replace worn-out lines; to make all single tracks double, excepting Beckett Street, which will remain single track, and be extended, via Burmantofts Street, to York Road.

ROUTE, AS PER ACT OF PARLIAMENT.	Track of Girder Type Rail, on Concrete.		Track of Non-Girder Type Rail.				Street Length.
			On Concrete.		Not Concreted.		
	Double. Miles.	Single. Miles.	Double. Miles.	Single. Miles.	Double. Miles.	Single. Miles.	Miles.
HEADINGLEY to BOAR LANE	·28	·075	...	...	1·42	1·19	2·965
KIRKSTALL to BRIGGATE (including Wellington Street)	·75	...	...	·04	1·25	·94	2·980
CHAPELTOWN to BOAR LANE	·69	...	...	··	·64	1·64	2·970
MEANWOOD to SHEEPSCAR	·012	·02	...	...	·32	·39	·742
HUNSLET to BOAR LANE	No Girder Rails		·44	...	·89	·62	1·950
MARSH LANE (To be superseded by York St.)	No Girder Rails		·20	·25	·18	·13	·760
WORTLEY to WELLINGTON STREET ...	·66	·60	·40	...	...	...	1·660
ROUNDHAY to SHEEPSCAR ... ... } BECKETT ST. to ROUNDHAY ROAD }	2·06	1·23	...	...	...	...	3·290
	4·452	1·925	1·04	·29	4·70	4·91	17·317
	10·829 Miles of Single Track.		2·37 Miles of Single Track. 33·36 Miles of Old Rails.		14·31 Miles of Single Track.		

Total Length of Present Tramway taken as a Single Track, 27·509 Miles.

TRAMWAYS (TAKEN AS SINGLE LINES) REQUIRING CONSTRUCTION.

Extension of Beckett Street, as single line to York Road, with passing places ... ·385
Perfect Single line to be made double ... ... 1·455
Imperfect worn-out single line, totally re-constructed as double line ... ... 9·820
"   "   double   "   "   ... ... 9·400
Junctions at York Road, &c. ... ... ·360
Say 21½ Miles. — 21·420

Imperfect worn-out single line, to be re-constructed, except as to concrete ... ·58
"   "   double   "   "   ... ... 2·08
Say 2⅔ Miles. — 2·660

Total Miles of Needful Construction ... ... 24·080
Say 24¼ Miles.

A page from the City Engineer's Report of 1895 indicating the state of the track.   *Courtesy Leeds Corporation.*

All tramway rails used by the Corporation at first were of the Gowan's girder type laid on a concrete foundation. The tramway to Roundhay, however, laid in 1889, was on a 9" concrete foundation with girder rails weighing 98 lbs per yard supplied by H. Koenigs and Co. of Bochum, Germany, at a cost of £3,571 5s. 6d. The extension of the Roundhay route to the Canal Gardens and reconstruction of the Kirkstall tramway in 1896-7 used rails supplied by Walter Scott Ltd. of the Leeds Steel Works, Hunslet. The rails were to Gowan's pattern and Walter Scott's code W.S.5 and 6., W.S.5 weighing 98 lbs per yard and W.S.6 100 lbs.

Track construction at Kirkstall Abbey in 1897. The rails were to Gowan's pattern and supplied by Walter Scott Ltd. of Leeds.   *Courtesy "The Railway World."*

Much of the work of relaying and reconstruction of the tramway tracks and road works in Leeds, in both the Company and early Corporation days, was carried out by two local firms, Towler and Speight and Joseph Speight, probably related. In the early 'nineties William Towler invented a new form of rail construction. It consisted of a lower and top section, the top section being removable for easy renewal. According to Towler, if his rail was adopted over the whole of the

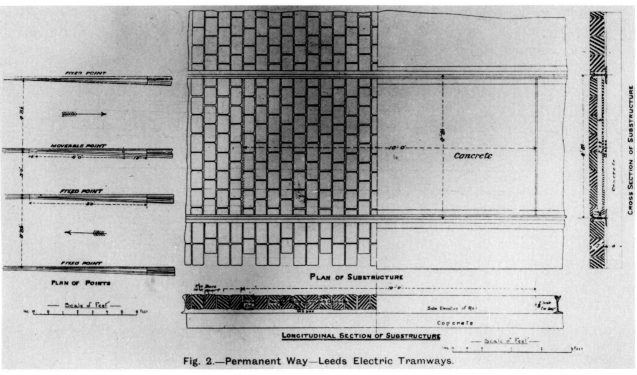

Fig. 2.—Permanent Way—Leeds Electric Tramways.

Track construction of the Roundhay and Kirkstall Electric Tramways, 1897.   *Courtesy "The Railway World."*

tramways in Leeds, a saving of £40,000 to the Corporation would be effected. In October 1894 he approached the Highways Committee and it agreed to allow him to lay down, at his own cost, a short length of rail as a trial. It was apparently successful, for he was allowed to lay a further stretch, again at his own expense, in North Street, in December 1895. The Highways Committee said it was satisfied with the results and in April 1896 ordered a mile of single track from Towler at £6 per ton for use on the new Roundhay to Kirkstall tramway. This was presumably laid down, but must have been unsatisfactory as no further mention has been found of Towler's rails in Leeds. In June 1898 a man named Deakin approached the Highways Committee and asked for permission for a trial of his patent rail. The request was referred to a sub-committee, but no further action appears to have been taken.

Over the next few years the new tramways laid down all used rails supplied by Walter Scott Ltd. Scott's supplied over 10,000 tons of rails to Leeds at costs varying from £6 to £7 5s. 0d. per ton in the period 1897 to 1903, all apparently to their W.S.6 section. The rails used were 60'-0" long and were joined by fish and sole plates, the former weighing 40 lbs and the latter 47 lbs per pair. The rails were electrically bonded with double Chicago bonds with cross bonds. The paving was of granite setts except in Briggate and Boar Lane where wood paving was used. The old iron and steel rails, used by the Tramways Company, were mainly sold to Thomas W. Ward, scrap merchants, at £2 per ton for steel and £1 17s. 6d. for iron rails.

Although Leeds adopted W.S.6 section as standard, other local authorities and tramway companies had their own sections and specifications which were dependent upon the whim of their own engineer in charge. In July 1901 the "Tramway and Railway World" listed no fewer than 71 different types of girder rail in current use, of

Track relaying at Briggate Junction in 1899 using Gowan's pattern rails. *Courtesy "The Tramway and Railway World."*

which Walter Scott Ltd. manufactured 21. With all these different sizes and types of rail sections, the rail makers found it impossible to stock rails, and in the case of a small order for repairs or extensions, the price was liable to be high and there was a likelihood of delay on account of the rolls having to be picked out, re-turned, and refixed in the mills.

A commission of experts was formed early in 1903, which later in the year issued a Standard Specification and Sections. Hence the British Standard section was born and was universally adopted. A choice of five sections was given in order to suit various conditions of traffic:−

No. 1	$6\frac{1}{2}'' \times 6\frac{1}{2}''$	90 lbs per yard
No. 2	$6\frac{1}{2}'' \times 7''$	95 lbs per yard
No. 3	$6\frac{1}{2}'' \times 7''$	100 lbs per yard
No. 4	$7'' \times 7''$	105 lbs per yard
No. 5	$7'' \times 7''$	110 lbs per yard

For a number of years Leeds adopted B.S. No. 4 as its standard rail section, in rails of 60'-0" lengths.

Newly laid Briggate junction with B.T.H. car No. 145, 1901.   *Courtesy "The Tramway and Railway World".*

Kitson engine No. 7 in Wellington Street about 1890.
Courtesy Science Museum, South Kensington, London, Whitcombe Collection.

Briggate junction with a Green engine and Milnes trailer No. 36. A Kitson engine with a converted single deck trailer is in the background.
Courtesy "Tramway and Railway World".

CHAPTER TWENTY-TWO

The Staff

The Depot Staff, probably Headingley Depot, about 1899. The car in the background is possibly one of the Milnes single-deck cars of the 111-120 series.

Courtesy West Yorkshire P. T. E.

The reader will have noted that the early omnibus proprietors, or members of their families, frequently drove or conducted their own vehicles. In many cases, however, staff were employed. A conductor, frequently a boy, and a driver, were required for each 'bus and the bigger proprietors also employed horsekeepers, blacksmiths, etc. Boys, known as "tip lads", looked after the "chain" horses – the extra horses required to pull a 'bus or tram up a gradient. Some staff were illiterate or semi-literate, but the following driver, unfortunately not named, certainly got the message across to his master:–

"The Coach cem hear this day, and it all brok. The off side of both Pannals are smashed inn. The Dore on that side along with the window are Brok to Buts. The fore-

Boot are also smashed along with lamp post. the Pannal off the near side Dore are also Brok. the Toung are brok, the under carriage are concidurably Damage. In Fack it is that much Broken and Damage that I do believes that the same coach can never be mended".

(Leeds Intelligencer 13th April 1861, quoting the Inverness Courier).

In 1869 when it became necessary for drivers and conductors to be licensed, the Hackney Carriages Committee insisted that they be literate. At their meeting on 2nd February 1882, the Committee ordered that 'bus drivers Richard Almond, John Guest and Thomas Kay should learn to read and write within the ensuing six months.

215

The average wage of a 'bus driver or conductor in the 'fifties and 'sixties was probably about 15s. 0d. per week. He was expected to be on duty from his first journey in the morning to the last at night – never more than 12 hours in this period. There were long waits at the termini for touting of passengers and the job was considered a leisurely one. With the introduction of later 'buses and trams in the 'sixties and 'seventies, the hours of the staff became longer and frequently varied from 14 to 17 hours per day on seven days per week. Wages, however, increased and were now between 20s. 0d. and 25s. 0d. per week for a 'bus driver or conductor. A tram conductor in 1875 earned 25s. 0d. per week, but drivers were better paid. In 1880 a driver on appointment received 4s. 3d. per day and this increased with long service up to 5s. 0d. A tram driver could therefore earn a maximum of 35s. 0d. per week as a full day's pay was paid for Sundays regardless of the number of hours worked. This was a good wage for the period, and William Turton said in 1882 that the tram drivers and conductors were better paid than those in any other town in the country. The wage compared favourably with the remuneration of the average skilled labourer and was much higher than the average earnings of accomplished clerks who worked long hours.

The Tramways Company Cash Books give details of the total wages bills and individual salaries paid, but no information on wages of other staff. Of the salaried employees, William Bulmer received £25 per month on appointment as General Manager in 1873 and retained this for the whole of his stay with the Company. The Secretary, William Wharam, received £12 10s. 0d. monthly, increased to £16 13s. 4d. in August 1875. The short-lived General Manager, Matthias Smith, received the same salary as Wharam. Wharam was promoted to Manager in December 1877 and received £25 per month, increased to £37 10s. 0d. (£450 per annum) in January 1882. Inflation was non-existent in these times and Wharam remained on this salary for the whole of his remaining 21 years with the Tramways Company and Corporation.

Details of the wages paid to platform staff were given in the local press in 1889 and these showed that there were variations according to the type of car used and route operated. Drivers on the "easiest" routes, Meanwood and York Road, where single-deck horse cars were usually employed, received the lowest wages. Wages were as follows:–

Headingley
   drivers 4s. 3d. to 5s. 4d. per day
   guards 3s. 0d. to 3s. 9d. per day
Hunslet and Kirkstall
   drivers 4s. 3d. to 5s. 0d. per day
   guards 3s. 6d. per day.
Chapeltown
   drivers 5s. 0d. per day
   guards 3s. 0d. to 3s. 9d. per day
York Road and Meanwood
   drivers 4s. 3d. per day.
   guards 3s. 6d. per day
Wortley
   drivers 4s. 8d. to 5s. 2d. per day
   guards 3s. 6d. per day

A horse keeper earned an average of 3s. 4½d. per day. There were no paid holidays and if a man was absent from work on account of sickness he received no payment, but every three weeks he was allowed a day off, for which he received pay.

The Tramways Company Staff Records illustrate some of the conditions under which their employees worked. The Company and some of the omnibus proprietors had a system whereby the staff were fined if they committed a minor offence and, if they were to blame, platform staff also had to pay the cost of any damage that was caused to their vehicles. The Tramways Company did not allow any time for meals and staff had to eat their meals on their vehicles. A driver or conductor had little leisure time and it is not surprising that many frequently called in for refreshment at the inn situated at the tram or 'bus terminus. Cases of drunkenness were common and innumerable instances are recorded. The following extracts from the Staff Record Books illustrate some of the above points:–

Entry No. 1,481 28th March 1884
Kelly, Joseph, Driver, Kirkstall section.
Discharged. Kelly was frequently in a half-muddled condition, brought on through drink, and consequently had, on several occasions, his horses falling. A few weeks ago his horses bolted off through the pin not being put in the socket, and previous to this he allowed his horses to run away from Kirkstall terminus, and were captured on the Bradford Road. Again on 25th and 26th March he had his horses down. Had been cautioned by the Manager.

Entry No. 478 5th June 1880
Hill, James, Conductor, Kirkstall car.
Conductor of No. 41 Kirkstall car, due in Leeds at 9.20 pm was worse for drink when he paid in his money. Note: I was at Boar Lane office when Hill came in, and noticed that he had something to drink. I spoke to him on the suggestion of the Manager who was there, and he said "I have had only two glasses of beer, I am all right, it's this infernal cap that is so heavy." I noticed he was no worse so let him proceed.

Entry No. 1,909 23rd November 1886
Licence, Charles, Guard, Headingley.
Negligence in calling his driver (Robinson) to come on single line at Carlton Hill, and not being at the points top of Cookridge Street to stop No. 10 engine from going over the points, and meeting on the single line. It was foggy at the time. Fined 2s. 6d.

Entry No. 1,541 26th June 1884
Nixon, George, Ex-Driver, Headingley.
To breaking six squares glass, 30s. 0d. 2 lbs india rubber, 15s. 0d. workmen's time 23s. 9d. Total £3 8s. 9d. (damage to car No. 51). Paid in nine payments.

Entry No. 1,228 11th October 1882
Mack, Edward, Driver, Beeston Hill section
Resigned same night, saying, "the hours were too long, when driving for Mr. Turton, he had ¼ hour allowed for dinner, but here it was all work and no rest, and he could not stand it. I am going to drive a cab on Monday." Mack was re-instated a few weeks after leaving – he could do no better, besides he is a good 'bus driver.

Many passengers did not like the practice of eating meals on trams and 'buses. Families or friends handed in basins or baskets and the conductor had to dispose of their contents with the "greatest celerity" and, at the same time collect fares, watch out for passengers and stop and start the tram when necessary. This practice continued until the first decade of the 20th century when messrooms were erected at the various depots.

Staff were liable to be cautioned, reprimanded or suspended instead of a fine for minor offences. In July 1884 S. Garth, a guard on the Kirkstall route, was suspended for a day for the unusual offence of allowing a passenger to carry a bucket of blood on his car. Passengers were allowed to carry carcases of meat although no authorisation for this was included in the Company's Bye-Laws. The carcases were presumably regarded as luggage. William Turton is recorded as regularly carrying carcases on his Beeston Hill 'buses, much to the annoyance of passengers.

A Kitson engine provides the background for the Wellington Bridge Depot Staff, transferred to Kirkstall Road Depot. The Foreman, James Wade is on the right. Wade drove the last steam tram on the Wortley route in 1902.
Courtesy The late J. Wade.

The drivers and conductors were said, generally speaking, to be an "obliging set of men" and did not grumble about their conditions of work as they were less arduous than those of employees in other industries and the job was regarded as an "easy" one. Turton said that the Tramways Company never had a word of complaint from its servants and observed that when a vacancy occurred there were more than 50 applicants for it. He said that staff were not "stewed up in a workshop or mill but had plenty of fresh air and much pleasure and amusement". However, throughout the late 'eighties and 'nineties, there was, in Europe and Britain, a reaction against, what were considered, the harsh conditions of working people. In Leeds the reaction or "agitation" resulted from the activities of the Leeds Trades Council, the Co-operative Society, several clergymen and "charitably disposed" people who lived mainly in the Headingley area. The "agitation" reached Leeds in the autumn of 1889 and the local press was mystified:-

"Whatever the influences at work be they occult, subterrene, pre-concerted, imitative or spontaneous, signs are everywhere visible of an upheaval of the labour elements of society. The undulations of the agitation are reaching Leeds and the West Riding and if further indication were needed of the extensive character of the ferment if will be found in the restlessness manifested among such diverse trades as the tailoresses in the ready-made clothing industry of Leeds, the Leeds tramwaymen, the Leeds gas stokers, and the employees on the railways converging at Leeds such as the North Eastern and the Great Northern Railways."
(Yorkshire Post, 21st October 1889).

In August 1889 the reaction affected the tramway workers of Liverpool who formed a Tramways Employees' Association or Union. Many were dismissed by their Company and there was a threat of a strike. The tramway mechanics at Bradford went on strike at the same time and were promptly dismissed. In an apparent endeavour to discourage its employees from attempting to form an association, in October 1889 the Leeds Tramways Company announced that it was improving the conditions for its workmen. At that time the men worked on six weekdays each week and on alternate Sundays. Staff were to be allowed one full day off per week. Pay was to be deducted for the days off, but a bonus of 5s. 0d. per month was payable provided that the employee did not forfeit his claim to the money by serious misconduct. The aggregate earnings of all classes of men were, therefore, to be reduced, but effectively they would be paid more per hour.

Saturday, 19th October 1889, was an important day for the tramwaymen of Leeds for at midnight, at the invitation of a number of ladies and gentlemen who had been "interesting themselves in their welfare," a number of the tram drivers and conductors met in the People's Hall, Albion Street, to discuss their grievances and to devise ways and means of remedying them. The meeting was chaired by Talbot Baines, a leading Liberal in the town, who said that public feeling in Leeds had been moved by the grievances of the tramwaymen. The public felt it very keenly and it was difficult for them to use the tramways without being participants in a system "which inflicted such great hardships on the men."

The meeting was held in a friendly spirit and it was agreed to appoint a committee representing all the sections of the tramway to try and reduce their working hours and improve conditions generally. A further midnight meeting was held on 27th October. The problem was complicated by the variation in wages and conditions on the different routes. The Company made some small concessions to Headingley and Wortley staff, but showed no interest in those who worked the horse trams and 'buses. Talbot Baines said that he failed to see how the position of the drivers and guards on any line could be made secure without a union. While the public learned with pleasure that concessions had been made to the drivers and conductors on what he called the "favoured lines", it was a matter of regret that the men who had got what they wanted, were content to sit down, interesting themselves no further in the fate of their less fortunate brethren on other routes. He advocated that a strong union be formed and added that no arrangement could be regarded as satisfactory which required a man to drive a steam car for 14 hours per day.

Baines' speech was greeted with applause and the meeting resolved to form a union. Within a week the Tramways Company had agreed to reduce the working hours from a scale varying from 13¾ to 14¼ hours per day to 12½ and the conditions of the staff on the horse car routes were improved. Drivers and guards generally were to have a paid day off once a fortnight. The Company made no comments on the proposals to form a union, but promptly dismissed the six men who formed the committee. Guards J. W. Pickersgill and T. C.

Metcalfe of the Headingley route were dismissed for minor offences, M.McGinley of York Road for "continually drinking and being in a boozy state" and guards S. R. North, G. Taylor and driver H. Danser, all of the Chapeltown route, "by orders of the Board". These dismissals upset the Leeds Trades Council and Co-operative Society, who organised a subscription and appeal on behalf of the men until they could find alternative employment.

Driver Billy Cain poses with oil can and Green engine No. 19 at Wortley in August 1892.   *Courtesy The late W. E. Cain.*

The action of the Tramways Company effectively put a stop locally to any further attempts to form a union for a considerable time, but meanwhile, efforts were made nationally to try and form a union for 'bus and tram men. A meeting convened by the Associated Unions of the United Kingdom was held in Birmingham in September 1890. There were no representatives from Leeds. The Chairman, named Suthbert, the President of the London and Counties tram and Bus Employees' Union, said that 100,000 of their fellow workers were working from 16 to 18 hours a day. A man was obliged on entering the service to sign an agreement that he could be dismissed at any moment without any reason being given, although he had to give a week's notice if he wished to leave.

A union known as the Amalgamated Omnibus and Tram Workers' Union was formed and, in June, 1891, organised a week's strike in London and obtained substantial concessions from the tramway and omnibus companies. Flushed with the success of their "weeks holiday", Fred Hammill of the Union visited Leeds in November 1891 to try and persuade the Leeds tramwaymen and 'bus workers to join. He made reference to a "recent badly managed strike" of tram workers in

Leeds, but no mention of this has been found in the local newspapers or staff records. The London strike had procured a reduction of from 16 to 12 hours in the working day and the 'bus men now received 6d. per hour. It was stated that there were some 'bus men in Leeds who were receiving only 2½d. to 4d. or 4½d. per hour. Two meetings were held and were largely attended by 'bus workers. It was said that there were fears of "spies" at the meeting and the tramway men were "frightened to come." It appears that a number of men joined the union, the terms of membership being 6d. per week for men under 40 and 3d. per week for men over that age.

Apparently the Tramways Company did have "spies," for the Staff Records show that T. Clark, driver of a Dewsbury Road 'bus, resigned on 20th November 1891, saying he would not pay a fine for being late at the depot. "Clark was one of the men attending the meeting of 'bus and tram men", and his deposit was returned the same day. Staff had to pay a deposit of 25s. 0d. when entering the service of the Company and this was returned when they left. It was not unknown for a guard to abscond with his fare box and pounds worth of change money, and in cases like this the deposit was forfeited. The system of staff fines and paying for damage to rolling stock was imposed to a lesser extent when the Corporation took over the tramways.

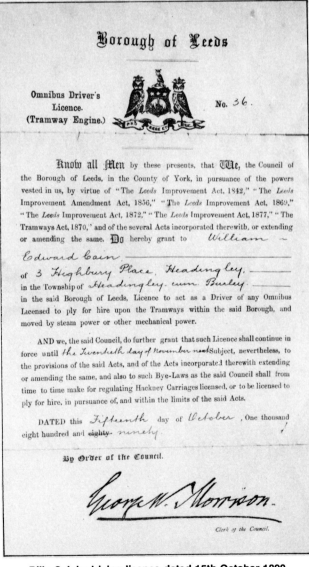

Billy Cain's driving licence dated 15th October 1890. *Courtesy The late W. E. Cain.*

Following the failures of 1889 and 1891, no further attempts were made to form a union during the time of the Leeds Tramways Company. On 2nd February 1894 the whole of the tramways staff was taken over by the Corporation and the first action of the Highways Committee was a restriction in that it insisted that every driver and conductor sign a declaration that they would not enter a public house while on duty. This was felt by many to be a great hardship as the only place of shelter at the terminus was the inn, where platform staff sometimes ate their meals and drank a glass of beer. Some councillors were opposed to the restriction, referring to it as "an unjustifiable interference with the liberty of the subject" or an "antiquated piece of bigotry", but it was approved. Of more significance was the Committee's attempt to reduce the hours and improve the working conditions of the employees. On 2nd February 1894, 57 drivers and 57 guards were employed on the tramways and, in order to provide an improved tramway service, within a fortnight an additional nine drivers and nine guards were appointed. It was said that the average time worked per day was 12 hours 27 minutes, and to reduce this to eight to ten hours a total of 83 men of each class was required. The hours worked on the various routes differed widely and the Committee aimed to reduce this to about 65 hours weekly for all staff. There were many anomalies due to the differing wage rates paid by the former Tramways Company as shown in the table below.

Staff were now paid by the hour and the drivers and conductors of the small horse cars on the Meanwood Road route were much better off working 26 hours less each week and receiving an increase in wages. On all the other routes the reduction in hours meant smaller wages. The lowest wage was earned by a steam car conductor on the Wortley route who, for his first three months employment, earned 16s. 7d. for a six day week. With the exception of Meanwood Road, which preceded it by a few days, the revised hours and wages came into operation on 1st May 1894. Under the old arrangement the weekly wages bill for platform staff was £132 2s. 6d., but was now £168 5s. 7d.

In the meantime, the Leeds Trades and Labour Council met and considered that the time was opportune for "organising" the tramwaymen. There was little fear that the men would be dismissed by the City Council, their new employers. Accordingly, a midnight meeting was held on 15th April, which resulted in the formation of a branch of the awkwardly worded "North Counties Amalgamated Association of Tramway and Hackney Carriage Employees and Horsemen in General", whose headquarters were in Manchester. 80 to 100 employees were present at the meeting, and it was said by George T. Jackson, General Secretary, that

the union had been in existence for five years, had 24 branches and a membership of 4,000. The entrance fee was 1s. 0d., the weekly subscription 6d. per member and the union had a capital of £3,000. Several employees enrolled and others at future union meetings. 20 drivers of the steam cars joined another union, the Amalgamated Society of Enginemen, Cranemen, Boilermen and Firemen.

The improved conditions for staff resulted in a large number of applicants and the Highways Committee soon had the required 166 men to work the new arrangements. The older drivers were pleased at not having so many hours to work but were dissatisfied with their reduced wages. Feeling that they now had the security of a union, the engine drivers applied for a wage increase. They asked for a minimum of 6d. per hour rising to 6½d. after six months. The horse car drivers did not apply for a specific increase, but asked the Committee to consider the matter. The Manager contacted the proprietors of the Manchester, Birmingham, Glasgow, Edinburgh, Bradford and other tramways and found that the Leeds employees were "fully as well off" as their counterparts in other towns, but the Committee agreed to increase the wages of the engine drivers to 6d. per hour and give all staff one clear day off in seven.

In January 1895, following representations from a new member of the Highways Committee, Councillor Ringrose, the Committee considered the question of conductors wages, but took no action. A bone of contention on the part of staff was that they had to pay their own fares to and from work which could cost 1s. 6d. to 2s. 0d. per week; a large slice out of a wage of from 17s. 0d. to £1 per week. The horse car staff were generally dissatisfied with their wages and conditions and, in February 1896, asked for a penny an hour increase. The men complained that they were better off under the old Tramways Company. Although they were working less hours, their leisure time came at an awkward time of the day; they could not use it and some asked to be allowed to work longer hours. Comparisons were made with the conductors of the Roundhay Electric Tramway, who received 4d. per hour when first taking up employment, as compared with the Corporation wage of 3½d. The proprietors of the Electric Tramway also paid one third of the cost of their employees uniforms, whereas Corporation conductors had to stand the whole cost. The wage increase of 20 to 25% would cost the Corporation £40 to £50 a week and was said to be too much to hope for. At the Highways Committee meeting on 11th February 1896 the staff's request was referred to a sub-committee.

The union, which many of the tramwaymen had joined, had taken little action with regard to the men's complaints and the representatives of another union –

LEEDS CITY TRAMWAYS						
HOURS WORKED WEEKLY AND RATES OF WAGES OF PLATFORM STAFF			1894			
ROUTE	before 1-5-1894 hours worked	driver's wages weekly	guard's wages weekly	after 1-5-1894 hours worked	driver's wages weekly	guard's wages weekly
HEADINGLEY & CHAPELTOWN	77 hrs. 30 mins.	£1 9s. 6d.	£1 1s. 5d.	66 hrs. 16 mins.	£1 7s. 7d.	£1 0s. 8d.
HUNSLET	81 hrs. 6 mins.	£1 8s. 2d.	£1 1s. 8d.	64 hrs. 50 mins.	£1 5s. 8d.	£1 0s. 3d.
MEANWOOD	91 hrs. 26 mins.	£1 4s. 11d.	£1 0s. 7d.	64 hrs. 50 mins.	£1 5s. 8d.	£1 0s. 8d.
YORK ROAD	83 hrs. 35 mins.	£1 4s. 11d.	£1 0s. 7d.	64 hrs.	£1 2s. 8d.	£1 0s. 0d.
KIRKSTALL	74 hrs. 42 mins.	£1 11s. 3d.	£1 2s. 0d.	67 hrs.	£1 10s. 8d.	£1 2s. 4d.
WORTLEY	79 hrs. 46 mins.	£1 13s. 0d.	£1 1s. 6d.	67 hrs.	£1 10s. 8d.	£1 2s. 4d.

the Gasworkers' and General Labourers' Union – appeared on the scene. On 20th April 1896, at a meeting held at the rooms of the Labour Party in New Briggate, it was decided to form a branch of this union, and it appears that many of the tramwaymen severed their connection with their old union. Shortly afterwards the Highways Committee announced that they would grant a farthing an hour increase to drivers and conductors (about 1s. 6d. per week). The probation period was altered and the deposit money, payable as security, was reduced from 25s. 0d. to 15s. 0d. On 20th May the Committee decided to allow drivers and conductors to travel free when going to or leaving duty. The men were said to be thankful for the "small mercy" offered by the Corporation "for the time being".

The concession to the platform staff resulted in an immediate clamour from other members of the Tramways Department. The horsekeepers, tip lads, engine drivers, pointsmen, cleaners, smiths, tinners and strikers asked for an increase of wages; drivers of one-horse cars wanted to be paid as much as two-horse drivers and the chopmen in the stables said that they now had to cut hay for 410 horses for the same wages as they did for 250 horses 12 months previously. The Gasworkers' and General Labourers' Union, which claimed that it had induced 150 of the tramways staff to join, was asked to approach the Tramways Sub-Committee. In August an application for an increase of wages for the whole of the tramways staff of about ½d. to ¾d. per hour was received by the Tramways Sub-Committee. A special committee was appointed and, on 7th September 1896, it decided to grant the smiths and foreman tinner an additional 3s. 0d. per week and the other tinners and strikers 1s. 0d. per week. It was less enthusiastic over granting increases to other staff which would create an additional expenditure of £2,364 a year. It rejected the application of the drivers and conductors, but in October granted 1s. 4d. a week increase to the stablemen and cleaners. At a union meeting on 21st October it was agreed to accept "for the time being the small concession offered by the Tramways Committee on the distinct understanding that the Committee be requested to reconsider the question at the earliest opportunity".

The Committee did not reconsider the question, but at the Council Meeting on 5th May 1897 it was agreed that free uniforms would be provided for staff. A month later the Gasworkers' and General Labourers' Union made a further application for increased wages and improved conditions. The increases requested varied from ½d. to 1¼d. per hour for most of the staff, and at a meeting on 9th July, the Tramways Sub-Committee yielded to the pressure. The steam car conductors received a penny, one-horse drivers a halfpenny and other drivers and conductors a farthing per hour increase. The depot men, comprising 45 horsekeepers, nine car washers, four chopmen, two harness cleaners and one drayman also received increases which took effect from 23rd July and cost the Corporation an additional yearly sum of £1,171. The ten shoeing smiths received a wage increase the following month.

During the mismanagement complaints of 1897 it was revealed that certain departments of the tramways were understaffed. It was said that on one night a single lad had all 19 engines to clean and two fitters had to do at night the servicing of the engines for work the next day. It appears that the labour force was soon increased.

On 23rd October 1897 Leeds experienced its first tramway strike. The previous week a breakdown had occurred at the generating station and the electric cars were unable to run. The electric car drivers and conductors were sent home and William Wharam, the Manager, accordingly deducted five hours from their wages. The electric car staff were incensed at this decision and the electric service was suspended from the early morning to 4.0 pm in the afternoon. The strike decision was made on the spur of the moment without reference to the union. Following the intervention of the Chairman of the Highways Committee, Councillor Hannam, when it was admitted that an "official mistake" had been made by Wharam, the men returned to work and received payment for the five hours when they were idle. Before their return, however, they asked the Committee to reconsider their application for a wage increase. A meeting of the Highways Committee was held on 25th October. The electric car drivers were represented and asked for an additional halfpenny per hour. Many were former Thomson-Houston Company employees and it transpired that this Company not only paid their drivers 5½d. per hour, but also gave them a bonus of £2 per year and half pay during sickness. Hannam said the Committee was not aware of this and immediately granted the drivers their halfpenny. The Committee asked that in future drivers should give or receive a fortnight's notice on terminating an engagement. At a meeting a few days later the men refused to accept this and passed a resolution in favour of 24 hours' notice on either side.

In Company days, in the event of an accident, employees simply made a verbal report to the clerks in the Boar Lane office. The management now required the men to prepare reports of accidents and other occurrences in their leisure time. At first the staff decided not to conform with the new regulation, but later agreed to abide by the new rule for a trial period. There was dissatisfaction that the recent wage increases had not applied to all staff, but no action was taken, and it was to be two years before another wage increase was requested.

The Gasworkers' and General Labourers' Union had represented the men successfully, but the union it displaced, the Amalgamated Association of Tramway and Hackney Carriage Employees and Horsemen in General, now reappeared. A small number of staff had remained members and in June 1899 it claimed that it was the "largest and most wealthy society of drivers in England", and intimated that it would serve the staff better than the Gasworkers' Union. The officials of the latter Union naturally objected, but a number of the men, mainly drivers and conductors, changed unions. The tramway employees were now represented by two unions who tended to work together. Both unions applied to the Tramways Committee for a wage increase of ½d. per hour for all staff. The Committee was surprised at the applications as it felt that the Leeds tramwaymen were paid the top rate of wages, but the unions said that the Halifax, Birmingham and Hull undertakings paid more. The application was allowed to stand over due to the Council elections in November 1899 and was considered by the Tramways Committee in February 1900. It recommended that the wages of steam, electric and horse car drivers and steam car conductors be increased by ¼d. an hour. All other conductors, viz. horse car, electric car, trailer and trailer brakesmen were to receive ½d. an hour extra, the chopmen an additional 1s. 0d. per week and inspectors were to have a commencing wage of 30s. 0d. per week rising to

40s. 0d. The increases added £2,000 per year to the running costs of the Tramways Department. These were the last wage increases to be granted to staff prior to electrification, and the final rates for the various classes of drivers and conductors were therefore as follows:–

Steam Car Drivers
First six months 6¼d./hr. after six months 6¾d./hr.
Electric Car Drivers
First six months 5¾d./hr. after six months 6¼d./hr.
3-horse Car Drivers
First six months 5¼d./hr. after six months 5¾d./hr.
2-horse Car Drivers
First six months 5d./hr. after six months 5½d./hr.
Trailer brakesmen
First six months 4¼d./hr. after six months 4½d./hr.
Steam Conductors
First six months 4¾d./hr. after six months 5¼d./hr.
Horse Conductors
First six months 4½d./hr. after six months 5d./hr.
Electric Conductors
First six months 4½d./hr. after six months 5d./hr.
Trailer Conductors
First six months 4½d./hr. after six months 5d./hr.

A bonus of 20s. 0d. per half year was to be paid to each driver who was free from blame for accident during the period.

On 2nd February 1901 a second tramway strike occurred on the occasion of the funeral of Queen Victoria. The staff had been instructed to work, but no cars ran as the tramwaymen felt that they should take part in the mourning for the Queen. After an apology by the men the incident was soon forgotten.

A major concession to the tramwaymen was made in September 1901, when they asked for payment of a time and a half on Sundays and double pay on Christmas Day and Good Fridays. The Committee already gave double pay on Christmas Day as a favour to the men, but would not entertain agreed extra pay on Sundays or holidays. They offered a week's annual holiday with pay in lieu.

In the early days of the horse 'buses and throughout the period of the Leeds Tramways Company, it was the practice of charitable people to obtain subscriptions from passengers at Christmas to give to drivers and conductors on the various routes. Staff were employed on the same route, and frequently the same vehicle, year in and year out, and became well known to passengers. They took a pride in their tram or 'bus and were responsible for polishing the brasswork. Usually, shopkeepers on the route collected subscriptions and they were then distributed among the platform staff. Grateful staff frequently advertised their thanks in the local newspaper:–

"On behalf of the driver and conductor of the Chapeltown and West Street 'bus, 'The Gem', I beg respectfully to thank the passengers for the Christmas gifts amounting to £8, and to wish one and all a happy and prosperous New Year. Yours etc, James Briggs".
(Yorkshire Post, 4th January, 1884).

The Tramways Company used to allow the organisers to fix a notice in the cars listing the shops where subscriptions could be paid, but when the Corporation took over this was discontinued at Christmas 1894, but allowed in later years. Predictably, the passengers on the wealthy Chapeltown and Headingley routes were the most generous. At Christmas 1898, for example, the amount collected on the through route was £73 6s. 8d. This sum was divided among 73 drivers and guards in sums proportionate to their respective length of service, during the year, as follows:– 42 men who were on the through route each received £1 5s. 6d.; ten men who were on the through "Oak" to Reginald Terrace service, each 19s. 1d.; the remainder being split among 21 men who had been on the route less than 12 months.

With the expansion of the tramways in the period 1894 to 1900, the number of staff employed doubled. On 29th September 1894 there were 314 staff, on the same date in 1898, 588 and by 1900, almost 700. With this large increase in staff and revised traffic conditions which led to drivers and conductors working different routes, staff were not as well known to passengers, and the practice of collecting subscriptions became less frequent. It remained on the Chapeltown and Headingley routes until Christmas 1912. In December 1913 a strike of the tramwaymen put the public off collecting and the practice does not appear to have been resumed.

Staff worked on average 64 hours per week and on alternate Sundays. A reduction in hours and the six day week was to come later. In 1902 the "Amalgamated Association of Tramway and Hackney Carriage Employees and Horsemen in General" became known as the "Amalgamated Association of Tramway and Vehicle Workers" and many years later joined forces with the "Gasworkers' and General Labourers' Union" and others to form the "Transport and General Workers' Union", which still exists today.

1888

2220 Dacre A.   Guard   Dewsbury Road
Nov 30 Suspended for 7 days for being repeatedly
late at depôt, and told if late again will
be discharged

2221 Tansley J.   Guard   Wortley
Nov 27 Did with considerable damage to horse car, by
letting it down to the Bogue at the Star, &
by so doing, the one of the brakes not acting
properly, it ran with great force into the Engine
  Tansley was suspended for a day & brought
before the Manager, who severely reprimanded
Tansley, & told him he would have to pay the
whole damage done – The Manager further
considers this a gross piece of neglect of risking
life & limb –
        Tansley agrees to pay damages & 7/6 per week

2222 Furnage J Conductor Chapeltown line   and
Dec 15 Bowers driver late at Reginald Terrace
from Chapeltown due in Leeds at 7 PM did
not stop more than a moment and in
spite of the Manager & Brampths Bus
driver who happened to be at Reginald
Terrace, & several other men shouting
neither Conductor nor drivers attention
could be attracted and a passenger
on the top of the car shouted "theres a
Bus yonder."

2223 Powell J.   Guard   Wortley
Nov 22 This man has been reported several times for
negligence in not collecting his fares at the proper
places, his receipts when looked at shewed it very
badly, and when spoken to about them, replied "how
can you expect me to keep my family on 3/- a day".
He also absconded with his change money, for which
his deposit was forfeited – Nov 1888

A typical page from the Leeds Tramways Company Staff Records for 1888. Entry No. 2222 dated December 15th 1888 is in the hand of the General Manager, William Wharam.
Courtesy Leeds City Transport Department.

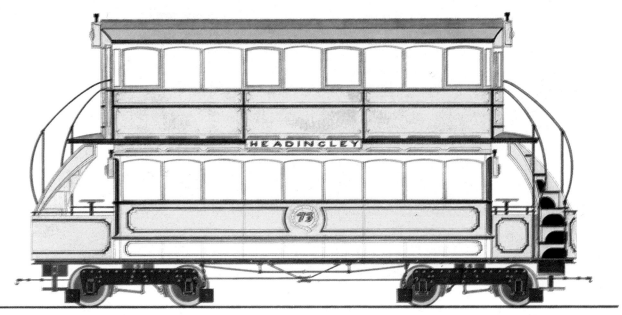

LEEDS TRAMWAYS COMPANY   ASHBURY TRAILER   1887

LEEDS CITY TRAMWAYS   MILNES TRAILER   1897 LIVERY

KITSON TRAM ENGINE

GREEN TRAM ENGINE

J Soper March 1985

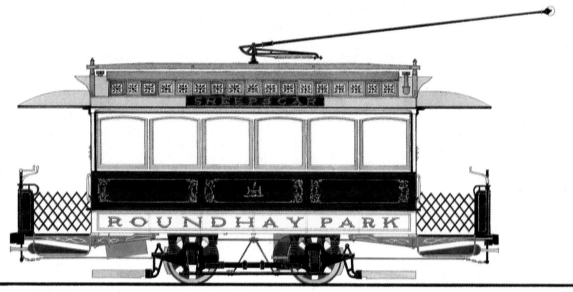

ROUNDHAY ELECTRIC TRAMWAY   1891

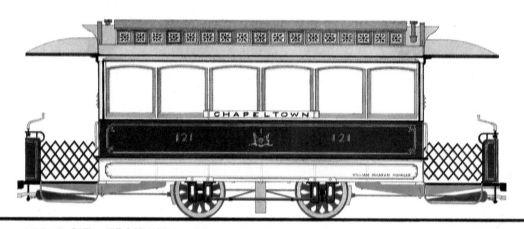

LEEDS CITY TRAMWAYS TRAILER CAR   1898

1891 LIVERY

1898 LIVERY

J Soper February 1985

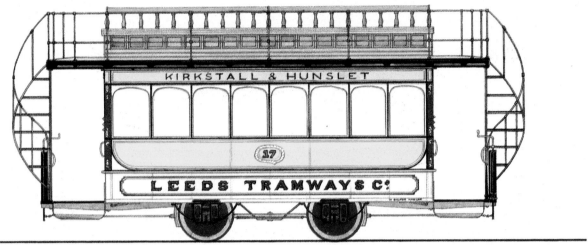

LEEDS TRAMWAYS COMPANY
DOUBLE DECK HORSE CAR   1871-73

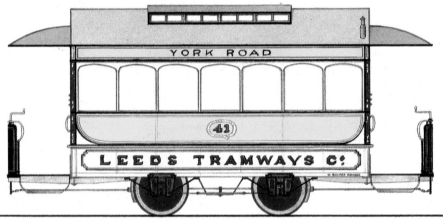

LEEDS TRAMWAYS COMPANY
SINGLE DECK HORSE CAR   1874-75

LEEDS CITY TRAMWAYS
DOUBLE DECK REBUILT HORSE CAR   1899 LIVERY

J. Soper February 1985

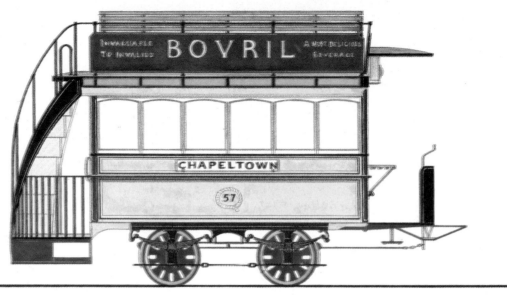

LEEDS TRAMWAYS COMPANY   EADES REVERSIBLE CAR   1883

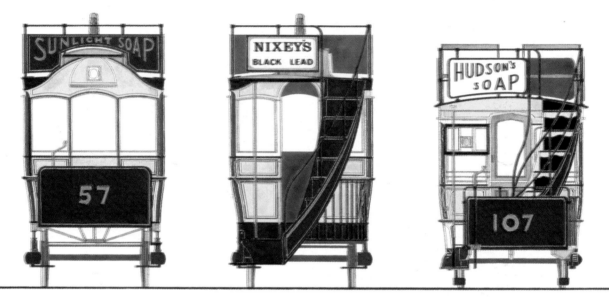

EADES CAR FRONT   EADES CAR REAR   MILNES CAR   1898

LEEDS CITY TRAMWAYS   MILNES CAR 1898   1899 LIVERY

J Soper March 1985

CHAPTER TWENTY-THREE

The Horses

Of great importance to the successful operation of a horse 'bus or tramway service were the horses themselves. Prior to the 'eighties all suburban transport in Leeds was horse-drawn and the selection of suitable horses was essential. The Leeds Tramways Company was fortunate in that its Chairman, William Turton, and Manager, William Wharam, both had a good eye for a horse. Turton was particularly skilful in the purchase of sound horses, and at the Company meeting on 23rd August 1879, he was complimented. In 1876 the cost of horse renewals was £2,633; in 1877 £3,104; in 1878, when Turton became Company Chairman, £1,874 and in 1879 only £1,443. Turton and Wharam purchased most of the horses used on the tramways.

'Bus and tram horses were from the harness breeds, usually of the "heavy hackney" type. Those in Leeds were principally Irish, short, clean-legged, powerful, 15½ to 16½ hands high and about five or six years old when bought. They had a useful turn of speed for their moderate weight and had a higher, more stylish action than the heavy draught horses still used by breweries today. In the early days of the Tramways Company, Daniel Busby supplied several of the horses, but dealers usually brought horses for inspection and subsequent purchase by the Company. Some of the principal suppliers in the 'seventies and 'eighties were W. Balding, H. Decelle, P. Gilholy, C. Palmer and C. Williamson. Latterly, J. Bleasby, Booth, Dawson and G. Williamson supplied horses, but the biggest supplier in the late 'nineties was horse dealer and omnibus proprietor, John William Wilks of Leeds, who between 1895 and 1900 sold 438 horses to the Corporation for a total of £13,205, an average of about £30 each. Usually the purchase of an animal was subject to a short trial period for fear it was found to be prone to lameness, short of wind, of a vicious nature, a "shiverer" or otherwise defective.

When the Corporation took over the tramways a Horse and Corn Purchasing Sub-Committee of the Tramways Sub-Committee was formed to take over the job of buying and selling horses. The four members were the Chairman, Councillor Hannam, Alderman North, Councillor Metcalfe and the Manager. They continued to buy horses in the same manner as the old company but occasionally went further afield. On 16th June 1896 they visited Boroughbridge Fair and bought 13 horses, as follows:–

Seven horses from
Barker, Thirsk for £193 0s. 0d.
One horse from
John Whittaker for £20 0s. 0d.
One horse from
T. Hutchinson for £29 10s. 0d.
One horse from
George Williamson for £27 10s. 0d.
One horse from
R. Watson for £27 0s. 0d.
Two horses from
Booth Dawson for £59 0s. 0d.

Some of these were bargains as the normal price paid for a tram horse was between £30 and £35. On 14th December 1900 the Corporation bought its last tram horses – 13 from Wilks for £429.

The major factor in horse traction and the principal item of cost was what was termed horse keep. The animals ate their way through 20% of the receipts whether they were working or not and the purchase of provender at the most economical price was very important. The Tramways Company was again fortunate in its Chairman, Turton, who was in business as a corn merchant and gave good advice. Most of the corn or maize was bought at the ports of Hull and Liverpool, which were said to be the cheapest places. In 1875 horse keep on the tramways amounted to £1 1s. 5d. per horse per week made up as follows:– corn and hay 15s. 6d.; straw and moss litter for bedding 6d; wages for stablemen, foremen and utensils such as brushes etc. 3s. 11d.; shoeing and wages of blacksmiths 1s. 3d.; veterinary surgeon and medicine 5d.

Hay was usually bought locally from farmers and tenders were invited for the supply of hay every six months. The consumption was five tons of meadow hay and five tons of clover and seed hay per week. If the hay harvest was poor the Company had to obtain it elsewhere and in 1876 hay was imported from Ireland. As well as corn and hay the diet of the horses also included various types of oats – white, black, English, Russian, Old Russian etc; Konigsberg beans, English beans, Canadian peas and barley. Horses of delicate constitution were fed with expensive linseed meal. Linseed, oats and barley were frequently boiled before serving to the horses. Feedstuffs were normally bought through local farmers such as John Revis of Scarcroft and John Rollinson of Halton.

A useful source of income from the horses was the sale of manure and tenders were invited annually for its collection from the various depots. Local farmers collected the manure and the income from this source varied from 2d. to 5d. per horse per week. It cost about

£50 per annum to keep a tramway horse, much more than its purchase price. There were also other costs. Gravel had to be spread on smooth granite setts to prevent horses slipping and in winter salt was used on the tram lines.

A tram or 'bus horse had a hard life. A fully loaded double-deck horse tram weighed about five tons and, as trams and 'buses were hailed like taxis, the frequent starting and stopping took a heavy toll of the horses. Horses which were past their best were put on the short York Road route. Charles Lake, a former conductor, reminiscing in 1930, said that one horse was nicknamed "Puffing Billy", who used to make unscheduled stops to catch his wind. Sometimes the slight incline of Marsh Lane was too much for him and passengers had to get out and walk up the hill and, more than once, male passengers were asked to get out and push the tram.

The York Road tram horse. Could this be "Puffing Billy?" *Courtesy A. K. Terry.*

Most horses had a working life of only four or five years. There were exceptions and there was a lot of luck as well as judgement required in the selection of horses. Some only lived for a week or two after purchase, others remained in service for ten to 15 years, the record being held by horse No. 262, purchased about August 1877 and sold in January 1900 – an incredible 22½ years service.

Horses were usually bought and sold from Hunslet Depot and the following list records a typical batch of horses sold on 18th June 1896 with their respective purchase dates:–

No. 878
  bought December 1886, and sold for £5 5s. 0d.
No. 879
  bought January 1887, and sold for £6 0s. 0d.
No. 888
  bought March 1887, and sold for £5 10s. 0d.
No. 1032
  bought June 1889, and sold for £6 10s. 0d.
No. 1064
  bought January 1890, and sold for £5 10s. 0d.
No. 1168
  bought August 1891, and sold for £5 5s. 0d.
No. 1253
  bought May 1892, and sold for £10 0s. 0d.
No. 1396
  bought June 1894, and sold for £6 0s. 0d.
No. 1411
  bought July 1894, and sold for £6 0s. 0d.
No. 1428
  bought September 1894, and sold for £5 0s 0d.

It can be seen that horses were given a number. Up to 1878 when a horse was sold or died the next horse purchased occupied a vacant number. Some numbers were re-used frequently; for example between 1873 and 1878 there were five horses numbered 255. This practice was discontinued after horse No. 294 in 1878 and it is easy from the Tramways Company Cash Books to trace the "history" of each horse. After 1889 horses numbered over 1,000 were also given an abbreviated number. Those numbered between 1001-99 also bore Nos. 01-99; 1101-99 Nos. X1-99; 1201-99 Nos. C1-99; 1301-99 Nos. D1-99 etc. up to 2001-99 which took Nos. L1-99. (omitting the letter I). Some towns branded the horse number on the fore hoof and Leeds probably adopted the same system. There would not be room for four digits on the hoof. After 1896 the later system of numbering was generally used. Details of horse disposals are not complete for the years 1900-01 when large numbers were sold. The highest numbered horse that has been traced is No. 2090 (L90) which died in January 1900. This horse had been in the possession of the Corporation for less than a month and as 31 horses were bought in 1900, the numbers appear to have reached the 2120's. The horses also had names, but few are recorded. 'Maggie' is mentioned later and there are some records of the names of 'bus horses. The five horses that Turton used with his Meanwood 'bus when sold in 1878 were listed as 'Tom', 'Charlie', 'Jet', 'Duke' and 'Polly'. Elizabeth Riley, when she sold her Hunslet 'buses, referred to her horses as 'Doctor', 'Jimmy', 'Paddy', 'Prince', 'Johnny', 'Roger' and 'Barney'. The tram horses presumably had similar names.

A horse carcase was sold for about 30s. 0d. compared with £5 or £6 for a live horse, the latter usually going to more gentle work on farms. Horses died from many causes, as shown in the illustration listing the horses that died between June 1894 and January 1895. Their carcases would finish up at the tannery or glue factory.

N°	Description	Years of age	Date	Cause
1361	Brown horse	8	1894 June 9	Pleurisy
874	Brown mare	14	July 18	Rupture of the diaphragm
1302	Grey mare	7	August 3	Fracture of the pedal bone (accident)
1394	Black horse	5	August 4	Fell and broke its leg on Meanwood Road
1104	Grey mare	11	October 18	Congestion of the lungs and heart disease
1420	Black horse	6	October 31	Pneumonia
1333	Bay mare	7	Dec 11	enteric inflamation of the bowels
1071	Brown mare	9	Dec 11	Inflamation of the bowels
1096	Roan mare	15	Dec 18	Bilious fever
896	Black mare	15	1895 Jany 30	Inflamation of the bowels

An illustration from the minutes of the Horse and Corn Purchasing Sub-Committee listing the horses that died between June 1894 and January 1895. *Courtesy Leeds Corporation.*

Probably two or three of the horses died in the street. This was bad publicity for the Tramways Company, but dead horses were a common sight, the carcase being winched ignobly into the knacker's cart.

To keep losses through deaths to a minimum and the horses in good condition, competent veterinary surgeons were employed and, during the latter days of the horse trams, the surgeon was Samuel Wharam, the son of the General Manager. Horses were subject to infectious diseases such as 'glanders' and 'pink eye' — a type of influenza — and in cases such as these slaughter was sometimes the only course of action. The Tramways Company lost six horses through 'pink eye' in 1890 and some omnibus proprietors, such as Matthew Jackson and Henry Harrison, mentioned in previous chapters, lost almost all of their animals through disease.

For the first year or two of tramway operation, the leading tram horses carried bells, but for "economic" reasons this procedure was abandoned. The Tramways Company and some of the omnibus proprietors, notably Bramfitt, Turton and Walker, prided themselves on their horses. The horses were to be seen, carefully groomed, matched for colour and gaily caparisoned on May Day and other parades. The tram horses were generally considered to be among the best in Leeds. The public was very horse conscious and the R.S.P.C.A. was keen to prosecute anyone who cruelly treated an animal. Many of the omnibus proprietors offended, but rarely the Tramways Company. When a horse was unfit for further service, it was sold and it was the responsibility of the depot foreman to ensure that his horses were in good condition and that a lame or sick horse was never used with a car. In November 1896 Foreman Barrow of Hunslet Depot was dismissed for allowing a lame horse to be worked and was also fined by the local magistrates. One passenger had the audacity to complain about the tramway horses:—

"I had occasion to go to Chapeltown and rode on a car leaving Leeds at 12.15 and a more painful 40 minutes I never spent. The car was drawn by three horses. The wheelers it is impossible to describe — not an ounce of flesh on them, their manes, tails and skin filthy, their legs a mass of humour, and I doubt very much if they would fetch a sovereign apiece at the knackers. The leader was in a better condition, but worn out, and as the driver had to depend on him to do the greater part of the work, needless to say he was done for before we got half way to Chapeltown, especially as he was twice down on the road.

Shortly after leaving Reginald Terrace a fourth horse was yoked, but this poor brute was dead lame. Two fellow passengers informed me that this kind of thing had been common for some months past, and that only by this means, combined with continuous flogging and yells from the driver were they able to get to the far end of the journey." wrote E. Sydney Horton.

(Yorkshire Post, 8th October 1892).

The Tramways Company was very upset and took Horton to Court for libel. It won its case.

With their greatly reduced rolling resistance trams did not strain the horses as much as 'buses. The trams also had very effective brakes but in the case of the 'bus this was frequently an old boot tied with a piece of string. A feature of the 'bus terminus at Headingley "Oak" was the collection of discarded boots at the base of the oak tree. The 'bus driver had to rely on the team to stop his vehicle pulling their heads up as the weight was thrown on to their collars. The handbrake on a tram could usually stop a car from a full speed of six to eight m.p.h. in twice its own length thus relieving the horses of the weight of the car. A careless driver might sometimes rely on the horses and, in order to prevent this, in February 1899 the Tramways Committee decided to replace the rigid haulage poles by ordinary traces. The drivers objected and were supported by members of the Hackney Carriages Committee. It was said that there had been an accident due to the lack of poles. Councillor Smithson maintained that the accident was due to the fault of the driver and pointed out that poles were not used on the extensive Glasgow horse tramways. The City Council decided in favour of the Tramways Committee.

The harness used on the three-horse, pair-horse or one-horse car consisted simply of a well fitting collar and bridle with leather traces from the harness fitted to the collar and a spreader bar or swingle-tree, one of which was provided for each horse. On the Headingley and Chapeltown tramway routes trace or "chain" horses were used to assist the regular team up gradients such as Cookridge Street or Mitchell Hill. Chain horses are known to have been used in the following locations:—

Headingley route:
St. Anne's Cathedral to College Road.

Chapeltown route:
St. Martin's Church to "Queen's Arms".

Hunslet route:
Salem Chapel to "Star and Garter," Call Lane.

York Road route:
"Woodpecker Inn" to terminus at Victoria Avenue.

Woodhouse Street route:
Top of Cambridge Road to the "Grapes Inn".

The "chain" horse was in the charge of the "tip lad", who rode on the horse on its return journey. A horse knew every inch of its route and could almost manage without its driver:—

"I see a good deal of the 'bus horse, and I find in him an animal who well repays watching. Most people know that he understands the conductor's bell; but few know how well he understands it. The 'bus driver is a very clever Jehu, but his cattle need very little driving. I see them start when the bell rings, and I see them stop when the bell rings again, even when it does so within two seconds. Yet when the 'bus is in full roll, the conductor rings twice to show the driver he is "full inside", and the horses know the double ring and never pause in their stride. Again the 'bus horse knows the policeman's signal. I am driving down Oxford Street. At the corner of Bond Street an old lady wants to cross the road. The policeman holds up his white gloved hand and the horses stop — automatically, not pulled up by Jehu. The lady is safely across; the policeman jerks his thumb forward, and the horses start again. A heavy dray is in front. Without a sign the horses swerve to circumvent it. I sometimes think the conductor might drive by merely pulling his bell cord, and so save the driver's wages. Further, these sagacious beasts know all their stopping corners and they know the clatter of the released brake. Observe too, how skilfully the 'bus horse picks out the drier portions of the wet and slippery wood pavings. And see him cleverly skate down Waterloo Place after a shower of rain or of a water cart, with the heavy 'bus behind him. What other animal could do the like? To me there is a character in the jerk of a 'bus horse's ears and the flourish of his tail; and I believe that a horse is capable of higher training than

any dog or rat that has ever learned a trick."
(Yorkshire Post, 29th August 1885, referring to a London 'bus.)

On one occasion the Leeds Tramways Company experimented with the use of mules. Three, Nos. 459 to 461, were bought for £114 4s. 0d. on 9th June 1879. Inspector W. C. Taylor, reminiscing in 1916, remembered them:–

"I was driving two of these one day, and had just loosed them off to take them to the other end of the car when they bolted and ran through the old toll bar at Hunslet. They would not have been caught yet had they not gone one at each side of a telegraph post, and of course as they had the traces on, that brought them to a full stop."
(From lecture by J. B. Hamilton, 1916)

The Company made a profit on the mules. On 16th July 1879 they were sold for £117 0s. 0d. Joseph Walker, omnibus proprietor, also experimented with mules at about the same time as the Tramways Company, but they were unpredictable and, following complaints from the Hackney Carriages Committee, they were soon taken off the road.

On a sadder note Inspector Taylor recalled an instance of the attachment which staff had for their horses.

"I had grown quite fond of a horse called "Maggie" and it was a great trouble to me when, one day, the vet found she was suffering from "pink eye" and ordered her to be slaughtered. Her stablekeeper blackened her hoofs and brushed her down on that sad morning when he had to take her to the slaughter-house. But when he got to the gate with her the poor fellow could not go any further, but just sat down and wept."

To keep a three-horse car on the road with a daily mileage of 70 needed 16 horses, five teams on duty plus a spare. The one and two-horse cars needed fewer horses and the overall average number of horses required per car was nine. After the completion of the Chapeltown tramway, the Tramways Company had about 280 horses. The construction of the Meanwood Road and Wortley tramways in 1878-9 increased this to 342, and the purchase of Turton's omnibus business in 1882 brought the number to about 440. The withdrawal of the horse 'buses and the introduction of steam traction brought a gradual reduction and by February 1887, the stud totalled only 265 horses. In the late 'eighties improvements in services increased the number until by February 1892 there were 302, and the withdrawal of the Headlingley steam trams led to a further growth in the number. At the time of the Corporation takeover in February 1894 there were 368 horses valued at £35 each, or £12,880. The horses were worth more than the rolling stock, the latter being valued at only £8,900.

The improvements to services and additional rolling stock purchased by the Corporation increased the number of horses still further. In November 1899 they reached their maximum of 645 and then, with the introduction of electric traction, the number declined.

Like other horse owning concerns, the Tramways Department registered horses with the War Office under the Military Mounts Scheme of 1888. 200 horses were registered and the War Office paid 7s. 6d. per horse per annum for the privilege of claiming the horses at any time. When horses were required for the Boer War in 1899 and 1900 a number were requisitioned by the Army. 40 were sold to the Army authorities in November 1899 for £45 each and a further 61 in April 1900 for £50 apiece – a substantial profit for the Corporation.

The War and natural wastage were insufficient to reduce the stud quickly enough and on 24th and 25th April 1901, 250 horses were auctioned by Hepper and Son and fetched an average price of £21 15s. 0d. each. These were followed by a further 80 on 14th August and a final sale of 59 on 23rd October the same year. On 16th January 1902 a clearance sale was held at North Street Depot and comprised *"75 pairs of strong harness and traces, 5 sets of breast harness, 62 pairs of harness, 530 capital harness collars, 170 winkler bridles, 100 skeleton bridles, 200 harness bits, 70 pairs of harness reins, 400 leather head collars, 25 neck straps, 450 canvas night rugs, 80 surcingles, 20 stable pails, 25 corn sieves, 36 feeding baskets, 100 dung skeps, 30 stable rakes, 360 iron manger logs, 180 chop bags, 1,000 corn sacks, 400 rack chains, 2 large fomenting sheets, 2 sets of horse slings, sundry harness etc. Also 7 new brown leather harness collars, 36 new winkler bridles, and a quantity of new wood pails, rakes, dung skeps, feeding baskets, corn sieves, curry combs etc."*
(Leeds Mercury, 11th January 1902)

Within two years the horses and the extensive equipment required for their welfare had disappeared. Only 14 horses were left to be used on 'bus duties for a few more years.

Two worn-out horses wait in Lower Briggate to haul the Hunslet 'bus in 1890.
Courtesy The late D. Hunt, Photographer.

CHAPTER TWENTY-FOUR

The Depots and Stables

The local children pose with Roundhay Electric Car No. 77 at Beckett Street Depot in 1894.
Courtesy The late W. Nichols, Photographer, Leeds City Libraries.

Centralisation of depot accommodation was a feature of electric traction, but with horse tramways was of no advantage. A horse tram travelled slowly and to avoid loss of time and energy, unnecessary or "dead" mileage had to be reduced to a minimum. Horses were subject to disease and dispersal of the stables was essential to reduce cross infection. In Leeds each major route had its own depot and stables.

The first buildings used for tramway purposes in Leeds by Busby's, the tramway promoters, were of a temporary nature and few details have been traced. They were rented from private individuals and appear to have consisted simply of a yard and stables. With the exception of Harrison Street, no evidence has been found of any covered accommodation for tramcars and for the first few years of their existence many probably spent the whole of their time in the open air. There must, however, have been a covered area for the repair and overhaul of cars and this was probably adjacent to the Hyde Park Stables.

The exact location of the Hyde Park Stables has not been determined, but it is recorded that to serve the Boar Lane to Headingley "Oak" tramway, a track connection was made from Headingley Lane to a yard at Hyde Park. The car yard was rented from a Joshua Nussey at £60 per annum, and apparently came into use in September 1871. About ten cars and 60 to 80 horses were accommodated. In 1874 a new depot was opened at the "Three Horse Shoes" terminus and the property at Hyde Park was vacated. On the instructions of the Highways Committee the tramway access was almost immediately removed.

The Kirkstall tramway was served initially by stables rented from a Joseph Clarkson and situated adjacent to the "Cardigan Arms", Kirkstall Road. Clarkson charged a rental of £8 16s. 0d. per month and, in addition, charged rent for grazing the tramway horses. There does not appear to have been a track connection for cars and the stables went out of use when a permanent depot was opened at Kirkstall in 1876.

Some stables in Harrison Street, off Briggate, formerly used by Atkinson's and later Turton's 'buses, were rented from William Turton at £71 per annum. The stables were apparently first used by the Tramways Company on 16th June 1873 and a track access from Briggate was made in late 1874. This building was used for the Chapeltown cars until the opening of Chapeltown Depot, and appears to have been vacated by the Company in August 1876. It was demolished shortly afterwards as it occupied the site of the new Grand Theatre which opened in 1878.

From 1st March 1874 some stables and stores in High Court Lane, off Marsh Lane, were rented from William Turton at £100 per annum, increased to £114 in 1877. 48 horses were accommodated there at first and the premises were the principal store for feedstuffs for the Company's horses. The number of horses kept there was reduced to 21 in 1876, but later increased to 30. The building was superseded by North Street Depot and went out of use in early 1883. There was apparently no tramway access, but it is recorded that some of the Company's 'buses were operated from there for a time.

A yard and stables, referred to as the "Hunslet Car Yard" and situated near the "Black Bull Inn", Hunslet Road, was rented from a John Scott at £1 per week. A track connection was made and the premises appear to have been used for the first time on 19th April 1874 when 12 horses moved in. This number was increased to 24 on 1st May. The buildings were vacated when a permanent depot was opened at Thwaite Gate, Hunslet, in 1875. The temporary track was still in position in February 1878, but, at the request of the Highways Committee, was probably removed soon afterwards.

The Tramways Company accounts indicate that other buildings and stables were rented from various individuals for short spells up to about 1876. Stables at the "Royal Hotel", Briggate, for example, were rented from the spring of 1873 to the summer of 1874. There were others but their location is not known.

In accordance with its policy of keeping "dead" mileage to a minimum, the Leeds Tramways Company endeavoured to erect depots and stables at the outer termini of its routes. Each route had its own depot with the exception of the short York Road and Meanwood Road tramways. Apart from a small depot at Kirkstall the first tramway depots were built to a standard design. Horse traction was subject to infections and odours and the car sheds were provided with a large amount of ventilation. The sheds each had three tracks and the front and one long side were open to the elements. Adjacent to the open side was a large yard around which were grouped the stables. The stables were all of a standard size, 28'-0" × 28'-0", containing ten stalls. They were well lit and ventilated and had access only from the yard, thus minimising the risk of spreading disease. Central in the yard or contiguous were the blacksmith's shop, a small building for boiling feedstuffs – linseed, barley and oats, a manure pit and a privy. Set apart at one end of the yard was a small stable with loose boxes for the treatment of sick horses. The depot foreman lived on the premises in a detached house situated near the depot entrance, and incorporating a waiting room for passengers. The construction of the car sheds was of brickwork and iron with a pitched slate roof and a floor covering of York stone flags or granite setts. The smithies and small workshops were generally floored with granite setts and the yards were of ash. The foreman's house was of brickwork with a slate roof.

The first depot site to be purchased by the Tramways Company was adjacent to the "Three Horse Shoes" at Headingley, 5,587 square yards of land being purchased from the trustees of Lord Cardigan for £1,267 4s. 10d. in 1873.

John Kincaid, the company's engineer, was commissioned to design the depot and it was the only one of the company's buildings with any architectural pretensions. Although the main buildings were simple sheds like those that were to follow, the brick front elevation was relatively imposing with three flattened gothic arches, the centre of which was the depot entrance with the words "Leeds Tramways Company" around it. A weather vane in the form of a horse tram was placed over the top of the gable. The depot was of the standard three track layout and held, officially, 12 cars and 124 horses. The drawings, however, indicate that 18 cars could be squeezed in and this must have been done as

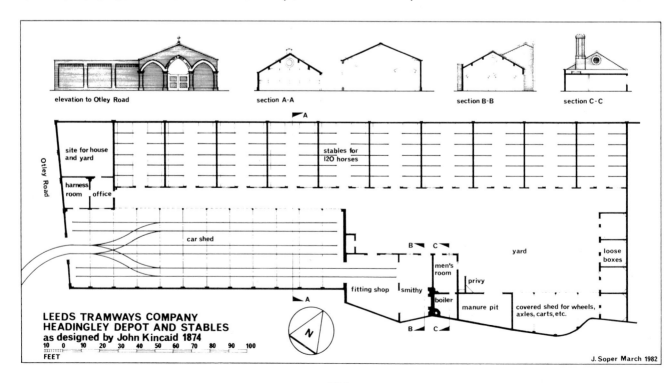

elevation to Otley Road   section A-A   section B-B   section C-C

LEEDS TRAMWAYS COMPANY
HEADINGLEY DEPOT AND STABLES
as designed by John Kincaid 1874
10 0 10 20 30 40 50 60 70 80 90 100
FEET

site for house and yard

harness room   office

stables for 120 horses

car shed

fitting shop   smithy   boiler   men's room   privy   manure pit   yard   loose boxes   covered shed for wheels, axles, carts, etc.

Otley Road

N

J. Soper March 1982

the Company's total depot accommodation in the later 1870's would not have held the 51 cars that were in the fleet. It is not certain whether the depot was built exactly to the original plans as a later drawing has not been found, but photographs indicate that it was very similar.

The building was erected by A. M. Child, the contractor for the Hunslet tramway, under the direction of the Continental and General Tramway Company, and appears to have cost about £2,000. It was opened on 25th May 1874, but the Tramways Company stated that there was no reduction in rental payments. This was due to the opening of new tramways to Hunslet, York Road and Chapeltown which required depots and stables. The depot was used as the main workshops of the Company and a small extension to the workshops was made in 1879 at a cost of £61. The building was modified in late 1883 and early 1884 for the use of steam engines, the cost being £394. A new street and five cottages were built at the rear of the depot for the Company's employees and were occupied from November 1885. The cost was £742. Ten more cottages were added and in use from April 1887 at a further cost of £1,463. To cater for the increased number of tramway engines on the Headingley route, the Company entered into a contract with J. Tomlinson and Sons, contractors, to convert the stables into an engine shed. The work was carried out between March and September 1886, and the "commodious car shed" was completed at a cost of about £1,100. In addition to the trams, the Adel horse 'bus was stabled at Headingley Depot.

Following the withdrawal of the Headingley steam trams in 1892, temporary stables were erected, but the depot continued to be used as the main repair shop for tram engines until the opening of the large depot and works for electric cars in Kirkstall Road in 1897.

The Company's inventory of 1893 valued the depot at £9,000 and stated that it comprised a "car shed, engine sheds, painting shop, fitting shops, store rooms, yard, smithy, and dwelling houses." After the Corporation takeover wooden stables for 16 horses were built in 1894 and the paint shop was also converted into stables. When electrification took place considerable alterations were carried out. The roof was raised, pits added and the building increased in size. The work was carried out by William Irwin and Co. of Leeds from about August 1900 to early 1902.

Green engine No. 27 and a Milnes trailer at Headingley Depot about 1890. *Courtesy The late W. E. Cain.*

The building was demolished in the 1930's and replaced by a new structure. Of the various depots owned by the Leeds Tramways Company, this is the only site still in use. It has seen continuous use by public service vehicles for over 100 years.

The Continental and General Tramway Company agreed to construct all the depots and stables for the Leeds Tramways Company. They completed Headingley Depot and, in August 1874, acquired 4,840 square yards of land at Thwaite Gate, Hunslet, from the trustees of J. Atkinson for £968. Thereafter, they failed to take any action and the Leeds Company let the contract for the construction of a tramway depot to Longley Bros., contractors, of Leeds. The design work was carried out by C. S. and A. J. Nelson, Architects, of Leeds. Construction began in April 1875 and was completed in October at a total cost of £2,832 5s. 2d. and the depot opened on 12th October 1875. The standard three track layout was used and the car shed, 135'-0" long by 40'-0" wide, accommodated 15 cars. Stables for 40 horses, a smithy and manure pit were also provided. Almost immediately, Nelson's were commissioned to design an extension to the depot. This consisted of a small two track fitting shop with pits, a boiling place, further stables for 50 horses, loose boxes, a waiting room with a clock tower and a house for the depot foreman. M. A. Plows, contractor, undertook the work from February to October 1876 at a total cost of £3,189 9s. 0d. The use of the waiting room with its seats and

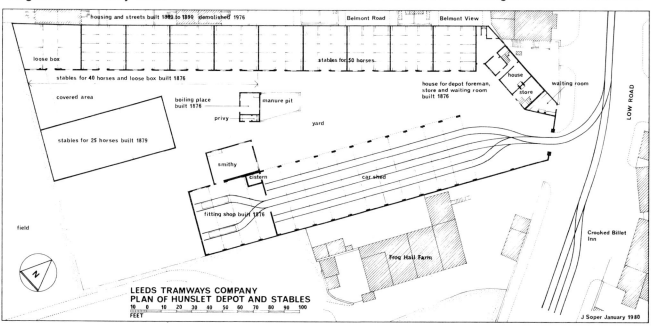

LEEDS TRAMWAYS COMPANY
PLAN OF HUNSLET DEPOT AND STABLES

comfortable open fire was apparently abused and it went out of use after a few years, but was re-opened in 1895 after the Corporation takeover.

An additional stable for 25 horses was built during the spring of 1879 for £828, the total stable accommodation being increased to 115 horses. During the 'eighties the number of horses stabled at Hunslet rarely exceeded 100. As mentioned in the last chapter, horses, cast for sale, were usually sold from Hunslet Depot and dealers brought fresh horses for inspection and prospective purchase by the Tramways Company. The new stables were probably used for this purpose. In February 1898 the Tramways Committee decided to erect further stabling, but no record has been found of this work being carried out.

When built, the depot was situated in rural surroundings with fields on two sides and a farm to the south west. The area to the north west became built up in 1889 and 1890 when a large area of housing and streets was built between New Pepper Road and the depot. In addition to serving the Hunslet route, the Wortley horse trams, cars on the York Road service, and the Hunslet Carr 'bus were also operated from the depot. During 1898 and 1899 the Reservoir Street to Reginald Terrace through service was also worked from Hunslet Depot.

It was necessary to strengthen the walls and raise the roof for electric cars and the building was lengthened, pits and two tracks added. The work was carried out by Isaac Gould Ltd. and Clayton Son and Co. Ltd. (steel-work) from September 1900 to September 1901 at a cost of £5,061. The fitting shop, smithy, two of the

original stables, the stables built in 1879, boiling place and manure pit were demolished. A mess room was added during the latter part of 1901. The building still exists and is used by John Waddington Ltd., printers.

The clock tower of Hunslet Depot demolished in November 1982. *Courtesy J. Soper.*

In accordance with its policy of building depots at termini, in September 1874, the Tramways Company applied for permission to build a tramway depot in Back Lane (later re-named Woodland Lane), Chapeltown. The depot was to be constructed on land to the right of a small church school and would have necessitated a track 300 yards long and a very sharp curve to form a connection with the terminus at the "Queen's Arms". The Highways Committee refused the application due

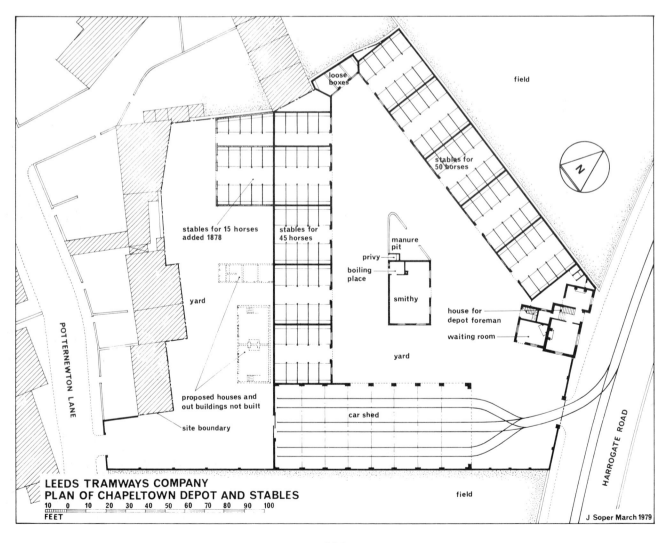

LEEDS TRAMWAYS COMPANY
PLAN OF CHAPELTOWN DEPOT AND STABLES

230

to the narrowness of the road as they felt it would endanger the lives of the public. The Company had to be content with another site just below the "Mexborough Arms" and about a mile from the terminus. 3,970 square yards of land were bought from the Earl of Mexborough for £1,985 in July 1875. Nelson's were again the Architects and the arrangement was very similar to that of Hunslet Depot. The three track layout was employed and there was accommodation for 12 cars and 95 horses plus loose boxes, smithy, boiling place, manure pit, waiting room and house for the depot foreman. The buildings were erected from January to August 1876 by Longley Bros. at a total cost of £5,217 16s. 11d. A contract to remove manure from the depot started on 14th August 1876 and the depot was apparently occupied from this time. The building served the Chapeltown and, from 1878, the Meanwood Road horse car routes, the first car leaving the depot in the morning running on the latter service. To accommodate the additional horses required for the Meanwood Road trams, stables and a shed with access from Potternewton Lane were built during the summer of 1878 at a cost of £433. The stables were for 15 horses and the shed was apparently used by the Moortown 'bus. The exact location of the shed is not certain. Other stables were rented from John Wilson at the "Chained Bull Inn", Moortown for some of the 'bus horses.

In 1878 drawings were prepared for two houses to be built in the yard used by the Meanwood horses, but permission was refused by the Corporation and they were not constructed. A small stable for about ten horses was built under the directions of the Chairman of the Tramways Committee in 1896 and was situated at the side of the stable for the Meanwood horses. The Deputy Chairman and General Manager were asked to look into the question of additional loose box accommodation in 1897, and a shed backing on to the open side of the depot was built. This was apparently used for loose boxes.

Upon electrification a pit was formed and, from September to November 1899, the roof of the car shed was raised, the work being carried out by Isaac Gould Ltd. at a cost of £237 16s. 0d. With its small capacity the depot was not of much use for electric traction and was completely rebuilt in 1907-8.

As early as January 1874 the Tramways Company had advertised for land between the "Cardigan Arms" and Kirkstall terminus, but were unsuccessful. In July 1875, however, they managed to obtain 523 square yards of land on a 299 years lease from the Leeds Corporation at the rear of the police station at Kirkstall terminus. The site was not ideal, being restricted and close to the mill race from the River Aire. During August and September 1875 a retaining wall adjacent to the mill race was built by a contractor, John Wilson. The land was rented from the Corporation at £30 per annum and a start was made on the construction of a small two track depot for five cars, and stables for 15 horses, in May 1876. The Architects were again Nelson's and their original plans show that three tracks were intended, but there was inadequate clearance at the sides and two tracks only were installed. A harness room, waiting room, manure pit and privy were included. The contractor was again John Wilson, and the work was completed in November at a total cost of £1,437 3s. 6d. (including a cost of £170 for the mill race wall). Manure

Sketch showing interior of Chapeltown Depot, based on original Architect's drawing.

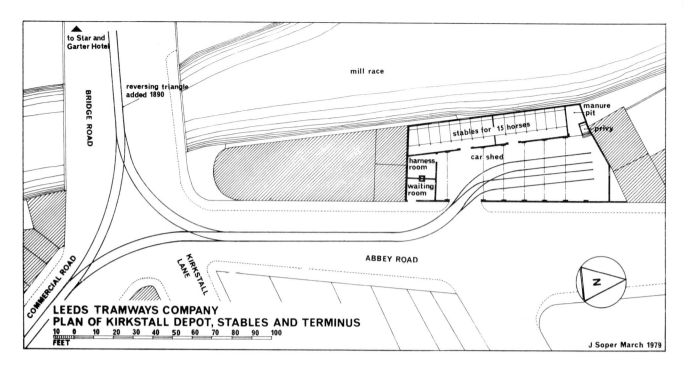

to Star and
Garter Hotel

BRIDGE ROAD

reversing triangle
added 1890

mill race

stables for 15 horses

manure
pit

privy

harness
room

car shed

waiting
room

COMMERCIAL ROAD

KIRKSTALL LANE

ABBEY ROAD

N

LEEDS TRAMWAYS COMPANY
PLAN OF KIRKSTALL DEPOT, STABLES AND TERMINUS

10 0   10 20 30 40 50 60 70 80 90 100
FEET

J Soper March 1979

was removed from the stables for the first time on 4th November 1876 and presumably the depot opened on this day. Approval was given by the Corporation for a small alteration to the stables in 1887, but no details have been traced. The horses were removed in March 1892, when the Kirkstall route became steam operated, and the building was disused. Being close to the river the external wall was subject to subsidence, and at the arbitration in 1893 the depot was valued for the Tramways Company by John Hepper at £918. The Corporation contended that it was of no value as the buildings had got into fearful disrepair and were so dangerous that they could not be occupied. They had not been used for some time and could slip into the river at any moment. William Wharam admitted that there had been a "little giving away of the depot" and it had shown a "weakness of foundation", but denied that it was dangerous. After the Corporation takeover, the Tramways Sub-Committee, in April 1894, decided to carry out repairs and the building was temporarily occupied by steam cars. When the tramway extension to Kirkstall Abbey was constructed in April and May 1897 the access track was disconnected and the depot abandoned. In November 1901 it was proposed that it be transferred to the Sanitary Committee in exchange for land which the Tramways Committee required for the extension of the depot in Stanley Road. The transfer did not take place, however, as in February 1903 the Tramways Committee was approached by J. W. Aspey, a monumental mason who wished to rent a portion of it. The building was later demolished and the site, complete with tram rails of 1876 vintage, still exists, and is in use as a builder's merchant's yard.

Another depot used by the Leeds Tramways Company was situated in North Street. The history of this depot goes back to December 1874 when an estate of 1,724 square yards in area, in North Street, the property of the late William Sheepshanks, was auctioned. The bulk of the property appears to have been bought by William Turton. There was a spacious yard behind and in June 1878 Turton applied to the Corporation for permission to build stables, a workshop, office and cottage on the site. The application was granted by the Building Clauses Committee and the premises were constructed shortly afterwards, and used by Turton for his expanding omnibus business.

In 1882 the depot passed into the hands of the Tramways Company when they bought Turton's undertaking, the building being rented from Turton at £300 per annum (increased to £345 in 1888). In addition to being used for the storage and overhaul of 'buses and stabling for 100 horses, the depot was used as the main stores for feedstuffs for horses, and included a food preparation house. In January 1888 the Company were granted permission to lay a track along Sheepshanks Yard to the tramway in North Street. All the 'bus services, with the exception of Adel and Moortown, were worked from the depot and, after 1888, it was jointly used with Hunslet Depot to house the York Road cars. The repair of horse trams was carried out at North Street in lieu of Headingley Depot, the low height at North Street precluding the use of steam trams. On electrification of the Headingley, Chapeltown and Hunslet routes, North Street became the principal depot for horse trams, and all horse services appear to have operated from there. It was never electrified and on 31st May 1902 the Corporation's tenancy of the property expired. The building was still referred to as the "Leeds Tramway Stables" for many years afterwards and was used for the sale of horses. It was demolished in 1967 due to the construction of the Inner Ring Road in Leeds.

Looking down Sheepshanks Yard to the entrance to North Street Depot shortly before demolition in 1967.
Courtesy J. Soper.

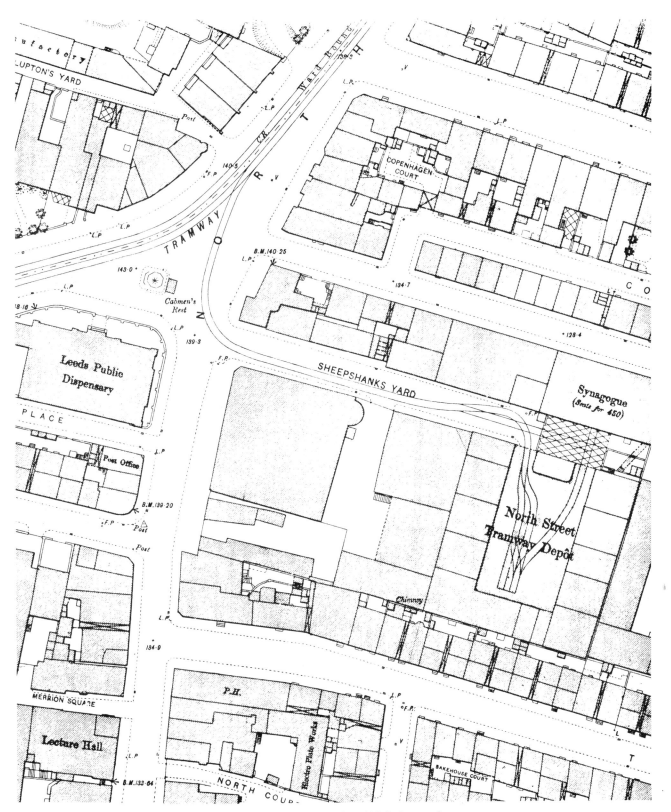

Plan of North Street Depot from the 1890 Ordnance Survey map.

After finding that steam traction was successful, the Directors of the Tramways Company selected a site for a depot near to the town centre at Wellington Bridge, at the junction of the Wortley and Kirkstall tramways. The necessity of providing a depot at the terminus of the route was not so important with mechanical traction.

On 8th December 1882 the Company obtained approval for the construction of an engine and car shed on a site 3,560 square yards in area. Nelson's were again the Architects and a four track depot of cheap construction 100'-0" long was built. Also included were

a store room, office, tool shed and coke shed. A "land furnace", apparently for the production of live coals for the firing of tram engines, was situated at the rear of the shed and there were also two pits for the servicing of engines. Construction began in late 1882 and a track connection made from Wellington Street. The depot was in use by 2nd April 1883, although it does not appear to have been completely finished until about two months later.

From 31st October 1881 the Company had rented a yard in Wellington Street at 10s. 0d. per week from

233

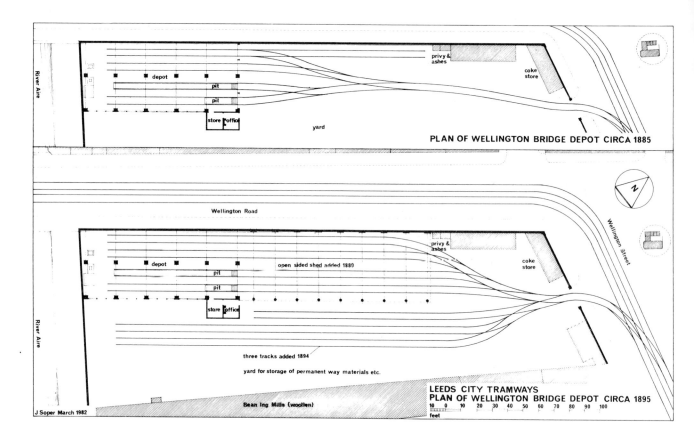

PLAN OF WELLINGTON BRIDGE DEPOT CIRCA 1885

LEEDS CITY TRAMWAYS
PLAN OF WELLINGTON BRIDGE DEPOT CIRCA 1895

J Soper March 1982

Illingworth, Ingham and Co. and it appears that it was this yard that was employed. By October 1888 the land was in the possession of Joshua Wilson and Sons who charged the Tramways Company a ground rental of £125 per annum.

In February 1889 Nelson's designed an extension to the car shed, doubling its size. This was of temporary construction, open on one side, with cast iron columns and corrugated iron roof, and cost £504. The construction of this extension necessitated alterations to the track layout in the yard; the siding was removed and the pointwork modified.

One of the first actions of the Highways Committee, after the Corporation took over the tramways, was a decision in February 1894 to lay additional lines at the depot for the storage of engines and cars and provide further pits. Three tracks were added and Wilson's promptly increased the ground rental to £215 per annum, which the Highways Committee reluctantly agreed to pay. On 9th December 1896 they decided to terminate their tenancy but took no immediate action.

It was the practice to change engines and cars at Wellington Bridge, frequently in the middle of a journey, and this was a source of annoyance to passengers. On 7th February 1898 a deputation representing 200 Wortley ratepayers made a formal protest to the Tramways Sub-Committee, complaining about the practice and the irregular service of cars on the Wortley route. They requested that the depot be dispensed with as soon as possible and a new depot erected at Wortley terminus. The new depot was not built but Wellington Bridge Depot was closed soon afterwards. The Staff Records indicate that it was still in use in May 1898 and in January 1899 the Corporation made their last rental payment to Wilson's.

The rapidly increasing tramway network in 1900-1 demanded a yard for the storage of permanent way materials. A Highways Department yard in Whitehall Road was used for this purpose, but it was restricted in size and was not connected to the tramways. The Highways Committee was interested in the abandoned Wellington Bridge Depot and, in December 1901, approached the owners, represented by Newsum and Gott, estate agents. In January 1902 an agreement to lease the land at £200 per annum was made. Some workshops were erected by Banks, Mawson, contractor, for £815 10s. 0d. but the corrugated iron shed was retained. A simplified track layout was employed and permanent way plant installed during the summer of 1902. The depot and its staff of tramway platelayers was run under the auspices of the Highways Committee, but this was transferred to the Tramways Committee in February 1903.

The last depot to be described was used by the Roundhay Electric Tramway. It was situated on land owned by the Leeds Corporation Sanitary Committee in Stanley Road, off Beckett Street. At first it was known as Beckett Street Depot, but later as Stanley Road Depot. It was built to the designs of the Leeds Borough Engineer and erected by William Irwin and Co. of Leeds for the sum of £683 between March and September 1891. It was of brick and iron construction with a pitched slate roof. There were four tracks with pits at the rear and it was built for a capacity of eight cars, although it could accommodate 12 cars of the length used by the Roundhay Company. Adjacent was a brick built stock room leading to the engine room and boiler house at the rear, these being of temporary corrugated iron construction.

When the Roundhay electric cars ceased to run in 1896 the building was disused for about two years. In December 1897 the Tramways Sub-Committee decided to buy the corrugated iron shed from the British Thomson-Houston Company for £60, and it was converted into stables for 25 horses. The depot came into use again when the Beckett Street horse car service was instituted in April 1898. In October of that year it was decided to improve the service on the York Road tram-

Re-built Kitson engine No. 4 and Milnes trailer No. 5 in Wellington Bridge Depot Yard about 1895.
Courtesy Science Museum, South Kensington, London, Whitcombe Collection.

way and, to achieve this, to erect further stable accommodation for 30 horses at Beckett Street. This was done and from mid-January 1899 the working of the York Road horse cars was transferred from Hunslet Depot to Beckett Street. The building remained in this condition until 1902, when extensive reconstruction for electric cars took place. The original depot was retained but extended to the rear to the full depth of the site – 296'-0". Tenders totalling £2,579 8s. 4d. for the extensions were approved by the Tramways Committee in October 1901, W. H. Dews and Co. being the main contractor. The work was carried out between January and November 1902. The depot was later further extended by the addition of three tracks to the right and a two-storey office, mess and stores block.

The tramway offices of the Leeds Tramways Company were situated in Boar Lane adjacent to Trinity Church and were on land rented from John Thomas Beer, clothier, at £55 per annum. The offices (two small rooms) were erected by Busby's in 1871-2, and contiguous was a waiting room with a facade of ornamental glass and cast iron and a large imposing clock. Part of the building was on land owned by Beer and part on land rented from the Trustees of Trinity Church. For the waiting room the Company paid Beer £20 and the Church £30 annually. A store room and a small cash receiving office were added later. An old horse car body was also used as a store at the rear of the building. On 14th November 1896 the horse car was destroyed by fire, but unfortunately no further details are known.

In May 1896 some members of the Tramways Sub-Committee considered the advisability of enlarging and rebuilding the "stuffy little structure", but decided instead to abandon part of the building. On 9th Decem-

ber 1896 they resolved to terminate the tenancy of the office, retaining only the cash receiving office, but changed their mind, for a year later they decided to increase the office space. An extension was built on Holy Trinity land at a cost of £350 in 1898 and a ten years agreement for the site rental was signed, the Corporation being allowed to sub-let to a suitable tenant if they decided to vacate before the expiration of the term.

A Conductor carries his fare box from the Boar Lane Office. In the background are B. T. H. car No. 139, a Green engine and Milnes trailer. *Courtesy Leeds City Libraries.*

The system of conductors handing in their fare boxes at the cash receiving office was a source of considerable complaint due to congestion in Boar Lane. Following a visit to Glasgow in January 1898, the Tramways Sub-Committee found that the conductors there handed in

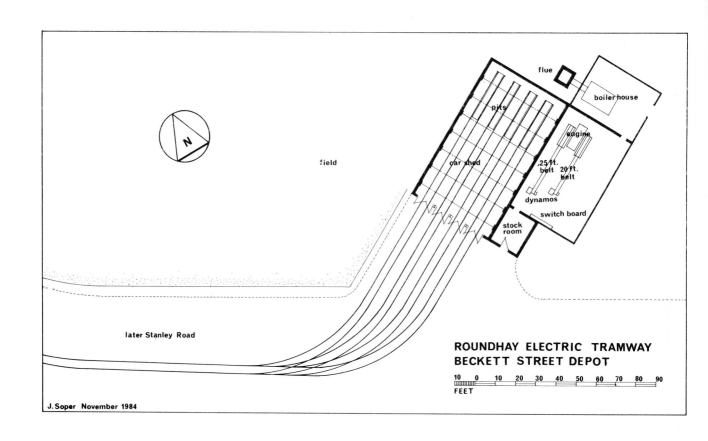

ROUNDHAY ELECTRIC TRAMWAY
BECKETT STREET DEPOT

flue
boiler house
pits
engine
car shed
25 ft. belt
20 ft. belt
dynamos
switch board
stock room
field
later Stanley Road

10 0 10 20 30 40 50 60 70 80 90
FEET

J. Soper November 1984

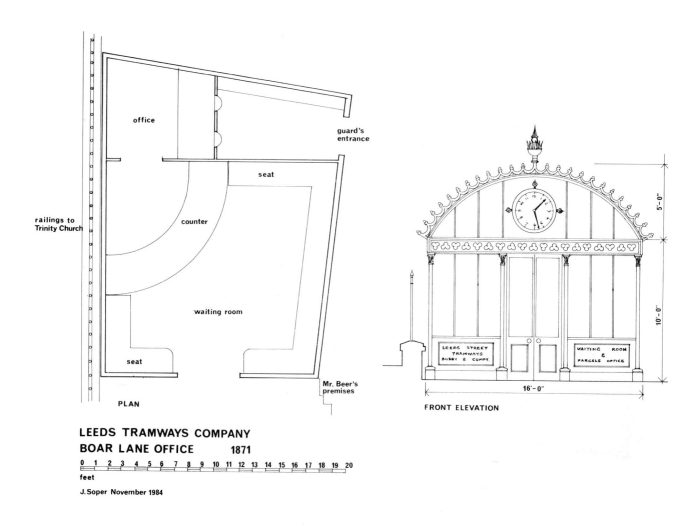

office
guard's entrance
seat
counter
railings to Trinity Church
waiting room
seat
Mr. Beer's premises

PLAN

LEEDS TRAMWAYS COMPANY
BOAR LANE OFFICE   1871

0 1 2 3 4 5 6 7 8 9 10 11 12 13 14 15 16 17 18 19 20
feet

J. Soper November 1984

5'-0"
10'-0"

LEEDS STREET
TRAMWAYS
BUSBY & COMPY.

WAITING ROOM
&
PARCELS OFFICE

16'-0"

FRONT ELEVATION

236

their cash at receiving offices at the outer termini of routes. The following month they decided to build a cash receiving office at the Canal Gardens terminus, Round-hay, which also incorporated a waiting room. The following year a cash receiving office was provided near the "Oak", Headingley to serve the Headingley and Chapeltown through service, and in 1900 similar facilities were provided near the Corn Exchange.

With electrification and expansion of the tramways, the office accommodation was inadequate and two additional rooms were rented from Beer at £55 per annum (later increased to £60) from January 1900. The office area was now at its maximum possible on the site, but the demand for increased space continued to grow.

In November 1901 the Tramways Committee decided to rent rooms in the basement of the newly erected Standard Insurance Buildings in City Square and a seven years lease at £350 per annum was agreed. The lease took effect from February 1902. Additional rooms were rented in July 1902, June 1904 and June 1905. In July and August 1905 the Boar Lane office was vacated by the Tramways Department. It was sub-let for the unexpired period of the ten year term.

Others had cashed in on the old tramway office as, adjacent to the waiting room, was Samuel Lee's "Tramway Restaurant", which offered a "substantial dinner" for 10d. and a tea for 4d. In 1887 it was renamed the "Silver Grid".

The Canal Gardens Waiting Room and Cash Office provide the background for Greenwood and Batley car No. 21 in 1899. *Courtesy "Tramway and Railway World".*

A seven window Starbuck double-deck car stands on the reversing triangle outside Headingley Depot about 1895. *Courtesy J. Soper Collection.*

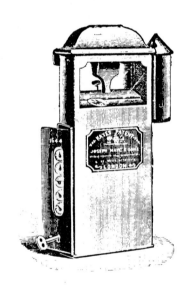

CHAPTER TWENTY-FIVE

Fare Collection

In the early horse 'bus days fares were collected by hand and there was little or no check on the amount received. Dishonesty was common but the boy conductors, who were usually employed, could no doubt be coerced into parting with all the money they received.

In the 'seventies and 'eighties the fare box system patented by Joseph Kaye and Sons, locksmiths, of South Accommodation Road, Hunslet, Leeds, came into general use on both the 'buses and trams in Leeds. Kaye's patent fare box first made its appearance in 1874 and was immediately used on the Leeds tramways. The locked box consisted of two compartments, an upper and lower, and the passenger placed his fare in a slot situated in the top of the box. Underneath was the top compartment, glazed on both sides, and through which both the conductor and passenger could observe the coins. If correct the conductor pressed a plunger which allowed the coins to pass into the locked compartment below. Incorporated in the fare box was a "tell-tale" known as a "bullet" which came out of a socket if the box was tampered with. It could also come out if the box was dropped or severely knocked and if a conductor did not have a witness he was liable to a fine if his "bullet" was dislodged. Also supplied with the fare box was a fare box lamp and a lamp case for use at night.

A conductor was given his 20 shillings worth of change and was not allowed to handle fares or allow coins to remain on the platform in the top of the box. These were offences which could result in a fine or dismissal. By using a piece of wire, a dishonest conductor could remove a coin from the platform of his box and, to prevent this, in January 1881, the fare boxes were returned in batches to Kaye's and modified. A fare box cost 28s. 0d. and if one was stolen or lost the conductor was liable to half the cost. Again if his lamp and lamp case were mislaid he had to pay the replacement cost of 1s. 6d. The fare box lamps were kept in a lamp cabin adjacent to the Boar Lane office and were in the charge of a lamp boy. He was responsible for seeing that the lamps were filled with oil and the wicks properly adjusted. It was the responsibility of the conductor to collect the lamp and light it.

The fare boxes had hooks on the back and there was a tendency by some conductors to hang them inside the cars with the consequent danger of the box falling on passengers. In July 1885 Kaye's brought out a new type of box with the hooks omitted and this became generally adopted on the Leeds tramways. The cost of the new box was 30s. 0d.

The Kaye children and their friends frequently travelled on the Hunslet tram and became notorious "spies". In July 1874, shortly after the introduction of the fare box, conductor William Runton was reported to the Manager by one of the Kaye's for collecting fares in his hand. It was found that he had 25s. 2d. in his change bag instead of 20s. 0d. He could not account for the difference and was sentenced to three months imprisonment.

Some of the reports made by the Kaye's were justifiable, but some were doubtful. In one such case in November 1898, Hunslet conductor Albert Minter was dismissed and later, backed by his trade union, sued Kaye's for damages for slander. He won his case and Kaye's had to pay £75 damages. The "spying" ceased.

Kaye's farebox system was used on the Leeds tramways up to 1903, when the new General Manager, J. B. Hamilton, introduced the Bell Punch ticket system. In 1881 another type of fare box with a clockwork dial had been tried out, but no further details have been traced and it was presumably unsuccessful. There was a brief encounter with a type of ticket system in 1874, described at the beginning of Chapter 8, but no other tickets were apparently employed by the Leeds Tramways Company.

Shortly after the Corporation takeover, Alderman Firth announced that the Tramways Sub-Committee had made inquiries in various towns and found that in all cases the Bell Punch ticket system was preferred to the fare box system. In April 1894 the Sub-Committee decided to adopt the Bell Punch system on the short York Road route. Four "Bailey's" bell punching machines were obtained and the following month the system came into use. It does not appear to have lasted long and was probably discontinued when the stock of tickets ran out.

In December 1895 some members of the Tramways Sub-Committee were appointed to consider the question of issuing workmen's return tickets, but no action was taken.

Certain members of the tramways staff had free passes for use on the cars. The Directors and Manager of the Leeds Tramways Company had free passes which they produced if asked by the conductor, and the horse-keepers, blacksmiths, sand boys etc. had tin passes which they carried on a leather strap tied round their neck. If the pass was not displayed a fare had to be paid.

A way-bill was used by the conductors to record the number of passengers and the conductor had to make up the difference if there was a discrepancy between his way-bill and the contents of the fare box. Inside and outside passengers, and passengers holding free passes were shown on the way-bill. Parcels and luggage also had to be paid for and indicated. According to philatelist David Stirling, the Leeds Tramways Company issued parcels stamps of the values 2d., 3d. and 4d. but no copies have been seen by the writer. Parcels of newspapers were carried, but these were usually paid for in advance. It is recorded, for example, that the rate for the carriage of one parcel of newspapers from Leeds to Chapeltown was 3s. 0d. per month. Dogs were not allowed on the cars. When the conductor presented his cash at the receiving office, the amount was entered on the way-bill by the cashiers and the conductor then signed the way bill.

> # PLEASE PAY YOUR FARE INTO THE BOX ONLY
>
> Any Complaints to be addressed to
> 81, CHAPELTOWN ROAD.
>
> J. WHITEHEAD & SON, Printers, 17 Lower Head Row, Leeds

Walker Bros. traffic notice relating to the payment of fares. *Courtesy Leeds City Museums.*

Kenneth E. Smith in his book "Catalogue of World Transportation Tokens and Passes, except North America", published in 1967, lists a token issued by the Leeds Tramways Company. It was of brass, circular, and measured 23 mm. in diameter. On one side were the words "LEEDS TRAMWAYS COY." and a numeral. On the reverse side were the words "THIS MUST BE PAID IN THE FAREBOX." It is not clear which group of workers used the token.

In July 1894 the Tramways Sub-Committee agreed that postmen be given tickets to put in the fare box equivalent to 1d. per journey. These did not last long and the following year were replaced by tokens. The penny tokens used by the postmen came into use on 18th November 1895. Later, in the Hamilton era, tokens became used by other groups of workmen in Leeds.

The fare box system was generally considered to be cumbersome and inadequate and, in August 1899, a new type of fare collection system appeared. It was known as "Ohmer's Patent System" and consisted of an automatic ticket recording machine measuring only $5\frac{3}{4}'' \times 1\frac{3}{4}''$ and weighing about the same as a bell punch machine. For every penny handed to the conductor he had to strike a "recording plunger" which not only rang

out aloud the amount of money paid, but also indicated it by figures on an automatic wheel. At the same time the conductor was required to touch a lever which automatically printed and delivered a small paper ticket to the passenger, and exposed to view on another counting wheel the exact number of passengers carried. A time clock was also included on the face of the machine and this enabled the ticket to be issued (again automatically) with the exact hour and minute of issue printed upon it. The great advantage claimed was the abolition of an elaborate system of office checking, the machine itself registering all that was necessary.

The Tramways Committee was sufficiently impressed to give an order for 250 of the machines, 50 to be delivered as soon as possible. The balance of the order was to be cancelled if the 50 machines were not satisfactory. The rental was apparently to be paid in French currency at the rate of not more than 50 centimes per machine per day. However, Ohmer's system was not immediately introduced as the inventor made certain modifications and improvements to the mechanism. On 17th December 1900 Ohmer demonstrated the modifications to the Tramways Committee and they confirmed their original order. Thereafter, no record has been traced of the machine and no payments were apparently made to Ohmer. Probably the machine was too sophisticated for the rough usage it would receive in the hands of the Leeds tram conductors.

A transfer ticket system was briefly used on the Dewsbury Road service when the route was severed due to the reconstruction of the bridge in Dewsbury Road. At the same time, probably, the Armley and Beeston Hill routes also used transfer tickets due to bridge construction. The transfer tickets were supplied to the conductors in books and were printed by Goodall and Suddick of Leeds.

Two of Walker Bros. Tickets. *Courtesy The late M. Walker*

The introduction of the "Bell Punch" ticket system on the Leeds Corporation tramways is covered by the next volume of this work, but the system was latterly employed by Walker Bros., omnibus proprietors. Two of their tickets are known to survive, a 1d. white Moorland

Road and a 3d. brown Roundhay, and are illustrated. The Roundhay Electric Tramway also used the "Bell Punch" system and a set of their tickets was preserved in the Leeds Reference Library until they "disappeared" some time ago. Fortunately, the writer obtained a photostat but did not record the colours. The photostat is illustrated and shows that the tickets consisted of a variety of types. The 1d. and 2d. at the top largely consisted of advertisements, of which the upper portion was apparently cut off by the conductor. From memory, the 2d. A2745 was brown in colour. The tickets in the middle were of the geographical type and each punch hole indicated that a penny fare was paid. Again from memory, the central 2d. ticket 4672 was white in colour and the lower 1d. ticket 5664 was on heavy white card and was probably used by postmen, who were allowed to travel free on the tramway. The ticket on the left is a Liverpool ticket which was included in the Reference Library collection.

NOTICE.

EACH passenger is requested to see that the TICKET given by the Conductor in exchange for the Fare denotes the amount paid, and is punched in the section showing the place to which the passenger is entitled to travel.

All Tickets must be punched by the Conductor IMMEDIATELY on receipt of the Fare, and in the presence of the passenger paying.

ALL COMPLAINTS TO BE ADDRESSED

WALKER BROS., 81, CHAPELTOWN RD.

TELEPHONE No. 28

The Roundhay Electric Tramway also used contract tickets and a white blank ticket is illustrated. The contract tickets were stuck in small rexine bound card folders with a small window indicating the name of the holder. Six folders were used for the various sections as follows:– Roundhay Park and Sheepscar, dark brown; Harehills Road and Sheepscar, red; Harehills Avenue and Sheepscar, light brown; Roundhay Park and Harehills Road, dark green, Roundhay Park and Beckett Street, pale buff, and Harehills Road and Beckett Street, blue.

THE ROUNDHAY ELECTRIC TRAMWAY.

No.....................   Entered ....

CONTRACT TICKET,

Between ....   and ....

From ....   to ....

This Ticket is forfeited if transferred, and only available for the journey when produced to the proper officers of the Company on demand, and is issued subject to the same regulations as are applicable to other passengers, and the holder by accepting it agrees that the Company is not to be liable for any loss, damage, injury, delay, or detention caused or arising off their cars.

Signature of Holder ....

....

                                        Managers,
                           1, Roseville Rd., Roundhay Rd., Leeds.

Contract Ticket used by the Roundhay Electric Tramway.
Courtesy A. E. Burbridge.

An annual pass was also issued. Kenneth E. Smith lists a pierced aluminium pass, measuring 39 mm. in diameter, with the words "ROUNDHAY ELECTRIC TRAMWAY LEEDS" and the City Coat of Arms on one side. On the other side were the words "ANNUAL PASS NON-TRANSFERABLE No. ...." The year was also stamped on this side. The pass was referred to in the "Rules for Employees" for the Company, Rule 27. for Conductors, Appendix 3 of this volume.

Punch	No.		Tickets	1900
Time	MOORLAND ROAD	Time	BRIGGATE	
8.30		8.50		
9.10		9.30		
9.50		10.10		
10.30		10.50		
11.10		11.30		
11.50		12.10		
12.30		12.50		
1.10		1.30		
1.50		2.10		
2.30		2.50		
3.10		3.30		
3.50		4.10		
4.30		4.50		
5.10		5.30		
5.50		6.10		
6.30		6.50		
7.10		7.30		
7.50		8.10		
8.30		8.50		
9.10		9.30		
9.50		10.10		
10.30		10.50		

Walker Bros. Way Bill for the Moorland Road 'bus route, 1900
Courtesy Leeds City Museum.

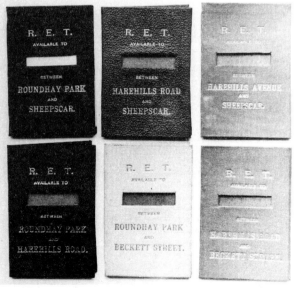

Contract Ticket Folders used by the Roundhay Electric Tramway.   *Courtesy A. E. Burbridge.*

ROUNDHAY
ELECTRIC TRAMWAY.

2d. D 4672 2d.

This Ticket is issued subject to the Company's Bye-Laws, and must be produced or delivered up on demand.

'Busses meet each Car at Green Road and Sheepscar to take up passengers.

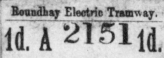

Roundhay Electric Tramway.

1d. A 2895 1d.

This Ticket is issued subject to the Company's Bye-Laws, and must be produced or delivered up on demand.

Roundhay Electric Tramway.

1d. A 2151 1d.

This Ticket is issued subject to the Company's Bye-Laws, and must be produced or delivered up on demand.

ACKNOWLEDGED
DYSONS
Are the Best and Cheapest for
GUARANTEED WATCHES,
GUARANTEED RINGS,
GUARANTEED CLOCKS,
GUARANTEED REPAIRS.
TIME-BALL BUILDINGS,
24, 25, 26, BRIGGATE, LEEDS
HATS & UMBRELLAS
THOROUGHLY RELIABLE IN WEAR
S.TIMMS 128.KIRGATE.

SAY!
Say you had two shillings
Say you wanted a pound of Tea.
Say it was at No 11 Boar Lane, Leeds
Say it was a Tea Shop.
Say you ventured to buy a pound there
Say you liked it exceedingly.
Say you told your friends.
Say it was BROOKE, BOND'S TEA.
SAY NO MORE.

ROUNDHAY ELECTRIC TRAMWAY.

1d. 5664 1d.

This Ticket is the property of the Company, and must be shown or given up on demand.

Bishop, Stationer, 81 & 82, Briggate, Leeds.

Appendix One

Acts of Parliament, 1871 to 1899

THE LEEDS TRAMWAYS ORDER, 1871.
14th August 1871

This Order authorised William and Daniel Busby and Co. to construct the following tramways:–

Tramway No. 1
From the junction of Briggate and Boar Lane, via Boar Lane, Wellington Street and Kirkstall Road to a point near the "Star and Garter Inn", Kirkstall.
Total length of line 2m. 7f. 3ch.
In addition there were four lengths of tramway, double track or loop lines, Tramways Nos. 1A to 1D.

Tramway No. 2
From the junction of Briggate and Boar Lane, via Boar Lane, Park Row, Cookridge Street, Woodhouse Lane, Headingley Lane and Otley Road terminating near the "Three Horse Shoes Inn", Headingley.
Total length of line 3m. 3.7ch.
In addition there were seven lengths of tramway, double track or loop lines, Tramways Nos. 2A to 2G.

Tramway No. 3
From the junction of Briggate and Boar Lane via Briggate, North Street. Chapeltown Road and Harrogate Road to the "Queen's Arms", Chapeltown.
Total length of line 2m 6f. 3ch.
In addition there were six lengths of tramway, double track or loop lines, Tramways Nos. 3A to 3F.

Tramway No. 4
From the junction of Briggate and Boar Lane via Briggate, Hunslet Lane, Hunslet Road and Low Road to Thwaite Gate, Hunslet.
Total length of line 1m. 7f. 3.5ch.
In addition there were five lengths of tramway, double track or loop lines, Tramways Nos. 4A to 4E.

Tramway No. 5
From the junction of Briggate and Boar Lane via Duncan Street, Call Lane, Kirkgate and Marsh Lane to the "Shoulder of Mutton Inn".
Total length of line 5f. 9ch.
In addition there were two lengths of tramway, double track or loop lines, Tramways Nos. 5A to 5B.

THE LEEDS TRAMWAYS ACT, 1872
6th August 1872

This Act authorised the transfer of the interests of William and Daniel Busby in the Leeds tramways to a new company, the "Leeds Tramways Company", which was incorporated.

THE LEEDS TRAMWAYS ACT, 1877
2nd August 1877

This Act authorised the Leeds Tramways Company to construct the following tramways:–

Tramway No. 1
From the existing tramway in Wellington Street via Wellington Road to the "Crown Inn", New Wortley.
Total length of line 5f. 8.3ch.

Tramway No. 1C
From the "Crown Inn", New Wortley, via Tong Road to the "Star Inn", Upper Wortley.
Total length of line 6f. 8.85ch.
In addition there were two lengths of tramway, double track or loop lines, Tramways Nos. 1A to 1B.

Tramway No. 2
From the existing tramway in North Street via Meanwood Road to the "Primrose Inn".
Total length of line 5f. 8.4ch.
In addition there was one length of double track, Tramway No. 2A.

THE LEEDS TRAMWAYS ACT, 1881
18th July 1881

This Act authorised the Leeds Tramways Company to run steam tramcars on its lines and to build, purchase, hire, provide, work, use and run omnibuses and hackney carriages in Leeds.

LEEDS CORPORATION TRAMWAYS ORDER, 1888
28th June 1888

This Order authorised the Leeds Corporation to construct the following tramways:–

Tramway No. 1
From the existing tramway at Sheepscar via Roundhay Road to Gledhow Lane, Roundhay. Double track.
Total length of line 1m. 6f. 5.5ch.
In addition there was a turning circle at the terminus, Tramway No. 1A.

Tramway No. 2
From the existing tramway in Kirkgate and Call Lane via York Street and Marsh Lane to connect with the existing tramway in Marsh Lane. Single track with passing places.
Total length of line. .690 miles

Tramway No. 3
From Marsh Lane via Burmantofts Street, Beckett Street, and Harehills Road to the junction with Roundhay Road. Single track with passing places.
Total length of line. 1.615 miles

LEEDS CORPORATION TRAMWAYS ACT, 1896   2nd July 1896

This Act gave the Leeds Corporation legal authority to work the tramways and authorised the renewal of the 1888 Act to construct a tramway from Kirkgate via York Street, Burmantofts Street and Beckett Street to Green Road, Beckett Street. (Tramway No. 2 and part of Tramway No. 3 of 1888 Act.) It also authorised the construction of the following tramways:–

Tramway No. 1
Extension of the Roundhay tramway from Gledhow Lane, via Prince's Avenue to the Canal Gardens, Roundhay Park. Double track.
Total length of line. 7f. 7.36ch.

Tramway No. 2
From the existing tramway in Marsh Lane via York Road to Victoria Avenue. Double track.
Total length of line. 6f. 4.27ch.

Tramway No. 3
From the existing tramway terminus in Meanwood Road via Meanwood Road to the "Beckett's Arms", Meanwood. Double track.
Total length of line. 1m. 2f. 2.77ch.

Tramway No. 4
From the "Star Inn", Tong Road, via Tong Road to the "New Inn". Double track.
Total length of line. 2f. 6.21ch.

Tramway No. 5
From a connection with Tramway No. 4 at Whingate Junction via Whingate to Town Street, Armley. Double track.
Total length of line. 3f. 7.48ch.

Tramway No. 6
From Wellington Road via Armley Road to the "Nelson Hotel", Armley. Double track.
Total length of line. 1m. 0.75ch.

Tramway No. 7
From the terminus of the existing tramway at Kirkstall via Abbey Road to Kirkstall Abbey. Double track.
Total length of line. 2f. 4.77ch.

Tramway No. 8
From the existing tramway at Bridge End via Meadow Lane and Dewsbury Road to the "New Inn", Dewsbury Road. Double track.
Total length of line. 1m. 2f. 9.67ch.

LEEDS CORPORATION ACT, 1897
     6th August 1897

This Act authorised the Leeds Corporation to construct the following tramways:–

Tramway No. 1
A small extension of Tramway No. 4 authorised by the 1896 Act, the Tong Road tramway, to a point about 50 yards past the "New Inn". Double track.
Total length of line. 1.97ch.

Tramway No. 2
A connection of the Tong Road tramway near to the "Crown Hotel" and "Star Inn", via Oldfield Lane and Upper Wortley Road to form a circular route. Single track with passing places.
Total length of line. 1m. 1f. 0.96ch.

Tramway No. 3
From City Square via Aire Street, Whitehall Road and Gelderd Road to a terminus in Gelderd Road near the Cattle Market. Double track throughout apart from Aire Street, single track.
Total length of line. 1m. 1f. 2.4ch.

Tramway No. 4
An extension of the Dewsbury Road tramway from the "New Inn", via Dewsbury Road to Cross Flatts Park. Double track.
Total length of line. 3f. 8.54ch.

Tramway No. 5
From the Hunslet tramway at the "Swan Junction", via Waterloo Road, Church Street, Balm Road and Moor Road to the junction with Arthington Avenue. Single track with passing places.
Total length of line. 1m 1f. 1.5ch.

Tramway No. 6
From the existing tramway in Duncan Street, via New Market Street, Vicar Lane and North Street to connect with the existing tramway in North Street. Double track.
Total length of line. 3f. 0.5ch.

Tramway No. 7
From Park Row, via Infirmary Street, East Parade, Calverley Street, Great George Street, Clarendon Road, Moorland Road and Hyde Park Road to Hyde Park. Double track.
Total length of line 1m. 6f. 9.15ch.
In addition Tramway No. 7A formed a connection with the Headingley tramway at Hyde Park. 1.05ch. in length.

Tramway No. 8
From a junction with Tramway No. 7 in East Parade, via Park Lane, Burley Street, Burley Road, Cardigan Road and St. Michael's Road to form a connection with the Headingley tramway in Otley Road. Circular route. Single track with passing places.
Total length of line. 2m. 3f. 6.2ch.

Tramway No. 9
From the existing tramway in Headingley Lane, via Victoria Road to Tramway No. 8 in Cardigan Road. Double track.
Total length of line. 4f. 7.18ch.

Tramway No. 9A
From the existing tramway in Headingley Lane, via Woodhouse Street and Cambridge Road to form a connection with the Meanwood tramway in Meanwood Road. Single and double track.
Total length of line. 7f. 0.1ch.

Tramway No. 10
From a junction in Meadow Lane with Tramway No. 8 authorised by the 1896 Act (Dewsbury Road) via Meadow Road, Beeston Road and Town Street and terminating in Town Street. Single track with passing places.
Total length of line. 1m. 6f. 2.3ch.

Tramway No. 11
From a junction with Tramway No. 10 in Meadow Road, via Elland Road to a terminus in Elland Road. Double track.
Total length of line. 1m 0f. 4.75ch.

Tramway No. 12

From the existing tramway in Marsh Lane, via East Street, Cross Green Lane, Easy Road, Dial Street and Upper Accommodation Road to form a connection in York Road with Tramway No. 2 authorised by the 1896 Act. Circular route. Single track with passing places.
Total length of line. 1 m. 2 f. 3.03 ch.

LEEDS CORPORATION ACT, 1899
9th August 1899

Tramway

From a junction with Tramway No. 6, authorised by the Leeds Corporation Tramways Act, 1896, at Armley via Stanningley Road and Bramley to the City Boundary at Town Street, Stanningley. Double track with single track in Town Street, Stanningley.
Total length of line. 3 m. 3 f. 7.17 ch.

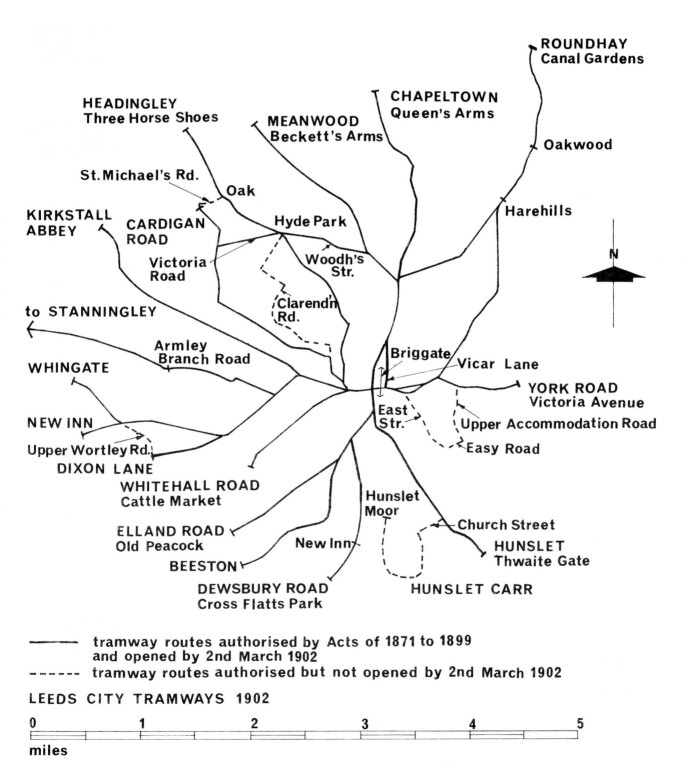

——— tramway routes authorised by Acts of 1871 to 1899 and opened by 2nd March 1902

- - - - tramway routes authorised but not opened by 2nd March 1902

LEEDS CITY TRAMWAYS 1902

0   1   2   3   4   5

miles

Appendix Two

RULES AND REGULATIONS FOR THE DRIVERS AND CONDUCTORS OF THE LEEDS TRAMWAYS COMPANY

SPECIAL RULES

Applying to
DRIVERS AND CONDUCTORS

---

1. Conductors or Drivers must deposit all money or articles left in their Cars or Omnibuses with the Clerk on duty, at the receiving office, on their first arrival after such articles are found, and the Clerk will enter them in a book which is kept for that purpose.

2. In all cases of absence through illness, notice to that effect must be sent to the Yard Superintendents at their respective yards before 7.30 in the morning, to enable them to procure other men. If absent more than two days a medical certificate must be forwarded to the Manager or Superintendent, or the vacancy will be filled up.

3. If the Car is three or more minutes late, or out of place, a report must be made in the office, giving a reason. The fact of any car meeting another car on a single line must likewise be reported by the Conductor.

4. Cars must be started and stopped by the bell signal only, and when cars are brought to a full stop the driver must hold his horses well in hand, and keep the car perfectly still by the break till the bell is rung.

5. In all cases of accidents, however trivial, Conductors must endeavour to obtain the full names and addresses of several witnesses, and make a report in the office on their arrival in Boar Lane. In case of accidents, be it known that Tackle for Cars and Tip Horses can be had at the Offices in Boar Lane. Every Driver must have upon his Car daily, an extra trace chain, bolt, and S link.

MODE OF COLLECTING FARES

6. **Conductors must give change all round if required, before commencing to collect fares, and then receive each fare separately into the fare box, and after examining the coin to see that it is good and the amount correct, let it down into the lower compartment of the box. In no case will they be excused if detected in allowing any fares to remain on the platform of the fare box, or in taking any fares otherwise than in the fare boxes.**

7. Giving Change and Collecting Fares:–

Headingley Section – Give Change between Great George Street and Woodhouse Lane, and Collect Fares on Woodhouse Moor, Cars not to start away from Hyde Park Corner until all the Fares have been collected. Down Journey – Give Change on Woodhouse Moor, and Collect Fares at St. Mark's Street.

Chapeltown Section – Give Change in New Briggate and Leopold Street, Collect Fares at Cowper Street Loop. Down Journey – Give Change between Newton Lane and Cowper Street, Collect at Barrack Street.

GIVING CHANGE AND COLLECTING OF FARES

LEEDS TO HUNSLET. (1d. Stages)

1d. For St. Jude's Church. – Give Change, and Collect the 1d. Fares at or near Salem Chapel, in Hunslet Lane.

1d. For Church Street. – Second Collection to take place at the Mechanics' Institute.

1d. For Thwaite Gate. – Third and Last Collection immediately after passing Church Street.

HUNSLET TO LEEDS.

1d. For Church Street. – Give Change, and Collect the 1d. Fares before arriving at Church Street.

1d. For St. Jude's Church. – Second Collection to take place at, or near the Mechanics' Institute.

1d. For Boar Lane. – Third Collection at or near Salem Chapel, in Hunslet Lane.

Through Passengers. – 2d. either way; but the Fares of such passengers to be Collected at each 1d. Stage.

LEEDS TO KIRKSTALL. (1d. Stages)

1d. For Wellington Street Junction, opposite St. Philip's Church. Give Change, and collect the 1d. Fares immediately after passing the Great Northern Railway Station.

1d. For Cardigan Arms. – Second Collection to take place at or near the Beckett Arms.

1d. For Kirkstall. – Third and Last Collection at the Clock.

KIRKSTALL TO LEEDS.

1d. For Cardigan Arms. – Give Change at the Clock, and immediately Collect the 1d. Fares.

1d. For Wellington Street Junction, opposite St. Philip's Church. Second Collection of 1d. Fares after passing the Beckett Arms.

1d. For Boar Lane. – Third collection to take place at or near Little Queen Street.

CHILDREN.

No child under Seven years of age shall be counted as a Passenger, but where there are two under Seven years of age they must be charged one full fare, and so on in the same proportion.

All Fares must be Collected as per instructions herein contained, and not on the Platform of any Car. Any deviation from this rule will subject the offender to suspension or dismissal.

GENERAL RULES

1. Drivers and Conductors are each to sign for a copy of these rules, and to have the book with them when on duty, so that in the event of any dispute the rule applicable to the point in question may be referred to.

2. The whole of the Drivers and Conductors are engaged by the day only, and they are liable to be discharged at the end of any day. The time books are made up to Thursday evening, and the wages are paid on each Friday.

3. Drivers and Conductors will be classified into first, second, and third class, and paid at the rates fixed for each class. They may be advanced for merit or reduced for any offences they may commit.

4. Drivers and Conductors may be suspended from duty by the Superintendent or the Inspector, for drunkenness or any other gross misconduct; but no man shall be dismissed from the service without an opportunity of representing his case to the Manager, who will give it a fair hearing.

5. Drivers and Conductors may have leave of absence almost any time by giving a few day's notice to the Manager or the Superintendent; and any one absenting himself without leave will run the risk of not being further employed.

6. Drivers and Conductors must attend regularly at the Company's Depots at the exact time appointed for their Cars to leave the respective yards.

7. Drivers and Conductors should work together in all matters of interest to the Company, and see that passengers are well treated and accommodated.

8. Drivers must see that their horses are properly harnessed before starting from the terminus.

9. Drivers will be held responsible for all damage caused by their neglect or carelessness, and the amount of damage will be stopped out of their wages.

10. Drivers must constantly keep hold of the break so as to be able to pull up the Car on the shortest notice, and so avoid collisions.

11. Drivers and Conductors will be fined or suspended if they are seen to let the pole drop when turning the horses.

12. Drivers must slacken speed when going into sidings.

13. Drivers must not stop their Cars where streets cross each other, if it can be avoided.

14. Drivers are not allowed under any circumstances to take money for carriage of boxes, parcels, etc; nor to receive fares from passengers.

15. Conductors must use the greatest care in taking up and setting down passengers, and when a Car has been stopped to set down a passenger, it must not be started again till such passenger is quite clear of the Car.

16. Conductors must keep a good look out for passengers, and announce the names of the principal streets and stopping places in a loud and distinct voice. Their position (except when collecting fares) must be with their backs to the cars, signalling all persons who may appear to wish to ride, a special care being taken to look down the side streets when passing them. Conductors must be uniformly respectful to all passengers, and answer all their enquiries, but not continue to converse with them.

17. Conductors must not allow any intoxicated person to enter or mount their Cars (Bye-Law 5). Should any have inadvertently been allowed to do so, the assistance of the police may be called to eject them at the first opportunity.

18. Conductors must exhibit the "full inside" signals whenever the Car is full, taking care to change it so soon as any passenger alights.

19. Conductors neglecting to deliver any parcels, note, letter, etc. to Foremen or Timekeepers, etc., when given them at the office, will be liable to a fine.

20. Conductors will be held responsible for all counterfeit or foreign coin they may take, and if it is proved that any Conductor has given such coin in change to passengers, he will be dismissed from the Company's service.

21. Conductors must see that their money is properly counted by the Cashiers in the receiving office, and the correct amount entered on their way-bills at the end of each journey. Conversation betwixt Conductors while paying in their receipts is not allowed.

22. Conductors must not read newspapers while the Car or Omnibus is running.

23. Conductors must not allow outside passengers to sit on the guard rail, or stand on the roof.

24. Conductors must not allow any person to ride free without a pass. Horsekeepers are permitted to ride free only when going to or coming from their work, **but they must wear their tin passes suspended round their necks by the leather strap, which has been attached to the passes for the purpose.** Directors and others having passes will show them on being asked in a respectful manner.

25. Conductors will be held responsible for the security and the proper state of the cushions and aprons. In wet weather Conductors must put the aprons on the tops of their Cars for the use of the passengers, and at the end of each journey put them in proper order.

26. Conductors must not allow large boxes, baskets, or barrels, or merchandise of any description inside the Car or Omnibus. All such articles are to be placed on the front platform, and none are to be taken up on the road unless a passenger accompanies them, and such articles are not to be put in the Cars or Omnibuses in Boar Lane or Briggate, without the party accompanying them first bringing them to the receiving office and having them booked and paid for.

27. **Drivers and Conductors will be required from time to time to show these books to the Manager or the Superintendent, and any man who is unable to produce his book will be supplied with another, for which he will be charged.**

W. WHARAM,
Secretary and Manager.

June 30th, 1880.

Appendix Three

Roundhay Electric Tramway
Rules for Employees

General Rules

1. All employees will be appointed by the Manager, and will be expected to sign the usual agreement.
2. They will report for duty promptly at the time designated by the Manager, or by the Foreman or Inspector, under whose immediate charge they may be.
3. They will be expected to perform their duties to the best of their ability, and in points not fully covered by instructions will use every endeavour to protect the interest of their employers.
4. The abuse, or neglect of tools or machinery will not be tolerated.
5. They will answer politely, and give any explanation in their power either to other employees or the general public; but will refrain from mentioning accidents, delays, or trouble of any kind except to the proper Officer. They will not talk of receipts, expenses, wages or other financial matters, nor make remarks about the probable actions of their employers to other than the proper Officers.
6. They will be expected to perform their duties in such a manner as not to unnecessarily interfere with the duties of others. This applies particularly to those whose duties are not clearly defined, or whose departments interlace in the control of men, use of tools, etc. A little consideration, patience and goodwill on the part of all will avoid all friction in this respect.
7. All employees in place of or in addition to their regular duties will be expected to perform such other duties, in cases of emergency; as the Manager, Inspector, or Foreman may see fit to direct.
8. On leaving the company's service, employees must return this book to the General Office, failing to do this 2s. 6d. will be deducted from their pay.
9. If any question or dispute should arise, upon the construction of these or the following Rules, or in reference to any matter not dealt with by them, the same shall be settled by the Manager whose decision shall be final.

Rules for Conductors and Motormen

1. All conductors and motormen will be appointed by the Manager and will be furnished with a copy of these Rules, with which they must become entirely familiar.
2. When appointed, a man's first duty will be to report at once for practice and instruction to the Inspector. He will be expected to learn thoroughly, under the instructions of a regular conductor and motorman, all the duties of both positions; for this he will receive no pay. When a man is approved by the Inspector he will be appointed last extra upon signing the usual agreement.
3. As extra he will work in the Car House under the Motor Inspector either during the day or night, and will be prepared to take the place of any regular motorman or conductor. As extra he will receive pay of 20 shillings per week, until such time as he is appointed to regular duty.
4. Conductors and motormen will report for duty at least five minutes before the schedule time that their car is to leave the house. They will take the car assigned to them by the Foreman in charge of the car house, and note carefully any instructions given them by the Manager, Inspector, or Foreman.
5. They must keep their uniform neat and clean, buttons and front plate of cap bright.
6. Any employee seen under the influence of liquor, entering or leaving a public house while on duty or in uniform, renders himself liable to prompt discharge.
7. Employees will answer all inquiries politely, but must refrain from conversation while on duty, and are strictly forbidden to talk to anyone except the proper Officers of the company about any accident, either to apparatus or persons that may occur on the line.
8. In event of accident, either to passengers or others or vehicles, no matter how slight, conductors shall obtain names and addresses of witnesses, and fill up blank forms provided for that purpose, and do all in their power to assist injured parties.
9. Any trouble either in the mechanical or electrical equipment of the cars, whether the result of accident or otherwise, **must** be reported to the Manager or Inspector at once, and entered in the book provided for that purpose in the office, and stating the time such trouble was discovered. Crews upon taking charge of cars will note condition of same, and report at once any defect or trouble to Inspector.

Failing to see Inspector at once, conductors must note such defect or trouble on back of trip slip, and show same to relieved crew. Any crew not complying with above are liable to be discharged.

10. Employees must bear in mind that the strictest politeness must be shown to everyone with whom they come in contact. We are fully aware of the many annoyances and even insults that they are liable to receive from the public, but we wish to impress upon them the absolute necessity of patience and politeness. Discourtesy to a passenger, no matter how great the provocation, will be regarded as a most serious offence.
11. Smoking while on duty is strictly prohibited.
12. Any crew backing a car without reversing the trolley render themselves to instant dismissal.

Rules for Conductors

1. Any conductors' failure to report for duty for two successive mornings will be sufficient cause for being placed last extra, at the discretion of the Manager.
2. The conductor must be familiar with detailed instructions under the head of "Rules for Motormen", as well as his own.
3. The conductor must report for duty in full uniform at least five minutes before the time for starting, having a sufficient supply of tickets and change, his trip slip, and accident blanks; and also inspect his car to see that everything is clean and in proper shape.
4. On approaching an overhead frog, motorman will warn conductor by single stroke of foot gong, the conductor will immediately take hold of trolley cord and retain same until trolley wheel has passed frog, and then give the signal to go ahead **promptly**.
5. In event of the trolley leaving the wire, ring one bell instantly, and hold it down clear of the wires by means of the trolley cord until the car stops. Then replace it on the wire and give the signal to go ahead.
6. He will see that the lamps are all right, by testing lamp circuit, before taking out car, and see that an extra lamp is in the car.
7. No conductor will absent himself from duty without the consent of the Manager. Those desiring to be absent will apply to him in person or by letter the day previous.
8. The motorman and car will be under his control, subject to the rules for motormen. He must carry a watch accurately adjusted to clock in general office and start the car promptly on time from the terminals of the road.
9. His position when on duty and not engaged in collecting fares is on the rear platform, so standing that he has a free view of the interior of the car, and can keep a lookout on both sides of the street and up and down side streets for passengers. He must not sit down in the car, nor engage his attention in reading, talking to passengers, his motorman, or other employees, or doing anything which will interfere with the correct, prompt and accurate performance of his duties. Failure to comply with the above will be sufficient cause for dismissal.
10. The conductor should always give the signal to stop the car so that the motorman will not be obliged to stop on curves, steep grades, or cross streets, except in cases of emergency; and will give starting signal **promptly** when passenger has boarded or left car.

11. The conductor will use the following signals:–
One bell – "Stop".
Two bells – "Go ahead".
While moving, three bells – "Danger! stop instantly".
While standing, three bells – "Back up".
12. When a passenger is getting on or off the car the conductor must not give the signal to start until he or she is safely on or off.
13. When a lady leaves the car, he will see that her dress is entirely clear, before giving the signal to start.
14. He must be ready at all times to give a hand to persons needing his assistance in getting on or off the car.
15. Conductors must always keep the right hand gate on car platform closed, and invariably caution the passengers against getting off the car while moving.
16. No smoking allowed on any part of the car.
17. Children must not be allowed to stand on the seats or to damage or in any way mutilate the cars.
18. Conductors will allow no one to ride on the rear platform, except regularly appointed extras while practising.
19. Any valise or parcel too large to be carried on the lap without inconveniencing other passengers must be placed on the front platform and a charge made therefore. Substances liable to injure the car or clothing of passengers, such as paints, oils, acids, etc, or having an offensive odour will not be carried.
20. He will in no case accept any package, parcel, or letter for delivery on the route, except by directions of some officer of the company.
21. He will immediately take in charge and leave at the main office all articles left on the cars by mistake, and note the same on trip slip.
22. Dogs, except in the case of small dogs held in the lap and not permitted to annoy passengers, will not be allowed on the car.
23. The conductors will promptly report all defects in roadbed or car to the Manager or Inspector. If a car passes over a stone or other obstruction, the car must be stopped and the obstruction removed.
24. Each conductor will be furnished with day slips, which he must fill out in accordance with instructions received from general office. Failure to do this will be considered sufficient cause for discharge.
25. The conductor must collect fare from each passenger, except police officers with badge in sight, postmen in uniform and on duty, and such other persons as may from time to time be specified by orders issued from the general office.
26. Fares will be as follows:– between Sheepscar and Harehills Road, one penny either way; between Harehills Road and Roundhay Park, one penny either way; between Roundhay Road and Green Road, one penny either way. One child under seven, accompanied by parents or guardians, not occupying a seat, free; two children, to pay one fare.
27. Passes in the shape of medals in white metal, and bearing on one side the "Leeds Arms" and the words "Roundhay Electric Tramway", and on the other side, the words "Annual Pass, non-transferable", with the date 1892, and a specific number have been issued. Conductors will honour these

passes, and will in each case enter the number of each pass on his trip slip. Conductors will also honour any written passes bearing the signature of the Manager, observing same closely, and if they have a time limit take same up when such limit has expired.

28. Employees will be carried free when going to or returning from their work, unless their seats are required for paying passengers.

29. Conductors will commence to collect fares within 200 yards of starting points, first proceeding through the car to the front end, and collecting fares from either side, as he returns to rear platform. He must collect the fares of any passenger getting on cars after leaving starting points promptly.

30. The conductor must keep himself properly supplied with change and tickets from the general office.

31. The conductor will be held to redeem all uncurrent money turned in by him at the office, and will neither give nor receive any such money, knowingly, upon the car.

32. The conductor is expected to collect every fare, and this can only be done by strict and prompt attention to that part of his duty.

33. The conductor must call out clearly, so that every passenger can understand, the names of principal streets crossing their lines, 150 feet before the car reaches them.

34. The conductor will give passengers such other information or aid in reaching their destinations as he can consistently with the rules, but must on no account talk about receipts or other business of the company, except to authorised persons.

35. The conductor will prevent all persons from peddling anything in or upon the car, and will not allow the distribution or placing of placards or advertisements of any kind in the car without special instructions from the office.

36. The conductor will use the utmost care and vigilance to prevent accidents.

37. Should an accident or collision, however slight, occur, or should the conductor have any trouble with passengers, he must immediately fill out two accident blanks, giving date, road, place, time, direction, car number, motorman's name, his own, the names and addresses of as many reliable witnesses as possible, and those of the party injured, together with a brief description of the accident, collision or trouble. These he must sign and must hand one to the Inspector or leave it at the station for him, and must bring or send the other, enclosed in proper envelope, to the main office at the earliest possible moment after the accident has taken place. If his car is moving up town (or away from the office) he should try to send the report down on a car going in the opposite direction as soon as it is filled out. Too much emphasis cannot be laid on the necessity of getting the names and addresses of the parties injured, and as many witnesses as possible, and getting the report to the office at once.

38. The conductor is forbidden to talk of any accident to any person except the proper officers of the company.

39. If any person is injured, however slightly, he must render all assistance in his power.

40. The conductor must at all times be neat and clean in person and dress. His position is a responsible one and a man filling it should take pride in the manner in which he performs his duty. Fitness for it is shown by honesty, a certain snap, vigour, and promptness in doing his work, by a polite firmness in insisting on his and the company's rights, by a patient treatment of disagreeable occurrences, and be a cheerful attention to the wants of the passengers. A conductor with the above qualifications will be appreciated by the company and the public. Any man who cannot display the above qualities will not be retained as conductor.

41. The conductor is, while on duty, to abstain from the use of intoxicating drinks, from smoking, and from using profane or obscene language.

42. Drunken and disorderly persons must not be allowed to ride. This does not apply to men who are slightly under the influence of liquor and who are orderly and quiet. The use of profane or obscene language, or improper or indecent conduct, must not be allowed on the cars.

43. When it becomes necessary to eject a passenger from the car for any of the above reasons, or for non-payment of fare, the conductor should call a policeman, if one is in sight, and request him to do it. If he refuses, the conductor should take his number and report him to the Manager. Should no policeman be at hand to eject the passenger the conductor must do so, calling on his motorman for assistance, if necessary, but using as little force as possible. In no case must anyone be ejected while the car is in motion, or in the absence of witnesses.

44. Any conductor failing to report to the Manager or Inspector any breach of the regulations for motormen by his motorman will be held equally responsible for any such breach.

45. Upon changing direction at the end of a trip, conductor will take particular notice to see that rear brake is off, and that track scrapers are securely fastened in place.

46. The conductor while on duty must always have a copy of these rules in his possession.

47. In all matters not fully covered by these rules, he is expected to use judgement and discretion in dealing with passengers.

48. Special rules will be found posted on the bulletin boards at the car house and in the office. Amendments or additions to these will be printed for pasting in the books.

49. Ignorance of these rules will not be accepted as an excuse for not observing them.

50. Wilful or careless violation of any of these rules will be sufficient cause for discharge.

Rules for Motormen

1. Failing to report for duty for two successive mornings will be sufficient cause for being placed last extra, at the discretion of the Superintendent.

2. They must become familiar with detailed instructions for conductors.

3. Report for duty in full uniform at least five minutes before the time for starting.

4. Before closing main switch always see that controller handle is turned hard against the stop.

5. Always release the brake before turning on any current.
6. In starting car turn controller handle one-half turn and stop, then turn the current on gradually.
7. Always turn slowly in shutting off current until current is nearly off; then throw controller handle quickly, but lightly against the stop.
8. Always be sure that the controlling handle is against the stop when the current is off.
9. Always turn the current off instantly when the trolley jumps the wire.
10. Always, in case of trouble, turn off the current, then throw off main motor switch.
11. Always apply brakes gradually.
12. Always apply the brakes before leaving the car.
13. Always use the brakes to stop the car.
14. Always turn current off before reversing the motor.
15. Always, in using the reversing switch, throw the handle hard over.
16. Always, when leaving car, take controller handle off and open both main switches.
17. Always report promptly and fully all trouble in report-book at car house or office.
18. On appoaching sharp curves and switches reduce speed to 2 m.p.h.; when wheels have entered curve this speed may be increased.
19. The speed of car must never exceed 8 m.p.h. under any circumstances. The speed must not exceed 6 m.p.h. on Roundhay Road between Whitfield Street and Bankside Street on the down trip. Speed must not exceed 4 m.p.h. when passing the Board Schools at the times when the children are entering or leaving schools. Speed must not exceed 2 m.p.h. when passing through points or under frogs.
20. Never stop on a sharp curve.
21. Never use the reversing switch to stop the car.
22. If it becomes necessary to use the reversing switch in order to save life, shut the current off by controller handle, throw the reversing handle hard, and turn the current on gradually until car stops.
23. Never allow the controller handle out of your possession while the car is in service.
24. Never start out without five extra safety fuses and screwdriver and all necessary tools belonging to the car; the motormen will be held responsible for same.
25. Before passing car that is receiving or letting off passengers always bring the car to a full stop, then start slowly, to avoid accident with passengers from opposite car.
26. The carriages shall be brought to a standstill immediately before reaching the following points:–
    a) The intersection of Whitfield Street with Round-hay Road on the inwards journey.
    b) The intersection of Glebe Street with Beckett Street on the inwards journey.
    c) The intersection of Arthur Street with Beckett Street on the inwards journey.
    d) The intersection of Granville Terrace with Beckett Street on the outwards journey.
27. Do not meet cars on cross streets, but slow up as to allow the car that is nearest the street to be fully 50 feet over the street before passing, then pass slowly looking carefully to avoid accident.
28. Do not approach nearer than 200 feet any car going in the same direction.
29. Current should always be off while the trolley wheel is passing under an overhead frog, and should not be turned on until signal is given by the conductor.
30. On approaching an overhead frog notify conductor by a single stroke of the foot gong.
31. In general, reckless running on curves, switches or grades, will be regarded as a most serious offence.
32. Change the headlight at the end of the line, and see that it is lighted before starting. Lift it into such a position as to light the car in the event of the loss of current for an unusual time. Motormen will be held responsible for the headlight, and no excuse will be accepted for neglecting it.
33. The motorman who takes out the car will be held responsible for its condition, and must notice its condition before assuming control of it. If it is in any way damaged, call the attention of the Manager or Inspector to it.
34. Ring gong twice on the up trip and three times on the down trip when passing other cars, or approaching streets, and also in rounding all curves, and to warn teamsters and pedestrians of danger.
35. Do not run over any wire, stones, sticks or coal, but always stop, pick up the obstruction, and remove it to a safe distance from the track.
36. You must learn all that is possible about the caring for and repairing of motors and machinery. All employees are welcome to our shop for this purpose. Do not hesitate to ask any questions.
37. One bell, "Stop". Two bells, "Go ahead". While moving, three bells, "Danger! stop instantly". When standing, three bells, "Back up".
38. Do not allow any one to run the car other than a properly qualified employee of the company.
39. Motormen are **strictly forbidden** to make any comment on the operation of their car, or talk of any accident, either in the station or on the car, to any one except the proper officers of the company.
40. Both gates on front platform **must** be kept closed.
41. A motorman's position is standing erect, one hand on controlling handle and one on brake, looking straight ahead. It will be regarded as a serious offence to take hands off brake or controller handle while car is in motion.
42. Motormen are forbidden to go inside of cars while waiting for time.
43. They will give careful attention to the sandbox; if sand does not run freely, stir up sand in box with switch stick. Care must be exercised in the use of sand. A very little will do the work.
44. They will exercise great care in the use of scrapers. Never run over five m.p.h. with them, and never attempt to use them on points or curves, and upon reversing a car, pay particular attention to see that the scrapers are clear, and **both** chains hooked in place and the handle securely fastened.
45. If a car will not run, try lamps; if they do not light, current is off line; leave them turned on until they light, then allow one minute to elapse before starting the car. If the current is on, and the car will not move, see that the main switches are closed, see that fuse is all right, see that reversing switch is thrown hard over, see that there is a good contact between the rail and wheel; if not make connection with piece of wire, wrench, or any metal. Examine all connections.

46. Motormen will be expected to become familiar with all the details of the cars, and be able to remedy any trouble that may occur on the road. Anyone who does not will not be retained as motormen. Any man taking interest enough in his work to ask intelligent questions with this view will be appreciated.

47. Ignorance of these rules will not be accepted as an excuse for not observing them.

48. Wilful or careless violation of any rules will be sufficient cause for instant discharge.

49. In passing a vehicle, the horse of which appears frightened, motormen will use the **greatest caution** bringing the car to a standstill if necessary.